ROME
AND
PERSIA

ROME
AND
PERSIA

THE SEVEN HUNDRED YEAR RIVALRY

ADRIAN GOLDSWORTHY

BASIC BOOKS

New York

Basic Books
Hachette Book Group
1290 Avenue of the Americas, New York, NY 10104
www.basicbooks.com

Printed in the United States of America

First Edition: September 2023

Published by Basic Books, an imprint of Hachette Book Group, Inc. The Basic
Books name and logo is a trademark of the Hachette Book Group.

The Hachette Speakers Bureau provides a wide range of authors for speaking
events. To find out more, go to hachettespeakersbureau.com or email
HachetteSpeakers@hbgusa.com.

Basic Books copies may be purchased in bulk for business, educational, or
promotional use. For more information, please contact your local bookseller
or the Hachette Book Group Special Markets Department at
special.markets@hbgusa.com.

The publisher is not responsible for websites (or their content) that are not owned
by the publisher.

Print book interior design by Jeff Williams.

Library of Congress Cataloging-in-Publication Data

Names: Goldsworthy, Adrian Keith, author.
Title: Rome and Persia : the seven hundred year rivalry / Adrian Goldsworthy.
Description: First edition. | New York : Basic Books, 2023. | Includes
bibliographical references and index.
Identifiers: LCCN 2022050483 | ISBN 9781541619968 (hardcover) | ISBN
9781541619944 (ebook)
Subjects: LCSH: Rome—Foreign relations—Iran. | Iran—Foreign relations—Rome. |
Rome—Military relations—Iran. | Iran—Military relations—Rome. | Rome—
Commerce—Iran | Iran—Commerce—Rome. | Rome—History. | Iran—History—
To 640. | Parthians. | Sassanids. | Romans.

Classification: LCC DG215.I7 G65 2023 | DDC 303.48/2370357—dc23/
eng/20221024

LC record available at https://lccn.loc.gov/2022050483

ISBNs: 9781541619968 (hardcover), 9781541619944 (ebook)

LSC-C

Printing 1, 2023

CONTENTS

KINGS AND EMPERORS

HOUSE OF ARSACES

Kings		Emperors
Arsaces I	c. 247–211 BC (217? 214?)	
Arsaces II	c. 211 (217? 214?)–191 BC	
Phriapatius	c. 191–176 BC (?)	
? short-lived king or kings?		
Phraates I	c. 168–164 BC	
Mithradates I	c. 165/4–132 BC	
Phraates II	c. 132–127 BC	
? short-lived king or kings?		
Artabanus I	c. 127–124 BC	
Mithradates II	c. 121–91 BC	
Gotarzes?	c. 91–87 BC	
Orodes I	c. 90–80 BC	
unknown	c. 80 BC	
unknown	c. 80–70 BC	
Sinatruces	c. 93/2–69/8 BC	
Phraates III	c. 70–57 BC	
Mithradates III	c. 57–54 BC	
Orodes II	c. 57–38 BC	

HOUSE OF ARSACES

KINGS		EMPERORS	
Phraates IV	c. 38–2 BC		
		31 BC–AD 14	Augustus
Tiridates I	c. 29–26 BC (as rival)		
Phraataces/Musa	c. 2 BC–AD 4		
Orodes III	c. 6		
Vonones I	c. 8–12		
Artabanus II	c. 10–38		
		14–37	Tiberius
Tiridates II	c. 35–36 (as rival)		
		37–41	Caligula
Vardanes I	c. 40–47		
Gotarzes II	c. 40–51		
		41–54	Claudius
Vonones II	c. 51		
Vologaeses I	c. 50–79		
		54–68	Nero
a son of Vardanes	c. 55–58 (as rival)		
		68–69	Galba
		69	Otho
		69	Vitellius
		70–79	Vespasian
Pacorus II	c. 75–110		
		79–81	Titus
Artabanus III	c. 80–82		
		81–96	Domitian
		96–98	Nerva
		98–117	Trajan
Vologaeses III	c. 105–147		
Osroes I	c. 109–129 (as rival/colleague?)		
Parthamaspates	c. 116 (crowned by Trajan)		

HOUSE OF ARSACES

KINGS		EMPERORS	
		117–138	Hadrian
Mithradates IV	c. 129–140 (as rival)		
		138–161	Antoninus Pius
Vologaeses IV	c. 147–191		
		161–180	Marcus Aurelius
		161–167	Lucius Verus (as colleague)
		180–192	Commodus
Vologaeses V	c. 191–208		
		193	Pertinax
		193–211	Septimius Severus
Vologaeses VI	c. 208–228? (223? 224?)		
		211–217	Caracalla
		211	Geta (as colleague)
Artabanus IV	c. 213–224		
		217–218	Macrinus
		218–222	Elagabalus
		222–235	Severus Alexander

HOUSE OF SASAN

KINGS		EMPERORS	
Ardashir I	224–240		
		235–238	Maximinus Thrax
		238–244	Gordian III
Shapur I	240–270?		
		244–249	Philip the Arab
		249–251	Decius
		251–253	Gallus

HOUSE OF SASAN

KINGS		EMPERORS	
		253–260	Valerian
		253–268	Gallienus (as colleague)
		268–270	Claudius II
Hormizd I	270–271		
		270–275	Aurelian
Bahrām I	271–274		
Bahrām II	274–293		
		275–276	Tacitus
		276–282	Probus
		282–283	Carus
		283–284	Carinus and Numerian
		284–305	Diocletian
		286–305	Maximian (as colleague)
		293–305	Constantius and Galerius (as junior colleagues)
Bahrām III	293		
Narses I	293–302		
Hormizd II	302–309		
		306–337	Constantine
Shapur II	309–379		
		337–340	Constantine II
		337–350	Constans (as colleague)
		337–361	Constantius II (as colleague)
		351–353	Gallus (as colleague)
		355–363	Julian (initially as colleague)

HOUSE OF SASAN

KINGS		EMPERORS	
		363–364	Jovian
		364–375	Valentinian
		364–378	Valens (as colleague)
		375–383	Gratian
		379–395	Theodosius
Ardashir II	379–383		
Shapur III	383–388		
		395–408	Arcadius in EAST
		395–423	Honorius in WEST
Bahrām IV	388–399		
Yazdgerd I	399–420		
		408–450	Theodosius II in EAST
Bahrām V	420–438		
		425–455	Valentinian III in WEST
Yazdgerd II	438–457		
		450–457	Marcian in EAST
		455	Petronius Maximus in WEST
		455–457	Avitus in WEST
Hormizd III	457–459?		
		457–474	Leo in EAST
		457–461	Majorian in WEST
Peroz	459–484		
		461–465	Libius Severus in WEST
		467–472	Anthemius in WEST
		473–474	Glycerius in WEST

HOUSE OF SASAN

KINGS		EMPERORS	
		474–491	Zeno in EAST
		475–476	Romulus Augustulus in WEST
Balash	484–488		
Kavadh I	488–496		
		491–518	Anastasius in EAST
Zamasp	496–498		
Kavadh I	498–531 (returned from exile)		
		518–527	Justin in EAST
		527–565	Justinian in EAST
Khusro I	531–579		
		565–578	Justin II in EAST
		574–582	Tiberius II in EAST
Hormizd IV	579–590		
		582–602	Maurice in EAST
Khusro II	590		
Bahrām Chobin	590–591		
Khusro II	591–628 (returned from exile)		
		602–610	Phocas in EAST
		610–641	Heraclius in EAST
Kavadh II	628		
Ardashir III	628–630 (629?)		
Shahrbaraz	630		
Khusro III	630		
Queen Boran	630–631		
Yazdgerd III	632–651		
		641	Constantine III in EAST
		641–668	Constans II in EAST

CHRONOLOGY

323 BC	Death of Alexander the Great
305 BC	Seleucus I creates the Seleucid empire
280s BC	Parni raid Seleucid province of Margiana but are defeated by Seleucids
264–241 BC	First Punic War between Rome and Carthage
c. 250 BC	Rebellions by satraps create independent regimes in Seleucid provinces of Bactria and Parthia
248–247 BC	Arsaces I gains power among the Parni
239 or 238 BC	Arsaces I attacks Parthia and overthrows its ruler, Andragoras. He begins to conquer Hyrcania and names himself ruler.
c. 235 BC	Seleucus II confronts Arsaces I and is defeated
218–201 BC	Second Punic War between Rome and Carthage
192–189 BC	War between Romans and Seleucids under Antiochus III
189 BC	Romans defeat Antiochus III at Battle of Magnesia
187 BC	Antiochus III prepares expedition to restore control in the east of his empire but dies before it can begin
c. 158–155 BC	Mithradates I of Parthia conquers Media
149–146 BC	Third Punic War between Rome and Carthage

146 BC	Carthage is razed to the ground and Corinth sacked by the Romans
c. 141 BC	Mithradates I's armies overrun Mesopotamia
133 BC	King Attalus III of Pergamon dies and bequeaths his kingdom to the Roman people. Political violence in Rome leads to killing of the tribune Tiberius Sempronius Gracchus and some supporters.
130 BC	The Seleucid Antiochus VII reconquers Mesopotamia, Babylonia, Media, and Elymais
129 BC	Roman province of Asia is created. Phraates II of Parthia defeats Antiochus VII.
c. 128/127 BC	Phraates II is defeated and killed by the Saka and other nomads
c. 123 BC	Artabanus I of Parthia is mortally wounded by nomads
121 BC	Caius Sempronius Gracchus, brother of Tiberius, is killed along with many allies in major outbreak of violence in Rome
c. 115 BC	Chinese envoys visit Parthia for the first time
104–100 BC	Caius Marius is elected consul for five consecutive years, violating all precedent
96, 94, or 92 BC	Sulla meets Mithradates II's envoy in Cappadocia
91–88 BC	Social War between Italian allies and the Romans
88–85 BC	First Mithridatic War between Mithridates VI of Pontus and the Romans
88 BC	Sulla and his legions seize Rome by force. Marius returns and storms Rome later in the year.
83–82 BC	Second Mithridatic War between Mithridates VI of Pontus and the Romans. Roman civil war is won by Sulla, although it continues for several years, notably in Spain under the leadership of Sertorius.

74–66 BC	Third Mithridatic War between Mithridates VI of Pontus and the Romans
73–71 BC	Spartacus leads slave army in rebellion and ravages Italy
72 BC	Assassination of Sertorius leads to conclusion of Roman civil war in Spain
70 BC	Crassus and Pompey hold first consulship
69 BC	Lucullus defeats Tigranes II of Armenia at Tigranocerta
67 BC	Mithridates VI of Pontus defeats Lucullus's subordinate commander at Zela. Pompey holds command against the pirates.
66–63 BC	Pompey holds extraordinary command in the eastern Mediterranean. He defeats Mithridates VI.
63–62 BC	Attempted coup led by Catiline leads to Roman civil war
c. 58–57 BC	Phraates III of Parthia is murdered in conspiracy led by two of his sons, Mithradates III and Orodes II. The brothers soon begin to fight each other.
55 BC	Pompey and Crassus hold second consulship. Pompey is given all of the Spanish provinces with their armies, while Crassus is allocated Syria and sets out from Rome late in the year.
54 BC	Orodes II defeats and executes his brother Mithradates III. Crassus begins expedition against Orodes II and crosses the Euphrates. Several cities surrender or are captured. Local satrap is defeated.
53 BC	Crassus is defeated at Carrhae by the Parthian army commanded by the Surena. Crassus is killed in the aftermath, and most of his men are killed or captured. His quaestor Cassius escapes to Syria. Armenia pulls out of the war and allies with Parthia. Surena is executed by Orodes II. Political violence prevents elections in Rome.

52 BC	Pompey holds third consulship, initially without a colleague. He restores order in Rome by force. Small groups of Parthians and allies raid Syria.
51–50 BC	Cicero serves as proconsul of Cilicia. His troops encounter Parthian detachments or allies. Cassius wins a victory over the Parthians in Syria.
49–45 BC	Roman civil war between Caesar and his enemies, including Pompey
44 BC	Assassination of Julius Caesar by conspirators led by Brutus and Cassius
44–31 BC	Succession of Roman civil wars culminating in the defeat of Antony by Octavian/Augustus
41 BC	Antony and Octavian defeat Brutus and Cassius at Philippi
41–40 BC	Parthians with Roman allies under Quintus Labienus overrun Syria and Judaea. Labienus advances into Asia Minor.
39 BC	Publius Ventidius Bassus is sent to Asia Minor to take command. He swiftly drives out Labienus, who flees but is eventually caught and killed. Ventidius defeats the Parthians.
38 BC	Ventidius defeats a Parthian army near Mount Gindarus and kills Pacorus, the favoured son of Orodes II. Antony returns to the east late in the year. Ventidius returns to Rome and celebrates triumph over the Parthians. Orodes II is dethroned by Phraates IV, who murders most of his brothers to secure himself from potential rivals.
37 BC	Antony goes to Italy to negotiate with Octavian
36 BC	Antony leads a major expedition through Armenia into Media. After initial success, his siege and baggage train is destroyed. He fails to capture Phraaspa or draw the Parthians and Medians into a decisive encounter. During the retreat, his army is harassed and suffers heavy losses.

34 BC	Antony marches into Armenia and deposes and arrests its king. He returns to Alexandria and stages the Donations, awarding much of the east to his children by Cleopatra.
31–30 BC	Antony and Octavian fall out, leading to civil war. Antony is defeated at Actium. He and Cleopatra take their own lives.
c. 31 BC	Phraates IV is challenged by Tiridates but manages to defeat him. Tiridates seeks refuge within the Roman empire and is sheltered by Augustus.
c. 26–25 BC	Tiridates makes another attempt to overthrow Phraates IV. He mints coins in Seleucia calling himself 'friend of the Romans' but is eventually defeated.
20 BC	Augustus visits Syria. Negotiations with Parthians lead to a declaration of peace. As part of this, the Parthians agree to return Roman prisoners of war and the eagles and other standards. Among the gifts given to Phraates IV at this point or later was the slave girl Musa, who becomes a favourite and then a wife.
19 BC	Parthian Arch is begun or an existing arch is modified to celebrate Augustus's 'victory' over the Parthians
11–10 BC	Phraates IV sends some of his sons and their families to Rome
2 BC	Phraates IV dies (perhaps murdered). Musa's son Phraataces becomes king of kings, and she is publicly involved with his government, appearing on coins.
AD 1	Temple of Mars Ultor in Augustan Forum is inaugurated, and the returned eagles are ceremonially installed in it. Caius Caesar is sent to the east with extraordinary command.
2	Caius and Phraataces meet at the Euphrates and confirm peace

3–4	Caius Caesar intervenes in Armenia. He is wounded and his health degenerates, leading to his death.
4	Phraataces and Musa are overthrown and flee to the Roman empire
8	Faction of Parthian nobles appeal to Augustus to send them Vonones I, son of Phraates IV. He returns and is crowned king of kings. He defeats Artabanus II.
12	Artabanus II returns and overthrows the now unpopular Vonones I, who flees to Roman empire
19	Tension over Armenia. Germanicus is sent to the east on extraordinary command. Vonones I tries to escape Roman supervision and is killed. Germanicus dies.
35	Artabanus II intervenes in Armenia. Another faction of Parthian nobles asks that Tiberius send another of Phraates IV's sons to them. The first choice dies before he gets there. Tiridates II is sent in his place and escorted to the border by the governor of Syria, Vitellius.
36	Tiridates II drives out Artabanus II. However, he alienates many supporters, and Artabanus II is able to return and expel him. Vitellius and Artabanus II meet at the Euphrates and confirm peace between Rome and Parthia.
c. 40–51	Division and civil wars in Parthia
43	Claudius invades Britain
52–53	Vonones II of Parthia invades Armenia to make his brother Tiridates its king
55	Corbulo appointed to eastern command
58	Corbulo invades Armenia and expels Tiridates
59	Corbulo captures Tigranocerta
60	Romans appoint Tigranes as king of Armenia
61	Tigranes of Armenia invades Adiabene. Vonones II threatens Syria.

62	Lucius Caesennius Paetus is given command in Cappadocia and advances into Armenia, where he is defeated at Rhandeia. The war is eventually resolved by negotiation.
66	Tigranes, brother of Vonones II, travels to Rome, where he is crowned as king of Armenia by Nero
66–74	The Jewish rebellion
68–69	Civil war: the Year of Four Emperors. Galba, Otho, and Vitellius seize the throne in rapid succession, but the war is eventually won by Vespasian.
72	Paetus is governor of Syria and annexes Cappadocia
c. 75	Alans raid Parthian territory. Vonones II appeals for Roman support, which is declined.
101–102	Trajan's First Dacian War
105–106	Trajan's Second Dacian War
c. 110–113	Pliny the Younger governs Bithynia
114–117	Trajan's Parthian war. Romans annex Armenia and advance into Media and Mesopotamia. Ctesiphon is captured. However, widespread rebellion breaks out in much of the captured territory.
115–117	Rebellion by Jewish population of Egypt, Cyrenaica, and Cyprus
117	Hadrian becomes emperor after the death of Trajan and abandons almost all of the conquered territory
131–135	Bar Kochba revolt in Judaea
151	Vologaeses IV of Parthia subdues Characene
161	Vologaeses IV appoints a king in Armenia. Tension with Rome leads to Parthian attacks against Cappadocia and Syria.
162–166	Lucius Verus is appointed to overall command of war with Parthia. Roman armies drive into

	Parthian territory, eventually taking Seleucia and Ctesiphon. Some territory in Mesopotamia is annexed and peace is imposed on Roman terms. Outbreak of plague follows the army as it returns home, beginning a series of terrible epidemics.
194–195	Septimius Severus's first campaign in the east. After his departure, Vologaeses V of Parthia counter-attacks.
197–202	Septimius Severus's second campaign in the east. The Romans once again march to the royal cities and take Ctesiphon. A new province of Mesopotamia is created.
208–213	Parthian civil war
215–217	Caracalla wages war against the Parthians
217–218	Caracalla is murdered, and Macrinus becomes emperor and continues war with Parthians. He fails to defeat them and may have suffered defeat himself, and he ends the war by making concessions. He is killed, and Elagabalus is proclaimed emperor.
224	Ardashir I defeats the Parthian king of kings Artabanus IV and founds the Sasanian dynasty
226	Ardashir I is crowned king of kings at Ctesiphon
227–230	Ardashir I launches a series of attacks on Roman provinces. He eventually overruns much of Mesopotamia.
231–232	Severus Alexander campaigns against Ardashir I with mixed fortunes but proclaims success and returns to Rome
235–237	Ardashir I makes further attacks on Roman provinces
239	Sasanian attack on Dura-Europos
c. 240–241	Shapur I succeeds Ardashir. He captures Hatra and launches attacks on Roman territory.

242–244	Gordian III leads expedition against Persians. After initial successes, he achieves little and dies. Philip becomes emperor and buys peace from Shapur I.
252	Tension over Armenia. Shapur I resumes attacks on Roman provinces, plundering many cities, including Antioch.
254	Shapur I captures Nisibis
256	Sasanians besiege and capture Dura-Europos
258	Septimius Odaenathus of Palmyra awarded consular rank
260	Valerian leads major attack on Persians, only to be captured and held prisoner by Shapur I for the rest of his life. Shapur I raids Roman territory.
261	Odaenathus of Palmyra given extraordinary command
262	Odaenathus wins victory over Persians and advances close to Ctesiphon
c. 266	Odaenathus raids towards Ctesiphon again
c. 266–267	Odaenathus murdered. Zenobia assumes command in name of their son Septimius Vaballathus.
269–270	Zenobia's armies gain control of much of the Roman east, including Egypt
271	Vaballathus openly proclaimed as emperor
272	Aurelian attacks and defeats Zenobia's regime
c. 272	Death of Shapur I
273	Revolt in Palmyra is quickly suppressed by Romans
282–283	Carus attacks Bahrām II of Persia and may have taken Ctesiphon but dies (or is murdered), and the campaign comes to nothing
296	Narses of Persia intervenes in Armenia and drives out its king

297	The Caesar Galerius is sent against the Sasanians but is defeated by them in Mesopotamia
298	Galerius defeats Narses in Armenia, capturing his harem
299	Treaty restores peace, with the terms heavily favouring the Romans
c. 336	Tension and some fighting on the eastern frontier. Constantine prepares for a major expedition against the Persians.
337	Death of Constantine and seizure of power by his sons
c. 377–338	Sasanians try and fail to take Nisibis
c. 339	Constantius II campaigns against Sasanians
c. 343	Constantius II attacks Persian territory
344	Indecisive battle is fought near Singara
346	Sasanians try and fail to take Nisibis
353–358	Uneasy peace between the empires
359	Shapur II leads major expedition into Roman territory. Amida is besieged and captured.
360	Shapur II leads new expedition and captures Singara and Bezabde. Constantius II counterattacks but achieves very little.
361	Julian's proclamation as Augustus forces Constantius II to refrain from further offensives against the Sasanians
363	Julian leads a major expedition to Ctesiphon but does not try to besiege it. His army begins to withdraw, and he is killed in a skirmish. Jovian becomes emperor and negotiates a peace treaty favouring the Sasanians.
c. 367–370	Tension between the empires
c. 376	Queen Mavia attacks Roman territory until peace is concluded
381–387	Tension and skirmishing, but prolonged negotiation leads to a peace treaty between the empires, partitioning Armenia

	he then fights a battle at Callinicum and is defeated. Belisarius is sacked by Justinian.
532	Prolonged negotiations lead to declaration of 'eternal peace'
538	First contact between Romans and Avars
540	Khusro I leads grand expedition into Roman Syria and sacks Antioch
541	Romans raid Persian territory but achieve little. Justinianic plague has first outbreak, which rapidly spreads.
542	Khusro I again leads expedition through Roman territory
543	Khusro I attacks again. He fails to capture Edessa but extorts money before leaving.
545	Five-year truce declared
547–549	War in Lazica with both Romans and Persians taking part. This does not lead to a full resumption of war elsewhere.
551	The truce is extended, but fighting continues in Lazica for next decade
c. 552	Monks smuggle silkworms into Roman empire
562	Romans and Persians agree to fifty-year peace
c. 568	Embassy from Western Turks arrives at Constantinople as this group becomes a major force on Persia's frontier
569	Justin II refuses to pay Persians the next instalment of the subsidy agreed to in the treaty
c. 570	Khusro I at war with Western Turks
c. 570	Birth of Muhammed (although an earlier date is possible)
571	Rebellion in Persian-held Armenia
572	Justin II openly makes war on Persians
573	Persians capture Dara. Justin II has mental breakdown.

574	Truce between Romans and Persians, initially for one year, then extended for four years. It does not include Armenia.
576	Khusro I suffers bad defeat in Armenia
578	Attempts to turn truce into a treaty fail. War resumes in Mesopotamia and continues with attacks and counter-attacks from both sides and their allies.
586	Avars besiege Thessalonica
589–590	Rebellion against Khusro II by his commander Bahrām Chobin. Khusro II flees to Roman territory. Maurice gives him military aid to regain power.
591	Khusro II, having dealt with the challenger, negotiates a peace treaty with Maurice, bringing the long war to an end
c. 595–601	Khusro II is faced with rebellion by former ally. He eventually wins.
602	Maurice and family are murdered and Phocas becomes emperor
603	Khusro II begins his war against the Romans
604	Persians capture Dara and win victories in Armenia
605	More Persian victories
607	Persian successes in Armenia
608	Heraclius rebels against Phocas
609	More Persian successes. Heraclius's forces take Egypt.
610	Heraclius takes Constantinople. Phocas is executed. Persians take Antioch and win other victories. Muhammed begins to preach at Mecca.
611	Persians take Caesarea in Asia Minor
613	Heraclius leads army against Persians and is defeated. Persians take Damascus.

614	Persians take Jerusalem
615	Persians reach Bosporus. Roman Senate sends letter to Khusro II asking for peace negotiations. He rejects this approach.
616–617	More Persian victories
619	Persians overrun Egypt and take Alexandria
622	Heraclius leads small-scale offensive in Asia Minor and wins a victory. Muhammed and followers are expelled from Mecca and travel to Medina.
623	Heraclius barely escapes ambush when Avars attack during negotiation. Nevertheless, he buys peace from them.
624	Heraclius launches larger-scale offensive through Armenia into Atropatene, destroying fire temple at Thebarmais.
624–625	Heraclius winters in Caucasus. Persians hold negotiations with Western Turks.
625	Heraclius raids more widely in Persian territory. He defeats three Sasanian armies in succession.
626	Heraclius withdraws to Roman territory. A major Persian offensive to the Bosporus is co-ordinated with an Avar attack on Constantinople. The siege of the city fails, and the Avars withdraw. Western Turks begin to attack Persians.
627	Heraclius launches another major offensive, beginning in Lazica, and meets Turkish army led by their khan/king. Roman-Turkish alliance is confirmed. Siege of Tiflis.
627–628	Late in year Heraclius defeats Persian army and drives towards Ctesiphon. Khusro II retreats. Palace coup overthrows Khusro II and names Kavadh II in his place. Peace negotiations begin.
629	Roman troops defeat Muslim Arab band
629–630	Rebellion of Shahrbaraz against Khusro II. Romans support the rebels. Although

Shahrbaraz's reign proves short, the peace between Romans and Persians is confirmed and Persian armies withdraw from the lands they have occupied.

630   Heraclius takes fragment of true cross and other relics back to Jerusalem. Muhammed and followers take Mecca. Many cities defect to them or are captured.

c. 632   Death of Muhammed

632–633   Growing number of Arab raids strike Roman territory. Heraclius orders troops moved from Africa to the eastern frontier, but local authorities refuse to obey.

634   Raids into Roman and Persian territory by followers of Muhammed

636   Arabs win decisive victory over the Romans in the Yarmuk campaign

638   Muslims win huge victory over Sasanians at Qadisiyya. Jerusalem surrenders to Arabs.

640–642   Arab armies overrun Egypt and take Alexandria

641   Arabs storm Caesarea Maritima. Other forces take Tripolitania in North Africa.

645   Attempt by Roman fleet to retake Alexandria is defeated by Arabs

c. 650–653   Constans II is unable to repulse Arab raids from Syria and has to pay them to secure peace

651   Yazdgerd III is killed in civil war

654   Arab fleet attacks Constantinople

656–661   Muslim internal disputes lead to civil war

663   Arabs attack Asia Minor

665–666   Major Arab raid on Roman Africa inflicts damage and forces Romans to agree to pay a subsidy. Peace is short-lived, and over the following decades the Arabs overrun the rest of Roman Africa.

711   Arab armies launch invasion of Spain

LIST OF MAPS

FOREWORD

HISTORY FASCINATES ME, AND WHILE I CAN READILY GET excited by almost any era or topic, the Romans have always had a particular draw for me—as those familiar with my writing will know. In one sense this is another book about the Romans because there is so much to learn and understand about their story, piecing together the surviving literature, the fragments of texts, and the inscriptions, coins, and archaeological remains of this lost era. I have been studying the Romans for all my adult life and I am still learning, and not simply because new discoveries are made all the time.

This is also a book about another empire, that of the Parthians and Sasanian Persians, and for a change some of the story can be told from a different point of view from the Roman sources. The Parthians appeared in the third century BC, carving out a great kingdom that included what is now Iran and Iraq, most of Syria, and at times some of Afghanistan, Turkmenistan, Azerbaijan, and Georgia, as well as wielding influence beyond, notably in the Arabian Peninsula. For more than three hundred years, the Parthians were neighbours and rivals of the Roman empire, and when the Parthian dynasty fell in 224, they were supplanted by the Sasanians, who ruled for four more centuries over what was for all intents and purposes the same empire. Neither the Parthians nor Persians were ever conquered by Rome, and both inflicted some devastating defeats on Roman armies.

Although this is a story of imperial competition which often led to war, it is also a story of coexistence and peace between these two empires. At its height the Roman empire was far larger than the Parthian-Persian empire, not only in sheer size but in population and wealth. Yet the Parthian-Persian empire was still bigger by a considerable order of magnitude than any other state or people nearby. China was an exception, but it was too distant from Parthia-Persia for substantial contact and even further away from Rome. Parthia-Persia was also more sophisticated than any other neighbour when it came to government, economy, and military efficiency. Fairly early on, the Romans realized that the Parthians had to be treated differently from other states and granted them more respect as a result. The Parthians, and later the Persians, realized the same about the Romans.

For more than seven centuries the rival empires lived side by side, and it is vital to understand what happened from the Parthian-Sasanians' point of view as well as the Romans'. As important is the part played by all the other states caught up in the competition between the empires. All were active players; even small states often did their best to turn the rivalry between the great powers to their own advantage. For all their might, neither the Romans nor the Parthians-Sasanians were ever in full control of their allies, let alone other leaders and groups beyond the frontiers.

Seven centuries represents an immense span of time. If thirty years is taken to represent a generation, then some two dozen generations passed from the first encounter between Roman and Parthian representatives to the sudden fall of the Sasanian empire and the shrinking of Roman power in the face of the Arab conquests. Going back a similar period from today would take us to the medieval world before it was ravaged by the Black Death. Inevitably, one book cannot recount in detail everything that happened in seven centuries, or even all the encounters between the two empires. Sometimes it is necessary to summarize, sometimes to simplify, unless the subject is critical to our understanding. On the whole, I have omitted names of people and places, as well as technical terms, whenever these are not essential. The works cited in the references will help the interested reader to explore some of these topics in more detail and discover more about the structures of the Roman and Parthian-Persian states and armies.

The aim has been to make the story clear and simple, while still understanding what happened and why. Narrative history is important, and I have done my best to cover as much as possible and have gone into considerable detail for certain key events. Narrative history is not fashionable in academic circles, but it acts as a check on any thematic approach to a subject, let alone any theoretical analysis. Any idea, any theory, any insight can only be valid if it fits with what the evidence suggests is most likely to have happened—a test that many elegant academic theories fail, which is why so few of their advocates embrace it. Only once the story is fully understood is it valid to search for lessons. Understanding this story—or any other episode in human history—requires an appreciation of the human beings, both the individuals and the groups, who played their parts in all that happened.

There is a good deal of warfare in the pages that follow. The Romans and the Parthians-Sasanians spent far more time at peace than fighting each other, but inevitably, sources tell us far more about the great and dramatic events, including wars, than the quiet times when no stirring or terrible deeds were done. Yet there were still plenty of wars and some periods of prolonged warfare. With a handful of possible exceptions, neither empire ever brought all its resources to bear in a life-and-death struggle against the other. Although they fought on many occasions, this was always in the expectation that the other would still exist at the end of hostilities. In the past, the Romans in particular were inclined to persist in a war until the enemy was absorbed or permanently neutralized, becoming a loyal ally or ceasing to exist as a political entity. This did not happen with Parthia or Persia, and there is little sign that the Romans ever tried to make it happen. This does not mean that the Romans or their opponents did not fight these wars with immense determination. Victory remained important, but the ambitions for what victory meant were more modest than the total and permanent defeat of the other side. The striking thing about these wars is their limited nature—in scale, duration, and consequences.

In the West there is now a tendency to expect warfare to be decisive. Partly this is a legacy of society becoming less and less military, so that few commentators or leaders seem to have much idea of what armies and military force can and cannot achieve. Even more, it is because of the ongoing fascination with and influence on memory of the world wars, and especially the Second World War. The Great War is often seen as somehow pointless because it led to another global conflict twenty-one years later. In the popular mind, not only was the First World War not the war to end war as proclaimed, but the Allies did not really win—which ironically enough is close to what Hitler claimed. National Socialist Germany and Imperial Japan then launched a war which produced savagery, death, and destruction on an unprecedented scale, but this time the Allies did the job properly. Roosevelt declared his intention to fight until the unconditional surrender of the enemy, and that is what the Allies did. Japan and Germany (admittedly only part of Germany at first) were turned into peaceful democracies, in no position to go to war again. Both countries continued to exist—if, in the case of Germany, partitioned for several decades.

The extent of change in Germany and Japan was more drastic than the consequences of most wars in human history, just as the world wars were different in their scale and rapidly evolving technology. Sometimes a markedly stronger, more ruthless society has destroyed or, more often, absorbed a weaker community. Peoples have been conquered, sometimes permanently, sometimes only for a few decades. Yet organized states have tended to go to war with the same opponents over many generations, as geography turned them into competitors and rivals. The roots of the European Union came from a desire to make it hard, even impossible, for Germany and France ever to go to war again by linking key aspects of their economy. Before that, France and various German states had fought each other many times over the centuries. Occasionally they were allies, when they joined forces against other states around them jockeying for position. A war might destroy a regime—for instance, Napoleon's empire in 1814 and again after his return in 1815—but it was not intended to destroy a country. France remained, deprived of some territory but still largely the same and very powerful. Most wars throughout history have been limited wars, fought not to extinction but to a less permanent outcome, usually in the form of a negotiated settlement. Advantage was sought to make this agreement as favourable as possible and shift the balance of power in the longer or shorter term.

Sadly, at the time of writing, the war in the Ukraine has been going on for several months, reminding those who preferred not to think of such things that wars still happen in the modern world, and can even happen in Europe. One of the many surprising aspects of the initial reaction to the war in Ukraine was how quickly many commentators and politicians seem to have forgotten the conflicts following the breakup of Yugoslavia, which produced a dreadful death toll even if the terrain and forces involved gave less sense of massed battle. At the moment, Russian forces are making slow but steady progress in eastern Ukraine, in circumstances where they can gain more advantage from the destructive power of their artillery and other supporting arms and fight in a way that better suits their strengths than the initial operations of the war.

The United States and its NATO allies, and to a lesser extent the EU, have imposed economic sanctions on Russia and are assisting the Ukrainian forces with weapons, equipment, money, training, and apparently intelligence, while stating that they will not join directly in the fighting. Yet different voices in different countries make various claims about objectives, and if there is more unity than the months before the war suggested was likely, there is also a good deal of division. Russia has responded with economic measures of its own, leading to soaring costs of fuel in Europe, while the consequence of a war involving two of the world's largest grain producers has forced up the price of food and may well lead to shortages, even famine, in countries thousands of miles from the war zone.

This is a limited war, most obviously because Russia possesses a large arsenal of nuclear weapons, none of which have been used and hopefully will not be used. It is also a war which Russia had hoped would swiftly be resolved in its favour with little or no fighting, following on from the 2014 occupation of Crimea and other districts. Western leaders are acting on the basis that they can impose sanctions on both Russia as a country and individual Russians, and give major military assistance to the Ukrainians, while remaining spectators, not directly involved and not suffering too many consequences. The perspective is naturally different for states further away than for those bordering Russia or Ukraine, most of them former Soviet republics. Another major factor in all that is happening is the personality of the various leaders involved, as well as the domestic politics in which each one operates. No one yet knows how well the enthusiastic support for Ukraine will endure in the face of high costs and likely shortages of energy over the coming winter—although by the time this book is released, these months will have become history, and everyone will know what has happened.

All of this offers a reminder of how the events of history play out, including those so many centuries ago about which we know far less. History never stops, and human nature has not fundamentally changed since the Stone Age. People are as smart and stupid, kind and callous, generous and mean, courageous and timid, efficient and incompetent as they have always been, just as leaders are capable or not, realistic or not, lucky or not. Other factors remain constant, such as the weather, which determines if the ground is hard enough to permit off-road movement, or the state and extent of the road infrastructure itself.

History is valuable because it helps us to understand our own world a little better. It would be absurd to claim that studying the rivalry between Rome and Parthia-Persia shows us exactly how to interpret a conflict in the twenty-first century. Yet it may help a little to understand human nature, and it is certainly a good principle when trying to learn lessons from the past to examine as much history as possible. The fascination with the Second World War tends to mean that at times like this, every leader is labelled as either a Churchill or a Chamberlain. Similarly, talk of the dangers of appeasement is common, if less often accompanied by reasoned proposals of what to do instead. Not every situation is fundamentally the same as the late 1930s, and not every leader perceived to be hostile is a Hitler, let alone one with the military and industrial might of National Socialist Germany behind him. That does not mean that threats need not be taken seriously. It only means that each situation must be looked at as what it actually is, not as a simple replay of one or two familiar episodes in the past. There is much to gain from examining many more eras of history.

In the case of the Romans and the Parthians and Sasanians, there are loose parallels in the restrictions placed on warfare by both empires. This was a mixture of respect for—even fear of—the enemy's potential power and a sense of how broad a conflict was really advantageous, even in the best possible circumstances. These were self-imposed restrictions on ambition and behaviour—including the deterrent created by the acceptance that the enemy might prove very dangerous if pressed too far. These limits worked, most of the time at least, so that conflicts were fought without turning into life-or-death struggles between the rival empires. One of the great uncertainties at the moment is that none of those involved in the conflict in Ukraine are quite sure what the rules are and what limits should be placed on their actions if the war is not to escalate in ways none of them want. There is a particular mental adaptation for those wedded to the idea of 'a rules-based international system' (or similar concepts) to accept that such things work only when everyone understands and accepts the same rules, which is far from guaranteed when there is no means of enforcing them. After all, making murder a crime has never meant that there are no more murders, and it requires other measures, including investigation and punishment, to make the act as rare as possible. Even efficient measures of controlling such crimes reduce rather than eradicate them.

The Romans, the Parthians, and the Persians lived long ago and were products of very different societies and cultures to our own. Yet they were still human beings like us, both flawed and wonderful. To study them is to help understand ourselves and our world.

INTRODUCTION

THIS IS THE STORY OF ANCIENT ROME AND ITS RIVALRY WITH the Parthian and Sasanian Persian dynasties that presided over an empire with its heartland in modern Iran. Nowhere else did the Romans share a border with a state anywhere near as large or sophisticated for such a long period of time. Rome's earlier confrontation with Carthage spanned a century or so and ended in the latter's political extinction. In contrast, the Romans first encountered the Parthians at the start of the first century BC, and although the Parthian line of kings was eventually overthrown in the third century AD, it was replaced by the Sasanian dynasty that lasted into the seventh century. The ruling family changed, as did some aspects of government, but this was essentially the same Iranian empire, bringing together the same regions and peoples. There was more continuity than change, and if the two dynasties are considered phases in the history of the same entity, then this empire lasted for well over eight hundred years. For some seven centuries, the Parthians-Persians were in direct contact with the Romans, sometimes at war and sometimes at peace, always wary of each other and in competition. This book is about that long rivalry, which with hindsight seems to have achieved very little and was brought to an end by the sudden emergence of a new, unexpected factor, when Arab warriors appeared under the banners of Islam to challenge both empires. Within a couple of decades, they had conquered the Sasanian empire as well as most of the remaining provinces of the eastern Roman empire. Seven centuries of confrontation were over and the world had changed, suddenly and profoundly—so much so that the story of the preceding rivalry is rarely told and is unfamiliar to most people today.

Yet this is strange, for this was a major episode in Roman history, and Rome and its empire continue to fascinate us in a way that no other ancient culture ever quite manages to match, even those better remembered than the Parthians-Sasanians. Egypt of the pharaohs comes closest in popularity to Rome, judging from the quantities of books, articles, and most of all television documentaries to appear each year. By comparison, there is far less on the Greeks or the other peoples of Europe (unless we move later to the Vikings), and very little indeed on the cultures of the rest of Africa, Asia, and the Americas. The Romans score even better when it comes to drama, largely because the evidence we have for the pharaohs offers far less material for such stories. Cleopatra VII is the exception for a reason, though she was at best tenuously connected with what most people think of as truly ancient Egypt. She lived closer to us in time than she did to the building of the great pyramids, and her story was dominated by Rome and bound up with the stories of famous Romans like Julius Caesar and Mark Antony. For all its drama, Cleopatra's career ended in failure, and neither the queen nor her Egypt had much of an influence on subsequent history.

By contrast, the story of Rome is one of staggering success, and Greco-Roman culture played a central role in shaping the development of the Western world, whether in matters of ideas, government and law, architecture, or simply the symbols of power—eagles and triumphal arches and the rest. Popular memory portrays the Romans as very advanced, as great engineers who built towering aqueducts, immense monuments, practical things like the extensive network of all-weather roads, and indulgent and expensive luxuries like bathhouses. It is a sign of a society's wealth and stability that it can devote so much ingenuity and resources to things that do no more than make life comfortable or entertaining. All in all, the Romans' achievements were many and impressive, their history filled with larger-than-life characters and deeds both great and terrible. Alongside all the admiration is the sense of a darker side, of the mad and bad emperors and a world of slavery, gladiatorial games, repression, and crucifixion.

The sheer scale of Roman success is undeniable. In 160,* the elderly Antoninus Pius ruled an empire stretching from the Atlantic coast to the Rhine and Danube, from the north of Britain to the Sahara desert and the Euphrates. Even by a cautious estimate, some sixty million people lived within this territory, making up perhaps a fifth of the entire population of the world at that time. These people were not all alike, for there was a good deal of diversity from region to region, and province to province, in terms of language, beliefs, and rituals, often based on traditions stretching back before the arrival of Rome. Yet everywhere this was obviously the Roman empire, with its currency, laws, institutions of government (however distant), and many aspects of a common culture which extended even to fashion in art, food, clothes, and hairstyles. This was a vast state—all the more so in an age of slow communication—and it lasted a very long time before it declined and fell. At the end of the fourth century, the greater part of the lands ruled by Antoninus Pius remained under Roman rule, if in some cases only just, and it was now an empire divided into eastern and western halves. One hundred years later, the western Roman empire was gone. The eastern empire survived for another thousand years, albeit eventually much reduced in size. Understanding how and why the Roman empire eventually fell is an important question because it had been so successful for so very long.

Roman success meant the destruction or absorption of many other states and regimes. Some, like the Carthaginian empire or the Hellenistic kingdoms, were large, and many were far smaller. Because the Romans won, we will never know how the world might have developed had things been different, for instance if Hannibal had broken the Roman Republic. The impact of Rome on subsequent history remains so great and so multifaceted that we can never get any real sense of what might have happened if it had failed early in its rise. The Romans left their mark on Western Europe, North Africa, and the Near East, not necessarily making

---

*All dates are AD unless specifically given as BC.

everyone Roman in any strict sense but changing them nonetheless. Greek culture morphed into Greco-Roman culture, while the Christian Church, most of all in its Catholic and Orthodox forms, was shaped by Roman society.

The Roman empire that did all this was created and maintained by military might. That did not mean that everyone who ended up under the Romans' rule had first fought against them. Many leaders saw the growing power of Rome as something they could harness and employ against closer rivals, who were perceived as much more threatening. Cleopatra's family, the Ptolemies, allied with Rome's republic at an early stage and never fought against the Romans; her bad luck was to end up on the losing side in a Roman civil war. There were plenty of other communities and leaders who saw the encroachment of the Romans as an opportunity to strengthen their own position, and more who were pragmatic and judged that they could not hope to protect themselves from an aggressor as strong as the Romans and so had better accept their dominance. In each case, some would change their mind when faced with the reality of a permanent Roman presence, while others from the start were determined to resist whatever the cost. Julius Caesar, who conquered Gaul in eight years of bloody warfare, saw this as entirely justified for the good of the republic and himself. At the same time, he accepted that it was natural for the Gauls to fight for their freedom against him.[1]

The Romans were usually at war somewhere, although as the empire expanded, campaigns were fought far away from Rome itself. The Pax Romana was a reality for much of the empire, especially in the first and second centuries, in the sense that Italy and most of the provinces were almost free from warfare for generations at a time. Yet there was nearly always fighting somewhere on or beyond the frontiers. Years when the Roman people were not formally at war with anyone, anywhere in the world, were so rare that they were marked by the ceremonial closing of the doors of the Temple of Janus in Rome.* This ritual was only performed on

---

*Janus was depicted with two faces, one looking to the front and one behind. The month of January was named after him since it was the beginning of the political and religious year.

a handful of occasions, but with such a vast empire, one or several conflicts could rage without directly touching the lives of the overwhelming majority of the population.

Wars were common but tended to be local affairs, and the enemies were tribes, states, or kingdoms whose resources were dwarfed by those of the empire. These were not wars between well-matched powers in the wider sense, which did not mean that they were necessarily easy or foregone conclusions, since one tribe never had to fight against the entire might of Rome. Antoninus Pius had in theory some 350,000 military personnel at his command, so that soldiers and sailors represented around 1 in 170 of the overall population (if the estimate for the empire's population is more or less right). Conflicts requiring even a tenth of this force to be committed to the theatre of operations were rare indeed, and larger-scale operations truly exceptional. Most campaigns involved far smaller numbers of troops. In 60, a major rebellion in Britain was defeated in a battle where the Roman commander had barely ten thousand men in his army (although admittedly he had hoped to gather more). The Romans were good at fighting, which, combined with a talent for dominating and controlling others, made their empire possible. They did not always win every war, let alone every battle, but they did win most battles and the vast majority of wars.

The Romans were conquerors, but after the death of the Emperor Augustus in 14, new conquests were rare. Although Britain (which Augustus had decided was not worth taking) was invaded in 43 and most of the island subsequently occupied, the Romans never established a permanent presence in the very north over much of what became Scotland. The tribes of Ireland were left unmolested altogether. Augustus had created a German province stretching as far east as the river Elbe, and then lost it when three legions and their commander were ambushed and slaughtered in 9. It was never recovered, and centuries later tribes from this area were among the German-speaking peoples who broke into the western Roman empire and dismembered it.

Greco-Roman literature and history dominated education in the modern West until very recently, and plenty of powers have liked to see themselves as successors to all that they felt was best about the Roman empire and Roman civilization. Connections with the Romans were greatly prized, which was one of the driving forces behind the growth of archaeology in the nineteenth century. Alongside this pride in the distant past, some found particular pleasure in the thought that 'they' had stood up to the might of Rome, whether the Scots because the Romans had never conquered all of what became Scotland or the Irish because the Romans did not even try to conquer them. In an ugly form, the claim that Germans were different from other Europeans because they had thrown off the Roman yoke was a common theme for the leaders pressing for German unification in the second half of the nineteenth century, carrying with it a sense of racial uniqueness and superiority that would bear ghastly fruit under the Nazis. The narrative relied heavily on Roman perceptions of the Germanic tribes as distinct from the Gauls and other peoples and on their stereotypes of simple, virtuous barbarians—exaggerated for political and literary reasons, if they reflected reality at all. It was also the Romans looking from the outside who saw these tribes as related to each other, developing the idea of *the* Germans, or for that matter *the* Gauls or *the* Britons. Unity in any sense, let alone political, was not a feature of Iron Age peoples at this level. Thus, most of the time, the neighbours in contact with the Roman empire were divided into many different tribes and communities, with many individual leaders.[2]

The Parthians and Sasanians were different. Their ruler was called the king of kings, because within his empire there were distinct kingdoms ruled by lesser, regional kings. Sometimes these local leaders resisted central authority, fuelling civil war, but this was always the exception rather than the rule. For most of the period of contact with Rome, the Parthian-Sasanian empire covered essentially the same area, stretching from the Caspian Sea in the north to the Arabian Gulf in the south, from what is now Afghanistan in the east to the Tigris and Euphrates in the west. Much of it was defined by mountain ranges, with the Caucasus in the very north, the Elburz and Zagros ranges to the east, the edge of the Hindu Kush in the Far East, and the Taurus range in the west. These mountains were not all the same. Some blocked communication, some not, while others channelled it along particular routes; trade and especially campaigning armies had to go with the grain of the landscape, a constant factor in all that follows. Within this wider area were extensive stretches of desert, high plateaus, mountain valleys, and wide areas of steppe land where cultivation was easier. To the north and east it touched the great steppes of Eurasia, reaching all the way to China.

At the time of Antoninus Pius, the Han emperor of China may well have presided over territory as populous and extensive as his Roman counterpart. The Parthian-Sasanian empire was smaller, although still far, far larger than any other state in contact with Rome. There was some distant diplomatic contact between Parthians-Sasanians and the Chinese, although it was limited and varied as the fortunes of Chinese emperors waxed and waned and the distance between their lands widened or shrank. The Romans and Chinese were aware of each other's existence, but too far away for any significant political contact.

Unlike the Roman empire, which grew around the Mediterranean, a central sea was not a feature of the Parthian-Sasanian state. For all the variety of landscapes and climate encompassed in the Roman provinces, there were greater, more extreme contrasts in the lands subject to the king of kings. Populations can only grow in proportion to their capacity to generate food, which in turn depends on availability of water to grow plants, whether as fodder for animals or food for people. In the desert areas, this was extremely limited. Pastoralism tends to be more practical in arid conditions than farming, but it is the latter that allows communities to grow in size. Agriculture was easiest where there was sufficient natural rainfall, although this put farmers at the mercy of the weather, as too little or too much rain at the wrong times had a drastic impact on the harvest. Greater effort, organization, and resources were required to draw water from the rivers to irrigate as wide an area of land as possible. Although more expensive and difficult, this had the advantage of creating a predictable water supply, making it easier to support a larger population in the long term.

Cultivating the soil—like civilization, organized government, and indeed empire—had far more ancient roots in many of the lands ruled by the king of kings than it did in most of the Roman provinces (with the exception of Egypt and some other lands in the east). Under the Parthians and especially the Sasanians, irrigation systems were extended over wider areas than ever before, while the relative stability created by these regimes, as with earlier empires like the Achaemenid Persians, helped to foster population growth. There were many cities, some very old indeed, some new foundations, and some very big. Yet they tended to concentrate in particular regions, and large swathes of the Parthian-Sasanian empire could not support and feed such densely inhabited communities.

In contrast, the Roman empire was a world of cities, for it controlled far more land where climate and other conditions helped agricultural production. To put it simply, more of their provinces had plenty of rainfall and less extreme heat in summer and cold in winter. If the Roman empire at its height was double the size of its Parthian-Sasanian neighbour, the difference in population was significantly greater, although even rough precision is impossible. The estimate of sixty million for the age of Antoninus Pius reflects scholarly consensus and a good deal of guesswork, which may or may not be correct. There is even less evidence for the Parthians and Sasanians, but the same sort of estimation might suggest a range of nine to fourteen million—with the possibility that it was somewhat less or more, and may have varied considerably over the period.[3]

The Roman empire was larger than the Parthian-Sasanian empire, and its wealth and resources of manpower and most raw materials was much greater. When the western empire collapsed in the fifth century, this advantage was reduced to a smaller margin, although still not to parity. Resources and size were never the whole story, since by their nature each empire had many other commitments and ambitions and could not devote everything to competition with the other. The two powers would fight many wars, but with a few possible exceptions, these were not wars fought to the death, intended to destroy the enemy. At no point was there the remotest possibility of a Parthian or Persian army driving deep enough into Roman territory to reach Italy or Rome. Only at the very end of our period did a Sasanian Persian army come within sight of Constantinople, and it proved unable to cross the Bosporus into Europe in any strength. In contrast, successive Roman armies went down the Euphrates and Tigris valleys to sack the great Parthian and Sasanian royal cities of the region. Yet the Romans never stayed there for long, and the eastern Iranian heartlands of the rival empire never saw a legion under arms.

Rome was larger and stronger, an aggressive imperial power which had conquered a large part of the three continents known to the Greeks and Romans. Yet it did not conquer the Parthian-Sasanian empire or destroy it as it had destroyed Carthage, and alongside some much trumpeted Roman victories came humiliating defeats. The Parthians killed Caesar's associate Marcus Licinius Crassus and humbled Mark Antony. The Sasanians captured the emperor Valerian in 260—the only time a Roman emperor was ever taken prisoner by a foreign enemy. They also sacked Antioch in Syria—after Rome and Alexandria, the largest city in the empire—on multiple occasions, as well as many other cities large and small. There was glory and humiliation on both sides, without either securing a big enough advantage to dominate the other permanently, let alone to conquer or destroy it.

There was also a good deal of peaceful coexistence between these rival, aggressive empires, even if this figures less prominently in our sources than the inherently more dramatic disputes and conflicts. This book is about the contact and rivalry between the two empires, but it must also be about the many leaders and communities of the wider region caught up in their competition. These were no mere pawns in the greater struggle—nor simply pro or anti Roman or Parthian-Sasanian—but active participants with ambitions of their own. Both empires relied heavily on allies, even though they could prove difficult to control and at times were willing to play the Romans and Parthians-Sasanians against each other for their own advantage. There is much more to this story than simply the competition between the great powers.

Seven centuries of imperial competition and its context is a big topic. Inevitably, as with any aspect of the ancient world, the surviving sources of information are limited and often inadequate. As already noted, there are no truly reliable figures for populations, and in the same way there are no reliable statistics to reveal the economies of either empire or the impact of epidemics, natural disasters, and other phenomena mentioned in the literary accounts. All literary evidence reflects the authors' knowledge, which might be faulty, and to a greater or lesser extent their prejudices, as well as what they felt their readers wanted to know. For most aspects of Classical history there are only Greco-Roman voices to tell the story, since the peoples who fought against the Romans left no accounts at all.

For a change this is less true for the Parthians-Sasanians. While written narratives from the Roman side still provide the vast majority of the sources, there are other traditions—for instance, from Armenia and Arabic histories written much later under the Muslim dynasties but covering earlier periods. The fullest narratives are medieval, making it difficult to judge how much reliable information was still available. One interesting feature is that the Sasanians had managed to suppress memory of their Parthian predecessors so effectively that much less was known about them, while the list of their rulers was reduced in the literary tradition and the four and a half centuries of their dominance shortened to barely a third of this time.

There is some sense of the Parthian-Sasanian perspective, but even so this remains a story told predominantly through Roman evidence because otherwise it could not be told at all. It helps that the Parthians and Sasanians produced coins, which help to trace the rule of successive monarchs, and that some monuments and inscriptions survive, giving glimpses of how rulers wished to present recent events to their subjects. More generally archaeology provides information about settlements, fortifications, trade, and industry, while the names and titles on clay seals that once held official documents provide glimpses into Sasanian administration. Over time, more will be learned and more data gathered to give at least a little more confidence to the reconstruction of settlement patterns and population levels from period to period and region to region. Yet all this evidence is patchy, reflecting the chance of discovery and the levels of work possible given the physical and political environments in different countries. As an example, far more is known about the Roman civilian and military settlements in Israel than in Turkey or Syria, simply because more survey and excavation has occurred there. This means that even on the Roman side there are substantial gaps in our knowledge, whether because of lack of fieldwork in a region or because the literary accounts are few and unreliable. Much remains unknown, and it can be difficult to judge how far information from an inscription or literary account can be seen to reflect a wider experience.

There will be places where it is impossible to be sure just what happened, and most of the story must be told from Roman sources, which to a greater or lesser extent saw the Parthians and Sasanians as foreign and often as enemies. It is not difficult to find dismissive comments and generalizations about Asians or easterners in Greek and Roman literature or similar stereotyping in art. Yet it would be dangerous to see everything as part of the wider history of rivalry between east and west, which invariably focuses on the last few centuries and projects back assumptions according to an individual's preconceptions and politics. Greeks and Romans alike were equally disparaging about all other outsiders, such as the 'barbarians' to the west, north, and south—and about each other. This changed only a little as the empire grew and an ever higher proportion of the population became legally Roman citizens or more generally identified themselves as Romans. Stereotypes of Gauls, Germans, Syrians, Egyptians, former slaves and their descendants, rural peasants, and urban poor all remained strong, even when people from all these groups rose to high office.[4]

There is no reason to believe that the Parthians and the Sasanians did not have a similar sense of their own superiority over all foreigners and plenty of groups within the empire. They certainly did not think of themselves as 'easterners'—any more than Romans thought of themselves as 'westerners' in any strong sense. Zoroastrian religion encouraged the Sasanians in particular to see themselves as at the centre of the world, physically as well as spiritually and morally. Once again, this is the natural belief of most peoples, not least great empires. The Romans and the Parthians-Sasanians were imperialist, aggressive powers who cherished military glory and conquered and controlled many other peoples, suppressing by force—often brutal force—any challenges to their rule. They also both brought stability, peace, the rule of law, and prosperity over wide areas for long periods.

The historian must aim to understand the past, to piece together as well as possible what happened and why. Rushing to judge an era, a state, or a leader and to depict them as good or evil, as victims or oppressors, rarely helps in this process. If it must be done, then it must follow analysis of what actually took place. This requires examining all of the available evidence, treating it with care, and weighing as carefully as possible its likely accuracy. Admitting what is not known is as important as stating what is known, and making clear the likely levels of doubt or certainty in each case. Some may not care for a narrative that at times is tentative, even cautious, but anything else would be dishonest and likely to lead to conclusions that are dubious at best. The aim is to treat both sides in the same way, to view these empires as equals, asking the same questions about their intentions, capacity, strengths, and weaknesses and treating evidence from either side with matching care. These questions are worth asking even when there cannot be a definitive answer, because they show the issues at stake.

Since the focus is on the rivalry between two great empires, this book cannot hope to be a full history of either the Roman or Parthian-Sasanian empire. It would be possible to write a book of this length on the theme of any single chapter—and in some cases, such works exist and are listed in the notes. Also, for reasons of space, not all of the story can be described in the same detail, even when fuller accounts exist, and anything that is not central to the theme can receive no more than cursory treatment—for instance, religion when it did not impinge directly on foreign relations. Far more could be written about Zoroastrianism and the difficulties of understanding its development and role under the Parthians and greater prominence under the Sasanians than is possible here. Similarly, the theological disputes and schisms within the Christian Church after Constantine made it the faith of the empire—and in particular the bitter disagreements over how to define the Trinity and Christ's specific nature—are mentioned only when they affected the politics of an era. Such topics are highly complex; the Latin craving for legal precision collided with Greek enthusiasm for the abstract and tradition of philosophical debate, all fuelled by a sense of urgency since getting to the truth was seen as essential to proper worship, faith, and hence eternal life. Describing these developments would have required considerable space while adding nothing to the overall theme; hence it is better to be as brief as possible. The same is true of political, administrative, and military structures, where only the essential points can be covered.

Yet one of the advantages of taking such a long perspective and following the competition between the two empires over so many centuries is that some of the great debates between scholars working closely on aspects of the period soon fade in importance. The Romans encountered the Parthians when both were well-established, expansionist powers. Thus, there is less need to explain the development and reasons behind either side's imperialism—something discussed with great passion in the case of the Romans. Leading on from this is an equally heated debate over the question of how the Romans viewed their frontiers: whether their intentions were predominantly or ever defensive, and whether they were more concerned with future aggression or maintaining control of the existing provinces. Official pronouncements, and the more enthusiastic poets, spoke of empire without limit or end and of Rome's right and destiny to rule. Certainly, conquest could often be seen by many Romans as an unambiguously good and desirable thing.[5]

Stepping back and studying what happened over such a long period immediately encourages caution about assuming that attitudes were simple and unchanging. A major weakness of these debates is that they have tended to speak of *Roman* imperialism and *Roman* frontiers while ignoring the part played by other states. The Romans were often aggressors, but sometimes they were not, and wars began when they were attacked. Nor was their aggression constant or always of the same nature. There were plenty of occasions, even during the great periods of expansion, when they chose not to seize territory or even to wage war when a pretext existed. Most of all, despite so many centuries of competition, they made very little effort to conquer the Parthians and the Sasanians.

Some territory was taken and held for a long period, but this stopped far short of the Romans' ruthless determination to destroy Carthage as a rival—a conflict which only gathered momentum in the buildup to the final clash in 149 BC and reflected Roman insecurity rather than Carthage's actual power at the time. If the Romans are viewed as determined to dominate and expand wherever possible, always seeking empire without limit, then the central question becomes: Why did they fail in the east? Explanations are sought on the political and especially the military side, ranging from low-level tactics to strategy.

Yet is the question the right one to ask? Once again, it is focused solely on the Romans and assumes, firstly, that they were driven to conquer at every opportunity and, secondly, that they were only prevented from doing this by their own limitations. From the start, the Parthians and Sasanians are reduced to a passive role, simply resisting Rome rather than having aims of their own. Beginning with such fixed assumptions about what should have happened is never wise. Instead, the aim is to trace what actually occurred and only at the end return to such big issues. As importantly, every situation must be viewed from the Parthian-Sasanian standpoint as well as the Roman one, in addition to the point of view of everyone else involved, while bearing in mind the simple yet all too easily forgotten truth that no one knew what was going to happen.

More than seven centuries of contact, confrontation, and negotiation makes for a long and complex story, involving many actors, places, and regions. Detail is needed at many points, since it is essential to understand the narrative on which any conclusion is based and the doubts that surround it. Therefore, there is a lot of information and qualifications based on the strengths and weaknesses of our sources. I have done my best to make the chapters as easy to follow as possible, avoiding too many names of individuals or places and of details that are not essential. Unfortunately, that does mean passing over many remarkable characters and incidents. Some may find certain passages repetitive, as the rival empires wage yet another limited war in much the same area. In the later chapters, cities like Nisibis, Amida, and Dara will figure again and again. The very repetition, of contest after contest for the same key locations, is at the heart of the story and needs to be done in order to understand the nature of most of the rivalry and especially the warfare.

This is a book about Rome's empire* and the only power large enough and strong enough to be a serious rival over many centuries. The Parthians and the Sasanians were among the most successful dynasties in antiquity, and the scale of their power and longevity is too often forgotten. The story of their encounters with Rome helps to give some sense of their success, while presenting the Romans in a different manner from more familiar studies of the empire. Two great powers—one stronger than the other, but not to such an extent that the encounter was unbalanced—lived alongside each other for an immensely long time. How this happened, how the balance was maintained, and how the experience changed each side and those around them is our theme. To understand all this means tracing the entire history of contact—something not done in any detail before—and following a path through some unfamiliar territory and leading to more than a few surprising conclusions.

---

* Throughout the book I will refer to Rome and the Roman empire, extending this to include the eastern empire with its capital at Constantinople which continued after the fall of the western empire in the fifth century. Although it has been conventional to describe this entity as the Byzantine empire, its leaders and inhabitants thought of themselves as Roman—as did neighbours, including the Sasanians.

I

FELIX

90S BC

Romans loved spectacle. The same was true of most societies in the ancient world, and, whatever else Hollywood has got wrong, the fondness of historical epics for grand processions, parades, and casts of thousands reflects something of this reality. Important events in the life of a community or leader were marked publicly and choreographed with great care, usually following well-established traditions. Thus, when for the first time a representative of the Parthian king met a representative of the Roman Republic, the occasion had to be marked by a ceremony where discussions were held in plain view, even if some or most of the real negotiation happened behind the scenes. A willingness to bargain in public was seen as a sign of good faith.

The Parthian envoy was called Orobazus, and other than this incident and its aftermath, nothing else is known of him. He came across the Euphrates because he had heard that a Roman governor was in the closest part of Cappadocia (in today's eastern Turkey). Orobazus sought to make contact with the Romans as they came closer to the lands ruled by the Parthian king. His purpose was to weigh up the newcomers and establish a more-or-less formal friendship between Rome and Parthia. As yet, the lands directly

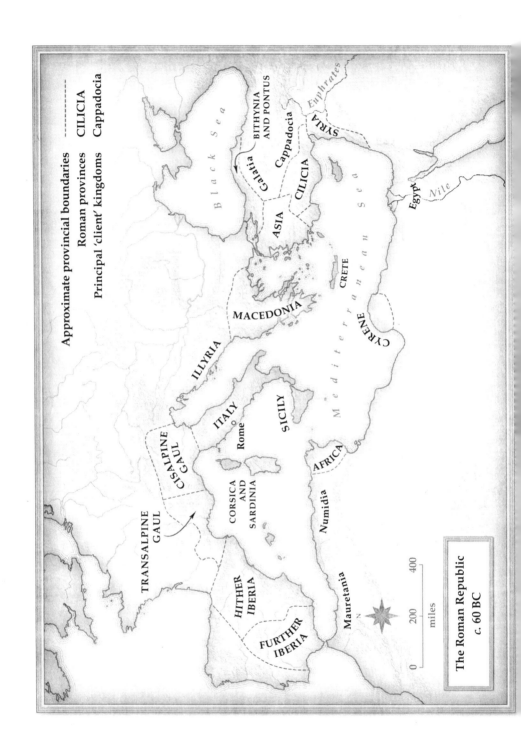

Approximate provincial boundaries - - - - -
Roman provinces CILICIA
Principal 'client' kingdoms Cappadocia

Black Sea

Euphrates

BITHYNIA AND PONTUS

Galatia

Cappadocia

SYRIA

ASIA

CILICIA

Egypt

Nile

CRETE

Mediterranean Sea

MACEDONIA

CYRENE

ILLYRIA

ITALY

Rome

SICILY

CISALPINE GAUL

AFRICA

CORSICA AND SARDINIA

Numidia

TRANSALPINE GAUL

HITHER IBERIA

FURTHER IBERIA

Mauretania

N

0   200   400
miles

The Roman Republic
c. 60 BC

ruled by each power stood at a considerable distance from each other, but the regions in which they took some interest were just starting to coincide. Both sides knew of the other by report, and formal contact was the next logical step.

Presumably Orobazus had an entourage, but there is no suggestion that he was accompanied by any significant number of soldiers. In contrast, the Roman was at the head of an army and had marched into Cappadocia to restore to power a king whose claim to rule had been supported over his rivals' by Rome's Senate. The favoured Cappadocian king, as an interested party as well as an important man, was present at the meeting. So was the army, for the Roman convention was to mark such occasions with a parade, ideally with serried ranks of legionaries providing a backdrop as well as a reminder of Rome's might. Armour was cleaned and polished, shields uncovered to show their brightly painted decoration, crests mounted on helmets, and, at the front, massed standards held high and surrounded by trumpeters.

The aim was to display Roman power, and how the visitors were treated was an important part of the whole process of diplomacy, for it reflected each side's status in relation to the other. Defeated enemies suing for peace—and even the representatives of minor kingdoms, cities, or tribes—might well be brought before a Roman commander sitting on a high podium and thus looking down at them. In this case, there was no such crude assertion of superiority; instead, three chairs were placed on the same level. Yet when the Roman took his seat in the middle, with the Parthian on one side and the king on the other, this was seen as a slight to the ambassador and an assertion of Rome's superiority over Parthia. Perhaps something of this tone extended into the negotiations and whatever was agreed, for when the ambassador returned to report to his own king, the latter was displeased and had Orobazus executed.

At least that is the story told by Plutarch, a Greek and also a Roman citizen who wrote some two hundred years after the event. Otherwise, this first formal encounter between Roman and Parthian is barely mentioned in the surviving sources, and none of the other accounts name Orobazus or his supposed fate. There is a reasonable chance that the story of the ambassador's execution is untrue, whether invented to demonstrate the supposed—from a Greek or Roman perspective—inherent despotism of eastern monarchs, and the Parthians in particular, or as part of an attack on the Roman commander by one of his many personal enemies. Plutarch claims that the governor was subsequently criticized for his poor manners and arrogance, while noting that others felt the seating arrangement was only appropriate and the best way to treat foreigners. Some of the details Plutarch records may have come from the Roman commander's own memoirs, which were obviously highly favourable to him. Equally, if Orobazus was executed, this may have had far less to do with his alleged mistakes on his mission than with the politics and personal relationships at the Parthian royal court, about which next to nothing is known.[1]

This first formal diplomatic encounter between Rome and Parthia assumed far greater significance in hindsight than it deserved. Plutarch thought it notable because he knew of the events and conflicts to follow, some of which he wrote about in great detail elsewhere. More generally, his account and the other sources for the meeting illustrate many of the problems faced in understanding the history of the two powers, not least that the only surviving records come from the Roman side and there is nothing directly from the Parthian perspective. Incidents such as Orobazus's execution are based on what Greco-Roman sources thought had happened in Parthia and why, based on information that may not have been wholly reliable.

Where detailed narrative histories survive in Greek or Latin—and that is always the exception rather than the rule—first encounters of this sort between Romans and foreign ambassadors tend to get mentioned, especially if the delegation came from a reasonably powerful ruler or people. Meeting another people for the first time and establishing a relationship in keeping with Rome's dignity and majesty was a worthy accomplishment for a Roman governor. If it could be portrayed as a formidable, barbarous tribe acknowledging the superior might and moral worth of the Romans, then it reached something of the prestige, if not the full martial glory, of defeating them in war.

Apart from being so overwhelmingly Greco-Roman, the surviving record is influenced by another important factor. Plutarch describes the incident in his biography of the Roman governor Lucius Cornelius Sulla, which means that compared to Orobazus far more is known about him. The incident occurs early in Plutarch's *Life of Sulla* as a minor episode, and if Sulla had not gone on to play such a pivotal role in Roman history, then he would not have been chosen as a subject by Plutarch and the details in his account would not have been preserved. A postscript to the diplomatic meeting is the claim that a 'Chaldean' accompanied Orobazus and, using ancient Babylonian lore to assess Sulla's appearance and character, predicted that the Roman commander would become the greatest man in the world. In this way, the episode allowed Plutarch to highlight Sulla's talent in resolving the situation in Cappadocia, his good fortune in being the first Roman approached by a Parthian embassy, his arrogance in insulting the envoy, and this prophecy of a grand future. The author does not bother to record the details of what was discussed or the type of friendship agreed, for his focus was on the character and fortunes of his subject, not history in general. On balance, it seems most likely that no formal treaty was agreed beyond some expressions of mutual goodwill between the Roman people and the Parthian monarch.[2]

Naturally enough, famous and important figures attracted the attention of authors, so that whenever they were involved in diplomacy or contact with Parthia or Persia there is a far greater chance that this is recorded in our sources than when the less famous were involved. This is not infallible. A lot was written at the time and subsequently about the Parthian wars of Trajan and Lucius Verus in the second century, for instance, but all that has survived is brief, fragmentary, and confused or distorted. So much of the literature of the Roman era has been lost that many major events are very hard for us to reconstruct even at a rudimentary level. Yet there is a greater chance that at least something has been preserved if an important man—and it was almost always a man—was involved. Even then there are likely to be gaps, and no firm date is preserved for the meeting between Orobazus and Sulla; it may have happened in 96, 94, or 92 BC. Only hindsight made the encounter appear important because of what Sulla was to do in just a few years. It is easy to forget that, when it occurred, he was not yet one of the republic's leading men.

Family mattered in Roman public life, almost to the exclusion of everything else. Once ruled by kings, Rome had become a republic at the very end of the sixth century BC and developed a constitution designed to prevent one section of society, let alone one individual, from gaining permanent supreme power. Rome's magistrates, the men who led the state in peace and war, were elected and held office for a set period, usually a year, and were barred from reelection to the same post before a ten-year interval had passed. The two most important magistrates were the annually elected consuls who gave their name to the year. Individuals rarely held the post more than once, but the same family names appear again and again in the lists of consuls, as brothers, sons, nephews, and grandsons followed in due course. These were the aristocratic clans with the fame, influence, connections, and money to sway the voters. Romans tended to expect the latest generation of a family to live up to the great deeds of their ancestors, while the families went to a good deal of trouble to advertise their past achievements and honours. A boy born into one of the well-established families was almost guaranteed the consulship—assuming he lived long enough, for no one was permitted to seek the office before his forty-second year.

Sulla was not born into this golden circle. His family was ancient, for the Licinii were patricians, members of the oldest aristocracy which had dominated the early years of the republic. Over the centuries, some of the patrician clans and many family branches dwindled, dying out or fading into obscurity, while men from the wider population, the far more numerous plebians, forced their way into high office and created a new aristocracy. By the beginning of the first century BC, the important plebian families dominated public life and only a few patrician lines remained significant. Success tended to reinforce itself, for it brought high office and distinguished commands in war, which in turn brought glory and great wealth and helped to win election to further offices for the individual and his descendants.[3]

There were some three hundred senators, members of the permanent council where affairs of state were discussed. Magistrates, including consuls and praetors, were senators and spent far more of their political career as a member of the Senate than they did in office, although their former rank mattered because it determined their status within the Senate, which in turn dictated how often their opinion was sought in debates and the weight it was given. With only two consulships each year, simple arithmetic ensured that the vast majority of senators never held this prestigious post. A man with a consul or consuls among his ancestors was a *nobilis* (or noble), and the distinction greatly increased his own chances of winning the post, but the value of the status faded over time. The most recent consulship held by anyone in Sulla's family had been in the early third century BC, too long ago to sway any voter. Since then, the family do not appear to have had much success even with lesser magistracies and steadily dropped to the fringes of public life.

By aristocratic standards, Sulla was poor and obscure. Instead of a grand house in one of the prestigious areas of Rome—best of all on the lower slopes of the Palatine Hill close to the Forum—in his youth Sulla lived in an apartment in a moderately shabby block of flats. Later in life he boasted of his good luck, taking the nickname Felix or 'lucky'. One of the earliest examples was when he inherited substantial sums, some from his stepmother and the rest from a wealthy lover. This gave him the funds to embark on a political career, albeit when perhaps a few years older than usual. In 107 BC he became quaestor, one of twelve of these most junior magistrates. First and foremost financial officials, quaestors, when sent to assist a provincial governor, undertook a wide range of commands as the only other elected official in the province. Sulla went to Africa, where the consul Caius Marius was waging war against Jugurtha, king of Numidia. Another ruler, up until now an ally of Jugurtha, agreed to switch sides and hand over the Numidian king as a prisoner, and Sulla was sent on this mission, which he managed successfully, bringing the war to an end. This was a great coup and another example of both his talent and luck. A few years later, Sulla served as a senior subordinate in the bitter campaigns which finally ended the threat posed to Italy by the migrating Celtic or Germanic Cimbri and Teutones, who had slaughtered a succession of Roman armies in the last decade.[4]

Sulla's record was decent, but plenty of other ambitious senators could boast of such achievements and had far better connections. He tried and failed to win one of the six posts as praetor, probably for 98 BC, the first year when he was old enough to be eligible. He succeeded twelve months later and was allocated the prestigious post of *praetor urbanus*, responsible for many aspects of running the city of Rome itself. During that year he staged lavish and expensive public entertainments, and promising to do this may well have eased his election. After this, Sulla was sent abroad.[5]

Governing its empire posed considerable problems for the Roman Republic, straining its political and military systems. There were two consuls and six praetors elected each year, giving eight magistrates senior enough in rank to govern a province, which in many cases involved command of an army as well as a civil role. Yet consuls sometimes needed to spend weeks or months legislating in Rome before they set out, while several of the praetors, like Sulla, were allocated responsibilities that kept them in the city for all or most of their year of office. In addition, a small but significant minority of magistrates did not want a province or were too infirm for the task, reducing the pool of available governors even more.[6]

For the Romans, a province (*provincia*) originally meant something like sphere of responsibility: for instance, 'the war with the Jugurtha', which might or might not have an implied or specified geographical component. Only gradually did it acquire a stricter association with a specific region as the republic established direct rule over territory outside Italy. Each year, the Senate decided which provinces were necessary and allocated military and financial resources as they felt appropriate, and then the specific tasks were assigned by lot. By the early third century BC, Rome had expanded to control all of the Italian Peninsula south of the river Po. These conquests had rarely required more than two provinces per year, one for each of the consuls, and at that stage there was only a single praetor, who remained in Rome.

The great struggle with Carthage was fought on a huge scale over an ever-widening theatre of operations. Rome's victory in the First Punic War (264–241 BC) brought the first permanent overseas province in Sicily, and a second praetor was added to provide a governor. Corsica and Sardinia were seized a little later and administered as one province. The Second Punic War (218–201 BC) brought two provinces in the Iberian Peninsula, and the Third Punic War (149–146 BC), one in Africa. At the same time, attempts to rule the former Macedonian kingdom were abandoned and a province of Macedonia created. In addition, the creation of permanent provinces in Cisalpine Gaul (south of the Alps) and Transalpine Gaul (north of the Alps roughly equivalent to modern-day Provence) formalized a trend that had often seen two magistrates and large numbers of troops sent to northern Italy. In 129 BC, the province of Asia was created, bringing the total number of provinces to nine—all more or less based on a well-defined region—and sometimes the total was increased as emergencies occurred elsewhere. As the number of provinces rose, the college of praetors expanded, eventually to six, but did not keep pace with the requirements of Rome's empire.

Since there were more provinces than the supply of annually elected magistrates could meet, the Senate made increasing use of extended commands, so that a consul or praetor appointed to a province remained in command after his year of office as a proconsul or propraetor. This did not require fresh elections and was at the Senate's discretion, so like everything else reflected the influence and concerns of individual members—not least the current magistrates—as much as practical concerns. The same was true when it came to allocating resources to a task. Consuls could expect the most important and prestigious provinces and command in the most important wars, as well as the troops, money, and supplies required for success. Several conflicts occurring at the same time stretched all of these, with praetors getting the lesser tasks and often minimal manpower and funds because that was all that could be spared.[7]

Sulla's provincial command is a good example of this. In the past, the Senate had often adjudicated dynastic squabbles in allied kingdoms by issuing a decree and expecting all those involved to follow it. Sending a governor with an army to enforce the decision was a step taken only with great reluctance and was not a major task compared to other provincial commands. Sulla was sent to govern Asia (or possibly Cilicia, which may have become a regular province around this time) because he was not especially important and neither was the posting. No one expected this to turn into a major war likely to involve substantial forces or the opportunity for fame and glory. Therefore, the Senate gave Sulla little in the way of military strength and expected him to employ contingents supplied by Rome's allies in Asia Minor. This meant that when he paraded his army to impress Orobazus, the majority of soldiers were locally raised. He is very unlikely to have had more than a few thousand troops from Italy, and even these may well have been contingents from the Latin cities rather than actual legionaries (although admittedly these were unlikely to appear very different to all but the most experienced eye). With this mixed bag, Sulla defeated the Cappadocian faction and its Armenian allies opposed to the king approved by the Senate, and with this same predominantly Asian army he did his best to impress the Parthian envoy with the might of Rome.[8]

On only a handful of occasions had a large, genuinely Roman army gone to Asia Minor. Diplomatic contacts between Rome and many of the monarchs and states bordering the eastern Mediterranean began in the third century BC and became even more numerous in the second century, but a permanent presence of any sort came very late in the day. The struggle with Carthage led to war between Rome and Macedon. This shifted the balance of power in Greece, prompting subsequent intervention there by Antiochus III, the Seleucid king whose empire covered a large part of the eastern conquests of Alexander the Great. The Romans defeated his expedition to Greece, but a few years later war resumed and a consul with a large army was sent to Asia Minor, winning victory at the great Battle of Magnesia in 189 BC. By the time the new year's consul arrived to take over this command, peace had been made. Determined to fight a war and win glory somehow or other, this man, Cnaeus Manlius Vulso, tried and failed to provoke

Antiochus to resume hostilities before attacking the three Galatian tribes, descendants of migrants from Gaul who had carved out territories in central Asia Minor from which they preyed on their neighbours. Vulso got his war, his glory, and his rich plunder before leading his legions back home. No province was established, no garrison left behind, and for most of the second century BC Rome's attention was focused on the west.[9]

The Roman Republic was rarely at peace with its neighbours. In northern Italy, Gallic and Ligurian tribes resisted the encroachment of Roman colonists for a generation, so that major armies, and in many years both consuls, went to the region. The Iberian Peninsula required as great or greater commitment for even longer, with several cycles of major conflict. Even when there was no active campaigning, substantial garrisons were maintained in the provinces there throughout the second century BC and beyond. Similarly, once conquered, Cisalpine Gaul had to be defended, and friction with the tribes of the Alps and Illyricum led to raids and counter raids and eventually expansion into Transalpine Gaul. Defeating Macedonia took considerable effort, and when the Senate finally decided to establish a province, this meant another permanent garrison to secure the former kingdom from its traditional enemies among the Balkan peoples.[10]

The Roman Republic had defeated the Carthaginian republic because it had been able and willing to suffer casualties on an appalling scale; more than one hundred thousand Roman and Italian soldiers and a third of the Roman Senate died in the first three seasons of the war against Hannibal. No other ancient community could have coped with losses on this scale and continued to wage war, but the Romans were unique in their capacity for absorbing other peoples. Where other city-states were jealous of their citizenship, the Romans granted it in full to many former enemies in Italy and suggested to the rest that there was a pathway from the lesser rights of Latin or merely allied status to the full franchise. All male citizens registered as owning sufficient property to equip themselves as soldiers were eligible to serve in the legions whenever called upon by the republic, and a similar obligation was part of Latin and allied status. In the field, each Roman legion was accompanied by a similarly sized *ala* of allies from Italy, and sometimes—as was probably the case with Sulla—these non-citizen formations were sent on their own for lesser campaigns. The total military manpower available to the Roman Republic when Hannibal invaded Italy in 218 BC was estimated at more than seven hundred thousand, ten or even twenty times more than the resources of any other city-state and substantially larger than any kingdom. In addition, these soldiers were highly motivated, willing to subject themselves to harsh discipline, and, given competent leadership and time to train, the equals of any opponent.

Rome's military manpower was huge, but it was not unlimited. The growth in the number of garrisons being maintained overseas proved a strain. Nor was it possible to maintain the level of mobilization needed during the Second Punic War permanently. The typical legionary was a farmer with a small farm, serving the state out of a sense of duty and because it was expected of him by the rest of the community. In the old days, when wars were fought in Italy, campaigns were relatively brief interruptions to normal life and the agricultural cycle, and their purpose was obvious. Spending up to a decade stationed somewhere in Spain or chasing Thracian raids away from Macedonian settlements was a different matter, separating a man from his home and family for a long time with little chance of glory or lavish plunder and a significant risk of death at the hands of enemies or from disease. At the same time, decades of victories overseas flooded Italy with slaves and brought staggeringly huge profits to the commanders fortunate enough to lead the major campaigns, as well as to the men who profited from state contracts supporting each war. By the second half of the second century BC, there was a widespread belief that the old class of farmer-soldiers was in decline. Too many men went off with the legions for too long, so that their families struggled to keep the farm going, while there were plenty of rich men able to buy up land from those falling into debt, either turning the occupants into poor tenants or replacing them with slave labourers. Emergencies were one thing, and no one suggested withdrawal from existing provincial commitments, but there was a general reluctance on the part of the Senate to take on permanent responsibility for garrisoning any more territory.[11]

This was the context for Rome's dealings with the eastern Mediterranean. As far as possible, here and elsewhere, the Senate preferred to protect Roman interests through alliances with local leaders and powers rather than by direct military intervention. Allies were seldom hard to find and more often than not sought Roman friendship. There was a long tradition in the Hellenistic world where disputing communities went to a third party and asked them to arbitrate. Usually the third party was stronger, so that it was a mark of respect to approach them and offered a potentially peaceful means of resolving disputes that honoured all those involved. Like any system, it was open to manipulation—such as by influencing the third party—and there was never a guarantee that any decision would be followed. It was very rare for the arbitrator to attempt to impose its ruling by force.[12]

Rome was often asked to act as arbitrator, especially after the creation of the province of Macedonia, since this allowed embassies to approach the governor before travelling all the way to Rome itself. Treaties could only be ratified in Rome after debate in the Senate, but governors could make recommendations, ease the journey and reception given to a request, and deal with lesser matters. The republic was also seen as a prestigious and useful ally because of Roman might, not least because it was better to ally with Rome than to let a neighbouring rival become a closer friend of the Romans, letting them receive Roman support in any dispute. The Hasmonean Jewish kingdom, which emerged from the revolt of the Maccabees against Seleucid rule, reached out for and received Roman recognition at a very early stage in its existence. There was little tangible gain from an alliance with Rome, but there was prestige and the hope that Rome would favour its closest friends in any dispute.

Even though no Roman army was likely to appear in Asia Minor or beyond, Roman envoys—individual senators or, most often, boards of three senators—were far more frequent visitors. They were sent by the Senate—for otherwise no senator was permitted to travel outside Italy save as a governor or a member of his staff—and given a specific task. Sending such a delegation was the next step if simply issuing a ruling had not led to the locals' obeying. If the delegation failed, then the Senate might take direct action, as when Sulla was sent to Cappadocia. Roman senators came to view themselves as at the very least the equal of any king and expected to be received in grand style and with great honour. They did not always show much consideration to their hosts. Buoyed by news of Roman victory in the Third Macedonian War, the leader of a board of three senators sent to Egypt bluntly demanded that the Seleucid king and his invading army withdraw. When the surprised Seleucid hesitated, the Roman used his staff to draw a circle around the king and told him to make up his mind before he stepped outside the ring. The king backed down and retreated to his own kingdom rather than risk angering Rome. By comparison, Sulla's arrangement of chairs was mild.[13]

The Romans could be blunt, even brutal in their diplomacy, but it is a profound mistake to see them as the dominant force in the affairs of the Near East or to forget that only hindsight makes their eventual expansion into the area seem in any way inevitable. Their envoys were occasional visitors, and most were far more moderate in their behaviour. One former consul was murdered without provoking any reprisals, and while this was an extreme case, the Senate often had plenty of other matters to consider apart from foreign affairs—let alone dealings with just one area—and usually defined Roman interests vaguely. The states and kings of the eastern Mediterranean understood this well, so that Rome's view was rarely more than a minor concern in planning and taking action. Even when the Romans decided against a ruler, there was a decent chance they would never bother to check whether their decision was implemented and might well come to accept an alternative over time.[14]

Competition between the major states and kingdoms of the eastern Mediterranean went on throughout the era. Few kings were safe from assassination or coups, while any doubts about succession tended to spawn rival claimants. Whenever strong enough, leaders were eager to expand their own power and territory, often by backing one of the rivals in a power struggle within a neighbouring kingdom. Sometimes this extended to direct military support, although more often it was a matter of money and covert aid. Rome, preoccupied with more immediate concerns, rarely responded swiftly and might not even respond at all. All major states and leaders in the region were allied with the Roman Republic, but this allegiance did not mean that they could not fight each other or that the Romans were bound to intervene—or even likely to do so.

This changed only a little with the creation of the Asian province, which in itself came as a surprise to everyone, including the Romans. In 133 BC, King Attalus III of Pergamum died and bequeathed his kingdom to Rome. The king was young and had not yet produced an heir, but his death was wholly unexpected and the clause in his will may well have been temporary and intended to deter anyone from murdering him, since taking his place was likely to be made more complicated by Roman involvement. Had he lived on and fathered a son, he might have altered the terms, something unlikely to irritate the Romans as long as he and his successors continued to be loyal allies. In the event, he died, and the Senate was faced with a problem, which was swiftly complicated when an ambitious young magistrate named Tiberius Gracchus proposed using the wealth of the kingdom to fund his controversial programme of land redistribution. Tempers flared and a mob of other senators, including Gracchus's cousin, clubbed him and a number of his supporters to death.[15]

A power vacuum was never likely to endure long in the fiercely competitive environment of Asia Minor—or for that matter anywhere in the ancient world—and while Rome's elite turned inwards, a popular leader emerged in Pergamum and was soon rallying support from the wider area. Rome's allies were asked to deal with him and failed. In 131 BC, a consul finally went out with an army, only to be defeated and killed. One of the next year's consuls did better, although it took several more years of campaigning to destroy the rising altogether. Substantial parts of the former kingdom were ceded to Cappadocia and Pontus, leaving only a small rump to become the directly governed Roman province, which was expected to manage without a significant garrison.[16]

The destruction of Carthage and Corinth in 146 BC had pro-claimed Roman dominance throughout the Greek world, and hindsight tells us that Rome's power would continue to grow and that the empire would endure for a very long time. Yet an outside observer of Rome in the early first century BC would have been unlikely to predict all of this. The defeat and death of a consul in Asia was part of a wider pattern of battlefield disasters and wars won only after great effort. The series of defeats at the hands of the migrating Cimbri and Teutones inflicted losses on a scale not seen since Hannibal's day, made worse when around the same time another army was massacred by the Thracians. The Romans re-sorted to extraordinary measures as the migrating tribes appeared poised to invade Italy, ordering a human sacrifice for the last time in their history and electing Marius, the victor over Jugurtha, to five successive consulships between 104 and 100 BC. This broke all precedent and was especially surprising since Marius was a new man, the first of his family to become a senator. What he lacked in ancestry he made up for with a proven—and much trumpeted—record of military competence, so that voters wanted him to lead the war against the tribes. He lived up to their expectations, crush-ing the migrants in two battles.[17]

A decade later, a widespread sense among the Italian allies that they no longer were treated sufficiently well by Rome prompted a revolt known as the Social War (from *socii* or allies), and once again defeats were common and the losses appalling. Both sides were as frightened as they were determined, and since both fought with the same tactics, weapons, and ferocity, battles tended to turn into costly slogging matches. The Romans won, as much by the rapid granting of full citizenship to the loyal allies and to rebels once they capitulated as by fighting. Marius, by now in his late six-ties, took the field once more and, if less aggressive and active than in the past, continued his habit of winning.[18]

The Social War was good for Sulla. On his return from the east, perhaps in 92 or 91 BC, he was charged with corruption during his governorship and, although this did not come to a full trial, the ac-cusation damaged his prestige. Celebration of his role in Numidia all those years before helped raise his profile again while angering

Marius. It was unlikely to have been enough to give him a chance of winning the consulship against better-connected opponents. Then he was given a command as a pro-magistrate in the Social War and did exceptionally well. Late in 89 BC he won election as consul for the next year. By this time, war had broken out in Asia Minor against King Mithridates VI of Pontus, who had routed the locally raised armies sent against him. Freed from the dire threat posed by the Social War, the Senate decided to send a consul to Asia to deal with the king, and Sulla was allotted the task.[19] Within less than a decade, he was due to return to the east, this time with a strong army of six legions.*

Marius was jealous. Historians are trained to look past personal emotions in reconstructing the past, but what followed began with personal rivalry. His own career had broken many of the rules of public life and was a symptom of the wider strain on a political system once admired by the Greeks for its remarkable stability. The mob violence that had seen senators bludgeoned to death in 133 BC was repeated on a far larger and more organized scale in 121 BC and again in 100 BC, in the last case encouraged and then suppressed by Marius as consul. Now Marius arranged for a vote in the popular assembly to strip the command from Sulla and transfer it to himself as a pro-magistrate. This was legal, in the sense that the assembly could legislate on any matter, but it threw traditional conventions out the window with no justification other than Marius's ambition.

Sulla refused to accept the decision and went to the army he had already formed for the Asian war. He found that almost all the officers and men resented the change, suspecting that Marius would want to raise his own legions to take to the probably highly lucrative struggle against Pontus. For the first time in history, a Roman consul led Roman legions against the city of Rome, killing anyone who stood in their path. Marius and many of his

---

*After the Social War, virtually all Italians became Roman citizens. One consequence was the disappearance of the ala, the legion-size formation composed of allies. Instead, all Italians were formed into legions. In the past, a standard consular army consisted of two legions and two alae. Now it consisted of four legions. Sulla's army was unusually large at six legions.

supporters fled, while others were executed. After a while, Sulla left for the east, but the killing did not stop. Within a year Marius returned, and Rome was stormed for a second time, with the fighting and atrocities even more bloody. The old man died within days of assuming a seventh consulship, but once again the violence continued. Leading senators fought for power, and some prepared to defeat Sulla when—or if—he returned. Rome's republic appeared to be on the brink of self-destruction.[20]

2

KING OF KINGS

247–C.70 BC

As the leaders of the Roman Republic began waging war against each other, it is doubtful that anyone in Parthia followed events closely. Rome was still a long way away, a potential rather than a major concern, and its interests had not yet directly interfered with those of Parthia. More importantly, by one of those strange coincidences of history, at almost the same time the Parthians were also divided among themselves, as rival claimants for the throne fought for power. Political violence, coups, and civil wars plagued many communities in the ancient world, not least the city-states of Greece and more recently the kingdoms of Asia Minor—hence the bequest of King Attalus and Sulla's mission to Cappadocia. Rome had been unusual, and much admired by Greek observers, for its centuries of internal stability. Up until this point, the Parthians also appear to have avoided the power struggles so common in other kingdoms. Inevitably, while we can trace the Roman Republic's descent into chaos, our sources do not provide the details of how and why stability in Parthia broke down.

There is much that remains mysterious about the Parthians and their history, so that any survey of their origins and rise raises far more questions than it can answer. The region named Parthia

(Parthava) existed long before the people the Greeks and Romans—
and subsequent history—knew as the Parthians appeared. It was
a northern satrapy of the Achaemenid Persian empire from the
sixth century BC onwards, a region of cities and organized cultivation of the land. Parthians answered the call of Achaemenid kings
to invade Greece in 480 BC and to defend against the onslaught
of Alexander's Macedonians in the 330s, but these were troops
raised from the established population of the area; the Parthians
we know had yet to appear.[1]

In barely a decade, Alexander the Great overthrew Achaemenid
Persia, creating a vast empire stretching from Macedonia to what
is now Pakistan. He was about to embark on an Arabian campaign when he fell ill and died at Babylon, only a few weeks before
his thirty-third birthday in 323 BC. There was no obvious heir,
and after acrimonious debate, a compromise was found naming
his brother, until now considered mentally incapable of a public
role, as joint king along with the child being carried by one of
Alexander's wives. Although the baby was born healthy—and,
most conveniently, a boy—neither he nor his uncle were ever
more than figureheads as senior Macedonian officers fought for
power. Alexander's 'funeral games', as they were dubbed, lasted
for decades and were marked by murder, execution, treachery, and
warfare on a vast scale.

Alexander's empire convulsed and eventually fragmented, and
the three biggest Successor dynasties to emerge were the Antigonids
in Macedonia, the Ptolemies in Egypt, and the Seleucids in Syria
and the east, each line named after its founder. While it is doubtful that the entire empire could have remained united even if
Alexander had lived longer and left a capable heir, the dream of
one great realm persisted. Each dynasty presented itself as the true
heirs to Alexander, who had ruled as king of Macedon and by
right of conquest. Even if the dynasties' heartlands remained essentially stable for generations, the desire to take more of the old
empire remained strong. In that sense, the funeral games ended
only with the demise of all the kingdoms and were simply waged
more sporadically and with lesser resources as time passed and the
successor kingdoms decayed.

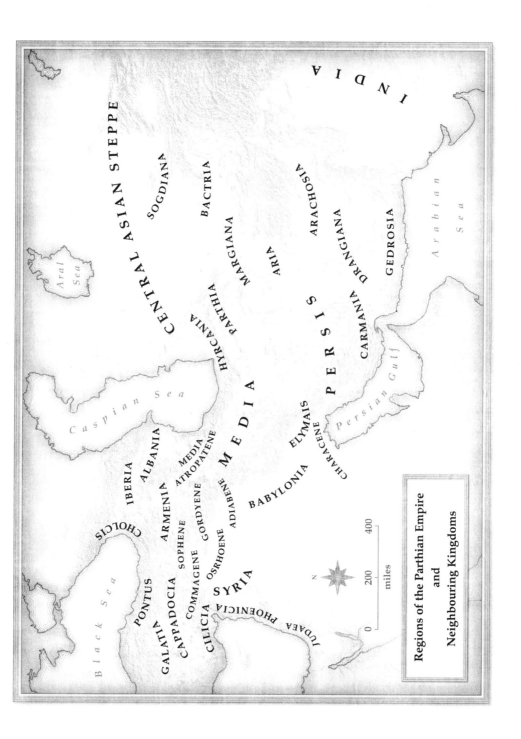

INDIA

CENTRAL ASIAN STEPPE

SOGDIANA

BACTRIA

MARGIANA

ARACHOSIA

Aral
Sea

ARIA

DRANGIANA

PARTHIA

HYRCANIA

GEDROSIA

CARMANIA

Arabian
Sea

PERSIS

Caspian Sea

MEDIA

IBERIA

ALBANIA

MEDIA
ATROPATENE

ELYMAIS

Persian Gulf

ARMENIA

CHOLCIS

SOPHENE

GORDYENE

CHARACENE

COMMAGENE

OSRHOENE

ADIABENE

BABYLONIA

PONTUS

GALATIA

CAPPADOCIA

CILICIA

SYRIA

Black Sea

JUDAEA PHOENICIA

N

0   200   400

miles

Regions of the Parthian Empire
and
Neighbouring Kingdoms

45

At their strongest, the Seleucids ruled from the Mediterranean coast of Syria all the way to the parts of India reached by Alexander. They struggled to control Anatolia (in modern Turkey)—where other kingdoms rose and fell and no single state dominated permanently—but long maintained an interest in and some influence on what happened there. Seleucus I was the only one of Alexander's senior officers not to repudiate the Persian wife he had been given at the mass marriage arranged by the conqueror in 324 BC, and he later named several cities Apamea in her memory. This—and his service in Alexander's conquering army—was Seleucus's only connection to the lands that he ruled. Like Ptolemy in Egypt, Seleucus seized by force the territory that he turned into a kingdom, building on Alexander's original—and still recent—conquest.

None of these lands were strangers to empire. Alexander defeated the Persians, who were themselves the most recent in a series of dynasties and empires to rise and fall, ruling for a while, sometimes centuries, over great swathes of this broad area. The Persians had overthrown the Medes, and before them came Babylonians, Assyrians, and others. Even deeper than empire lay a tradition of civilization: of walled cities, strong leaders, organized farming, laws, writing, and record keeping. In the fertile crescent of the Euphrates and Tigris—as in the Nile valley, the Yellow River in China, and on the Indus—before the end of the fourth millennium BC communities had organized to irrigate the land by diverting water from the great rivers. The result was a far greater yield, which in turn encouraged prosperity and population growth, coupled with a desire to protect this bounty from predators from outside the community. None of this was to happen in Europe to anything like the same degree or scale until much, much later. Alexander lived closer in time to us than he did to these earliest civilizations, but in many of the lands he conquered, there were communities living and farming just as they had done for many, many centuries. In Babylon, temple cults recorded astrological observations and significant events reaching back many generations, and other groups such as the Jewish community preserved their own sense of identity and history. Civilization and central authority were deeply rooted in many parts of Asia in a way that was simply not the case in Europe.

Successful empires all began with military might and often with dynamic leaders, whether Cyrus for the Persians or Philip and Alexander for the Macedonians. Conquest was often brutal; at times the Assyrians appeared to relish savagery in their war making. By their nature all of these empires were aggressive and subsequently ruled their subjects through fear. Imperial expansion did not always involve great waves of population movement, and sometimes the conquerors were never more than a small minority of the population within their empires. Alexander settled some tens of thousands of colonists, most of them former Macedonian or Greek soldiers, in his new empire. There were already some Greeks in the region, and more arrived under the Successor dynasties, but added together these still amounted to a tiny fraction of the population, and they were largely concentrated in overtly Greek cities founded or refounded by Alexander or one of the Seleucids. The overwhelming majority of the people within the Seleucid empire were descendants of the indigenous peoples, just as they were in Ptolemaic Egypt and the kingdoms of Asia Minor, and languages, cults, and traditions were deeply entrenched.

Communications were slow in the ancient world, with news and orders travelling only as fast as a horse could gallop or, where feasible, a ship could sail. Government officials, let alone the king and his court or an army of any size, moved much slower than this. The Achaemenid Persian kings ruled more territory than any of the earlier empires, and sheer distance limited the capacity of central authority to govern. This meant a compromise between the king himself—who spent most of his time at one of several royal cities, such as Persepolis in Persis or Susa in Media—and his representatives in each district. The most important of these were satraps appointed to control, govern, and defend each region, backed by local dynasties and other regional elites, including the leaders, priests, and magistrates in cities. The lines between these various groups were often blurred and their behaviour similar. On the whole, all of them did what the king required most of the time, although refusal was possible, as was outright rebellion. Publicly, most of all in grand ceremonies at Persepolis, representatives came from all over the empire to show submission and bring tribute to the great king. Practically, leaders and communities enjoyed a good deal of local autonomy, their traditions were respected, and the demands of central government were light. When all these conditions applied, any resentment of rule by a foreign dynasty was far less likely to boil over into rebellion.

Alexander had to rely on essentially the same system as he overran Persia because he was in even less of a position to impose his own administration at all levels. He, too, appointed satraps, and while most were Macedonians or Greeks, quite a few were Persians or from the aristocracy of the region. Local dynasties and leaders and the nobility in general were allowed to transfer their loyalty to him, as long as they did it in a timely manner and with suitable respect. A fragmentary cuneiform tablet from a Babylonian temple says a good deal about the attitude of one local elite. In early autumn 331 BC, it describes Darius III of Persia as 'the king of the world'. Without apparent emotion, it recounts Darius's defeat at Gaugamela and the desertion of most of his army. Then, a little later, 'Alexander, the king of the world, entered Babylon.' The identity, even nationality, of the king was far less important than the respect he showed to local traditions and rights and the scale of his demands. As long as the former was sufficient and the latter not unbearable, then fear of his military might normally deterred any thoughts of open resistance. This is not to pretend that conquest was not often traumatic for the occupied communities. Some formal structures, most of all the Zoroastrian ritual and belief centred around the Achaemenid great king, were not—and could not be—transferred to a new, foreign monarch. Macedonian and Greek ideas of religion, power, and the public symbols of both were different. This meant that some priesthoods, temple cults, and groups associated with them fared badly under the new regime, but there were not enough of them to provoke active military and political resistance.[2]

The Seleucids adopted the same approach to ruling their kingdom. Greeks and Macedonians—a distinction increasingly cultural rather than ethnic—were privileged, as were the cities where most lived, but they only owned a small fraction of the land. In most areas, day-to-day life continued as it had always done, communities following their own customs, speaking their own language, following their own laws, and worshipping their own gods. Commands occasionally came from the Seleucid king—demands for tax or tribute more often—and petitions could be taken to him. Plenty of local leaders joined the new regime, and this required a good knowledge of Greek, for this was the language of the court and administration, just as the Persians had employed Aramaic as the lingua franca for their empire. The king needed the collaboration of regional leaders to maintain control, just like the Persians and indeed most empires in the ancient world.[3]

One change was a question of focus. Seleucus I founded Seleucia on the Tigris, a Greek city not far from Babylon, to be his capital, but the ongoing competition with the other Successor states tended to draw attention west towards rivals in Egypt, Asia Minor, and Macedonia itself. Later, the effective capital of the Seleucid empire moved to Antioch in Syria, close to the Mediterranean shore and another overtly Greek city in Asia. In time, Seleucia, Antioch, and Alexandria in Egypt (or next to Egypt, as it was known and considered separate from the wider country) grew in size to dwarf Athens or any of the cities of old Greece, with populations numbering several hundred thousand. Each was highly cosmopolitan but remained militantly Greek in appearance, law, and official ritual.

A high proportion of revolts against the central authority of the Achaemenid kings had come from regions on the fringes of their empire. Whether this was because the populations and especially the elites in these areas felt neglected, preserved their separate identity more strongly, feared the king's might less, or simply felt that independence would offer greater opportunities is difficult to say. This did mean that trying to rule an Asian empire from close to the Mediterranean coast was always likely to be difficult. Territory in India was lost early on, in part through a deal between Seleucus I and Chandragupta, the charismatic creator of an empire in central and northern India. The Seleucids withdrew voluntarily from the lands around the Indus and in return were supplied with war elephants to employ in the funeral games. Even so, the dream of reviving Alexander's entire empire remained and extended to the eastern territories even when those in the west attracted more attention. Kings sent armies and commanders to the east or went in person, but no ruler could be everywhere at once, nor were resources of manpower, supplies, and money sufficient to garrison the entire empire in any strength. Ultimately, the ability and wider fortunes of individual Seleucid kings determined how well the empire held together at any time.

In the west, fortunes swayed back and forth in the first half of the third century BC. Seleucus I (305–281 BC) more than held his own, and although his older son Antiochus I (281–261 BC) had to face down a series of rebellions to secure his own position, he did much to consolidate the empire carved out by his father. His son, Antiochus II (261–246 BC), did less well, and his divorce from his first wife to marry a Ptolemaic princess and cement an alliance with Egypt provoked a violent power struggle after his death. Around this time, Andragoras, the satrap of Parthia, and Diodotus, the satrap of Bactria to the east (in the area of modern Afghanistan), both declared themselves as independent rulers of their own kingdoms. Andragoras may have been a local man, while Diodotus was of Greek or Macedonian extraction, but in neither case was this in any sense a nationalist or Asian rebellion against Hellenic rule. Both men minted coins inscribed in Greek and used similar symbols of power to the Seleucids, and there is no sign of sudden cultural change.[4]

In 248 or 247 BC to the north of the province of Parthia, beyond the territory claimed by the Seleucids in what is today Turkmenistan southeast of the Caspian Sea, a leader took power among a people known to outsiders as the Parni. They were nomadic, one of many groups living on the great steppes stretching from eastern Europe to China whose lives were poorly understood by the settled peoples of the Classical world. Transient herdsmen and hunters, the Parni had a relationship with farming communities that varied from friendly trade and exchange to predation. Greek and Roman sources believed that the Parni were part of a broader people called the Dahae, who, like the neighbouring Saka, had fought for Darius against Alexander, against Alexander in their own right, and also for Alexander in his later campaigns. Their harsh lifestyle made them superb riders and archers and formidable warriors, whether as raiders, allies, or mercenaries. Groups, tribes, and rival leaders within them often fought each other for power and to dominate the best grazing land or give better access to trade and resources. To the Greeks and Romans, they and all the other nomadic peoples of the steppes were often known as Scythians because of their similar lifestyle—another example of outsiders grouping a large and diverse population together as a single ethnic group.

In the 280s BC, bands of Parni had attacked the province of Margiana (in modern Turkmenistan) until they were driven out by a Seleucid general. Such onslaughts were nothing new, and it is difficult to determine what prompted such bursts of aggression from the nomads, although it is possible that Alexander's and Seleucus I's strengthening of the Bactrian frontier disrupted the established relationship between farmers and herdsmen in the wider region, increasing tension. Yet the rulers did not create the problem, and attacks from steppe nomads had long been a potential or real threat in this region and were to remain so throughout our period and beyond.[5]

The new leader of the Parni was called Arsaces ('Ruling over Heroes') and was to give his name to the dynasty of monarchs subsequently known as the Parthians. Less clear is whether this was at first a personal name or if it was a title from the very start, but every legitimate Parthian king was called Arsaces on his coins and most official documents, which often makes these very hard to date and associate with specific monarchs. Almost nothing is known of the first Arsaces, and a tradition telling of two brothers is almost certainly a later embellishment. There was just one war-leader who managed to unite a substantial number of tribesmen under his leadership and ultimately create a new kingdom. He may have been one of the Parni or perhaps an aristocrat from Bactria. Both may be true, since intermarriage between leaders was a common form of diplomacy. He probably led raids and may also have served as a mercenary or ally in the initial struggles to set up the Bactrian and Parthian kingdoms.[6]

In 239 or 238 BC, Arsaces led his army into Parthia and overthrew Andragoras. Soon he had also taken Hyrcania to the west (on the shores of the Caspian Sea and partly in modern Georgia), carving out a new realm for himself. This was not a plundering raid or the spread of a nomadic band intent on imposing its way of life, but the emergence of a kingdom and a ruling dynasty similar to what had happened in Bactria and was happening in Pergamum and other parts of Asia Minor at much the same time. Just as other strong leaders did, Arsaces and his Parni seized power, but they remained only a small, if privileged, minority among the existing population. Within a generation or so they had adopted the local language of Parthia and were fostering the repair and expansion of irrigation systems and the growth of cities. Whether or not Arsaces had ever truly lived the nomadic lifestyle, he made the city of Nisa his capital. Coins minted there and elsewhere conformed to the standard of the drachma and bore his name in Greek characters, sometimes with the title *autokrator* (or autocrat/ruler). Sometimes clean-shaven, Arsaces was always shown wearing a soft, perhaps felt hat of nomadic or 'Scythian' style, and on the reverse of the coin a seated figure holds out—but does not use—a bow. While there are stylistic echoes of pre-Macedonian coins minted by Persian sa-traps, there is no sign of a sharp break with recent tradition or any hint of a local rejection, or wider 'Asian' resentment, of Greco-Macedonian occupation. This was a leader backed by military force who wanted to be acceptable to all elements and communities within the existing population. Parthia and Hyrcania were not a natural state or kingdom; they were simply what Arsaces had managed to take.[7]

Although Arsaces had overthrown a rebel satrap, this did not make him any more legitimate in the eyes of the Seleucid kings. Seleucus II (246–225 BC)—son of Antiochus II's first, subsequently repudiated, wife—had to fight for the throne against a half-brother backed by the Ptolemies before he could restore control over the kingdom. A rebellion in Babylonia was put down, but he had less success confronting Parthia and Bactria. Details are obscure, and it is possible that Arsaces defeated Seleucus II and may even have held him prisoner for a short time.

What is clear is that Parthia and Bactria remained independent of the Seleucids and that Seleucus II turned to deal with problems

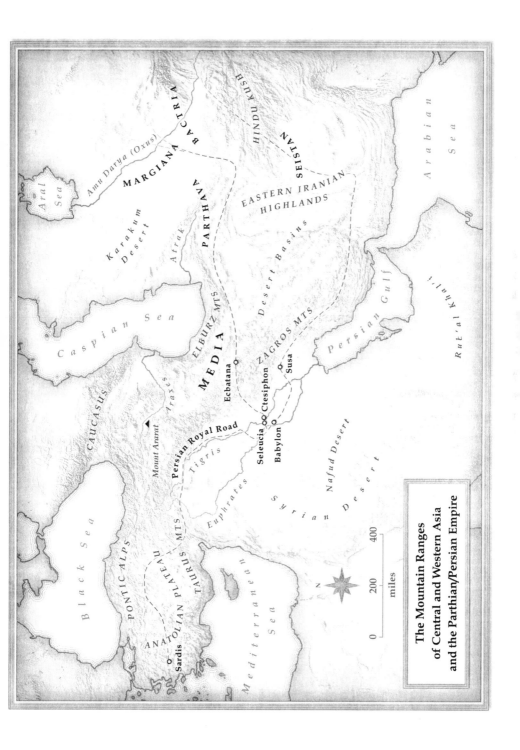

The Mountain Ranges
of Central and Western Asia
and the Parthian/Persian Empire

Aral
Sea

Amu Darya (Oxus)

MARGIANA

BACTRIA

HINDUKUSH

SEISTAN

Karakum
Desert

Atrak

PARTHAVA

EASTERN IRANIAN
HIGHLANDS

Desert Basins

Caspian Sea

ELBURZ MTS

MEDIA

ZAGROS MTS

Persian Gulf

Arabian
Sea

Rut'al Khali

CAUCASUS

Araxes

Ecbatana

Ctesiphon

Susa

Mount Ararat

Seleucia

Babylon

Persian Royal Road

Tigris

Nafud Desert

Black Sea

PONTIC ALPS

TAURUS MTS

Euphrates

Syrian   Desert

ANATOLIAN PLATEAU

Sardis

Mediterranean
Sea

N

0   200   400

miles

in the western part of his empire. His oldest son lasted just three years before he was murdered, but the younger brother, Antiochus III (223–187 BC, the same man who fought against the Romans), did better when he attacked Arsaces's son Arsaces II. This time the Seleucids won several victories over Parthian armies and forced the kings of Parthia and Bactria to seek peace. Neither king was deposed, and instead they accepted subordinate status as vassals of Antiochus. Arsaces II appears also to have lost most of Hyrcania and some territory in Parthia itself. He was weakened, but he had survived the severe test of facing the main might of the Seleucid empire.[8]

Antiochus was soon called away to deal with other problems in his great empire, and it is fair to say that Arsaces II and Parthia was a lesser concern to him than threats elsewhere. Antiochus was known in his lifetime as 'the great' (*megas*), and although he suffered battlefield defeats at the hands of the Ptolemies and the Romans, he had done much to reassert central control and return the Seleucid empire to something like the pinnacle of its power, recovering Syria, restoring his dominance throughout the central and eastern satrapies, and even pushing into India. Yet in the ancient world, power seldom went unchallenged for long, and late in his reign he prepared for another eastern expedition, but he died in 187 BC and the campaign was abandoned.

His son Seleucus IV (187–175 BC) was more concerned with Asia Minor and the west, giving the Arsacids a chance to recover and pursue an ever more independent policy. The same was true of other dynasts. The Bactrian kingdom lost ground to another part-Greek, part-Indian dynasty that had emerged as a rival and had little time left to challenge Parthia. The next Seleucid king, Antiochus IV (175–164 BC), was also drawn towards the Mediterranean; he was the one forced to withdraw from Egypt by Roman ambassadors. He was also the king whose drive to Hellenize the population of Judaea prompted the rebellion of the Maccabees, which in turn created the Hasmonean dynasty of Jewish kings. This might not have happened had Antiochus IV been able to devote all his resources to suppressing the revolt, but like other Seleucid kings he often had to act as a firefighter, rushing from one part of his empire to another. A major campaign to restore order in the central and eastern satrapies was planned and once again abandoned when the king unexpectedly died before it could be launched in 164 BC.

Arsacid Parthia was already expanding by this time, which was one of the reasons Antiochus IV had grown concerned about the region. The lost territories of Parthia and Hyrcania were once again brought under Parthian control. About 165 or 164 BC, Mithradates I became the Arsacid king (and like all the others is simply Arsaces on his coins). He exploited the weakening power of Bactria to seize Margiana and Aria (in what is now western Afghanistan). Later, while the Seleucids were busy with a series of civil wars, he took wealthy Media despite stubborn resistance by local Seleucid commanders.

The Parthians were not the only ones expanding at the expense of the Seleucids. The king of Elymais (Elam of the Bible, situated around the Persian Gulf) rebelled and made his territory independent. Another leader may have appeared in Babylonia. Opposition to the Seleucids did not create any fellow feeling between these new regimes. Mithradates I of Parthia seized Babylonia, probably defeating both the Seleucid forces and those of the local leader. The king of Elymais also attacked Babylonia, and the Parthians managed to defeat his army. Mithradates I then attacked Elymais itself but failed to conquer it.[9]

This massive expansion by the Arsacid king presented a serious challenge to the Seleucids. They continued to be divided, and Demetrius II (145–138, 129–126 BC), grandson of Seleucus IV, was faced with a rival claimant to the throne. In spite of this direct challenge to his rule, Demetrius II decided that he could not accept the damage to his prestige caused by the success of Mithradates I of Parthia, as well as the serious loss of revenue from the seizure of so much territory. After more than a year of preparation, he advanced into Babylonia in 138 BC. Mithradates I was elsewhere and the defence in the hands of his brother, who seems to have acted as his governor for this area and Media. The choice proved good, for the Seleucids were badly defeated and Demetrius II taken prisoner and paraded through the major cities of the area, riding on a donkey. After this humiliation, Demetrius II was not otherwise mistreated and was settled in comfortable confinement and given one of Mithradates's daughters as a bride. The Romans had also held hostages from the Seleucid royal family, including Demetrius's father and namesake, who had managed to escape and return to claim the throne. The son was less successful in his escape attempts and better supervised. Once, Demetrius II almost reached the edge of Parthian territory before he was caught, admonished, and sent back to his wife and the several children they had had together.[10]

Mithradates I fell ill not long after his defeat of Demetrius II, although he seems to have lingered for several years before finally succumbing. There is little sense that this weakened his kingdom, for the transition towards his successor did not tear the regime apart. There was more conflict with regional rivals, as Elymais once again attacked Babylonia, only to be driven out and this time conquered by the Parthians. More and more territory was added to the Arsacid kingdom, whether directly or through submission of other kings. By this time the descendants of the original Parni horsemen were a very small minority. They may still have formed an important, probably the most important, component of the army and dominated the court and some senior positions. As landlords they presided over a great deal of territory, especially in the less urbanized eastern regions of the empire, but the kingdom came to an accommodation with the elites and wider population in each region. These, and especially the nobility, accepted Arsacid rule because it meant that they were no longer subject to Parthian attack. The Parthians would protect them from others and not only impose bearable demands but even let them share in some of the benefits of belonging to a strong kingdom.

In little more than two decades, Mithradates I had made the Arsacids the dominant power in the central and eastern districts of what had been the Seleucid empire through a combination of near constant successful warfare and the ability to retain control of conquered territory. The imagery on his coins developed along the way. Early issues have much in common with those of his predecessors, but after a while he is always shown as heavily bearded, like the kings and satraps of Achaemenid Persia and within a broader and deeper eastern tradition. Over time the soft cap of the nomad altered in shape, combining with and then being replaced

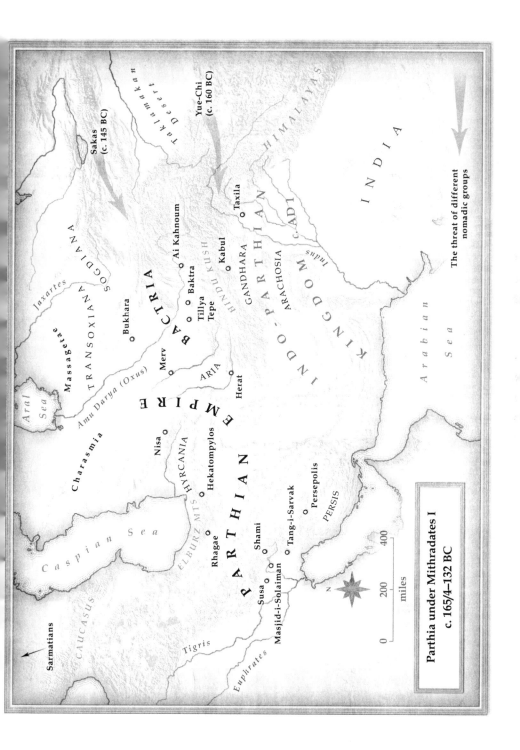

Sakas
(c. 145 BC)

Taklamakan Desert

Yue-Chi
(c. 160 BC)

HIMALAYAS

INDIA

Taxila

Jaxartes

SOGDIANA

Massagetae

TRANSOXIANA

Bukhara

B A C T R I A

Ai Kahnoum

Baktra

Tillya Tepe

HINDU KUSH

Kabul

GANDHARA

ARACHOSIA

Indus

I N D O - P A R T H I A N

Merv

K I N G D O M c. AD 1

Aral Sea

Amu Darya (Oxus)

Charasmia

ARIA

Herat

E M P I R E

Arabian Sea

Nisa

HYRCANIA

Hekatompylos

P A R T H I A N

ELBURZ MTS

Caspian Sea

Rhagae

Shami

Tang-i-Sarvak

Persepolis

PERSIS

Susa

Masjid-i-Solaiman

CAUCASUS

Sarmatians

Tigris

Euphrates

The threat of different nomadic groups

N

0   200   400

miles

**Parthia under Mithradates I
c. 165/4–132 BC**

by a diadem with Hellenistic associations. Coins 'of Arsaces' become 'of King Arsaces', and then 'of the Great King Arsaces', and sometimes 'whose father is a god'. On coins struck at Seleucia on the Tigris, he is also 'the Philhellene', and instead of the seated archer there were designs more familiar to Greek eyes, such as a seated Zeus bearing symbols of power. The archer could be conflated with Apollo, and instead of a chair, in some issues he sat on the omphalos, the navel of the world which Greek tradition claimed lay at the god's shrine in Delphi. Mithradates I did not impose a new uniform culture on the territories he gained and instead did his best to appeal to all the different communities, convincing them of his might and relative benevolence, so that accepting his rule was more appealing than resisting it.[11]

Yet ultimately, success rested on military supremacy, just as it had for Alexander and the Successors, for the empires of earlier centuries, and for all the other kingdoms emerging and competing to survive and grow. With Demetrius II a prisoner, his younger brother Antiochus VII (138–129 BC) had become king. After defeating a long-standing challenger for the throne and curbing the growth of the Hasmonean kingdom and other threats in the west, he mustered what was probably the biggest army seen for generations and headed east to deal with the Parthians. Many of the men were mercenaries, and all of them served for pay and had to be fed and supplied, so this was extraordinarily costly, especially for a king who had lost so much territory and the revenue that went with it. Antiochus VII's campaign shows just how critical a threat the Parthians had become and just how severe the loss of so much territory and so much prestige was to the Seleucid monarchy. Rome had never taken hostage a reigning king, but the Parthians had done just that.

In 130 BC, Antiochus VII marched into Mesopotamia. Babylon and Seleucia were retaken, and the advance pressed on into Media and Elymais. Three major battles were fought, and the Parthians were defeated in all of them. Campaigning then largely halted for the winter months as was the custom. The Arsacid king, Phraates II, reeling from this onslaught, sought to hire mercenaries from the steppe nomads and also decided to send Demetrius II back to

Syria. While Antiochus VII had proclaimed his intention of rescuing his brother, his designs for him were unclear, and the generally fractious family relationships among the Seleucids suggested that the older brother was more rival than ally.

Over the winter of 130–129 BC, the situation changed. Seleucid troops had been dispersed to billets in many of the reoccupied cities, partly as garrisons and even more so to make it easier to feed them. Too many troops misbehaved and too many demands were made on the communities, a situation encouraged by poor choice of governors and other officers. Seleucia and Babylon had welcomed the attackers, just as the latter had welcomed Alexander the Great. Yet while Alexander had made sure that the occupation was not too bitter, Antiochus VII failed to do this. The result was a nostalgia for gentler Parthian rule and a simultaneous, co-ordinated rebellion in many cities. Antiochus VII responded to the news by gathering all the forces close to him and rushing back to assist his beleaguered garrisons. En route, Phraates II caught him. The Seleucid king boldly attacked, only to find himself surrounded and isolated when the bulk of his troops failed to support him through a mix of inertia, caution, and in some cases treachery. Antiochus VII died fighting, and the Parthians who had captured one Seleucid king now killed a second while also capturing a son and daughter of the dead man. There was no public humiliation, and Antiochus's corpse was cremated with appropriate ceremony. Phraates II kept the son as hostage and married the daughter but was too late repenting his decision to release Demetrius II, who this time made good his escape and reestablished himself as king. That was unfortunate, for he understandably showed no love for the Parthians, but it did not matter too much, as the cost of the failed expedition rendered the Seleucids incapable of serious hostility in the immediate future.[12]

Phraates II already had other problems. The northern frontier with the steppe nomads was as much a concern for the Arsacids as it had been for the Seleucids and Persians. Warfare among the bands and tribes drove some groups who had fared badly in these struggles to seek new pastures elsewhere, while ambitious men who managed to unite several groups needed ongoing glory and plunder to maintain and expand their position. One safety valve for all regimes was to hire warriors and bands to fight in their armies, but even so there was always the danger that someone else would do what Arsaces I and the Parni had done. A contingent of Saka hired for the war against Antiochus VII arrived too late to take part, and their desire to be rewarded and Phraates II's mis-handling of the situation turned into a new war. Phraates II made use of prisoners from the Seleucid army, especially the mercenaries, to bolster his own forces as he moved against the Saka and other bands eager to exploit his apparent weakness. The former Seleucid troops proved unreliable, and Phraates II was badly defeated, dy-ing soon afterwards from an arrow wound. Perception of weakness was always likely to attract renewed attacks. This came from no-mads and also from other regional powers, notably the kingdom of Characene on the Arabian Gulf. A few years after Phraates II's death, another Arsacid king was killed fighting against yet another band of nomadic raiders.[13]

Kingdoms rose and fell quickly in this era, with sudden shifts as battles were won or lost and as gifted leaders died or emerged. Chance played a big role, and the Arsacids were very fortunate to be navigated through the rest of the second century BC by Mithradates II, who became king around 121 BC. Like his earlier namesake, most of his reign was spent in warfare, as the Parthians steadily re-gained territories they had overrun and then lost in recent decades. Sources are poor, especially for the years spent fighting against the nomadic tribes and other leaders of that region, but he not only recovered all lost regions but significantly expanded his empire. In time he began to advance in the west, turning Armenia into a sub-ordinate ally around 112 or 111 BC. Around the same time, the title 'king of kings' began to appear on his coins. This was a revival from the Achaemenid era, although it is unclear how far this was a deliberate invocation and, if so, how the memory of that earlier dy-nasty was preserved. More directly, it staked a claim for the Arsacid monarch to be the lord of a great empire, with other regional dy-nasts as his vassals.[14]

It was Mithradates II of Parthia who sent Orobazus to meet Sulla and subsequently, according to Plutarch, had the ambassador executed. When the king of Armenia died, Mithradates II released his son, who had spent most of his youth at the Parthian court as a hostage, to return home to Armenia and succeed his father as Tigranes II. The Seleucids were once again busy fighting among themselves over the succession, but in the late 90s BC, for the first time a rival member of the Arsacid family declared himself against the ruling king. This surviving son of Mithradates I rebelled and soon gained control of much of the eastern part of the Parthian empire. Mithradates II tried and failed to suppress the rebellion and died around 91 BC. Soon afterwards, or perhaps before this happened, another ruler, Gotarzes, who was probably Mithradates II's son and appears to have held high office during his father's lifetime, perhaps as satrap of satraps, emerged and reigned in Babylonia.[15]

In the decades that followed, there was often more than one claimant to the Arsacid throne, and it is not surprising that there was no repeat of the rapid expansion seen under Mithradates II. Permanently weakened by the loss of so much territory, and the revenue, manpower, and resources drawn from it, the Seleucids were also in no position to strike back. The Parthians killed another Seleucid king, then intervened in the ongoing power struggle, killing one claimant and sending troops to install another on the throne. In the east, the Bactrian kingdom crumbled, beset by nomadic tribes seeking new opportunities and split by internal divisions. At the opposite end of the Parthian empire, Tigranes II of Armenia, who had begun his reign by ceding lands to the Arsacids, exploited their weakness to take back this territory and more. He also expanded his realm into Syria, deporting people from cities captured there and elsewhere to populate his newly founded capital of Tigranocerta. Tigranes II styled himself king of kings, a title that no Arsacid any longer dared to claim. Armenia was growing quickly, just as the Parthians and others had expanded quickly when led under a capable and lucky leader. Tigranes II's closest rival was Mithridates VI of Pontus, and for the moment it suited these two leaders not to challenge each other, not least because Rome was seen as a greater threat.

Parthia—like Rome—would come through these first outbreaks of civil war. There were setbacks and times of weakness, but no rival state was able to inflict serious and permanent damage on either empire. In the case of Parthia, this was testament to the success of its early kings, most of all Mithradates II, who had managed to grab more of the old Seleucid empire than any other contemporary ruler. The Arsacids succeeded at first because they led highly effective and well-motivated armies, winning far more battles—and especially far more campaigns—than they lost. Then they absorbed communities, convincing enough of the local elites to collaborate with and join them. Once again, in both respects, the same could be said of the Romans, even if the details of how they did these things were different. Both states were strong enough not only to survive an era of frequent civil wars but even to thrive and continue to expand. This was the background for their first confrontation.

3

WARS AND RUMOURS OF WARS

70–54 BC

Mᴏʀᴇ ᴛʜᴀɴ ᴛᴡᴏ ᴅᴇᴄᴀᴅᴇs ᴘᴀssᴇᴅ ʙᴇᴛᴡᴇᴇɴ ᴛʜᴇ ᴍᴇᴇᴛɪɴɢ ᴏꜰ Sulla and Orobazus and the next diplomatic contact between Rome and Parthia. Ancient states did not maintain permanent embassies in each other's capitals or feel the need to be in constant touch, and instead sent ambassadors only when there was something that they wished to say. Preoccupied with bitter internal strife and with enemies and friends closer to their territory, neither the Romans nor Parthians chose to seek out the other.

The appalling devastation caused by Rome's first civil war can sometimes be played down compared to the later conflicts leading to Julius Caesar's dictatorship and ultimately the emergence of the first emperor, Caesar Augustus. Yet Sulla marched on Rome in 88 ʙᴄ when the last embers of the Social War had not yet been stamped out. Caius Marius and his allies stormed the city a year later, and Sulla returned to take it again in 82 ʙᴄ. The years in between were spent preparing for or actively waging civil war. In 78 ʙᴄ, one of the consuls tried to use his army to do what Sulla had done and had to be defeated in battle. From 73 to 71 ʙᴄ, Spartacus led his army of escaped slaves up and down the Italian Peninsula, routing one Roman army after another. This meant that large swathes of Italy were ravaged by war for the best part of twenty years. Civil war also spilled over into Sicily, North Africa, and most of Spain, where the charismatic Sertorius, an ally of Marius, fought against Sulla's supporters until he was assassinated in 72 BC. In the end he lost, but, as far as he was concerned, he was throughout his career a Roman magistrate serving the true republic.

Levels of savagery rapidly escalated over the course of the conflict. When Sulla took Rome for the second time and had himself made dictator, he ordered mass executions of captured enemy soldiers and introduced the proscriptions—death lists posted in the Forum. In constitutional terms, the regime he created before retiring to private life appeared highly conservative, emphasizing the role of the Senate in state affairs and regulating political careers, but this veiled the revolutionary nature of what he had done. The Senate he left to lead the republic was wholly his creation, doubled in size from three hundred to some six hundred members, consisting of men who had backed him in the civil war, many owing their elevation solely to him, as well as the few who had managed to remain neutral during the conflict. Sulla's opponents were dead or in exile, and the survivors and all their descendants were barred from public life.

Yet apart from having fought together against Sulla's enemies, his former partisans had little else to unite them. The aristocratic urge to compete was as strong as ever, with the prospect of violence now a very real threat. Ambitious men knew that their rivals might resort to riot, murder, or open war and had to consider whether it was better for them to strike first. The 60s and 50s BC have an air of stability about them, partly because the only open outbreak of civil war in 63–62 BC was ended by a single battle, and even more because the orator Cicero's voluminous correspondence provides so much day-to-day detail that the periods of calm between each crisis appear longer. Even so, Cicero had served during the Social War, kept a low enough profile to survive the subsequent civil war, first made his name in the courts attacking one of Sulla's henchmen for abuse of power, and claimed as his greatest triumph the defeat of Catiline's coup in 63 BC. Like most prominent senators of his generation, Cicero was to die a violent death at the hands of Roman enemies. Throughout his adult life the republic was unstable, prone to outbursts of shocking violence and sudden changes of power. For other kingdoms and states, this meant that Rome's republic was as unpredictable as it was dangerous.

In the eastern Mediterranean, the Romans had long felt concern about the growing power of Mithridates VI of Pontus (a kingdom in what is now eastern Turkey). Sulla's intervention in Cappadocia was meant to keep an eye on the king, while a little earlier Marius had met Mithridates VI and advised him to keep quiet and do whatever Rome asked. Yet in 89 BC a Roman proconsul, backed by other officials in Asia Minor, had provoked war with Pontus, relying primarily on local levies of troops. Mithridates VI responded promptly and efficiently, routing the invaders and overrunning the Asian province, where he ordered communities to massacre the Romans and Italians living among them. Tens of thousands died, although a few cities either let the Romans go or protected them. When Sulla at long last went east to confront Mithridates VI, he first met the Pontic armies in Greece, for they had crossed into Europe. The Romans won and after a hard struggle took back not just Greece but the lost territory in Asia Minor. Sulla was satisfied by the Pontic king's willingness to submit and accept loss of land and power. This was partly because he was eager to return to Italy and face his opponents there but also because turning an enemy into a suitably humble and subordinate ally was an entirely acceptable conclusion to a Roman war.[1]

The peace did not last, although the first attempt by an ambitious governor to restart the conflict was swiftly brought to an end. By 74 BC, the Senate considered Mithridates VI's behaviour to be once again that of an enemy, and one of the consuls, Lucius Licinius Lucullus, was given a wide-ranging command to deal with him. Lucullus had been Sulla's quaestor in 88 BC and was the only one of his senior officers to join him in the first march on Rome. He then served in the war against Mithridates VI and the subsequent civil war, his loyalty to Sulla and his obvious ability easing his rise. Lucullus's campaigns in the east mixed strategic aggression with very careful tactical judgement. In the first big confrontation with Mithridates VI, the Romans fortified themselves in a strong position and avoided battle, all the while cutting the Pontic army off from sources of supply—an approach nicknamed 'kicking the enemy in the guts'. Faced with starvation, Mithridates VI's army began to retreat, at which point Lucullus launched a merciless pursuit and inflicted huge casualties on the enemy. Next the Roman army marched into Pontus and again defeated the king, this time in his homeland.[2]

Mithridates VI fled to Armenia, where Tigranes II at first gave him a wary reception until eventually deciding to ally with him against the Romans. The two kings approached the Arsacid monarch, Phraates III, in the hope of persuading the Parthians to join them in the fight. At almost the same time, Lucullus also sent his envoy to the Arsacid court in the hope of enlisting aid for his own operations. For Phraates III, Armenia was a former subordinate ally now turned into a dangerous rival. He did not wish to see Tigranes II grow even stronger. Nor did he wish someone else to gain from Armenia's defeat, nor, still worse, to provoke Armenia only to see it win. Both sides in the war had to content themselves with Parthian neutrality, as Phraates III walked a careful line of promising friendship without getting directly involved.[3]

Lucullus's numerically small army confronted the Armenians near Tigranocerta around October 69 BC. Tigranes II dismissed them as 'too many for an embassy and too few for an army' and then watched as the Romans launched a rapid, highly coordinated attack and defeated his own host in detail. Neither king was willing to give in, and the war continued. Lucullus had achieved a great deal but had also already held his provincial command for an exceptionally long period. Some Romans had grown impatient for an end to the war, while some senators envied him the opportunity for winning glory. The influential companies who bought state contracts to collect taxes in the provinces resented Lucullus's restrictions on their activities, no matter that these were fair and also pragmatic, since otherwise there was a high risk of pushing an ever more desperate population to rebellion. Calls to bring Lucullus home and replace him with another commander gathered momentum. First, he was stripped of Asia and Cilicia, in

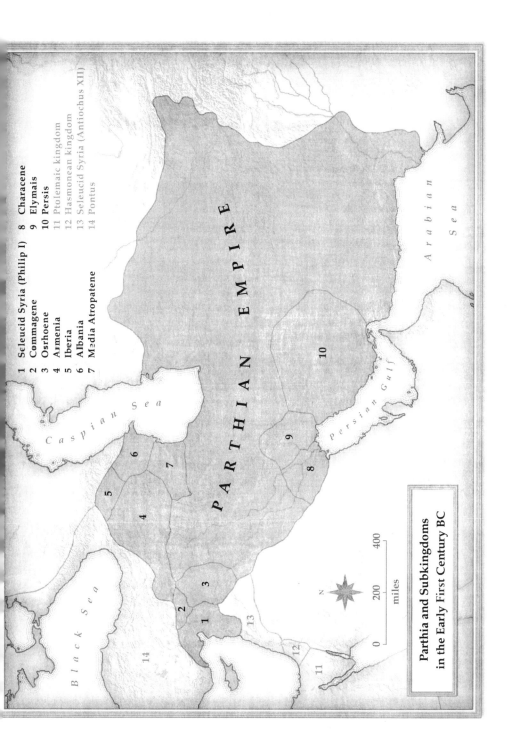

1 Seleucid Syria (Philip I)   8 Characene
2 Commagene   9 Elymais
3 Osrhoene   10 Persis
4 Armenia   11 Ptolemaic kingdom
5 Iberia   12 Hasmonean kingdom
6 Albania   13 Seleucid Syria (Antiochus XII)
7 Media Atropatene   14 Pontus

PARTHIAN EMPIRE

Caspian Sea

Black Sea

Arabian Sea

Persian Gulf

N

0   200   400
      miles

Parthia and Subkingdoms
in the Early First Century BC

the past separate provinces which had been added to his exceptional command. This markedly reduced his forces and his ability
to support them in the field, which in turn made it harder to complete the war against Armenia and Pontus. In 67 BC, Mithridates
VI outwitted and virtually destroyed a Roman army at Zela, and
although Lucullus was not present or responsible for the disaster,
it fuelled the sense that all his claims of imminent victory were
hollow. A year later, a tribune of the plebs introduced a law stripping Lucullus of his remaining command and replacing him with
Rome's most popular general, Cnaeus Pompeius Magnus—or as
we know him, Pompey the Great.

Pompey's career had begun in the civil war and broken almost
every law and convention of public life. Aged nineteen, he had
raised and funded three legions from his own estates, joining Sulla
and leading his 'private' army with great panache. Sulla dubbed
him 'the great'—possibly ironically—but preferred to employ
him rather than risk his defecting to the other side. The leaders of
the Senate thought the same way, using him to defeat the coup
in 78 BC and then sending him to Spain to deal with Sertorius. In
70 BC, aged just thirty-six, Pompey was elected consul and at long
last was enrolled in the Senate. In 67 BC, another tribune voted
Pompey an extraordinary command to deal with piracy all around
the Mediterranean. Given immense authority and matching resources, Pompey did the job quickly and very well, for throughout
his career he displayed a great talent for organization. The next
year he replaced Lucullus, and once again Pompey was granted
men, material, and powers far greater than his predecessor. He
could also be sure that no one would try to replace him before
the job was done, allowing him to take his time and prepare thoroughly for each operation.[4]

In just over four years Pompey ended the wars and reshaped the
Near East, spending as much or more time in diplomacy and administration as he did actually fighting. Mithridates VI of Pontus,
who had expanded his kingdom and then struggled with Rome
for so long, was finally beaten and ordered a bodyguard to kill
him, having famously dosed himself with antidotes for so long that
he proved immune to poison. He was about fifty-seven. Pontus

survived as a kingdom, albeit with substantial loss of territory, and was ruled by one of Mithridates VI's sons, who pledged himself to be a loyal ally of Rome. Tigranes II did even better, surrendering to Pompey in a suitably humble manner and being confirmed as king of an Armenia that was still an important regional power, even if extensive districts were stripped away from his control. In contrast, the last Seleucid king was deposed, Pompey having judged that he was too weak and irrelevant to be useful to Rome's interests. In Judaea, Pompey intervened in a dispute between rival leaders, besieging one of them in the Temple in Jerusalem and eventually storming it. He confirmed as high priest and effective ruler Hyrcanus, who was felt to be more reliable from a Roman point of view. Wherever possible, local leaders were left in place, so that allied kingdoms made up more of the region than directly ruled Roman provinces. Even so, Pompey expanded Asia and Cilicia and created a new province of Syria.[5]

In the relatively recent past, the Parthians had intervened in Syria. Under Mithradates II they had taken Mesopotamia, Gordyene, Osrhoene, and Adiabene, only to lose some or all of this territory and parts of Media as Tigranes II of Armenia expanded. In the future, all of this area would once again come under Arsacid rule, but to understand the relationship between Rome and Parthia in these years it is essential to remember that this was not the case at the time. Lucullus marched through territory that had been—and later would again be—Parthian but was either dominated by Armenia or more or less independent at the time. Similarly, Pompey sent columns led by subordinates over a wide area. In one case, Parthian forces, lately arrived to reclaim the region, withdrew before the Roman advance, most likely without any fighting occurring.[6]

Pompey, like Lucullus, negotiated with Phraates III with the aim of securing aid to defeat Armenia and Pontus or at the very least of assuring his neutrality. Again the outcome was similar, with the Parthian king doing his best to appease both sides without getting sucked into the war. However, he did choose to intervene when Tigranes II of Armenia's son and namesake fled to him and asked for backing to take Armenia from his father. Phraates III led an invasion with the exiled prince but soon tired of the siege of Artaxata, the second city of the kingdom, and returned home, although he left some of his troops behind to support the younger Tigranes. Tigranes II then attacked and routed his son, who fled to Pompey, collaborated with the Romans, and for a short time was made ruler of Sophene, another of the neighbouring districts, until a failure to obey Roman instructions led to his arrest. Phraates III, who had married one of his daughters to the prince, asked for his release, only to be told that the younger Tigranes was closer kin to his father than to his father-in-law.[7]

Allegiances in this area were fluid, with few well-established borders for the lands of any of the rival kings, so that some of Pompey's arrangements were always likely to prove temporary. Yet in most respects Pompey's settlement of the wider region proved highly successful, with some of his regulations enforced for centuries. That does not mean that putting it all together was simple or quick. Rulers with an interest lobbied hard and manoeuvred as best they could to shape events to their own benefit. Phraates III came to meet with Pompey, as did many other monarchs. The Roman treated the Parthian ruler with respect and addressed him as 'king', but not as 'king of kings'. An earlier request by Parthian envoys to establish the Euphrates as the boundary between Roman and Parthian lands was not granted, and instead Pompey would impose whatever boundaries were just. Gordyene, where the Parthians had been ejected by Roman troops, was allocated to Tigranes II of Armenia. The decision on other disputed territories was placed in the hands of three Roman commissioners, who appear to have been fairly even-handed. Phraates III regained some of the territory formerly seized by Tigranes II and was not forced to give up anything else that he actually held.[8]

Plutarch claims that Lucullus had planned an invasion of Parthia, only to be prevented when his army refused to obey him, and it is hard to know whether there is any truth in the story and, if there is, then just what was planned. Pompey is said to have discarded more quickly any thoughts of leading an army against the Parthians. He had already achieved plenty of glory from his activities in the east, as well as acquired a huge amount of wealth and even more political influence and prestige among the kings and communities of the area. As importantly, Phraates III had shown respect for Rome and Pompey as the republic's representative. Throughout these initial contacts between the Arsacids and a succession of Roman governors, there is no sign that either side was eager for confrontation. As with Sulla, the evidence is unclear whether formal treaties were made between the two sides. At the very least, recognition of Phraates III—and quite possibly earlier of Mithradates II—as 'friends' of the Roman people seem likely, since establishing such relationships with powers lying beyond Roman provinces was common practice. Only a very late source claims that there was a formal treaty with stronger terms than this, and academic opinion remains divided on the question of whether such an alliance was actually formed.[9]

Around 58 or 57 BC, Phraates III was murdered in a conspiracy led by two of his sons, Mithradates III and Orodes II, who promptly turned on each other. Initially successful, Mithradates III lost support among the noble families and fled to Syria and the current Roman governor, Aulus Gabinius. As tribune, Gabinius had introduced the law granting command against the pirates to Pompey and then served him as a senior subordinate in that campaign and subsequently in the east. He was the first former consul to be sent to the province of Syria, the previous governors all having been ex-praetors, and he secured a three-year command with considerable resources and a sizeable army. Probably his target was expected by the Senate to be the Arabian kingdom with its capital at Petra, which had been raiding widely into allied territory. Instead, Gabinius welcomed Mithradates III and prepared to reinstall the exiled monarch. However, before the invasion started, he was approached by Ptolemy XII (the father of the famous Cleopatra), who had been thrown out of his own kingdom in favour of his eldest daughter and had spent the last few years trying to get the Romans to restore him. Pompey wrote in support, encouraged by promises of immense sums of money as payment. Gabinius was given similar incentives, so turned around and went to Egypt instead of Parthia. Ptolemy XII was restored and his eldest daughter executed (and allegedly the teenage Cleopatra saw a dashing Mark Antony in charge of Gabinius's cavalry and fell in love). On his return to Rome, Gabinius was prosecuted for his illegal intervention and was acquitted in the first trial and condemned in the second. His cause was not helped because, like Lucullus, he had restrained Roman tax-collecting companies and investors from abusing their association with the imperial power.[10]

Early in 54 BC, a new governor arrived in Syria who was not simply a former consul, but one of the most influential men in Rome. Marcus Licinius Crassus's father and brother had both been executed by Marius's allies in the civil war, while he fled to Spain. There, he is supposed to have spent time hiding in a cave with just a few companions, a client of his family providing meals and two slave girls for the young man's other requirements. Later he joined Sulla and fought with great distinction in the battle to capture Rome. Crassus did very well from the confiscation of property from proscribed victims of Sulla's purge, being given or buying cheaply many houses and blocks of apartments in the city itself. It was the beginning of a property empire, which he steadily expanded. Crassus bought and trained slave engineers and craftsmen to maintain and improve his buildings, and he also formed a fire brigade, something Rome lacked. With narrow streets and poorly built, high apartments ignoring the rarely enforced planning laws, the city was prone to frequent, devastating fires. Crassus worked out that he could wait for a fire to start, snap up as bargains buildings in its path, then bring in his men to make a fire break and afterwards repair or rebuild on the cleared land.

Crassus was rich, and he boasted that no man who could not raise and pay for his own legion could ever call himself rich. Yet he had a reputation for personal thrift and extreme care when it came to expenditure on those in his employ. He did not hoard his money for the sake of it but was very free with loans, especially to other senators, and often was generous in the terms of these, because the political influence to be gained was far more important to him than the money itself. Similarly, he was very active and extremely diligent as a legal advocate, especially in defence, and won far more cases than he lost, once again putting plenty of people in his debt. Crassus had immense influence. No one dared to attack him in the courts or push criticism too far in the Senate. That did not mean that he could always get what he wanted. Crassus had tried and failed to arrange the restoration of Ptolemy XII years before Gabinius had succeeded.[11]

Built into the Roman system was the belief that competition between great men—and the more numerous middle-ranking aristocrats—would help to counterbalance their influence. Crassus had wealth and had put large numbers of senators under obligation to him in one way or another, but this stopped far short of control of the republic. He had fought well in the civil war, and in 72 BC he had been given command against Spartacus after so many others had failed. Crassus organized well, planned carefully, and was ruthless in the execution of his strategy. Within a year Spartacus was dead; his armies captured, killed, or dispersed; and five thousand of his men had been crucified all along the Appian Way from Rome to Capua as a horrific warning. This had been a difficult task well performed but lacked the glory of defeating a foreign enemy, and once the danger was past, most Romans were eager to forget the whole grim and frightening affair. Crassus was awarded an ovation, a lesser honour than the prized triumph, and when it came to military glory he was overshadowed by the victors in foreign wars, such as Lucullus and, most of all, Pompey.[12]

Pompey and Crassus never really got on, even though both had fought for Sulla. Crassus was some ten years older and lacked the dash and charisma of the younger man. Pompey had actually raised an army at his own expense—Crassus's supposed definition of a rich man—and had inherited a fortune rather than having to make one, leaving him free to concentrate on military adventures, which in turn brought plenty of profit from plunder. In 71 BC, Pompey returned to Italy from Spain and managed to catch and destroy a fragment of the slave army, allowing him to boast that he had completed the war. Like a lot of highly successful commanders, Pompey had a petty streak that made it difficult for him to accept that others might win victories without him. The two men buried their differences to become consuls for 70 BC, although cooperation was limited, and for much of the next decade they did their best to ignore each other, apart from occasional rivalry.

However, by 60 BC both men were frustrated. Pompey had failed to get approval for the settlement he had made in the east, demanding that the Senate rule on the entire programme rather than each provision. This was partly a question of his prestige, but also, because the scheme was carefully balanced, it might easily unravel if picked apart. Crassus had heavy—if officially invisible—investments in tax-collecting companies and investors in the region, and he wanted the relaxation of some unwise commitments the former had made to the state. Having tried and failed to secure these objectives for several years, the two wealthiest and most influential men in Rome came to a private arrangement with Caius Julius Caesar, a member of an old but recently unimportant aristocratic family. Crassus had backed Caesar in the past by covering his huge debts, but we do not know who initiated or played the key role in forming a political alliance between the three men.* With Crassus and Pompey as backers, Caesar was elected as consul for 59 BC and proceeded to pass laws ratifying the eastern settlement and giving relief to Crassus's allies. Opposition was shouted down, intimidated by organized crowds, pelted with dung, or manhandled. Caesar secured an exceptional five-year proconsular command in an expanded Gallic province, where he would fight the long series of aggressive campaigns described with calm, plain, and skilfully partisan words in his famous *Commentaries*.

Caesar went to Gaul in 58 BC, and after his departure Pompey and Crassus got on less well, while public life became ever more volatile and violent and there were moves to recall Caesar from his provincial command. In 56 BC, the two older men travelled to Luca in Cisalpine Gaul for a series of meetings renewing their cooperation.** Crassus and Pompey were elected to a second consulship, and among other things passed a law extending Caesar's command for five more years. Pompey was to follow his consulship

---

*Scholars refer to this as the first triumvirate, and this is convenient even though it implies an official and open arrangement where none existed. Probably the most visible mark of the arrangement was the marriage of Caesar's daughter, Julia, to Pompey.

**Caesar could not leave his province without laying down the command, which meant that they had to come to him.

with five years in control of all the Spanish provinces, while Crassus was given a similar command in Syria. The measures gave each of the three allies control of substantial armies and immunity from prosecution for the duration of the command. Caesar was busy winning glory and making himself a very rich man. Pompey already possessed sufficient martial achievements for the present, so planned to stay just outside Rome in a comfortable villa and govern his provinces through subordinates (or legates) on the spot. In contrast, Crassus was eager to head out to Syria and to wage victorious war. Before he left Rome, there was clearly talk of a war against the Parthians, even though the task was not explicitly allotted to him by the Senate.[13]

There is little doubt that Parthia was vulnerable at this time. Disappointed by Gabinius, Mithradates III of Parthia had subsequently returned home without the backing of a Roman army and challenged his brother. Significant factions in Babylonia either welcomed him or were willing to accept his rule for the moment, and he gained control of Seleucia, where coins were minted in his name. Orodes II struck back, but the fact that he did not appear in person may suggest that this conflict spread more widely than our slim records state, requiring him to fight for other parts of his empire. Instead, he sent a senior subordinate to isolate and besiege Seleucia. This was the Surena, head of the Suren, one of the seven most important noble families of the Arsacid empire. (The name was a hereditary title, like that of the chief of a Scottish clan, and we do not know his personal name.) He was in his twenties, tall, handsome even by the standards of the proverbially beautiful peoples of ancient Iran, and charismatic. He was also brave and capable. Seleucia was taken by storm, with the Surena allegedly the first of the attackers up onto the city wall. Mithradates III was arrested and taken to his brother, who promptly had him executed. The coins minted for Mithradates III were overstruck by Orodes II with his own name.

The chronology of this war is as uncertain as many of its details, but it is unlikely to have been over soon enough for news to reach Rome during Crassus's consulship. This means that, like Gabinius, Crassus may have felt that he could intervene in Parthia in support of the 'true' Arsacid king, thus supporting a Roman friend or even ally rather than attacking one. Caesar's *Commentaries* provide ample examples of how an aggressive governor could justify interventions over an ever wider area of Gaul and beyond as in the interest of the republic, because these campaigns protected Rome's interests or those of friendly leaders and communities. While there would always be some critics, most Romans readily accepted such justification for new wars, as long as they were successful. Caesar was said to have written from Gaul to encourage Crassus in his plans for Parthia, and Pompey also appears to have accepted the planned war, even with his knowledge and connections in the area.[14]

Yet not everyone accepted either the dominance of Crassus, Pompey, and Caesar or their plans. There was far more violence during Pompey and Crassus's election campaign and during their year of office than there had been a few years earlier when Caesar was consul. On one occasion, Pompey came home from a riotous public meeting spattered with someone else's blood, a sight that so shocked his wife Julia that she miscarried. Money, influence, and brute force (including the use of furloughed centurions and perhaps soldiers from Caesar's legions) meant that they won, but not without a fight. One of the ten tribunes of the plebs declared that the omens for Crassus's departure and planned war were bad. The technique was not a new one. Caesar's consular colleague Bibulus had spent much of the year barricaded in his house, repeatedly announcing that he had seen signs of divine displeasure, which meant that public business ought to cease and in turn that anything Caesar did was invalid. The tribune tried to use his veto (an ancient privilege of the tribunate) to forbid Crassus from leaving the city but was prevented by his colleagues. However, there were clearly sufficient people who sympathized with his view to make Crassus fear for disruptions when he left. Pompey, still overwhelmingly a favourite with the crowd, accompanied Crassus, and his presence was sufficient to prevent a mass protest. Yet, according to Plutarch, the tribune was unrelenting. Rushing ahead of the procession to the gateway, he had prepared a brazier and flung incense onto the burning coals. Then he cursed Crassus, employing archaic verses and language and invoking half-forgotten and sinister deities and powers.[15]

Cicero, who was in Rome at the time, does not mention this. He later cited the observation of bad omens and notes that these were subsequently vindicated when Crassus lost his war and his life. In a letter written in November 55 BC, very soon after the departure, Cicero wryly commented that 'our Crassus made a less dignified start in his military cloak than Lucius Paullus, his equal in age and a second consulship.' (Paullus had won the Third Macedonian War in his second term as consul.) Crassus was a 'worthless man' (*O hominem nequam*), but this may have been a judgement on his character rather than his ambitions. Crassus was about sixty but came across as older, well past the prime of life. Plutarch claims that he was already making ridiculous, almost childish boasts about his forthcoming success, and perhaps this is what Cicero had in mind. It was sixteen years since Crassus had led his army against the slaves, and until his second consulship he had shown no inclination for further military service. He had never governed a province or fought a foreign war, and it was late in life to begin doing such things. His motives for this are impossible to know, although it is hard to avoid the conclusion that, at least in part, he was jealous of Pompey and Caesar and their military reputations.[16]

Mithradates III may well already have been dead by the time that Crassus reached Syria, but it is possible that he was not. If the civil war between Mithradates III and Orodes II was still ongoing, then none of our sources for Crassus's operations mention it, which does not mean that it did not play a role in his thinking. Even if the war was over, at the very least it suggested an opportunity to intervene while the Arsacid king was weak, so that he might be willing to submit and leaders in some regions could be willing to abandon him and ally with Rome. Ideas can readily become entrenched in people's minds, even when circumstances have changed.[17]

Unfortunately, our sources say little of the context of Crassus's war, explaining events instead through reference to his character. For Plutarch, whose account is by far the most detailed, this was an almost inevitable disaster, with an unjustified war motivated solely by the ambition of a man who had always been greedy for money but was now greedy for glory as well, and too old to achieve what he wanted. A sense of tragedy pervades the narrative and makes it hard to understand what was truly intended. Folly there may well have been, but things are unlikely to have been as simple as Plutarch suggests. Crassus had been voted considerable resources and granted leeway and powers beyond those normally permitted a proconsul. These included the right to operate outside his province and make war at his own discretion, and he would surely have produced a justification for any action he took.[18]

Whatever the motives and aims, a major war could not be prepared quickly. Crassus was permitted an army of seven legions, and while these may have included two already stationed in Syria, the rest had to be raised from scratch. This was no easy task when Caesar was on the lookout for men to feed his Gallic campaigns, Pompey was recruiting for his Spanish command, and other governors in other provinces were also in need of soldiers. Campaigns in the east were widely believed to be lucrative and less dangerous than wars elsewhere, which helped, and Crassus managed to find some experienced officers, including some who had served with Pompey in the wider region. The odds are that the majority of eager and talented centurions, tribunes, and other senior officers were already in service elsewhere. Ordinary recruits were also hard to find, especially any with experience, and Crassus was unable to recruit his legions to full strength. There were also losses during the voyage across the Adriatic, when some ships foundered and the soldiers aboard them were drowned. On balance, it is unlikely that Crassus's legions averaged more than four thousand men per unit in the field, and they may have been significantly smaller than this. This gave him some twenty-eight thousand legionaries, to which he added around four thousand light infantry, including some archers, and three thousand cavalry recruited locally. Another one thousand horsemen, led by his younger son, Publius, were sent to him by Caesar. These were Gauls, with perhaps some Germans, and were highly thought of but did not arrive until late in 54 BC.[19]

The Romans did not possess a permanent army in this era. Once each legion was raised, it had to be drilled and trained, and then in turn become accustomed to working with the other components of the army. All this took time and effort, and the sources suggest that Crassus largely delegated the task to his subordinates and instead busied himself with the logistical and financial preparations for war. Operations in his first campaigning season were limited. He bridged the Euphrates, probably at Zeugma, and pushed into Osrhoene. Silaces, the Parthian satrap in charge of the area, engaged him with the forces immediately available and was beaten. This was the first definite military engagement between Romans and Parthians and was a small affair. The whole region had been lost to the Parthians for a generation and only gradually recovered in the aftermath of Pompey's defeat of Armenia. Unsure who would prevail, and not deeply committed to the Arsacid cause, virtually all the cities of the area welcomed the Romans and accepted Roman garrisons. The sole exception was Zenodotia (which cannot be located), where the local tyrant admitted one hundred soldiers and then had them massacred. Crassus besieged the city and captured it, a project which likely took weeks or even months. Then he withdrew the main force to spend the winter in Syria, leaving behind seven thousand infantry and one thousand cavalry to control and protect the communities in the newly occupied area.[20]

Both Plutarch and the early third-century historian Dio Cassius criticized Crassus for not continuing the offensive straightaway, but this was impractical. The winter was spent in preparation, training soldiers and raising funds to pay his troops and buy the supplies and transport they needed. Sources criticize Crassus for greed: he demanded contingents of troops from local allies and then readily accepted the money they offered to be relieved of the responsibility, making it clear that he was more interested in cash than soldiers. He took gold from the Temple in Jerusalem—which Pompey had not done, although he had gone into the holy of holies and thus violated its sanctity. Antiochus III and other Seleucid kings had been criticized for confiscating treasures from sanctuaries to fund campaigns, and this was given as reason for Antiochus III's sudden death and other kings' failures. The list of bad omens surrounding Crassus is long even by the standards of ancient historians and no doubt largely invented after the fact. Greedy or not—and the bar for Roman provincial governors in this era was not high—Crassus had made a reasonable start, creating a base for operations and giving his young soldiers some experience and easy victories.[21]

It is worth remembering that Crassus had immense freedom of action as proconsul of Syria. He was a magistrate of the Roman Republic, and like any other governor operated too far away for the Senate to micromanage his conduct. They had given him instructions, and there were the precedents set by earlier governors to help shape his actions, but on the whole it was up to the man on the spot to decide what to do with the power given to him. If enough senators disapproved of how he chose to use this freedom, then they could vote to replace him, deprive him of military resources, or prosecute him once he returned home. For the moment, Crassus and his allies were confident that their influence would prevent any restrictions being imposed on his behaviour while in his province and ensure that no one was sufficiently unwise as to take him to court on his return.

Rome's elite knew Crassus, understood his status, and were aware that for the moment he was not a man to cross. Yet to Orodes II and his senior advisors, Crassus remained a largely unknown quantity. They did not know how he was likely to act, and earlier contact with the Romans reinforced the sense that each new governor might behave in unexpected ways, while neither side had had much chance to measure each other's military potential. Rome's republican system posed a problem to its neighbours, for individual ambitions and domestic concerns meant that each new governor might act in a radically different way to his predecessors. It was hard for a king of kings to know the Romans and sense how the latest of their many leaders would behave compared to a state led by a monarch. At the same time, Roman governors arrived with little—or in Crassus's case no—personal experience of the region. All this added to the unpredictability of encounters between the two powers during these years.

4

THE BATTLE

53–50 BC

Orodes II did not know what Crassus wanted or how easily he might be brought to terms. The Romans had advanced, intervening in a civil war that was now over. The invaders had made some initial gains and clearly possessed a substantial army, even if it was impossible to judge just how dangerous this might prove. Neither side really understood the other's strength, determination, or true aim, making everything that followed highly unpredictable.

In 53 BC, Crassus prepared for a bolder campaign. His son Publius had brought his Gallic horsemen, substantially increasing his cavalry force. However, expected reinforcement from Armenia came to nothing. King Artavasdes II, son and successor of Tigranes II, had arrived with six thousand fine cavalry and the promise of more but took them back to his own kingdom when he learned that Crassus was unwilling to advance via Armenia. While that route had some attractions, it would have meant a long detour to reach the starting position—something likely to infringe on the authority of the Roman governor of Cilicia—and ignoring the previous year's gains. Instead, Crassus planned to make use of his garrisons in northern Mesopotamia to protect his supply lines.[1]

Before the campaign began, Parthian envoys arrived, pointedly asking the reason for Crassus's attack. Plutarch claims that they told him that if Rome had settled on war with them, then they would resist with all their strength and courage. However, if this was a private expedition unsanctioned by the Senate, then they were willing to take pity on the folly of an old man and permit the soldiers he led to march back home without molestation. Caesar claims that a Germanic war-leader had some knowledge of Roman politics, so it is quite possible that something along these lines was said, although this may also be invention to stress Crassus's sole responsibility for the war. The Parthians did appear willing to negotiate, as they had done in the past, understanding that both sides were inclined to posture and threaten. Orodes II demanded the territory recently occupied by the Romans, but he might have been willing to compromise a little, as his father had done in negotiations with the Romans. Crassus may have seen the Parthians' assertion of strength and confidence as empty, while the Parthian envoys may in turn have expected the Romans to threaten, only to draw back from full-scale war. Neither side had any particular reason to fear the other's military strength, and no doubt each felt confident should it come to war.

Crassus was not about to back down, and he told the ambassadors that he would answer their questions in Seleucia. Forcing Orodes II to submit to Rome would be a proper conclusion for a Roman war. He could then be left to rule, just as Tigranes II had been left to rule Armenia. If Orodes II was unwilling, then experience elsewhere suggested that there would be other candidates for the throne agreeable to taking power with the aid of a foreign army. Permanent occupation was not at all necessary for a Roman victory, and Plutarch's claim that Crassus had earlier talked of outdoing Alexander the Great and pressing on to India may be pure invention. There is certainly no sign that this shaped his plans in 54–53 BC.

Yet the Parthian envoys were not impressed by Crassus's bluster. One held up his right hand, palm open, and gestured towards it. 'Hair will grow here, before you see Seleucia', he told the Roman proconsul, and the meeting ended. The Parthians were far better prepared than they had been the year before. Their empire was large, and there was no permanent standing army at the king's immediate disposal. There were some more or less full-time soldiers in royal service, in garrison, and in the households of satraps and other noblemen. For a major war, the king summoned his nobles, who in turn summoned the lesser nobles and soldiers drawn from the communities under obligation to them. It took time for these contingents to muster, and then more time for them to gather and travel to wherever they were needed. Orodes II had assembled loyal forces for the civil war against his brother. By 53 BC, Mithradates III was defeated and killed, which meant that the king was free to concentrate on the threat posed by the Romans and their allies.[2]

In the campaign that followed, Plutarch never mentions any Parthian infantrymen. Other sources, such as Dio, dismissed Parthian foot soldiers as of poor quality and little more than skirmishers. This exaggerated the situation, and there were occasions, most obviously in the attack on Seleucia or in defence of fortified towns, where infantry, or cavalrymen fighting dismounted, played the key role. However, in field armies it was the cavalry that mattered, and these consisted of two types. The most common—and the one that captured the Romans' imagination as the quintessential Parthian— was the horse-archer. Riding a sturdy mount with good stamina and wielding a powerful recurved composite bow, the horse-archers combined speed with the ability to strike from a distance.* They did not wear armour or encumber the horse with any unnecessary weight and avoided incoming missiles by keeping on the move and making themselves a difficult target. Paradoxically to the Greeks and Romans, who saw martial virtue very much in terms of going toe-to-toe and trading blows with the enemy, the horse-archer could twist round so that he shot at the enemy while galloping away, the famous Parthian shot (often corrupted these days to 'parting shot').

---

* A composite bow meant that it was made from more than one type of wood glued together, providing a stronger mixture of strength and flexibility than a bow shaped from a single piece of wood. Recurved meant that, when unstrung, the two arms of the bow bent forward in the opposite direction, forming a mirror image of the usual C shape.

Horse-archers might charge down a scattered or wavering enemy but saw no virtue in putting themselves at unnecessary risk for the sake of martial display, especially since this reduced the advantage they gained from their bows.[3]

Closer to Greco-Roman ideas of fighting was the cataphract, who did charge home against his foes. The rider did not carry a shield but was heavily protected by a helmet and armour covering the body, arms, and legs. This could be mail or iron or bronze scales, or sometimes of laminate construction. His horse was also armoured—at least for those in the front ranks—with protection for head, neck, and body, sometimes in the form of metallic scales. The principal weapon was the *kontos*, a slim-shafted spear up to twelve feet long and wielded with both hands. If this broke, then the cataphract was equally adept in using a long, slashing sword. In later periods many also carried bows, and from hunting as well as the prestige of this weapon it is likely that most knew how to shoot, but it is unclear whether bows were commonly carried in battle in the first century BC. Fighting with a kontos and shooting a bow each required the use of both hands and demanded very high standards of horsemanship. Stirrups had not yet been invented, but riders were aided by the horned saddle, which seems to have originated among the steppe nomads sometime in the fourth century BC.[4]

In warfare, the steppe origins of the early Parthians seems particularly obvious, but some caution is necessary. The Achaemenid Persians and many early cultures within the wider region had prized horses and horsemanship very highly indeed and made great use of cavalry in war. While some Scythians and other nomads wore heavy armour and may have ridden armoured horses, it is less clear that these men fought en masse. The Persians did use formations of heavily armoured cavalry, while the Seleucids developed and employed cataphracts, so we cannot say whether the Parthian version had as much or more to do with this tradition than the warfare of the steppes. Similarly, archery was of great importance to the Persians, and the symbol of the bow was often associated with the king or his representatives such as satraps.[5]

The Parthians drew on a range of traditions to shape their way of waging war. The dominance and prowess of the horse-archer was far greater for them than the Persians. Another change from both Persian and Seleucid traditions was the degree to which the quality of troops in an army was preferred to their sheer quantity. To fight well as a horse-archer or a cataphract required considerable skill which could only come from long practice. Noblemen and the better-off tended to serve as cataphracts, not least because of the cost of the equipment. Greco-Roman sources saw Parthian society as strictly divided between a small minority of free men, largely the nobility, and the mass of dependents, who were wrongly described as slaves. (Caesar said much the same about contemporary Gallic society, so some of this is simple disdain for 'inferior' foreigners added to the old Greek stereotype of easterners as slave-like.) The 'free' men went everywhere on horseback, but their dependents included men raised and thoroughly trained for war. According to Plutarch, the Surena routinely called upon some ten thousand warriors to follow him to war, including kin, lesser nobles, and dependents. Of these, one thousand fought as cataphracts and the rest as horse-archers.[6]

In 53 BC, Orodes II decided to lead an invasion of Armenia in person—news of this may have encouraged Artavasdes II of Armenia to hurry home once he had decided against accompanying Crassus. The Armenians were a known quantity, their style of fighting and political inclinations better understood than those of the Romans. They were also Crassus's most important local ally and, if ever they joined up with him, would have greatly increased his cavalry strength. Therefore, Orodes II chose to deal with this enemy and sent Surena to face the Romans. No source tells us how large either Parthian army was. Oddly, many scholars mistake Plutarch's comment on the size of Surena's personal entourage to state that he had just ten thousand men with which to face Crassus, even though there is no justification for this. Plutarch also tells us that Silaces, the satrap defeated in 54 BC, was with Surena, and there is no reason to believe that other noblemen and their retainers were not also present. In the past, subordinate commanders had been employed by Arsacid kings to deal with major invasions, for instance when Mithradates I sent his brother to meet Demetrius II. Sending Surena against Crassus was well within the Parthian tradition, and not in any way a token gesture, a delaying force, or the sacrifice of a distinguished nobleman but part of a co-ordinated plan for fighting the war. The chronology is unclear, but it is possible that Artavasdes II of Armenia only left Crassus when he became aware of the Parthian threat to his kingdom or of the actual invasion.[7]

Crassus crossed the Euphrates at Zeugma early in the spring. Once he was across, a storm blew up and wrecked the bridge of boats, as just one of a host of bad omens throughout the campaign. One of his horses jumped into the river and drowned, while the eagle standard of a legion had to be prised out of the ground and another turned back to face away from the enemy. Later, Crassus absent-mindedly appeared in a black cloak, as if in mourning, rather than the deep red cloak of a general. Perhaps Crassus did upset a parade by dismissing the loss of the bridge as unimportant because no one would need it again, which was taken as a sign that all would die rather than an explanation that he planned to retire by a different route. Even practiced orators sometimes make mistakes. There had been skirmishes around some of the garrisoned cities during the winter months, and rumours began to circulate of the ferocious skill of the Parthians. (Once again, there is an echo of an episode in Caesar's *Commentaries*, where stories of the size and strength of Germanic warriors for a time dismayed his legionaries.)[8]

The Romans pushed on, initially planning to follow the direct route towards Seleucia, until scouts spotted the tracks of many horses. There were reports of a Parthian army to the east, beyond Carrhae (Harran of the Old Testament), one of the cities to welcome the Romans in the previous year and a stopping place on one of the other main trade routes through the region. Reasonably enough, Crassus decided to deal with this force. At the very least, this would protect his communications and the cities who had joined him, and better still might offer a battlefield victory to inspire his men and dismay the enemy. Our sources are full of accusations of treachery on the part of local allies, who wilfully misled the naive Crassus and lured him into a trap. While duplicity is possible, there may have been nothing more at work than human error, or the stories were later inventions intended to excuse the subsequent Roman defeat. One tradition was especially favourable to Crassus's quaestor Caius Cassius Longinus (who nine years later with Brutus would lead the conspiracy to murder Julius Caesar).* In this version, time and again Cassius gave sage advice and saw through the professions of loyalty of the traitors, only to be overruled.[9]

Within a week he had passed Carrhae and approached the river Balissus (Balik), which lay somewhere between that city and Ichneae, the next major stopping place on the trade route. This was not desert country—despite the dramatic descriptions in our sources—but arid, rolling grassland. In early June, when the campaign took place, temperatures are in the high nineties Fahrenheit (or midthirties centigrade) in daytime and can go higher. The marching was hard—the track probably unsuitable for so many marching men, let alone the baggage train—and this was still a relatively inexperienced army, not yet accustomed to hard campaigning. The bulk of the garrisons appear to have remained in the cities, so that the field army may have mustered some twenty thousand or so legionaries, four thousand light infantry, and three thousand cavalry (or four thousand if the majority of these were taken back from the garrisons). These figures are rough estimates, and the total may have been larger or even smaller; either way it would have been increased by slaves and other servants and camp followers. The only figures given in our sources are for losses and survivors and are of questionable reliability and at best rounded up. There is a good chance that the Romans outnumbered the force under Surena, perhaps by a substantial margin, but the only certainty is that the Parthians were greatly superior in cavalry.[10]

Reports came that Artavasdes II was fighting Orodes II, but Crassus decided that he was too far away to join the king and that there was no other reason to move closer to Armenia. Instead,

---

*Cassius was probably elected quaestor for 54 BC. Rioting at Rome prevented the elections for the next year from being held until too late in the year for a successor to have reached Crassus's army. This would suggest that he was about thirty-one at the time of the battle.

he pressed on. His scouts bumped into enemy patrols, who killed many of them, but the survivors came back to report that they had seen a very large Parthian army advancing boldly towards them. The Romans deployed into battle line, with cavalry on the flanks, and waited. After a while, Crassus re-formed the army into a great hollow square, twelve cohorts on each side, supported by formations of cavalry. This was a version of the *agmen quadratum* often employed by Roman armies who were unsure from which direction the enemy was likely to attack. There may have been additional reserves, depending on how many cohorts there were in total, and the usual practice was to shelter the baggage train in the centre. Although still cumbersome, this was a far better formation for continuing the advance than the extended line.[11]

There was still no more sign of the enemy, so Crassus pushed on until he reached the Balissus river. Roman commanders were expected to discuss important decisions with their *consilium*, the council of senior officers, before making up their own mind. Some of Crassus's officers suggested camping on the spot, with ready access to water. Marching camps were a well-established feature of Roman warfare and offered some protection from direct assault, giving the army opportunity to rest and prepare and providing a base for operations in the area, not least where the baggage train could be left and protected by the servants and a small detachment of soldiers. Setting up camp would have been well within reasonable Roman practice, but the decision was not simple. Bold commanders could press on and seize the initiative, even building a camp in the face of the enemy if they chose not to risk battle immediately. Judging from subsequent events, it was early in the day, and this may well have persuaded Crassus that it was too soon to stop. Publius Crassus was said to be especially eager to press on, and after discussion, the order was issued for a short rest to drink and take some food before resuming the march.[12]

Surena was waiting for the Romans. All large armies raise clouds of dust on the march, especially in the hot Mesopotamian summer, and even more when they consist of so many cavalrymen. The Romans did not see a cloud of dust ahead of them, which strongly suggests that the Parthians were already in position, ready to meet the enemy as they came along the familiar track. Crassus forced the pace as much as possible, eager for battle, although he was still encumbered with his baggage train, and keeping the four sides of the square aligned also slowed him down. At last, the enemy were sighted, and encouragingly they did not seem as numerous as reports had claimed. The Surena had deployed his forces with care, with only a narrow front line formed in plain view and the bulk of his men either stationed behind these units or hidden in the many folds of the rolling landscape. The cataphracts had covered their armour with cloth or skins to prevent reflected sunlight from betraying their position and no doubt also to keep them as cool as possible in the heat.[13]

Suddenly drums began to pound, deluging the Romans with sound; Plutarch noted that the Parthians understood that noise can have a powerful effect on emotions. To sound, they added sight. Men pulled the covers off helmets and armour, and then the cataphracts led the advance in a glittering line. Surena had meant to launch them in a charge, hoping that their sudden and dramatic appearance would make the Romans waver. Instead, the square showed every sign of good order and steadiness, no matter the inner feelings of the legionaries confronted by such a daunting sight. This generation of Parthians had no real experience of facing disciplined infantry in battle, but neither had the Romans any experience of facing a large and well-led Parthian army. The cataphracts held back, while horse-archers raced out and soon threatened the square on all sides. Crassus countered by sending his infantry skirmishers ahead of the main line of cohorts. Outnumbered, many with javelins so that they had to get within thirty yards or so of their target, the light troops were met with showers of arrows. A few were cut down, and the remainder recoiled back into the shelter offered by the legionaries. The Parthians closed in.[14]

Plutarch says that the Parthians did not bother to aim at individual targets and simply bombarded the area occupied by the Roman formation, since they were almost bound to hit something. This was an arrow storm, like that produced by English and Welsh longbowmen in the fourteenth and fifteenth centuries—albeit less regular, for they were archers on foot in massed formation. Parthian horse-archers made best use of their speed, heading towards the enemy, shooting as they went, then turning to the right, since a right-handed man struggles to aim a bow to his own right and naturally shoots to the left. Riding parallel along the enemy line he shot again, before turning back and heading away, perhaps sending a Parthian shot at the enemy as he withdrew. Accurate shooting on the move is not easy, and a speeding horse is not the most stable platform. Surviving Saracen manuals on horse-archery from the Middle Ages recommended loosing the arrow when a galloping horse was in midstride and believed that an accomplished archer could shoot well three times in 1.5 seconds. All of this needed space and was not suited to neat ranks. More likely, horse-archers went in files, one behind the other, rushing forward and shooting before turning, followed a moment or two later by the next man, and so on. Rather than a near constant rain of arrows, there were surges forward up and down the Roman lines, with intensive bursts of shooting at one particular spot, then at another.[15]

The Romans had helmets, mail armour, and long, broadly oval, semi-cylindrical shields made from three layers of plywood and covered in calfskin. All would stop an arrow, except at extremely close range. Faces, right arms, and legs were unprotected, since greaves were rare in this period except for officers, so the only way to protect these areas was to crouch behind the shield. Archers on foot stood a chance of outranging horse-archers, at least as regards accurate aimed shots, but there were too few of these to keep the Parthians back everywhere along the sides of the square. Each legionary carried a single pilum, a heavy javelin with a maximum range of some thirty yards and an effective range of half that. Many of the skirmishers carried a bundle of lighter javelins, with a better effective range, but the fast-moving horse-archers were difficult targets and must soon have worked out how to stay just out of range. Local attacks by the infantry, running forward close enough to throw pila or javelins, or even less probably catching the horse-archers and cutting them down, were almost as easily evaded. The attackers simply made themselves better targets for the Parthians, for it was hard to advance, let alone run, and shelter fully behind a shield.

Slowly, the Parthians began to wear down the Roman army. This was less a question of killing a lot of men than of robbing the Roman infantry of spirit and confidence. There were bound to be hits: arrows striking the lower legs under the shield or, still worse, hitting the face. An arrow is visible in the air, the velocity slow enough for a man with good reactions to dodge, but it is harder to dodge every missile when many are in the air. There would always be occasional gaps in a wall of shields or an arrow coming at just the right angle to go past the edge. Fatalities were few at this stage, although an arrow hit might well take the man out of the fighting line, if in some cases only until the arrow was removed and the wound bound up. Yet the combat was one-sided, with the Romans having to wait in ranks, crouched behind their shields, as now and again a comrade was hit and more often arrows banged into a man's own shield. After a civil war battle a few years later, 120 arrow strikes were counted in one centurion's shield. Attempts to hurt the enemy failed and were often costly, and still the arrows kept coming, noisy in flight and sometimes wounding. In some ways the experience was akin to that of soldiers under an artillery bombardment in more recent centuries.[16]

Crassus and his men hoped that so heavy a barrage of missiles would empty the Parthians' quivers, so that then the enemy must either withdraw or fight at close quarters, something always likely to favour the Romans. However, there proved to be no let-up, because Surena had stationed baggage camels carrying bundles of arrows not far from the fighting line, and men simply went back to replenish their stocks. Although sometimes put forward as a mark of Surena's personal genius, there is no reason to believe that this was anything other than good practice in any competently led Parthian army. As some horse-archers were reloading, others were always available to shoot at the square.[17]

Realizing that time would not end this slow torment on its own, Crassus sent a dispatch rider to his son, ordering Publius to launch a major attack and see whether this could break the enemy's hold. Taking eight cohorts, five hundred archers, and 1,300 cavalry, including his Gauls, Publius did as he was told.* Publius had done well in Gaul, using his initiative to make bold—and happily, correct—decisions in a major battle and being trusted with a prolonged independent command. He attacked quickly, and the Parthians gave way. In one engagement in Gaul, his cavalry advance guard had been ambushed, but by reinforcing them rapidly he had fought his way to victory. When the Parthians fled before him now, he eagerly gave chase. The pressure all around the square was quickly relieved, as substantial numbers of the horse-archers surrounding it also withdrew.[18]

Publius kept going, his infantry hurrying to keep up with the faster horsemen. The pursuit led him several miles away. Distance, combined with folds in the ground, meant that he and his men disappeared from view. This was the critical moment of the battle and led to probably Crassus's biggest mistake. Camping by the river earlier that day and waiting until he had a better idea of enemy strength and intentions would have been prudent. Once he engaged in battle, he had to co-ordinate the different components of his army and make sure that they supported each other. When his son vanished over the horizon, he ought either to have recalled him or, better yet, re-formed the square and followed, however slowly. Instead, he used the slackening of the enemy attack to withdraw and re-form on some high ground. Then he waited.[19]

Possessing ground on a battlefield mattered little to a Parthian commander. In this respect at least, there was a hint of the old nomadic tradition, for there was always more steppe and no sense in dying for the sake of this particular stretch of grassland. The Greeks and Romans thought it important to control the ground at the end of a battle, not least to bury the dead and tend the wounded, hence a long tradition of erecting battlefield trophies. When Publius Crassus attacked in strength, it was natural and entirely reasonable for the Parthians facing him to give way and flee. When the situation changed back in their favour, it was equally natural for them to rally. Someone, whether Surena or a

---

*Plutarch does not say whether these men were part of the square—perhaps a corner or two-thirds of one side—or had been in some form of reserve up until now.

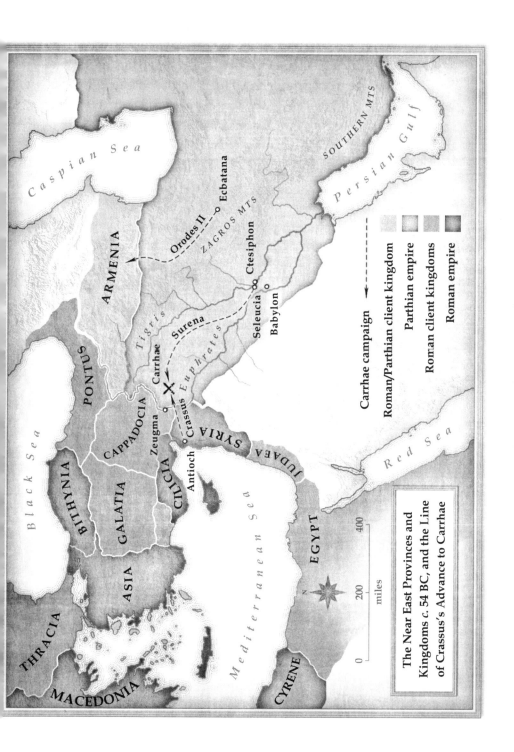

The Near East Provinces and
Kingdoms c. 54 BC, and the Line
of Crassus's Advance to Carrhae

Roman empire

Roman client kingdoms

Parthian empire

Roman/Parthian client kingdom

Carrhae campaign

subordinate, made sure that the situation did change, for Publius Crassus and his men found themselves facing fresh troops as well as rallying fugitives. A formed body of cataphracts anchored the Parthian position, threatening to charge, but not charging, while horse-archers swiftly surrounded the Romans. Galloping horses threw up great clouds of dust, and through the haze horse-archers darted forward, shooting and then retreating. The same pattern as before was repeated, but this time the Romans were isolated and heavily outnumbered.

Publius Crassus started sending messengers back to his father, but the first ones were all intercepted and killed. In the meantime, casualties mounted among his isolated force, although once again wounds were far more common than fatalities. Publius led his cavalry in a charge. The horse-archers evaded, but the cataphracts met them. The Gauls had shields, helmets, and mail shirts, far less protection than their opponents. They fell to thrusts of the kontos or blows from swords but struggled in turn to penetrate the Parthians' armour. A few desperate men wrestled cataphracts from their saddles or dismounted and dived low to hamstring the enemy horses. This was brave and skilful but could not possibly tip the balance against opponents who were brave, skilful, and far better equipped. The attack was driven back, and the survivors dismounted and together with the legionaries formed a circle on a low hill, the remaining horses in the centre. Yet the slope only exposed the rear ranks, the wounded, and the horses to the arrows that kept on coming. Publius took an arrow through one hand but was believed to have refused to abandon his men in a bid to escape. Eventually he ordered an attendant to run him through with a sword, since his injury meant that he could not do it himself. Two of his close friends died with him, one assisted because he was also wounded and the other by his own hand. The Romans had no long tradition of suicide in foreign wars, but it became common in the civil wars and seems to have exerted a particular hold on this generation of aristocrats. Their leader dead, the remnants struggled on, as more and more were hit by arrows. In the end, their wall of shields was in ruin and the cataphracts charged in to ride them down. Barely five hundred survived to go into captivity.[20]

Publius's attack, pursuit, check, and last stand cannot have happened quickly. An hour had passed, perhaps two or even more, since he had disappeared from view, and it was only near the end of this time that a message requesting help finally got through to Crassus. By then it was too late, and having misread the situation for so long, the Roman commander continued to dither. If he had followed his son's attack with the main force, then he might have reached Publius's detachment in time to prevent its extermination. That does not mean that the Romans would necessarily have won the battle, but they might have achieved some sort of draw or at least avoided such a serious defeat. Eventually, Crassus decided to advance in the hope of reaching his son. Instead, more and more Parthians came back into view, their drums pounding once again. A few rode close to the Roman army, parading Publius's severed head and allegedly calling out—presumably in Greek, although Plutarch does say some of Surena's men also spoke Latin—to ask who this brave hero had been, since he obviously could not be related to the craven Crassus.[21]

Roman generals were not supposed to despair, even when their armies went down to rout or were slaughtered by the enemy. For the moment Crassus lived up to the ideals of his class, and he rode around the square, telling his men that the sorrow was personal and for another day, but that now they all must fight on and prevail. Yet the heart had gone out of his men, and when their officers tried to raise a battle-cry, it sounded feeble and unconvincing. The Parthians resumed their harassment, relying on the horse-archers to bombard the mass of Romans, nibbling away at them. The cataphracts waited in close support, charging only on the rare occasion the Romans launched a local counter-attack. Plutarch claims some cataphracts managed to spit two Romans with the same thrust of a kontos. Dio alleges that some of Rome's local allies switched sides and attacked the legions in the rear.[22]

It was getting late, and gradually the onslaught slackened until it ended at sunset. Parthians preferred to camp at a safe distance from the enemy, for their chief tactical advantages were lost at night, and a camp full of horses and baggage animals was hard to protect and highly vulnerable to a surprise attack. After many hours of riding and fighting, men and mounts were bound to be weary, and after so many hours of shooting even the supply of ammunition provided by the baggage camels was probably running low. It remained to be seen whether they would have to fight another pitched battle the next day, but Surena and his men could be well content with what they had achieved.[23]

The Romans were just as tired but also depressed because they knew that they had come off badly. Some four thousand men were wounded, others dead, but the army began to fall apart, and hardly anyone bothered to look after them. Nor is there any sign that they had begun to fortify the rough camp they had made. Crassus's spirit snapped, and Plutarch says he lay alone and silent in the dark, his face covered. Cassius and a man named Octavius, probably a legate, eventually organized a withdrawal under cover of darkness, managed without any of the usual trumpet signals or other signs. They decided to abandon all the wounded unable to keep up, whether from loss of blood or arrow hits to the legs. When the injured men realized what was happening, they cried out, begging to be taken along. There was chaos and panic, but the fit men left them and began the march to Carrhae. Order largely fell apart, as the army broke up into lots of separate groups, and many of these got lost during the night. An otherwise unknown officer named Egnatius sped away with three hundred horsemen. He reached Carrhae, perhaps some twenty miles away, and shouted up to the sentries on the walls that there had been a great battle with the Parthians. Then he and his men rode on and made their own way back to Syria. However, the meagre news was enough to convince the garrison's commander that something had gone badly wrong, and he sent out patrols who brought in large numbers of retreating men, including Crassus and Cassius.[24]

The next morning, Surena began by overrunning the Roman camp and massacring all the wounded. His men launched a careful pursuit, surrounding and destroying isolated groups of Romans whenever they discovered them. The remnants of four cohorts made a last stand on an isolated hill, only to be shot down. At the end, a few tried to break out, and the Parthians—according to Plutarch, impressed by their courage—let twenty men go. Surena was unsure where Crassus himself had gone and wanted to secure him as a captive. Worried when he received a report that the Roman was well on his way back to Syria, he sent men to Carrhae with orders to say that he wanted to negotiate, but only with Crassus or Cassius in person. The Romans agreed, and local tribesmen who had previously been in the Romans' camp confirmed that they had seen the quaestor. The next morning, large formations of Parthians showed themselves outside the city walls and demanded the surrender of Crassus.[25]

Instead, the Romans once again waited for nightfall and then sneaked out, trusting in the enemy's unwillingness to fight in the dark. Mistakes were made, and a guide may have been false, for several contingents, including the one with Crassus, got lost. Cassius ended up back at Carrhae where he had started, but then turned around and at the head of five hundred cavalry struck off on his own and made it back to Syria. Octavius, with the strongest group, reached some hilly country to the west, which offered a decent position. But when the sun rose next morning they spotted Crassus in the plains, and the loyal legate marched down to join him. When the Parthians caught up, the Romans were still in open country, ideally suited to cavalry. Yet Surena was reluctant to fight. His men had fought a long and arduous battle, as well as skirmishes, including at least one fairly large one, in the last few days. For all his care over supply, there is a good chance that they lacked sufficient arrows for another long fight. Preferring to talk, he sent word asking for parley. Crassus was reluctant, but his officers were eager to snap at this chance of survival, and neither they nor the men were in the mood to fight. In the end he agreed.

The Romans went to the meeting on foot, according to their custom, and the Parthians on horseback, according to theirs. Surena felt this was unbecoming and ordered a horse brought for Crassus. He is said to have refused to mount, only to be lifted bodily onto the animal. At that point, fighting broke out and Crassus was killed in the confusion. Octavius ran one Parthian through before he and the others were cut down. In situations of this sort, it is impossible to know whether there was deliberate treachery or some terrible accident between nervous and naturally suspicious men.

Crassus as a captive would have been a considerable prize, even if he lacked the status of the Seleucid kings captured in the past. A dead Crassus was also valuable. Surena ordered his head and hand cut off. Some of the main force of Romans surrendered, but the Parthians did not launch a serious attack to destroy the rest, which again suggests that they were worn out and low on arrows. The remaining Romans split up and tried to get back across the Euphrates, but many were hunted down by Arabs from the local tribes and kingdoms rather than by the main Parthian army.[26]

Before Crassus was defeated, Orodes II had put sufficient pressure on the Armenian king to persuade him to negotiate. Artavasdes II agreed to an alliance with Parthia, ending hostilities, although not obliging the Armenians to fight against the Romans. Orodes II gave his new ally one of his daughters in marriage to cement the agreement, and the occasion was celebrated in grand style. Both kings were fluent in Greek and very fond of Hellenic culture, and Plutarch claims that they were watching a performance of Euripides's play The Bacchae when news of Surena's victory arrived. With the report came Crassus's head as trophy and proof of the victory. In the play—by coincidence written and probably first performed in Macedonia—a king of Thebes is torn to pieces by women devotees of the god Bacchus as punishment for having doubted his power and divinity. One of these women brought the king's head back to the city, and Plutarch tells us that the actor snatched up Crassus's head and used it as a prop. It is a good story and bears repeating but is more than likely an invention. Dio says that the Surena had ordered molten gold poured into the mouth of Crassus's corpse (the same degradation allegedly inflicted on a Roman by Mithridates VI of Pontus). It seems unlikely that both stories could be true.[27]

In the meantime, Surena had gone to Seleucia, where he staged a triumphal procession through the city. A Roman captive who resembled the dead proconsul was put in a woman's dress and told to declare that he was Crassus; he was accompanied by a few surviving lictors and other ceremonial attendants of a Roman magistrate. Professional female singers, entertainers, and prostitutes from the city joined the procession, singing bawdy songs about the dead man. No doubt the display of these trophies and the humiliation of Rome was intended to impress the citizens and their leaders, and it may hint that they were still suspected of disloyalty for having so recently supported Mithradates III, who had sought Roman backing. Now Mithradates III was dead, as was Crassus, and a Roman army shattered. Surena was supposed to have mocked the Romans, pointedly showing the council of Seleucia pornographic books captured among the baggage of a senior officer.[28]

The war had gone very well for Orodes II, but perhaps it was unfortunate that a subordinate had won such a complete victory and celebrated it in public and with such ostentation. Within a few months, Surena was accused of disloyalty and executed. Orodes II, who after all had come to power through the murder of his father and then fought a civil war against his own brother, may have had concerns about the reliability of other noblemen and communities within his empire. This helps explain why he made no effort to follow up the victory in the remainder of the year. He may also have hoped to negotiate a favourable peace with the Romans, capitalizing on his recent success, but, with Crassus dead, there was no one with whom to negotiate. Cassius was the most senior Roman to reach Syria and the only one holding an elected magistracy. By default he became the temporary governor of the province, acting as pro-quaestor. This was an improvisation, meant only to provide some stability until a new, far more senior governor was sent out. Yet time passed and no replacement for Crassus arrived. Cassius governed Syria for the best part of two years, commanding an army formed from the survivors of the Carrhae campaign. Eventually this force numbered somewhere between five thousand and ten thousand, for it seems that most of the garrisons were able to withdraw back across the Euphrates. No reinforcements were sent by the Senate, just as they chose to appoint no proper governor for Syria.[29]

At first sight, this indifference on the part of Rome's leaders is even more surprising than the delay before Orodes II pushed his advantage in the conflict. Today, Carrhae is seen as one of the worst disasters ever suffered by the Romans, and as showing that the legions had met their match in another, very different, tactical system. There is little evidence that this was the way it was viewed by Romans at the time or later. It is certainly one of the best described Roman defeats, which gives it prominence, and Crassus was the most famous senator in this era to die in the aftermath of a battle against foreign opponents. Yet Carrhae was far from unique. Other Roman armies were defeated or almost destroyed, and sometimes the proconsul in charge died with his men. Half a century earlier, the Cimbri and Teutones had shattered a far larger Roman army at Arausio, killing eighty thousand men according to Livy. More recently, Mithridates VI of Pontus had routed a Roman army at Zela in 67 BC, while Caesar himself had lost a legion and a half just a few months before Carrhae. The Romans fought a lot of battles, and while they won far more often than they lost, there were defeats, and some of these were costly. In the Social War and civil wars, the casualties were very high among soldiers from Italy. In the aftermath of one of these disasters, blame tended to be placed on a failure to recognize bad auspices and omens, on the poor decisions of a commander, and on the treachery of allies—all features of the later accounts of Carrhae. Crassus was dead and could not tell his version, and while he had occupied a key place in public life, his removal simply meant that relationships among Rome's elite would begin to reset.[30]

From Syria, the power of the Parthian king was frightening, and it was natural to expect Orodes II to wish to strike back after Crassus's invasion of his territory. For those in Rome, the Euphrates was a long way away, and there was no reason to think that the Romans could not deal with the Parthians whenever they chose to do so. For the moment other threats and other concerns were far more immediate and important. During 53 BC, public life in Rome degenerated into chaos. Political rioting became ever more frequent, on a grander scale, and far more organized, as did bribery and coercion during elections. In the event, no elections could be held that year because of rioting and intimidation, while the Senate house was burned down after the wounding and subsequent murder of a prominent senator just outside the city. Fifty-two BC began with no consuls in office until the Senate gave Pompey extraordinary powers to restore order. This he did, bringing troops into the city, and eventually he was elected as sole consul, although he subsequently chose a colleague.[31]

As this crisis passed, fresh ones loomed, most of all the thought of what would happen when Caesar's ten-year command in Gaul came to an end and he returned home. Opponents wanted the chance to prosecute him, which could only happen if he became a private citizen. He wanted to go straight to a second consulship and then another province to prevent this. With Pompey's assistance this would surely have been possible, but Pompey had always been a difficult man to read, and his intentions now were highly ambiguous. Caesar's bitterest enemies sensed an opportunity to prise the two men apart. Crassus was gone, weakening the alliance, and Julia had died in childbirth. Scorning the offer of other female relatives, Pompey had married Cornelia, the widow of Publius Crassus and an attractive, intelligent, and much admired young woman but also the daughter of a harsh critic of Caesar. Plenty of people saw tension growing between the two former allies, and perhaps the poet Lucan summed it up best when he declared that 'Pompey could not tolerate an equal, nor Caesar a superior.'[32]

The next few years were dominated by this impending crisis, although as always there were plenty of other rivalries and ambitions playing out at the same time. Ultimately it led to the civil war, but at this stage many senators believed reasonably enough that actual confrontation could be avoided. There was talk of sending either Pompey or Caesar against the Parthians. Each commander was required to give up a legion to form the basis of an army to go to the east. Pompey generously chose a unit he had loaned to Caesar a few years earlier, so that the latter effectively lost two from his command. These went to Italy and stayed there, where they formed the most experienced element of Pompey's army in the civil war. Syria was left to make do with the remnants of Crassus's army and an acting and inexperienced governor whose decision to abandon his commander in the aftermath of Carrhae was questionable. Only in 51 BC was a proconsul appointed to the Syrian command. This was Bibulus, Caesar's consular colleague in 59 BC, who had not wanted a province afterwards and now was in no hurry to take up his appointment.[33]

Also appointed, but in this case to Cilicia, was Cicero, another senator who up to this point had managed to avoid being given a provincial command. His letters give wonderful insight into this period, not least showing how little was known in Rome about events in the east. Cicero knew of the Parthian threat but did not know how likely it was to develop. From the start, he was desperate to ensure that he held his province for no more than the year required by law as long as a successor was appointed. Arriving in Cilicia, he discovered that the two legions of its garrison were badly under-strength and low spirited to the point of mutiny. Rumour said that some of his cavalry had been badly cut up by a band of Parthians. Reports and his own observation told him that neighbouring kingdoms like Cappadocia, as well as communities within the province, had been so badly treated by past governors (especially his immediate predecessor) and Roman businessmen and tax collectors that it was unreasonable to expect them to fight well on Rome's behalf.[34]

In 52 BC, small groups of Parthians or their allies had crossed into Syria. Cassius concentrated on defending Antioch and managed to hold his own against them. In 51 BC, Cicero received reports that Orodes II's son Pacorus, along with a senior general, had again invaded Syria, this time with a stronger force. To support Cassius and block the route into his own province, Cicero concentrated his army to close the narrow mountain passes at the border. A detachment of his troops cut up a Parthian band, but soon it was clear that the main enemy force was not heading in his direction. Instead, they closed around Antioch, but Cassius refused to be drawn out into the open, and the Parthians were in no mood for a long siege. They went to another city, and in wooded country nearby Cassius managed to lure some of them into an ambush. The Parthian general took a wound which proved mortal, and Pacorus withdrew his remaining forces for the winter. At this point, late in the year, Bibulus arrived and Cassius was at last able to return home, having defended Syria with sufficient heroism to balance his dubious role in the Carrhae campaign.[35]

Greatly relieved that the Parthians had not attacked him, Cicero launched an offensive against the communities of Mount

Amanus, who were fiercely independent and prone to raiding. This was partly to exercise his troops and partly to give a display of Roman strength to the mountain tribes and allies in the wider area. The orator and highly reluctant governor, let alone soldier, did well enough to hope for a triumph. Soon afterwards, Bibulus tried to copy him but suffered a serious defeat, losing most of the First Cohort of one legion. Although it is possible that this was in an engagement with the Parthians, the more natural reading is that this was during a punitive expedition against the mountain communities. Dio says that Bibulus did engage in negotiations, trying to split some of the Parthians' allies away from them and even turn Pacorus against his father.[36]

Whatever the details, Cicero greatly feared a renewed invasion in the spring or summer of 50 BC and was desperate that this not happen before he could leave his province. He got his wish, although soon after Cicero reached Italy, Caesar crossed the Rubicon and they were all caught up in the civil war. Once again, Parthia became a minor concern for Rome's leaders as they did their best to kill each other.

Carrhae was important as the first significant battlefield encounter between the Romans and Parthians, and it is revealing because it is described in far more detail than any other battle between the two powers. This means that it has needed to be considered in depth, because far too often sweeping conclusions are drawn which do not actually fit with the evidence. Equally important is the aftermath, when neither side seemed all that keen to wage the war started by Crassus. Our sources show why the Romans were preoccupied during these years and remind us that Parthia was only one of many concerns for the Roman Senate—and subsequently for the emperors—and even at times of conflict not necessarily their greatest or most immediate priority. This is an important lesson to remember for the less well-documented periods of Roman history. Equally, although we know far less about Parthian domestic affairs, we must remember that the Arsacids often had far greater concerns than their dealings with the Romans. Still, it is safe to say that as civil war engulfed the republic, the Romans continued to be one of the least predictable concerns of the king of kings and his advisors.

5

INVASIONS

49–30 BC

'The die is cast.' People said that those were Julius Caesar's words as he led the Thirteenth Legion out of his province, where he was legally entitled to command, into Italy, where he was not. A gambler's tag was certainly appropriate, and no one knew how the dice would fall as Caesar confronted Pompey and his allies. Fighting soon engulfed Italy, Spain, Sicily, and North Africa, then spread to Macedonia and Greece, where Caesar's legions shattered Pompey's legions at the Battle of Pharsalus in August 48 BC. Pompey fled to Egypt, hoping for sanctuary and support from Ptolemy XIII, son of the king restored to power by Gabinius just a few years earlier. The teenage monarch and his advisors felt that the wind was blowing the other way and lured Pompey the Great onto the shore, where he was stabbed to death and beheaded. Cornelia, widow of Publius Crassus, watched from aboard the ship as her second husband met this violent end.[1]

The civil war continued, helped because Caesar followed Pompey to Alexandria, where he and Ptolemy XIII's sister Cleopatra became lovers and the small Roman army got caught up in a Ptolemaic civil war. Caesar prevailed in the end, as he always did in war, then had to defeat a Pontus resurgent under Mithridates VI's son in a swift campaign, later prompting the famous boast '*Veni, vidi, vici*' (I came, I saw, I conquered). More campaigns against Pompeians followed in Africa and Spain. Caesar had been named dictator for life by a Senate and people who did not have a great deal of choice, but the ongoing campaigns of the civil war meant that he spent little time in Rome. Always an energetic, even restless, character, he did a lot in a short time—for instance introducing the Julian calendar, which apart from minor adjustments is the one we use today—but everything was hurried, and much simply could not be done. For while Caesar had beaten all his enemies on the battlefield, and in marked contrast to Sulla pardoned all those willing to surrender, there were many aristocrats who loathed the fact that one man held supreme, permanent power in the republic. Led by Brutus and Cassius, the man who had held Antioch after Carrhae, a group of conspirators stabbed Caesar to death on 15 March 44 BC.

Civil war swiftly resumed. Mark Antony, fellow consul with Caesar for the year and one of the most high-born of his supporters, soon rallied as many of the dead dictator's former soldiers as he could. Others backed Caesar's great-nephew and heir to his name and fortune, who is conventionally called Octavian in modern accounts. At the same time, several of the conspirators started to raise their own legions, as did other magistrates. Antony and Octavian started as adversaries, then decided that this was only helping their enemies and joined forces, seizing Rome. Once in control they copied Sulla rather than Caesar, posting proscription lists, making it legal to kill the men named on them and seize their property.

Brutus and Cassius went to the eastern Mediterranean, the latter seizing Syria, where he was already known. When Antony and Octavian confronted Brutus and Cassius outside Philippi in Macedonia in 41 BC, their combined armies were almost double the size of the forces that had been engaged at Pharsalus. In two battles, the conspirators—or 'liberators' as they styled themselves—were defeated and took their own lives. Sextus, son of Pompey the Great, continued to fight, his powerful fleet based in and around Sicily, and less successful leaders popped up elsewhere. In the long run, Sextus Pompey was defeated and fled to Asia to rebuild his strength. It was not until 35 BC that he was finally killed. Four years later, Octavian and Antony, whose alliance had come under strain before, turned on each other. Antony lost and took his own life in 30 BC.

For the best part of two decades Rome's republic, along with its provinces and allies, had lived with the reality or imminent threat of civil war, spreading death and destruction over a wide area. For the Parthians, this made the Romans even less predictable, but for the moment less of a danger. Pompey sent a senator as envoy to Orodes II, apparently asking for military support in his struggle against Caesar. Given the recent hostilities prompted by Crassus's attack, this was strange and rather suggests a very Roman assumption that all neighbouring peoples were inferior, of use only as allies. Orodes II imprisoned the envoy and sent no assistance but did not see the Romans' preoccupation as an opportunity for a new attack on Syria. Parthia remained neutral. After Pharsalus, Pompey is supposed to have considered fleeing to Parthia rather than Egypt, before deciding that the court of Orodes II was no place to take the beautiful and dignified Cornelia. The source does not say that this was because of her connection with Crassus and his son, instead relying on the well-established Greek and Roman stereotype of Persians and Parthians as good-looking, sensuous, and lustful. More probably the whole tale was invented to blacken Pompey's memory by suggesting that he was unpatriotic enough to consider running away to the Parthian enemy.[2]

Caesar spoke of a reckoning with Parthia during his short visit to Syria in 47 BC before he hurried back west to deal with his enemies in North Africa. There was clearly tension in the east, and a year later the man Caesar had left to govern Syria wrote to Cicero that he was worried about a Parthian invasion. When some former Pompeian soldiers serving in Syria rebelled, a force of Parthians came to help them. Orodes II's son Pacorus may have been involved, although it is not certain whether these men were sent by the Parthian king or were mercenaries—or perhaps even from one of the kingdoms broadly under Arsacid control rather than, strictly speaking, Parthians. Later Cassius sent a delegation to Orodes II's court asking for military aid in the coming struggle with Antony and Octavian, but once again this was not forthcoming. Although there were a few Parthians with Cassius's army, these seem to have been mercenaries, men from an allied kingdom, or exiles, rather than a contingent sent to him by the Arsacid king.[3]

On the whole, Orodes II avoided direct involvement in the Roman civil wars of the forties BC, and, while it is possible that he had more pressing concerns elsewhere, this was clearly through choice. Rome's provinces and closer allies did not enjoy this luxury. Cicero had informed the Senate that Cilicia and the neighbouring kingdoms and communities had suffered so badly from the rapacity of Roman governors, moneylenders, and businessmen in recent years that they lacked not only the capacity but even the will to resist any Parthian attack. Soon afterwards, Pompey combed the entire east for money, material, and manpower for the war effort against Caesar, calling in all the many favours and debts owed to him in a region he had done so much to shape. After Pompey's defeat, Caesar needed to assert control over these provinces and was desperate for cash to pay his soldiers, so once again the demands went out. Brutus and Cassius squeezed the provinces and communities even tighter, selling into slavery city leaders who failed to meet their demands and sacking any cities who resisted. After they were defeated, Antony wrote to provincial communities claiming that he wanted 'to let our allies also participate in the peace' granted to them by divine favour, and claiming that 'the body of Asia is now recovering, as it were, from a serious illness'. Yet all the while he needed money to reward loyal supporters and most of all to pay the huge armies needed to survive as a warlord in this era; that meant that provincials and allies were expected to pay once again.[4]

Loyalty to Rome was a hard thing to manage in these years. Dutiful obedience and support for one leader became suspicious enthusiasm for the wrong side when that leader fell. Pompey went to an east already shaped by his decisions and favours. Caesar reduced and enlarged kingdoms and city-states, favouring some monarchs and regimes and penalizing or even dismissing others. Something similar happened under Brutus and Cassius, and there was an even more thorough reorganization by Antony starting in the winter of 41–40 BC. Cleopatra, who had honoured her family's obligation to Pompey, afterwards embraced Caesar politically as well as physically, then obeyed Cassius's instructions and later came to Antony eager to win his favour. As Plutarch described, and Shakespeare so wonderfully evoked, she arrived at Tarsus in spectacular fashion, sailing on a lavish barge, and her style, charm, and political skill had the desired effect. Antony had already appointed a new king for Cappadocia over a rival claimant because he was having an affair with the youth's mother. He was certainly susceptible to physical charm, but this should not obscure the fact that, as well as her love, Cleopatra brought a willingness to exploit the great wealth of Egypt on Antony's behalf. The leaders who survived and prospered in these years were the ones who gave the Roman warlords what they wanted, regardless of the cost to the communities under their rule. If they were reluctant to do this, then there were almost always competitors who would replace them. Cleopatra had disposed of her remaining brother soon after Caesar's assassination. Having proved herself to Antony, he ordered the liquidation of her final sibling, her sister Arsinoe.[5]

The Romans were powerful and made unpredictable by their civil wars, but in spite of all the demands and levies, their presence was occasional and their focus often elsewhere. Local politics, ambitions, and rivalries were by their very nature more immediate and constant. Given that ideology played little part in Rome's civil wars, when even the liberators swiftly started to act like all the other warlords and base their power on military might, there was even less reason for provincials or allies to feel strong commitment to any side. Roman power was simply a reality—important, but far from the sole factor as individuals sought to gain rank, status, and wealth in and beyond their communities and to deny these to rivals. Competition within a city, let alone within and between dynasties, was endemic, and the instability caused by Roman civil wars created even more opportunities for change than usual.

Directly administered provinces still covered only a small minority of the eastern lands dominated by the Roman Republic. Even within these areas, the small staffs of Roman governors had to leave most day-to-day administration to communities, especially city-states with their own magistrates, laws, and institutions.

Beyond were the kingdoms, few of any great antiquity. Even fewer were so well-established that their territory was clear, permanent, and universally recognized as it had been in the second century BC, when both Parthia and Rome started to become involved in the area. Succession in each kingdom was rarely straightforward, even when one ruling dynasty managed to cling to power, with challenges often coming from within the family and sometimes beyond. Within their realms, noblemen and self-governing cities were sometimes powerful enough to resist or even defy a monarch and certainly capable of backing a rival. At all levels, the ambitious did their best to play the game and do as well for themselves—or simply keep themselves as safe—as possible, and competition was often murderous or made use of riot and warfare.

The empire of Arsacid Parthia was in many ways a network of such kingdoms, as well as more or less substantial cities in some areas. From the start consciously a dynasty, Parthian kings did their best to control the subkingdoms by encouraging the succession of kings they favoured and forming marriage alliances, as when Orodes II married his son Pacorus to a daughter of the Armenian king. The connection did not prevent Armenia from remaining an ally of Rome, and perception of the strength of everyone involved—from Armenia itself to the Arsacid king to the Romans—did much to determine how each would act. Although several sources claim that Parthian envoys to Sulla, Lucullus, and Pompey discussed recognizing the Euphrates as the boundary between Rome and Parthia, at this early stage very little was fixed. Within living memory, Pontus and Armenia had dominated over wide areas; Parthia had expanded and retreated and, like the Romans, had gone through periods of vicious infighting and weakness. Similarly, the fortunes of other kingdoms and monarchs had waxed and waned, so that no one could be sure how the balance of power would develop in the future.

Orodes II had demonstrated his strength by defeating Crassus, encouraging the communities and kingdoms of Mesopotamia and the wider area to respect him. The attacks into Syria had added to this, and any defeat suffered there was too small to weaken his reputation significantly. Whether or not Dio was right to claim that

Bibulus had undermined trust between Pacorus and his father, the prince remained very influential. Even though Orodes II had some thirty other sons considered potential monarchs, Pacorus was clearly the crown prince, marked out as successor, and may even have minted coins bearing his own image. Whether this prominence was due to Pacorus's talents, substantial support from the noble houses, his father's genuine favour, or a combination of all these things is hard to say.[6]

There were always losers in competitions for power in each kingdom and community, and most of them were eager to find friends sufficiently rich and powerful to help them regain what they had lost. Rome's civil wars greatly swelled the numbers of such fugitives. Some went to the Roman rivals of whoever was backing their own opponents, hoping to win their favour. Others turned to Parthia. At the Parthian court was Cassius's envoy, who had failed to secure support for the Philippi campaign and then remained after it was over, fearing for his own life if he returned. His name was Quintus Labienus, and little is really known about him. His father, Titus Labienus, had been Julius Caesar's ablest subordinate in the Gallic campaigns, only to side with Pompey during the civil war, perhaps honouring an older friendship, and fighting hard until he died in the Spanish campaign of 45 BC. Exiled aristocrats were a common enough feature of many royal courts in the ancient world, and they were often willing to seek vengeance on enemies in their former home. Yet in the past, such behaviour was unheard of in a Roman senator, for whom the only valid competition for power and glory could occur within the republic.

Labienus encouraged Orodes II to believe that the Roman east was vulnerable. Roman hostility was clear. In 44 BC, Caesar had been days from setting out for major campaigns against Dacia and Parthia when he was murdered. Preparations, including the massing of legions and resources in the eastern provinces, were carried out in plain sight. The knives of the conspirators ensured that the expeditions did not happen, and soon afterwards Antony and others had called the soldiers away to fight in the civil war, but none of that meant that some Roman would not at some point choose to avenge Crassus. Late in 41 BC, Antony raided Palmyra, partly for money but also, it was rumoured, because the city on the fringes of Syria might be useful in a future offensive against Parthia. Everything suggested that the Romans were still enemies, even if they were currently preoccupied. As far as we can tell, Orodes II had no other major conflicts anywhere else in his empire, which may have convinced him and other leading Parthians that it was better to strike at the Romans sooner rather than later and not wait for the Romans to attack him at a time of their choosing.[7]

In 40 BC, Pacorus and Labienus jointly led an expeditionary force into Syria. At first the bulk of the army was composed of Parthian and allied soldiers, for it is unlikely that Labienus had more than a few Romans with him. However, the legions garrisoning Syria and the neighbouring provinces appear to have included many men who had little attachment to Antony and the commanders he had appointed, and who in many cases had once served Pompey or the liberators. Encouraged by pamphlets, most mutinied and joined Labienus, so that soon he led a Roman army. Resistance swiftly collapsed in Syria. The city of Apamea resisted the initial attack, but most other communities submitted without fighting. While Pacorus completed the subjugation of Syria, Labienus took his men into Asia Minor, and once again many legionaries defected to join him. A few communities were willing to fight, and some managed to hold off the attackers, but organized resistance collapsed as Antony's governors were killed or fled.

Labienus presented himself as a Roman magistrate, minting coins with appropriate symbols of office. He did not hide his Parthian connection, dubbing himself Parthicus, which was odd because traditionally Roman generals only took the name of peoples they had subdued and never of allies. Even so, Labienus's advance could be seen as no more than a fresh round in Rome's civil wars, his foreign allies as subordinate and inferior to Rome, as all such allies must be. No significant Parthian forces accompanied him once he left Syria, so the provinces and kingdoms of Asia Minor submitted to a Roman commander at the head of a Roman army rather than to a representative of the Arsacids.[8]

This was not true in Syria, but Pacorus and his Parthians similarly found that very few communities were willing to fight him.

Antioch, which a decade earlier had resisted under Cassius and then Bibulus, now opened its gates. Before long, the Parthians split into several columns, because there was no organized threat to their presence. The coastal cities capitulated, except for Tyre, and Pacorus did not attempt to besiege it, since without a fleet of his own there was no way to cut off supplies and other aid coming in by sea. Returning exiles, factions in each community eager for change, and leaders who switched allegiance because they felt that without Roman aid there was no way to defeat the invaders all helped to speed the advance.

By this time, Judaea did not have a king and was ruled by the high priest Hyrcanus, although the brothers Phaesel and Herod, his nominal supporters, had gained considerable power. Hyrcanus's nephew Antigonus appealed via allies to Pacorus, promising a thousand talents in money and five hundred women as payment for overthrowing his uncle. The women were intended for the royal harem, were mainly of noble birth, and notably included all the key members of the households of the high priest and his supporters. This was a very traditional aspect of international relations in the wider region. Such women served as hostages, and the more distinguished they were, the more they enhanced the king's status. As concubines, sometimes even wives, they might also produce potential heirs to regional kingdoms.

The offer was a good one, not matched by any placatory moves from Hyrcanus, and Pacorus accepted, sending a courtier—his cup-bearer, also named Pacorus—with a force of five hundred cavalry to Jerusalem. This was not a huge number, and the bulk of the fighting was done by Antigonus and his partisans, but the aid and limited intervention by the Parthian soldiers tipped the balance. Hyrcanus and Phaesel accepted an offer to negotiate, only to find themselves prisoners. Antigonus mutilated his uncle, in one source biting his ears, because only a man who was physically perfect could serve as high priest. After that he was sent to Orodes II as a hostage. Phaesel managed to commit suicide. His brother Herod, never the most trusting of men, avoided the trap and then managed to escape with his followers from Jerusalem, fighting off any pursuers, including some of the Parthians. He escaped, taking with him many of the women promised for the harem, and it is not clear how many of the five hundred Antigonus was able to provide as he was proclaimed king in Jerusalem.[9]

Apart from Tyre, virtually all of the former Seleucid kingdom in Syria and the surrounding area was now controlled by regimes supported by the Parthians. It had happened very quickly and been achieved at little or no cost in Parthian lives. Apart from a desire to present Labienus as a genuinely independent Roman commander, Pacorus's refusal so far to push beyond this territory into Asia Minor, or for that matter Egypt, is significant. The Arsacids had overthrown the Seleucids, and this latest success gave them control of almost all the latter's empire. If the Roman defence had been feeble and the collapse unexpectedly rapid, the same had been true of some of the surges of conquest by earlier Parthian kings. It was reasonable enough to suppose that Roman power in the east had already peaked and was doomed to decline, just as that of Pontus or Armenia, or indeed the Seleucids, had done. If the Romans did try to return, then the example of Carrhae suggested that they would be no match for a competently led Parthian army. Pacorus had good reason to believe that the lands he had overrun could stay under Arsacid influence, even control, in the long term.

The Parthian offensive had caught the Romans by surprise. After Philippi, Antony was placed in charge of the eastern provinces, and he threw himself into raising money as he reorganized the region before revelling in a winter spent in Cleopatra's Alexandria. Yet all the while his attention remained focused on Italy. Sextus Pompey was strong, imposing a tight blockade on the food supplies on which Rome and the other cities relied, adding to the unpopularity of Octavian—already high as he confiscated land to give to his veteran soldiers. Antony's younger brother Lucius added to the tension which eventually erupted in war against Octavian. Lucius Antonius lost, and managed to lose fast enough that it was easier for Mark Antony to avoid a permanent breach with Octavian, something neither man wanted at this stage. Nevertheless, after a brief stop at Tyre in the spring of 40 BC, Antony headed west because the situation in Italy was what really mattered. It was another year before he took concrete action to deal with Labienus and Pacorus, and even then he sent a subordinate.[10]

Publius Ventidius Bassus's story is a remarkable one, for as an infant he was carried or walked beside his mother as a captive in a triumphal procession through Rome celebrated by Pompey's father for a victory over the Italian rebels in the Social War. As an adult, he bred mules, always a more profitable business in mountainous Italy than raising horses, and over time came to be a major supplier of the Roman army. Julius Caesar sensed something of his talent, employing him to assist in the logistics of his Gallic campaigns and steadily promoting him to ever more senior roles. Rallying to Antony after the dictator's murder, he was rewarded with a consulship in 43 BC and in 39 BC was sent to deal with the invaders.[11]

Ventidius had an army of several legions along with allies. Probably he outnumbered Labienus, and perhaps his men were better drilled and disciplined, for the chaotic changes of loyalty for many soldiers and officers in the eastern provinces during these years did not make for efficiency. With little or no fighting, Ventidius advanced and Labienus withdrew, concentrating his forces but still retreating in the hope of reaching his Parthian allies, who had come to the edge of Syria near the Cilician Gates pass in the Taurus mountains—the same area defended by Cicero. Ventidius seized the pass, then managed to convince the Parthians to attack him in a position of his own choosing and without arranging for Labienus's men to support them. The Parthians were routed with heavy losses, after which Labienus's army fell apart even faster than it had been created. The soldiers defected again or deserted. Their leader tried to evade capture, employing disguises, but was eventually caught and executed.

A second battle followed the first, and Ventidius repeated his tactics and success. Pacorus was not there, but in 38 BC he came with a larger army. Roman sources boast that Ventidius deceived him, feeding false information to an allied dynast because he knew the man would pass it on to the enemy. This is supposed to have convinced Pacorus to advance by a slower route and given the legions time to concentrate from their winter quarters. Whether or not this was so, Ventidius eventually confronted Pacorus near Mount Gindarus and once again routed the Parthians, killing the prince in the process.[12]

History is proverbially written by the victors, yet one of the many oddities of our sources for Roman conflicts with Parthia is that there are no detailed accounts of any of the battles where the Romans won—yet another factor reinforcing the false impression that Carrhae was typical of the warfare between the rivals. By comparison, details of Ventidius's victories are meagre, although they do suggest several common threads. The first was that he only fought on ground of his own choosing. In each case, he defended and the Parthians were willing to attack, only to discover that the Roman commander had concealed his intentions and often many of his troops. Secondly, the Romans did not employ a static defence but counter-attacked with their legionaries and other troops and were able to move to hand-to-hand combat and win. Thirdly, Ventidius supported his legionaries with large numbers of light infantrymen armed with missile weapons. His slingers are singled out for their effectiveness, and it is claimed that they outranged the Parthians' horse-archers. This may well be true for accurate shooting, and sling bullets or stones were harder to see in flight than arrows, hence harder to dodge, and if they struck a helmet they could incapacitate the wearer through concussion, without needing to penetrate.

The victory at Carrhae had naturally given the Parthians great confidence, and the sense of their superiority grew when they overran Syria so easily, making them disdainful of the Romans. This meant that by the time they encountered Ventidius, they were all too willing to attack in expectation of an easy victory. Instead in 39 and 38 BC, the Romans under Ventidius outfought and outgeneralled the Parthians just as Surena and his forces had done to Crassus. The Parthians attacked the Romans, committing so heavily that they suffered badly when the Romans struck back and they could not easily disengage in their traditional manner. Thus, admittedly with far more fighting, all the gains of 40 BC were lost in just two campaigns. Pacorus's corpse was beheaded and paraded on a tour of the Syrian cities, just as the Surena had shown off the trophies of Crassus's defeat. The majority of communities were no more committed to the Parthian cause than they had been to the Roman, so they capitulated readily, accepting that for the moment the Romans were stronger. There was a little fighting, especially in Judaea, on the part of leaders who doubted that the Romans would accept them. Ventidius sent more troops to support Herod than the Parthians had done to aid Antigonus in 39 BC, although even then the bulk of the fighting fell to Herod's own army.

The Parthians made no move to reverse the outcome of the war. Orodes II was said to be broken-hearted at the news of his son's defeat and death, and his physical and mental health rapidly declined. Pacorus had been the acknowledged successor, but now that he was out of the way, another son named Phraates decided to act. Rumour said that he tried and failed to poison his father. Either then or soon after, he had his thirty brothers murdered and his father strangled, and he named himself Phraates IV. Not everyone was happy, and a wider purge of the nobility followed. One aristocrat, who may have served in the attack on Syria, fled to the Romans.[13]

Phraates IV was too busy securing his rule to consider attacks outside his empire. By the late summer of 38 BC, Antony had finally arrived in the region, sending Ventidius home to hold the first triumph ever celebrated over the Parthians. Many felt that this went a long way towards avenging Crassus and his legions, which had remained a stain on Roman honour, whatever the context of that earlier war. It was claimed that the Battle of Gindarus was fought on the same date as Carrhae, or at least close enough to make no difference. Antony's subordinate had done very well indeed, perhaps too well, for after this Ventidius appears to have retired and was certainly never given any other office.[14]

Antony and his other subordinate commanders were active trying to reassert Roman authority even more clearly, especially in the allied kingdoms, but in 37 BC he once again travelled to Italy to meet with Octavian, for the struggle with Sextus Pompey was going badly. Antony agreed to lend his ally warships in return for getting soldiers sometime in the future, and it was clear that he was planning even larger operations in the east. In the meantime, one of his commanders put on a show of force in Armenia and subdued the Albani and Iberi, kingdoms in the Caucasus between the Black Sea and the Caspian Sea. Antony prepared a grand expedition for the following year. Plutarch claims that, when concentrated, he had sixty thousand legionaries, ten thousand Gallic and Iberian (whether Spanish Iberians or eastern Iberians is unclear), and another thirty thousand allies, including six thousand cavalry and seven thousand infantry supplied by King Artavasdes II of Armenia. If correct, this total, which does not include camp followers, would have made this the largest Roman field force assembled up to this date. Ancient authors were prone to exaggeration, so caution is needed, but it is safe to say that this was an exceptionally big force.[15]

Antony was forty-seven, and although he had always styled himself as a new Hercules, and as a bluff, hard-fighting soldier, his actual military record was less impressive than most imagine. Although he had served for a year and a half under Caesar in Gaul and commanded the left wing at Pharsalus, the dictator had employed Antony more often in political roles than in military ones. Antony had spent more time fighting other Romans than foreign enemies, and even then had done badly in Italy in 43 BC. His greatest success was at Philippi, and most awarded him the chief credit for the victory rather than Octavian. That campaign had been fought on a vast scale in terms of numbers but had involved few manoeuvres, the action being confined to a limited area between two clumsy and inexperienced opponents. Antony had never commanded an army as big as the one assembled in 36 BC, and in turn the troops composing it had had little time to train and practice together. Nor had Antony ever planned and conducted an operation over such huge distances. At the very least, his army was twice the size of the one Crassus had led, perhaps even larger, although similar in scale to the force Julius Caesar had planned to employ for his Parthian expedition.

Caution is needed in accepting just what objectives Caesar had in mind for his campaign, since so much rumour surrounds his plans. Suetonius wrote that Caesar intended to advance through Armenia, where the country was less favourable to the Parthians, and to test the enemy's strength and qualities before risking a major battle. While it is possible that he hoped to annex new provinces, an equally glorious success would have been the submission of the Arsacid king or helping to install a new and friendly man on the throne. Antony's ultimate goals are equally hard to reconstruct, for with any major eastern war our sources tend to invoke Alexander the Great—as they do in the cases of Crassus and Caesar—and suggest that permanent sweeping conquest was the goal. In this case, it is better to examine what happened and then try to deduce the purpose of it all.[16]

Antony began with negotiation, demanding the return of the standards and prisoners lost by Crassus, before concentrating a major part of his army near the usual Euphrates crossing at Zeugma. Phraates IV mustered an army on the opposite side of the river and was in no mood to give in to a show of force. He was stronger now, having calmed the mood of many aristocrats, for instance convincing the exile with Antony to return home and serve him. The speed of the Parthian response may have surprised the Romans. After all, Crassus had crossed unopposed, and it had taken some time for the Parthians to muster a force to meet him. On the other hand, Antony may always have intended this as a feint, doing what the enemy expected before surprising them. What is certain is that he then led his army on a march, taking them past the mountains into Armenia and through the valleys running west to east in that kingdom—for that was the grain of the country—to strike against the neighbouring kingdom of Media Atropatene. Some of his forces appear already to have been in Armenia, and perhaps this had been his plan all along, but it did mean that a large part of the campaigning season was spent simply reaching his initial objective. Plutarch claims that the legions marched over a thousand miles.[17]

Antony targeted Media's main city, Phraaspa (Phraata), which housed the king's treasury and harem. The site has not been located but was deep within the country and well-fortified. Antony had brought with him a siege train carried on three hundred wagons, including artillery and a great battering ram some eighty feet in length. Inevitably, the heavy carts moved slowly, most of them probably drawn by plodding oxen, and, equally inevitably, the pace slowed even further whenever the roads were poor or the country steep. Antony grew impatient, and leaving two legions to escort the siege train, he force marched the bulk of the army in the hope that their sudden appearance would convince the defenders of Phraaspa to give in. They did not, and the city was too well-defended to be stormed. By this time Phraates IV had also had time to come to the region with a large army, suggesting that if the initial moves of the campaign were intended as a feint, any benefit was short-lived.[18]

Learning that the siege train was isolated, the highly mobile Parthians and Medians avoided Antony's main force and struck. Two legions, even if they mustered anything like their full complement of ten thousand men and had allied support, were too few to protect such a long and cumbersome convoy from any serious attack. The result was a massacre more than a battle, with the legionaries slaughtered, the siege train plundered, and whatever could not be carried off burned or otherwise destroyed. The Armenian contingent may have been close enough to help but did not do so, and in the aftermath of the disaster their king led them home. In 53 BC the Parthians had launched their main effort against Armenia, so it was not unreasonable to worry about this now. Antony led a column to rescue his men but arrived to find them dead or led off as prisoners.[19]

Roman commanders were expected to be determined, and Antony refused to abandon the siege, even though he was without heavy equipment or good supplies of timber. His men were reduced to the old-fashioned method of constructing simple siege mounds from earth. The Parthians and Medians hovered nearby, making it difficult to forage from the surrounding land. Hoping to provoke a battle, Antony led out the greater part of his army in a supply-gathering expedition. As they returned, they marched close to a great crescent-shaped line of enemies, so close that at a given signal the legionaries suddenly wheeled to face them and charged. Shocked, the Parthians held against Antony's cavalry, who reached them first, but then gave way as the legionaries came up, shouting their war cries and banging weapons against shields in the hope of frightening the enemy horses. The Parthians galloped away, chased

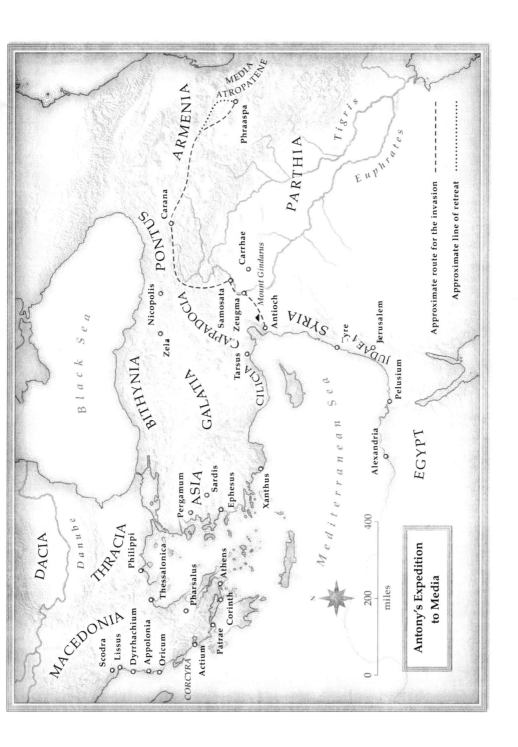

Antony's Expedition
to Media

for miles by the legionaries and even further by the cavalry. They did not rally (and the incident does raise the question of what would have happened at Carrhae had Crassus followed Publius Crassus's attack with the rest of the army). However, at the end of the day the Romans had captured just thirty prisoners and counted eighty enemy corpses. Unlike Ventidius, Antony had not been able to force the Parthians to stay and fight, so the result was that the opposing army was effectively intact. By the time he marched back to Phraaspa, Antony found that the defenders had sallied out, panicking the besiegers and inflicting damage on the siege-works. Antony was so angry that he decimated several cohorts, executing one man in ten and feeding the rest on barley rather than wheat. It is a depressing thought that he may have killed more of his own men than he managed to kill of the Parthians in the recent engagement.[20]

It was now autumn, very late in the year for campaigning, and the siege showed no sign of progress, while both sides were finding it harder and harder to supply themselves. Phraates and Antony alike wanted a way out but also wanted to save face. There were negotiations, and Dio described Phraates receiving the envoys. He sat on his throne, toying with the string of a composite bow, an image familiar from many Arsacid coins. A demand for the return of Roman prisoners and standards was once again refused. However, Phraates offered the Romans safe passage if they retreated to Armenia.

Reluctantly Antony accepted, but mistrust remained strong on both sides, and when the Romans followed a different route than the one agreed—allegedly because they had been warned of treachery—the Medians and Parthians began to harry their march. Learning from Ventidius's experience, Antony had brought large numbers of slingers and other missile-armed skirmishers. Forming the army into the rectangular agmen quadratum, the remaining baggage protected in the middle of the hollow square, the Romans proceeded slowly. If the horse-archers came close, the skirmishers engaged them, retreating behind the formed units of legionaries whenever the pressure became too great, at which point Gallic or other auxiliary cavalry charged out to drive the enemy off. They did not pursue far, and the key was for all the elements of the army to act in mutual support, staying close enough so that no one had to fight the enemy on their own. There was a trickle of casualties on both sides, and step by step the Romans went on their way.[21]

After four days, Antony let himself be persuaded by an officer who was convinced that he could do the enemy more harm. Given command of part of the rear guard, the officer counterattacked the Parthians and this time kept following until he was left some way behind the army, facing ever growing numbers of enemies. Reinforcements were sent piecemeal, without the numbers at any one time to make a difference, and it was only when Antony marched back with the whole army that the Parthians gave way. The officer died of his wounds, and his experiment cost the Romans three thousand dead and five thousand wounded, at least according to Plutarch. It was a blow to morale, and only the sight of horse-archers shooting down stragglers deterred many of the disheartened men from deserting.[22]

Reverting to their original tactics, the Romans resumed their march the next day. The Parthians and Medians pressed them, encouraged by their success, but could not repeat it. When one group of horse-archers pressed especially close, the legionaries formed testudo: shields held as a wall by the front rank and the rest holding them up over their heads to interlock. Never having seen this before, the Parthians misunderstood the sight of the front rank kneeling down better to shelter behind their shields and the movement within the whole formation as a sign of disorder, even submission. The horse-archers charged and, as had happened in the battles against Ventidius, suffered severely in hand-to-hand combat before they managed to break away and escape.[23]

The Romans resumed their march. With a well-balanced army like this, kept under tight control and discipline, the Parthians were unable to prevent them from going where they wished and incapable of inflicting serious casualties. Conversely, the Romans could not make the Parthians fight a massed battle, and, if they attacked, the enemy retreated without suffering significant losses. This essential balance—almost standoff—between the two sides characterized all the campaigns to come. When one of the armies was of poor quality or badly led, then things were different. Otherwise, from a tactical point of view, it was a question of waiting for one side or the other to make a mistake.

Antony's problem was that his supplies were running very low indeed, reduced by the long campaign and most likely the loss of stores with the siege train. Having to go slowly to fend off the Parthians simply made the problem worse. Pack and baggage animals had been slaughtered for food or had their loads removed to carry the wounded. There were still supplies of wheat, but far too few hand mills to grind it into flour for issue. Some hungry men died after eating any vegetables they could grub up. Most of the rest were malnourished, which helped disease to spread. A Roman army camp was a crowded place at the best of times, and infections readily passed from one man to another. That meant some deaths and even more sickly men who needed to be carried, slowing progress even more and adding to the problems of supply.[24]

Phraates IV sent men to say that he was willing to resume negotiations, during which he promised an end to hostilities if the Romans changed to a different route across easier country. Antony and his officers were suspicious and became convinced of treachery when someone from the Parthian camp sent word to them that the king intended to attack them while they were in this open country better suited to his cavalry. The informant varies in each source: the exiled nobleman who had been received by Antony a year earlier, another guide, or one of Crassus's legionaries, a prisoner now granted some freedom by his Parthian captors. Force marching from their camp, the Romans struggled for thirty miles, the water they had carried soon exhausted and their ranks harried by enemy cavalry. Men drank from the bad water in the first stream they reached and became ill. That night the camp was chaotic, as men plundered the baggage, first for food and then for anything of value, killing those who stood in their way. In the confusion an enemy attack was feared, so Antony prepared to commit suicide before realizing what was really going on. By dawn order was restored, and they marched for another day, keeping in formation to hold off the Parthian attacks. It was the last day of fighting, and at its end some Parthians symbolically unstrung their bows to show that they no longer chose to fight and shouted praise of the

Romans' courage before riding off. Yet the army was still not safe, and as they marched back through the mountains of Armenia the late autumn brought cold, rain, storms, and even snow. Thousands more Roman soldiers died of exposure or disease.[25]

Antony had utterly failed to take Media Atropatene or force the Parthians to submit to a negotiated settlement, which were clearly the main objectives of this first campaign, whatever he may have planned for the future. Failure came at a high price, for Plutarch claims that he had lost some thirty-two thousand soldiers. Other sources suggest different proportions, but since numbers for his initial strength vary this is not surprising. Estimates for his losses range from a quarter to a third of his troops, with even higher casualties among the camp followers. It is fair to say that Antony lost more men than Crassus in 53 BC. On top of this were the cavalry mounts, baggage animals and vehicles, and all the equipment, even if a greater proportion of his army survived, as did the commander and all his senior officers. Harder to replace was the blow to his prestige, although Antony's dispatches to Rome put a very rosy interpretation on the campaign, something Octavian was unwilling to contradict, at least for the moment. Even so, it steadily became apparent that this was no great triumph or conquest. Antony's career never really recovered from that moment, and it is quite possible that neither did his self-confidence.[26]

Phraates IV's situation was much stronger and helped the nobility to forget his bloody accession to the throne. In 36 BC he had seen off the attack of an enormous invading army, probably larger than anything in the area since the heyday of the Seleucids. Phraates IV's grip on power was strengthened, but the outcome was far from perfect and there was no clear victory to set alongside Carrhae, even though the king had been present with an army of forty thousand or more. For all the appalling Roman losses, Antony's resources remained immense, and there was no assurance that he would not return in the years to come and do better—or, if not him, then whoever next rose to prominence within the republic. Carrhae had encouraged the Parthians to believe that they were militarily superior, more skilful, perhaps even braver than the Romans. Ventidius's victories had persuaded the Romans to think the opposite. For both, this deep sense of their innate martial superiority over all outsiders was natural. Antony's expedition suggested something rather different. At a tactical level, the engagements tended to be a standoff. The Parthians could not break a Roman army or stop it marching where it wished unless the Romans made a mistake, but neither could the Romans do serious harm to the Parthians unless they in turn committed an unforced error.

In the years that followed, the balance of power shifted a little towards the Romans. In 34 BC, Antony led a force into Armenia and had its king arrested, seizing him under cover of negotiations. The man's son was proclaimed as successor by a group of nobles and escaped to Parthia to avoid capture. For the moment, the Armenian nobles were willing to respect the Romans' strength and not oppose them openly. Strikingly, apparently more worried by Phraates IV, the king of Media Atropatene allied with the Romans, the bond being confirmed by a marriage between Antony's older son by Cleopatra and the king's daughter. Since both were infants, this was for the future—and a future that did not in fact come to pass—but it suggested that the Romans were gaining influence in the major kingdoms of the region, while the Parthians were losing ground. The marriage alliance was well within the local tradition of diplomacy, if utterly unprecedented by Roman standards.[27]

Even more bizarre was the ceremony known later as the Donations of Alexandria, where Antony proclaimed Cleopatra 'Queen of Kings, whose sons are kings'. Great swathes of territory were 'given' to the queen and her children, with the six-year-old Alexander Helios, pledged to marry into the Median royal family, getting Armenia, Media, and Parthia. None of the arrangements announced at the ceremony appear to have had any practical consequences, but they helped Octavian to shift the mood in Rome against Antony. When war finally came, Antony's generalship was lethargic and clumsy. Worse still, at the naval battle of Actium he gave up too easily and sailed off with Cleopatra, abandoning the remainder of his fleet and his legions on shore. This was abhorrent behaviour for a Roman aristocrat, who was allowed to lose as long as he lost bravely and did his best to rally his men and prepare to fight another day. From that moment on, the war was irrevocably lost, even though it was not until late in the next year that Antony ordered an attendant to kill him. Cleopatra, who had been a loyal ally of Rome throughout her life, followed suit around a week later after failing to secure an acceptable deal with Octavian.[28]

No one in Rome—and least of all in Parthia or the wider world—knew that the civil wars were over or that a profound and permanent change would soon replace the republican system with a form of monarchy. For the moment, there was a new Roman leader, the heir to the Caesar who had planned a great expedition against Parthia. Phraates IV and his court did not know what to expect of Octavian, who until the struggle with Antony had never in his life been further east than Macedonia. There was no reason for the Parthians to think that the Romans would be any more predictable or easier to deal with in the future.

6

EAGLES AND PRINCES

30 BC–AD 4

THE END OF THE CONVULSIONS THAT HAD TORN APART THE
Roman Republic came surprisingly suddenly. In the longer run, this
led to far more stable relations between the two empires. Partly this
was because various factors combined to make both Romans and
Parthians less inclined towards large-scale aggression. The biggest
changes—at least in the short term—involved Rome's political system and leadership; a monarch and his advisors were inherently
more likely to show consistency in their attitude and policies than
a Senate composed of hundreds, where influence shifted on an almost daily basis. Quite simply, it was easier for successive kings of
kings to deal with successive emperors than it had been for them
to negotiate with the line of warlords and less influential governors that emerged during Rome's internal struggles. Yet the new
Roman monarchy was very different from the Arsacid system, and
this would also shape events. This means that it is important to
understand something of the change in the Roman state, and to do
that it is necessary to understand the leader who created the new
political system.

So far it has been convenient to refer to Antony's adversary as
Octavian, even though he never used the name. Great-nephew of

Julius Caesar, he was the principal heir in the dictator's will and, as was common, as part of this took his name, so that from then on he was Caius Julius Caesar. The dictator had not adopted him as his son, but Octavian decided that this had been his intention and had the adoption ratified posthumously, which by that time made him son of the divine Julius, since he had already deified Caesar. From the very start, Octavian, as we call him, called himself and insisted that everyone else call him Caesar. Antony at first dismissed the teenager as a 'boy who owes everything to a name' before being forced to accept that the inexperienced youth had political skill as well. Yet the name mattered a great deal, not least by helping to rally support from the dead dictator's supporters, and it is largely to avoid confusion that the convention is to call the heir Octavian. Similarly, for our purposes, following his victory over Antony, it is simplest to refer to him as Augustus, even though he did not in fact become Caesar Augustus until a few years later. Claiming to restore the res publica—better in this case rendered 'commonwealth' than 'republic'—he styled himself as princeps, first magistrate and servant of the republic. Creating this new regime was a gradual process and not always smooth, for there were problems and significant changes of direction along the way. While this is a fascinating story, the details need not concern us here, and instead what follows is a summary of the final form. This should not imply that Augustus and his allies were working to a fixed plan in this or any other area, including foreign relations.[1]

Augustus's power ultimately rested on control of the army. From the sixty or so legions in service in the aftermath of Actium, he formed twenty-eight permanent units. Legionaries took a sacred oath of loyalty to him as well as to the res publica, were paid by him, promoted and decorated by him, and, after twenty-five years of service, were discharged and given a farm or a substantial bounty by him. With only a handful of exceptions, the legions were stationed in provinces controlled by Augustus—beginning with Gaul, the Spains, and Syria, but later more—and administered on the spot by a senatorial governor acting as his legate (*legatus* or, literally, representative). In this way, senators still had opportunities to hold military command, as well as serve as proconsuls in the largely demilitarized senatorial provinces, just as they continued to serve in the consulship and other magistracies in Rome. Yet in reality, no one would rise very high without Augustus's favour, and the victories won by his legates were ascribed to their leader. After 19 BC, no one unrelated to the princeps was awarded a triumph.

Augustus's image was everywhere. Caesar had been the first living Roman to permit his likeness to appear on coins. Others, including Brutus and Cassius, did the same in the years after his death, but it was only under Augustus that the practice became almost universal. Apart from coins, there were statues and monuments to his achievements throughout Italy and the provinces, depicting a princeps who was handsome, serene, and ageless—all breaks in style with Roman tradition. The even greater break was the all-pervasive presence of Augustus's name, titles, honours, and face and the emphasis on physical and moral renewal. He boasted that he had 'found Rome mud-brick and left it marble', and the sheer scale and high quality of his building programmes reshaped the city and was reflected in similar outbursts of grand construction all over the empire.[2]

Peace was celebrated—notably in the Altar of Augustan Peace (Ara Pacis Augustae) in Rome—for with it came prosperity and stability. The civil wars were at an end, and this, more than anything else, was what the new peace meant. An ancient ceremony was revived to close the gates of the Temple of Janus whenever the Roman people were at peace everywhere in the world. Augustus performed the ceremony twice, for his forty-four-year reign saw almost constant warfare and a good deal of expansion. Some of this was unfinished business, often arduous and not especially profitable, such as the conquest of the Alps and the completion of the subjugation of the rugged north-western regions of the Iberian Peninsula. The Balkans were also overrun and the frontier settled on the Danube, and for a while the German tribes up to the Elbe were brought under direct Roman rule. The Augustan Peace—like the Pax Romana of which it formed a part—was the product of strength and victory rather than amicable coexistence with neighbours. Although in art the princeps was overwhelmingly depicted as a toga-clad civilian rather than a general, Augustus's conquests were on a vast scale, and plenty of monuments commemorated these achievements.

Augustus gave the Roman state stability, internal peace, and success abroad. None of this was instant, and in the aftermath of Actium few would have predicted that the victor would last so long, not least because he was not a robust man and suffered several bouts of illness so severe that he was not expected to survive. Hindsight too readily lends an inevitability to the course of events, so that we must always remind ourselves that contemporaries—whether Roman, provincial, allied, or Parthian—did not know what the future held and lived their lives and made key decisions day by day, month by month, and year by year. Augustus kept recovering whenever he was ill, and the handful of conspiracies failed, so much so that scholars can be inclined to doubt that they were real and not imagined. The princeps survived, modified his position without ever losing supreme power, and from early on started to groom successors, even if the favoured ones kept dying with a frequency that caused suspicion at the time and since, although it may have been no more than chance.

History has remembered Hadrian as the great traveller among the emperors of the first two centuries of the principate (the name scholars give the system created by Augustus), most of whom spent the bulk of their reigns in Italy. Yet this was not true of Augustus, who was more often to be found touring the provinces. Never a great or natural commander, within a few years he stopped leading his armies in person but did supervise campaigns from close to the theatre of operations. All major wars were fought by the men he most trusted, ideally relations: at the start, his old friend and subsequently son-in-law, Agrippa; then his stepsons Tiberius and Drusus; and ultimately the next generation, his grandsons Caius and Lucius and great-nephew Germanicus. In many ways the system relied not on a single leader or princeps doing everything but on a college of two or more principes, of which Augustus was always the unchallengeable senior, son of the divine Julius and with a list of honours no one could hope to match.

In addition to commanding or supervising major campaigns, listening to petitions and arbitrating local disputes took up an immense amount of time. A story is told of Hadrian (and once had been told of Alexander the Great) being carried in a litter through a city when an old woman called out to him asking that he hear her case. Hadrian replied that he did not have the time, prompting the challenge 'then stop being emperor', which made him halt and give her an audience. One of the main jobs of the princeps was to be the ultimate source of appeal, and even in a settled era this was time-consuming. In the wake of the civil wars—which had not only disrupted provincial government but also caused upheaval and sudden changes of regime in many communities, as whoever happened to control a province at the time exploited it for the war effort— there was a hefty backlog of problems and disputes. An advantage of the principate was that everyone knew that Augustus had the power and the willingness to deal with any problem, and one no longer had to go to Rome in the hope of finding a senator able to help. The long tours of the provinces helped even more, since it was cheaper and quicker to seek an audience as the emperor passed by than it was to travel to Rome and wait there for as long as was necessary. In the same way, the creation of the principate made it simpler for Parthian kings to deal with Rome, the attitude of an emperor being easier to understand and predict than that of the succession of provincial governors and warlords thrown up by the civil wars.[3]

Again, at the start, the Parthians had no more idea than anyone else that the rule of Augustus and the regime he created would endure. By 31 BC if not before, Phraates IV was more concerned by the immediate threat of a challenger for the throne, a man named Tiridates, than he was by the Romans. Both the king and the usurper sent envoys to Augustus before Actium, seeking friendship or perhaps just some assurance that he would not intervene on behalf of their rival. There is no record of whether they also contacted Antony. Either way, no Roman assistance was granted, Augustus being far too preoccupied to send anything while also taking satisfaction in the thought that the Parthians would be busy fighting each other and so unlikely to pose any threat to Rome's provinces.

Late in 30 BC, with Antony and Cleopatra both dead and Egypt occupied, Augustus made his first visit to Syria. His main concern

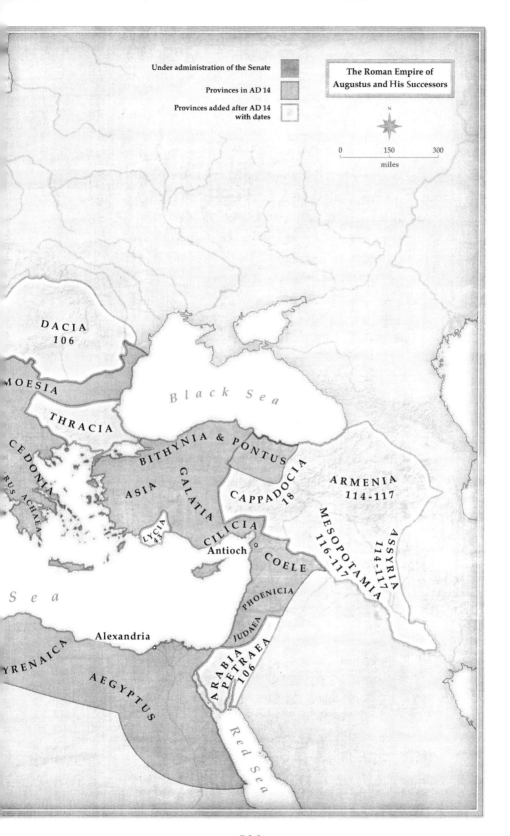

DACIA
106

MOESIA

Black Sea

THRACIA

CEDONIA

BITHYNIA & PONTUS

RUS ACHAEA

ASIA

GALATIA

CAPPADOCIA
18

ARMENIA
114-117

MESOPOTAMIA
116-117

ASSYRIA
114-117

LYCIA
43

CILICIA

Antioch

COELE

Sea

PHOENICIA

Alexandria

JUDAEA

ARABIA
PETRAEA
106

YRENAICA

AEGYPTUS

Red Sea

was to settle the province and neighbouring allied kingdoms of a region that had now backed the losing side for the third time in a Roman civil war. Often this was best served by confirming appointments made by Antony, including Herod's, and in the process placing the incumbents in Augustus's debt. Tiridates arrived, defeated in Parthia but bringing one of Phraates IV's sons with him. Once again, Augustus declined to back him but also for the moment refused to return the prince to his father. Tiridates was granted a comfortable exile within the Roman empire, while the young prince went to Rome with Augustus and was treated as a guest.[4]

A few years later, Tiridates went back to Parthia to renew the civil war, and for a while things went well for him. Phraates IV retreated and was pursued. At one point he became so desperate that he ordered the execution of his harem rather than risk their capture by Tiridates. A little later, a document shows that Phraates had four formal wives, so perhaps these and other royal woman were spared or were somewhere safer at the time, unless he married them in the aftermath. Clearly, the threat posed by Tiridates was serious, for soon Seleucia rallied to him, and he minted coins with the unprecedented slogan of 'friend of the Romans', as well as autokrator or 'sole ruler'. There is no sign that he received any active support from the Romans, so perhaps the boast was meant to show his strength or suggest that relations with Rome would be good once he was secure. After a hard struggle, Phraates IV once again expelled Tiridates, who took permanent refuge in the Roman provinces. Augustus sent Phraates IV's son back to his father, presumably as a gesture of goodwill. Relations with Parthia were just one concern for the emperor among many, most of them more urgent—one of the embassies had reached Augustus when he was in Spain.[5]

Other Romans may have felt differently. In the twenties BC, the poet Horace suggested that 'Augustus will be deemed a god on earth when the Britons and the deadly Parthians have been added to our empire.' He wondered whether there were soldiers captured at Carrhae, still alive decades later, married to 'barbarian wives' and living and serving as soldiers 'under the king of the Medes', forgetting their true names and the traditional toga and gods of Italy. Some ten thousand prisoners had been taken in 53 BC and more during later fighting. As far as we can tell, the bulk of them were sent to Margiana, far off in the east of the Parthian empire, where among other things they built fortifications for and probably garrisoned the city of Merv. There is little evidence that the fate of these men was a major issue in a Rome preoccupied by civil wars, but there was certainly a feeling that the Parthians had proven themselves to be enemies, even if many felt Crassus had been wrong to provoke them. Roman pride had been humbled, and while Ventidius's victories had done something to restore it, Antony's disappointing campaign had muddied the issue. Apart from Horace, other poets spoke with enthusiasm of humbling Parthia and restoring Roman supremacy throughout the world. Inevitably, talk of eastern wars tended to lead to Alexander the Great and predictions that Augustus might equal or surpass his conquests.[6]

Augustus did not neglect the eastern provinces. Syria, which remained a relatively small province geographically, was garrisoned by at least four legions, while there appear to have been two more in Galatia, at least for several decades. Legions tended to move around more in this period than later, as under the principate most established large permanent bases, almost taking root within a province and requiring considerable upheaval to shift them elsewhere. Under Augustus, legions were readily moved from one war zone to another, often several times, and there is evidence for the garrison of Galatia having been sent to Macedonia when there were problems on its borders. This mobility meant that, if necessary, the three legions stationed in Egypt could be considered a handy reserve for the forces in Syria. Uniquely, Augustus placed the legions in Egypt under a governor and commanders who were not senators but equestrians and titled prefects rather than legates. In addition, there were substantial numbers of auxiliaries, non-citizens serving in new units that were both professional and permanent. All in all, almost a third of the army, at least in legionary strength, was stationed where it could be concentrated to threaten Parthia or to meet any attack. That was not its only job. The region was too wealthy and important to risk defection to a

Roman rival, and its population had been exploited so thoroughly in recent years that it had little reason apart from fear to be loyal. Egypt, whose wheat supplied a good deal of the empire, and most of all Rome itself, was especially sensitive, hence Augustus's refusal to place it under the command of a senator or even permit an aristocrat to visit the province without his permission.[7]

Regular Roman forces were just part of the picture, for, as in the past, the region as a whole remained a patchwork of kingdoms, all with armies of their own or the ability to raise them. The Romans continued to expect allied leaders and communities to supply troops and resources whenever requested, so that a substantial part of any field force usually was composed of allies. Nor was it uncommon for allied kings to wage war against a neighbour on Rome's behalf in the hope that victory could be achieved without committing any Roman forces. Royal troops were also employed against raiders and bandits, as well as political insurgents, and indeed at times for unauthorized warfare against other kingdoms, who might themselves be allies of Rome. Sometimes this provoked a response from the Romans—or indeed, for the kingdoms within the Parthian sphere, from the Arsacid king—and sometimes it did not. In this respect little had changed since the arrival of each power in the wider region.[8]

After Antony switched his attention to the power struggle against Octavian, the son of the Armenian king returned from Parthia and took back control of his own kingdom. One source says that he killed all the Romans he found, although it is not clear how many there were or whether they were troops or civilian businessmen. The action does not appear to have provoked a Roman response. Around the same time, the king of Media Atropatene who had allied with Antony appears also to have confirmed his alliance with Phraates IV. In neither case did this mean that the monarch in question was seeking confrontation with Rome. One of the greatest hindrances to understanding the geopolitics of the era is to view everything in simplistic language, where a king is either pro or anti Roman or Parthian. Good relations, even firm alliance, with Rome did not mean that similarly good relations could not be maintained with Parthia, or vice versa. Allied kings were free agents, their day-to-day conduct subject to little or no scrutiny from outside. As long as they kept their own kingdoms fairly stable, did not disturb the wider region too much, and did not do anything in direct conflict with the important interests of Rome or Parthia, the two empires did not worry very much about what the kings did.[9]

As an example, Herod the Great, appointed by Antony and then Augustus as monarch of Judaea and several adjoining territories, spent a great deal of money and effort demonstrating his loyalty to Rome and its princeps, as well as his generosity to provincial communities, most of them Gentile. There were substantial Jewish communities within the Parthian empire, and pilgrims came regularly, especially to mark Passover in the great Temple in Jerusalem. Herod also sent ambassadors to Phraates IV and negotiated successfully for the return of Hyrcanus, the deposed high priest captured by Pacorus. Herod had married Hyrcanus's granddaughter, but the older man still represented the true line of the old Hasmonean royal family, something Herod—as an Idumean, semi-Jewish outsider—most certainly did not. There is no hint in the sources that Herod's negotiations were in any sense sponsored by Rome and intended to foster relations between the two great powers. As far as we can tell, Herod acted in this respect as an independent monarch, claiming that he acted for the prestige of his kingdom and in the interests of the family into which he had married. Both Hyrcanus and Herod's wife would subsequently be executed for alleged conspiracy, just two of many within his household to fall prey to the king's murderous suspicion. None of this prevented Herod from remaining a reliable ally of Rome. While maintaining that loyalty was one of his main priorities, it was still a means to the end of achieving personal security, success, wealth, and prestige.[10]

Augustus maintained substantial forces in the eastern provinces, backed by the armies of the kingdoms. However, he never massed troops in the same sort of numbers as Caesar had planned to do and Antony had actually done for his expedition in 36 BC. In Europe, at times in North Africa, on Egypt's southern borders, and in Arabia, Augustus's reign saw large-scale, aggressive warfare, which included taking large swathes of territory under direct rule. Ten legions were concentrated in Pannonia in AD 6 and similar numbers were deployed in the aftermath of the disaster in Germany in AD 9. Yet Augustus did not listen to the poets and launch a major war against Parthia—nor did he invade Britain for that matter. While no ancient source suggests this, scholars plausibly argue that this was a pragmatic judgement on the part of Augustus, who was a clever man, even if not a gifted general. The experience of Crassus and Antony showed that the Parthians were formidable opponents, so that fighting against them was considerably more risky than war against Iron Age tribes. Tribal opponents were less sophisticated tactically, their settlements less well-defended, and, even more importantly, they lacked political unity. This made it easier to defeat them one by one and made the risk of disaster less, or at the very least likely to be on a smaller, less embarrassing scale. In contrast, the Parthian king of kings could call on the men and resources of a great empire and wage war for a long time and on a large scale. At the same time, this relative political unity aided negotiation between the leader of Rome and the Arsacid king. In essence, it was easier to make and maintain peace with one leader of an empire than with many kings and chieftains of tribes and clans.[11]

The details of negotiations between Augustus and Phraates IV are impossible to reconstruct, even though the outcome was much celebrated throughout the Roman empire. In 20 BC, Augustus came to Syria as part of a wider tour of the eastern provinces. A faction from Armenia had already approached him, complaining about the current king and wanting to replace him with his brother, taken as a hostage by Antony and subsequently sent to Rome. Augustus agreed and was willing to back the change with force, giving the task to his stepson, the twenty-one-year-old Tiberius, no doubt with several more experienced advisors. A force was mustered, perhaps with fresh troops or perhaps from the region. However, before the Romans could act, the unpopular king was murdered, so Tiberius and his men simply escorted the brother into his kingdom without having to fight. Domestic politics was central in all of this, and to achieve their end, the faction involved was willing to accept Roman aid, just as at other times they might have sought Parthian aid. In this case, the new king could be expected to have goodwill towards Rome—and he certainly knew a good deal about Rome and its leaders from the years spent as hostage. At best this fostered some influence, even a strengthened alliance, but in no sense did it mean that the Romans controlled Armenia or had turned it into a satellite state or one hostile to Parthia. Around the same time, alliance was renewed with Media Atropatene, and similarly this did not sever ties between that kingdom and Parthia. Yet all in all Augustus could feel pleased with having strengthened alliances in the region.[12]

The princeps did not want a war with Parthia any more than Phraates IV—relieved of the challenge of Tiridates but never sure whether a new usurper might emerge—wanted to risk confrontation with Rome. The result was a treaty, advantageous to both sides, which could be presented to a home audience as a great success. Phraates IV freed himself from the prospect of a Roman invasion, at least for the immediate future. There was some talk of parts of the Euphrates as a boundary, although whether as a limit to Parthian claims or for both sides is less certain. In return, the Parthians handed over all the eagles and other standards they still possessed—for Antony had got back from the Medes those taken by them from his men. Phraates IV rounded up the surviving Roman hostages and returned them as well. Some men who had spent more of their lives within the Parthian empire than in their original homes hid rather than went back, and a few were even said to have committed suicide rather than leave the wives taken and children raised during their internment. The return of prisoners is noted in our sources and acknowledged as a good thing, but far more attention was paid to the lost standards. Marius, Sulla's rival, had made the eagle the primary standard of each legion, alongside the sixty signa of the *centuriae*, and while coins often showed an eagle with a signum on either side, the eagles were the greatest focus of pride.[13]

'I forced the Parthians to return to me the booty and standards of three Roman armies and to ask as suppliants for the friendship of the Roman People.' Thus Augustus himself described the event in a great inscription set up outside his mausoleum and copied around the empire. For him, the Parthians' action demonstrated that they acknowledged Rome's greater might and respected his own reputation as leader. In *The Aeneid*, the poet Virgil declared that Rome's destiny was 'to spare the conquered and overcome the proud in war'. Parthia had not been conquered in war, but the presence and visible determination of Augustus, Tiberius, and the legions and other troops in the eastern provinces were presented as the display of sheer power that had 'forced' the Parthians to return the eagles and seek peace as 'suppliants'. While there was always greatest glory attached to victory in battles where the enemy dead were numbered in thousands, a voluntary submission in the face of Roman power was entirely acceptable to a Roman audience. When the news reached Rome, the Senate voted Augustus a long list of fresh honours, including a triumph where his chariot could be drawn by elephants rather than horses. Augustus responded in his usual way, thanking them for their generosity while declining almost all the awards, especially the more extravagant ideas. When he eventually returned to Rome, he entered the city quietly and at night and did not celebrate this triumph, with or without elephants. Agrippa, who won victory after victory on his friend's behalf, also pointedly refused to accept a single one of the successive triumphs awarded him by the Senate.[14]

One reason such modesty had power was because even with what was left, the achievements and honours of Augustus outstripped those of any of Rome's great heroes. Eventually the eagles and other standards, along with those recaptured in other theatres, were installed with great ceremony in the newly built Temple of Mars Ultor (Mars the Avenger), which formed the centrepiece of the Forum of Augustus, an extension at right angles to the old Forum Romanum. In the precinct outside were statues of the greatest members of the Julian family and of the men who had celebrated triumphs in the past. Augustus's achievements were marked, among other things, by a statue of a four-horse chariot like that driven by a triumphing general. The natural way to see the monument was a celebration of Rome's great past as all leading towards, even culminating in, Augustus and his greatness.

Coins depicted every stage of the celebrations for the return of the eagles, including imaginings of monuments and events—even the elephants pulling the chariot—that were in fact declined by the princeps.[15]

Scholarly opinion is divided over whether the Parthian Arch awarded to him by the Senate was actually constructed or whether an existing arch, probably the one awarded for his victory at Actium, was enlarged and modified. Judging from coins, most likely the latter was the case, and the grand monument stood beside the tomb of the divine Julius on one of the main routes into the Forum Romanum. On top, Augustus was depicted in a four-horse chariot, and on either side and lower stood a Parthian, one presenting an eagle and the other waving his bow in a gesture of peace. The formidable nature of the Parthians seems to have been emphasized. On the breastplate of the famous Prima Porta statue of Augustus, a standing Parthian warrior hands over an eagle to a figure that probably represented the goddess Roma. Defeated nations were usually shown as female personifications, always suppliant and often seated and with wrists bound. Augustan art permitted the Parthians to appear more formidable even as they acknowledged Rome's superiority. This made the bloodless triumph of 20 BC all the greater an achievement, and one celebrated far more often than the many hard-fought battles won against the tribes of Europe.[16]

Through Augustus, Romans could believe that they had asserted their dominance over a proud and formidable enemy, and even, if they wished, that distant Phraates IV was a subordinate ally like other kings. The Parthians, in contrast, had no reason to see things in this way. While they had seen the importance the Romans invested in the eagles and other standards, we do not know how much the Parthians valued these trophies. From a personal point of view, Phraates IV had secured peace at a low price, handing over symbols without giving up any land he occupied at the time. That the Romans had been forced to ask for the standards taken in battle reminded a home audience of past victories. Ancient leaders and states were seldom inclined to see any treaty or agreement as permanent. Having just survived the challenge of

Tiridates, remaining in power and consolidating his position were Phraates IV's main priorities for the moment.

Like many diplomatic meetings, this one appears to have been accompanied by meetings of gifts, and it may well have been at this time that Augustus presented Phraates IV with a slave girl called Musa. Josephus, the only literary source to mention her, describes the girl as an Italian slave, although precisely what that means is unclear. Presumably she had been born to a slave mother in Italy, but that gives no clue as to her ethnicity; Musa was a fairly common slave name. Perhaps she was from the imperial household and well-educated, unless she was selected purely on the basis of her remarkable beauty. An attractive woman was doubtless considered a pleasing gift for a king who maintained a harem and who may have been in the process of replacing the concubines killed on his orders in the civil war. A mutual exchange of gifts was also a good way for Phraates IV to present the negotiations as a meeting of equals—not that he or Augustus ever met in person.[17]

Musa was clearly a remarkable woman, although the details of her story cannot be known, for Josephus's account is short, gossipy, and hostile. The bare-bones narrative makes it clear that she became one of Phraates IV's favourites, and after she bore him a son, he was moved to acknowledge her as one of his wives rather than an ordinary concubine. Josephus claims that she came to dominate and manipulate the king, who was now middle-aged or older.

Around 11 or 10 BC, according to Augustus, 'Phraates, son of Orodes, king of the Parthians, sent all his sons and grandsons to Italy, not because he had been beaten in war, but to win our friendship through using his sons as sureties.' Four sons with their wives and households, including grandchildren of the king of kings, went to live among the many foreign princes associated with Augustus's household. Josephus says that Musa was behind the decision, wishing to send away the most obvious rivals to her son. Another source suggests that Phraates IV actually wanted the young men out of the way to prevent them from challenging him or being used as figureheads by aristocrats opposed to him. Given that he had murdered his father, brothers, and possibly even one of his own sons to seize the throne in the first place, the suggestion is plausible enough. Yet there was surely also a risk in giving a foreign power so many potential heirs to the throne.[18]

The modern word 'hostage' carries a good deal of baggage not implied by its closest Latin and Greek equivalents. Foreign leaders had been held in Rome in the past, including the Seleucids mentioned earlier, and under Augustus and his successors the numbers would swell immensely. Even if these hostages were demanded as sureties for a treaty, it is highly significant that none were ever executed or punished in any way if such a treaty was subsequently broken. Many cultures in the ancient world had long traditions of guest friendship, forging bonds that were personal more than national. While in and around Rome, the Parthians, like other royalty and aristocrats, were given a Roman education and mixed socially with the princeps and his family. They were not allowed to leave but otherwise appear to have had considerable independence, luxury, and funds. One of Phraates IV's sons endowed a temple during his time in Italy. Augustus paraded them in public as signs of friendship, giving them good—and highly visible—seats at the games. The Ara Pacis Augustae has friezes on either side depicting Augustus, Agrippa, and other family members leading the Senate in a religious ceremony. A small boy in eastern garb clutches the cloak of Agrippa, while a woman whose bowed head has an unusual diadem comforts the lad. Some suggest that the figures may be one of Phraates IV's grandchildren and his mother, but little is certain about this monument, and the boy may be a generic representation of easterners, matching another barefoot and bare-bottomed child on the opposite side who may represent westerners.[19]

The Romans and Parthians remained at peace, with any moments of tension being settled by diplomacy. Agrippa had spent several years in the eastern provinces in the twenties and was there again from 16 to 13 BC, holding imperium, or power superior to all the governors of the region. A year later he was dead, followed in 9 BC by Augustus's stepson Drusus. This meant that a considerable burden fell upon Tiberius, and in 6 BC he was sent to supervise the east but instead chose to retire to private life on Rhodes in an episode that still defies easy comprehension of all its aspects. By this time, the king Tiberius had installed on the throne of Armenia had died, leading to a prolonged and violent power struggle, with at least six kings rising and falling in the next decade and a half.

In 2 BC, Phraates IV's long reign also came to an end when he was allegedly murdered by Musa so that her son Phraataces (or little Phraates) could succeed him while some of the older and more obvious heirs remained in Rome. In itself this did not change the relationship with Rome, but there was more concern when the young Phraataces offered support to a contender for the Armenian throne. Josephus portrays Musa as pulling the strings behind the scenes, even claiming an incestuous relationship between mother and son. Certainly she was important, and for the first time in Parthian history the image of a royal woman appeared on coins. Named as the 'Goddess Mousa', she was on one side and her son on the other, so that they were not shown together, as Antony had chosen to do on some issues depicting him with Cleopatra. Some scholars believe that the pair were married, but the evidence is too poor for any certainty, and we do not know enough about the context to judge how likely this was. The Parthians were not strict adherents to the mainstream Zoroastrian tradition as it developed after the fall of the Achaemenids, which embraced consanguine marriage. As one example, the Parthians buried their dead rather than exposing the bodies. They did revere some of the deities of the Zoroastrian pantheon, but they gave little emphasis to the supreme Ahura Mazda and more emphasis to other gods, notably Mithra— something obvious in several of the names employed since the second century BC. What they thought about marriage between close family members such as mother and son is simply impossible to know, so that we cannot be sure whether Musa flouted convention. Josephus does claim that the influence of the queen, whether as wife-lover or controlling mother, alienated many Parthians.[20]

In AD 1, Augustus sent his adopted son (and actual grandson) Caius Caesar to the east on another of these super-provincial commands, so that his imperium was greater than that of the provincial governors. Poets once again spoke of great wars and triumphs to come, helped by the fact that, as the youth set out, the Temple of Mars Ultor was dedicated with great ceremony and lavish celebration, including a re-enactment of the Battle of Salamis, the famous Greek naval victory over the Persians, by thousands of gladiators in dozens of ships on an artificial lake. Yet there is nothing to suggest that Augustus wanted to launch a major war in the east. Nineteen and inexperienced, Caius was provided with a large and experienced staff of advisors and presumably substantial military forces, although whether this meant reinforcing or simply concentrating the provincial armies is harder to say.

The expedition began with angry diplomatic exchanges, with the Romans refusing to address Phraataces as king of kings, thus casting doubt on his legitimacy. In return, Phraataces wanted his brothers in Rome to be sent back. Yet fairly quickly the mood softened, and a year later Caius and Phraataces met in a carefully orchestrated conference which suggests a good deal of prior planning and negotiation. On the first day, each leader accompanied by an equal number of companions met on an island in the Euphrates. The day after, the Parthian king came across to the Roman bank to dine, and the next day was host to Caius on the other bank. Years later, the author Velleius Paterculus, who was a tribune serving with Caius's forces, recalled 'the sheer spectacle of the Roman army parading on one side and the Parthian army on the other bank' as the two leaders met.[21]

Friendship between Rome and Parthia was reconfirmed, and from the Roman perspective any equality of ceremony was offset because Phraataces met Augustus's son and not Augustus himself. The Romans conceded nothing and refused to return Phraates IV's other sons who were in Rome, agreeing only to keep them there at the moment. The Parthian king informed Caius that one of his own senior advisors had been taking bribes on a grand scale, prompting the disgrace of the senator implicated, who was killed or committed suicide a few days later. On the other hand, the Romans had few demands. Parthian intervention in the Armenian civil war ended, leaving Caius to deal with the matter. This proved less straightforward than hoped, as the first man installed, a member of the royal house of Media Atropatene, was soon deposed by a rebellion. Caius unwisely agreed to meet one of the leaders of the rebels at a parley, only for the man to attack him. Badly wounded, he never fully recovered his physical and emotional health, and he died in February AD 4. Eventually, after further interventions backed by threats as much as force, a candidate acceptable to Augustus managed to survive long enough to be secure.[22]

Phraataces could consider the conference with Caius Caesar a success. The Romans had made formal recognition of his right to rule and treated him with dignity and respect, allowing him to appear as equal, especially for a home audience. If his brothers and nephews were not returned so that he could dispose of them permanently, then they were at least to stay far away in Italy, and the Romans were pledged not to launch any unprovoked attack upon him. Some have speculated that Musa may have schooled her son to deal with Romans with more sophistication and skill than any of his predecessors, and that may or may not be true. Either way, Phraataces's success was short-lived. By AD 4 he had been chased from Parthia by internal opponents, and, ironically enough, went to Syria, where the Romans gave him sanctuary. There is no sign that the change of regime in Parthia disturbed the peace with Rome, at least in the long run.[23]

The war of conquest poets imagined Augustus would wage—or later might bequeath to his sons—was never launched. While this appears a break with what Caesar planned and Antony attempted, in many ways this was a reversion to Roman behaviour under Lucullus and Pompey. As we have seen, there is no certainty that Caesar, Antony, or even Crassus had aimed at extensive conquests rather than an assertion of Rome's dominance and perhaps the installation of a friendly king on the Arsacid throne. Under Augustus, Roman interests were protected and Roman influence expanded, notably among the kingdoms of the region. The means employed were shows of strength and more or less direct threats, combined with a willingness to negotiate. As far as the Romans were concerned, asserting dominance was an acceptable alternative to warfare, and by their standards Augustus had more than achieved this. To Roman eyes, the Parthians had accepted the reality of Roman strength and behaved with appropriate respect to Rome. Whereas Arsacid princes and their families came to live in

Rome, no Roman of consequence, let alone a member of the princeps's family, went to Parthia. It would be centuries before anyone followed the example of Labienus and joined the Parthian court. Both sides had chosen peace rather than a conflict neither wanted at that time, and both benefitted. That did not mean that circumstances would not change, and assertions of dominance were always likely to be transitory.

7

BETWEEN TWO GREAT EMPIRES

5–68

AUGUSTUS'S CAREER RESHAPED ROMAN AND PARTHIAN RELA-
tions and in many ways shaped the boundaries between the two
empires for generations to come. Symbolism was at the heart of
this, with both sides able to present the agreements between them
as glorious—and, even better, bloodless—victories. Augustus assured Romans that the Parthians now understood and accepted
their proper place as subordinate to a Rome which did not really ask anything of them. Phraates IV no doubt assured his lesser
kings and noblemen that the empire to their west similarly understood and respected Parthia's greatness. It was important to
remain militarily strong in case a reminder was needed and for
all the other threats a ruler might face. The possibility of major
conflict between the empires had not vanished but was substantially diminished, allowing Augustus and Phraates IV to focus on
the many other aspects of maintaining their rule and ensuring the
strength and prosperity of their lands.

Sometime around 8, a deputation representing a group of
noblemen travelled from Parthia to Rome, asking Augustus to
give them Vonones, the eldest son of Phraates IV, as king. After
consulting with Tiberius—returned from his self-imposed exile

on Rhodes, rehabilitated, and adopted as the emperor's son and clear successor—Augustus was happy to oblige. Vonones left Italy after some eighteen years living in the imperial household and returned to his homeland, supported by a generous gift of money but without direct military support. At first things went well, and the returning prince was proclaimed king and greeted with enthusiasm. Gradually the mood changed, for inevitably there were noblemen who did not do so well under the new regime. The Roman senator and historian Tacitus, writing about a century later, blamed Vonones's long stay abroad, which meant that he no longer revelled in horses and the chase, preferred a litter to riding, and was fond of Greek courtiers of the sort fashionable in Rome. A man who had been away for so long was bound to have lost touch with the politics and rivalries—and perhaps culture—of his homeland.

Artabanus II, king of Media Atropatene and an Arsacid from a different branch of the family, appeared as rival. The disaffected and those eager for a change rallied to his cause, as did many from the eastern regions of the Parthian empire and beyond, for he appears to have had family connections among the Dahae. Vonones's forces defeated the challenger's first attempt to seize power, after which the Parthian king minted coins proclaiming his victory. In 12, Artabanus II returned and this time drove out Vonones, who fled to Armenia, where the king had lately been deposed. Vonones managed to establish himself as Armenia's ruler and clearly cherished hopes of a return to Parthia one day. Modern scholars tend to agree with Tacitus and see Vonones's failure as almost inevitable, given the stigma of having lived in a foreign—and in the past hostile—capital, adopting the manners of Rome, and being backed by the Romans. While this was surely a factor, perhaps a very important one, to set against this is the fact that he did rule for some four years; plenty of men who had lived all their lives in Parthia failed to hold on to the royal diadem for as long as that before they were murdered or deposed. The newly crowned Artabanus II was a formidable opponent and a gifted and determined leader, so the story can equally be told as his success rather than Vonones's failure. For a few years the rivals watched each other warily, until

Artabanus II was able to encourage discontent among enough Armenian aristocrats and threatened invasion.[1]

Vonones sought Roman support, but there was no enthusiasm for direct conflict with Parthia, so the legate of Syria persuaded him to flee to the Roman empire. The former king was treated with respect and allowed to maintain his court in exile but was also kept under guard. By this time Augustus was dead, having outlived almost all his contemporaries as well as anyone who could remember the days when the Roman republican system had functioned well. Tiberius succeeded him and—while honouring the name of Augustus and presenting most of his own actions as following his precepts—adopted a very different style of leadership. Fifty-four, with a long record of successful campaigns and diplomacy on the frontiers, the new princeps was not inclined to tour the empire and grew weary of the task of listening to endless petitions, appeals, and speeches. After some years, he retreated from Rome to the country and eventually to his villa on the isle of Capri.

At first, he copied Augustus by using family members to go out and deal with major problems. Thus, when Artabanus II moved to install a brother as the new king of Armenia, Tiberius dispatched Germanicus, his nephew and adopted son, to the east, with powers similar to those once held by Caius. Once again, a Roman force marched into Armenia, and at Artaxata Germanicus appointed a son of the king of Pontus to the vacant throne. The new king was seen as well-disposed to Rome and, as importantly, had lived for some time in Armenia and was popular with a good proportion of the nobility. Artabanus II sent envoys, accepting the situation in Armenia, at least for the moment, and asking to renew the alliance with Rome, ideally by holding another face-to-face summit at the Euphrates like the one between Caius and Phraataces. This did not happen, although this may have had nothing to do with willingness on either side. Artabanus II did complain that Vonones was still trying to win over supporters inside Parthia, prompting Germanicus to have the exile sent from Syria to Cilicia, where he would be a little further away.

In 19 Vonones tried to escape, making off during a hunting trip— ironic, given Tacitus's claim that he showed too little enthusiasm for the chase. Word quickly went out, and messages were sent ordering bridges to be broken on the most likely route from Cilicia to Armenia. Recaptured by a cavalry patrol, Vonones was placed back in the charge of the former officer or soldier who had guarded him in the past, who promptly killed him. Tacitus repeats the suspicion that the jailer had been bribed to let the king escape and was covering his own guilt. Corruption on the part of Roman officers, even senior advisors, was a feature of Germanicus's command, just as it had been of Caius's time in the east. There were plenty of locals eager to influence those with authority and plenty of Romans looking to profit and hopeful that the young commander would not notice or care overmuch. In this case, things were made worse by the open hostility between Germanicus and Piso, the legate of Syria, until the latter was sacked. Before the end of 19, Germanicus had fallen ill and died amid rumours of poisoning. Piso was prosecuted for inciting civil war by returning to reclaim 'his' province after the death. He committed suicide before being found guilty, and the Senate issued a decree to be published around the empire which condemned his conduct in considerable detail.[2]

Gossip at the time and later speculation hinted at mistrust between Tiberius and the dashing Germanicus, who had campaigned with considerable success beyond the Rhine before being sent to the east. Whether or not there was any truth in this, his loss and the subsequent death of Tiberius's actual son, Drusus, meant that there were no longer any male relations that the princeps was willing to trust with major commands. Unwilling to go to the provinces himself, Tiberius had to rely on provincial legates on their own. Augustus had left written advice to him suggesting that the empire should be kept at its current size, which added the now deified first emperor's approval to a reluctance to wage aggressive wars. Tiberius's reign was largely one of consolidation, and his dealings in the east, and with Parthia in particular, aimed at avoiding direct Roman involvement and especially military conflict.[3]

Artabanus II had other problems and was equally content to keep the peace with Rome. No king had lasted more than a few years since the death of Phraates IV, and although Artabanus II would manage to break this trend, no one knew this at the time, and it was only to be achieved through considerable effort. There is some sign that territories were lost in the far east of his empire to regional competitors. As ever, the Arsacid king had to find a delicate balance among local kings, the wider nobility, and especially the seven big families—including the Suren, Karen, and Mihran—that held large estates, giving them access to considerable manpower. These men provided almost all of his senior commanders, ministers, and courtiers, as well as much of the manpower for field armies. Also important were the many self-governing communities. A Greek inscription from Susa consists of a letter written by the king, confirming the election of a local magistrate. The result had been contested because the new magistrate had not conformed to a city law stipulating that a number of years should pass between spells in post. Artabanus II backed his claim, praising the man's ability and loyalty to him personally. A king of kings needed to satisfy all these different groups while still asserting sufficient control to make his rule secure and effective.[4]

This was often difficult, for the empire was large and the resources of central government limited, so that no king of kings could hope to impose his will by force everywhere at the same time. Josephus tells a strange story of these years, and it is tempting to see it as illustrating the weakness of central—and some local—authority in the aftermath of a long period of power struggles. Two Jewish brothers, Asinaeus and Anilaeus, part of a substantial Jewish community in Babylonia, were apprenticed to a weaver but found some weapons and fled when the weaver threatened to have them beaten. They turned to banditry and over time gathered large numbers of followers, the majority also Jewish, so that eventually they built strongholds and extracted protection money from farms, villages, and even larger communities. News spread, and the satrap of Babylonia gathered a force and moved against them. Hoping that religious scruple would give him an easy victory, he attacked on the Sabbath, when many Jews held that it was against the law of God to fight. The brothers and their men broke the rule and routed the attackers, inflicting heavy losses.

When reports of the battle reached Artabanus II, he sent trusted messengers from his household to summon the brothers to him.

One brother agreed and got such a favourable reception that he persuaded his sibling to join him, for Artabanus II had decided to make use of the bandits rather than try to suppress them. Therefore, he appointed the two brothers to govern the region they had seized, but from now on they were to be his representatives. The decision was not universally popular at court, but opposition remained personal and disunited. According to Josephus, for fifteen years the brothers governed over a large district, with Parthian aristocrats showing them every honour in public. Their rule was based on force, which allowed them to extort money whenever it was not willingly surrendered. Then Anilaeus became infatuated with the famously beautiful wife of one nobleman, so that he declared the husband an outlaw, attacked and killed him in battle, and married the widow. She remained a pagan, presumably a Zoroastrian of some form, and when this was resented by the brothers' followers, her new husband refused to listen to their concerns. Josephus claims that she poisoned Asinaeus so that her man was in sole charge.

The bandit turned governor began to prey on some villages in the territory of a nobleman named Mithridates, taking people as slaves as well as livestock and money. Mithridates was married to a daughter of Artabanus II but clearly felt it right and proper to defend his own lands without seeking royal support, so he gathered warriors from his household. He moved to attack but rested on the Sabbath on the basis that, while Jews might defend themselves on that day, they would not attack. Again, the bandits broke the rules, attacking during the night and routing their surprised enemies. Mithridates was captured and promptly paraded around, naked and riding a donkey. He was then released, on the basis that humiliation was something the king might ignore, whereas he would be bound to seek vengeance if a son-in-law was killed and most likely would attack the wider Jewish population rather than the bandits themselves. However, spurred on by his royal wife, Mithridates gathered a far stronger force and attacked for a second time, catching the overconfident bandits when they were weary and thirsty as they marched to meet him. Josephus claims that tens of thousands were slaughtered, but he was often inclined to exaggerate these sorts of numbers.

Anilaeus escaped and started to rebuild his band, albeit with far less experienced and confident replacements compared to the men he had lost. The bandits were weaker and probably made more vicious by desperation, so the wider population wondered whether it was better to tolerate them or resist them. Gentile communities tried to persuade the Jewish population to give them up. The approach failed, but a locally raised force discovered where Anilaeus was. Approaching stealthily, they found the bandits drunk and helpless. All were slaughtered, including their leader. In the aftermath there was a period of bloody intercommunal violence—something always lurking beneath the surface in many ancient communities—and hatred of the bandits was turned against the Jewish population in general.

Josephus recounts the story to describe the fortunes of the Jewish population in Babylonia and because it fits with many of the broader themes of his work, notably the role of bandit leaders in Judaea's great rebellion in 66. Banditry was a common enough problem in much of the Roman empire, as it was in the wider ancient world. Yet even if only the broad picture is accurate, it suggests that in these years large and important areas of Parthia were under, at best, the loose control of a king who preferred to back anyone with armed force behind them rather than try to suppress them. The attack on Mithridates's territory does not appear to have prompted Artabanus II to intervene, and at the second attempt the nobleman defeated his enemies through his own efforts. Any man of status maintained warriors in his household and others upon whom he could call as necessary, and there is no evidence that any ethnic groups were wholly excluded from becoming part of this elite. A little earlier, Josephus mentions a Jewish man who brought his family and five hundred cavalrymen when he fled to the Roman empire and was eventually given land by Herod the Great. What is striking is the importance of possessing soldiers not simply as a symbol of duty but to confirm the reality of power. This is in marked contrast to the Roman empire under the principate and in other periods of stability. There, at least in normal times—though less so during civil wars—men like Asinaeus and Anilaeus could not hope to raise a private army, prey on the lands around, and eventually gain formal recognition as local governors.[5]

Tiberius described the job of princeps as like 'holding a wolf by the ears', as the ruler had to keep a tight grip to avoid being savaged. This was surely even more true of the Arsacid king of kings. In Rome as in Parthia, prolonged periods of instability and civil war made the task even harder, so that the success of Artabanus II is all the more striking, even if this was sometimes achieved by letting local strongmen, be they noblemen or successful bandits, enjoy considerable freedom as long as they did not turn against him. Gradually, he grew stronger. When the Armenian king appointed by Germanicus died, Artabanus II managed to place his son on the vacant throne and sent a deputation to Tiberius, demanding the substantial treasury that had been left by Vonones and making grand comments about his right and intention to reclaim all the lands once ruled by Achaemenid Persia and Alexander and his successors.[6]

A king of kings so confident in his own strength was not necessarily popular with noblemen worried that he might move against them or at the very least curb their independence. One group banded together and opened secret negotiations with Tiberius, with an aristocrat and a senior eunuch from the court acting as spokesmen. Once again, a Roman princeps was asked to send a Parthian prince back home so that he could become king. Tiberius chose Phraates IV's last surviving son, who then most inconveniently died when he got to Syria. In the meantime, the princeps asked the king of Iberia to intervene in Armenia, encouraged by generous gifts of funds. Artabanus II's son was assassinated and replaced on the throne of Armenia by the Iberian king's brother, yet another man named Mithridates.

Artabanus II responded by sending another of his sons, Orodes, with money and troops to regain Armenia. Both sides did their best to hire mercenaries from the Sarmatian Alan tribes to the north, but since the Iberians controlled the routes through the Caucasus, they managed to prevent any bands from joining their opponents in Armenia. It is another sign that the easiest way to raise soldiers quickly for an Arsacid king, and indeed most leaders of the wider region, was to look to the fierce horsemen of the steppes. Presumably there were Armenians on both sides. Mithridates also had infantry from the Iberians and the Albani and mounted Sarmatians, while Orodes had Parthians, which as usual might often include men from Media Atropatene and the other regions. The latter's strength was in their cavalry, and they were more effective horse-archers than the Sarmatians, who, although they used bows, favoured hand-to-hand combat. Mithridates's men charged to close the distance, and Orodes's men tried to prevent this and rely on their shooting, but the terrain and the better mix of troop types worked against the Parthians. Sighting the enemy leader, the king of the Iberians galloped at Orodes, wounding him, but was unable to turn back and finish the job before the Parthian bodyguards ushered their leader to safety. Even so, rumour spread that the commander was dead and not simply wounded, and his army broke and fled, seeing no sense in fighting to place a dead man on the throne. No Roman had taken part in the battle, and even the Parthian contingent did not represent the royal army as such. However, the defeat prompted Artabanus II to intervene, striking first at Iberia.[7]

With his first-choice candidate for the throne of Parthia dead, Tiberius then sent a prince from the next generation, Tiridates, a grandson of Phraates IV. Tiridates was escorted to the Euphrates by the legate of Syria and his army. The Romans postured, threatening invasion, which helped persuade Artabanus II that this was a far greater threat. Before he could move to deal with it, significant numbers of his noblemen openly declared themselves against him and for the challenger. Worried, Artabanus II withdrew to the eastern part of his empire and tried to regather his strength, but his supporters trickled away. The legions threw a bridge of boats across the Euphrates, most likely near Zeugma, but then sent Tiridates on his way to be greeted by supporters, including the king of Osrhoene, the nobleman who had negotiated with Tiberius, and another who had spent some time in Roman service leading a Parthian contingent and being rewarded with Roman citizenship. No doubt there were others with the franchise, such as the prince and prominent members of his court, but there were no units of

Roman soldiers with the army. This was a Parthian prince claiming his rightful inheritance, and the communities in his path welcomed him as he marched to Seleucia on the Tigris. Whether the people saw him as favouring their community more than Artabanus II—who had stopped putting the slogan 'philhellene' on his coins early on in his reign—or simply felt that it was better to back a likely winner is hard to say.

Calculation went alongside sentiment, and this was clearly demonstrated when two prominent noblemen sent excuses to explain that they were delayed in coming to acclaim Tiridates as king of kings. Deciding that he could wait no longer, the new king had the diadem placed on his head by the current Surena, as was traditional, but in the aftermath felt unable to move directly against Artabanus II. Instead, the new king besieged a stronghold where his rival had left his harem and a large part of his treasury. Money was essential for any ruler, and once again the prestige and important connections of the royal women were highlighted. Josephus stressed that the Mithridates who fought Asinaeus was married to Artabanus II's daughter, and how this connection marked his status and meant that he had to be treated differently from a nobleman who lacked a similar family tie. There is a good chance that Artabanus II himself carried Arsacid blood from the alliance between a king's daughter and a prince of the Dahae.

Tiridates was grandson of Phraates IV, although he had spent most of his life in Rome. This upbringing may have counted against him—and made it harder for him to understand his new subjects—but more than anything else he was blamed for lacking urgency and a killer instinct. As he waited, more and more noblemen decided that Artabanus II was the better option. This included the two men who had failed to turn up for the coronation. A romantic story claims that some noblemen tracked down Artabanus II and found the former king on the distant fringes of Hyrcania, living the basic life of a hunter. In the campaign that followed, he stayed in this dirt-stained and simple garb rather than donning the silks and splendour of the palace. First he recruited strong contingents of Dahae and Saka—again demonstrating the importance of warriors from outside the empire proper. Then he launched a rapid attack, arriving at Seleucia far earlier than expected. Tiridates seemed weak, he dithered, and his supporters deserted him, the trickle becoming a rushing stream as he retreated. There were only a handful of people still with him when he crossed the Euphrates again and reached the sanctuary offered by Syria.[8]

Artabanus II was a survivor, and once again his success had as much to do with his own talent, skill, and luck as it did with his rival's failings. While the Romans had funded and encouraged Tiridates and—at slightly more of a distance—backed rivals in Armenia, no Roman soldiers or formal representatives of Rome had taken part in any of the campaigns. Neither Artabanus II nor Tiberius wanted direct confrontation, so peaceful relations and past treaties were confirmed at a meeting with the legate of Syria, held this time at the centre on a bridge over the Euphrates, where Herod Antipas, the ruler of Galilee and Peraea, staged a lavish feast for the king and the governor. Artabanus II sent a son and other family members to live as guests of the emperor in Rome. Among the presents to be sent to Tiberius was a Jewish man of exceptional size, if perhaps less tall than the ten feet six claimed by Josephus.[9]

There was another plot against Artabanus II soon afterwards, which forced him to seek refuge with a regional king, whose backing helped him raise enough troops to regain power yet again. This was his last success, for he died within a year or so, at which point his remaining sons fought and murdered each other to succeed him, and other contenders may also have appeared. Then for several years, two of Artabanus II's sons split the empire, one ruling in the west and the other in the east. Although there was brief talk of striking against the Roman provinces, presumably as a show of strength for the home audience as much as anything else, nothing much came of it. Raiders plundered a couple of villages near Zeugma and within the Roman province and may have occupied them, prompting the provincial legate to complain. This was enough to make the attackers withdraw, and we cannot tell whether they were freelancers or men under orders of a local king or one of the claimants to the throne.[10]

Tiberius died in 37, his last years blighted after narrowly suppressing a coup headed by a trusted friend, the commander of his Praetorian Guard. Many leading Romans fell victim to the purge that followed, and then to the suspicions of a fearful emperor. There was great enthusiasm for his successor, the surviving son of Germanicus. Caius—who is normally known by the nickname Caligula, or 'little boots', given to him by his father's soldiers because the family dressed him up in a miniature version of a legionary's uniform—proved a disappointment. Within four years he was assassinated by that rarest of things, a successful conspiracy organized by senators. For a few hours, the Senate debated whether it was time to do away with emperors and return to annually elected leaders, but this was dismissed as impractical, and instead they talked about who among them should succeed. It was already too late, for in the meantime the praetorians had discovered the emperor's uncle Claudius hiding behind a curtain in the palace and had proclaimed him as princeps. Lacking troops of their own, the Senate accepted this with as much grace as they could muster.

Unlike Tiberius, let alone Augustus, neither Caligula nor Claudius could boast of any military exploits before they became emperor. This made them more inclined to be aggressive than Tiberius, but neither looked to the eastern frontier for glory, although Caligula deposed Mithridates the Iberian as king of Armenia. The appointment, dismissal, and even transfer of allied monarchs was not unusual. Tiberius had deposed the king of nearby Commagene and taken the area under direct Roman rule. Caligula restored him, then changed his mind and deposed him again. Later the decision was again reversed, and the king was sent back to Commagene by Claudius and ruled for a considerable time as a loyal ally of Rome. He also sent Mithridates the Iberian back to Armenia with a small escort of Roman troops, but his main ambitions lay elsewhere. In 43, Claudius sent an army of four legions and auxiliaries to invade Britain, visited twice by Julius Caesar almost a century before. The elderly and infirm emperor bothered to pay a brief visit to the island in person and celebrated the victory with great ceremony, naming his young son Britannicus.[11]

In Parthia, one of Artabanus's sons was murdered, encouraging the surviving brother to bring the entire empire under his sole control. For a third time, a group of aristocrats went to Rome's leader, in this case Claudius, and requested that a descendent of Phraates IV be sent back to them. As before, the legate of Syria—interestingly, a descendant of Cassius, Crassus's quaestor and Caesar's assassin—escorted the prince to the crossing point of the Euphrates but went no further. With an army of local nobles and kings, including in time the head of the great Karen clan, this grandson of Phraates was persuaded to take the route through the mountains of Armenia. It was a while before the two sides met in battle, and before that several important allies had defected to the other side. The great clash was confused, but it was decided when the Karen, in an echo of the fate of Publius Crassus, pursued too far and he and his men were overwhelmed and killed. As his army dissolved in despair, the challenger was betrayed by an ally, but the victor contented himself with cutting off the prince's ears and keeping him in comfortable captivity.[12]

Around 50, Artabanus II's remaining son died, whether naturally or through misadventure is unclear. The king of Media Atropatene was crowned but was dead within the year, and next to nothing is known of him. Succession appears to have been smooth, and a relative—either brother or son and supposedly the child of a Greek concubine, Vologaeses I—was crowned as king of kings. There were two brothers, or perhaps half-brothers, who were strong in his affections or too powerful to ignore. One was made king of Media Atropatene, and Vologaeses I hoped to install the other in Armenia, which was in the throes of civil war. Mithridates of Iberia's nephew Rhadamistus had come to live at his uncle's court in Armenia and responded to his warm hospitality by encouraging disaffection among the nobles of the country. Eventually, backed by his father, the king of Iberia, Rhadamistus openly revolted, besieging the king and the Roman troops still acting as his escort. The prefect in charge was bribed to persuade Mithridates to capitulate and helped to undermine the enthusiasm of his soldiers for protecting the king. Mithridates reluctantly gave in to their wishes, and he and his family surrendered and were murdered by the rebels. Rhadamistus proclaimed himself king of Armenia.[13]

In 52, Vologaeses I invaded Armenia on behalf of his brother, whose name was Tiridates. Rhadamistus fled and the Parthians and those Armenians who joined them besieged Artaxata, until winter weather meant that there was not enough fodder for the army's horses. The bulk of the Parthian troops withdrew, leaving Tiridates with a significantly weaker army. Rhadamistus came back and drove him out of Armenia, dealing savagely with his rival's supporters. Vologaeses I was unable to return for some time, first intervening in Adiabene, where a significant body of the nobility had turned against the local ruler, and after that having to go to the east because of raids, even an invasion, by large numbers of steppe nomads. However, internal rebellion soon forced Rhadamistus to flee from Armenia for a second time. He was accompanied by his pregnant wife, Zenobia, who was unable to ride fast enough to keep ahead of their pursuers. Apparently at her bidding, to give her an honourable death, Rhadamistus stabbed her and departed. Yet the queen was not dead and was found by shepherds, tended until she recovered, and taken to the Parthians, who treated her with great courtesy.[14]

Claudius died in the autumn of 54 and was succeeded by his stepson, the seventeen-year-old Nero. Rule was supposed to be joint with Britannicus, who was three years younger, but he conveniently died and was widely assumed to have been murdered. One of the first challenges to confront the youngest and least-experienced emperor up to this point was Armenia, for Tiridates had returned and assumed the kingship without at any point seeking Roman approval. The response began, in the best tradition of Augustus and the other emperors, with a build-up of force to provide an edge to diplomatic activity.

Distance, and especially topography, made it extremely difficult for the Syrian legate to watch the border with Mesopotamia and simultaneously direct operations on the border with and inside Armenia. Therefore, a new provincial command was created for as long as was necessary in Cappadocia and Galatia, and the four legions in Syria split into two armies, so that there were two legions in each area. This number was soon increased as units were brought from elsewhere, so that each of the legates had three legions under his command, supplemented by auxiliaries and strong forces supplied by the allied kings of the region. A recruiting drive took place in the provinces, perhaps including a measure of con-scription among the citizen population, as the legions were brought up to strength and those soldiers who were no longer fit for active service were weeded out.[15]

The new command was given to Cnaeus Domitius Corbulo, who had made a name for himself as legate on the Rhine under Claudius. One of his first tasks was to muster his forces and lead them in a rigorous training programme, keeping them in tents throughout the winter and getting them accustomed to operating in the mountains and dealing with snow and the cold—all likely if they ended up campaigning in Armenia. Discipline was harshly enforced. Recaptured deserters were executed for the first offence, rather than getting a second or third chance as was more normal. At the same time, Corbulo was no mere martinet and led by ex-ample, sharing the hardships, 'praising the hardy, encouraging the weary, acting as an example for everyone to see'. Middle-aged like any Roman commander of this era who was not from the imperial family, he was a good-looking, physically fit, and vigorous man with a good deal of charm and great skill as an orator.

For all his many virtues, like many successful commanders throughout history, Corbulo had an extremely high opinion of himself, was inclined to be dismissive of other senior officers, and could be jealous of his reputation, even to the point of pettiness. The negotiations with Tiridates, Vologaeses I's brother, opened with bickering between the officers sent by Corbulo and the Syrian legate over who should escort the king's envoys. This was unfor-tunate, but more seriously the subsequent negotiations failed to resolve the issue, which was essentially a question of reputation and saving face. Nero and the Romans were prepared to accept Tiridates as king of Armenia, but only if he appeared as a suppliant who was granted his throne by the emperor. At this stage, confident in his own ability and his brother's support, Tiridates did not wish to be seen as so weak that he was dependent on Rome. Armenia was not an easy kingdom to control at any time, let alone after the overthrow of a succession of kings. Its nobility were fiercely independent, aided by the fact that many of them could retreat to strongholds in the high valleys which were difficult to capture.[16]

Tiridates had both supporters and opponents among the Armenian nobility, and no doubt there were plenty more watching and reluctant to commit themselves fully until it was clear whether he would win. In order to persuade everyone that he was here to stay, Tiridates began attacking his opponents, using a mixture of Armenian troops, his own household, and others supplied by his brother. Corbulo had stationed most of his forces near the border with Armenia, including several auxiliary units in a row of forts. He had placed an officer—a former *primus pilus*, the senior centurion of a legion—as overall commander of these outposts, and was dismayed when the man disobeyed his instructions and attacked a detachment of Tiridates's men, only to be routed. This was a bad start for a largely inexperienced army. A story was told that the prefect in charge of one cavalry ala had neglected the care and discipline of his men so badly that Corbulo ordered a public humiliation. The prefect was told to report to the general's tent, where he was stripped naked and ordered to stand to attention for hours. The defeated soldiers were also shamed by being ordered to set up tent lines outside the camp's ramparts and sleep there while receiving barley—the food of animals, the poor, and slaves—for their grain ration rather than wheat. After a while, a petition from the army, or perhaps the officers, asked for pardon for them all. Corbulo had made his point about the importance of obeying his orders and granted the request.[17]

Discipline, tight control, and a methodical advance were the keys to Corbulo's style of warfare in the campaigns to come. In the following spring, he marched into Armenia to face Tiridates. When the Romans kept in good order—units placed so that each troop type could support the rest—the enemy could not inflict significant harm on them. Yet, in reverse, the mobile enemy could not be forced into fighting and withdrew ahead of them. There was a face-to-face meeting, with Corbulo ignoring his opponent's request to attend with only unarmoured soldiers and instead bringing a legion supplemented by men from another to suggest that each one under his command was larger than was actually the case. Neither side was willing to compromise enough to satisfy the other, so fighting resumed. Unable to provoke a battle, the Romans split into four independent columns, and Corbulo instructed allied kings to lead their own attacks in support. Targets were the strongholds of the nobles who supported Tiridates.

The Roman army excelled at siege-craft, as long as they took care to prepare and protect the equipment and supplies needed for these operations. Antony's fatal error in 36 BC had been to let the enemy destroy his main siege and baggage train. Corbulo took care not to repeat this mistake and set up forts along key supply lines and ensured that escorts for any convoy were adequate to protect it. It is particularly striking that the relatively small columns formed by Corbulo proved perfectly capable of acting on their own. This was partly because they were composed of a good balance of soldiers and partly through competent leadership at all levels. As important was the rugged nature of much of the terrain and the relative weakness of Tiridates, whose brother was once again directing his main energies to fighting in the east of his empire and so was in no position to send major reinforcement.

Stronghold after stronghold fell to the Romans, sometimes to rapid and sometimes to more careful assaults. Corbulo's attitude towards atrocity was pragmatic rather than moral, which is to say characteristically Roman. At one major settlement he staged a deliberate act of terror: all adult males were massacred, and the rest of the population given to the troops for sale as slaves. Horrified by the news—and balancing protecting their families and property against loyalty to a king who appeared very weak—more and more communities chose to surrender rather than resist the seemingly unstoppable and ruthless enemy. Those who did capitulate were treated generously by the standards of ancient warfare.[18]

The fall of these communities made Tiridates seem vulnerable, so he felt obliged to mass his forces and confront Corbulo, who had concentrated much of his army and was marching on Artaxata. Yet again, the result was a standoff, with neither side able to harm the other as long as neither made a mistake. This was highlighted when the officer commanding a troop of auxiliary cavalry led a reckless charge and was shot down by arrows. Otherwise, Corbulo kept his army under tight control, and steadily their hollow square continued its advance. Disappointed, and not seeing what else he could do, Tiridates withdrew under cover of darkness. The Romans closed on Artaxata and surrounded it, prompting an immediate surrender from citizens unwilling to fight for a king who had abandoned them. Corbulo spared the population but slighted the defences and burned some of the city. The army hailed Nero as imperator, for Corbulo was his representative and the true victory was attributed to the emperor, a couple of thousand miles away. The Senate eagerly approved and added many more honours.[19]

Corbulo then undertook the long march to Tigranocerta, the other main city of the kingdom. It was a risk, for supplies ran short, and for a while the soldiers had to eat a diet almost solely of meat before they reached land where they were able to forage more successfully. Tigranocerta chose to resist, and the Romans started to construct siege-works to capture it. In the meantime, a young nobleman was killed, and his head was shot by a ballista over the walls. 'By chance it fell in the midst of the council being held by the most important barbarians: the sight of this object, which seemed almost an omen, so stunned them that they rushed out to surrender.' Once again, to encourage others to follow the example, the city and its population were spared. In the meantime, Rome's allies continued to raid. One was the king of the Iberi, who had prudently executed his son Rhadamistus, the man who had overthrown his uncle, made himself king of Armenia, and so alienated his subjects that he was twice chased out. Around this time, envoys came to the Romans from 'Hyrcania', which may mean no more than the far east of the Arsacid empire, where leaders were in arms against Vologaeses I. They asked for alliance with Rome, and—whether or not this was granted and any practical assistance offered—Corbulo took great care to have them sent home via the Caspian Sea to avoid going through Parthia.[20]

The Romans continued to take stronghold after stronghold, and when Tiridates launched an offensive the following year he quickly withdrew when the Romans marched against him. To replace him, Nero named Tigranes—son of the king of Cappadocia, descendant of Herod the Great, and someone who had spent most of his youth with the imperial family in Rome—as the new king of Armenia. Corbulo placed a garrison of several thousand

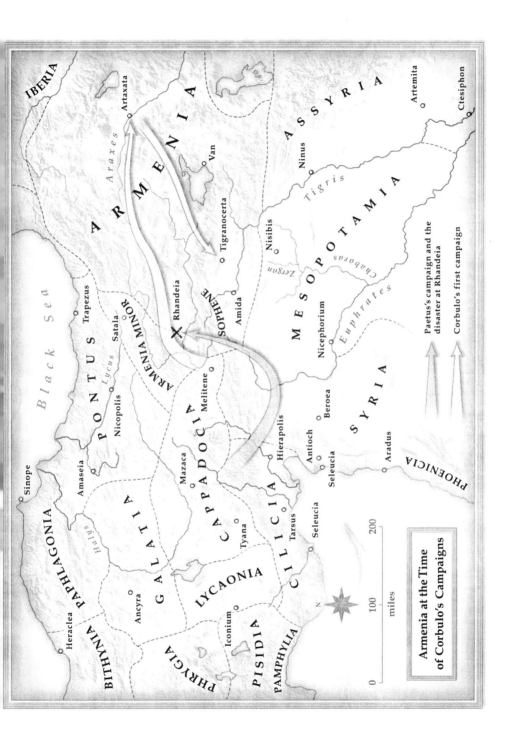

Armenia at the Time
of Corbulo's Campaigns

Paetus's campaign and the
disaster at Rhandeia

Corbulo's first campaign

IBERIA

Black Sea

Sinope

Heraclea PAPHLAGONIA

BITHYNIA

PHRYGIA

PISIDIA

PAMPHYLIA

Iconium

LYCAONIA

Ancyra

GALATIA

Tyana

Mazaca

CAPPADOCIA

CILICIA

Tarsus

Seleucia

Amaseia

Halys

Nicopolis

Lycus

PONTUS

Satala

Trapezus

ARMENIA MINOR

Melitene

SOPHENE

Rhandeia

Amida

Hierapolis

Antioch

Beroea

Seleucia

SYRIA

Aradus

PHOENICIA

ARMENIA

Araxes

Artaxata

Van

Tigranocerta

Nisibis

Ninus

ASSYRIA

Tigris

Zergan

Chaboras

Nicephorium

Euphrates

MESOPOTAMIA

Artemita

Ctesiphon

N

miles

0   100   200

169

legionaries and auxiliaries in Tigranocerta and took the rest of his army back to the Roman provinces. Since the legate of Syria had died of natural causes, Corbulo took his place, reuniting the provincial command split at the start of the crisis.[21]

So things might have settled, had the newly installed king of Armenia not decided to raid Adiabene in circumstances that are not recorded, and done it so well that he threatened to take permanent control of territory on the border. Unfortunately for him, Vologaeses I felt that this justified his return from his eastern campaign, not least because the king of Adiabene complained of lack of protection from the king of kings, while Tiridates was also accusing his brother of weakness. Plenty of Parthian kings had been deposed when they were perceived to be weak or unreliable, so for his own safety as much as anything else Vologaeses I decided to make Armenia his immediate priority. The king of Adiabene was reinforced with troops. Tigranes of Armenia withdrew at this threat and soon found himself besieged in Tigranocerta. Corbulo demonstrated by massing an army by the Euphrates. A formal complaint was sent to Vologaeses I, and eventually it was agreed that the invaders would withdraw and an embassy be sent to negotiate at Rome itself. Part of the deal also appears to have led to the withdrawal of the Roman troops in Tigranocerta.[22]

As at the start of the confrontation, it clearly would have been very difficult for one legate to protect Syria and supervise operations on the Cappadocian border with Armenia, let alone Armenia itself. Therefore, Corbulo requested another legate be sent for the command he had formerly held, while he remained in Syria. Nero chose Lucius Caesennius Paetus, but, when the Parthian envoys came to Rome, negotiations failed to resolve the dispute. War resumed, with Paetus marching into Armenia, hoping to reach Tigranocerta. Unlike Corbulo, he does not appear to have come to the post with an existing military reputation, and he was not a careful commander. His units were under-strength from detachments and furloughs. In addition, his attention to supply was inadequate, so that as the winter closed in he was unable to reach his goal and instead built camps near Rhandeia, close to the river Arsanias, which flowed into the Euphrates.[23]

Corbulo remained near Zeugma, where he constructed a bridge of boats across the Euphrates itself. He used catapults to cover the work, since these had a longer effective range and greater force than any bow. Parthian riders watched but were unable to slow, let alone prevent, the construction. Once complete, the Romans built forts on the far bank to protect the bridgehead but made no other aggressive move. Corbulo wanted to make clear that he could advance if he chose, but that, with his army in position, it would be very difficult for the Parthians to cross into the Roman province.[24]

Blocked from threatening Syria, Vologaeses I sensed better opportunities in Armenia and took a considerable part of his royal forces to assist his brother in regaining the kingdom. Paetus swung between overconfidence—advancing to meet this force and bragging about great victories—and nervousness, retreating when the enemy grew close. He split his forces, isolating several thousand men in outposts that were quickly overrun. The rest holed up in the main camp at Rhandeia while he sent messengers asking Corbulo to march to his aid. Before this arrived, Paetus despaired and surrendered. The Romans handed over their camp, heavy equipment, and supplies and built a bridge over the Arsanias for the Parthians to cross, with Vologaeses I riding an elephant to make the event all the more spectacular. There was a rumour that the legionaries went under the yoke—an ancient humiliation where each man had to duck his head to pass under a frame of spears—before they were allowed to depart. Whether this happened or not, the episode was designed to show Parthian might and Roman weakness, and Paetus made matters far worse by retreating so quickly that he abandoned any of the wounded unable to keep up. The fugitives soon ran into Corbulo's relief army, marching fast, its supplies carried on pack camels, just a few days too late.[25]

Negotiations followed, and Vologaeses I agreed to withdraw his own forces from Armenia, leaving his brother to look after himself, and in return the Roman outposts across the Euphrates were demolished and the troops withdrawn. Envoys went to Rome once again, but as before agreement proved impossible. Nero demanded that Tiridates travel to Rome to receive the royal diadem and official acknowledgement of his right to rule Armenia.

Tiridates was one of the magi, a Zoroastrian priestly caste, and it was claimed that he was forbidden from crossing water.* Instead, he offered to show submission to an image of Nero rather than in person. As the next spring approached, Corbulo mustered a field force, taking care to make no use of the troops still demoralized from the debacle at Rhandeia. He marched into Armenia, capturing any stronghold offering resistance. This was enough to prompt Vologaeses I and Tiridates to meet for fresh talks, and to make a point they arranged for these to happen at Rhandeia as a reminder of their recent success. Pride and face were very important, and neither side wanted to prolong the struggle or let it escalate into full-scale war between Rome and Parthia.[26]

When the talks were over, Tiridates symbolically took off the royal diadem and laid it down in front of an image of Nero. Setting aside his scruples, he agreed to go to Rome in person and ask Nero for the throne. No one was in a hurry, and it was the best part of four years before he set off on this journey, accompanied by three thousand horsemen as well as a large part of the royal court. Vologaeses I had insisted that every honour be paid to his brother. Nero's governors greeted him with all the respect and pomp appropriate for a senior Roman magistrate as he made his way, avoiding crossing water whenever possible, so that it took months to reach Rome. Nero paid all the expenses as well, ensuring that the whole thing was grandly stage-managed. Simply to feed and care for the royal party cost some eight hundred thousand sesterces per day.** The visitors were entertained with games and other spectacles, culminating in a ceremony where Tiridates bowed before Nero. A proud man from a proud race, he was unwilling to do this unarmed, so instead had very visibly nailed his

---

*The magi are most familiar from Matthew's account of the Nativity, although it is unclear whether the visitors from the east were formally part of this caste or this was a generic term. Very little is known about this group during the Arsacid Parthian period, other than that they were important and were represented in at least some royal councils.

**There were four sesterces in a denarius (the penny of the Authorized Bible). As a rough guide, the minimum property qualification for the Senate was one million sesterces, although most had far, far more than this. In Nero's day, a legionary earned nine hundred sesterces in a year.

sword into its scabbard. Still, he claimed to worship Nero as he did Mithras (the Latinized name for Mithra and one of the most important of the Zoroastrian gods) and declared himself subject to whatever judgement the emperor chose to make, even though the business was already settled. Nero crowned him king, stressing that no one else had the power to do this; only he could give a kingdom or take it away. Publicly grateful, the Romans aided the rebuilding of Artaxata, partly destroyed by Corbulo, by a gift to the king worth two hundred million sesterces, and for a while the city was renamed Neronia in the emperor's honour.[27]

The ceremony occurred in 66, and the sheer scale of it all was symptomatic of Nero's reckless spending that did so much to drain the imperial coffers. The dispute had started almost a decade earlier and sputtered along, so the precise chronology of the campaigns is uncertain. During that time there had been quite a lot of fighting, as different claimants to the Armenian throne struggled to impose their rule on unwilling subjects, and as allied kings raided and burned for their own ends or with encouragement from the Roman emperor or Arsacid king. Corbulo's men had stormed numerous walled settlements, had captured both Artaxata and Tigranocerta, and had killed or enslaved the populations of other communities. Parthian cavalry—a vague term since it said little about the horsemen's ethnicity and meant no more than contingents from the royal household or the households of noblemen in the empire or warriors employed as mercenaries—had joined with Armenians and other local troops to besiege Tigranocerta and its partly Roman garrison and more directly strike at Paetus's outposts and blockade his camp. Few numbers are given, but the Romans appear never to have employed more than three legions and auxiliaries in one place. Even if all units were close to full strength, Corbulo probably never had a field army as big as the one Crassus had led into Mesopotamia, and even if all the soldiers in the wider theatre are included, the total was nowhere near as great as the host gathered by Antony in 36 BC. The Parthians seem similarly to have committed less than their full might.

These years of confrontation are also striking for what did not happen. There was no major pitched battle between Romans

and Parthians. Corbulo deliberately went only a short distance—
perhaps a mile or so at most and probably less—after crossing
to the far bank of the Euphrates. No Parthians or allies attacked
into any of the Roman provinces, most notably Syria, and instead
nearly all the fighting took place in Armenia. In addition, for all the
confrontations that did occur, both the Romans and the Parthians
were careful to avoid escalating a dispute over who would rule
Armenia into a full-scale clash between them. There was negotiation at the start and frequent, often prolonged, lulls in operations
to allow further talks. Both sides postured and threatened but
never pressed the other too hard. The limited nature of the fighting meant that neither side was backed into a corner and made
desperate or committed to a war they could not afford. Given that
this was the most direct confrontation to occur in the century after Augustus's death, its relatively small scale and tentative nature
stand out. The first century was overwhelmingly a time of peace
between Rome and Parthia.[28]

In AD 66, the brother of a Parthian king of kings was proclaimed
as ruler of Armenia by a Roman emperor. From then on, Armenia
was ruled by Arsacids, with perhaps a few short-lived challengers.
Thus, for many scholars, this is seen as a major Parthian success,
which the Romans chose to veil by an assertion of theoretical
rather than actual might and dominance. Too often the familiar
cold war language dominates, as Armenian factions are described
as pro or anti Roman or Parthian, but the truth is a good deal
more complicated. Rome's aim was to dominate, and much of this
had more to do with image than physical force, let alone control
on the ground. Even in this respect, the achievement of Nero's
regime is significant. An Armenia racked by civil war and instability was an uncomfortable neighbour to the Roman provinces
and allied kingdoms. For all the immense expense of the journey,
Tiridates's visit to Rome marked him as an ally. The Romans did
not demand much from allied kings beyond a suitably submissive
attitude. Tiridates left behind in Rome family members, along with
those from other noble families, as another mark of Roman dominance. There was no reciprocal exchange of hostages.

In recent years, Roman armies had shown that they were fully capable of driving into Armenia and capturing any settlement, including the kingdom's two biggest cities. There was no reason to believe that they could not do it again if they chose. Another lesson of these years was the degree of balance between the professional Roman army of the principate and Parthian-style armies. Perhaps this would be different in a less rugged country than Armenia, but there had been no Carrhae-like victories for the Parthians and their allies, and on the whole the Romans had held off any Armenian or Parthian attacks far better even than Antony's men. The Romans could march where they wished, and if they could not force a decently led Parthian-style army into battle, they could go on and take almost any stronghold. The balance depended on good leadership. Paetus had made a series of poor decisions and been punished accordingly, but neither the Parthians nor the Romans could rely on the opponent making enough mistakes to hand them a victory.[29]

For all the talk of reclaiming the Persian or Seleucid empire, and indeed Rome's boast of imperium—power, rather than empire as physically held territory—without limit, neither side sought to conquer the other. The tactical balance shown in these campaigns reflected a broader strategic balance. Both sides realized that waging all-out war against the other was a major enterprise and likely to be a risky one. Neither the Roman emperors nor Arsacid kings were eager to take that chance unless there was no other choice. Instead, they wanted to save face and ensure that the other continued to be wary of them in private and to behave in public in a way that was acceptable. The latter mattered both for their home audiences and for the monarchs and leading men of the kingdoms on the borders.

Tacitus described Armenia as 'between two great empires'. Even though Vologaeses I had with great effort managed to secure the throne of the kingdom for his brother, it is well worth considering what this really meant, rather than seeing everything as part of a wider rivalry so that Armenia was now more Parthian than Roman. Arsacid history, as indeed the history of just about every dynasty in the wider region, showed that a brother or any other relative was almost as naturally a rival as an ally, as Tiridates seems to have proved when he complained about his brother's failure to support him. In a sense, the younger brother was less of a threat if he was kept busy controlling the unruly nobles of Armenia, and ideally he would want to keep Vologaeses I's support and thus be more willing to be persuaded in any dispute with neighbouring monarchs. The king of kings was better off as a result of the settlement culminating in the ceremony of 66, but that was not to say that he now controlled Armenia in any real sense.[30]

The Near East remained a patchwork of kingdoms and communities whose internal politics could be volatile. In 66, discontent with the Roman governor of the minor province of Judaea erupted into a rebellion, and the knee-jerk Roman response of sending a hastily gathered army led to disaster outside Jerusalem. The Romans suffered more than five thousand dead, while one of the legions that had taken part in Paetus's debacle lost its eagle. For a few years there was an independent Jewish state, minting its own coins and doing its best to rein in the violent competition between different factions among the rebels. An army of three legions, later increased to four, as well as substantial numbers of auxiliaries and allies took three years to crush the rebellion, and smaller forces were engaged for several years after that. Some of this was because of political distractions. By 68, Nero's poor government had alienated so many senators and other members of society that he was forced from power and fled, eventually telling a faithful slave to kill him. There followed what is known as the Year of Four Emperors, with a renewal of outright civil war for the first time since 30 BC. Eventually it was won by Vespasian, the man sent by Nero to deal with the Jewish rebellion. He managed to restore stability and was uniquely remembered as the only man whose character improved rather than degenerated after becoming princeps.

Vologaeses I might have been expected to exploit the chaos of civil war or, for that matter, given the large Jewish population in his empire, to intervene when Judaea rebelled. He chose to do neither and instead offered military aid on the alleged, if unlikely, scale of forty thousand cavalry to Vespasian in his bid for power. The Roman declined, both because he did not need the assistance and because it would surely have discredited him to have such obvious foreign backing. Vologaeses I's attitude testifies again to the preference for good relations with Rome whenever this was achievable without damaging his own interests.[31]

Paetus happened to be related to Vespasian so, in spite of his humiliation at Rhandeia, was appointed legate of Syria. Corbulo did not live to choose sides in the civil war. Although always scrupulously loyal, he had come under suspicion and been ordered by Nero to commit suicide. A stickler for discipline, the man who had held such prolonged command on the eastern frontier obeyed this final order and took his own life.[32]

Corbulo's career exemplified the new realities of the principate and more specifically the relationship between Romans and Parthians created under Augustus. For around a decade he had held a command, and usually the overall command in the theatre, in the Armenian conflict. This involved extensive operations in Armenia and some fighting and even more negotiating with the Parthians. Objectives on both sides were limited, and care was taken not to turn this dispute into an all-out war between the two empires. Instead, they threatened, discussed, and sometimes fought to create, preserve, or restore each empire's influence in volatile Armenia. The limited scale and scope of the conflict did not mean that either side was less determined when they actually came to blows, for these limited aims were vital and the symbolic nature of the final settlement far more than empty words. The odd compromise of the visit to Rome for coronation by Nero—indeed, of the sword nailed to its scabbard—mattered because it confirmed the essence of the relationship. Each empire needed to show respect to the other's sensibilities. Pushing too hard risked bringing on a far more serious war, something that neither side wanted.

8

GOOD AT BUSINESS

First and Second Centuries

Arsacid Parthia and Rome were each wary of the other's power and jealous of their reputation and prestige. Even so, conflict of any sort between them was rare, and posturing only a little more common. They talked far more than they fought, although even this is only sometimes reported in our sources, making it hard to judge how often diplomatic contact occurred. The grand occasions were rare indeed, when an Arsacid king or prince met with the emperor's representative, usually in the form of the provincial legate of Syria. These events were carefully stage-managed and choreographed, with public negotiations on a bridge, platform, or island and the occasion marked by formal parades and lavish feasts. While on a smaller scale, Parthian embassies to Rome were accompanied by ceremony at each stage of the journey and especially on arrival.

Less is known of the reception given to Roman envoys visiting the Arsacid king of kings or, for that matter, one of the regional rulers. Such men were not senators or anyone from the imperial household and instead appear always to have been army officers, which perhaps meant that less fanfare was felt appropriate. The vast majority were centurions, which was a grade of officer rather than a specific rank. There were about sixty in each legion and perhaps four thousand in the entire empire, including auxiliaries, naval squadrons, and other units. Some enlisted in the ranks and rose through merit, favour, or—in time of war—conspicuous valour. Others were directly commissioned into the centurionate, and among these were some equestrians who chose this career path over the one created by Augustus and his successors for their class. The persistent belief that centurions were essentially sergeant-majors has never really been justified by the evidence. Whatever their origins, they required a high level of education to carry out their duties, and this was especially true of the centurions seconded from their units to serve on the governor's staff, let alone those selected as envoys to neighbours as important as the Arsacids.[1]

Centurions, or the equestrian prefects sometimes sent in their stead, represented the princeps but lacked the authority to make major decisions. They were reliable conduits for communication between the two sides, whose use implied that there would be time for messages to go back and forth and for both sides to deliberate. In Tacitus's detailed narratives, they were sent reasonably often, but since these describe periods of tension this may not be representative. We simply do not know how often provincial legates sent a mission to the Arsacid king or how often Parthian envoys came to them. Similarly, we can only guess at the amount of information routinely gathered by Roman governors about the activities and attitudes of the Parthians or vice versa.

When Cicero was proconsul of Cilicia in 51 and 50 BC, much of his information about the Parthian threat to Syria and his own province came from allied kings, which meant that he had to gauge its accuracy in terms of their loyalty, individual agendas, and ability to know in the first place. Such allies remained a key source of political and military intelligence for governors under the principate. The greater permanence of provinces and garrisons under the emperors did mean that there were far more likely to be officers with a good deal of local experience on which to draw. However, we know very little about how much was done or how well it was done, or how much of this information was routinely sent to the princeps.[2]

In 72, Lucius Caesennius Paetus, as legate of Syria, wrote to Vespasian to report that the king of Commagene and one of his sons were planning to break away from Rome and ally themselves more closely with the Arsacids. Josephus, who reports the incident, states that no one was ever sure whether the governor believed what he was saying or had invented it because he had a grudge against the king, perhaps dating back to Paetus's ignominious intervention in Armenia. The allegations were serious, and Vespasian does not appear to have had any convincing source to contradict them. Commagene was sensitive, not least because the main city of Samosata lay on the Euphrates and 'would afford the Parthians, if they harboured any such designs, a most easy passage and an assured reception'. Therefore, Paetus was given authority to act as he felt necessary, and he promptly marched into Commagene at the head of a column based around Legio VI Ferrata, along with some auxiliaries and allied troops supplied by the rulers of Emesa and Chalcidice. The king was caught by surprise and fled with his wife and family. Paetus occupied Samosata and chased the king, who still refused to fight. Two of his sons, including the one Paetus had accused, did muster a small force, but after some indecisive fighting they abandoned their men, who promptly dispersed.[3]

Commagene once again became directly governed, this time permanently, being added to the Syrian command. From the start (or in the near future), it gained a garrison of a legion supported by auxiliaries, although it is unclear whether this was meant to control the population or protect it from other perceived threats. Commagene's king had reached Cilicia before he was caught by a centurion sent by Paetus. Taken to Rome in chains, he was granted comfortable exile in Sparta by Vespasian. The two princes who had chosen to fight crossed the Euphrates with the mere ten soldiers left as their escort and went to the Arsacid king of kings, who welcomed them as guests. Eventually, having heard that their father was not a prisoner and preferring to live within the Roman empire, they returned and were taken to Italy. The deposed king soon joined them, and the reunited household settled in or near Rome itself. Perhaps this allowed the princeps to keep a close eye on them, or perhaps it was an acknowledgement that the whole episode was based on a misunderstanding. We shall never know whether it was all a ghastly mistake or whether Paetus was shrewd, an honest fool, or a knave. Either way, he crowned his badly tarnished career with a successful military intervention.[4]

Vologaeses I was kind to the fleeing princes but at no stage acted to support them. Yet Josephus states unambiguously that the possibility of Commagene aligning itself more closely with Parthia than Rome, and the risk that this might one day allow a Parthian army easy access across the Euphrates, was an important concern for the Romans, even though there had been no Parthian invasion for over a century. It is revealing that Paetus acted only after getting express permission from Vespasian, with the exchange of messages taking several months at the very least. That imperial permission was based on limited, perhaps deliberately misleading, information about the current situation, supplemented by the princeps's personal experience of the wider area and the knowledge of those able to advise him. These included the foreign princes and guests living in Rome, soon to be joined by the royal family of Commagene, but their impressions were likely to be dated and their opinions shaped by their own political and personal concerns. Allied kingdoms were a cheaper and easier way for the Romans to secure their interests—primarily, maintaining a level of dominance and keeping the peace—in an area, but they were inevitably less stable than directly governed provinces. Mistakes, misinformation, and individual ambition on the part of a governor were nothing new when it came to Roman interventions, although the creation of the principate did at least make it harder for governors to act on their own.[5]

The potential threat of a fresh Parthian attack on Syria and beyond was a concern for the emperor and the Syrian legate, but it remained one concern among many. The last few embers of the Jewish rebellion had not yet been stamped out at the time Paetus marched into Commagene: the fortress of Masada near the Dead Sea still held out. Judaea had been upgraded from a minor province governed by an equestrian procurator with only auxiliaries at his disposal into a larger region, including parts of former allied kingdoms, commanded by a senator as legate with a legion as its main garrison. The long-term trend was to increase the number of troops stationed in the wider east and reduce the area controlled by allies in favour of directly ruled provinces. While this did mean that the Romans were in a generally stronger position should it ever come to a major confrontation with the Parthians, there is no sign of unusual tension or sabre-rattling on either side. The allied territories taken under direct rule had been under Roman hegemony for generations. There were also plenty of other reasons for the growth in military presence. The Jewish rebellion had taken seven years and considerable effort to suppress and had also unleashed a wave of intercommunal violence between and within cities throughout the wider area. Internal security was an ongoing concern, another of the multiple roles, including construction projects and policing, required of the army.

In time, more and more permanent bases were established near the Euphrates or along routes in frontier areas. Yet it is important to remember that most bases were essentially depots, where the administration of the unit was conducted and where most of its personnel would spend time when not needed in other places for other duties. Roman army bases in this period were not castles in the sense that they were primarily designed to hold a position. They were places to accommodate men and animals and keep them in reasonable training and health. They were not positioned where the army expected to fight but where it was as convenient as possible for them to muster and move to wherever they were required to operate.[6]

Although some scholars have argued that the Roman empire lacked clearly defined frontiers, this runs against the grain of the evidence. Roman governors knew where their authority and responsibility extended and where it did not. In this period, there was not a common frontier between Rome and Parthia because no Roman province bordered territory under the direct rule of the Arsacid king. Yet the place where Roman territory met kingdoms like Armenia or Osrhoene was universally understood. For a considerable distance this was marked by the Euphrates, but whatever the precise form of the boundary, crossing it with a body of troops in either direction was perceived as a violation and not something that could occur unconsciously.[7]

That is not to say that these were militarized zones under constant close watch, still less that travel was restricted or that this was a closed frontier. Before discussing the careers of Asinaeus and Anilaeus, Josephus noted that the wider Jewish population of Babylonia used the cities of Nisibis and Nearda to gather and protect the special two-drachma silver coins sent as offerings to the Great Temple in Jerusalem. Until the Temple's destruction in 70, the author claims that many 'tens of thousands' helped to escort the convoys carrying the money to Jerusalem. These were only some of the families and individuals who journeyed from inside and outside the Roman empire for the great festivals until the Temple was destroyed and the great public rituals and sacrifices surrounding it lapsed. Others travelled for their own reasons. According to Matthew's Gospel, wise men or magi 'from the east', which can only mean territory under the Arsacids and most likely Babylonia, went to Jerusalem and then Bethlehem soon after the birth of Jesus. The much later Apocryphal Gospel of Thomas and Philostratus's biography of the philosopher and miracle-worker Apollonius of Tyana both tell stories of men going from the empire through the lands of the Parthians and beyond to India. Whatever their historical accuracy, these narratives suggest that most people believed that such travel was perfectly possible, even routine. Individuals could and did cross between the empires and were not hindered or automatically treated as subversives and spies on either side.[8]

For all the pilgrims, missionaries, philosophers, and wanderers, most travellers went on business. The Silk Road is a modern name, and, if wonderfully evocative, does simplify the vast network of trade patterns stretching from Europe to China, from the steppes to India, Sri Lanka, Arabia, and the east coast of Africa. Most of this trade is difficult to quantify and trace in detail, but the literary and archaeological evidence reveals some of the broader patterns and makes clear its sheer scale. Given that transporting any goods was faster and cheaper by water than overland, the probability is that the busiest of all these routes in terms of sheer bulk was the one across the Indian Ocean. Of great antiquity, this was developed from the first century BC onwards, first by the Ptolemies and then by the Romans, as sailors learned to make use of the monsoon winds and time their voyages according to the seasons. The ports on the Red Sea coast of Egypt were developed under Roman rule, with roads to them through the desert policed and monitored by the army. This was not just a question of security and protection, for tolls were levied by the empire as trade passed through. Thus, the military presence made it safer for those travelling the roads while also making sure that they paid the required levies, mainly on goods, which in the ancient world did include human beings in the form of slaves. The same priority is visible on all the other routes.[9]

The Arabian Peninsula was a source of spices and incense, the latter much used in religious rites and extremely common for funerals, and so was in great demand. Some of this was carried across the Gulf to the Red Sea ports, but a significant amount, if probably still a fraction of the overall trade, went by caravan over-land. This was the only land trade route which in the main avoided crossing Parthian territory, although some convoys do appear to have gone up the Euphrates through Mesopotamia. Palmyra, the city raided by Antony, grew into an extremely prosperous place by organizing trade and protecting caravans. So effective were its escorts and leadership that a good many merchants and travellers chose to take the path via the city, even though this was never the shortest route. By the time of the principate, Palmyra was a Roman ally, considered part of the empire but granted a good deal of autonomy because this was to the advantage of both Rome and the Palmyrenes, whose soldiers escorted trains of camels and carts through Roman and Parthian territory alike.[10]

Caravans protected by large numbers of armed escorts crossed back and forth between Roman provinces and kingdoms allied to Rome, others allied to the Arsacids, and to directly ruled Parthian territory as a matter of routine. Perhaps they stopped or avoided the areas where there was fighting during a war, although this is not certain, and in the first century AD, conflict was rare and mainly limited to Armenia. Otherwise, the authorities monitored travellers so that they could levy tolls and taxes, welcoming them for this reason and not seeing them as a threat, even though it was well-understood that such travellers could also be a source of military and political information. The advantages of the trade far outweighed other concerns. The Roman state charged around 25 percent of the value on goods being brought into the empire from outside.[11]

Some of these items had come a very long way before they reached Roman territory. Most famous is true silk, the secret of which was still known only to the Chinese. Wild silk was produced on Cos and some of the other Greek islands but was coarser and far harder to produce than the real thing, so it was not available in the quantities desired by the increasingly prosperous communities of the empire. In China, the practice of cultivating silkworms was already ancient, its discovery lost in myth, and the secret was carefully guarded from outsiders. There were other areas where Chinese civilization was far in advance of the Greco-Roman world and its neighbours, most notably turning iron into high-quality steel. Yet iron was by its very nature heavy, which meant that although such steel was prized, there was never a long-distance trade on it in any great scale. Some was carried vast distances, and Parthia's elite cherished weapons or armour made from 'Margian steel', but overall the quantities were small. Very little ever reached Rome.[12]

In this era, China was not only technologically sophisticated but also politically united under the Han dynasty, which had risen to power at the close of the third century BC. While civil war and rebellion did happen on occasion, on the whole this was a time of strength and expansion, not least under the famous Emperor Wu-Ti (or Wudi, c. 141–87 BC). The nomadic horse tribes were perennial enemies of the settled communities in the heartland of the Chinese empire and countered by defensive measures, not least the complex of forts and fortifications that would be developed and refined over centuries and eventually become known as the Great Wall. As important was aggressive campaigning by the emperor's disciplined armies. Fighting was often hard, and defeats occurred, but during the course of the second century BC the Han expanded westwards until they controlled land bordering on the Hindu Kush. They encountered the Bactrian kingdom, first as its

Greek dynasty and then after the region was overrun by nomadic invaders, more than likely bands pushed out of their old pasture-lands by other bands driven onto them by Chinese conquests. Chinese reports showed some awareness of the declining power of the Seleucids and of the growth of the Parthians, referring to the latter as Anxi, derived from the name Arsaces.[13]

Near the end of the second century BC, when Mithradates II had greatly expanded Parthian power, Chinese envoys—probably men sent by the leader of an expedition to the west around 115 BC—came to Parthia. They were received in some style, although the claim that the leader sent to greet them was escorted by twenty thousand cavalry sounds like an exaggeration. The Chinese were escorted to the king of the Anxi's capital, perhaps Ecbatana, and there was an exchange of courtesies, gifts, and expressions of friendship. Chinese sources were much taken with presents of ostriches and ostrich eggs as well as other unfamiliar curiosities, including a hornless unicorn, which probably was some form of gazelle. They noted the importance of magicians in the land, presumably the magi, and had some idea of the extent of the Parthian empire and its rule over other kingdoms and communities. As with all travellers, they had a tendency to interpret what they saw or heard in the context of their own assumptions. Peoples who cultivated crops were given more respect than pastoralists and generally assumed to grow rice as well as cereals, even though the former was very rare in most of the Arsacid empire. The coins of the Parthians were noted as bearing the head of the king, the image replaced by that of the new king when the first died. More puzzling is a claim that the queen was depicted on the reverse of each coin, since as far as we know this only happened at the time of Musa as Thea Mousa. Perhaps it is a later addition to the text, sparked by someone who happened to come across coins bearing her image.[14]

Diplomatic contact was not solely or even primarily about trade, but it did encourage it, and comments about goods available, freedom of movement for caravans, and the locals' willingness to buy and sell are prominent in the Chinese sources. One writer noted that many of the inhabitants on the route between China and the Anxi were 'good at business and will haggle over the fraction of a cent'. Active diplomatic contact helped foster trade, and even more important was the security offered by the relatively stable kingdoms, especially once Chinese expansion had brought their borders nearer to the Hindu Kush, granting access to India and central Asia. For a while, a partly Greek kingdom flourished in the Indus valley, followed by an Indo-Parthian dynasty of Arsacid kings separate from the main line. During the first century, the Kushan empire was created when one of the nomadic groups became dominant in Bactria and then expanded to the surrounding lands, at times challenging the Indo-Parthian dynasty of the Indus valley. All in all, it was easier for caravans to pass through these regions, paying tolls or protection money as appropriate as the price of relative security. No doubt the journeys were often arduous—the climate and landscape of mountain and desert alone assured this—as well as dangerous, from natural phenomena, animals, and human predators, but many people made these trips. Few appear to have gone all the way from China to Rome or vice versa, especially overland. In the second century, one source noted that a merchant from the Roman empire, perhaps from Antioch in Syria, sent employees a long way east, even to the edge of Chinese territory, but this appears exceptional. More people made the voyage to and from India, and there is evidence for Roman traders living in Sri Lanka and India and merchants from the subcontinent in the Red Sea ports of Roman Egypt.[15]

Silk was an exciting, spectacular luxury for Rome's wealthy in the first century BC. Under the principate, vastly more silk—and spices, incense, and pepper from distant lands—was available, as what had passed for wealth under the republic was far outstripped. Some Romans worried about the cost of all this, both its consequences for public and private morals and the financial ramifications. Pliny the Elder once claimed that fifty million sesterces went each year to purchase goods from India, many of them selling for a hundred times their basic value. At another point he lumped together all the imports from China, India, and Arabia and estimated that as one hundred million sesterces per annum.[16]

There was a long literary tradition of lamenting the moral decline supposedly visible in ever-growing luxury, with the clothes, perfumes, and jewellery of wealthy women a favourite target. This means that we need to be careful in taking Pliny's complaints at face value. Even if his figures are correct, he does not tell us whether he was estimating the totals spent by Romans inside the empire on these imports or the amount it cost to bring these goods to the empire in the first place. Substantial quantities of gold and silver currency left the Roman empire year after year and was not replaced by foreign coins or bullion. This was a concern, even if we do not know how many shared Pliny's worries, although it still represented a tiny fraction of the empire's overall economic activity. However, if all this money actually represented the amount spent by Romans on goods from the Far East, then much of the profit was actually going to businesses within the empire and the authorities, including the imperial government, which taxed imports and levied tolls on commercial deals.[17]

The Roman appetite for eastern imports was considerable, and under the principate a far larger section of society than simply the elite could afford some of them. Inevitably, the literary and archaeological evidence is fuller for Rome's role in all this, especially as consumer, but, as always, we must be aware that this is only part of the story. Similarly, the natural tendency to stress the links between the two great civilizations of the era, China and Rome, can obscure the wider picture, which is far more interesting. Silk made in China might go to India before being shipped across the Indian Ocean to a port in Egypt or the Arabian Gulf, before travelling overland to a Mediterranean harbour and another ship. Or it might follow one of the land routes all the way to the Roman empire, passing through tribal lands and kingdoms, including Arsacid territory.

Whatever the route, this was a journey of thousands of miles, broken into many different stages, and the silk changed hands time and time again in the process. The traders involved were not simply middlemen, wholly dependent on the great cultural and economic powers at either end of the long journey. Just as the kingdoms allied to Rome and Parthia were independent actors with their own political agendas, so this trade was only one component in many great and small trade networks. There were plenty of profitable markets for silk and other luxuries at many stages along the path to the Roman empire. There were also plenty of other goods to trade and profits to make in these places. To see only the very long-distance trade is to miss the reality of many communities doing their best to benefit from commerce. Probably the biggest beneficiaries of the long-distance trade in luxuries were communities in India, and there were dangers enough sailing across the Indian Ocean, even if it lacks the romance of lines of laden ponies and camels trudging over mountain passes and through deserts. Yet the truth is that trade by sea and land both flourished, especially in the first and second centuries, and to a lesser extent before and reasonably well afterwards.[18]

The trade was not all in one direction, for all the concerns of Pliny and others. Apart from the local networks all along the routes, goods went back east from the Roman empire; many scholars have a curious reluctance to note that someone who has transported items to sell in a distant market will usually want to replace them with something to carry back and sell during the journey home. Roman coins were just part of this, in many cases seen as bullion rather than tokens. China lacked sufficient sources of precious metals to supply all its needs, as did substantial parts of India and, indeed, the Parthian empire. Coral, commonplace and unregarded in the Mediterranean world, was exotic and much prized by many in China. Like the Chinese, the Romans also had their inventions. Glass-making was unknown in Han China, which meant that there was great profit to be made in the careful transport of the delicate, blue-green vessels made in workshops in Rome's provinces.

Other goods passed through the Roman empire as part of their journey. Ivory came from Africa, extending the trade network down the east coast of the continent to lands wholly independent of Rome or Parthia, and was passed on, often after being carved by Roman craftsmen. Amber came from Scandinavia through the Roman empire on its long journey to the empire of China. Even more strangely, Chinese silk was brought to Syria and other Roman provinces, carefully unravelled, and then reworked into a finer thread and dyed. There was a market for this especially gauzy and colourful silk within the empire, but a great deal was sent back and sold in Chinese markets, where everyone assumed that the Romans produced their own, distinct type of silk, never guessing the truth.[19]

While the Romans and Chinese were dimly aware of the other's existence, knowledge was limited. Late in the first century, a Chinese envoy reached the coast somewhere, most likely in Characene, the kingdom around the mouths of the Tigris and Euphrates and subject to Arsacid overlordship. Hoping to reach the Roman empire and make contact with its ruler, the envoy was dissuaded when the local sailors assured him that the voyage was extremely long and very perilous. This may have been based on misunderstanding, perhaps even the assumption that the envoy wanted to sail around the Horn of Africa, hence the claim that the journey could take two whole years. In 166, the Han emperor's court was visited by an embassy who said that they were sent by An-tun, king of Ta-ch'in—surely Marcus Aurelius Antoninus, the famous philosopher-emperor of Rome, or his predecessor Antoninus Pius. They brought gifts, including ivory, rhinoceros horn, and tortoise-shell, none of them originating from the empire, although as we have seen this did not mean that they had not passed through it. Whether they were a genuine delegation or merchants wishing to impress and knowing that no one could disprove their claims, nothing lasting came of the encounter. Rome and China, for all their similar size and sophistication, were simply too far apart to establish any real relationship.[20]

Now and again, a few traders may have gone from one empire all the way to the other, but it was rare. There was also an appetite in China for entertainers from far afield, so slaves trained as musicians, dancers, jugglers, and in other novelties went there from the Roman provinces, although as with any other 'goods', they may well have been bought and sold by many different owners on their journey. This great web of markets and trade networks stretched across Europe and Asia and reached into Africa, touching the lives of many people in many different communities while only bringing them into contact with folk from closer to hand—if still from some way away and speaking a different language and having different customs. A piece of amber from the Baltic could make its way to be admired at the Han court without anyone along the way having much sense of its origin and final destination, any more than a Roman dressed in silk understood how far the material had travelled or how it had been modified on the way. There was a good deal of mutual benefit for communities and especially individuals all along the route, which did not need to create more than a vague sense of connection with a wider world. At every stage, people sought their own advantage, as seen by the great diversity of routes followed so that no major commodity was only carried along a single path. Much ingenuity was spent trying to find fresh opportunities, for instance, when Chinese sources mention alternative routes avoiding some kingdoms. Those involved directly in trading were a small minority, but even so, over such a wide area with such a big combined population, trade could become a major, even prime concern of some cities. None of this alters the fact that the vast majority of people in the ancient world tilled the fields or tended herds to produce food and rarely travelled very far. Yet even some of these, varying from region to region, had a little contact with the wider world through goods from far afield, whether glimpsed in the possession of the wealthy or even owned.[21]

Ancient economies are not well-understood because the evidence is difficult to assess. In essence, much depends on whether the literary mentions represent the entire understanding of trade, taxation, and finance on the part of the Roman elite, including emperors and their advisors, or were simply the way these were presented in literary form. There is very little—some sceptics would say none at all—unambiguous evidence of detailed, rational, and routine consideration of commerce and economic factors in the judgements made by the Senate and later by emperors. Yet it is not really tenable to push this view to an extreme and deny that trade and commerce ever played a part in decision-making by Rome's Senate under the republic or by the emperors under the principate. Money was important to all ancient leaders, especially those of the Roman state tasked with paying for a professional army, among other things.

It is abundantly clear that there was an awareness that trade, including long-distance trade from beyond the borders of the empire, was a good, profitable thing, deserving encouragement if nothing else. Individuals did very well from this and some of these individuals involved directly, or indirectly through investment, were members of Rome's ruling elite. The state also did well from levies and taxes on goods. Within the empire, the government developed and encouraged the development of infrastructure to foster travel, from roads and canals to harbours, while making some moves to prevent piracy and banditry from getting out of hand. Even when some of these measures were primarily created to support military deployment or supply the state issue of grain and other commodities to the people of Rome itself, their existence helped travel and trade more generally.[22]

Parthia's attitude appears to have been similar. Some Chinese sources hint that the Parthians discouraged them from making direct contact with Rome to maintain a monopoly on trade through their own lands, and more than a few modern scholars have felt that this was likely. Yet even if true, this may have been the attitude of the merchants as much as the Arsacid king and his court, which is not to say that he was not influenced by them. The king of kings—and all the great families, the rulers of the smaller kingdoms, and leaders of the main cities—benefitted from having the trade routes passing through his lands. Like the Romans—and for that matter the Kushans and everyone else—there was income from taxes as well as readier access to the goods being transported and anything else traders realized would win them a welcome from local powers. Commerce was a good thing, worth protecting and encouraging, as well as exploiting, ideally enough for the greatest gain short of deterring the merchants from seeking an alternative route.[23]

Rome's empire functioned with a tiny civilian bureaucracy, backed in some areas by military clerks but relying on devolving considerable power and day-to-day administration to local communities and leaders. This limited its capacity to intervene in any dramatic way in what we might call economic policy (and scholars will argue at length about just what sort of economy existed in this era and whether emperors had policies by modern standards). Ancient governments did not claim to intervene in as many fields as those of the modern world, although it is worth noting that the generally common aspirations of local leaders and communities encouraged each other. Thus, when Herod the Great invested money and effort into constructing an artificial harbour at Caesarea Maritima on the Mediterranean coast, this created a route through which trade could flow more easily than before and benefitted many beyond his kingdom. He went to the trouble in expectation that the cost would bring substantial benefit. There was competition between regions, communities, and individuals, and a widespread desire to have access to and profit from commerce, which overall helped to foster and expand such trade.[24]

The Arsacid kings had even less of a formal bureaucracy than the Romans and relied more heavily on devolved authority to maintain their empire. Once again, it was in the interest of regional kings, aristocrats, and city authorities to promote trade. Far more than most of Rome's emperors after Augustus, the king of kings moved around his empire, probably according to the seasons of the year. The original capital of Nisa was supplanted by Hecatompylos before the end of the third century BC, although Nisa continued to have ceremonial and ritual importance. Later Rhagae, Ecbatana, and Ctesiphon grew in importance. Ctesiphon was constructed as a formally Parthian companion to nearby Greek Seleucia on the Tigris, where the king could hold court and his garrison could live throughout the year without worrying about Hellenic custom and sensibilities or the other city's often violent factional and ethnic rivalries. In the first century, Vologaeses I—the same man who had kept waging war until he gained a beneficial compromise with Nero—founded Vologasia as another royal city near Babylon, which seems to have drawn some trade away from Seleucia, becoming a frequent destination of caravans from Palmyra.[25]

The king of kings and his court moved during the year, visiting some or all of these royal cities. This had the benefit of letting him see different parts of his empire, especially his subordinates in each region and the local royalty, nobility, and other leaders, and in turn gave more of his subjects the opportunity to see their ruler. News and instructions were passed on by oral and written communication to reach the rest of the empire. A good monarch was supposed to listen to advice from the inner council of family, including the royal women, and from a more formal council of the kings, leaders of the great houses, and other senior nobles, joined by representatives of the magi. Little is known about this body, such as how often it was convened and whether decisions could be made with only some of its members present. Under the principate, more and more Roman senators were drawn from the well-to-do families in the provinces, but all were required to own property in Italy and not allowed to go anywhere else unless on public duty or with express permission of the emperor. This meant that the Senate met regularly, with at least a large proportion of its current membership, many times in each year and was always available for an emperor to consult, even if this was little more than a show. Arsacid Parthia lacked such a single political and social centre, but while its system was less formal, it was well-suited to an empire of so many more or less independent kingdoms, regions, and cities. It did limit the extent to which a king of kings could directly intervene in aspects of life throughout the empire. Probably there was little desire to do this in the first place, beyond developing infrastructure, especially irrigation systems to improve agricultural productivity.

Parthian rulers had some contact with China and were closer so better placed to obtain silk and other luxuries. The relationship with the Indo-Parthian empire to the east is unclear and may well have involved periods of tension and conflict. This was also true of the Kushans, just as it was true of Parthia and Rome. Such episodes and ongoing mistrust in no way prevented the commerce which everyone desired. Goods moved, and so did people—the communities and individual agents, seeking their own advantage and not simply working for their states. Ideas also spread because people wanted to spread them. Whatever the historicity of the tradition about the Apostle Thomas, Christians appeared in Bactria and the Indus valley during the first century. There were also Buddhists, who enjoyed great success carrying their message into Bactria and all the way to China. Enough folk travelled in this era of ancient history beyond their homeland to carry beliefs, thoughts, images, and styles to others, who in turn might pass them on and on. Recipients took what they wanted, often adapting it, as is famously seen in the blending of styles and ideas of Gandharan art.[26]

Rome and Parthia had different cultures, political systems, and traditions. They were rivals for power, especially in the lands that had once formed part of the Seleucid empire, and to a lesser extent the great conquests of Alexander. Even so, the rivalry was cautious for the first century of the principate, helped by the fact that there was no ideological basis to the competition. Neither society was closed to the other, not least because they naturally assumed their own traditions to be superior. In the Roman empire, the cult of Mithras built up a significant following, devotees attracted by its secret rituals, initiating them over time to higher grades within the order. Mithra was an Iranian god of great antiquity, within the Zoroastrian pantheon and much revered by many Parthians, especially among the nobility. The Roman cult drew inspiration from this tradition, since the distant and exotic has a natural appeal for many people, so the god was depicted in eastern dress and temples built to resemble caves to invoke old stories about the god. Yet the details were garbled, probably beyond recognition for traditional worshippers of Mithra, and everything tailored to suit the tastes of the Greco-Roman world. Plenty of the followers of Mithras were equestrians, including army officers, and there was never the slightest suggestion that their cult made them anything other than patriotic Romans. Similarly, reverence for the Greek tradition did not make subjects of the Arsacids automatically disloyal.[27]

Rivalry for power and dominance did not make either Rome or Parthia closed to the other. They were wary, jealous of anything taken as a slight, but on the whole content to coexist for generations, emperors and kings of kings alike realizing that this was wiser, since it gave them time and the resources to address other threats and problems in their empires. Wars were expensive and risky against so powerful an adversary, and for a long time rulers on both sides judged that peace was preferable. However, in the second century AD, this coexistence became harder to maintain.

9

GLORY AND TEARS

70–198

Instability within either empire tended to make their behaviour less predictable to the other as they waited and watched to see who would emerge as the new ruler. Crassus was encouraged to attack by the apparent weakness of the Arsacids at a time when brother was fighting brother, while the most serious invasion of Roman territory came from the Parthian-backed Labienus when Rome's republic was deeply divided. The principate established by Augustus had created stability for a long time, making it a far more predictable and easier neighbour from a Parthian point of view. At the same time, successive emperors remained reluctant to intervene too heavily in Arsacid internal struggles. They would back an individual claimant felt to be favourable to them but not to the extent of waging war on his behalf. Even at these times of upheaval, it proved in both sides' interests to maintain good relations with each other.

The principate had done much to restore stability to the Roman state. Yet the senator and historian Tacitus wrote that the civil war after Nero's death revealed a 'secret of empire', that a princeps could be made in the provinces through support of the army rather than in Rome by the Senate. When Vespasian's victory was secure and he came to the city in the late summer of 70, the Senate voted him the powers and privileges of a princeps in a single law. In the past, men had acquired the rank in stages and, in a well-ordered succession, already possessed some of the status under the rule of their predecessor. Vespasian was legally confirmed as emperor over a year after being proclaimed as such by his own legions, soon followed by others in the east and beyond, as well as key provincial governors and allied monarchs. The Senate had no real choice in the matter—Rome itself had been captured by forces loyal to Vespasian in the previous year—and passed a law making legal what was already a reality in every other respect.[1]

On the whole, Vespasian and his older son Titus, who assisted and then succeeded him, were admired in our sources. There was disdain for their background, for their family were not aristocrats but were instead something akin to minor country gentry. Vespasian's parents were equestrians, and apart from his mother's brother, he was the first of the family to achieve admission to the Senate. Funding his career in part through breeding and selling mules—an echo of Publius Ventidius Bassus—he did reasonably well, although in normal circumstances he would not have been among those senators considered suitable for elevation to princeps. Nero chose him for the Judaean command in part because his background made his competence less of a threat to a suspicious emperor. Only this, and the rapid demise of the first two men to succeed Nero, put him at the head of an army in a position to make his bid for power. Suetonius, an equestrian and imperial official who wrote biographies of Julius Caesar, Augustus, and the ten rulers who followed them, uniquely depicted Vespasian as a man whose character improved rather than deteriorated once he had become princeps. Titus fares almost as well in the tradition, although he was princeps for little more than two years before he died and was succeeded by Domitian, his younger brother, who was remembered as one of the bad emperors.[2]

Suetonius completed his series of biographies with Domitian. Tacitus's *Histories* also covered the years up to Domitian's death in 96, although only a handful of fragments survive for the period after 70. For the remainder of the first century and the whole of the second century, we have no detailed narrative history, let alone one that is reasonably contemporary and reliable. This era is often seen as the golden age of the Roman empire—not least by Dio, looking back as the third century turned sour—and can boast many of the greatest achievements of architecture and art. Most likely this was the time when the population of the empire was at its largest, prosperity highest, and famous emperors like Trajan, Hadrian, and Marcus Aurelius led the state. Yet very little is known about many of the great events of these years, let alone the smaller incidents. Predictably, the evidence for Arsacid Parthia is even worse, and its history has to be reconstructed largely through the coin series issued by successive monarchs. Much of this is guesswork, since dating and sequence are rarely certain, and the relationship between the men issuing the coins even less clear. Contemporary issues by more than one king of kings suggest civil conflict, without giving much idea of who some of these rulers were or how much support they enjoyed and for how long. We simply cannot know whether these men were permanently at war or came to some form of accommodation and divided the empire. All of this makes the period especially hard to understand, which is all the more frustrating since it saw three major conflicts between the Romans and Parthians and no doubt other tensions as well. The change from the century or so of generally peaceful relations initiated by Augustus is marked, and we must do our best to explain it with the threadbare evidence we have.[3]

On the whole, Vespasian and his sons appear to have continued the practices of earlier emperors with regard to Parthia. As we saw, Commagene was taken under direct rule because of fears that its king was becoming dangerously friendly to the Parthians. Lucius Caesennius Paetus was replaced as legate of Syria within a year, although we do not know whether this was a sign that Vespasian no longer had full confidence in him or just the routine turnover of governors. His successor was Marcus Ulpius Traianus, who had commanded a legion with great distinction under Vespasian and then Titus during the Jewish war. His family came from Spain, partly descended from Roman colonists sent out under the republic, and he was an example of the widening of the ranks of the

Senate to include members from the provinces. During Traianus's spell as legate of Syria, there appears to have been some friction with Vologaeses I of Parthia, which led to a demonstration of Roman military strength, possibly even some fighting, before the Romans decided that enough had been done to assert their dominance and claim success. There are no details, and more than likely this was a continuation of the sabre-rattling that so often accompanied diplomacy between the two empires.[4]

One curiosity of this period was the appearance in the eastern provinces of a number of men claiming to be Nero. At least two gained some following, for the Hellenophile emperor was fondly remembered by some in the region, and perhaps the pretenders simply had a lot of charisma helping them to appeal to the disaffected. Neither raised anything more than a crowd of unarmed supporters, and both fled to the Arsacid court when the provincial authorities started to take an interest in them. The king of kings gave them a welcome, for the peace settlement with the real Nero had been an honourable one for both sides. This was the closest thing to a member of the imperial family ever escaping to the Arsacids or ending up at their court as a result of diplomacy. Vologaeses I may have been a good host, but he made no move to back either 'Nero' with force or even active diplomacy. The first man was revealed as a fraud and promptly executed, and the second sent back as a prisoner when Domitian demanded his return. In neither case did the matter become a major issue. Perhaps Domitian spoke of ambitions for a great eastern expedition later in his reign, but nothing actually happened.[5]

The peace endured, as did the mutual suspicion. The annexation of Commagene was part of a wider reorganization of administration and Roman military deployment in the area, much of which may well have occurred during the governorship of Traianus. Vespasian had personal knowledge of the eastern Mediterranean from the Judaean command and from securing support in the region during his bid for power. In his career he had also served in Thrace, Crete, the Rhineland, Britain, and North Africa. Postings were rarely made on the basis of past experience in that area, so that serving in the same province more than once was the exception rather than the rule. The senior men chosen from the Senate to advise the princeps would have brought a similar range of direct knowledge of different parts of the empire. In addition, there were the letters and reports from current and past governors, as well as rulers and communities in the wider area and perhaps hostages and guests in Rome. Detailed, thorough mapping of territory is a relatively modern phenomenon; in Britain the Ordnance Survey was set up to map the country as a response to the threat of invasion by Napoleonic France, and the process was not completed until decades after Waterloo. The Romans had nothing like this, but then neither did many highly organized states throughout the world in the eighteenth and nineteenth centuries. Scholars inclined to minimize the Romans' ability to plan and make decisions rationally often impose far too high a standard on what is required of any state to do this.[6]

However the decision was made by Vespasian and his advisors and then implemented by his legates on the spot, two of the four legions stationed in Syria were soon moved to permanent bases in the former kingdom of Commagene, one at Zeugma and the other at Samosata, each on the western bank of the Euphrates. Around the same time, a new military province of Cappadocia was formed, encompassing Galatia and also parts of Pontus and the region known as Lesser Armenia. The governor was an imperial legate and former consul who commanded two legions and auxiliaries. The legions were stationed at Melitene and Satala, the two principal cities of Cappadocia. Under Vespasian and his sons there was also a programme of road building in this and the wider area and indeed much of the empire, easing the movement of supplies and troops across the Black Sea and improving the connection between Asia Minor and Europe.

The obvious consequence of all this was that four legions and supporting troops were stationed close to the key routes into and out of Armenia and the stretch of Euphrates most accessible to Syria. There are echoes of Corbulo's campaigns in the reorganization, most of all his consistent opinion that one man could not simultaneously command in the Galatian-Cappadocian region and in Syria. Whether the experience of those years and the opinion of a distinguished commander—and a man Vespasian had known, at least as an acquaintance and fellow senator—was a factor in shaping the new arrangement is impossible to say. The physical as well as the political geography made this division of command sensible, even if the legate of Syria was still left with a very wide range of other duties apart from supervising the troops on the Euphrates, which is one reason why it remained such a prestigious command held only by those most favoured by the princeps.

The four legions were well-positioned to confront an attack launched across the Euphrates or from Armenia. Equally, they secured these routes for any Roman offensives, and there is no real need to judge the deployment as primarily defensive or aggressive when it provided either option depending on the situation. Nor were the garrisons fixed to their bases, and just as they could be reinforced by troops from the rest of Syria—and in time from the Danube, Egypt, or even further afield—so they could be sent elsewhere as detachments or whole units to deal with disturbances, rebellion, or external wars on other fronts. While the Arsacid king of kings and the nearest regional monarchs, especially the king of Armenia, may have felt that the large, highly visible Roman bases on their borders were threatening, this remained well within the long-standing experience of negotiation backed by force and posturing. Diplomacy continued, and the Romans and Parthians alike backed allies in the kingdoms of the region, doing their best to advance their own interests. Vespasian sent engineers to strengthen the fortifications of the capital of the Iberian king, while under Domitian an inscription records that a centurion from one of the legions in Cappadocia was among the Albani, perhaps acting as an ambassador.[7]

As always, the princeps and the king of kings had plenty of more pressing concerns than rivalry with the other. Sometime around 75, groups of Alans, a Sarmatian people, raided widely into eastern Armenia and Media, defeating both of their kings in battle. Vologaeses I of Parthia asked Vespasian for military aid, but the Roman declined, feeling that this was not any of his business. There is no sign that these tribes posed any threat to the Roman provinces, at least at present, and even though there had been some cooperation between the raiders and Roman allies among the Iberi and Albani, there is no hint that this was done with Roman encouragement. Vologaeses I accepted the answer and was probably not surprised, since none of the treaties had ever required alliance against other threats.

In the latter half of his reign, Domitian was preoccupied with his European frontiers, especially a series of hard campaigns against Dacia (very roughly equivalent to modern Romania), led by the able king Decebalus. A Roman province was raided, its governor killed, and his army defeated, and the first major expedition sent in reprisal also marched to disaster. Another force did better, even if the resultant peace fell short of outright Roman victory, although it may not have been quite as much of a sham as our sources claim. Senators remembered Domitian as cruel, a man who had executed members of their order and others around him, and the criticism became more vocal after he was murdered in a palace conspiracy. For the first time, the Senate met and chose a new princeps, significantly selecting from their own ranks the elderly Nerva, who had never displayed any conspicuous talent other than for getting along with a succession of emperors.[8]

Nerva was childless, in his early sixties, and did not appear robust. To calm doubts about the future, and perhaps to placate factions within the aristocracy, he decided to adopt an adult son as his successor and selected the current legate of Upper Germany. This was a military province and—although a lesser command than Syria, Britain, or Pannonia—meant that the new heir came with an army. The legate is known to us as Trajan and was the son of Traianus, who had served Vespasian and Titus in the Jewish war and subsequently governed Syria. Trajan had yet to match the fine military record of his father, although he showed exceptional enthusiasm for military life, spending more time with the legions than was required for a career. He had also proven his dedication to Vespasian and his family, not least when a governor in the Rhineland rebelled against Domitian, and Trajan marched his legion all the way from Spain to help suppress the rising. Such a man was unlikely to prove vindictive towards others who had done well under the old dynasty.[9]

Early in 98, Nerva fell into a fever and died. Trajan was still in his province and waited, corresponding with leading men and other army commanders in case there was resistance to his rule. In the event, there was none, but this may not have been as predictable as it appears with hindsight. The chaos of the Year of Four Emperors was in living memory of many adults, but this time no one was sufficiently ambitious and confident in their own support to challenge an emperor who was clearly prepared to fight if necessary. Trajan was about forty-five and would prove to be one of the most fondly remembered and admired of all emperors, not least because he was respectful and lenient in his treatment of senators. Surviving replies to petitions and especially the collection of letters to and from Pliny the Younger—who was sent as special legate to Bithynia around 110–112/3—show a serious-minded man who tried to rule well, fairly, and with respect to the law.[10]

Reputation as a good princeps mattered to Trajan, and for many Romans the greatest glory came from defeating foreign enemies. In 101, Trajan went in person to lead a major campaign against Decebalus of Dacia. Troops were drawn from all over the empire, and at some point two new legions formed to raise the total number in service to thirty. A year later, Decebalus sued for peace and was granted terms that left him as an independent but subordinate ally of Rome. War resumed in 105, catching Trajan by surprise, for he did not reach the Danube until months after hostilities had broken out. The mountainous terrain and sophisticated Dacian fortifications tested the Romans' siege-craft and determination, but by the end of 106 the strongholds had fallen and Decebalus had been hunted down until he took his own life rather than be captured. Dacia was annexed as a province and the victory celebrated throughout the empire and especially in Rome, helped by the immense profits of gold looted from the wealthy kingdom. Some of Trajan's Forum in Rome is still visible to this day and gives an idea of the scale of commemoration. Within it is Trajan's Column, covered in spiral scenes depicting the wars and its height a marker to show the original height of the slope before it was excavated to make the site for the new complex.[11]

Just as the Second Dacian War was coming to an end, the king of Nabataea died without an heir. Roman troops marched into the kingdom, and at some point—perhaps a few years later—the decision was made to create the new province of Arabia in its place, governed by a legate with a legion and auxiliaries at his disposal. The details are obscure, so that it is unclear whether no suitable candidate for the throne was available or there was a conscious preference for direct rule. This was a sensitive area, used by a good deal of the overland traffic in spices and other luxuries, and had a long history of fighting between leaders and tribes and with neighbours, as well as straightforward banditry. Perhaps there was no suitable candidate available to appoint as king, or perhaps this was another example of a growing preference for replacing allied monarchs with direct rule.[12]

The situation in Parthia is even more unclear. Vologaeses I died around 79. In his later years, he may have appointed his son Pacorus II as co-ruler. Pacorus II was young and is shown beardless on his early coins, and it is just possible that he had a regent or guardian for a while, unless the man named Artabanus who minted coins circa 80 was a rival or a regional governor granted or assuming the licence to mint his own currency. Pacorus II lived until around 110, but near the end of his reign a rival appeared named Vologaeses III.* Before Pacorus II died, a son named Osroes I either was made joint monarch or proclaimed himself as king of kings. Osroes I and Vologaeses III were rivals, each claiming supremacy for some twenty years, although it is not known how often the rivalry spilled into warfare or which regions were loyal to each one at any moment. (The Romans appear to have viewed Osroes I as the king of kings and do not mention his rival, which may suggest that the former held the lands in the west closest to the Roman empire.) At the same time, the Kushan kingdom was thriving, and Bactria and Hyrcania were both ruled by strong and independent dynasties, while central authority over Characene in the south appears

---

*There is now considerable doubt among specialists over whether there was ever a Vologaeses II, but it would be confusing to change the convention. As always, these numerals are modern inventions.

limited at best. All in all, Arsacid Parthia was not at its strongest in the early second century, but it had survived similar disorders and upheavals in the past and gone on to recover.[13]

In the autumn of 113, Trajan set out from Rome for the eastern Mediterranean, stopping at Athens en route to Antioch. By this time, drafts of troops were concentrating in Syria and Cappadocia, along with the matériel to support a major war effort. Modern estimates set the eventual concentration of military might at some ten to twelve legions, some at full strength and others as detachments.* Debate continues over just when Trajan began to make preparations for such a major effort, and some have even tried to connect the annexation of Arabia or Pliny the Younger's special mission to Bithynia with a premeditated plan for a great eastern expedition. Yet the immediate source of friction was, as so often, the rule of Armenia. Vologaeses I's brother Tiridates—the man who had carried a sword nailed to its scabbard when he bowed before Nero in Rome—had held power until his death in the late 80s. It is presumed that his successors went through the charade of waiting for Roman approval. Late in 112 or early in 113, Osroes I deposed the current king, a man who was probably his brother, and replaced him with another sibling named Parthamasiris. More than likely this was part of the wider power struggle within the Parthian empire, and perhaps preoccupation with this explains why he failed to go through the diplomatic niceties and seek Roman approval.[14]

A Parthian embassy came to Trajan at Athens asking for this recognition rather late in the day and claiming that the previous king had not been pleasing to either the Romans or the Parthians. Trajan refused to negotiate or even accept the gifts which as usual had been brought by the ambassadors. He went to Antioch, where envoys and letters came from many of the region's kings. Osroes I sent delegates again and, once again, received no answer other

---

*These detachments were known as vexillations (*vexillationes*) by the Romans after the square flag or *vexillum* they carried in place of a legion's eagle. There was no fixed size to such detachments, which varied from several dozen to several thousand soldiers, but vexillations of five hundred to one thousand appear common in major campaigns. Thus, the presence of a legion in a theatre of operations might mean that only 20 percent or less of its full strength took part.

than sweeping statements that Trajan would do what he thought fitting—an echo of Pompey so many years earlier. In the spring of 114, the emperor went from Syria to Cappadocia, where a large force was mustering near Satala. Along the way, he watched the troops parade and joined in their training, showing the vigour of a much younger man, just as Pompey had done before his last campaign. Trajan was sixty or sixty-one, a similar age to Pompey at that time—or indeed Crassus when he made his ill-omened march across the Euphrates.[15]

Parthamasiris sent a letter which Trajan refused to answer because it had styled its author as king of Armenia. Afterwards he wrote again without claiming any title and asked for the legate of Cappadocia to be sent to negotiate with him in person. Trajan ordered the legate's son to go instead. In the meantime, Trajan marched unopposed into Armenia and occupied Arsamosata before continuing on to Elegeia, where Parthamasiris was to meet him, only to find that the latter was late. When Parthamasiris arrived, he behaved in a suitably humble manner, taking off his royal diadem and laying it at the emperor's feet, confidently expecting the performance to end with Trajan restoring the crown to him—again, just as Pompey had done with Tigranes II of Armenia. The king waited and the emperor did not move, and then his parading soldiers hailed him as imperator—victor over the enemy. Parthamasiris was angry, but in subsequent talks, largely conducted in public so that he could make his case openly, he got nowhere. Trajan announced that Armenia was from now on to become a Roman province. The deposed king left the camp and was killed by his Roman escort. Trajan claimed that Parthamasiris had broken his word and was trying to escape.[16]

What happened from then onwards can only be glimpsed in the fragments of our meagre sources—something made all the more frustrating because among the many lost accounts was a detailed narrative by Arrian, more famous for the thoroughness of his surviving account of Alexander's campaigns. Most of 114 was taken up in overrunning all of Armenia and beginning to organize it as a province. During the remainder of the year there were also expeditions into neighbouring territories. Columns attacked the Mardi,

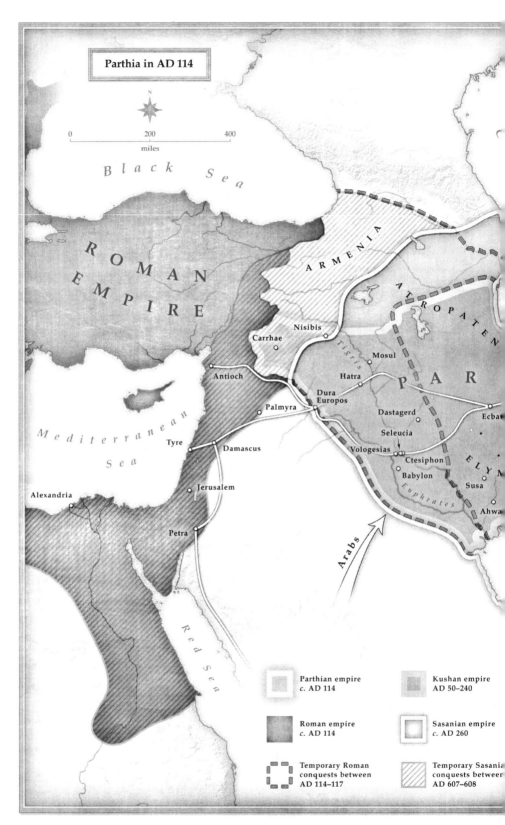

Parthia in AD 114

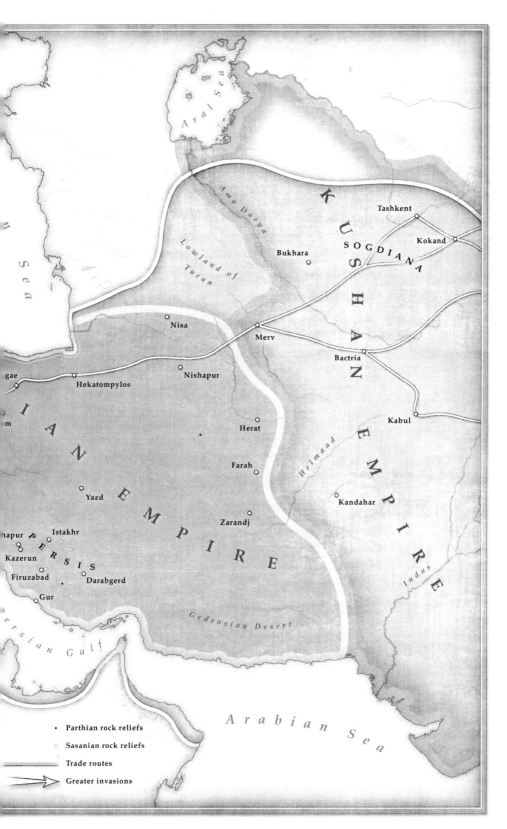

Aral Sea

Amu Darya

n Sea

S e a

K U S H A N

Tashkent

SOGDIANA

Kokand

Bukhara

Lowland of Turan

Nisa

Merv

Bactria

gae

Hekatompylos

Nishapur

Kabul

m

Herat

Helmand

E M P I R E

Farah

Yazd

Kandahar

Zarandj

hapur

Istakhr

Indus

Kazerun

P E R S I S

I A N   E M P I R E

Firuzabad

Darabgerd

Gur

Gedrosian Desert

rsian Gulf

A r a b i a n   S e a

• Parthian rock reliefs

◦ Sasanian rock reliefs

Trade routes

Greater invasions

a people living to the south of Lake Van, another pushed to the shore of the Caspian Sea, while a third operated in the mountains of Armenia, where the legate had his men don a form of snowshoe to be able to walk and fight in the winter conditions. Trajan did not take much direct part in these operations and instead was busy with diplomacy, summoning the nobles of Armenia to him and receiving delegations from the nearby kingdoms. For the moment, most were willing to accept the reality of Roman might, and the men promised allegiance and brought gifts, such as a horse taught to bow down. Around this time, Trajan appointed or formally recognized several new kings, including one for the Albani.[17]

Operations appear to have continued for much of the winter and into the following year. A victory arch was erected outside Dura-Europos, and this combined with the sequence of three large marching camps have been plausibly interpreted as signs of a victory won by a battle group based around Legio III Cyrenaica, the only unit named on the arch's inscription. Adiabene was overrun and its king defeated in another battle as the war spread. Although something like a quarter of the entire Roman army had gathered for these campaigns, there is little suggestion that they spent much time concentrated in any one place, in contrast to Antony and his great host. Instead, several commanders are named, apparently leading columns based on one or two legions along with detachments and auxiliaries, suggesting typical forces of some ten thousand to twenty thousand combat soldiers, although slaves and other camp followers would have increased the numbers of each force. Once again, there are similarities with Nero's Armenian war, where Corbulo and Paetus led similar-sized field armies. This reflected the terrain and also the political organization of the opposition, which in turn dictated the scale of the opposing forces. There is not the slightest hint of a massed Arsacid army taking the field against Trajan's men. Instead, individual leaders, usually the regional kings, fought their own individual wars against independent Roman columns, and at this stage were usually defeated. Much of northern Mesopotamia was occupied by the Romans. One city, its location uncertain, fell when a centurion sent as ambassador was imprisoned but managed to escape, kill the garrison commander, and open the gates to the Romans outside. Victory followed victory, submission followed submission, and as the news reached Rome, the Senate awarded Trajan six acclamations as imperator, bringing the right to hold a triumph. The emperor was even more pleased with the title of Optimus—'the best'—voted to him late in 115.[18]

The tide of success appeared to be with the Romans, and more and more local leaders recognized this. The king of Osrhoene initially tried to be neutral, fearing to anger either Parthia or Rome, but eventually came to terms with Trajan, the awkward negotiations allegedly eased because the emperor was charmed by the king's handsome young son. By the end of 115, Trajan was back at Antioch, for the job of being emperor continued even during a war, and deputations came to him from all over the empire as well as the theatre of operations. This made the violent series of earthquakes that struck Antioch even more of a disaster. Trajan narrowly survived, stories circulating that he was led out of a collapsing building by a miraculous being. Many more died, including an ex-consul and other distinguished men, some killed in the initial shock, others from injuries or trapped in the ruins. Dio noted that a woman and baby were found alive several days later as the wreckage was cleared, having survived by drinking her milk, but that in another case the rescuers found a live baby still trying to suckle at the breast of its dead mother.[19]

In 116, Trajan played more of an active role, which may suggest a greater degree of concentration as major columns moved closer to each other and operated in mutual support. In the main offensive, the emperor led one large force down the line of the Euphrates while another followed the Tigris. Staying close to the river made it easier for bulky supplies to be carried on boats, and the Romans also made use of a prefabricated bridging train. Trajan's men marched into Babylon, meeting no resistance. Barges and other boats were dragged overland from the Euphrates to the Tigris so that he could continue down to Seleucia on its west bank and Ctesiphon on its east bank, and both fell, once again without any fighting. Osroes I fled from Ctesiphon but left behind a daughter and the golden throne of the Arsacid king of kings for the Romans to take. The ease of the Roman advance suggests that rivalry with Vologaeses III preoccupied Osroes, who was devoting his energies to subduing one of the lesser kings as the Romans advanced. It was a far cry from the scorn that had met Crassus's boasts of dictating terms in Seleucia. As well as Armenia, a province of Mesopotamia and another of Assyria—a region hard to define closely—were created. The Romans were clearly planning to stay.[20]

Trajan took the title Parthicus and sailed downriver to the Persian Gulf in a flotilla of ships, including one ornate vessel meant for negotiations. There was no opposition, although there was nearly a disaster when the Romans misread the currents. Characene, long a reluctant member of Parthia's empire, welcomed the Romans. Roman might was triumphant, and Trajan had gone far beyond anything achieved by Pompey, Lucullus, or any other Roman. The emperor is said to have watched a ship setting sail for India and wept because he was too old to follow in the footsteps of Alexander. Trajan was now around sixty-three. He had made a show of doing what a Roman commander should do, riding and marching bare-headed in all weathers, sharing the hardships of campaign with his men, but in spite of, or perhaps because of, this his health now began to fail. In reverence for the famous Macedonian conqueror, and perhaps because he needed somewhere to receive delegations, he travelled back to Babylon and even visited the house where Alexander the Great had died.[21]

By this time, it had all started to go wrong. Rebellions broke out all over the newly conquered territory in Armenia, Osrhoene, Adiabene, and Mesopotamia. Roman garrisons, most likely token forces since they had overrun so much territory so quickly, were massacred. At long last a strong contingent sent by Osroes I appears in our sources, operating against the Romans. The episode was reminiscent of the winter of 130–129 BC, when the formerly successful army of Antiochus VII was suddenly attacked from all sides, and apparent victory turned into disaster. Both can be seen as a characteristically Parthian way of warfare, giving way when hard-pressed, trading ground for time to regroup, and then striking back hard at a time and place where the enemy was least prepared.

It is unclear how much co-ordination and planning underlay the risings in 116, because the details are obscure, making it impossible to say what happened by chance and what was design. Perhaps the Romans had provoked local communities by their excessive demands and arrogance, just as the Seleucid mercenaries had done, or perhaps fear of the invader's strength had lessened as the main armies moved on, allowing resentment to grow.

To make matters worse for the Romans, reports soon came of trouble elsewhere, notably on the Danube and in Britain. Worse still, sectarian problems between Gentile and Jewish communities in Egypt, Cyrene in North Africa, and Cyprus had been building for some time and now erupted into open war. A charismatic, perhaps messianic, leader appeared in Cyrene, and the rebellion grew as initial attempts to suppress it failed. Atrocities escalated on both sides, and even if talk of cannibalism and hundreds of thousands of civilian casualties was probably exaggerated, this was a brutal and hard-fought war. There is no direct evidence of a connection between the rebels and the Jewish community in Babylonia, perhaps even with Osroes I's government, although this is possible.[22]

The Roman response to rebellion was to counter-attack as soon as possible. This was risky, for sometimes it meant taking the field with comparatively small and poorly supplied armies, but could overawe the rebels before these had gathered momentum and widespread support. One commander did well initially before suffering defeat and death. Yet there were more successes, with Nisibis recaptured and Edessa, the main city of Osrhoene, sacked and its king killed in the aftermath. Seleucia, which had declared against the Romans, was also stormed, and large parts of the city were set on fire. The Parthian war effort was not always well co-ordinated and there was friction, perhaps even open fighting, between rival commanders, something that Trajan's envoys did their very best to encourage. At Ctesiphon, Trajan summoned a gathering of all nobles willing to attend and proclaimed Parthamaspates, son of Osroes I, as king of kings and ally of Rome—coins proclaimed that 'a king was given to the Parthians', in yet another first for a Roman.[23]

Late in 116, Trajan in person led a column to besiege Hatra, a city rich from trade, strongly fortified, and well supplied with water and food, both of which were hard to find in the surrounding lands. Dressing as an ordinary soldier so as not to stand out, the elderly Trajan was still targeted by the defenders, and the cavalry trooper standing next to him was killed. The siege failed, and the Romans retreated to prepare for a campaign in the coming spring. Yet it was not to be. Trajan's deteriorating health finally collapsed, and he seems to have suffered a severe stroke. One of his ablest subordinates had already been posted to govern Judaea and, since its Jewish population did not join in the wider rebellion on any great scale, appears to have done his job effectively. With so many problems elsewhere and the emperor incapable of coping with active command, the impetus went out of any plans to renew the war. Trajan set out for Rome, only to die in Asia Minor in the summer of 117. He was succeeded by a cousin, Hadrian, currently legate of Syria, after it was announced that the dying emperor had adopted him. Whether this was true or, as rumour claimed, an invention of Trajan's widow and other members of his staff, Hadrian and his close supporters acted quickly. Several senior senators were arrested, including the recently appointed legate of Judaea. Early on, Hadrian announced that the new provinces of Mesopotamia, Armenia, and Assyria were all to be abandoned. Trajan's appointee as king of kings was given Roman protection rather than support and had to content himself with becoming ruler of the kingdom of Osrhoene instead. It was not the end of Roman influence in the areas overrun by Trajan; Characene remained a Roman ally and independent of Parthia for some time. Even so, this abandonment of conquests and even more the arrest and subsequent execution of prominent figures was unpopular with many in the Senate, contributing to a lasting dislike of Hadrian.[24]

Since Trajan's ambitions were cut short, it is uncertain what he intended in the long term and whether his goals were achievable. Hadrian argued that the new provinces would be a burden rather than a benefit, and throughout his reign he would generally display a cautious, consolidatory approach to the empire's frontiers. No aggressive wars were fought during his reign, but it should be noted that in this respect it was Trajan who was unusual in his willingness to add so much territory to the empire. As important were the circumstances of Hadrian's accession. Although he had received some signs of favour, most recently a second consulship, Hadrian had in no way been marked down as Trajan's successor. Nor had anyone else. With doubts over the story of adoption, there was little appeal for Hadrian in spending years fighting a difficult war to secure the new provinces, where any defeats would reflect badly on him. In the event, peace and stability were achieved relatively quickly in the region. Kings raised or restored to power in the abandoned provinces were allies, often Roman appointees. There was no effort by the Parthians to continue the war, which would have been reasonable enough after the Roman invasion, and instead they turned back to their civil war.

The biggest mystery surrounding these wars remains Trajan's motives. Dio claimed that the dispute over Armenia was a pretext and that Trajan fought the war to win glory. Certainly, the mustering of so many troops in time for the emperor's arrival reveals a degree of premeditation. The question is how much, and whether this was simply the standard desire to parade military might and negotiate from strength or a conscious intention to fight rather than talk. Modern scholars have suggested other motives, such as a desire to make Syria and Asia Minor secure against any potential threat or, less plausibly, a quest to take over large areas of the trade routes to the Far East. Ultimately, we know too little about the details of what was happening in Armenia, and especially about the actions of Parthamasiris and Osroes I in the lead-up to the war, to judge how provocative this had really been from a Roman standpoint. Equally, there is no way of knowing whether Trajan was carried away with dreams of Alexander the Great from the start or whether the events happened in stages, his plans expanding from an assertion of power to the decision to make Armenia a province, then widening operations into Adiabene and Mesopotamia, and eventually pushing on to Babylonia and the sea.[25]

Trajan certainly had a taste for warfare and victory. No other event in his reign was celebrated as much as the Dacian victory, and at heart military success validated the rule of a man adopted by an appointee of the Senate, but with no blood link to the Julio-Claudian family or even connection to the old aristocracy. The fact that Trajan did not mark out a clear successor may also be revealing, given that by the time he went east he was much the same age as Nerva had been on succession. Trajan never had any children, and it seems unlikely that he still dreamed of fathering a son, even ignoring the gossip that held that he was far more interested in boys than women. True or not, he was discreet, so that Rome's elite were content to pass this, like his fondness for heavy drinking, off as an unimportant vice. On the other hand, it may be wrong to assume that he was expected to mark out an heir, and perhaps he was willing to entrust the task to the Senate. Thus, while it is possible to see Trajan as an ageing man unwilling to confront his mortality and eager to recapture his best years by winning a new victory, this is not the only way to reconstruct the evidence.[26]

Scholars are apt to see pursuit of glory as incompatible with rational decision-making. Yet for Rome's elite, seeking glory was entirely as honourable and reasonable as other concerns, not least because the greatest glory came from the greatest service to the state. Julius Caesar depicted his campaigns in Gaul as entirely for the good of the res publica and explained how he became sucked into operations over an ever-widening area to protect Rome's interests. The message was that he and his soldiers won glory serving the good of Rome. That was the ideal, whether or not everyone agreed that Caesar's actions lived up to such a standard. Trajan most likely did seek glory when he went to the east, but that does not mean that it was his only or even first concern or that his plans did not develop as the situation changed. For all Trajan's emphasis on his Dacian victory, in 102 Dacia was left as an independent kingdom and only became a province after the second war several years later. Trajan need not have planned to create new provinces in the east before he went to Armenia. Whatever his ambitions, the emperor did not anticipate the scale of rebellions in the conquered territory nor the collapse of his own health.[27]

There was one strange sequel to this conflict. The Senate had voted Trajan a triumph over Parthia, and Hadrian had the ceremony performed with great pomp through the heart of Rome. No dead man had ever triumphed before, and a chariot carrying an effigy of the now deified Trajan joined the procession to the acclamation of the crowds. Hadrian never celebrated a triumph, although he was awarded the right by the Senate on a single occasion. He spent the greater part of his reign touring the provinces, especially the frontier provinces with their large garrisons. Keenly interested in equipment and drill, he inspected troops, observed manoeuvres, and ordered the construction of frontier installations, most famously Hadrian's Wall in northern Britain. There were wars during his reign in several areas. Arrian was legate of Cappadocia when the Alans raided the province for the first time, and he won praise through driving them out. The most serious conflict was provoked by Hadrian's decision to turn Jerusalem into a Roman *colonia* and construct a temple to Jupiter on the foundations of the Jewish Temple destroyed by Titus in 70. Inspired by one Simeon bar Kosiba, nicknamed 'the son of the star' (bar Kochba in Aramaic), the rebels made great progress, and for a few years, as under Nero, there was an independent Jewish state in Judaea. Roman losses were heavy, perhaps including the massacre of an entire legion, and it took years of brutal, attritional fighting, as one fortified village and town after another had to be besieged in order to suppress the rebellion. This was the victory for which Hadrian was voted a triumph, but it was celebrated far less in propaganda than might have been expected.[28]

Hadrian comes across as a good ruler, although he never managed to make the senatorial class like him, something not helped by his fondness for parading his own intelligence, as well as his very public affair with the youth Antinous and extravagant mourning when this lover died. Perhaps because of the doubts about his own succession, Hadrian was careful to mark out an heir. When his first choice died, he not only adopted another senator, Antoninus Pius, but made him in turn adopt two young aristocrats, Marcus Aurelius and Lucius Verus, thus securing the succession for two generations.* Hadrian's plans worked this time, for when he died in 137, Antoninus Pius succeeded. One tradition claimed that the name Pius was given to him because he insisted that his 'father' be

---

*These are the names familiar to us. The younger men in particular had a succession of names during their lives, but this is not important for our topic.

honoured with deification in the teeth of resistance from a Senate now free to express its dislike of Hadrian.[29]

Antoninus Pius had little or no military experience and even less taste for travel and warfare. The frontier was advanced in northern Britain with the construction of the Antonine Wall, but he never visited this province or any other and instead trusted his provincial legates to deal with any problems. There were moments of friction with Parthia under Hadrian and again under Antoninus Pius which were settled with threats and diplomacy, but near the end of the latter's reign the rule of Armenia once again became a problem. By this time, the king of kings was Vologaeses IV, son of one of the unsuccessful challengers of Vologaeses III. How he came to power circa 147 is unknown, but he appears to have overcome any rivals fairly quickly and then began to reassert central control over the regional kingdoms. Characene was invaded and its king driven out in 151, a victory proclaimed in an inscription carved into a bronze statue of Herakles taken back as a trophy to Seleucia. A decade later, Vologaeses IV was willing to use force to place his own choice on the throne of Armenia, regardless of Roman feelings on the matter.[30]

Antoninus Pius died in 161, and this challenge came as his heirs had only just taken over. Hadrian appears to have planned for both men to rule, and Marcus Aurelius, who was older than his adopted brother, insisted on respecting this and ruling as coequal with Lucius Verus. This was an innovation, for previous attempts at having more than one heir had led to the rapid liquidation of the younger partner amid accusations of conspiracy. Yet it worked, and for all their contrasting temperaments (probably exaggerated in our sources), the two men worked well together and showed every sign of mutual trust.[31]

In 161, the Parthians initiated the war by overrunning Armenia. Many scholars consider this as the only occasion when they began a conflict with Rome, although this does mean viewing the invasion in 40 BC as a continuation of the war begun by Crassus, which is not really tenable. What it certainly meant is that the Romans were not prepared for major conflict, which in turn meant that it took time to react and to mass an army of suitable size. This was even true of the garrisons of Cappadocia and Syria. The legate of Cappadocia reacted to the invasion of Armenia aggressively, as was the Roman way, demanding immediate withdrawal. He advanced into Armenia with at most a battle group based around a single legion, but possibly a much smaller force since the Greek word used to describe it in our source is ambiguous. Whatever his actual strength, the legate and his men were swiftly surrounded by a superior enemy and took shelter within the walls of a city but, like Paetus, were not supplied or mentally prepared to stand siege. The legate died, probably by his own hand, and his soldiers were massacred. Vologaeses IV followed this by launching an attack on Syria—the first in two centuries. Although this force was eventually driven back, or chose to retreat, this was an even greater slight to Roman honour and Rome's sense of power than the fighting in Armenia, and it had to be answered.[32]

In 162, Lucius Verus was sent east to supervise the Roman response amid a mobilization of troops on a scale similar to Trajan's campaign. Sadly, surviving sources for what followed are even worse than for the earlier conflict. Many accounts were written at the time, prompting the satirist Lucian of Samosata to write a work mocking their exaggeration and sloppiness. It is a sign of just how meagre the evidence is that scholars try to glean facts from this work intended to entertain and amuse rather than record. In broad terms, the course of the war appears similar. Verus spent most of his time near Antioch, and one tradition mocked him for feasting and dallying with his mistress while he sent others off to wage war. This was not entirely just, since an emperor's job was to listen to petitions and receive envoys just as Trajan had done, but it is probably fair to say that he lacked Trajan's enthusiasm for army life.

As before, rather than one great army, the Romans operated as several field forces, whose commanders appear by name in our sources and who seem to have operated with considerable independence. Victories were won in Armenia and Mesopotamia, and as Roman strength grew there was no repeat of the Parthian attack into Syria. Cities surrendered or were taken by siege, among them Nisibis, Edessa, and Dura-Europos, and eventually the Romans pushed on to take Ctesiphon and Seleucia in 165. Then they

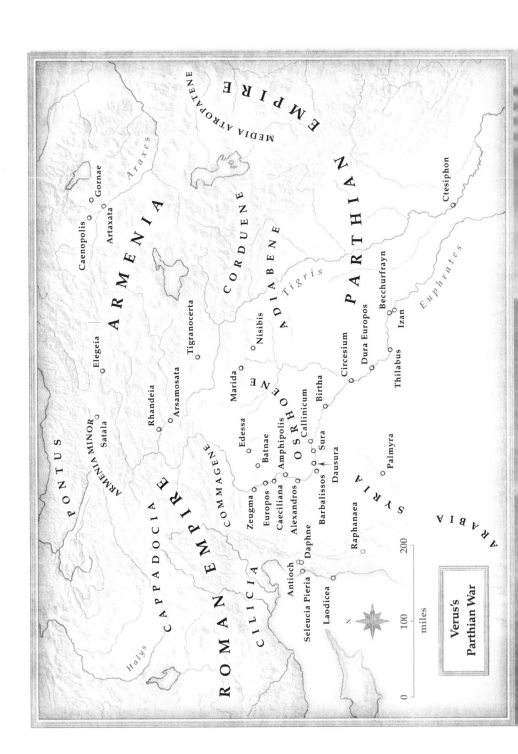

MEDIA ATROPATENE

PARTHIAN EMPIRE

Araxes

Gornae

Caenopolis

Artaxata

ARMENIA

Elegeia

CORDUENE

ADIABENE

Tigris

Ctesiphon

Euphrates

Tigranocerta

Nisibis

Becchurfrayn

Arsamosata

Izan

Marida

Circesium

Dura Europos

Thilabus

Rhandeia

ARMENIA MINOR

Satala

Edessa

OSRHOENE

Birtha

PONTUS

Batnae

Callinicum

Amphipolis

Sura

Palmyra

Zeugma

Dausura

Europos

SYRIA

Caeciliana

Barbalissos

Alexandros

CAPPADOCIA

COMMAGENE

Raphanaea

ARABIA

ROMAN EMPIRE

Antioch

Daphne

CILICIA

Seleucia Pieria

Laodicea

Halys

200

N

100

0

miles

Verus's
Parthian War

withdrew, probably after negotiation. Some territory was taken under direct rule, for instance Dura-Europos and Nisibis, but there were no new provinces nor talk of giving a king to the Parthians. Roman dominance and power had been reasserted unequivocally, but this had not done fatal damage to Vologaeses IV's prestige, for he continued to rule for decades.[33]

Lucius Verus returned to Rome to celebrate a triumph, which he shared with Marcus Aurelius. A worse legacy of the conflict was the spread of an epidemic throughout the empire in what is known today as the Antonine plague. Detachments of soldiers returning to their garrisons in other provinces were blamed and may well have spread the disease, which also was carried along the trade routes and by other travellers. Long-distance travel and commerce between thriving communities carried this risk alongside the benefits. Rumour spread that the pestilence was first unleashed during the sack of Seleucia, when soldiers ransacked the Temple of Apollo, but there is some evidence for earlier outbreaks in India and beyond. The disease itself cannot be identified. Smallpox is often suggested, even though no ancient source mentions facial scarring, and smallpox is unlikely to have simultaneously affected livestock, as is claimed in our sources. Measles is another possibility, although since either disease or any other might well have mutated over the centuries, this is really little more than guesswork. Without statistics, we cannot estimate the loss of life in the years that followed as successive waves passed through the empire—and presumably also swept through Parthian territory. An estimate of deaths totalling a quarter of the population of the empire is more than plausible, and sources note that the disease was naturally more devastating in crowded cities and army bases than in rural areas with small, scattered populations.[34]

The long-term impact of the Antonine plague, and subsequent epidemics over the next century, was surely serious, even if it cannot be traced in any detail. At the time it was an appalling cataclysm, which struck some and not others in a way difficult to understand. The physician Galen, who provides the best information about the disease, lost his entire household of slaves. On another occasion, he persuaded the two emperors to leave an army camp where the epidemic was raging. On their journey away from this, Lucius Verus fell ill and died—though not of the plague. He was in his thirty-ninth year, son of the man Hadrian had first chosen as heir, who had died at a similarly young age. Marcus Aurelius, never considered a vigorous or athletic man, survived and ruled for another eleven years, the latter part spent overseeing brutal campaigns against Germanic tribes from beyond the Danube. He was succeeded by his son, Commodus, only eighteen, but already co-ruler. He boasted that he was the first emperor born to the purple, and his record was not good, like that of most men who came to the throne when they were young. Twelve years later, he was strangled in his bath during a palace conspiracy. The Senate's choice was murdered by a mob of praetorian guardsmen just three months later, having failed to pay them all of the bounty he had promised when first acclaimed.[35]

Civil war followed, raging as intensely as it had done after the death of Nero. One senator outbid a competitor in Rome and bought the loyalty of the Praetorian Guard but enjoyed little support in the wider empire, especially among the legions. The three main contenders were the commanders of the major military provinces: Pannonia, Syria, and Britain. In 193, the legate of Pannonia, Lucius Septimius Severus, occupied Rome and disposed of the pretender there. Making a settlement to share power with the governor of Britain, he headed east and defeated the legate of Syria. This man had sought military support from kingdoms beyond the empire, notably Osrhoene and Adiabene and perhaps Parthia. Although he gained some allied soldiers in this way, most of the monarchs instead took the opportunity to attack Roman territory while the self-declared emperor's attentions were elsewhere. In 195, Severus fought a campaign against them to reassert Rome's dominance but then had to return to Europe after a breach with his ally, the governor of Britain. Victorious once again, Severus returned to the east in 197, for in the meantime the king of kings Vologaeses V had sensed the chance to exploit Roman divisions. The Parthians overran much of allied Mesopotamia (although Nisibis held out under siege) and may have launched a big raid into the Roman province of Syria.[36]

Severus's subsequent campaign followed a familiar pattern. He had a big army, combining his own troops with men who had recently opposed them, giving him a chance to reward both groups and cement their loyalty to him. (Later in his reign he campaigned in northern Britain, and it was no coincidence that his major foreign wars were waged in areas that had been loyal to his rivals; in each case there were provincial armies to win over, while the distractions of civil war had weakened the frontiers and provided good reason for fighting to restore Roman dominance.) As usual, this great force spent little time concentrated in one army and operated as several field forces under subordinate commanders. The strength and obvious determination of the now reunited Roman empire prompted the kings of Armenia and Osrhoene to send gifts and assurances of loyalty. Momentum was with the Romans as they advanced, and Severus followed much the same route as Trajan down the Euphrates. Babylon and the largely ruined Seleucia were taken, and Ctesiphon was sacked once again after a major battle in which Vologaeses V was defeated. Then, like Verus's army, the Romans marched away before their supplies ran out altogether and before resentment could grow into rebellion, although this time plague did not travel with them. Like Trajan, Severus besieged Hatra, and when his first poorly prepared attempt failed, he returned the following year only to fail again. Hatra remained independent, if wary of Rome.[37]

Like Trajan and unlike Verus, Severus added two new provinces, Mesopotamia and Osrhoene, to the empire, although significantly, he left Armenia as an allied kingdom and did not attempt to turn it into a province, so this was not a simple revival of earlier ambitions. Dio tells us that Severus called his new provinces a bulwark to shield Syria from attack. Dio dismissed the boast, claiming that in fact the garrisons were expensive to maintain for little return in revenue, while forcing the Romans to get involved with disputes and conflict in the communities bordering on them and provoking Parthia. At the very least, this illustrates the range of opinion that could be held on frontier matters by Rome's elite. It is harder to say which of them was right, for, despite Dio's scepticism, the frontier line established by Severus remained broadly in place for centuries. Two legions newly raised by Severus formed the garrison of this 'bulwark', adding to the forces stationed in the east.[38]

THIS CHAPTER HAS covered more than a century of events. Partly this is because of the similarities between these three great wars between Romans and Parthians and even more because of the paucity of sources which leaves so much unclear. Some broad conclusions can be drawn. For whatever reason, Trajan decided to settle his differences with Parthia by the direct use of massive military force, and this example was copied on several occasions by other emperors willing to campaign in person. As a result, Roman armies reached far further than they had ever done under the republic and repeatedly captured the great cities of Ctesiphon and Seleucia. These conflicts witnessed Roman defeats, some of them serious, but significantly more Roman victories. None of the Parthian kings in these years were able to stop the Romans from advancing deep into their empire, although there was never any question of their going even further into its eastern heartland. Whether the Romans could have suppressed the rebellions and kept control of the conquered territory in the long term if Trajan's health had not failed cannot ever be known. None of these wars were waged to destroy or conquer the Parthian empire altogether, and the territorial claims made were limited, even if significant acts of expansion.

The second century suggested that, for the moment, the balance of power had shifted in Rome's direction, or at the very least that Rome's emperors were more willing to exert their strength. Yet Arsacid Parthia remained powerful, despite periods of infighting. For all that the great wars stand out, there were decades of peace between each outbreak of conflict, and the picture was primarily one of coexistence. While the Romans spoke of limitless empire and power and saw conquest as a good thing, these were not overwhelming concerns to most emperors. As always, they and their Parthian counterparts had other priorities, including rebellions and problems on other frontiers, let alone the devastating plagues that began in this era. The third century AD would prove a time of immense, violent change for both Rome and Parthia; Dio wrote of the Roman world moving from an age of gold to one of iron and rust. Meagre though our sources are, there is little sense that what happened was inevitable, still less that it could have been predicted by anyone. Human beings—and empires—tend to live in the here and now. They assume that things are as they should be, and per-haps always will be, in spite of the lessons of history.[39]

10

DYNASTIES

199–240

THE STABILITY OF THE PRINCIPATE SUCCUMBED ONLY TWICE TO serious disruption in the first and second centuries. If the prolonged peace between Romans and Parthians was broken more often in the second century, this still stopped far short of creating permanent hostility. The Romans took and then lost new territory under Trajan, gained a little under Marcus Aurelius and Lucius Verus, and captured substantially more under Septimius Severus. Even so, the gains were no more than a small fraction of the Parthian empire. More frequent conflict surely made each side warier and more suspicious of the other, without turning into unrelenting—or even frequent—hostility. There was still much more to be gained by restraint than all-out conflict. However, over the next few decades other problems convulsed both empires, creating an environment where a major war against the other often seemed attractive, even unavoidable, to successive emperors and kings of kings.

On 4 February 211, Septimius Severus succumbed to illness and died at Eboracum (modern York) after three years of tough campaigning in what is now Scotland. He had two sons, Caracalla and Geta, and wanted them both to succeed him and rule as equals, just as Marcus Aurelius and Lucius Verus had done. Caracalla was almost twenty-three, his brother a little over a year younger, and both, along with their mother, Julia Domna, had accompanied Severus to Britain and been given duties to give them some experience. Severus's final advice to them was supposedly the rather grim 'love one another, indulge the soldiers, and despise everyone else.'[1]

Love was in short supply, and within a year Caracalla had arranged the murder of his brother, who was stabbed to death by centurions of the Praetorian Guard, his blood supposedly spattering the horrified Julia Domna. Caracalla claimed that Geta had been plotting against him and announced a bonus for the troops as a reward for their loyalty. The praetorians readily acquiesced. The legionaries of II Parthica, raised by Severus and stationed at Alba Longa close to Rome, took a little more persuading before they accepted what had happened. The arrest and execution of senators alleged to have conspired with Geta was sufficient to ensure the Senate's acceptance of the situation without the need for bribery. The dead Caesar was condemned posthumously, and all over the empire Geta's statues were removed and his name chiselled off inscriptions.[2]

Caracalla flouted many conventions and rarely bothered to treat the Senate with respect. The nickname Caracalla came from his fondness for a colourful hooded cloak, seen as Gallic or Germanic in style. More bizarrely, he tried to rape a vestal virgin—one of the aristocratic women who sacrificed their youth to serving the goddess—and then had her and three of her fellow priestesses executed for breaking their vow of chastity. All of them were entombed alive, even though the one attacked by Caracalla staunchly defended herself and said that she remained a virgin, despite the emperor's best efforts. Caracalla's health may have been poor, apart from this alleged impotence, which perhaps contributed to his hot temper. Dio, who had judged Marcus Aurelius's son Commodus to be stupid rather than fundamentally evil, was less kind to Caracalla and portrays him as bright and capable but also lazy, irascible, and dangerously, often murderously, unpredictable. As a senator who lived through and survived these years while seeing plenty of colleagues fall, Dio was apt to judge everything that the young emperor did in the most negative of lights. In 212, Caracalla extended Roman citizenship to all those within the empire who were already citizens of a recognized city or other community. This meant that the majority of people in the provinces were now legally Romans, a status that brought considerable privileges, albeit somewhat reduced from earlier periods. Dio claimed that the emperor only did this to make more people liable for certain taxes, most notably those on inheritance.[3]

Even making allowance for hostile sources, there is much that remains puzzling about Caracalla's behaviour. In 215 he visited Egypt and at Alexandria ordered his soldiers to massacre a crowd in an incident none of our sources seem able to explain. There was also tension over Armenia, although again the details are obscure. Caracalla invited the king of Armenia to visit him and then ordered his arrest. Soon afterwards he did the same to the king of Edessa, who ruled just a fraction of the old kingdom now that Osrhoene had become a province. Caracalla had come to the eastern provinces with substantial reinforcements to add to the armies of the region—as well as two massive, prefabricated siege engines—suggesting that he planned to do far more. Dio claims that the Roman emperor asked to marry a daughter of the Arsacid king of kings and used the refusal of his request as a pretext for war. The generally less well-informed and less reliable Herodian, in contrast, wrote that the offer was accepted, but that when the Parthian royal party came to celebrate the betrothal, Caracalla had most of them murdered during the feast, and only a few, including the king of kings, managed to escape. If this was surely no more than gossip, even the suggestion of Rome's emperor marrying a foreign princess must have been shocking, invoking Antony and Cleopatra (who at least was an ally and may or may not ever have been his wife). Caracalla also demanded the return of a philosopher and former favourite who had fallen from grace, and a man named Tiridates—perhaps a prince from one of the kingdoms—who had taken shelter with the king of kings, which also seems a flimsy pretext for war.[4]

In the summer of 216, Caracalla advanced into Media. There is no suggestion of a major battle, and either the Parthians were preoccupied with their own disputes or preferred to watch and wait until they were better prepared to deal with the invaders.

Caracalla revered Alexander the Great, and had even raised his own Macedonian-style phalanx, so he was no doubt pleased to tread in the famous conqueror's footsteps when he took Arbela. He also sent men to the tombs of the Arsacid royal family, which were broken open and the bones scattered in symbolic humiliation. An attack into Babylonia may also have happened, although if it occurred, it does not seem to have amounted to much. With the year spent, Caracalla retired to winter in Mesopotamia before renewing the war in the spring. On 8 April 217, the emperor was near Carrhae—now well within Roman territory—and journeyed to visit a shrine to a deity associated with the moon. Dismounting and disappearing behind some bushes to relieve himself, the twenty-nine-year-old was stabbed by a soldier in his household and died moments later.[5]

The assassin was swiftly killed by loyal bodyguards, but he had only ever been a tool in a conspiracy planned by Macrinus, the senior of the two praetorian prefects. Having discovered that a letter condemning him was on its way to the emperor, Macrinus had decided to act rather than wait for execution. After waiting a few days to make sure that he was not suspected of involvement in the murder, the praetorian prefect declared himself emperor, promising a bounty to the nearest troops. This worked, and the army in the area pledged its loyalty. A letter went to Rome, where the Senate felt obliged to recognize him, since he had an army and they did not, and there was no other claimant. Macrinus was not a member of the senatorial order but an equestrian and, worse than that from a traditional point of view, a Mauretanian from North Africa who had one ear pierced for the earring fashionable in that region. Praetorian prefects had always been equestrians, precisely because it was felt unwise to permit any senator to command the soldiers closest to the emperor, lest he seek to replace him. At first, the prefects' duties were restricted to controlling the guard, but over time these expanded as emperors chose to rely on them, using them as administrators and legal advisors. Macrinus was first and foremost a lawyer, and he had little direct military experience.[6]

In the meantime, Artabanus IV of Parthia had mustered a large army to confront the anticipated offensive from Caracalla. Sensing a chance to avenge the humiliation of the last year and strengthen his own position, he advanced, and a battle was fought over several days near Nisibis. Losses do not appear to have been very high, so perhaps the combat was tentative, as each side sought an advantage before really committing, hoping all along to negotiate from a position of strength. Herodian claims that the fighting was a draw, while Dio depicts it as a defeat for the Romans, which seems more likely since Macrinus paid the Parthians two hundred million sesterces and agreed to return captives and plunder as the price of peace.[7]

Macrinus proclaimed the settlement as a victory but soon faced a different sort of challenge. Julia Domna was now dead, but her sister, Julia Maesa, and the older of her nieces, Julia Soaemias, announced that the latter's fourteen-year-old son was actually the bastard child of Caracalla rather than her late husband's offspring. They were all at Emesa in Syria, where the lad, despite being the son of a man adlected to the Senate by Severus, was serving as priest to the god Elagabalus, perhaps through family tradition or simply because this was prestigious for a local aristocrat. The nearest legion was convinced of his claim, especially after being lavished with gifts and promises, and declared him as emperor. Others copied, for Caracalla was remembered with more fondness in the army than elsewhere, while Macrinus was largely unknown and does not appear to have been able to inspire much enthusiasm for his leadership. In 218, a battle was fought between relatively small armies supporting the rivals. Macrinus lost, fled, and was subsequently killed.[8]

Once again, the Senate accepted the judgement of the armies, condemning the defeated and praising the victor, even though this meant acknowledging as princeps an utterly inexperienced child alleged to be the illegitimate son of an emperor. The boy—known to us as Elagabalus after the name of his favoured deity—proved more of a surprise when he arrived in Rome, for he showed no respect for tradition and even less interest in the duties of his new role. Strangest of all was his fondness for dancing in public, a legacy of the rituals for his—to traditional Roman eyes—outlandish god, and his marriage to a succession of brides in a very short time. Two were vestal virgins, and another the priestess of a North African goddess, so that their union was in a sense a physical manifestation of a marriage between the two deities. Appointments were made for apparently whimsical, even scandalous, reasons, with rumour saying that the new emperor favoured the candidate with the largest penis; so much of the material in our sources is bizarre that it is hard to know how much of it is true, but it is clear that men like Dio were appalled. In the meantime, real power lay elsewhere, notably with Julia Maesa and her eldest daughter, who vied with each other for control, as well as with anyone able to influence the young ruler. The result was a sense of weakness at the centre of the empire. Armies in several provinces mutinied, and a succession of men were declared emperor only to be swiftly murdered.[9]

Julia Maesa had another daughter who in turn had a son, and in 222 they together arranged the murder of Julia Soaemias and Elagabalus. In his place they raised the thirteen-year-old Severus Alexander and made sure that he was closely supervised, traditional in his manners and behaviour, and, most of all, courteous in his dealings with the Senate. While this left a better impression on the elite—so that in our sources Alexander is treated far more favourably, in deliberate contrast to his cousin Elagabalus— it proved hard for the new emperor to seem anything more than a puppet. Elements in the army remained unruly, the praetorians most of all, and Severus Alexander struggled to control them. The highly distinguished jurist Ulpian, famed for his work codifying Roman law, proved unpopular with the guard when appointed as praetorian prefect, and Alexander could not prevent his murder.[10]

The sense of Rome's weakness spread to the wider world, and in 227 the king of kings Ardashir I was confident enough to attack the eastern provinces. Mesopotamia was overrun, both Nisibis and Carrhae falling, and there may well have been big raids into Syria and Cappadocia. By 231 Severus Alexander had gone to Antioch and gathered a large army, as some of the lost ground was recovered. The next year, the Romans took the offensive, employing three field armies, one of them led by the emperor, but later there were stories that he had proved overcautious and had not supported the other columns adequately. One column may have suffered a reverse. At best this was a limited success, although enough for victory to be declared and the emperor to celebrate a triumph in Rome in 233. Alexander was soon called away to deal with trouble in the Rhineland, and the discontent rumbling in some sections of the military eventually culminated in his murder in 235. The conspiracy was led by Julius Verus Maximinus, and once again a man from outside the Senate, without the slightest real or imagined blood link to an imperial family, was proclaimed as emperor. By the time of his elevation, he was an equestrian, having won this rank and a series of promotions in the army ever since Septimius Severus spotted his strength, courage, and ability. Rumours circulated that he had been born as a peasant in Pannonia, but there is a good chance that this was a considerable exaggeration. Whatever the truth, what was clear was that he had risen far higher than would ever have been possible in the first or second centuries, had become emperor through murder, and would only remain emperor as long as sufficient soldiers backed him.[11]

Ardashir I was another man who had come to power through civil war, killing Artabanus IV in 224 to take his throne.* This was the culmination of decades of civil strife, all of it far harder to trace than the contemporary power struggles within the Roman empire. So much is shrouded in mystery, even though the rise of Ardashir I is seen as ending the Parthian empire and replacing it with Sasanian Persia, which is universally depicted as a far more centralized and powerful state. For historians of Rome, the rise of Persia helps to explain the chaos of the third century, where emperors rose and fell rapidly and defeats were frequent on all frontiers. For specialists in the history of Iran, the Sasanians represent the return of a consciously Iranian dynasty, as opposed to the Arsacid Parthian outsiders. Roman sources claim that Ardashir I even asserted his right to retake all of the old Achaemenid empire overthrown by Alexander the Great, something not mentioned since the early first-century negotiations with Tiberius. For both, the transition is

---

*In earlier works he is referred to as Artabanus V, but reassessment of the Arsacid dynasty has led to the belief that an earlier Artabanus did not rule.

seen as sudden and dramatic, fundamentally altering the balance of power.[12]

The truth is a good deal more nuanced and raises more questions than can readily be answered. Ardashir I did not belong to any of the royal Arsacid houses who had ruled the Parthian empire since its creation four and a half centuries earlier. One of the reasons so little is known of the Arsacids is that the Sasanian kings did their best to suppress the memory of their predecessors. The tradition about the Sasanians is fuller, even if it mainly only survives in medieval form, sometimes misunderstood, often embellished or deliberately distorted as later kings rewrote the past to suit their own agendas. As a result, the earlier periods are especially problematic, including such vital questions as who Ardashir I was, and why he and his successors took the name Sasan, for it is not at all clear whether Sasan was a specific ancestor, some broader identity, or even a god.

Ardashir I's power base was in Persis (the modern Fars province of Iran), the heartland of the old Achaemenid Persian empire, where the still spectacular ruins of the vast palace complex at Persepolis was just one reminder of former greatness. Alexander had burned the palaces in 330 BC, some said on a drunken whim, over five hundred years before Ardashir was born. Since then, the Seleucids had ruled, and after them the Arsacids, both dynasties founded by outsiders with their own language and beliefs. Yet in each case, day-to-day governance remained in the hands of local leaders, kings of small kingdoms. In some periods one king was overall ruler of Persis, overlord of the petty dynasts of each district, just as the Seleucid or Arsacid king was his overlord and that of all the other regional kings and satraps. In Persis as elsewhere, the old language of the area, in this case Persian, survived, as did traditions, styles, and beliefs. None of these were static, and each developed naturally and under the influence of the current overlords. Coins minted in Persis show kings wearing traditional Persian headdress but also styling themselves as divine, after the manner of the Seleucids and some Arsacids. Rebellions against Arsacid rule had occurred in Persis, although less often than in other areas. There is no good evidence of resentment, let alone active resistance to rule by outsiders, lasting over the centuries, and it is very hard to say how much was truly known about the days of Cyrus and Darius and the glories of the Achaemenid empire. Some scholars are inclined to see Ardashir I's claims of recovering the old territories as inventions by Roman observers trying to understand the world through the prism of the history familiar to them from Herodotus and other accounts of the distant past.[13]

The Greco-Roman sources also tell some odd tales of Ardashir I's origins, claiming that a man named Papak, an obscure leather worker or cobbler with a gift for prophecy, foretold that the child of a soldier billeted in his house would grow up to win fame and power. Since he had no daughters, Papak arranged for his wife to sleep with the visitor, and in due course she gave birth to Ardashir (or Artaxares, as these sources tend to style him). Later, as the boy grew and showed promise, Papak and the soldier, sometimes called Sasanus, argued over who would raise him but agreed that he would be known as the son of Papak. Claims that future greatness was foretold are very common in ancient literature, although this is a more scurrilous story than most, even though one author asserted that it was based upon the official record in the Persian archives. The names, though garbled, are recognizable as the real names Pabag and Sasan. Sources going back to the Sasanian tradition vary in their presentation, with the simplest making Ardashir the son of Pabag who was the son of Sasan. Another makes Ardashir's mother the daughter of Sasan, but there is no consistency.[14]

Ardashir I describes himself on an inscription as son of King Pabag but is vaguer regarding his actual relationship to Sasan and does not call him king. Instead, he describes himself as from the house or family of Sasan. One tradition has Sasan as a priest, keeper of a Zoroastrian fire temple in Istakhr in Persis, but another has Pabag as the priest. He was probably not a local man. The name Sasan does not appear in Persis until after Ardashir I's rise but does occur further to the east. Recently, a good case has been made that he came from the lands ruled by the Indo-Parthian dynasties, whose rulers were Arsacids, although from a separate line from the families who had ruled Parthia itself. The division may go back to the earliest generations who had carved out the Parthian empire. Whether he was one of these eastern Arsacids is impossible to say, although since he never paraded any connection with kings other than Pabag, the chances are that he was not or was from a minor branch at best. Never once does he mention another king from the relatively recent past as ancestor, and it seems unlikely that he would not have made such a claim if it were even vaguely plausible. Ardashir I clearly had a talent for leadership and war and may have risen on his own ability, luck, and determination. Plenty of other leaders in the ancient world started this way, and while most ultimately failed, some did not. Most likely he came from the minor nobility rather than any royal house.[15]

Pabag became king of Istakhr, along with his son Shapur, minting coins depicting them both. Their rise was almost certainly through raising troops and overthrowing the existing incumbent. Perhaps there was a religious element, if Pabag was indeed a priest. Such local contests for power mirrored the wider struggles for the Arsacid throne and were nothing new—for instance, the extreme case of Asinaeus and Anilaeus, the bandits in Babylonia who had managed to win formal recognition. In most cases, a king of kings was willing to accept changes of regime at lower levels as long as the new leader offered their loyalty. No doubt the opportunity for such revolutions was more common at times of central weakness. In the later second and early third century, it was rare indeed for there not to be at least two men claiming to be king of kings. Artabanus IV's main rival was Vologaeses VI, and the struggle between the two may well explain Artabanus IV's slow response to Caracalla's attack.[16]

Ardashir I appears to have made himself the local ruler in another district of Persis by overthrowing the existing dynast. While he later styles himself son of the divine Pabag, there is a good chance that this was by adoption rather than birth. Around the same time, Pabag built on his initial success by attacking other neighbouring dynasts, steadily increasing his own territory. Ardashir did the same, and there is no assurance that the relationship between the two men was always good. Instead, they may have become rivals and even fought against each other. Shapur was clearly marked out as the favoured heir, but both he and Pabag may well have been defeated by Ardashir, perhaps even killed by him. In one tradition, Shapur died when a wall fell on him, apparently an accident. Perhaps Pabag was left with no alternative to accepting Ardashir in his place or was simply displaced by the younger man. In time, perhaps in the second decade of the third century, Ardashir I came to control most of Persis.

Once he had achieved overlordship of Persis, Ardashir I decided to aim for higher things and bring a wider area under his control. Perhaps Artabanus IV refused to recognize him as a major regional ruler, or perhaps Ardashir I sensed an opportunity. Vologaeses VI disappears from the record in the early 220s, whether having simply died or been defeated by Artabanus IV or Ardashir I himself. Afterwards, in 224, Ardashir I defeated the king of kings in several battles or a single great battle. One rock sculpture produced soon afterwards depicts Ardashir I running his rival through with a lance, both of them on horseback and equipped as cataphracts. Another shows the corpse of Artabanus IV being trampled beneath the hoofs of Ardashir I's horse. Two years after this victory, Ardashir took Ctesiphon, where he—and later most of the other Sasanian monarchs—was crowned king of kings. Notably this was a city created by the Arsacid Parthians, not somewhere associated with the Achaemenids.[17]

This conflict was a civil war, the latest in a long succession as the Arsacid throne changed hands through violence. There is no good evidence to suggest that it was primarily a rebellion of indigenous Persians against Parthian oppressors, or even that this dynamic played any significant role, but then almost nothing is known about individual communities' sense of their own identity. It is clear that there was considerable variation in beliefs and customs from region to region. The Zoroastrianism of the Achaemenid Persians could not function as it had done after their empire fell to Alexander the Great, so it had to change. Fire temples remained important cult sites throughout the era of the Seleucids and the Arsacids. How many of these cult sites conformed strictly to earlier traditions—or what would subsequently emerge as orthodox Zoroastrianism under the Sasanians—is impossible to say. There is a good chance that ideas of orthodox, state-sponsored, and controlled religion under the Sasanians in fact need to be revised, for there was probably quite a bit of variety. All this makes it impossible to say whether, after four and a half centuries, the Arsacid monarchs were considered outsiders and not of the true religion by significant groups within the empire, especially in Persis.

What is certain is that other than in the earliest days, only a minority of the men who fought for Ardashir I could be categorized as Persians, distinct from Parthians. As his fortunes rose, Ardashir I gained allies among the great Parthian noble houses, including the Suren, Karen, and Andegan, all with their heartlands in the east of the empire. More joined him as his success made his final victory ever more likely. These men brought their households and other warriors to fight on his behalf, just as earlier generations had done for other claimants to the throne, and just as other clans and local groups chose to fight for Artabanus IV. Making himself king of kings did not guarantee that Ardashir I's rule would endure, let alone that his heirs would succeed him. Plenty of members of the established royal house remained at large, not least the king of Armenia and his family. Challenges remained, and it took more fighting to drive open opponents to seek sanctuary in Armenia. One of the great ironies of the rise of the house of Sasan was that it forced Armenia to align more with Rome. Another was that Hatra was willing to accept a Roman garrison after Ardashir I tried to capture the city and failed, just like Trajan and Severus.[18]

In the fourth century AD, the Roman historian and former army officer Ammianus Marcellinus asserted that an Arsacid was always preferred as ruler of Persia. This has usually been dismissed as an absurd anachronism by a historian who used Persian and Parthian as synonyms, and a reflection of the tendency of Greco-Roman authors to shape their narratives to fit with familiar assumptions based on the Classical past. Yet it may contain more than a germ of truth, and the house of Sasan may have been in origin Arsacid, if from an obscure, previously unimportant line separated from the main houses of Parthia proper for centuries. In a wider sense, there were probably few local monarchs who did not possess some Arsacid blood, given the royal culture of polygamy and the harem and the use of the king of king's daughters as brides to cement relationships within the empire. In addition, over the generations brothers and other relatives had been appointed to rule the regional kingdoms, so that plenty of men, including some who supported Ardashir I, may have possessed a claim, however slight, to membership to the royal lines, and thus to the throne. How such men—and women—viewed themselves and their identity is impossible to say.[19]

Ardashir I's claim may have been distant, even tenuous, but for the moment he had seized power and there were well-established methods to consolidate this. Early on, he had appointed a son and namesake as king of one of the regions of Persis and later may have elevated him to be king of Sakastan and marked him out as heir, although the prince did not in fact succeed him. This use of relatives was well within Arsacid tradition, as was rewarding clans and leaders who had backed him. Some of Ardashir I's self-presentation was new. On several monuments, he had himself depicted being recognized as king of kings by Ahura Mazda, the god at the heart of the Zoroastrian pantheon. Achaemenid kings had similarly claimed to be the earthly agents of the great god, but the Parthians had not to any large degree, so this could be seen as a revival of traditional belief. However, the way the god is represented—as a human, the same size as the king of kings, sometimes riding a horse and dressed in broadly the same way apart from a few important details to show his identity—has no precedent. The god hands a royal diadem to the king, sometimes over a fire altar. There is nothing quite the same from the Achaemenids, although the influence of Greek images—for instance of Nike, goddess of victory, handing a circular wreath to a Seleucid or Parthian king—seems likely.

There were obvious advantages for a successful usurper to present his rise as divinely inspired and approved, thus providing a legitimacy even more convincing than success on the battlefield. The stories associating Pabag and Sasan with priesthood in a fire temple might suggest that there was a strong religious element to the rise of the former, and from the start Ardashir I may have seen himself as both king and priest. Persis was the heartland of the Achaemenids, and it maintained aspects of old beliefs and rituals as part of the population's identity. Given that half a millennium had passed, it would not be surprising if the traditions had developed and changed. Perhaps, whatever his actual origins, Ardashir I adopted ideas and beliefs common in Persis or behaved in a way intended to win support there, although even then this could represent only one strand of several in the religion of the area. This might reflect his own beliefs or those of key supporters. Politicians can easily come to believe their own speeches and proclamations, especially when they enjoy so much success.

Yet caution is necessary, since Ardashir I may well have taken ideas from a wider area than Persis. What may have appeared was just a different form of Zoroastrianism, perhaps more common not just in Persis but in the eastern parts of the empire and among the Indo-Parthians than the type largely seen under the Arsacids up to this point. Hindsight tells us that the Sasanian kings would rule for four centuries, almost as long as the Arsacids. Thus, it is the convention to speak of Parthia and Parthians up to 224 and Persia and Persians afterwards. The tendency is to see Ardashir I as a very clear break with the past, not simply in religion but in government, culture, and military practices. Certainly, under the Sasanians many aspects of the state appear to be different compared to Arsacid Parthia. Royal authority seems much more centralized, sanctioned by a 'state' religion, differences in language, and the symbolism of power. Change occurred, although since some things are not attested for generations, it is much harder to say when and why they changed. Similarly, the records for the Arsacid period are so poor, most of all for the century or so before the rise of Ardashir I, that it is possible that some apparent innovations were much older, perhaps part of a gradual evolution. So little is known about the Parthian empire at all, and especially in its last century and a half, that it is uncertain how the empire operated.[20]

Ardashir I claimed divine approval. Whether he presented himself as a revolutionary or instead as the king of kings whom recent Arsacids ought to have been but were not cannot be known. The centralization of royal power seen as characteristically Sasanian may have been no more than a reflection of how a strong king of kings asserted himself. Regional kings, and sub-kings below them, continued in many areas throughout the Sasanian era, and if Sasanian kings appointed many relatives to these thrones, this was following Arsacid tradition. In a military context, the Sasanians are judged by modern scholars to have been significantly better organized and disciplined than the Parthians and also to have displayed far more skill in siege-craft. In battle, they fielded more infantry than in earlier periods but relied principally on heavily armoured cavalry—some primarily archers, some more conventional cataphracts—while light horse-archers appear to have played a secondary role. In addition, they employed war elephants, something never reliably attested for the Arsacids on the battlefield—although Tacitus claimed that after Lucius Caesennius Paetus's surrender in Armenia, the king of kings rode on an elephant over the bridge constructed for him by the legionaries. While these developments may have come from a military revolution presided over by Ardashir I and his immediate successors, there is also the chance that they had evolved gradually. Once again, there is no detailed description of a Parthian army in the field after the campaigns of Corbulo, making it guesswork whether these changes were already under way in the big campaigns of the second century.[21]

The empire ruled by Ardashir I and his successors covered essentially the same area as Arsacid Parthia. Stronger kings, like Ardashir, were able to exert greater control and regain territory that had been lost from the fringes of the empire during periods of weakness. Yet overall, these were the same lands occupied by the same communities in both eras. Over time, individual dynasts changed, cities flourished or declined, and communities grew or emerged as more important. An army raised by a Sasanian king of kings was no more homogenous than one raised by an Arsacid Parthian king of kings and instead consisted of some royal troops, often some hired soldiers, and a majority of contingents raised by regional and local monarchs, as well as key aristocrats. The mechanism of raising, maintaining, motivating, and controlling such an army remained essentially the same. Change tends to stand out, especially when the historical record is so poor, but the continuity is just as important. Noble families like the Karen and Suren, who had emerged in the early days of the Arsacid state, remained important right through the Sasanian period and in some cases beyond. No doubt there were marriage links between them and the Sasanian royal house, and members of each clan perceived as loyal were given precedence and came to lead their people. Individual leaders fell in and out of favour or backed the wrong side at times of civil war or during disputes over the succession. Yet it is striking that the same noble houses remained in control of their traditional lands for so many centuries.[22]

Scholars tend always to look for underlying causes and explanations of change and can neglect the role of individuals, their talents, and their personalities. While the character of Ardashir I remains unknowable, it is safe to say that he was an extremely capable war-leader who spent nearly all his adult life in conflict. He began by raising followers and gaining control of part of one of the five main regions of Persis, albeit one far from the centre of the province. We do not know quite how he did this, but some degree of early acceptance and support from Pabag is likely. The latter was one of a number of ambitious men fighting to increase their own power. Ardashir I played the same game and played it so well that he eventually fought his way to dominate all of Persis, supplanting Pabag and the favoured heir, probably by around 212. From there he expanded, and his coins show a progression from 'king' to 'king of the Iranians' (Aryans) and probably only with the defeat of Artabanus IV or the fall of Ctesiphon and his own coronation there does he become 'king of kings'.

The fighting did not stop, for Ardashir I faced rivals at large, foreign threats, and the need to assert his dominance over as much of the old empire as possible. Aggression against the Romans was a display of strength, intended to impress his new subjects and contrast with the weakness of Artabanus IV, who had let the tombs of his ancestors be desecrated. The Romans were proven and prestigious enemies and, better still, were less united and strong than had been the case for a long time, with two very young emperors in rapid succession and stories of mutinies and indiscipline in the armies. Attacking Mesopotamia and capturing strongholds, as well as raiding further afield, brought glory and plunder in the form of treasure or captives. The early Sasanians would make considerable use of captives as a royal-controlled labour force, and this may have begun under Ardashir I. Apart from the prisoners, the Roman civil wars made some choose to leave the empire and seek a new life beyond. Changes in the style and quality of the series of rock carvings commemorating Ardashir I's career may well reflect an influx of craftsmen from the Roman provinces.[23]

Ardashir I did well in the early stages of the war, and at the very least held his own when Severus Alexander invaded his territory. Whether or not one of the Roman columns was beaten, everyone could see that afterwards all the Romans withdrew and did not return. They seem never to have got anywhere near Ctesiphon. If the gains made in Mesopotamia proved fleeting, Ardashir I does not appear to have lost any ground held by the Parthians before he came to power. All in all, he had stood up to the Romans and defended his newly acquired empire better than anyone had managed for a long time. More successes came in the east, and he may well have launched at least two major campaigns, firstly overrunning territories largely lost to the empire in recent years and then pushing into Bactria. There also appear to have been later attacks on the Roman provinces. Again, this was a message of his strength and right to rule for the audience formed by his subjects, especially the nobles, and a statement of renewed power meant for all his neighbours.[24]

The greatest change brought by Ardashir I was not replacing the current dynasty with the house of Sasan but the simple fact that he was a strong leader. This was a man who fought and won war after war and never appears to have suffered a serious defeat in the course of his campaigns. That suggests luck, talent, and a leader and followers who were very good at fighting and became used to winning, just like Cyrus and Darius, Mithradates I and II, or, for that matter, Philip and Alexander the Great. Success fed off success but also became so bound up with the right to rule that it encouraged more warfare, and it was hard for such leaders to stop fighting and expanding their territory and power. After generations of more or less weak Arsacid kings of kings, suddenly there was a new, far more capable and aggressive ruler. That he came from outside the traditional royal line and founded a new dynasty was secondary, at least in the short term. His achievement, like that of the first Arsacids, was to create a regime where only members of his line could hope to inherit, and it took time before this was certain. Not everything turned out quite as he had expected. The favoured heir, Ardashir, for whatever reason did not succeed him, and instead in 240 another son, Shapur I, became co-ruler with his ailing father. How this happened is unclear, but Shapur I was to prove as able and strong a leader as Ardashir himself. Within a year, Ardashir I had died and Shapur I ruled alone.

All successful leaders tend to be lucky; as we have seen, Romans like Sulla and Caesar openly boasted of their good luck. Ardashir I rose through talent but was fortunate to live at a time when there was ongoing civil war in Parthia and plenty of opportunities for the ambitious to rise. As important was relative weakness among the empire's neighbours, probably generally but easiest to trace in Rome. Scholars argue over the duration of what is known as the Third Century Crisis, with many inclined to limit this to the decades of greatest chaos. Yet from the murder of Caracalla onwards, the Roman empire was rarely free from the reality, or at least the shadow, of civil war in a way that had not been true since the collapse of the republic.

Septimius Severus had been able to fight and win a civil war because he happened to command one of the largest provincial armies at the right moment and was already an established and successful member of the Senate. Macrinus was neither of these things, simply a member of the imperial entourage—or court in most senses of the term—who had arranged the assassination of the emperor and was able to win support from the officers commanding the army in the east, at least in the short term. Elagabalus was a mere child, improbably proclaimed as Caracalla's bastard even though such offspring had no real rights under Roman law, and Severus Alexander was his cousin—both of them actually descended from Septimius Severus's sister-in-law. Though the claim to rule was based on being Severans by blood, this was flimsy at best. Maximinus had no such link whatsoever, nor a senatorial pedigree, and based his power solely on support from an army.

This was the pattern of the decades to come. Any man able to persuade substantial numbers of soldiers to back him was in a position to proclaim himself as emperor. Sometimes these soldiers were the praetorians and other guard units and sometimes troops in the provinces. Only rarely did the Senate play an active role, and never successfully unless sufficient soldiers could be persuaded to back their choice. Becoming emperor was far easier and open to far more men than ever before, since membership of the Senate was no longer essential. Marcus Aurelius had promoted quite a few equestrians to the Senate on the basis of their military talent—and because the plague had thinned the ranks of the senatorial order, especially ones capable enough to be trusted with command of a legion or army. Severus did the same but also chose to give important commands to equestrians instead of senators. His new province of Mesopotamia was governed by an equestrian prefect, and equestrians commanded the two newly formed legions stationed as its garrison. The trend continued, which meant that more equestrians came to hold senior positions in command of provincial armies.

Becoming emperor was much easier, but at the same time holding on to power was far more difficult, for challenges could come from so many different people. The armies benefitted, receiving bounties and other rewards, and officers benefitted most of all, so that they tended to be the kingmakers in such situations. Men were proclaimed as emperor and then not much later murdered by the same troops because someone else had made them a better offer. Individuals rose and fell, usually violently, and with each new claimant to the imperial purple there were executions to instil fear and bribes to win support. The need to win over and placate the legions and their officers took precedence over almost every other priority for an emperor, for only by doing this could he survive. It was not conducive to good discipline or maintaining high levels of training and efficiency. Time and again, Roman armies fought each other in battle. Whoever won, the casualties took a toll on the confidence and collective experience of the military.

All of this was beginning during Ardashir I's career, and he benefitted from it. For Shapur I, it offered even greater opportunities.

The Romans were self-evidently weak and vulnerable in a way that had not been true since the late republic and perhaps not even then. Attacks on Roman territory stood a good chance of success, bringing plunder and glory—and glory all the greater because for so long Rome had appeared so mighty. The Sasanians won victories, showing themselves as stronger in war, and thus more legitimate, than the decadent Arsacids. These attacks invited reprisals, but the ongoing weakness and internal divisions of the Romans meant that such counterblows were unlikely to have the strength, determination, and willingness to persist expected in the first and second centuries. Civil wars rendered Rome weaker at the very moment a Parthian civil war created the Sasanian dynasty and made Ardashir I and his successor eager for clean glory against a foreign power to legitimize their own rule. It was a recipe for war.

11

AND THE CAESAR LIED AGAIN

C. 240–265

SHAPUR I NEEDED TO PROVE THAT HE WAS A WORTHY SUCCES-
sor to his father and confirm that the house of Sasan deserved to
rule the empire—and was fully capable of enforcing its will against
foreign enemies and domestic rivals alike. If the Romans had not
been so obviously vulnerable, the new king of kings might have focused his attentions elsewhere, and he in fact did spend many years
winning victories on other frontiers. The Romans were weak, and
they were also seeking vengeance, as individual emperors sought
to justify their rule by winning a great victory in the east.

Shapur I left a large number of the surviving monuments raised
by Sasanian monarchs. Their tone is assertive, listing his many
great successes. Partly this a reflection of the sheer scale of what
he did, but it is also a sign of his need to prove his legitimacy. On
one he states: 'I am the Mazda-worshipping divine Shapur, King of
Kings of Aryans and non Aryans, of the race of the gods, son of the
Mazda-worshipping divine Ardashir, King of Kings of the Aryans,
of the race of the gods, grandson of King Papak, I am the Lord of
the Aryan nation.' Thus, near the end of his life, Shapur I chose to
open an account of his achievements. The text was subsequently
carved onto the walls of the Zoroastrian fire temple at a place now

known as Naqsh-i Rustam in Persis. This was an ancient, much revered shrine, closely overlooked by the rock-cut tombs of great Achaemenid rulers such as Cyrus and Darius.

The Achaemenids are never mentioned by Shapur I, in contrast to the Roman sources that claim Ardashir I boasted of his intention to recover the lands once ruled by the old dynasty before the coming of Alexander. Yet the decision to set up the inscription here, adding to rock carvings celebrating his father's and his own victories, cannot have been a coincidence. Having supplanted the Arsacids, the first Sasanian kings distanced themselves from the defeated dynasty and in time suppressed their memory. Instead, they associated themselves with the glories of a more distant past—both the Achaemenids and the more or less mythical great and just kings of far older Iranian tradition—but this connection was rarely explicit or actively promoted. History, vaguely remembered or largely imagined, offered a backdrop to present glory rather than something to be revived or matched. The present was what mattered, the spectacular might and success of Shapur I himself—whose monument this was—which rebounded to his glory and proved his divine right to rule. No one, past or present, could compete with him, and the text was not concerned with the future, even though it was probably set up by his son after his death.[1]

Shapur I's grandfather was 'merely' a king, his father named as king of kings of the Aryans, but significantly not also of the non-Aryans. Shapur was king of Aryans and non-Aryans, thus of the whole world, a claim similar to Roman boasts of power without limit. Shapur I was the rightful successor to a father who, like him, revered and was special to Ahura Mazda and, like him, was divine. Ardashir and Shapur were both called gods, echoing many Parthian and Hellenistic rulers rather than the Achaemenids, showing a blend of traditions. Ahura Mazda was the great god, overlord of all the other deities, representative of goodness and truth, who struggled for—and would eventually achieve—total victory over the demon Ahriman, lord of evil and lies. As his servants on earth, Shapur I and his father fought the same fight.

The text was carved on three of the temple's four walls, in Middle Persian and also translated into Parthian and Greek, the three main languages of Shapur I's empire, or at least of its nobility. There was a good chance that foreign emissaries would be able to understand at least one of these tongues, should they ever have been brought to an audience with the king of kings in the vicinity. They could read of the breadth of Shapur I's empire—which included so many named regions, his rule backed by loyal local kings—and the long catalogue of victories he had won over foreign enemies. Greatest of all—and given by far the most space in the account—were his triumphs over the Romans.[2]

For the first time in this story, the surviving sources are actually fuller from a Sasanian perspective than from a Greco-Roman one. The greatest single piece of evidence is this inscription, backed by other monuments that are similarly close in time to the events, while even the medieval Arabic tradition is fuller for this period. In contrast, the Roman sources are exceptionally poor, contradicting each other as well as the Sasanian version. While it is pleasant to reverse the usual bias, even taken as a whole, the evidence for a period of major conflict remains very poor, with large gaps and problems that are not easy to resolve. Tempting though it is to favour the Sasanian view over the all-too-familiar Roman perspective, all sources should be treated with the same caution. Parallels are often drawn between Shapur I's monument and *The Deeds of the Divine Augustus*. Both represent how the leader in question wanted to be seen and remembered. Exaggerations are easier to spot in Augustus's version than Shapur's, since we possess far more information about the former. Both probably represent a basically factual—if boastful, selective, and skilfully presented—version of the actual events. Like those of Augustus, Shapur I's achievements were exceptional, never really matched by any successor.[3]

A young Shapur was depicted defeating an Arsacid prince on the same rock sculpture that showed Ardashir I driving his two-handed lance into Artabanus IV. If Shapur was old enough to fight in 224, then the probability is that he played a role in many of his father's campaigns, learning how to fight and how to lead and at the same time becoming well-known to prominent men in the army. Elevated to joint rule late in Ardashir I's reign, Shapur took an army to attack Hatra. This time, the city that had defied Trajan,

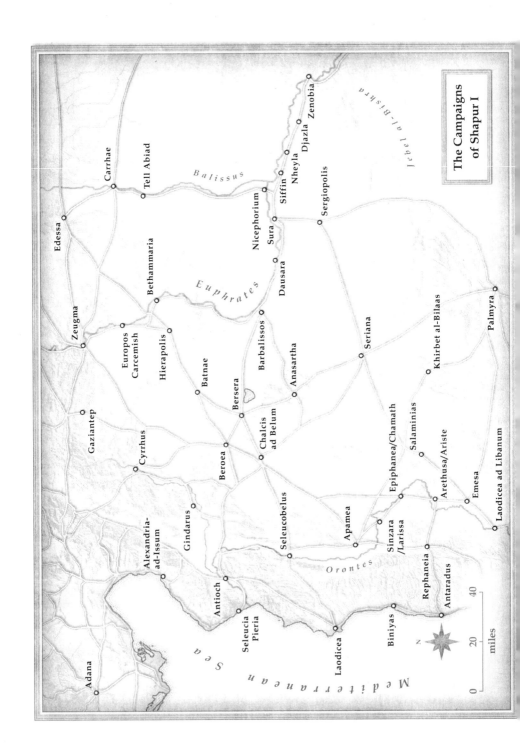

The Campaigns
of Shapur I

Mediterranean Sea

Orontes

Euphrates

Balissus

Jebel al-Bishra

Adana
Alexandria-ad-Issum
Antioch
Seleucia Pieria
Laodicea
Biniyas
Rephaneia
Antaradus
Gindarus
Gaziantep
Cyrhus
Beroea
Seleucobelus
Apamea
Sinzara/Larissa
Arethusa/Ariste
Emesa
Laodicea ad Libanum
Salaminias
Epiphanea/Chamath
Zeugma
Europos Carcemish
Hierapolis
Batnae
Bersera
Chalcis ad Belum
Anasartha
Seriana
Khirbet al-Bilaas
Palmyra
Barbalissos
Edessa
Bethammaria
Nicephorium
Sura
Dausara
Sergiopolis
Carrhae
Tell Abiad
Siffin
Nheyla
Djazla
Zenobia

N

0   20   40
         miles

Severus, and his own father was taken, after a long siege by a large and well-organized army. Perhaps in the end it fell through treachery—the commonest reason for the fall of a city for most of the ancient period. Hatra was destroyed as a stronghold and a kingdom, the city and its walls left in ruins, never to grow again.[4]

Roman troops had helped to garrison Hatra for some time and were no doubt caught up in its fall. The attack was part of a renewal of hostilities in the later 230s where the initiative lay with the Persians. Graffito scratched onto the plaster wall of a house in Dura-Europos recorded that on 20 April 239, the Persians 'descended upon us'. The excavators connected this with an epitaph painted and inscribed on stone and found on the floor of a private house, but it was probably originally set up on a memorial in the necropolis outside the town.* This was to Julius Terentius, tribune commanding the Twentieth Cohort of Palmyrenes, who was 'brave in campaigns, mighty in wars', but now dead and mourned by his wife, who set up this memorial.[5]

By a coincidence rare even for the wonderfully preserved remains of Dura-Europos, a portrait of Julius Terentius was among the earliest discoveries. His dark hair having receded up his forehead, perhaps a sign of age, and with a neatly trimmed beard, he is shown parading with the officers of his cohort to make an offering to the gods. Their uniforms are those of the third-century army, with enclosed boots, snug-fitting, drab-coloured trousers, long-sleeved white tunics, and cloaks. The colours of the cloaks vary, and there are rings on some of the sleeves and other distinctions hinting at some form of insignia, although we cannot discern the system. Most of the men are bearded, but the faces vary enough to show an attempt at representing the individuals. Julius Terentius, tribune, is named in Latin, as is only one other, the regimental priest, Thermes, son of Mocimus, although in his case the

---

*Although the original excavators assumed that the stone had been part of the house—and I and many others have repeated this—recent reassessment makes the house most unlikely to have been the residence of the tribune and his household. Not only was it very small for someone of equestrian status, but it was adjacent to another building identified as a military-owned brothel. As noted, the stone was not part of a wall, but loose in the rubble, which means that it might have been moved from elsewhere. Tombs and memorials to the dead were usually placed outside a city's walls.

label was painted in Greek. Presumably anyone interested enough to look was expected to be able to read both languages, at least to some extent, just as it was assumed that they would recognize the others without needing to be told. Watched by statues of the guardian spirits of Dura-Europos and Palmyra, with the vexillum flag of the cohort held by a standard-bearer (depicted as smaller than the others, no doubt because of his lesser rank), Terentius pours incense onto the flame of an altar, making an offering to three gods, who may be Palmyrene or represent the three emperors who briefly ruled together in 238.[6]

Excavations at Dura-Europos uncovered one of the richest finds of papyri anywhere in the Roman empire. Many of the texts are military, and of these most relate to Terentius's unit, *cohors XX Palmyrenorum*, apparently because someone dumped a load of their records when they were no longer needed. Terentius's name does not appear in any of the surviving documents, but on 27–28 May 239 a morning report reveals that the cohort was under the command of a senior centurion from a legion rather than its tribune. This was usually a temporary measure, appointing a centurion as *praepositus* or acting commander because no equestrian officer was available. This would all fit with a Persian attack early in the year or late in the preceding year, resulting in the death of Terentius and the cohort being given another commander until someone following the standard equestrian career could be found and dispatched to take charge. In addition, comparing this with an earlier morning report suggests a substantial drop in the number of soldiers available for duty. This could reflect casualties, although there could well be other reasons for this change. It looks as if the cohort remained under a temporary commander for several years, most likely a reflection of the dislocation of normal career assignments during this troubled period.[7]

After a brief occupation under Trajan, the Romans held Dura-Europos from the time of Lucius Verus's eastern campaign and appear to have maintained a substantial garrison throughout, numbering some two thousand men. The Palmyrenes may have been there for generations, for there were long-standing links with Palmyra, and the city was also one of the closest sources of recruits. The Twentieth were a mixed unit, with troops of cavalry and centuries of infantryman, as well as a small number of *dromedarii* riding camels. For much of the time, they provided around half of the soldiers stationed at Dura. In the early days, another auxiliary unit was routinely stationed with them, and by the third century there were also substantial detachments of legionaries. By this time, the distinction was more one of prestige, possibly pay, and unit tradition than anything else, since Caracalla's edict meant that the majority of recruits to the auxilia were already Roman citizens when they enlisted. A substantially complete nominal roll of the Twentieth Palmyrenes lists every man as Aurelius, in addition to his other names. (Septimius Severus had adopted himself into the family of Marcus Aurelius to add to his legitimacy, which meant that Caracalla was Marcus Aurelius Antoninus when he gave the franchise and his name to most of the empire's population.) Most soldiers were now citizens, and the archaeology from Dura-Europos and the wider empire suggests that patterns of equipment were no longer distinct. Legionaries and auxiliaries alike were equipped with the spatha (a long, slim sword, the blade often pattern-welded), spears and javelins rather than the pilum, and helmets of identical pattern and ornamentation. Mail and scale armour were the norm, and the famous banded armour known to us as *lorica segmentata* was very rare indeed. A Roman soldier in full equipment remained obviously a Roman soldier, but it would have taken more attention to the little details to discern his unit.[8]

Along with the soldiers came many dependents. Terentius was commemorated by his wife, Aurelia Arria, who may have gained her citizenship in 212 given her name. Like many wives of senior officers, she had accompanied her husband to his posting, bringing any children and supervising the household of slaves and freedmen. The standard auxiliary forts so well-attested in other parts of the empire invariably contained a house for the commander, which compared favourably in size to many of the grander houses in Pompeii. From the days of Augustus, ordinary soldiers as opposed to officers were not permitted to form a legal marriage, even though many did so. Hadrian was one of several emperors who made it easier for soldiers to bequeath property and status to the wives and children they were not supposed to have, while Septimius Severus either removed the ban altogether or at least greatly relaxed any restrictions. Therefore, the long-term presence of two thousand soldiers meant as many more dependents, whether women, children, or freedmen and slaves, including slaves owned by the army who were uniformed, given some training, and tasked with duties other than fighting. In addition were those who earned a living selling goods and services to the soldiers. The military zone at Dura-Europos encompassed rather more than a quarter of the city's overall area.[9]

The relationship between the soldiers and civilians in Dura-Europos was probably not simple. The garrison was imposed by the empire and not something over which any of Dura's citizens had any say. Parts of the city were requisitioned to provide billets and administrative and other facilities for the troops, with buildings being divided and streets closed off to demarcate the military zone. Over time, the soldiers added facilities for their needs, including a small amphitheatre and a brothel. Soldiers had special status under law, not least that they were tried only in military courts, which could give them an advantage over civilians if the latter did not have influential friends. Yet the evidence does not suggest wholly separate communities, but rather that the soldiers were one more element in a very mixed population—one where plenty of people, soldiers and civilians alike, passed through at one time or another.[10]

Apart from the wide range of gods attested by temples, altars, and statues, the excavations at Dura uncovered a synagogue that clearly thrived in the Roman period, its walls richly decorated with paintings, including some depicting scenes from the scriptures, such as the crossing of the river Jordan. Clearly, this Jewish community had no reluctance about portraying images of human beings and animals in spite of earlier tradition. The equipment of the warriors in these scenes was influenced by contemporary Roman army styles, albeit in a stylized form. Also discovered at Dura-Europos was the earliest definitely identified Christian house church, with a baptistry and wall paintings of Jesus walking on water and images of the Good Shepherd. Christianity was an illegal cult, although the ban was often ignored. At Dura, the church and the synagogue lay close to the city walls, which were routinely guarded by sentries from the garrison, and the communities attending them did so in plain view. There is no hint of tension or suspicion, and as far as we can tell they were simply accepted as part of the fabric of city life. Perhaps at times different sections of the population were hostile towards each other, for such things appear common enough in many cities in the Greco-Roman world—and indeed in Seleucia under the Parthians. Perhaps there were also times when soldiers abused their position or grew unruly, for again such things occur in the sources. That does not mean that they were everyday occurrences, and the odds are that soldiers, civilians, and the various races and faiths within these groups rubbed along well enough on a day-to-day basis.[11]

Dura-Europos was a garrison town almost on the edge of the Roman empire. There were small forts and detachments stationed to the north and south, mainly on or near the Euphrates and its tributary the Khabur. The Twentieth Palmyrenes contributed troops to the garrisons of several of these places, so that a significant number of its soldiers were away from the main base for months, even years, just as the legionaries at Dura itself were detached from the main bodies of their legions for long periods. Major campaigning under Septimius Severus, Caracalla, and Severus Alexander and the robust response by Ardashir I ensured that these decades saw more conflict in the wider region than had been the case since the first century BC. Most of it is impossible to trace in any detail, especially smaller-scale attacks or skirmishes, such as the one on Dura-Europos in 239. This makes the context of the big campaigns difficult to understand. Shapur I inherited a throne from a father who had seized it by force and begun a new dynasty. One of the reasons both men stressed their divine legitimacy in their monuments was because their rule was based on military success. Neither could afford serious failure against either domestic or foreign opponents, nor to be seen as weak. Simultaneously, Rome's emperors were the products of civil wars or coups, and their rule was precarious. Dio claimed that under Severus Alexander the armies of Syria were frequently mutinous, even murdering one provincial legate. Routine administrative documents of the sort found at Dura are unlikely to show something like this, although some scholars claim to have seen hints. Overall, it is fair to say that the frequent civil wars made the Roman empire weaker, less co-ordinated, and less predictable in its relations with its neighbours, and this gave Shapur I an opportunity to put pressure on the frontier areas, reclaiming some ground lost in the past. However, in the first years of Shapur I's reign, Roman attention was elsewhere, and this also allowed the king of kings to deal with other challenges.[12]

This changed in 242–243 when yet another Roman emperor came to the east at the head of a large expedition. This was the teenage Gordian III, whose grandfather and father had proclaimed themselves emperors in defiance of Maximinus. Lacking any significant military support, they and their supporters perished within a matter of months, but in 238 the then thirteen-year-old Gordian was proclaimed emperor with two mature senators as his colleagues. (If the Terentius wall painting depicts the cohort taking part in the imperial cult, then this was the trio of emperors being revered.) The older men were murdered by the praetorians within a matter of weeks, leaving the young Gordian III as sole emperor guided by more-experienced advisors, most of all the praetorian prefect Timesitheus. These advisors decided that an assertion of Roman strength was needed in the eastern provinces, but first the emperor needed to go in person to 'supervise' operations on the Danube. This took several years, by which time preparations were under way for an expedition against the Persians. Organizing a campaign on this scale was a slow process, as troops and supplies were drawn from a wide area to reinforce those already in the region. Shapur I claimed that men from the whole of the Roman empire, and from the Germans and Goths beyond its frontiers, were arrayed against him. This is one of the earliest mentions of the Goths as distinct from other Germanic tribes, although it is hard to say whether Shapur I understood the term any more accurately than the Greeks and Romans understood the names of peoples living to the east of Persia.[13]

In 243, Gordian III and his army crossed the Euphrates at Zeugma. Much of the Roman province of Mesopotamia appears to have been in Persian hands, and there was a battle at Rhesaina which ended in a clear Roman victory. Shapur I does not mention this, whether because any failure was unsuitable for inclusion in a list of achievements or because he was not present and had not yet mustered his main army and brought it to the theatre of operations. Carrhae and other cities were brought back under Roman control. Coins bearing Gordian III's image were produced at Nisibis after an apparent break in production which may well have occurred because of Persian occupation. At the same time, a mint appears to have been established at Singara, and there was some reorganization of other communities. In the following year, the Roman army advanced along the familiar route down the Euphrates, passing Dura-Europos.

Little else is certain. Timesitheus died, apparently of dysentery, and a man named Philip became the senior of the two praetorian prefects. Shapur I states that he met the Romans in battle on the borders of Assyria at Meshike and won a great victory, leaving Gordian III and most of his army dead. In contrast, the Roman sources speak of a Roman victory that went wrong in its aftermath. In some versions, the teenager fell from his horse and was injured or wounded, perhaps in battle. The vast majority attribute his death to Philip, claiming that he had the already weakened Gordian III finished off or straightforwardly murdered him and then declared himself emperor. From all this, the basic facts are that Gordian died and that, whatever losses were suffered by the Romans, the bulk of their army remained intact, giving Philip sufficient military support to make a successful bid for the throne. Like Macrinus before him, he negotiated and bought peace, although for five hundred thousand denarii (two million sesterces), which was a tenth of the sum paid in 217.* There may have been other conditions as well, but the result was peace and the retreat of the Roman army. Tactically, the fighting and any pitched battle may have been a draw, or even favoured the Romans. Strategically, this was a stunning Sasanian

---

*The amount comes from Shapur I's inscription, and some prefer to read it as Persian gold coins or dinars rather than Roman denarii. If this is correct then the sum was substantially larger, although still less than the amount promised by Macrinus.

victory, for a Roman army had failed to reach Ctesiphon or any of the other great cities and had been turned back with one emperor dead and another forced to beg for peace.¹⁴

Shapur I paraded this spectacular triumph as yet another proof of the divine favour that made clear his right to rule. Ahura Mazda had granted the throne to Ardashir I and his son because they were his earthly counterparts. In the rock relief showing Ardashir I's horse trampling the corpse of Artabanus IV as Ahura Mazda hands him the royal diadem, the god's mount treads on the body of the demon Ahriman, leader of those who seek to plunge the universe into chaos and overthrow the truth with the lie. Victory on earth thus matches cosmic victory, with order, good, and the truth prevailing in both. The message when Shapur I was depicted with Gordian III prostrate beneath his horse was equally clear without needing to show the god and his demonic foe. Philip was added, crouching or kneeling as he implores the king of kings for mercy. If Augustus in the *Res Gestae* could boast of suppliants coming from India and portray the return of the eagles as a great victory, Shapur I had at least as much, perhaps more, justification in claiming the Romans as subjects.¹⁵

The new Roman emperor is known in history as Philip the Arab, for although a citizen and an equestrian—his full name was Marcus Julius Philippus—he came from a small city near Damascus. He ruled for five years, minting coins boasting of the peace made with Persia, and later staged grand celebrations in Rome to commemorate the city's supposed thousandth year. Yet there were problems on the frontiers and challenges from other men claiming the throne. In 249, he was defeated and killed by Decius, a senator from Pannonia who had been given a provincial command on the Danube. Decius took the name Trajan to invoke the military glories of the past and spent much of his reign campaigning against the Carpi and Goths. In 251, he attacked a Gothic army in broken and marshy terrain near Abrittus and was defeated, earning the dubious distinction of becoming the first Roman emperor to be killed in battle by a foreign enemy.¹⁶

In contrast to the Roman principate, Shapur I's regime continued to grow in strength, even if the details and chronology are

The Forum. The Forum Romanum was the centre of Rome's political life under the republic. The Senate house—rebuilt by Augustus—is on the left.

Sulla. Sulla dubbed himself Felix —'the lucky'—and was envied for his good fortune in being the first Roman governor to encounter the Parthians.

Horse Archer. This terracotta statue depicts a Parthian horse-archer. A superb horseman armed with a powerful composite bow, he was a formidable warrior.

Roman legionaries. Rome's empire was conquered by armies dominated by legionaries fighting on foot. In the first century BC they were equipped like these men.

Horse armour. As well as horse-archers, Parthian armies included cataphracts with both horse and rider heavily armoured. This horse armour was excavated at Dura-Europos.

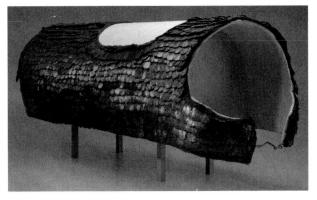

Sarmatian cataphracts. Cataphracts with their gleaming armour made a great impression on the Romans, even if Roman artists, as here, did not understand how the armour worked.

Crassus. Crassus was rich and powerful from his alliance with Pompey and Caesar, but by 54 BC he was older than was usual for a Roman commander.

Orodes II. Orodes II became king of kings after overthrowing his father and then defeating his brother but still led a determined and successful response to Crassus's invasion.

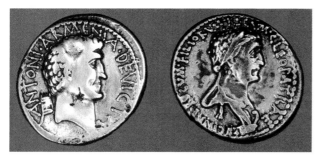

Antony and Cleopatra. Through civil war, Antony came to control Rome's eastern territory and began the famous affair with Cleopatra, who is shown on the reverse of this coin.

Ara Pacis. Several Parthian princes and their families were sent to Rome. The boy clutching the cloak of Agrippa on the left may be one of them.

Temple of Mars Ultor. Augustus made the Temple of Mars Ultor—Mars the Avenger—the centrepiece of his new Forum complex. Standards returned by the Parthians were installed there.

Thea Mousa. Musa was a slave from Italy who became mistress, favourite, and wife of Phraates IV and later ruled jointly with her son, Phraataces.

Parthian prince. This bronze statue is known as the 'prince of Shami', a Parthian nobleman in the characteristic open tunic and loose trousers of his people.

Trajan as general. Trajan celebrated his Dacian victories on Trajan's Column, the centrepiece of his Forum. Here the emperor sits as auxiliary soldiers approach to receive rewards.

Roman troops. Trajan's Column is heavily stylized but emphasizes the diverse range of troops serving in the Roman army, from citizen legionaries to auxiliaries, including archers.

Herakles. This bronze statue of Herakles is inscribed with matching inscriptions in Greek and Parthian recording the defeat of Characene by Vologaeses IV in 151.

Praetorian Guard. Augustus formed the Praetorian Guard to provide troops immediately at his disposal, but later emperors sometimes found them more of a threat than protection.

Arch of Severus relief. The Arch of Septimius Severus is carved with scenes depicting his campaigns against the Parthians. Sadly, these were heavily stylized and are poorly preserved.

Arch of Severus. Septimius Severus became emperor through civil war, so he was eager to celebrate his foreign victories. His arch stands in the heart of the Forum.

Firuzabad cliff. Ardashir I overthrew the last Parthian king of kings and founded a new dynasty. Propaganda such as the carvings on this cliff at Firuzabad emphasized his victories.

Firuzabad victory scene. On the right of this scene, Ardashir throws down Artabanus IV, while on the left his son, Shapur, defeats the Parthian's chief minister.

Cavalry tombstone. The tombstone of Bassus shows a typical auxiliary cavalryman of the principate. He is more heavily equipped than a horse-archer but lighter than a cataphract.

Investiture of Ardashir I from relief at Naqsh-i Rustam. In this relief from Naqsh-i Rustam, Ardashir I on the left is appointed as king by Ahura Mazda. Their horses each trample a defeated enemy.

Ctesiphon as it looks from an aeroplane

R.A.F. Official Photograph

Palace at Ctesiphon. The great Sasanian palace at Ctesiphon was built in traditional Parthian style, highlighting both in style and location the continuity between the two dynasties.

Dura-Europos. The site of Dura-Europos was discovered just after the First World War. The city was abandoned after its capture by the Sasanians in 256.

Wall painting from Dura-Europos. In this painting from Dura-Europos, the tribune Terentius sacrifices at the head of his cohort. He was killed during a Sasanian attack in 239.

Rock relief from Darabgerd. Shapur I won great victories over the Romans and took care to celebrate them. Here one emperor lies beneath him while another begs for peace.

Paris cameo. This cameo most likely depicts Shapur I seizing Valerian by the wrist when he captured the emperor in 260.

Rock relief from Naqsh-i Rustam. Another celebration of Shapur I's victories combined into one scene. He grabs Valerian by the wrist while a kneeling Philip begs for mercy.

The Tetrarchs from Venice. Diocletian created a new system called the tetrarchy, where four emperors ruled together. The harmony promoted in this image proved temporary.

Scene from the Arch of Galerius. Both empires celebrated their successes. This scene from the Arch of Galerius shows him addressing his victorious soldiers in 298.

Palmyrene gods. Palmyra was a city of travellers and traders but retained its own distinctive culture and language, expressed in this depiction of its three most important deities.

Qasr Bashir in Jordan. Built by Diocletian, the remarkably well-preserved Roman outpost at Qasr Bashir in Jordan shows how Roman bases became smaller but better defended in this era.

Coin of Heraclius. Heraclius encouraged his soldiers in the desperate fight back against the Sasanians by extensive use of Christian language and symbols and promises of rewards in heaven.

Taq-i Bustan carving. One of the few Sasanian victory monuments to survive from the later centuries, this scene shows Khusro II as a cataphract or clibanarius.

The dome of Hagia Sophia. Justinian's church of Hagia Sophia with its magnificent dome remains one of the most remarkable and beautiful constructions from the ancient world.

Sasanian frontier outpost. In recent years, the sheer scale and complexity of Sasanian defences on their northern frontiers have been revealed.

Theodosian Walls. Constantinople was heavily fortified. Protected by sea from the Sasanians, the high Theodosian Walls proved strong enough to hold back the Avars in 636.

Jerusalem. Jerusalem was captured by the Sasanians in 614. Heraclius recovered the city, only for it to fall again in 638, this time to the Arabs.

vague. Both he and his father were very active in the area around the Arabian Gulf. Characene, a kingdom that had more than once loosened its ties or broken away from the Arsacids, was brought under permanent direct control. In addition, territory further south was conquered and communities beyond that impressed with the might of the Sasanian king of kings. In the east, the Kushan empire was defeated and the ruling dynasty replaced with a new Kushano-Sasanian line of kings. On one of Shapur I's monuments, diminutive Kushans and Romans are shown bringing tribute to the king of kings. The Kushans have an elephant, while the Romans bring a carriage of the type reserved for emperors.[17]

Around 252, Shapur I once again turned his attention to his borders with Rome. As he put it, 'And Caesar lied again and did injustice to Armenia.' Other sources suggest that the Sasanians engineered the murder of the Arsacid king of Armenia. Perhaps Caesar's lie was to involve himself in the fortunes of Armenia in defiance of the agreement reached in 244, but it is unclear how justified Shapur I was, since ancient states so readily went to war whenever they felt it was to their advantage. He appears to have brought under his control or at least dominance both Armenia and neighbouring Iberia in these years. These successes were followed by leading a grand army up the Euphrates. Nisibis probably fell, and it looks as if Dura-Europos was occupied by the Persians for a while, perhaps without a fight. There is no evidence of a siege at this point, and the houses of many of the wealthier inhabitants show signs of having been evacuated in an orderly way, the owners taking all the valuables, which suggests plenty of warning. The emperor Trebonius was far away in the west, dealing with problems on the frontiers, while another epidemic was raging in a number of Roman provinces. To meet the Sasanian attack, all available troops appear to have been gathered to form a field army. Shapur I claimed that it numbered sixty thousand and that he met it and smashed it at Barbalissos. The number needs to be treated with the same suspicion as Roman claims for the vast hosts arrayed against them, but it is clear that this was a major Persian victory.[18]

Shapur I lists the names of cities taken by his armies, and from the order in which these appear, scholars have reconstructed the routes of two or three successive campaigning seasons, and perhaps of more than one column operating at the same time. His first offensive overran Mesopotamia and much of Syria. Antioch, probably the third largest city in the Roman empire after Rome and Alexandria, fell to the Persians. Folk memory spoke of treachery by a discredited local aristocrat who had sought refuge at the Sasanian court. Others claimed a surprise attack, even that people were watching a performance in a theatre by a husband and wife, when the latter suddenly called out to ask whether she was dreaming or whether the Persians were here. There may have been a few setbacks. Tradition maintained that a local leader at Emesa rallied people to defeat the Persian attack, but in the main resistance failed and cities were taken by assault or siege if they did not surrender.[19]

Syria fell, but Shapur I was not interested in permanent occupation. Cities were looted for treasure and other useful resources, and tens of thousands of captives were taken. Then the Persians withdrew, taking the spoils with them. The value of wealth was obvious, and the human beings were taken deep within the empire and settled in communities where they would till the fields, labour, and craft for the benefit of the king of kings. Shapur I, like his father, was a great founder and refounder of cities. The place closest to where he had made Philip negotiate was renamed Bishapur—the victory of Shapur. This was the other side of the coin to the destruction of cities, notably Hatra, and displayed Shapur I's power to destroy and create communities.

Dura-Europos was abandoned after a short time, leaving little more than graffiti as a trace of the Persian occupation. The Romans returned, although not necessarily the same units as before and with perhaps a greatly reduced civilian population. Before long, preparations were made to mount a better defence and strengthen the old Hellenistic stone walls. On three sides, the Euphrates and steep cliffs offered ample protection from assault, but the fourth, western wall stood open to a plain, the limestone surface rock making it impossible to put a ditch in front of it. The Romans toiled to build an earth reinforcement on the front of the wall, angling this to deflect missiles and make it much harder to batter through with a ram. Behind the wall they piled more earth to strengthen it further and buried buildings next to it. This improvisation covered parts of the adjacent street, including the synagogue and house church, sealing them off and, as a consequence, preserving them so well. A slope was fashioned on top of the mound created in this way, making it easier for reinforcing soldiers to run up from the city onto the top of the rampart. Since this would also have made it easier for attackers to swarm down into the streets, this expressed a confidence that the defenders could reinforce any spot much faster than the attackers.[20]

In 256, a large Sasanian army attacked Dura-Europos in an episode not described by any of our literary sources and known only through archaeology. The Persians camped outside and began to construct siege-works, notably an assault ramp, which the Romans countered by raising the height of the walls and towers as best they could. A Persian tunnel was dug underneath one of the towers, and the timber supports fired when it was complete, bringing down enough of the roof to collapse the front of the tower. It was rendered useless as a fighting platform, although it still functioned as a barrier, for it had not created a breach. Another tunnel was begun, starting from part of the necropolis where the ground rock had been broken through to make the tombs. Inevitably, tunnelling produced a lot of spoil, and there was nowhere on the open plain to hide this for very long. The Romans guessed where the tunnel was heading and dug their own gallery and mine to counter it. Days and nights of listening and calculating progress followed, each side trying to outwit the other. Eventually the Romans broke into the Persian tunnel and attacked, some of the men armed, armoured, and carrying shields, and others probably with tools to destroy the work the Persians had done.

The enemy was waiting for them. Perhaps nineteen Roman soldiers died in a crowded, poorly lit, and vicious little battle fought in a tunnel where a tall man could not stand upright. An intriguing theory argues that they were asphyxiated, the Persians blowing the smoke from naphtha, bitumen, and other combustibles into the tunnel, and the Roman's own mine, higher up, acting as a chimney and sucking the fumes through. However these Romans died, their corpses were then heaped up in a mound to get them out of the way and perhaps to act as a barricade. At the same time, perhaps unbeknown to the Persians, the defenders were frantically sealing up their end of the tunnel. The Persians fired the supports, but this time the collapse was less successful. The wall and tower above sank down several feet, but did not break, held together by the earth reinforcements built on both sides of it before the siege. One Persian skeleton was found not far from the Romans, his high helmet probably set down because the ceiling was too low. He—or someone else—had lifted his mail shirt as if trying to take it off. The man may have been a casualty in the fighting, or was perhaps the one chosen to ignite the combustibles meant to bring down the roof and was caught by the fumes before he could escape.[21]

None of the siege-works found during the excavations succeeded fully to the extent of opening a path into the city for a Persian assault. Yet Dura fell, perhaps to escalade, which would leave no archaeological trace; or from a breakthrough near the area of the River Gate, where the remains have been lost to erosion; or even because the defenders surrendered. Whatever the cause, the city was abandoned, for the Persians did not choose to stay, and the garrison and population had fled or were captives. Never again was this a thriving, vibrant city, although in later centuries a few hermits sought solitude among the ruins. Over the centuries, the city became buried and was forgotten. Dura-Europos was rediscovered after the First World War when some sepoys from Britain's Indian Army began digging a machine-gun pit during operations against local tribesmen and uncovered a wall painting. Excavation by an American and French team in the years that followed uncovered many of the city's mysteries, as did more recent expeditions. Sadly, Syria's ongoing civil war brought an end to this, while deliberate destruction and looting ordered by ISIS has inflicted terrible damage on the surviving remains as Dura-Europos once again became caught up in conflict.

Shapur I mentions the capture of Dura, although without giving any details or a clear indication of when the place was taken. Only the archaeology tells us of the sophisticated methods of siege-craft employed by his soldiers, thus helping to explain his success against so many well-fortified strongholds. His army was efficient, large—judging from the size of the siege camp—and determined enough to persist even when some projects failed to create a breach. Dio mentions desertions from the Roman army and provinces, so some engineering specialists may have defected or been among those captured and perhaps acted as experts and instructors. Most of the techniques had developed in the Hellenistic era, and there were plenty of manuals in Greek available for those willing and able to learn, so this is not the only way that the Sasanians could have acquired these skills, nor should human ingenuity and the capacity to work things out from first principles ever be underestimated. The skills were learned in some way or other, and, whether this occurred wholly under Ardashir I and Shapur I or had a longer development, Sasanian armies from this era onwards displayed considerable engineering prowess. On its own this was not enough, and their success also relied on organization of the work on mines and ramps and of the supply system to feed men and animals for weeks or months. In addition, it required numbers of determined infantrymen, perhaps led or supplemented by cavalrymen willing to fight in close combat on foot, to storm the breaches created by craft or attack from the mobile assault towers attested in the fourth century and probably already in use.

A strongly fortified, well-led and well-supplied city was difficult to take, whether for Romans or Persians, but whereas in the first centuries BC and AD the former had been good at sieges and the Parthians markedly inferior, the difference had now become slight, perhaps non-existent. Part of this was a confidence on the part of the Persians to advance into enemy territory in considerable strength and accept the challenge to massed battle, at least if the circumstances were favourable. Sieges and battles were the most decisive but also the riskiest ways of warfare, and over the long term there was a clear shift in the tactical balance of Sasanian armies compared to their Parthian predecessors. Far less reliance was placed on light horse-archers, and less and less use made of the tactics of retreating to tire and scatter their enemies before isolating and destroying them piecemeal.

Instead, Persian armies came to contain a much higher proportion of close-order heavy cavalry, many of them heavily armoured
and riding armoured horses. As well as cataphracts, we hear of
clibanarii—a nickname meaning 'bread ovens', apparently because the Romans were amazed that anyone could bear such
heavy equipment in the summer heat. The distinction between
the two is uncertain. Both were willing to close with formed enemies, sometimes after weakening them with volleys of arrows,
and their armour, skill, and determination made them a threat
even to Roman legionaries. The increased numbers of such troops
reflected a tactical change but also had a social element. Such warriors needed to train to accustom themselves and their horses to
moving and fighting while bearing the burden of this equipment
and to doing this in close formation. This meant that they were
usually landowners or favoured members of an aristocrat's household, hence able to afford the equipment and time required. The
profits from long-distance trade may well have helped to fund
the growth of this class of warriors under the Arsacids and early
Sasanians, for heavy cavalry equipment was expensive. Over the
long term, Sasanian armies came to contain ever larger numbers of
professional or semi-professional soldiers, many of them paid or
in direct service to the monarch. Unfortunately, how and when this
developed is impossible to trace.

In the past, a well-handled and properly balanced Roman
army had been able to march almost at will through Parthian
territory, safe from serious loss unless its leaders made a mistake.
The Sasanian willingness to meet strength with strength may well
have emerged as a response to this and from their determination to overwhelm the Arsacids and supplant them. Cataphracts
and clibanarii were not agile and manoeuvrable like light horse-
archers, which meant that, once they had closed with the enemy,
it was harder for them to retreat unscathed. The same was true
of formed infantry and even more of war elephants. All were intended to pin their enemies and smash them, not to evade and
harass. There were still plenty of unarmoured or lightly equipped
horsemen, mostly archers, in Sasanian armies, but their role was
essentially a supporting one in large engagements. On campaign,

they fulfilled a wide range of roles as scouts and raiders, moving fast to surprise and terrify, much like Cossacks in Russian armies of the eighteenth and nineteenth centuries. Shapur I's forces could fight in more than one way and at more than one level to a degree not seen in earlier periods.

As always, this was not a one-sided process but an ongoing competition for advantage. In sieges, the Romans did their best to counter Persian ingenuity with engineering skill of their own. As legionaries and auxiliaries came to be equipped almost identically in the late second and third century, there was a trend towards heavier equipment, for instance with some infantry and cavalry wearing greaves to protect their legs. Trajan had formed a cavalry ala of lancers or *contarii*, equipped with the two-handed kontos used by Parthian and some Persian cataphracts. Hadrian formed the first recorded ala of cataphracts, and more units of these very heavy cavalry were raised in due course. There is also evidence that other auxiliary cavalry had some men, whether those in the front rank of the formation or a specific *turma* (troop), equipped as cataphracts. Horse armour was found in Roman stores at Dura, apparently under repair. While these trends were empire wide and not solely a response to problems faced on the eastern frontier, the challenge posed by the Parthians and subsequently Persians was surely one motive. In the coming years, sources describe Roman infantry spreading caltrops—iron spikes welded together so that however they fell one prong pointed upwards—in front of their position to injure the feet of attacking heavy cavalry.[22]

Nothing was static, but it is fair to say that the Roman empire faced so many crises that it was not in the best position to innovate and meet the challenge posed by Ardashir I and Shapur I. In 253, Valerian (Publius Licinius Valerianus) was sent to Raetia to raise forces to aid the current emperor against a challenger. Before he could return, the challenger had defeated and killed the man who sent him, so Valerian declared himself emperor and in turn killed the challenger. Already in his sixties, the new ruler was a senator, so a more traditional princeps than many of those who had held power in recent years. He appointed his son Gallienus as co-ruler, both of them titled Augustus. In 254, Valerian went east, but before he could think of facing Shapur I, he had to spend several years dealing with large-scale raiding by Goths and other tribesmen, first around the Black Sea and then more widely in Greece and Asia Minor. Gallienus was busy in the west, which meant that fending off Persian attacks was left to provincial governors and as often local leaders. There were successes, most likely over small detachments of Shapur I's army or perhaps allies acting more or less independently.[23]

By the end of 259, Valerian had moved to the eastern frontier, bringing troops with him and summoning others from over a wide area. Mustering this great army and arranging its supply took time, and Shapur I moved first, laying siege to Nisibis, which seems to have once again been in Roman hands, and Carrhae. Valerian responded and advanced into Mesopotamia. Shapur I claimed that the Romans had some seventy thousand soldiers, listing twenty-eight 'nations' or provinces that had supplied troops. As before, the alleged size of the enemy's army must be treated with similar caution to Roman claims about the Persians and other enemies. Notably, it is larger than the army of sixty thousand Shapur says that he had defeated at Barbalissos and may mean no more than that there was a substantial Roman force in each case. In an odd way, the numbers probably offer more of a guide to Shapur I's own army, since the natural urge for Roman and Persian alike was to claim that they won battles in spite of being heavily outnumbered. Therefore, the Persian army is unlikely to have been as large as sixty thousand, although it is hard to say any more than that—for instance, whether we should think of Shapur I at the head of thirty, forty, or fifty thousand warriors. The Sasanian camp outside Dura-Europos is very large, suggesting a substantial field army.[24]

If Valerian had anything like the numbers attributed to him, then this was also a very large, but not inconceivable, size for a Roman army, although past experience suggested that it was usually more efficient to split such a host into two or more columns operating independently. The record for large Roman armies concentrated in one place was not especially good, for they tended to become clumsy and hard to supply. On the other hand, some civil war battles were fought on such a grand or even grander scale, not least because with no inherent tactical or organizational advantage over another Roman army, it was natural to seek a numerical advantage. This encouraged more reliance on brute force and numbers on the part of the Romans in this period compared to earlier centuries, an attitude that may well have spread to campaigns against foreign opponents.

Shapur I claims to have fought and won a great battle, although his account is a brief summary. Other sources suggest a prolonged campaign, with numerous smaller actions and manoeuvring, but are equally vague. At some point, Valerian was captured, probably along with most of his senior staff and courtiers, perhaps falling to an ambush or treachery during negotiations. On a succession of monuments, Shapur I depicted himself grasping the wrists of the Roman emperor, who stands beside the king of kings' horse. Despite one tradition that says Valerian was swiftly killed, the majority of sources describe how he lived on as a captive for many years, the first emperor ever to be taken prisoner by a foreign enemy. Some claim that he was treated with ignominy by Shapur I, who would make him kneel down as a mounting block whenever he wanted to get on his horse. Then when Valerian eventually died, his skin was supposedly flayed from his body, dyed red, and set up in a temple as a victory trophy. These may be no more than rumours or later inventions, for Christian authors in particular had no love for Valerian, who had actively persecuted their faith.

Whether or not his army had already been beaten in battle, Valerian's capture destroyed any momentum left in the Roman campaign. There are no figures for Roman losses, whether the number killed or wounded in battle or the large contingent marched into permanent captivity. What was left of the army scattered or dispersed, and it is not entirely clear how long it took for the inevitable usurper to emerge at the head of some of the remnants. Fragments of the army do appear to have rallied and won some small victories. Gallienus was too busy dealing with other threats closer to Italy to seek either revenge or the ransom of his father. For the moment, Roman military strength in the region was shattered, and Shapur I drove deep into the Roman provinces, going through Syria into Cappadocia and Cilicia, taking city after city.

No Parthian army had ever done anything like this, although their ally, the younger Labienus, had led his troops into the same area some three centuries earlier in 40 BC.

As before, Shapur I's army, probably dividing into a number of columns, advanced, captured cities, plundered, took prisoners, and then withdrew. Although they were overrunning lands once ruled by Achaemenid Persia, there was no attempt at permanent occupation anywhere beyond Mesopotamia, where some Roman strongholds were garrisoned by the Persians and others destroyed. Shapur I had demonstrated his might to the Romans, just as Roman campaigns in the past had asserted their power, but it only resulted in limited territorial expansion. He had defeated three emperors, marched at will through Roman provinces, and—at least so far—not suffered any serious reverse. The message to allied communities and monarchs in the wider area was clear.

If anything, it was even clearer to Shapur I's subjects. One famous rock carving showed Gordian III's corpse being trampled, Philip begging for mercy, and Valerian held by the arm by the victorious king of kings. More often just two Romans were depicted, but the scale of the triumph remained unquestionable. No one could doubt Shapur I's right to rule, when the approval of the gods, and especially Ahura Mazda, was so clearly manifest. His victories were spectacular in terms of glory and tangible benefits. The spoils rewarded his faithful soldiers and especially the nobles. Roman gold and silver helped fund great royal projects, and tens of thousands of captives provided a large and skilled labour force under the king's direct control. Shapur I had them construct a palace, bridges, and aqueducts and develop and expand irrigation systems. This contributed towards substantial growth in agricultural produce and over time population and wealth.

Such things had been encouraged by the Arsacids, but under Ardashir and Shapur this was far more organized and had the time and resources to take deeper root. The king of kings became wealthier as a result, which in turn permitted more royal projects and helped to maintain a large campaigning army and to pay garrison troops. Settled far from the Roman empire's frontier, and never more than an alien minority, the captives were unlikely to desert or rebel. Ultimately, they could be made to do whatever the Persians wished, much like slaves within the Roman empire, and victors in the ancient world were often cruel. A fourth-century source describes the trail of dead and dying left behind one convoy of captives taken by the Persians in a later campaign, as those unable to keep up were hamstrung and left to perish.[25]

Like all successful leaders in the ancient world, Shapur I fought and won a lot of wars and was ruthless in achieving victory and putting down foreign enemies and any internal rivals. He was lucky because his reign coincided with a time of civil war and weakness in the Roman empire, just as Augustus was fortunate to live when he did. Both men demonstrated immense talent in the way they made the most of every opportunity, for their success was never inevitable and each one might have failed. If they chose to exaggerate their achievements when recounting their deeds, the truth was still remarkable and should not be taken for granted. Hindsight lends familiarity to what they achieved and can blind us to how surprising, even shocking, their careers were to contemporaries.

Shapur I's need to prove himself reinforced Ardashir I's decision to assert his power in the face of Roman encroachment. Little territory was gained, and instead the outcome was to alter perceptions on both sides about the balance of power between the two empires. Not simply standing up to the Romans but winning spectacular victories over them did a great deal to confirm the Sasanians as the new royal dynasty; they were not challenged for centuries to come by rivals from outside the line, and even then the attempt failed. At the same time, the Romans suffered, the disasters in the east fuelling the ongoing turmoil within the empire. For the moment, the pattern seemed set for frequent conflict, since the Romans were bound to try to shift the balance of power, both real and perceived, back in their favour whenever they felt that there was an opportunity to do this.

12

A BRILLIANT QUEEN AND THE RESTORER OF THE WORLD

C. 265–282

AN ASSERTIVE SASANIAN EMPIRE FACED WITH A WEAK ROMAN neighbour scented opportunities for successful war-making and took them. Yet all the chaos and infighting in the Roman empire—and even the humiliation of having an emperor captured and others humbled—did not fatally cripple its strength. Temporary crises should eventually end, and, whatever form the empire took in the aftermath, it would be large and have considerable resources of money and manpower. It would also want revenge, both for the sake of it and, more importantly, to reassert its strength and—at least as far as the home audience was concerned—superiority over its eastern neighbour. Less certain was how long it would take for this to occur and how well the Sasanians would deal with a more united Roman empire.

For Shapur I, so much success had left far less need for him to prove himself as rightful king of kings. He may also have been failing in strength through age. Shapur I boasted of few achievements definitely dateable to the years after his triumph over Valerian in 260. Since he had played an active role in his father's rise to power, by this time the king of kings was at least in his fifties and perhaps much older and less inclined to lead his army to war. This was likely a time for consolidation as the spoils of his victory were put to good use. On the other hand, he may have been active on his eastern and southern borders, since the chronology of his expansion in these areas is hazy at best. Hostilities continued between Rome and Persia over the next decade, but there is no evidence that this was ever again Shapur I's main focus.

Roman sources for this period are poor and often raise more questions than they answer. An officer named Ballista (or Callistus) won victories over Persian forces in Cilicia and Syria. Macrianus, a senior staff officer in charge of organizing supplies for Valerian's army, allied with him and at some point declared his two sons as emperors—apparently because he was lame and felt himself to be an unsuitable candidate. Other successes were won by Septimius Odaenathus, a Palmyrene and a Roman citizen of senatorial rank. Withdrawing after a successful invasion was always a difficult task, especially since the Persians had advanced so far and so quickly. The Persian army was scattered in detachments, tired, and eager to return home, but at the same time forced to go slower to carry the spoils and escort their captives along routes that were simple to predict. All this made it far easier for Roman leaders to pick the time and place for an attack or ambush. Some pride was restored, captives released, and plunder recovered, but such victories did not alter the overall outcome of the war. The Persians withdrew through choice—just as Roman armies under Lucius Verus and Septimius Severus had withdrawn from Ctesiphon—and any losses they suffered were small compared to the victories they had won so recently.[1]

Valerian's humiliating capture soon prompted other usurpations apart from Macrianus's sons, as several men assumed the imperial purple only to be killed within weeks or months. More seriously, a certain Postumus established himself in control of the Rhineland, Britain, most of Gaul, and parts of Spain. Although this area was often referred to as the Gallic empire, Postumus considered himself a legitimate Roman emperor. His supporters saw themselves as Romans, separatist only in the sense that Postumus had not been appointed with the approval of Gallienus. Hoping for recognition in due course, Postumus never launched an offensive designed to destroy Gallienus and take over the territory still loyal to him. Both emperors were kept very busy dealing with threats from beyond the frontiers. Gallienus also had to deal with Macrianus, who crossed to Europe with one of his sons. Their campaign ended in defeat and death, and the brother who had remained in the east was soon dealt with by Odaenathus. Ballista's fate is unclear, although there is a good chance that he also perished at this time.[2]

There is not space in a book like this to cover in detail the many civil wars, mutinies, and murders within the third-century Roman empire, or for that matter in the years that followed, even though this makes it harder to convey just how chaotic and weak the empire was at this time. The external threats faced by the Romans were certainly serious. Ardashir I and Shapur I were far stronger, more determined, and more capable than any of the Arsacids for many generations. Beyond the Rhine and the Danube, peoples like the Goths, Alamanni, and Franks appear in the third century, and many scholars continue to see this as a period of greater unity as smaller tribes combined into confederations under charismatic war-leaders, making them far more powerful and able to launch bigger raids into the rich provinces of the empire. Postumus's bid for power came in the wake of a victory over Germanic raiders on their way back from taking plunder and captives in Italy itself. Far more big attacks on and through the frontier provinces are recorded for these years, in spite of the poverty of our sources, and communities who had not needed to fear foreign attack for many generations suddenly faced the real possibility of this. Athens was attacked in 268 and some old monuments demolished so that the stone could be used for makeshift fortifications. Most cities in most provinces built or strengthened their walls during the third century.[3]

Bad luck—at least from the Roman point of view—played a role in the chaos of this era. Epidemics continued to sweep across the empire. There is a chance that Valerian's army was weakened by such an outbreak, or at least hindered in its concentration and preparation, before the clash with Shapur I. Much was beyond the control of the emperors who struggled to rule during these years. Yet caution is necessary. A pattern is visible throughout Roman history, and in the wider ancient world, that perception of weakness invited attack and that each successful and unpunished raid encouraged bigger and more frequent attacks. The Romans attempted to dominate the peoples beyond their frontiers with a mix of threats of force and actual violence, combined with diplomacy and bribery. When the façade of strength showed cracks or shattered, the carefully cultivated fear diminished, memories of past Roman violence were revived, and the sense of an opportunity for glory and revenge sprang up.

Civil wars drew Roman troops away from their usual bases, stripping strongly guarded frontier zones of soldiers, perhaps for years on end. Diplomacy and bribery were neglected or at least disturbed. Warriors from beyond the frontiers were often hired as mercenaries to bolster one man's attempt to make himself emperor, but these soldiers might easily find themselves on the losing side of a civil war, stranded deep in the empire. Once a frontier line was broken, and chieftains and warriors able to return home with tales of glory and plunder to show, it took concerted effort by strong Roman forces to restore a belief in Rome's overwhelming might. This meant catching and crushing bands of raiders and usually advancing beyond the frontiers to burn and massacre. In this way, warriors and their leaders might again become convinced that keeping the peace with Rome was preferable to the risk of attacking the provinces. This reliance on terror inevitably sowed the seeds for hostility whenever in the future the Romans came to seem vulnerable instead of strong. Breakdowns in the system had occurred in the past, notably on the Danube under Marcus Aurelius. In the third century, they became more and more common, cumulatively making it harder to reassert Roman might in each place.[4]

The Roman empire changed profoundly in the century or so following the accession of Septimius Severus, far more than had been the case at any other time since the creation of the principate by Augustus. In addition to establishing Mesopotamia and Osrhoene as new provinces, Severus divided Syria into two, Syria

Coele and Syria Phoenice, each with its own legate. Other military provinces, such as Britannia, were re-formed in the same way, in this case to Britannia Inferior and Superior. No governor of any province was left in command of more than two legions, while the emperor himself—having doubled the Praetorian Guard and Horse Guard and stationed a legion at Alba Longa—had at his immediate disposal in Italy a force comparable in size to any provincial army. Although most of the troops from Italy accompanied the emperor whenever he went to the provinces and thus provided the nucleus of a field army for large-scale warfare, there is not the slightest hint that these reforms were intended as a response to real or imagined threats from outside the empire. Instead, their purpose was to make it harder for a provincial governor to make a bid for the throne, as Severus and his two rivals had done in 193. In this respect, it failed utterly, but the trend continued, and by 300, nearly every province had been divided into smaller units. At the same time, military and civilian authority were separated and no longer in the hands of one governor.

Emperors clearly felt safer when their provincial governors commanded fewer soldiers and there were civil appointees controlling finances and access to food and other resources who might act as a check on their commanders' ambitions. That the experience of the third and indeed fourth centuries—with their numerous attempts to usurp the throne—gave the lie to this belief has not prevented many scholars from viewing all these reforms as sensible attempts to deal with a changing situation. Yet the most dangerous enemies for any emperor were other Romans. Valerian was the only emperor ever to be captured by a foreign enemy, while just a handful of others shared Decius's fate and died in foreign wars. Very many, the clear majority in the third century, died at the hands of other Romans, whether from their own court or men they had appointed to provincial or military commands.[5]

While this made fear and suspicion of subordinates natural for any emperor, it did not make for efficient government. Compared to earlier periods, frontier provinces now had governors with significantly smaller resources at their disposal. Large armies to deal with large threats could only be gathered and maintained through cooperation with neighbouring governors and other officials, something that was viewed with suspicion unless they were acting under direct imperial orders. Messages took time to travel from provinces to wherever the emperor was and back again, making it difficult to respond quickly to any major threat. More often than not, an emperor had to go in person to deal with any serious problem, which meant that he could only deal effectively with one crisis at a time.

Trajan, Lucius Verus, Marcus Aurelius, and Septimius Severus had led major wars in person, although most emperors after Augustus had chosen not to do this. By the third century, it was natural for emperors to preside over any major expedition, since they were unwilling to entrust such responsibility to anyone else, lest the appointed commander become too ambitious. This had the disadvantage of associating an emperor much more closely with any failure, as well as carrying the risks of campaigning. More obviously, he could only be in one place at a time. Even having a colleague, as when Valerian made Gallienus co-ruler, only helped to some extent. One reason for the success of Postumus and the 'Gallic empire' was that having an emperor in the Rhineland made it much easier to restore some sort of security to the frontier. The desire to have someone dealing with immediate problems, as well as having a dispenser of favours and honours locally, encouraged regions to back usurpers whenever they felt neglected by the existing emperor.

Change in the structure and oversight of provinces was accompanied by and often linked to the transformation of the army. As we have seen, one aspect of this was the gradual exclusion of the senatorial order from military posts. In the early third century, it remained common for senators to serve as senior tribune in a legion around the age of twenty, as legate in charge of a legion around the age of thirty, and then perhaps as legate of one or a succession of imperial provinces with military garrisons after the age of forty. The junior posts appear to have fallen away first, as no more broad-stripe tribunes (as opposed to the narrow stripe of an equestrian tribune) occur in the record, followed by the senior posts. By the end of the century, senators did not command armies or serve in the military, although they continued to hold important civil posts, particularly in Italy and also in the remaining non-military provinces. As a body, the Senate continued to meet, but its influence on the emperor was reduced as emperors spent less and less time in or near Rome.[6]

Instead, the army's higher command was supplied by equestrians, whether men born into the order or those who had been admitted through service in junior positions, including the centurionate. By the end of the third century, only one of these men could realistically aspire to become emperor. The positive way of looking at this major shift is to claim that all this was necessary in such desperate times. Senators were amateur soldiers of limited experience and presumably limited talent. Now facing far more formidable enemies, the empire could simply not afford to rely on such men as commanders and instead needed hardened professional soldiers, whether to lead an army in the field or serve as emperors. Yet the record of these years is one of numerous defeats, so this line of reasoning helps to reinforce the belief in an empire beleaguered by far more numerous and more serious threats than in the past. That this occurred despite the supposed toughness and professionalism of equestrian commanders and emperors would then suggest that things might have been even worse if senatorial amateurs had remained in charge.[7]

Talent is often hard to judge, let alone for an era when sources are so poor, making it impossible to know whether the equestrians who filled the senior positions in the army by the end of the third century were on average any more competent than their senatorial predecessors. The Romans did not create a system to train officers of any status for high command and instead expected them to learn by doing, by observing others, and through natural ability. The status of 'protector' appears for officers who had started their careers before being admitted to the equestrian order, and who then served close to the emperor. How far admission to this rank, or any senior post, was based on perceived ability and track record is unclear, and caution is needed when any sources stress the humble origins of a man, for a decent level of education was essential to rise high. Loyalty to the emperor mattered, probably even more than in the past, since now an emperor's senior officers were the very men who might find it easiest to overthrow and replace him. Trust was precarious at best, on all sides, and conspicuous success by a subordinate commander was as likely to be rewarded with suspicion as faith.

The 'Gallic empire' was the clearest example of fragmentation, but plenty of other regimes emerged, even if they did not last very long. Detachments of units, especially the legions, found themselves owing loyalty to different, rival emperors. Under the principate, the steps of a military career often took a man from one end of the empire to another. Senators rarely served in the same province more than once, equestrians similarly moved around with each promotion, and legionary centurions might serve in units dotted all over the empire. However the system worked, the emergence of rival regimes dislocated it. While emperors from Severus onwards showed a growing suspicion of the senatorial order, the drop in the numbers of young aristocrats seeking tribunates and other posts may well have been voluntary. Service in a provincial army now carried a far greater risk than in the past of becoming caught up in a usurpation and civil war. While that offered a chance of rapid promotion, it carried a greater risk of death or disgrace, which might readily extend to the rest of the family if the victor felt vengeful.

Alongside the dislocation of career patterns, changes in administration and recruitment were bound to be significant. Much of our understanding of the Roman army from the first to the early third century comes from inscriptions and the archaeology of its bases. By the end of the third century, military inscriptions are far rarer, reducing the information we have about ranks, careers, unit titles, and garrisoning patterns. New army bases built in this period and afterwards tend to be much smaller in area and far better fortified than before, as well as designed in a way that appears to bear less obvious relation to their intended garrison. The big legionary fortresses fell out of use, and most were abandoned or occupied only on a far smaller scale by the fourth century. There is growing evidence that the forts of Hadrian's Wall rebuilt the barracks blocks inside them around the middle of the third century, reducing by about half the accommodation space they offered. The permanent bases maintained by the army into the fourth century appear individually and collectively intended to house significantly fewer soldiers.

Quite a few legions, auxiliary cohorts, and alae remained in existence from the early days of the principate into the fourth and even fifth centuries, keeping their title and perhaps traditions. Many more units were created, some having a brief existence and others surviving for generations. The evidence of the fixed bases combined with glimpses provided by papyri and mentions in our literary sources suggest that not only did patterns of equipment largely become standardized between legionaries and auxiliaries, but the size of units also became much the same. In Septimius Severus's time, a legion had a theoretical strength of over five thousand men, including many specialists and a significant amount of artillery. A hundred years on, a legion had on paper some 1,000 to 1,200 men, not much bigger than a milliary cohort in the auxilia. Overall, the army was still every bit as large as it had been. In theory it may even have been larger, although the claims by some scholars that there were far more soldiers ring rather hollow. There were certainly far more independent units, which meant more commissions bringing status and pay to their commanders. Smaller basic units suggest an organization primarily designed to deal with relatively small armies. Although it appears reasonably common by the fourth century to 'brigade' two units together on a semi-permanent basis, these were still significantly smaller building blocks for a field force than a legion of some five thousand men.[8]

By the end of the third century, military equipment tended to be less ornate and had a mass-produced, crude-but-functional quality. A Roman soldier remained well-equipped, with each man having a sword, armour, shield, helmet, and a range of javelins or spears (and sometimes weighted darts) to throw or thrust. Drill and discipline were not forgotten. This was still an army intended to keep formation, fight in groups, and obey orders issued by a clear hierarchy of commanders. The majority of soldiers served for many years, even if the details of military service are less clear. They were professional, full-time soldiers—although a higher proportion were conscripts rather than volunteers—and they served in an army that had the potential to be very effective on campaign and in battle when well-trained and competently led.[9]

A focus on institutions and organization can lead to a neglect of the human element in warfare. During the third century and afterwards, the army in many parts of the empire was not well-situated to fulfil its potential. The cycle of civil wars disrupted its training and preparation. If it gave some soldiers far more experience of actual combat than was typical in the earlier principate, some of this experience was inevitably of defeat or of mutinies, perhaps encouraged by senior officers, which ended with the death of the emperor to whom they had sworn loyalty. Neither was likely to improve discipline or confidence. At the same time, the abandonment of the old established bases meant the loss of purpose-built accommodation, workshops, military hospitals and bath houses, granaries and other stores, drill squares and training grounds, and stable facilities. Billeting troops in cities—especially when this was for a matter of weeks or months rather than the permanent arrangements at places like Dura-Europos—removed much of the organized infrastructure which trained, fed, clothed, and cared for soldiers, and also kept cavalry mounts, pack and draft animals, and gear in good condition.[10]

The army represented the biggest ongoing expense in the imperial budget. Non-military bureaucrats were few in number by comparison, although they proliferated during this period. In Hadrian's day there were perhaps a couple of thousand civil officials and clerks working for the emperor. By the end of the third century, there were some thirty thousand, although it is less clear whether this promoted any greater efficiency. Quantities of money—bearing the head of the emperor, symbols, and slogans of his successes—also increased and were the most visible aspect of government. The silver coinage in particular was adulterated, from 90 percent silver content to some 70 percent at times during the first and second centuries, and then down to less than 2 percent in the third century, as emperors made their precious metals go further. Data is lacking to trace the consequences of this, but the overall trend was inevitably towards inflation, perhaps in sudden rapid bursts, as seems to be shown at least once from the evidence of Egyptian papyri.[11]

During the course of the third century, the Roman state was considerably weaker than it had been in the past, and overall the empire was less prosperous. That does not mean that all aspects of government and life were uniformly bad throughout Italy and the provinces. Fewer great monuments were built during this period, but there were some that were every bit as grand and fine as those of the past. Trade levels declined, although again some routes and goods appear largely unaffected. Some cities and communities thrived. Much had to do with location, since those on the frontiers or who found themselves in the path of civil war armies were more likely to suffer than those in quieter areas. The Roman approach of leaving most day-to-day administration in the hands of provincial communities meant that many aspects of local affairs continued regardless of who the emperor was or what he was doing. Yet signs of this normality, even stability, should not blind us to the speed with which emperors appeared only to meet violent deaths, the constant power struggles, the cost of raising and maintaining the armies who fought them, or the defeats and invasions across the frontiers that reached deep into formerly peaceful provinces. This was a time of chaos and change, and it is hard to know just how contemporaries felt and what they expected the future to hold—something especially important when we come to examine events in the east of the empire after the capture of Valerian and try to understand the career of Odaenathus of Palmyra.

Odaenathus's background and early career are unknown. That he was called Septimius meant that an ancestor, most likely a father or grandfather, was granted Roman citizenship by Septimius Severus sometime before the universal grant made by Caracalla. There is no sign that Odaenathus belonged to one of the leading noble families at Palmyra, still less any hint of a royal ancestry if there was such a thing in his home city. From the later second century into the third century, several Palmyrene men are attested following the equestrian military career in command of Palmyrene and other units in turn. This may also have been true of Odaenathus, which would explain how he caught the eye of one of the emperors visiting the region and was rewarded with promotion to senatorial status. By 260, he may well have been the legate of one of the

Syrian provinces and at some point was named *dux*, or general, a title coming into use in this period. Thus, when he acted to harry the Persian withdrawal and a year later to suppress the remaining son of Macrianus, this was the case of a Roman governor doing his duty at the head of Roman troops, which may have included auxiliaries from his home city as well as levies raised during the crisis.[12]

According to one source, Gallienus rewarded Odaenathus either before or after his suppression of the usurper by appointing him *strategos* (commander). A good case has been made that the actual title was something like *corrector* (or perhaps *rector*) *totius orientis*, and that he was effectively granted a supervisory role over the provinces of the east. Not everyone is convinced, and certainty is impossible, but it does seem that Odaenathus was accepted as a loyal subordinate of Gallienus. The emperor in Italy continued to appoint governors and other officers to these regions, even if they then fell under the command of Odaenathus once they were there. In this respect, the arrangement was unlike the separate empire presided over by Postumus and his successors in the west. Yet Gallienus never went to the eastern provinces and seems to have been content to allow Odaenathus freedom to act as he wished. Like Corbulo—if on a larger scale, so perhaps more like Agrippa or Germanicus—one man was given command over more than a single standard province. While possessing considerable authority and independence, he remained a subordinate of the emperor, and this was a practical solution to large-scale problems, all the more so given that normal provinces were smaller than in the past.[13]

That, at least, is the best reading of the sources from the Roman perspective—save that the picture from Palmyrene sources, later tradition, and subsequent events appears to suggest something different. This may simply be a question of perspective and the intended audience, or simply hindsight, but is tied in with the enigmatic nature of Palmyra itself—another of those truly remarkable archaeological sites to suffer in Syria's civil war. In the 70s, Pliny the Elder described Palmyra as between the empires of Rome and Parthia yet distinct from both. Physically the city was nearer to the Roman provinces, and the connection was closer, even if scholarly opinion is divided over whether it became formally part of the

empire under Tiberius or considerably later. Roman troops are attested, presumably as garrison, from the second half of the second
century, and later the city was granted the status of a colony, which
brought legal privileges. During this time, the city acquired many
grand monuments and much artwork, interpreting Greco-Roman
styles in a distinctive way. Over three thousand inscriptions have
been found on the site, far more—and generally with much longer
texts—than from the entirety of Roman Britain.[14]

Palmyra existed because of water, a rare and precious resource
in a landscape described as desert or dry steppe depending on your
point of view. The inhabitants called the place Tadmor in their
own language, and, whether or not it was the Tadmor claimed to
have been founded by Solomon, settlement was very ancient. There
was enough water from the oasis, associated springs, and carefully
collected rainwater to permit cultivation of the lands around the
city, to support goats and sheep over a wider area, and beyond
that to support those who relied on camels. Neither the farmers,
pastoralists, nomads, nor even the craftsmen and traders of the
city itself appear numerous and wealthy enough to have produced
the success of Palmyra on their own, and the best explanation is
that the different groups found mutual benefit in cooperation. This
may well have produced a social structure very different from the
Greco-Roman city-state that Palmyra's grid plan and monuments
might suggest. Inscriptions refer to tribes, at least nineteen of them,
although perhaps there were four by the third century, even if sub-
groups remained. Ancestry was important, and men often refer
to themselves not simply as the son of but as the grandson and
great-grandson of a named individual.[15]

Memories were long—past friendships, favours, and perhaps
enmities remembered. Yet the overwhelming picture of Palmyrenes
is of a people able to cooperate and work with others. The tribal
system apparently linked those who dwelt mainly in the city together with the farmers from close by, the shepherds and goatherds
from a little further afield, those who raised camels and travelled
far more, and the traders and those associated with them. Long-
distance trade made the city and at least some of its inhabitants
very wealthy, but it required the support and participation of many

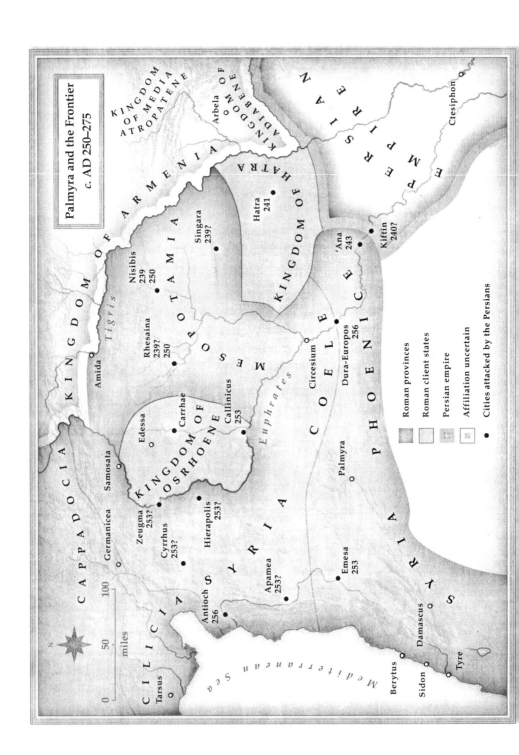

Palmyra and the Frontier
c. AD 250–275

KINGDOM
OF MEDIA
ATROPATENE

KINGDOM OF ARMENIA

KINGDOM OF
ADIABENE

Arbela ○

KINGDOM OF HATRA

Hatra
241 ●

Singara
239? ●

Nisibis
239
250 ●

Tigris

Amida ○

Rhesaina
239?
250 ○

M E S O P O T A M I A

Edessa ○

Carrhae ●

KINGDOM OF
OSRHOENE

Callinicus
253 ●

Euphrates

Circesium ○

'Ana
243 ●

Kiffin
240? ●

P E R S I A N   E M P I R E

Ctesiphon ○

Dura-Europos
256 ●

C O E L E

Samosata ○

Germanicea ○

Zeugma
253? ●

Cyrrhus
253? ●

Hierapolis
253? ●

Apamea
253? ○

Antioch
256 ●

S Y R I A

Palmyra ○

Emesa
253 ●

P H O E N I C E

S Y R I A

Damascus ○

Berytus ○

Sidon ○

Tyre ○

CAPPADOCIA

CILICIA

Tarsus ○

Mediterranean Sea

N

100

50

miles

0

Roman provinces

Roman client states

Persian empire

Affiliation uncertain

● Cities attacked by the Persians

of Palmyra's citizens, quite a few of whom took part and benefitted to some degree. Caravans, perhaps one or two a year going in each direction along the main routes, were most likely large, perhaps numbering thousands of pack animals, mostly camels. That meant many people earning their livelihood raising the beasts and keeping them in good condition when they were not on one of these great trading expeditions, as well as others to lead and care for them when they were. It meant some people never travelled far but supplied the food those in the caravans would carry as supplies, the clothes they wore, and the saddles, packs, and other equipment needed by men and animals. Then there were the guards needed to protect the caravans, since goods, animals, and people were all tempting targets for banditry by those so inclined, who for large parts of the route were nomads tough enough to thrive in such a harsh environment. It was better to placate such potential predators, winning over their leaders with gifts and respect, all aided by relationships forged and maintained over the generations. Yet there were plenty of competing groups and leaders, and agreement with one might provoke hostility from rivals or simply challengers eager to supplant them.[16]

Inscriptions express thanks to the men who organized the great caravans, sometimes on behalf of all or some of the wider community and its tribes, as well as the men who led them, guided them, escorted them, and protected them. Thus the council, people, and the four tribes honoured Ogelos, the son of Makkaios, grandson of Ogelos, great-grandson of Agegos, and great-great-grandson of Sewiras, for the assistance provided by his 'valour and courage' and 'because of his frequent expeditions against the nomads'. He had supervised and guarded caravans, spending his own wealth to serve the community with 'brilliance and glory'. The language is that of proclamations in many a Greco-Roman city, but whereas other inscriptions tended to praise a man for service as priest or magistrate or for paying for building works, staging games and festivals, or securing favourable decisions from governor or emperor, Palmyrenes valued more martial achievements, albeit in the service of commerce. Most inscriptions do not go into as much detail over the nature of the services required to protect the caravans.

One from the second century thanks a Roman centurion, without telling us how he had the opportunity to assist, whether he commanded a detachment in the area by chance or design, or even if he was an ambassador with his escort who accompanied a caravan for convenience.[17]

Palmyrenes organized themselves to fight if it was necessary to ensure the safety of the caravans. Sculptures depict warriors who rode camels and travelled well-armed to deal with any problems. The aim was not to fight for the sake of it but to ensure safe passage, and in scale this probably meant hundreds or at least no more than a couple of thousand fighting men willing to serve as guards some of the time. This was not an army or even militia, in either scale or intention, and instead gave the Palmyrenes protection that was under their control to a far greater degree than any Roman troops stationed in the city and the wider area. At least as important was the fact that these escorts could travel beyond the empire without being seen as invaders. The ability to get along with others, or at least convince them that it was more beneficial to cooperate than not, drove Palmyrene success, and it is amazing just how far afield people from this one city spread. Apart from the Palmyrenes living in Babylonia and Characene, there were Palmyrenes in the Arabian Gulf in communities independent of Parthia and Rome. Palmyrene merchants operated in the Red Sea ports of Egypt, where they hired passage in ships owned and captained by Palmyrenes to cross the waters to India. There are signs that the relationship between Palmyrenes and Jewish communities was often good, as one widely scattered population worked with another to oil the wheels of commerce. The rise of the Sasanian dynasty may have presented a challenge to Palmyrene interests, as a more forceful expression of central power and Ardashir I's and Shapur I's campaigns to bring Characene under direct control and expand into Arabia disrupted or shattered long-standing relationships. Trade did not stop, except probably during the times of open conflict between Rome and Persia, but it was surely disrupted.[18]

None of this had hindered Palmyra's integration into the Roman empire, although it surely gave many of its citizens and leaders a wider perspective on the world. Local customs, beliefs, and practices were never suppressed by the Romans unless they conflicted strongly with the empire's interests. Latin is rare in the inscriptions from the city, but Greek is as common as it was throughout the eastern provinces, and virtually all large public inscriptions were at the very least repeated in this language as well as Palmyrene. There is no sign that the presence of a Roman garrison produced tension or disruption, and Palmyrenes were entering imperial service and following the equestrian military career. Odaenathus is the only recorded example at this stage of a Palmyrene joining the senatorial order, but this would not be unusual for a single city—no senator is ever attested from Britain throughout its life as a province. From 260 onwards, Odaenathus rose to prominence first as a provincial governor and then because of the grant of additional authority by Gallienus. He was celebrated in his home city and drew support from it, perhaps easily because of his connection. Yet he led as a Roman magistrate, and in this capacity also drew on many other communities, and commanded troops from the regular Roman army, although he may have added allies and levies, including Palmyrenes, to these. None of this was unprecedented or in any deep sense abnormal, save that the disastrous failure of Valerian's campaign was an extreme situation.

Odaenathus responded with great boldness as well as ability, and by around 262 decided that a counter-attack against Persia was in order. Details are scanty, but he led an expedition close to Ctesiphon. Unless it was very small in scale, then Palmyrenes formed only a small minority of the troops involved, which is not to say that their knowledge and experience of crossing large distances and keeping supplied in this wider region did not play a significant role. Ctesiphon was not taken, and most likely it was never the intention to storm or besiege the city. There is no sign of a major confrontation with a big Sasanian army, or of the presence of Shapur I himself, which suggests that the king of kings and the bulk of his forces were elsewhere. Some sources claim that early on Odaenathus had negotiated with Shapur I, seeking some sort of recognition from the Persians. The approach was dismissed, prompting Odaenathus to make war. Most scholars are inclined to see this as preceding the loyal service to Valerian and Gallienus, but it may have occurred during the fighting as one of those frequent attempts to seek a diplomatic settlement alongside the use of force.[19]

Fighting took place over several years, and Odaenathus and his men are said to have reached the outskirts of Ctesiphon at least twice between 262 and 267. This was not a success on the scale of Shapur I's expeditions into the Roman provinces, for there is no hint that any major cities were captured or large battles won. Yet the attacks were statements of confidence in the wake of disaster, the beginning of a reassertion of the dominance the Romans—and, for that matter, the Sasanians—aimed to create on and beyond their frontiers. Gallienus took the title Persicus Maximus and celebrated a triumph in Rome on the back of his subordinate's victories. Odaenathus's prestige grew, and at some point—probably while he was in Babylonia—he had himself named not simply as king of Palmyra but king of kings, and extended this to his oldest son as well. The title never occurs in Latin or Greek, at least in surviving documents, only in Palmyrene. Throughout Odaenathus's life, coins minted in the provinces under his supervision loyally show Gallienus's head and imperial slogans without hint of another authority.[20]

Claiming to be king of kings was clearly a challenge to Shapur I, but it is very hard to say just what Odaenathus intended. Perhaps he hoped to weaken the prestige of the Sasanian monarch, adding to the blow suffered as the Romans were able to raid Babylonia unscathed. It still was little to set against all of Shapur I's achievements, and there is no direct evidence that anyone was persuaded to switch sides. Nor did the challenge provoke Shapur I to march against Odaenathus for a direct confrontation, if he had hoped to provoke one. Whatever kept Shapur occupied elsewhere continued to do so. It is possible that Odaenathus was thinking of the future, dreaming of leading a new empire based around his home city, including the Roman provinces he controlled and perhaps adding the closest regions of the Sasanian empire. After all, Postumus was showing what was possible in these chaotic times. If Odaenathus was pondering such a design, it is impossible to say whether he hoped for something similar to the Gallic empire— Roman in all important respects, notably law—or some sort of greater Palmyrene empire. As always, local leaders had their own ambitions and hopes, whether or not they seem realistic in hindsight. Whatever plans Odaenathus cherished came to an abrupt end when he was murdered in 267, apparently by a close relative motivated by politics or a personal grudge.

Something strange then happened, although it is unclear whether it reflected Odaenathus's plans or those of the people best placed to take advantage of his death. His oldest son, child of his first wife, was already dead. His second son, Septimius Vaballathus, was no more than a boy, and real control passed to his mother, Odaenathus's second wife, Zenobia. Acting as queen and regent and proclaiming the child as king was unexceptional, although in the past the right to appoint a successor was only granted to a few allied monarchs by Roman emperors. Zenobia also had her son awarded all of his father's Roman titles and positions, none of which was legal, for governors and generals did not pass command on death to their own heir. Only monarchs did this, whether regional kings or, at least to all intents and purposes, Roman emperors. Gallienus was in no position to challenge these claims, and it is significant that at the start the eastern mints continued to bear his name and image and those of his immediate successors. Gradually, Vaballathus also appeared on the reverse of the coin, suggesting a claim to the status of colleague, though still a subordinate one.[21]

Events moved quickly, and Gallienus was overthrown by the end of 267 by one of his own generals, who was in turn overthrown, and Claudius II named as emperor in 268. After a victory over the Goths, he took the name Gothicus and was remembered with fondness in our meagre sources, but he perished from plague in 270. A brother quickly succeeded him, was almost as quickly murdered, and Aurelian became emperor. Postumus was murdered around the same time, as was his successor. In the same year, Shapur I succumbed to old age, and for the next few years the nobility of his empire were more concerned with the issue of succession, as several of his sons were crowned only to be deposed within a short time.

Zenobia took advantage of the confusion to expand the territory under her son's control, sending troops to occupy Egypt around

270. There was a little fighting, but most officials, troops, and the wider provincial population were either overawed by the strength of the invaders or willing to accept their rule. Zenobia claimed descent from the Ptolemies, the Macedonian dynasty that had ruled the kingdom until its absorption by Augustus, and boasted the famous Cleopatra Thea, wife of three Seleucid kings in turn, as ancestor (although not Cleopatra VII, better known to us). There are echoes of the influence and public role of the Severan women in Zenobia's career, although in many ways she was to surpass them. Unusually for a woman playing a leading role in politics, let alone for a queen, the Greco-Roman sources for her are positive, influenced by the memory of Cleopatra VII but far kinder. Both women were remembered as linguists and scholars and as ambitious, but whereas Cleopatra was always the sensuous seductress, Zenobia was remembered for stern virtue. Supposedly, she would make love to her husband only for the purpose of having a child, and after each encounter she would wait to discover whether she was pregnant and only admit Odaenathus back into her bed if she was not. Able to ride and hunt as well as any man, she was also said to be extremely beautiful, dark eyed and dark skinned.[22]

How much, if any, of this is true is impossible to say, for Zenobia attracted romantic invention and at this distance in time might even be judged mythical were it not for the inscriptions and coins recording her career. Gradually, Vaballathus was presented more and more openly as an emperor, although at least at first all due respect was paid to Aurelian, and the aim was surely to gain formal recognition from the new emperor—or any successor should Aurelian swiftly go the way of his predecessors. Two generals, both Palmyrene from their names but also Roman citizens, appear leading the army in Egypt and elsewhere. Palmyra's population was too small to provide the majority of their soldiers unless the forces involved were modest. Although it is not specifically recorded, significantly more warriors might have been recruited from the peoples, especially the nomadic tribes, with whom the Palmyrenes had such long-standing connections. The wealth of the trading city would also have permitted the recruiting of mercenaries drawn from a wide area, although again there is no positive evidence for this. A significant force of cataphracts, as well as some armoured camel riders, are mentioned, but it is unlikely that these numbered more than a few thousand at most. Most probably the bulk of troops fighting for the young Vaballathus were units from the provincial Roman armies.[23]

Nor is there any indication that Zenobia acted differently from any other imperial authority, however she chose to present herself in Palmyra—and in all cases she was presented as acting on behalf of her son. Later tradition maintained that Christians from Antioch took a dispute to her for arbitration. She is said to have favoured Paul of Samosata, a bishop no longer acknowledged by the majority of the community because of doctrinal differences, but who continued to occupy a church building and dressed and acted almost like a civil magistrate, backed by a band of devoted followers. The stories may have been invented or distorted later to associate her memory with heresy and, much like the claim that Zenobia was Jewish, clearly come from a hostile source. There is evidence for a ruling protecting Jewish communities in Egypt, but this seems no more than the usual arbitration expected of Roman authorities, ideally impartial and just but, more importantly, intended to keep peace and stability in a province. Coming under the control of the young emperor-king from Palmyra does not appear to have involved any drastic changes in any province.[24]

Expansion appears limited to territory within the Roman empire, even though in some ways Palmyrenes and other peoples in the frontier provinces may have had as much or more in common with the nearest communities within the Persian empire. At this stage, there was no great religious divide between the two empires. There were Christians in Arsacid Parthia and Sasanian Persia from early on, their numbers then significantly boosted by the captives taken home by Shapur I. Although proclaiming their connection with Ahura Mazda and holding the priesthood once held by Pabag, Ardashir I and Shapur I both appear tolerant of other cults, as long as the adherents accepted and supported their rule. A priest of Zoroaster named Kirdir rose to great prominence under Shapur I's successors and set up an inscription boasting of many achievements. He claimed to have accompanied the Persian invasion of the Roman provinces, to Antioch and into Cilicia, and to have found Zoroastrians already established there. These he protected—for instance, from deportation to Persia—but also instructed in what he felt was the proper conduct of the religion, saying that this was all done on Shapur I's orders.[25]

Yet Shapur I also showed favour to other religious leaders. One was Mani, born into a community of Gnostic Christians.* As a youth he claimed to have had visions of a purer truth, and after travelling widely, including some time in India, he preached a new faith and found many adherents. He claimed that the universe was engaged in a struggle between light and darkness, and that darkness pervaded the physical world and all flesh, so individuals needed to struggle for purity and redemption. Kirdir rose high in the years after Shapur I's death and was able to persuade one of his successors to persecute the cult. Mani was arrested and executed in 276, but this did not prevent the persistence of the religion he had founded, which spread into the Roman provinces and eventually as far as China. With some irony, a generation later a Roman emperor ordered the suppression of the Manichaens because he was suspicious of their practices but also because he viewed them as representatives of Persia and potentially subversive.[26]

The position of Christians—who along with Jews and other minorities would also attract Kirdir's violent hostility—remained ambiguous in the Roman empire. In the first and second centuries, persecutions were occasional, starting when Nero made Christians scapegoats for the fire that had devastated Rome in 64, hoping to deflect the blame that was falling on him. He failed in this, and, in spite of the executions and the principle he established that being a Christian was illegal, the faith continued to spread. Persecutions broke out when local authorities became worried, usually after natural disasters or economic or social problems, seeing—or wanting other people to see—that these were the result of the neglect of

---

*Gnostic Christians were a diverse group who emerged in the second century as an offshoot of mainstream Christianity. To oversimplify, they viewed the physical world as wholly alien to God and bodies as prisons for souls, although the latter could be awakened spiritually by the divine message and, through correct teaching, ascend to heaven.

the cults of traditional gods and goddesses because of the spread of Christianity. Trajan approved Pliny the Younger's execution of unrepentant Christians in Bithynia, while Marcus Aurelius was more directly involved in an outbreak of arrests, trials, and executions in Gaul. Neither emperor embarked on any systematic campaign to suppress the religion, seeming to hold to the view expressed by Trajan that governors were not to go searching for Christians and were only to act when the local authorities demanded.[27]

The insecurity of the third century prompted a change, in one sense an extension of the desire to have someone to blame for recent disasters and also a reflection of emperors desperate to reinforce the loyalty of their people. In 249 or 250, Decius ordered the entire population of the empire to make public sacrifice on his behalf. Christians did not sacrifice but, unlike Jews, were not accepted and taxed as a recognized community, so their reaction depended on their individual consciences and the enthusiasm of local officials. Some obeyed and decided to forget what they had done, some gained exemption through bribery, some hid, and some found themselves arrested and imprisoned or executed. In 257, Valerian more directly targeted Christians and there were more deaths, but after his capture in 260 Gallienus issued an edict of toleration. This may explain why the dispute between Christians in Antioch was so public, although more likely the rarity of persecution over past generations meant that most church communities went about their lives fairly publicly. When persecutions occurred, the authorities appear to have had little difficulty finding leading Christians.[28]

Aurelian, whose coins would later proclaim him 'restorer of the world' (restitutor orbis), would promote 'the Unconquered Sun' (Sol Invictus) as divine supporter of his rule, but he does not appear to have acted with hostility to Christians or any other minority group. His focus was on political reunification of the empire and re-establishing its security. He defeated several large groups of Germanic raiders, then the current emperor in Gaul, and gave orders for the construction of the great city walls still visible in Rome to this day. Then he turned his attention to Zenobia and Vaballathus. Zenobia had stopped short of proclaiming her son as Augustus, but in all other respects depicted him as emperor. She also appeared on coins herself, while Aurelian's name and image were phased out. Egypt was retaken in Aurelian's name, and then in 272 he advanced on Antioch. A battle was fought, and interestingly Zenobia's cataphracts were exhausted chasing after cavalry who feigned flight before turning on their scattered and weary pursuers, an action reminiscent of Parthian tactics, not least at Carrhae. The sources emphasize the foreign nature of Zenobia's army, making it hard to know how many of the troops willing to fight for her son were regular Roman units. Aurelian was victorious and followed this success by marching to Palmyra and winning a second battle.[29]

Zenobia tried to escape beyond the empire but was caught. Several leaders were executed, and Vaballathus died or was killed soon afterwards, but although there was a tradition claiming that his mother was also put to death, most sources assert that she remained a prisoner. Taken back to Rome, she walked in Aurelian's triumph, so laden down with jewellery and golden fetters that she struggled to walk. Afterwards, she was released, married a senator, had children with him, and their descendants remained a prominent aristocratic family in Rome for over a century. Thus the end of Zenobia's story has her very much as the Roman lady rather than an eastern queen and highlights the complex cultural world she inhabited. Sources, no doubt encouraged by Aurelian, tend to depict the war she fought and lost as a rebellion by a provincial people seeking independence and an empire of their own, and many scholars are inclined to treat it in the same way. Perhaps there was an element of this, but equally there were many of the characteristics of a Roman civil war.[30]

Palmyra rebelled in 273, a rising that does not seem to have spread much more widely than the city itself. It was quickly crushed, and although sources talk of a siege, as far as we can tell the city had no fortified walls at this time. In the future it would be a garrison town of modest importance and wealth, with limited amounts of trade passing through. Within a year, Aurelian had also dealt with the last ruler of the Gallic empire, bringing all of the pre-260 Roman empire back under his control, apart from the

Dacian provinces beyond the Danube which he decided to abandon. His success was remarkable, not least for its sheer speed, but did not prevent his assassination in 275. At least six men made a bid for the throne in the next seven years, all of them dying violently. In 282, the emperor Carus felt sufficiently secure—or was eager for glory to legitimize his rule—to mount a major expedition against Persia. He reached Ctesiphon, may or may not have taken it, and then died. Sources say that he was struck by lightning. Many scholars are inclined to suspect that an assassin's knife was responsible. Either way, the army withdrew.[31]

Whatever the motivation of Carus, his campaign and the earlier successes under Odaenathus had shown that there had been little or no fundamental shift in the balance of power between Rome and Parthia-Persia. Decades of civil strife had meant that the Romans were unable to make full and effective use of their resources in the confrontations with the Sasanians. In spite of this, they had only lost a little territory, and for all the terrible cost of the Persian invasions to provinces like Syria, these would recover in time. Ardashir I and Shapur I had firmly established their dynasty, and the victories over the Romans had helped a good deal in achieving this. Once this was done, it was in most respects more in their interest to revert to a relationship with Rome similar to the one maintained by the Parthians in the first and second centuries. Yet this was easier said than done, since one price of their success was the fuelling of a Roman need to humble the Sasanians. Every fresh war left scars on both sides, encouraging a leader—especially of the side that did less well—to seek redress through armed force. The pattern continued to be one where war was far more common than it had been under the principate.

13

SIEGES AND EXPEDITIONS

Late Third to Fourth Centuries

Both empires were more jealous of their reputation, since the back and forth of successive campaigns had altered perceptions of each one's strength, not only among the Romans and Sasanians themselves but also among all the peoples of the area. The rapid rise and fall of Roman emperors left each new incumbent eager to prove his legitimacy, and the best way to do this remained through military success, whether in actual war or militant diplomacy to force submission from enemies. Similarly, Sasanian monarchs needed to live up to the high standard of success set by Ardashir I and Shapur I and were very likely to feel that provocation from Rome needed to be met with a strong response. There was little to encourage the resumption of the less prickly and generally peaceful relationship under Augustus and his successors.

Shapur I was probably dead by the time Aurelian had defeated Zenobia, although the record is so poor that it is just possible that he heard the news of this, and perhaps even of the final sack of Palmyra, before he died. Victor in so many wars, king of kings for three decades, and an important figure for much of his father's reign, the old man's death was bound to produce an air of uncertainty. The Sasanians were still a relatively young dynasty, not yet

having had the chance for the royal line to split and produce anything like the flocks of potential kings common in the Arsacid era.
Even so, each king of kings took several wives and also fathered
sons with members of the harem, and there was no rigid system of
succession based on age or prestige of the mother. The choice of a
new ruler was rarely simple.

Shapur I was succeeded by one of his sons, Hormizd I, in 270—
although some scholars still favour 273 as the date. The new king
of kings appears to have campaigned in the east, but he was dead
within a year, whether by accident, combat, or illness is unknown.
If he had any offspring, then these were passed over and another
of Shapur I's sons was crowned as Bahrām I (or Varahrān I in an
alternative transliteration). He appears to have lacked some of the
prestige of his predecessor and may have been the offspring of a
less distinguished mother. Bahrām I ruled for some three years, and
after his death in 274 his son was proclaimed as Bahrām II. He
was the king of kings faced with Carus's invasion and made some
concessions, giving up territory previously taken from Roman
Mesopotamia. A major challenge to his rule came from his uncle,
another son of Shapur I, who rallied considerable support in the
eastern provinces and proclaimed himself Kushan king of kings.
Eventually this rebellion was defeated, and Bahrām II ruled until
his death in 293. Someone named Vahunam appeared as ruler then
disappeared, then he was briefly succeeded by a son of his predecessor, Bahrām III, but the young king and his supporters alienated
much of the nobility, and attempts to terrify them into submission
with a number of executions led to open rebellion in favour of
Narses (or Narseh) I, another son of Shapur I who had also been
passed over up to this point. Narses I prevailed, presumably killing
his rival, although an inscription from early in his reign suggests
that at this stage he did not enjoy the active support of some of the
great clans, like the Karen and Suren.[1]

Scholars, especially those specializing in the later Roman empire, all too often depict the rise of the Sasanians as replacing
Arsacid Parthia with a new empire that was far, far stronger and
usually aggressive. Yet the spate of short reigns, internal struggles, and problems on the eastern borders that followed the death

of Shapur I show that the truth was a good deal more complex. There was change, certainly, much of it gradual. Projects begun by Ardashir I and Shapur I—such as moving populations over wide areas (for the Roman captives were surely not alone) and creating or enlarging cities—took time to develop. The same was true of the substantial extension of irrigation systems to allow wider and more efficient cultivation, and these projects continued under Shapur I's successors, reaping benefits over time. Similarly, the development of a more centralized administrative state was not instant but gradual, although the process is impossible to trace or date. Nor is it clear whether this was imposed by the stronger monarchs or more often by the court of weaker rulers, who were desperate to secure their hold on power.

Running parallel was the creation of a structure and hierarchy with the Zoroastrian religion, so that there was a clerical counterpart to civil administration, but again this is very hard to trace and date with any certainty. Kirdir the priest flourished under the rule of the Bahrāms, styling himself priest of priests (mobad of mobads) in obvious parallel to the king of kings. It was during these years that he was empowered to turn on Mani and his followers and other religious minorities. Again, his rise may reflect weakness rather than strength on the part of the king of kings, and Narses I proved far less susceptible to his influence, returning to the tolerant approach of the past.[2]

Ardashir I and Shapur I were gifted war-leaders and strong monarchs, and they also had the good fortune to rule at a time when the Roman empire was very weak and divided. If succession could prove difficult for the Sasanians, it remained even more a source of chaos and infighting within the Roman empire, where there was no royal family able to exclude all other candidates for imperial rule. Carus was succeeded in the eastern part of the empire by Numerian, who was murdered within a year or so, and an officer named Diocletian was proclaimed emperor. The latter secured his rule by promptly executing the man who had led the conspiracy to overthrow and kill his predecessor in his favour. Diocletian ruled for twenty years before voluntarily retiring—a unique decision in the history of the empire up to this point. He created a system known as the tetrarchy: the rule of four, as opposed to the principate, or rule of one. In its purest form, it lasted no more than a decade or so in the second half of his reign, dividing the empire for administrative purposes into an eastern and western half. In each, a senior emperor titled Augustus ruled with the assistance of a junior emperor with the title of Caesar, thus providing four leaders to deal with up to four major problems simultaneously. At the same time, many other trends—notably, increased bureaucracy and centralization of power, the dividing of provinces into smaller units, and the separation of military and civil power—were deliberately accelerated.[3]

Diocletian has on the whole been admired by scholars, especially in recent years, and seen as the man who consolidated the success of Aurelian and others, bringing the empire back under control of a college of emperors, restoring a good deal of stability and prosperity. Some of this is justified. Civil wars became less common than they had been for more than a generation. The reformed and centralized government functioned reasonably well, certainly better than it had done for some time, even if attempts to control inflation and prices had mixed success. On balance, the empire appeared more prosperous and stronger than at any time since the death of Caracalla and was better able to deal with threats from outside. Whether, as is sometimes claimed, this created a truly more efficient state than the earlier principate is harder to judge, for so much had changed, but generally claims for the robustness of the late third- and fourth-century empire are unconvincing. Although less frequent, usurpations and civil war remained common enough. Diocletian and the other tetrarchs spent a good deal of their time confronting Roman rivals, not least a regime that emerged in Britain under Carausius, who for a while also controlled northern Gaul. Within months of Diocletian's retirement in 305, his planned succession broke down, and it was some twenty years before Constantine brought the entire empire under his full control.[4]

As the third century drew to a close, the Roman empire was less weak and divided than it had been for several generations, while the Sasanian empire was less strong than it had been under

Ardashir I and Shapur I. Armenia was once again a source of contention between the two powers. For a long time, it was largely controlled by the Sasanians, as much because they feared a resurgence of the Arsacids as part of the ongoing contest to dominate the kingdom. However, the Romans backed an Arsacid who managed to gain control of a significant part of the kingdom. Narses I, who may have been a local king in Armenia before his elevation to king of kings, drove this Arsacid king out around 296. Diocletian sent his Caesar, Galerius, to deal with the matter. The first confrontation came in Mesopotamia in 297 and saw the Romans routed in a battle fought somewhere near Carrhae. A later tradition claimed that when Galerius reported to Diocletian, the Augustus made his Caesar jog on foot alongside his carriage for some distance as a public humiliation for this embarrassing failure. A year later, Galerius did much better, surprising Narses I's army in Armenia and capturing his harem and much of his treasury. A peace was concluded, heavily favouring the Romans, who recovered lost districts of Mesopotamia, extending Roman authority up to the Tigris. At the same time, the Romans' right to intervene and back their candidate in Armenia was recognized, albeit with a substantial part of the old kingdom remaining in Persian hands.[5]

Diocletian's reign saw an intensive building program in the eastern provinces. Cities were fortified or strengthened and a network of forts created. In keeping with military installations in this era, these were small but had high walls and towers projecting in front of the curtain wall to permit men to shoot or throw missiles into the flank of anyone attempting to attack. Many cities were close to a new road, the Strata Diocletiana, which provided a cordon along the frontier of steppe and desert facing the nomadic Arab tribes and kingdoms. This was not an impenetrable defensive line. Raiders could slip through but risked detection, which then allowed an attack to be reported and sufficient troops gathered to defeat the enemy or at least harry their retreat, laden down with plunder.[6]

Mobility remained important, although the army came to be divided into two sections: the *comitatenses*, who did not have fixed bases, and the *limetanei*, who did. Both groups were professional

BRITANNIAE

North Sea

GALLIAE

VIENNENSIS

ITALIA
ANNONARIA

PANNONI

ITALIA
SUBURBICARIA

Rome

HISPANIAE

Mediterranean

AFRICA

WESTERN ROMAN EMPIRE

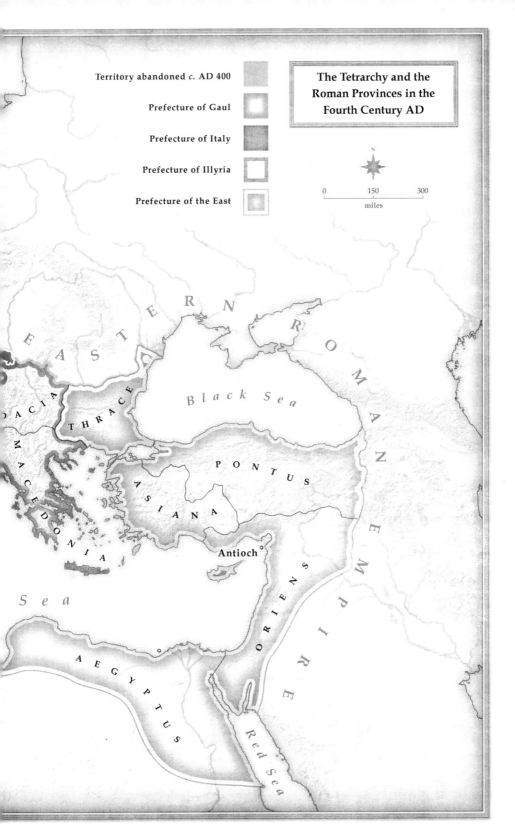

Territory abandoned *c.* AD 400

Prefecture of Gaul

Prefecture of Italy

Prefecture of Illyria

Prefecture of the East

The Tetrarchy and the Roman Provinces in the Fourth Century AD

N

0   150   300
miles

EASTERN ROMAN EMPIRE

DACIA

THRACE

Black Sea

MACEDONIA

ASIANA

PONTUS

Antioch

ORIENS

Sea

AEGYPTUS

Red Sea

soldiers, mainly conscripts in this era, but the limetanei provided permanent garrisons and were expected to remain in or near them. The comitatenses are often referred to by scholars as mobile field armies, although mobility depended a good deal on organized supply, which was helped by the well-guarded roads along and leading to the frontier. At times, especially in the east, comitatenses found themselves added to city garrisons, just as at times the limetanei were ordered to join a field force, which shows that the two types were not so different in training and equipment as to prevent cooperation. Additional command levels—grouping together the comitatenses of a region embracing numerous provinces or the limetanei in adjacent provinces—were created. However, the two hierarchies were kept separate, so that only in exceptional circumstances did one man have authority over both limetanei and comitatenses. The aim once again appears to have been to prevent potential usurpers from gaining control of all the soldiers in a wider area rather than any military utility.[7]

Diocletian left the eastern frontier far more heavily defended than it had ever been before in terms of the number of strong military outposts, and especially of well-fortified and garrisoned cities. As part of the treaty of 299, all trade coming into the empire from Persia had to pass through Nisibis, allowing the Romans to control and tax goods but also making it harder for spies to cross. Similar measures had long been in place on other frontiers, for instance, restricting members of certain tribes to specific entry points into a province. How effective this was in denying intelligence about defences and likely targets for raids is uncertain, but it does show an official desire to deal with a perceived problem. To a degree, this defensive mindset was matched by the Persians, with perhaps more reliance on cities than outposts, at least in this area. Overall, it is most striking just how similar the military thinking and practice of Romans and Persians had become by the fourth century. Armies could be large, and both had plenty of troops intended for close confrontation; the mention of war elephants in Sasanian armies becomes much more frequent in this era, while it is armoured horsemen rather than fast-moving archers who capture the attention of the Romans. Neither side possessed a clear tactical advantage in open battle unless they were able to fight in especially favourable conditions. As a result, pitched battles became rare, their result too uncertain to make the risk worthwhile, and there were to be no repeats of the stunning victories won by Shapur I over large Roman armies. Instead, warfare took the form of raiding, which offered a chance of profit and glory, and sieges, which were far harder but brought the chance of considerably greater and more permanent gains.[8]

Little is known of relations between Persia and Rome in the first decades of the fourth century. There is no evidence of major wars between them at this time, although raiding is possible and sometimes may have involved allies of each side acting more or less independently. Narses I was succeeded by his son Hormizd II, who ruled from 302 to 309. Following his death, one of his sons became king of kings, but he lasted less than a year before his cruelty aggravated enough of the nobility to depose him. Several of his siblings were killed or imprisoned during this coup, although one, also named Hormizd, managed to escape and found sanctuary with the Romans. The successful faction crowned an infant son of Hormizd II, Shapur II, as ruler, although real power rested with one or more regents for some time.[9]

As usual the power struggles within Persia are poorly documented, making them far harder to trace than those within the Roman empire. Constantine, son of one of the tetrarchs but not originally earmarked to join the imperial college, was proclaimed emperor by his army and spent much of his life fighting against Roman rivals. Famously, he attributed his victory at the Milvian Bridge outside Rome in 312 to the favour of the Christian God. During Constantine's long reign, Christianity ceased to be an illegal cult—periodically persecuted and forced into hiding—and openly became part of the fabric of the empire, with the emperor himself taking an interest in matters of doctrine. Constantine built and encouraged the building of churches, but he also endowed temples and made no move to suppress traditional, non-Christian beliefs. There is simply not enough evidence to estimate how many active Christians there were before Constantine embraced the faith, nor to what extent the numbers grew during his reign. At the very least, it was not politically damaging and was probably advantageous for Constantine to convert, which hints that there were rather more Christians or Christian sympathizers around than many scholars are apt to suggest. In a polytheistic culture, it is more than likely that many people revered the Christian God while continuing to follow older cults as well. One source claims that Severus Alexander added a statue of Jesus to the collection of deities especially important to him.[10]

Constantine was baptized in his last days, once he realized that he was dying, which was a common enough practice for those who feared sinning after undergoing the ceremony. If he had not quite made Christianity the official religion of the empire, this change was well under way by his death. At times, Constantine expressed concern for the welfare of Christians outside the empire, most of all those living under Sasanian rule. Later, the close identification between Christianity and the Roman empire created friction, with Persian Christians coming under suspicion of disloyalty. Constantine set officials to investigating the doctrines of Manichaeism, and probably other faiths such as Zoroastrianism, to learn whether adherents posed a threat to the empire. There is no evidence for systematic persecution as a result of this.

Near the end of his reign, Constantine began preparing for a major war against Persia, but this is unlikely to have been motivated by a desire to protect Christians living there. The alleged causes are unclear, and there is a good chance that foremost was a very traditional desire for the glory of defeating the greatest of all foreign states—a much cleaner glory than he had won fighting so successfully against fellow Romans. There was also a tradition that Constantine was encouraged by a charlatan named Metrodorus, who had returned to the empire after years successfully posing as a philosopher and miracle-worker in India. This individual brought the emperor a gift of gems but claimed that a far greater hoard had been sent overland by kings of India, only to be intercepted and confiscated by the Persians.[11]

Whatever the truth of Constantine's plans and motivations, he fell ill and died in May 337 before launching his Persian war. Power was supposed to be shared between his three remaining sons—the eldest had fallen from grace and been executed several years earlier—and two nephews, one of whom was named as king of Bithynia and Pontus rather than as an Augustus or Caesar. The arrangement did not suit Constantine's sons, who swiftly arrested and murdered their two cousins, and indeed all male relatives apart from two infant sons of their cousins. For a while the three brothers ruled as joint Augusti, until in 340 civil war broke out, leading to the death of the eldest. Ten years later, the youngest brother was overthrown and murdered by a conspiracy of his senior officers, and it took some time before the middle brother, Constantius II, was able to defeat the usurper who had replaced him in the west. Once this was done, he raised one of his cousin's sons to be Caesar, although this did not work out well, for this man was suspected of disloyalty and killed in 354. After a short rule as sole emperor, Constantius II appointed the remaining cousin's son, Julian, as Caesar in 355 and sent him to Gaul to secure the Rhine frontier. This permitted Constantius II to focus his attention on the Balkans and especially the east, where conflict with Persia was raging.

Shapur II had the longest reign of any Sasanian king—or indeed Roman emperor—being at least nominally king of kings from 309 to 379, albeit at first as an infant figurehead rather than actual ruler. By his late teens or early twenties, he began to throw off the controlling influence of guardians and rule in his own right, displaying both ambition and ability. He campaigned in Arabia, where Sasanian influence had been much diminished. Winning victories, Shapur II not only restored but expanded the Persian presence in the region. Later Arab sources remembered him for his might and as 'the piercer of shoulders' for his harsh treatment of prisoners.

Successful in these early campaigns, Shapur II turned his attention to Rome. One embassy revived old claims to the entire Achaemenid Persian empire, stretching all the way to Macedonia. More practically, the Persian envoy hinted that his monarch would be willing to settle for regaining the dominance in Armenia and ground in Mesopotamia lost in the treaty made with Galerius. This appears the key grievance, with a deep-seated belief that the terms had reflected temporary weakness rather than the actual balance of power between the two empires and that the agreement needed to change so that it reflected the true dignity and might of Persia. In this respect, the Persians followed the well-established pattern of asserting dominance.

Diplomatic exchanges were courteous but determined. 'I, Shapur, king of kings, partner of the stars, brother to the Sun and Moon, send many greetings to my brother Constantius' began one letter. It ended with an unambiguous threat to invade in the following spring, should 'his ambassadors return disappointed'. The Roman response was couched in similar terms. 'Victorious on land and sea, I, Constantius, Augustus forever, send many greetings to my brother Shapur.' However, the emperor refused to be intimidated and reminded the Persian that while the Romans sometimes— rarely—lost a battle, they never lost a war. In spite of this bluster, Constantius II sent envoys of his own to carry gifts and his desire for peace, not least because he had other problems elsewhere.[12]

This exchange occurred in 358, after a lull of several years between campaigns, but it reflects the high levels of courtesy already well-established in dealings between the two empires. This did not mean that either was less aggressive when it chose. In the decade or so before this particular exchange, the king of kings had led a succession of large expeditions into Roman Mesopotamia, only to discover that much had changed since the days of Shapur I. Constantine and especially Constantius II had continued the work of Diocletian, adding to the system of forts and supporting roads and strengthening the defences of cities on the main routes into the provinces. No longer was it the Romans' first instinct to muster as big a field army as could be gathered at short notice and then confront the invaders in the open. Only in 344 did Constantius II respond to the latest invasion by leading an army against it. The result was a confused encounter near Singara, with the Romans initially successful, driving back the Persians they encountered and overrunning their camp. However, as darkness fell and more Persians arrived, fortune shifted the other way, and in the heavy fighting during the night—something very rare in the ancient world—the Romans suffered far worse. Sources are poor and suggest a series of smaller engagements between sections of each army rather than a massed clash. Constantius II claimed a draw, or even a minor victory, although most Romans were inclined to see it as a setback. Sasanian views are not known. In the context of the campaign, it prompted a Roman withdrawal, but the losses inflicted were not sufficiently serious to prevent Constantius II from taking the field in strength in the future. However, as an emperor, he gained a reputation for caution and having more than his share of bad luck.[13]

Most of the time, neither side was willing to risk open battle in circumstances where the enemy was also willing to fight. From experience, both were nervous about succumbing to a surprise attack when the enemy was allowed to get close. Instead, Shapur II concentrated on besieging the main Roman strongholds. Singara fell at some point, although the Persians were unable to hold on to it. It was the furthest advanced and most exposed of the Romans' fortified cities, difficult for them to supply or reinforce when threatened by invaders. That made it vulnerable, but its very position tended to draw Persian attention, so that in a sense it served a useful purpose, delaying more than one Persian offensive long enough to give other strongholds valuable time to prepare.

Nisibis lay further back in the Roman province. It was still one of the more exposed positions, albeit one easier to supply and better protected by nature and human ingenuity. Shapur II attacked Nisibis no less than three times and failed on each occasion. This was not due to any lack of skill or determination. Each siege was mounted on a grand scale by a very large army led by the king of kings in person. Sources are meagre or so highly rhetorical that it is hard to separate fact from fiction and be sure about the details and even the dates of these campaigns. Nisibis was protected on two sides by rivers, and on more than one occasion the Persians are said to have dammed and diverted the water, whether to let engines mounted on ships approach the walls or to unleash a deluge and smash the walls down. Nisibis was a city with a large Christian population, and these devout believers, and especially their bishop, are said to have inspired the defenders—the bishop even being mistaken for the emperor in his dignity. Prayer was said to have increased the problems for the attackers—most notably with a plague of gnats, perhaps encouraged by the flooding, which tormented horses and elephants.[14]

The failure to capture Nisibis was in no sense a mark of poor siege-craft on the part of the Persians. All the evidence suggests that by this period there was no significant difference in the skill or methods used by Romans and Persians alike, whether to defend or attack a fortified city—yet another sign of just how well-matched and alike they had become militarily. In the past, the Romans had sometimes failed to capture a city, most obviously in Trajan's and Severus's attacks on Hatra, so the most advanced techniques had never guaranteed success. The difference now was that most cities were far better fortified than had previously been the case, shifting the balance significantly in favour of the defender. Even breaching the curtain wall did not guarantee success, and direct assault was often costly in lives and could and did fail. On each occasion, after months of toil and fighting, with the campaigning season running out, Shapur II decided that it was more prudent to abandon the siege of Nisibis for that year. Very large armies of the sort formed by the Persians for these attacks were inherently difficult to supply, swiftly consuming locally available food and fodder, which was little enough in the winter months. This meant that staying in one place for a considerable length of time was always a struggle, apart from the increased risk of disease. In similar circumstances the Romans faced the same problems and also struggled to deal with them. A siege might last for two or even three months but rarely any longer, with the attackers withdrawing if they had not taken the place within this time. Defenders were ordered to carry away, hide, or destroy crops and livestock in the path of an invasion to make the task as hard as possible for the invaders.[15]

The details and even the dates of the three attacks on Nisibis are uncertain. In due course, like so many Arsacid and Parthian monarchs, Shapur II went to the north-east of his empire to deal with urgently pressing threats. The most serious came from the Chionitae, the latest nomadic people in the long succession of those who had pushed into Bactria and Sogdiana (in modern Uzbekistan). These appear to have been Huns, although ethnic identity was fluid on the steppes, and there is a good chance that they had absorbed other communities as they migrated. The Kushano-Sasanian kingdom tried and largely failed to fight off these invaders, leaving the dynasty seriously weakened, although it is hard to say precisely when it disappeared. Shapur II was much more successful, forcing the Chionitae and other tribes to submit and become his allies, so that they supplied substantial contingents led by their own rulers for his next offensive against the Romans.[16]

Subsequent events are better attested than any other episode in the long struggle between Rome and its eastern neighbour, and this is overwhelmingly due to the survival of the relevant sections of Ammianus Marcellinus's history. Although supplemented by other Roman sources—with next to nothing from the Persian side—it is through Ammianus more than anyone else that we can describe the diplomacy and conflict between Constantius II, Julian, and Shapur II in far greater detail than is usually the case. Ammianus described himself as 'a soldier and a Greek', most likely from Antioch, although his duties and subsequent studies took him over large parts of the empire, and interestingly he chose to write in Latin.

Ammianus participated in several of the operations he describes and tends, for all his rhetorical flourishes, to provide a level of detail almost never found elsewhere. This is useful, although at the same time frustrating as we can never be sure whether the behaviour he describes was unique to his era or reflected practices at other periods as well. As with any source, care must be used, especially in his treatment of emperors and Roman senior commanders, some of whom he admired and some of whom he did not, let alone his descriptions of the Persian enemy, about whom he had less information. For all his interest in the past—and lost sections of his work covered the years from the murder of Domitian in 96—and strong identification with the Roman empire and its army, Ammianus does appear to have attempted to be fair and to explain how he understood events to occur. He describes the Romans and Persians as remarkably similar in the way they fought and in their ambitions.[17]

Before Shapur II returned from the east, the commander he had left in charge of the struggle with Rome planned a surprise attack, only to be thwarted when Persian deserters carried the news to the Romans. Subsequently a Roman senior officer named Antoninus, troubled by debt and beset by rivals, defected to the Persians, taking with him carefully gathered details of troop strengths and deployments in the provinces. Shapur II welcomed and rewarded him and, according to Ammianus, listened eagerly to his suggestions. The king of kings had decided to avoid yet another attempt at taking Nisibis and to follow a different route. Instead, Antoninus advised that he bypass the Roman strongholds and cross the Euphrates where the Romans least expected, so that the Persians could strike at the less heavily defended provinces of Syria. Ammianus was serving on the staff of Ursicinus, who until recently had been senior commander in the eastern provinces, the *magister equitum and peditum per Orientem*, one of the new grade of officers to appear by the fourth century. Posted away, and with some doubts raised over his loyalty, Ursicinus was sent back to the east late in 358 as it became clear that a major Persian offensive was brewing. However, command was divided with another general, a man dismissed by Ammianus for his sloth and incompetence. Whether or not this was fair, it probably reflected the opinion of Ursicinus, and the two men would not cooperate well.[18]

From the start the Romans were wrong-footed, not least because they expected Shapur II to advance on Nisibis. Instead, he followed the Tigris and sent ahead substantial cavalry columns to create confusion and make it harder for Roman patrols to work out what was happening. Refugees filled the roads, for the emperor's orders were for the countryfolk to take shelter in one of the walled cities. Ursicinus and his staff found 'a fine looking lad, about eight—so we judged—wearing a torc, weeping and abandoned in the middle of the road'. He had been left behind by his frightened mother in all the confusion. Out of kindness, spurred on by the boy's claim to be from a wealthy family, Ammianus was told to carry the lad to Nisibis on his horse. He rode fast, for there were signs of raiders everywhere, depositing the boy at a postern gate of the city before galloping away to rejoin his commander, whom he found near Amida, a city heavily fortified by Constantius II. Ammianus was then sent to the ruler of Corduene, a man educated in the Roman empire and sympathetic to Rome, although his state had largely returned to Persia's sphere of influence. The Roman officer was welcomed and given as much news as the Corduenes possessed. He claims to have seen the Persian host from a distance, and he learned that Shapur II was accompanied by the king of the Chionitae and the king of the Albani, among other allied rulers.[19]

According to Ammianus, the Persians intended to follow Antoninus's advice and make for the Euphrates and Syria, but they changed their plans when a report arrived that the water was too high for the army to ford the river—something that is possible, if uncommon, in the spring. The Romans were still uncertain about the enemy's plans, and Ursicinus and a small detachment making a reconnaissance were surprised by a larger force of Persian cavalry accompanied by Antoninus. On the verge of capture, the Romans fled, scattering in the process. Ammianus was one of a handful who managed to reach the refuge of Amida, spending much of the night half crushed in the crowd of fugitives pushing through the narrow ravine to reach safety, but was separated from Ursicinus and most of the others who eventually reached Melitene. Soon afterwards, Shapur and the main Persian force lumbered towards Amida.[20]

Amida occupied a strong position, protected by high ground and the river Tigris, and had its own spring to provide a constant supply of water. At the time of the siege, its garrison had expanded to include seven legions, some of them comitatenses, as well as a unit of archers and plenty of artillery. Perhaps this amounted to some five thousand to eight thousand soldiers, given the smaller size of legions in the fourth century compared to earlier. In addition, the city gave shelter to civilians from all over the wider area, and Ammianus claims that there were 120,000 of these, some able to fight, more of them able to offer labour, but all mouths to feed and bodies to be accommodated somewhere in the crowded houses and streets.[21]

Ammianus describes the sieges of these years as following a distinct sequence, and—presumably because of his own presence within the walls—recounts the events at Amida in greater detail than any other siege. It began with escalating levels of intimidation. Shapur II arrived, hoping that the sheer size of his army would dismay the defenders and persuade them to seek favourable terms of surrender. This was surely optimistic when facing a city as well-fortified and strongly garrisoned as Amida, and when the king of kings approached to summon the city, the Romans responded with bolt shooters mounted on the walls; one missile tore through Shapur II's cloak without harming more than his dignity. The next day, he sent King Grumbates of the Chionitae to make another attempt, and this time a bolt killed a prince, who was riding alongside his father. Seven days were spent in mourning, and the body was cremated on a pyre and the ashes gathered to take home—a custom of the tribe and a ritual alien to Zoroastrians, who exposed their dead.

The presence of the Chionitae and other allies was partly intended to confirm the loyalty of these former enemies to the king of kings, and this may explain why Grumbates had been sent to summon the city. However, the relationship worked both ways, and the overlord was expected to treat his subject allies with honour. In this case, it meant avenging the death of Grumbates's son. Ammianus claims that Shapur II had planned to bypass Amida if it refused to capitulate, sticking to Antoninus's plan to drive into Syria, but he was now obliged by honour and vengeance to capture and burn the city. This may or may not be true, since taking and destroying such a major fortress was an objective in itself. At the very least, the shooting of the prince of the Chionitae ensured that the siege was pressed with particular aggression and determination.

After a couple of days gathering food and supplies from the surrounding area, Shapur II had his entire army surround Amida, infantry formed five ranks deep, backed by cataphracts and elephants, all parading in silence. It gave the defenders a chance to count the vastly superior numbers of the enemy and sense their resolve. Dispersing for the night, the Persians and their allies reformed on the following day in exactly the same way and in the same unnerving silence, until Grumbates hurled a bloodstained spear—presumably one dipped in a sacrifice—against the walls, and the Persians at last advanced. Days of probing the defences followed, the Persians making best use of the very high proportion of archers in their ranks, while the Romans responded with their own bowmen, artillery, and, if anyone came close enough, stones and javelins thrown by hand. These exchanges confirmed that Amida's defences were formidable and unlikely to be rushed, so Shapur II's engineers began the task of planning siege-works and making or assembling prefabricated engines of their own. Although so far resisting, the city suffered from crowded conditions. This spawned an epidemic, which took many lives and left others weakened until, after ten days, a spate of heavy rain seemed to bring it to an end.

The Persians continued to press the defenders, edging ever closer to the walls, with their archers protected by mobile shields or mantlets, and gaining the space to construct ramps and assault mounds which would allow mobile siege towers to reach the wall and support the attack. Such towers mounted rams to begin pounding the wall, but they needed a stable path to reach it. Their height ideally also allowed archers and light artillery on the top to shoot down at the defenders on the wall. Similarly, mounds built by the besiegers were designed to be higher than the curtain wall to make the defenders vulnerable to missiles. As a response, the Romans toiled on a mound of their own, like the one at Dura-Europos, intended to strengthen the main wall as a buttress but also to make sure that their mound was higher than the ones built by the enemy, so that they would keep their advantage in the missile exchange.

Day after day, the two sides shot at each other and laboured at the siege-works. Casualties in this type of fighting tended to be relatively low and overwhelmingly involved men wounded rather than killed, but they helped to wear down the strength and stamina of the outnumbered defenders, whereas the attackers could rotate men in and out of the fighting. The Romans had mounted a few sallies early on, and Ammianus described the frustration of two legions raised in Gaul, originally by a rival to Constantius II, who had sent them to the east where they had fewer connections. These were comitatenses, more accustomed to a very different style of fighting against the Germanic tribes from beyond the Rhine, which meant that they had little skill or patience in the attritional siege warfare of the eastern frontier.

As the siege-works progressed, a deserter from inside Amida revealed the existence of a tunnel and permitted some seventy Persian archers to infiltrate the city and seize a tower. However, the Romans reacted swiftly, cordoning off the area and shifting heavy artillery to batter the archers into submission. All were killed or taken before they had provided sufficient distraction to weaken the defence of the main walls. This success encouraged the defenders, until morale dipped once again as the Persians paraded in front of the walls captives taken from smaller Roman strongholds they had managed to overrun. In an effort to revive spirits by giving the defenders a fresh victory, the two legions from Gaul were allowed to launch a major sally under cover of darkness. The main objectives were to damage the siege-works, thus delaying their progress, or to kill Shapur II himself. Neither was achieved, and the Romans suffered heavy losses even though they inflicted more on the Persians and caused considerable confusion in their camp. There was a lull for several days as the besiegers mourned their dead, which included a number of noblemen, but to set against this, the Romans decided that they could not afford to risk any more sorties.

After that, the Persians pressed the attack much more closely, accepting losses as they edged nearer to the walls and completed their ramps and mounds. By now, their siege towers were close enough to permit the bolt shooters mounted on top of them to strike defenders on the rampart. Once again, while the Romans probably inflicted heavier losses on the besiegers than they suffered in return, in the longer run the cost to the defenders was more severe, since they were so heavily outnumbered. The next day, the Persians pressed ever closer, inspired by the king of kings in person, riding around and urging his men on. Yet the Roman response remained fierce, and as the two assault towers were pushed towards the wall, they were smashed to pieces by the defenders' artillery.* The first all-out Persian assault was repulsed in a day of heavy fighting. Sadly for the Romans, their defensive mound, built

---

*At some point, the Romans had added the single-armed onager—known in the Middle Ages as the mangonel—to their armoury. These were more difficult to aim but threw a very heavy stone with considerable force. Interestingly, Ammianus notes that they were known to the soldiers as 'scorpions', a nickname which in earlier periods had been applied to the light bolt shooters capable of driving a bolt through any armour.

in haste to prevent the Persians gaining a height advantage, collapsed during the night. Most of the earth fell forward, covering the main wall and to all intents and purposes creating a wide ramp across it for the Persians to use. Still defiant, the Romans formed in close order to meet the enemy charge, but the final result was no longer in doubt, and, after heavy fighting, Amida was stormed by the Persians on the seventy-third day of the siege. Ammianus was among those who managed to escape in the chaos.[22]

The loss of Amida was a major blow to the Romans and to Constantius II personally, since he had turned the place into a fortress. It was also embarrassing that Ursicinus and his colleague had made no real effort to harass the besiegers, let alone relieve the city. Perhaps if the Romans' mound had not collapsed, the defenders might have managed to hold out. Summer was almost spent, and the approach of autumn and his heavy losses—Ammianus claimed these totalled some thirty thousand, but that is probably a considerable exaggeration—persuaded Shapur II to withdraw soon afterwards. Amida was sacked and burned, even more damage done to its fortifications, before it was abandoned by the Persians. This was a significant Persian victory, even if it had taken great effort and a good deal of time. Ammianus claimed that the siege had deflected the Persians from their true objective and then used up the campaigning season, preventing them from doing anything else that year. Even so, he did not try to hide the truth that this was a Roman defeat.

In 360, Shapur II returned to Mesopotamia and from the start appears to have focused on capturing strongholds rather than making an effort to go round them and attack into Syria, as Antoninus is still supposed to have urged. Such a plan was surely riskier than Ammianus suggests, since it would have meant leaving the bypassed garrisons in his rear, while taking fortresses offered longer-term gain. Singara fell, yet again, after a full-scale siege, with the Persians employing a particularly large and well-protected battering ram. This was directed at the same spot breached by the Persians in their last attack, which reminds us that these fortresses changed hands on numerous occasions. Major repair work tended to show clearly on a wall, making it easier to target, and a breach was made quickly and the city stormed. Survivors were sent as prisoners for settlement in Persia.[23]

No help had come from the Romans during the siege, for the bulk of units available for a field force remained watching Nisibis, once again having mistaken the Persians' intention. Shapur II moved next against Bezabde, near the Tigris, although its precise location is unknown. Garrisoned by three legions and some archers, the city was attacked in the familiar style. Once again, Shapur II was narrowly missed by a missile when he rode up to invite the defenders to surrender; after this incident, his envoys used captives from Singara as human shields whenever they approached the walls. The defenders proved resolute, so there were the same phases of demonstrations of strength, then skirmishing and missile barrages, and then proper siege-works to bring engines against the wall. In the end, a breach was made and the city stormed after heavy fighting, which led to a particularly brutal sack by the enraged stormers. This time, Shapur II decided to hold on to the city, providing a garrison and bringing in a population from his empire to replace those taken prisoner and transplanted. After this second success, he moved against a third city, but this time the siege failed, and with the autumn approaching, the Persians withdrew.[24]

At the end of 360, Constantius II was sufficiently free from other crises to devote personal attention to the struggle with Persia. There were worries that the king of Armenia might be drifting closer to Shapur II, in spite of his Arsacid blood, prompting a diplomatic offensive which included the marriage of a high-born Roman lady to the allied monarch. The king of Iberia also received encouragement and bribes to maintain his loyalty. After a while, the Augustus toured the scenes of recent operations, weeping at the sight of Amida in ruins. Anticipating a fresh Persian offensive, the Romans waited to meet it for most of the summer, and only as the campaign season was drawing to a close did Constantius II lead an army against Bezabde. Its defenders spurned the usual appeals to surrender and were unimpressed by displays of force, so the full-scale siege began, the Romans even using a battering ram that had been left behind by Shapur I's army after one of its invasions a century ago. All the Romans' efforts failed and, as autumn turned into winter, heavy rain drenched the siege-works and eventually persuaded Constantius II to withdraw. Bad news soon came from Gaul, where Julian had been proclaimed as Augustus by his soldiers.[25]

As the campaigning season approached in 361, Constantius II waited in the east, for there was news that Shapur II had massed another army near the border. Yet the Persians waited and did not attack and eventually dispersed, according to Ammianus because the omens were too unfavourable to risk a war. Once he was sure that the immediate threat was over, Constantius II moved against his relative and rival but fell ill and died before he could confront him. Lacking another heir, in his final days the dying emperor supported Julian's claim, and once again the Roman empire had just a single emperor.[26]

Julian was thirty years old, a small, not especially prepossessing man with a straggly, unkempt beard. A small child when most of the male members of his family were liquidated by Constantius II and his brothers, he had been raised in comfortable and very Christian captivity. Understandable resentment at the ruthlessness of his supposedly pious relations brought on a bitter—though at first concealed—rejection of their faith. Instead, he devised his own pagan religion, although plans for a structured organization suggest that his thinking was heavily influenced by his upbringing within the church. Julian was a clever man who had spent too much of his life frightened and unable to converse freely with others, so that he naturally assumed that his own inner thoughts and desires were always the right ones, shared by all good people. Perhaps to the surprise of many, he proved active and reasonably competent when appointed as Caesar, winning a major battle at Strasbourg in 357 and doing well in other operations, albeit all waged on a fairly modest scale. Ammianus greatly admired Julian—and not simply because he, too, was a pagan—but was also aware of his faults. Sole ruler for less than three years, Julian is better known to us because of Ammianus and also because many of the emperor's copious writings have survived. Yet his legacy was highly controversial, making a balanced assessment difficult and making it easy to forget that his rule was brief and did not change the empire's culture, beliefs, or structure in any significant way. Ultimately, Julian's memory became bound up with his decision to attack Persia in 363.[27]

Julian's true motives—like those of so many earlier emperors and kings—are as uncertain as the scale of his ambition. Constantius II was blamed for his mediocre, rather passive performance in the last few years, losing fortresses to the Persians, although in truth Shapur II's permanent gains were limited and fell far short of his ambition to recover ground and influence lost in 299. In its implementation, Julian's expedition was traditional, marching down the Euphrates to Ctesiphon, something no Roman army had attempted since Carus eighty years before. As traditional was the talk of even greater plans and the invocation of Alexander the Great. Julian had a romantic passion for the past and especially the heroes who best fitted his conception of a Greek and pagan ideal. At one point during the campaign, he and his companions consciously emulated the heroism of Scipio Aemilianus at the siege of Carthage in 146 BC. Such play-acting need not necessarily exclude plans and decisions based on more rational consideration, and in some ways the incident was within the range of acceptable and admirable conduct by a Roman—or indeed Persian—commander. Julian may have dreamed of being a new Scipio or a new Alexander, as so many other Romans had done, while still basing his strategy on more modest principles, or he may have let his romantic view of the past drive his decisions. Although nothing is mentioned directly, the exiled Hormizd, brother or half-brother of Shapur II, served as one of Julian's senior commanders, which makes it quite possible that the aim was to dethrone one king of kings and replace him with a man who had spent decades in Roman service.[28]

Our sources, knowing the outcome, focus on bad omens at the start of the campaign, including two accidents where buildings or piled stores collapsed to kill soldiers standing underneath. The force assembled for the expedition was substantial, probably more than had mustered for an eastern campaign for generations. Ammianus, who was part of the army, never gives a figure for its overall numbers, although he does mention a detached force of thirty thousand troops and claims some twenty thousand were needed to manage the fleet that carried supplies and equipment upriver. A later source says Julian had sixty-five thousand men in his field army. If these figures are remotely accurate in scale, then the expedition dwarfed anything he had done in Gaul, where rapid movement and boldness tended to pay off, not least because the enemy had no real fortifications requiring a formal siege. Julian had no experience of handling and planning at this level or in this region, and this was surely true of almost all of his senior officers, since nothing like this had been attempted for so long.[29]

There are also signs of political naivety and inexperience, most notably when Julian alienated the population of Antioch and then responded by mocking them in a pamphlet. Although he had concealed it during the struggle with Constantius II for fear of upsetting substantial numbers of his soldiers, once sole Augustus, Julian made plain his rejection of Christianity and his adoption of his distinct form of paganism. If it had made political sense for Constantine to adopt the new faith—and he may well have been sincere, whatever calculations he made—more than a generation ago, then it made far less to abandon it now. Nor was there a huge surge of enthusiasm on the part of all pagans for the emperor's unusual ideas. That does not mean that morale was low in all groups within the army, but much would depend on how the campaign went. In many ways, it offered the chance for Julian to prove himself and assert his right to rule by winning glory against a foreign enemy, something all Romans readily admired.[30]

Julian hoped to surprise the Persians, and a diversionary force, backed by Armenian allies, was to demonstrate and threaten in Mesopotamia, where all recent campaigns had been fought. To an extent it worked, just as the Romans had mistakenly concentrated on protecting Nisibis because that was where they had expected Shapur II to fight. In the meantime, Julian followed the line of the Euphrates, and his men passed the forlorn ruins of Dura-Europos—or perhaps a suburb on the left bank—and saw from afar the grand monument to Gordian III. There was little opposition at first, although the Persians did their best to destroy any crops or other useful resources that could not be carried away, just as the Romans had done in response to Sasanian attacks. Several walled towns and strongholds lay in the path of the army, which meant the familiar pattern of demands for surrender, escalating intimidation in the hope of convincing the defenders to give in, and then stages of attack building up to a final assault if necessary. Julian aped Scipio, and at another siege was almost killed when he and a handful of his staff were ambushed during a reconnaissance. The Augustus is supposed to have cut one Persian down before his officers surrounded him. Julian certainly took risks—arguably unnecessary, even foolhardy ones—but on the whole the operations were successful, and no single siege bogged down the advance for too long.[31]

Within a month, the Romans approached Ctesiphon, which was far larger and better fortified than anything encountered so far, and at this point Julian's decision-making became hard to understand, even for contemporaries. There was no sign of the diversionary army, assuming that it was supposed to rendezvous with the main force. Persian strength was growing, with the prospect that Shapur II himself might appear before too long with the bulk of the royal army. In addition, the defenders continued their scorched-earth strategy. Irrigation systems extending out from the river had created a network of canals, each of them an obstacle to an army, which had to find or make a suitable crossing point and file across. The promotion of such projects by the Sasanians may have meant that the route was harder for a big army to traverse than it had been in the days of Trajan, Verus, or Severus. This was increased by the willingness of the Persians to break down dams and otherwise destroy the system so that flooding slowed the Romans down even more.

After some dithering, Julian decided that a siege of Ctesiphon was impractical and chose instead to retreat. Rather than go back the way he had come, he ordered the army to march back along the Tigris. His supply fleet was set on fire, since it was felt too difficult to shift the barges and contents overland to the other great river. Then Julian changed his mind, countermanding the order, but by then it was too late. The episode was a serious blow to morale—and deprived the army of supplies. Julian does not seem to have been good at reading the mood of his troops on this and other occasions, and throughout history spirits have tended to sink when an advance turns into a retreat. Substantial forces of Persians began to threaten the Romans, although their movements were equally restricted by irrigation canals. The Roman army marched, as Romans armies had marched in the past, harassed but fully capable of going where they chose and driving off any heavy attack.

On 26 June 363, there was a succession of harassing strikes at different parts of the Roman column. Julian, whose personal courage was never in doubt, rode off to help organize the response in such haste that he did not bother to don a cuirass. In the midst of a whirling skirmish, made all the more confusing by the dust thrown up by the hoofs of so many horses, an Arab ally of the Persians drove his spear into the Augustus. The emperor was carried back to his tent and doctors summoned, but it was obvious that the wound was mortal. He died later that night, apparently calm and discussing philosophy with his intimates rather than the army's situation.[32]

The Roman army had lost its leader and was still deep in hostile territory. After some discussion and bartering, a man named Jovian, a protector, was proclaimed Augustus because the army and empire needed a ruler. He was a Christian, and Julian's plans for a new organized religion were immediately forgotten. There was a moment of farce when Jovian, who was unusually tall, had to wear one of the diminutive Julian's purple cloaks. Another was not available, since possession of a garment reserved for emperors was not safe in the suspicious political climate of the fourth century. Jovian took command and there was more fighting, but he was eager to secure his rule and did not want to risk a disaster. Shapur II sensed an opportunity and was equally averse to a decisive battle which might go either way and destroy his advantage. Instead, the king of kings achieved far more by negotiation than he had ever managed by invasion. In a reverse of 299, for now it was the Romans who were desperate for peace, Jovian promised that Rome would no longer intervene in Armenia. He also conceded parts of Mesopotamia, including the city of Singara. Most humiliating of all, Nisibis, the city that had thwarted Shapur II on three

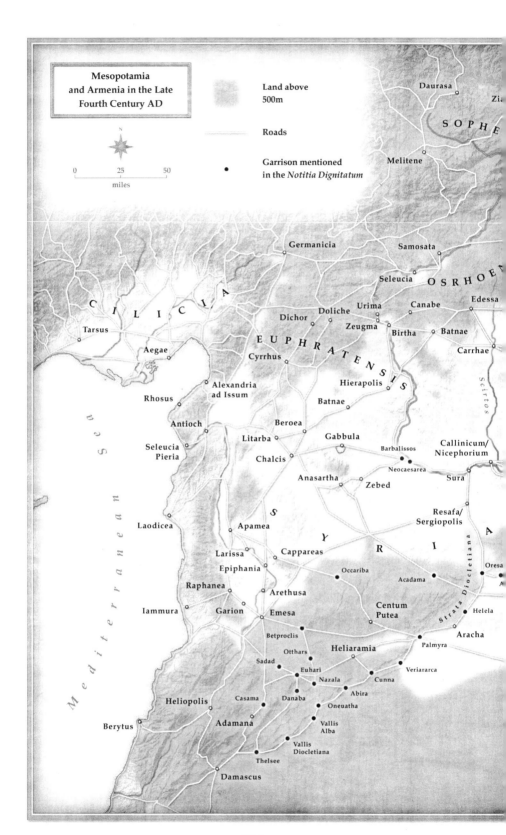

Mesopotamia
and Armenia in the Late
Fourth Century AD

Land above
500m

Roads

Garrison mentioned
in the *Notitia Dignitatum*

N

0   25   50
miles

Daurasa

Zi

S O P H E

Melitene

Germanicia

Samosata

Seleucia   O S R H O E

C I L I C I A

Tarsus

Dichor   Doliche   Urima   Canabe   Edessa

Zeugma   Birtha   Batnae

Aegae

Cyrrhus   E U P H R A T E N S I S

Carrhae

Scirtos

Alexandria
ad Issum

Hierapolis

Rhosus

Batnae

Antioch

Beroea

Litarba

Gabbula

Callinicum/
Nicephorium

Seleucia
Pieria

Barbalissos

Chalcis

Neocaesarea

Anasartha

Zebed

Sura

Resafa/
Sergiopolis

Laodicea

Apamea

S

A

Larissa

Cappareas

Y

R

I

Oresa

Epiphania

Occariba

Acadama

Strata Diocletiana

Raphanea

Arethusa

Iammura

Garion

Emesa

Centum
Putea

Helela

Betproclis

Aracha

Otthars

Heliaramia

Palmyra

Sadad

Euhari

Veriararca

Nazala

Cunna

Heliopolis

Casama

Danaba

Abira

Oneuatha

Berytus

Adamana

Vallis
Alba

Vallis
Diocletiana

Thelsee

Damascus

M e d i t e r r a n e a n   S e a

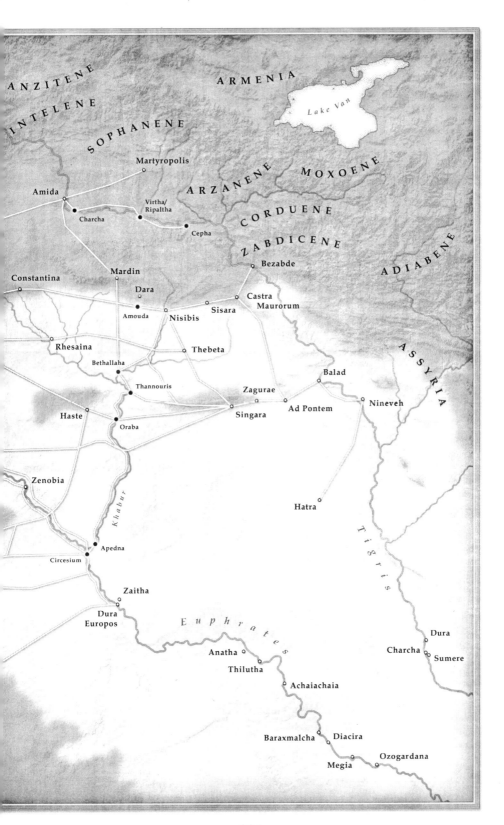

occasions, was handed over to the Persians. Its population, predominantly Christian, were allowed to leave with their portable possessions, which only added to the pathos and bitterness. Jovian was dead within a few months, perhaps from disease or accident, and the main blame fell on Julian's memory. He had attacked Persia hoping for glory, only to fail utterly and die a pointless death. Some Christians felt this was punishment for his rejection of their faith, and they even spread rumours that one of his own soldiers, a believer, had struck the fatal blow. While pagans like Ammianus did not accept such an explanation, they were equally saddened and distressed by the outcome of the war.[33]

Julian's expedition had been a disaster. For all the humiliation of the subsequent peace, the actual amount of territory given to the Sasanians was modest, even if of local strategic importance. Roman power remained considerable, especially during any prolonged interval from civil war, but the dangers inherent in a deep invasion of Persian territory and the difficulty of achieving anything tangible during such an expedition had been demonstrated very clearly. No emperor proved in a hurry to emulate Julian for a long while. At the same time, the ability of a Roman army to reach Ctesiphon and the other royal cities reminded the Sasanians of Rome's might. It had not been easy for them to repulse Julian. The risks of war were becoming more obvious, which did not mean that it was easy to break the cycle of mistrust and revenge, even when emperors and kings of kings would have preferred to concentrate on other problems.

14

THE TWO EYES OF THE WORLD

FIFTH CENTURY

By THE LATER FOURTH CENTURY, THE COSTS AND RISKS OF WAG-
ing war against each other tended to outweigh the likely benefits
for the Romans and Sasanians alike. Yet appearances and perceptions mattered, and it was vital for a Roman emperor to assert
Rome's superiority over every other nation and power, and for the
king of kings to proclaim a comparable superiority over all his
neighbours, including the Romans. This meant that considerable
care was required in how any peace treaty could be presented.
After more than a century of frequent warfare, it took time to create a workable system of etiquette for negotiations and agreement,
but over time this would lead to significant changes in the way the
relationship was presented.

Almost in passing, Ammianus Marcellinus mentioned that the
treaty negotiated between Jovian and Shapur II in 363 included a
declaration of a thirty-year peace between Romans and Persians.
The idea of a set period without hostilities was a very old one and
had been especially common in Classical Greece. Occasionally,
both sides lived up to their promise and the period passed without
a fresh war and sometimes even continued after that without formal renewal. Rather more often, one of the participants decided to

reopen hostilities long before the agreed peace had expired; there was almost always some real or imagined grudge, good enough by contemporary standards to justify violating the treaty. Thus, anyone agreeing to so many years of peace knew from the start that the odds were against fulfilment, and no one worried too much because it was simply part of how diplomacy worked and, like most protestations of friendship, not to be taken too seriously if circumstances changed.[1]

For many centuries, at least from the era of the Punic Wars, Roman attitudes had been different, expecting a more permanent conclusion to warfare. When Hannibal was defeated, Carthage was forced to make an annual payment to Rome for the next fifty years. Later, a Carthaginian offer of full repayment in one lump sum was refused, for this was meant as a reminder of defeat and subordination rather than valued for the money itself. It was no coincidence that the payment was completed in 151 BC, and just two years later Rome provoked the Third Punic War and destroyed its old rival.[2]

Carthage was an exception, for its sheer size and power and for the scale and cost of the conflicts waged against it. Plenty of other defeated enemies were obliged to pay the Romans in the aftermath of a war, whether a lump sum or ongoing payments. The latter tended to be a permanent obligation rather than for a set period of time, for the essential characteristic of these treaties was that they were not between equals, nor were they intended to be temporary cessations of hostilities. Rome had won, giving yet more proof of its inherent superiority, as once again the proud had been overcome in war, so that the humbled could be treated with leniency. Terms were supposed to be dictated by the Romans, who deigned to accept the submission of the vanquished, so that there was no point in setting a limit to peaceful relations. These would continue as long as the Romans decided that the other party was suitably submissive. If they were not, then force would be threatened or actually employed whenever it was convenient for the Romans. Roman victory, however long it took, was the natural outcome of any confrontation with another people or state.

Diplomacy was always couched in these terms, whether it was Sulla sitting in the centre between the king and the envoy or, more obviously, Pompey and Trajan having kings prostrate or bow in front of them before deciding whether to 'give' them back their kingdoms. Pomp and ceremony, not least parades of soldiers and massed standards, provided a backdrop representing the immense and unmatchable might of Rome, and most often the emperor or his representative sat on a raised platform. Any courtesy shown to the other side, and usually there was plenty on display, was a mark of condescension rather than necessity, and appropriate to the dignity of the Roman. In 375, the emperor Valentinian harangued the ambassadors of the Germanic Quadi at such length and with such passion that he had a stroke and died. While the rage was seen as excessive if characteristic of the man, no Roman doubted his right to speak to barbarians in this way.[3]

This makes the acceptance of a formally announced period of peace between Rome and Persia all the more striking. Since at least the time of Augustus, Arsacid Parthia and then Sasanian Persia had never quite fitted this traditional Roman image of foreign relations, just as Carthage, and to some extent the Macedonian and Seleucid kingdoms, had once been too large and powerful to be included with all the other foreign states. Distance helped to some extent, allowing Augustus or Nero in Rome to portray negotiations with considerable give and take on both sides as simple proof of Roman dominance. No one living in Rome, or indeed in most of the empire, was too worried about the reality of whether Roman might was in truth so overwhelmingly superior to its eastern neighbour. An identical attitude is on display in Shapur I's victory monuments, where he presents himself as king of all the peoples of the world and successive emperors as no more than liars who go very properly down in humiliating defeat, for that was simply the natural order of things. In his own heartland, just as in Rome, a leader's message could be simple.

By 363, when the two sides met in any formal way, the language and posturing was a good deal more subtle. The threats of force and protestations of utter confidence in their own military superiority continued. After all, Julian had just marched all the way to Ctesiphon, while as the talks began the Roman army was in a precarious position—although if Ammianus is to be believed, the Romans were still confident in their ability to defeat the enemy in a straight fight. Yet there was also a good deal more courtesy on both sides, something even more true when negotiations occurred in peaceful times. Just when the king of kings and Roman emperor began to address each other as brother is uncertain, but it appears to have been unremarkable by Ammianus's day and probably goes back at least to the late third century.

While it was not wholly new to portray the empires as well as the emperors as equals—after the manner of Velleius Paterculus and Justin—this sense had grown much stronger. A sixth-century source claims that Narses I sent a trusted advisor to Galerius around 299. This man compared the Roman and Persian empires to two lamps; like eyes, 'each one should be adorned by the brightness of the other', rather than seeking to destroy. The imagery may be genuine, for near the end of the sixth century a king of kings sent a letter to the emperor stating that it was the divine plan that 'the whole world should be illuminated . . . by two eyes, namely by the most powerful kingdom of the Romans and by the most prudent sceptre of the Persian state', who between them held down the wild tribes and guided and regulated mankind.[4]

The wheels of diplomacy have always been oiled by flattery, exaggeration, distortion, and straightforward falsehoods whenever convenient to one or both sides, so such blandishments need not be taken too seriously. Yet they reflect a greater willingness to acknowledge something like equality. Part of this was the cost to both sides of the intensive round of major wars lasting from the days of Ardashir I through to Shapur II. After all that effort, the rivals could show limited concrete gains, while each side had plenty of other threats to face. As they became more alike in the way they waged war, over time, especially in the century or so after the death of Julian, they also became much more closely balanced in terms of military strength and resources.

For all the novelty of a thirty-year peace, it broke down after barely six years. As so often in the past, the flashpoint was

Armenia. Shapur II overran much of the kingdom, captured the Arsacid king by treachery and, according to Ammianus, had him blinded and then tortured to death. Jovian had pledged not to support the Armenian king, but it is less clear whether Shapur II's actions were in violation of the treaty. Perhaps Persian and Roman interpretations of its details and spirit were different from the start or changed as time passed, especially for the Romans, who were no longer led by a newly proclaimed Jovian desperate to extricate his army. However, around the same time, the Sasanians also intervened in neighbouring Iberia, dethroning its king, who was a Roman ally, and this most certainly broke the peace. Then the Armenian king's son Pap escaped to Roman territory, appealing for aid.[5]

Two brothers jointly ruled the Roman empire at this time, for when Jovian died his only son was an infant, incapable of rule. Instead, an army officer named Valentinian was proclaimed as Augustus on 26 February 364 and swiftly appointed his brother Valens as colleague. At first they were busy elsewhere, but in 370 Valens came to Antioch and began making visible preparations for an offensive against Persia. There was little if any fighting on this front, and one source claims that negotiations led to the declaration of a seven-year peace. Armenia remained the real focus, where Roman troops were directly involved and clashed with Persian forces, even if most of the fighting was done by the allies of each side. Pap was placed back in control of some of Armenia, although to follow the letter rather than the spirit of the treaty he was not proclaimed king and did not don the diadem or other royal regalia. The restoration of the king of Iberia by another Roman army was done more openly. Shapur II attacked again but failed to achieve very much and may have suffered one or more defeats before both sides withdrew. In the years that followed, Pap struggled to control his kingdom and placate his powerful neighbours. Shapur II had tried to win him over early on or perhaps, as Ammianus alleged, wanted to make the Romans mistrust the young ruler. In the long run, Valens did become suspicious, encouraged by members of his court who held personal grudges against Pap. Summoned to the imperial presence, Pap managed to avoid arrest and escaped, only to be murdered on Roman orders with the connivance of some dis-gruntled Armenian noblemen.[6]

Valens appointed a new Armenian king, this time openly and in spite of diplomatic and military pressure from the Persians, led by the current Surena—a reminder that the old Parthian noble houses continued to flourish under the Sasanians. Roman prepara-tions for a major campaign were interrupted in 375 when Valens's attention switched to the Balkans and he left Antioch, never to return. Armenia remained turbulent as a rival emerged to chal-lenge the Roman appointee, and the Surena led an army into the country to support this man. In time, the traditional fractiousness of Armenia's aristocracy ensured that opposition to the Sasanians grew, and eventually even the man Surena had backed turned against him. Controlling Armenia was never easy for anyone. In 378, Valens sent ambassadors to discuss the situation with Shapur II, but their mission was overtaken by events.

Valentinian collapsed and died in November 375 in the mid-dle of haranguing the chieftains of the Quadi. His sixteen-year-old son, Gratian, had already been named as Augustus, giving the em-pire three rulers. With his father dead, this number dropped to two, then went back to three as army officers on the European frontier proclaimed Gratian's four-year-old brother, Valentinian II, as emperor. This was accepted, at least for the moment, and the child was given Africa and Italy to govern through his adult advi-sors, while Gratian took the rest of the west and Valens the east. The latter's first priority was to deal with a large-scale migration by a group of Goths, who had arrived on the Danube asking for admission to the empire and the grant of lands within it. They had been driven from their homeland directly or indirectly by the ar-rival of the Huns. Advised that these Germanic tribesmen could prove a valuable source of recruits for the army, Valens agreed to their petition, but in the months that followed the military and civilian officials tasked with bringing them into the empire badly mishandled the job. Through a mixture of corruption and incom-petence, the Goths were provoked into rebellion. In 376, fighting broke out, and a Roman commander decided to attack the mi-grants' camp and was ambushed and his men cut to pieces. A year later, another large Roman force attacked, only to withdraw after indecisive fighting. In 378, Valens went in person with the cream of the army of the eastern empire to defeat the Goths or convince them to submit. The ensuing Battle of Adrianople on 9 August 378 was an appalling disaster, which left the emperor dead along with the greater part of his army.[7]

In 379, Gratian appointed an officer named Theodosius as imperial colleague whose priority was to deal with the Goths. This took time and was achieved more by harassing them and wearing them down, after another pitched battle had ended in Roman defeat. Fortunately for the Romans, the enemy had neither the patience nor skill to take fortified cities; their leader declared after one failed attempt that he would 'keep peace with walls'. The Goths had nowhere to go and lacked the numbers to fight the Roman empire indefinitely, let alone win a war against it. In 382, a peace was agreed, with the Goths given land for settlement and pledging to serve as soldiers for Rome, albeit mainly in their own contingents and under their own leaders. A year later, an emperor was proclaimed in Britain, and Gratian died after most of his troops had defected to the usurper, Magnus Maximus. (It is a sign of how times and culture had changed that the name means Great the Greatest, something meaningless under the republic or principate.) By 387 Italy was his, but this prompted a response from Theodosius, who marched west, beat Maximus, and had him executed. A substantial contingent of Goths served in the victorious army. Valentinian II was left in charge of the western empire but was little more than a puppet of ambitious senior officers, and he died—perhaps from suicide, perhaps murder—in 392, aged just twenty-one. A usurper was raised to the imperial purple, and, after a lull, Theodosius mustered a strong army from the eastern provinces and defeated the challenger in 394 at the river Frigidus. Once again, the Goths played a conspicuous part in the success.[8]

Theodosius died in 395, leaving the empire in the charge of his two teenage sons, Arcadius in the east and Honorius in the west. These decades are poorly documented, not least because Ammianus Marcellinus ended his account in the aftermath of Adrianople, making it difficult to trace the relationship between Romans and

Persians. Shapur II died of natural causes in 379, having been king of kings for seventy years and a strong and successful ruler from the time he reached adulthood. Succession was always a difficult time, perhaps especially when the old monarch had been so formidable and lived so long. Ardashir II is said by some sources to have been Shapur II's brother, which seems unlikely since it would have meant that he became king as an old man. Perhaps he was a son, or some other relative, but either way he was deposed by a group of nobles four years later. Shapur III, a son of Shapur II, proved more popular with the aristocracy and was fondly remembered in later tradition, although his reign lasted only a little longer. He was murdered or perhaps the victim of an accident when a heavy tent collapsed on top of him. Bahrām IV was elevated from regional king to king of kings and ruled for eleven years before he was assassinated in 399.[9]

This was a confused period for Romans and Persians alike, with internal threats and problems on other frontiers drawing attention and resources away from Armenia and the rivalry between the two empires. The Goths were a major concern, especially for the emperor supervising the east, although at times troops and other resources from western provinces were also used to support the war effort. In spite of this, it took six years to bring the situation under some sort of control. During that time, of the four major battles fought against the migrants, the Romans lost three of them and managed no better than a draw in the fourth. Rome remained powerful, bound to win in the end, but it struggled to employ its wealth, sophisticated military, and logistic organization efficiently. Resources were stretched and not always well-managed.

Similar factors surely helped the rise of Queen Mavia, widow of one of the kings of the Arab groups living near the southern frontier in Syria and Palestine. Little is known about this intriguing figure, so that the reasons for her sudden hostility to Rome are mysterious. Faith played a part, for Valens was an Arian Christian, while Mavia held to more orthodox views about the nature of the Trinity, but this may have combined with political grievances. From around 376, as Valens transferred his attention to the Danube, she launched a series of attacks. Apparently leading her

army in person, Mavia raided into the Roman provinces, plundering villages and cities and brushing aside or avoiding any troops
who came against them. This was an area that had seen little warfare for some time, and, away from the main front line with Persia,
was less well-defended once past the outer line of forts. Eventually
the Romans persuaded Mavia to accept a peace and revert to being an ally. As part of the deal, she was sent an orthodox bishop to
tend to the spiritual needs of her people.[10]

The contest for Armenia continued for some time, although the
details are largely lost. In 387, the Romans and Sasanians agreed
to permanent partition of the kingdom, with some 80 percent going to the Persians. The remaining fifth was ruled for a while by
an allied king from the Arsacid line, until it was taken under direct
administration and treated as a Roman province. Similarly, in due
course the Sasanians replaced a local king with one chosen from
their own family. The earlier split of Iberia into two was revived,
all of which suggests that the Persians had greater influence for
the moment, if falling short of complete dominance. The disruption caused by competition between the two empires and rivalries
within the kingdoms may have contributed to events a few years
later, when in 395 a large band of Huns came through the passes
in the Caucasus. These were not Attila's people but one of a succession of nomadic groups to be drawn towards the two great
empires. Another band followed, or the same ones returned a few
years later, and each time they passed through Armenia and raided
into the Roman provinces and then parts of the Sasanian empire.
Like Queen Mavia, they struck at areas which had seen little or
no warfare for generations, and the raiders roamed almost at will.
Thousands of prisoners were taken as slaves, although some were
later rescued and those still fit enough sent home when a Persian
force defeated some of the Huns in Babylonia. However much real
damage and loss was inflicted, the trauma of this episode endured
for a very long time.[11]

In 399, Shapur III's son Yazdgerd I became king of kings and
would prove to be a strong ruler, wherever possible eager for peaceful relations with the Romans. At the start he was an unknown
quantity, but as time passed and he did not prove aggressive, there

was no doubt great relief. Neither of Theodosius's sons managed to assert themselves strongly, so they were figureheads while real power passed into the hands of senior courtiers, sometimes civilians in the east but usually generals in the west. These were kept busy outmanoeuvring rivals and dealing with the ever-present threat of usurpers from within and raids and invasions from outside the empire. In 396, the Goths under the leadership of Alaric felt discontented with their treatment by the authorities and began to plunder, and they became a major factor in a series of power struggles until they moved to Italy in 401 and became the problem of the western emperor and his advisors. The Huns were making their presence felt, both directly in raids on the empire and indirectly as they fought against other tribes. Goths from outside the empire launched a big raid across the Danube and reached northern Italy in 405. On New Year's Eve in 406 (or possibly in 405), a loose alliance of leaders among the Vandals, Suevi, and Alans crossed the frozen Rhine without apparent opposition.

In theory, the empire was guarded by a substantial, well-disciplined, and organized army. A famous document, the *Notitia Dignitatum*—which survives as medieval copies but originally dated from around this period—lists most of the elements of the Roman state. Most prominent is the regular army, listed by unit and command with the insignia each regiment painted on its shields and their usual station, whether limetanei or concentrated into field armies. While it is often forgotten that this document was a reference employed by the civil administration rather than the military, the detail is both remarkable and impressive. The problem is that there is little sign of this wonderfully organized and big army in these years, most especially in the western provinces. When the Vandals and allied groups crossed the Pyrenees around 409, they were unopposed, even though, at least according to the *Notitia Dignitatum*, there ought to have been sixteen field-army units stationed in the Iberian Peninsula. Numbers for armies, whether Roman or tribal, are hard to establish in this poorly documented period, but everything suggests that there were not vast hordes of invaders breaking into the Roman empire. An army of ten or twenty thousand warriors would have been large in this era, and many bands were probably smaller. Nor were their leaders bent on destroying Rome and all the symbols of its civilization. They wanted to support their warriors, through plunder and extortion at first but also, in time, in some more permanent and reliable method, which meant gaining formal recognition and employment from the Romans or taking permanent control of territory—or ideally both. Tribal warlords and their bands were thus simultaneously potential enemies and allies for the Roman authorities.[12]

As always, civil war was ever present and, more often than not, the most pressing concern for an emperor and his advisors. Britain produced no fewer than three usurpers in rapid succession, the last of whom, Constantine III, overran Gaul and Spain in the years the Vandals and others crossed the Rhine. It is hard to understand the sequence and relationship between these events. Constantine III's success brought him recognition by Honorius as a colleague, until another commander rebelled and defeated him, only to fall in turn. No emperor was strong or wholly secure in these years, whether they were new claimants to the imperial purple or the young and weak members of the house of Theodosius. In 408, Honorius's brother Arcadius died, aged thirty-one, and was succeeded by his seven-year-old son, Theodosius II. Inevitably, ministers and army commanders vied with each other to become the real power behind the throne, the rivalry bitter and often lethal for those involved. Personal advantage, or simply survival, guided most decisions, so that they were often short-term and rarely part of a concerted and co-ordinated plan.

The emperor Aurelian had abandoned the Dacian provinces to the east of the Danube in the third century, and there were signs that official imperial presence, primarily the army, had been run down for some time before this. Early in the fifth century, the British provinces were similarly abandoned. The traditional date for this was 410, although new currency stopped reaching the island in the preceding years, again suggesting that soldiers and officials were not being paid. Effectively, the imperial government gave up any direct rule in these regions, although in each case the population there may well have still considered themselves part of the empire and the civilization that it represented. In neither Dacia nor Britain were the Romans forced out by invaders, and the withdrawal—which may or may not have involved the actual exit of any troops or officials in the provinces—was essentially an admission that the imperial government no longer possessed the capacity or will to control these areas. If any soldiers or administrators stayed behind, they were no longer paid or given instructions by the imperial government. This weakness of central authority and its reduced ambition was felt especially in the western provinces, as the presence of Germanic warlords and their bands became a fact of life, since emperors and their commanders were unable to defeat them or preferred to use them against rivals, whether Romans or other barbarian warlords. Sometimes the war bands came into an area as allies, even as a recognized part of the Roman army, and sometimes they came because they could and no one was able to defy so many swords. For provincial populations, especially landowners who wanted to remain important locally and keep their wealth and status, it often made sense to come to an accommodation with a warlord rather than to flee or fight and die.[13]

New kingdoms emerged within the provinces as war-leaders were given or took control of land. There was a Gothic kingdom in Gaul, a Vandal kingdom in Spain, then one led by the Suevi, and later still another under Gothic kings. In 429, the main group of Vandals crossed from Spain to North Africa and eventually overran most of the Roman provinces there. In many cases, this meant the imposition of a foreign elite in place of the imperial authorities. Tax and other levies went to the kings and supported their warriors rather than to the emperor and his armies, but in day-to-day life little changed, at least at first. Usually, Roman law continued to be enforced, and rights of property were respected, apart from land confiscated to reward the king and his loyal followers. The attitude of emperors and their ministers to all this was much the same as their feelings towards provincial grandees, since they could not ignore these kings. Occasionally they felt strong enough to fight them, but they rarely if ever had the capacity to destroy any group. Instead, they played them against each other, did deals to accommodate them as advantageously as possible, and focused on the latest crisis. Apart from the groups already established, there were other tribal leaders attacking the frontiers. The Huns became more and more of a threat to Danubian provinces in particular, culminating in the reign of Attila, the charismatic and ruthless king who built up a confederation of subject tribes as well as his own clans and proved able to take cities and occupy land permanently. In time, he turned his attentions to the west.[14]

There were thus plenty of problems facing the emperors and their advisors, some of them crises on such a scale that it must have been hard to think about anything else. Probably the attitude was one of fighting each fire as it came along, surviving into the next week—and month and year—and trusting that if this could be achieved, in time the essential strength of the empire would recover and reassert itself. Rome and civilization were synonymous, and deep down few educated Romans could imagine a world without the empire. Under Rome there was the rule of law—laws that on the whole were considered fair, at least by the elite—and there was prosperity and comfort, security of rights of status and property, and more safety from violence than was the case in the wider world. None of the new kings offered an appealing alternative to this. Instead, each king became effectively a local emperor with the same duties as any Roman emperor, and thus there was the same call on their subjects' loyalty and the same obligations for the latter to pay taxes and to serve as required.

Nor was there any meaningful nationalism in the provinces, or indeed much memory of a time before the Romans. Britain was one of the last conquests, and one of the first surrendered, and the Romans had been there for three and a half centuries. No winds of change swept through the Roman empire in the fifth century that were comparable to the independence movements that hurried the retreat of the empires in the twentieth century after the Second World War. People, especially the wealthy and aristocratic, might back a usurper because they wanted an emperor who protected and favoured them and took an interest in local problems, but nowhere did they rebel because they saw the Romans as a foreign, occupying force and wanted to be free. If freedom meant anything, it was the freedom to live in a properly regulated society under just emperors, which naturally meant being Roman. The adoption of

Christianity had reinforced the sense that Rome and its civilization and empire were special, divinely ordained as best suited to spread and nurture the true faith.

No significant group inside the Roman empire wanted it to fail and fall, while the barbarian warlords within its old borders were eager to enjoy the wealth and security of Roman civilization, which meant doing their best to preserve all that made this possible. Tribes on the outside were different, and many viewed the empire as prey to be raided for plunder and glory. Attila's hostility was more direct, for he was a predator on a far bigger scale than any other warlord, intent on building an empire of his own, much of it at the expense of the Romans. Yet when he died, apparently having drunk to vast excess celebrating his latest wedding, no Hunnic leader ever managed to re-create his power, and the threat they posed rapidly diminished.

In 400, the Roman empire was rich and powerful. If it was not as rich or powerful as it had once been, it nevertheless was far greater by an immense order of magnitude than any neighbour apart from Sasanian Persia, where the difference was less, if still in the Romans' favour. Although there was an emperor controlling the western provinces and another ruling the east, it remained essentially still one empire. The law was the same everywhere, and in general rulings made in the name of one emperor were respected in the provinces administered by the other. At times, an emperor in the east aided one in the west and vice versa, even if at other times there was suspicion, rivalry, and even open war. The empire was so old, so well-established, that very few could truly imagine a world not dominated by Rome, and even fewer longed for such a world.

Yet for all that, before the fifth century was done, Roman rule had ceased in the western half of the empire. How this happened is too long a story to tell here, and why it happened remains contentious and equally too broad a topic to discuss in any detail. Easier to see is the succession of dramatic moments marking its fall, even if it is not always simple to gauge the true impact of each one. In 410, Goths under Alaric, successors and descendants of the victors at Adrianople, were so frustrated in their attempts to negotiate a favourable settlement with Honorius that they sacked the city of

Rome. The emperor was not there, as no emperor had resided in Rome for well over a century, and it was rare even for one to visit. The scale of the plundering, damage, and violence was limited, for this was still the largest city in the known world, with a population of several hundred thousand, and there were not that many Goths. Yet the news shocked the wider world, most famously moving Saint Augustine to begin work on his immense book *The City of God*, explaining to stunned Romans that as Christians their true capital city would be in heaven. That he felt the need reveals something of the horror he and many others throughout the empire had felt, even though the Goths left within days and did not return.[15]

In some ways, the end of imperial rule in Britain appears to have made less impact on emotions in the wider empire, even though this meant a permanent loss of territory and resources—and also of the costs of garrison and administration. As warlords carved out kingdoms in Gaul and then Spain, this in turn meant further drops in the revenue going into the imperial system, as the kings took over taxation in each region. While they might be allies, they could not be controlled or replaced in the same way as Roman commanders and administrators. Africa was the greatest single loss of all, for its well-irrigated rural estates produced a large agricultural surplus and with it great wealth, and its hardy population had for generations provided many recruits for the army. All of this was lost permanently, passing instead to the Vandal kings, and repeated attempts to recover the lost provinces failed, even when the Romans employed the combined resources of the eastern and western governments.

If the power and wealth of the Roman state in the west was to be measured on a graph, then it would resemble a series of steps down, as the sudden loss of a province caused an abrupt drop. After each disaster, imperial rule went along on a more or less even keel for a while until the next catastrophe. The overall trajectory was downward, and there was no significant recovery as the state grew weaker and weaker. In a sense this had been true since the problems of the third century, but by the fifth century the starting point was far lower and each step down substantially bigger. Sometimes, especially under the able leadership of commanders like Stilicho and Aetius, things were stable for a while until they fell from favour and were killed. Then there was weakness until another general grabbed sufficient power to stabilize the situation, but each new man started from a weaker position. As the state's wealth and infrastructure declined, institutions, especially the army, withered away. More and more reliance was placed on allied contingents serving under their own chiefs and warlords. A mark of the essentially administrative and idealized nature of the *Notitia Dignitatum* is that it made no mention of these bands, including the Goths, who were already a significant force. Aetius, one of the strongmen who kept the western half of the empire in being, had been a hostage of the Huns in his youth. This had the benefit that at times he was able to hire Hunnic allies, but the simple fact that he had had this experience says a good deal about the precarious balance of power in this era.[16]

The emperors in Italy—usually ruling from Ravenna in the north, because it was fairly well-defended by nature—took the brunt of the hard blows delivered to the empire in the fifth century, losing territory, revenue, and prestige. After taking Carthage in 439 and completing their conquest of North Africa, the Vandals overran Sicily, depriving the government of the revenues from yet another highly productive province. A combined invasion by the eastern and western navies and armies was prepared to recover the lost ground, but the emergence of other threats, notably tension with Persia, prevented it from being launched. In 442, a treaty grudgingly accepted the existence of the Vandal kingdom, although the unstable nature of Roman politics meant that the relationship was precarious. In 455, a Vandal army landed in Italy, killing an emperor (or usurper, since the man in question, Petronius Maximus, did not last long enough to gain widespread recognition) and subjecting Rome to a far more thorough sack than it had suffered at the hands of the Goths. More attempts were made to reconquer Africa from the Vandals, but again each ended in utter failure. Emperors rose and fell in rapid succession in the west, with the five-year reign of Anthemius between 467 and 472 proving unusually long. He was executed after losing a conflict with Ricimer, his army commander.[17]

The last emperor in the west lasted barely a year. He was a boy, ironically enough called Romulus after Rome's founder and soon nicknamed Augustulus or 'little Augustus'. Never more than a puppet, when his army commander father was killed in 476, he was deposed with little fuss and was not himself considered important enough to kill. The new commander of the army, Odoacer, did not appoint a replacement and instead made himself king, ruling in Italy since there was not really any other territory left. His authority rested on military might, and he and at least some of his soldiers were Germanic Sciri, although all had been in Roman service for some time. What was left of the state continued to function as well as possible, and in Rome the Senate still met. Odoacer sent the imperial regalia to Constantinople as a gesture of finality and in the hope of acceptance of his rule. In 489, King Theodoric of the Ostrogoths (or east Goths, one of the groups to emerge inside the empire) invaded Italy and eventually overthrew Odoacer. The imperial government in Constantinople had encouraged the attack, although all it meant was replacing one king and dominant group with another.[18]

By the end of the fifth century, the Roman empire in Italy and the western provinces was no more than a memory, while emperors continued to rule in Constantinople and would do so for another thousand years. This requires explanation, since at the beginning of the century there was little difference between the political and military systems in each area, but there was a marked contrast in fortunes. While the eastern provinces had suffered from the appearance of the Goths under Valens and the growing threat of the Huns until Attila decided to shift his attentions to the west, there had been far less permanent loss of territory. There was no equivalent in scale to the abandonment of Britain, and the subsequent loss of the other European provinces, or of Africa and Sicily. This meant that, in 500, the imperial government in Constantinople still controlled the bulk of the territory it had possessed in 400 and continued to have access to the revenue, manpower, and resources of these regions, even if these were diminished. The Sasanian Persians were a more organized and formidable opponent than any western warlord and his army—with the possible exception of Attila at the height of his powers, whose capacity for rapid and widespread destruction was considerable. Yet Persia was also a more stable neighbour, far more predictable, with whom it was easier to negotiate and deal. For much of the fifth century, successive Sasanian rulers were too busy managing threats to the east and north or internal disputes to seek major conflict with Rome. Peace with the neighbouring great power was desirable for both sides most of the time, so conflict was rare, brief, and did not involve major gains or losses of territory on either side.[19]

Much to everyone's surprise, the seven-year-old Theodosius II enjoyed a longer reign as emperor than anyone could remember, lasting until he died of injuries suffered when he fell from his horse in 450, aged forty-nine. Even as an adult, Theodosius II tended to let others make most of the key decisions, whether it was ministers, commanders, court favourites, or, allegedly, both his mother and his wife. One reason for his long success was surely his willingness to be little more than a figurehead. Individuals rose for a while to dominance but always felt the need to keep the emperor in power and to work in his name. Competition did not fatally weaken the regime, and much was achieved, notably the Theodosian law code, collecting and organizing past rulings. Twice there was conflict with Persia, in 420–421 and 440–441, neither involving heavy losses or expense, and the treaty ending each was capable of being presented as a victory. Attempts to aid the western emperors, notably in successive efforts to deal with the Vandals, were hindered by the need to confront Persia and later the Huns. The military did not perform especially well in these years and was badly mauled by the Huns, especially after 445 when Attila became their sole leader. Armies were defeated, provinces ravaged, and cities taken, but afterwards the army reformed and fortifications were rebuilt and improved. The 440s were a particularly difficult time, with earthquake and plague adding to the threats from outside. The imperial state survived—battered, sometimes bankrupt for the moment or militarily weak, but with its underlying structures more or less intact.

Theodosius II had no son, so troops eventually proclaimed an ageing officer named Marcian as emperor, who died in 457, again without a nominated heir. He was replaced by another senior officer in his fifties, Leo, who in turn was replaced by Zeno in 474, who ruled for seventeen years before dying of dysentery. All three were mature men when they were raised to the imperial purple, all had held military rank, and all managed to die of natural causes at an advanced age. This was in stark contrast to the emperors in the west, although it should not conceal the succession of failures, defeats, and challenges that the eastern government faced. Under Theodosius II's successors, competition to control the emperor escalated more often into murder, open violence, and civil war. Yet it never quite descended into the familiar cycle of usurpations, partly through luck and the ability of the emperors to survive.[20]

A Roman empire took shape in the eastern Mediterranean, and after 476 it was *the* Roman empire. At its heart was Constantinople, the new Rome founded by Constantine. It was a city of great splendour, with a population of several hundred thousand—smaller than Rome at its height, although still dwarfing anywhere apart from Alexandria and Antioch. In time, neither of these cities could quite compete with Constantinople's grandeur. Unlike Rome in later antiquity, emperors from the fifth century onwards chose to spend most of their lives in or near the city. In stark contrast to the pattern that had emerged under the Severans and crystallized under the tetrarchy, emperors no longer led their armies on campaign, instead entrusting this responsibility to their commanders. If it risked creating a rival with a loyal army at his back, it had the considerable advantage of distancing the emperor from any failure and also made it easier to wage war in more than one place at a time, assuming that troops and other resources were available.

Emperors resided in Constantinople, giving the city an importance that Rome had lost long ago. There was a Senate, although it was no more meaningfully independent than it had been since the early days of the principate. More importantly, there was the imperial court and the substantial bureaucracy surrounding it. A praetorian prefect, long since divorced from his military role, presided over deputies in five dioceses, which in turn were subdivided into more than forty provinces covering the remaining empire. Other senior ministers—notably the *magister officiorum*, whose duties included running the court and supervising the immediate imperial bodyguard units—dealt with administration, including finances, correspondence, and legal cases. Altogether, there were enough civilian bureaucrats to amount to a small army, dressed in military-style uniforms with very clear symbols of rank and status, each of which brought pay and set rights. At the head, at least nominally, was the emperor, whose life was surrounded by intricate protocol, with public occasions marked by orchestrated displays of loyalty and reverence. Silks, gems, gold embroidery, and other ornamentation were employed in elaborate costumes, highlighting the distinction between the emperor and all the grades of courtier. There was no longer any trace of the affable emperors like Augustus, who walked through the streets dressed like any other senator. Protocol and distinction were rigid and highly complex, especially to an outsider.[21]

This was also from the beginning a proudly Christian city, home of a Christian emperor who ruled a Christian empire. Many of the great buildings ornamenting Constantinople were churches, built as such from the start rather than converted like some of those in Rome. From early on, probably before Constantine adopted the new faith, some bishops had been inclined to embrace the ornate dress and ceremony of state officials, and again, this only became more pronounced with time. The claims to supremacy of the bishop of Rome were hard to maintain once he lived in a city ruled by a barbarian king, so that in most practical terms the bishop in Constantinople stood at the head of the church in general, with the exception of the emperor and perhaps his family. Constantine had set the precedent of intervening in doctrinal matters and church regulation when he felt this necessary, and emperors continued to do this, presenting themselves as God's representatives and ideally working in harmony with the church's hierarchy. Points of doctrine, most of all the nature of the Trinity, continued to create bitter divisions, not simply among bishops and priests but throughout society, since, after all, salvation depended on understanding the truth.

Constantinople's population could be volatile and violent, whether from disputes over matters of faith or other grievances.

Circus factions—'the Blues' and 'the Greens', originally supporters of teams of charioteers—grew into much larger organizations
who could sometimes take sides or protest or riot on their own
behalf. Tiberius's comment back in the first century that ruling
the empire was like 'holding a wolf by the ears' was never more
true than in the fifth century and afterwards for the emperors in
Constantinople, even though the system and society had in other
respects changed so much. Constantinople gave the empire a single
political, administrative, and religious centre—one that was, to all
intents and purposes, secure from threats from outside the empire.
The fortifications of the city, already formidable, were reinforced
under Theodosius II and improved again when they were repaired
after earthquakes in 437 and 447, when the circus factions organized massed labour to work on them in the face of the threat
posed by Attila. If the border in Thrace was never fully secure, over
time it became more and more heavily fortified, which reduced the
chance of an enemy army reaching the capital.[22]

Rome itself was lost, at least for the moment, as were all the
Latin-speaking provinces. The Roman empire was now overwhelmingly Greek speaking, at least in terms of the language of
the educated elite. Emperors and, as far as we can tell, most of
the population still thought of themselves as Roman, so that the
modern term 'Byzantine' is not really appropriate, at least until
the major changes that came after the great Arab conquests of
the seventh century. Certainly the Persians continued to see their
neighbours and rivals as Romans, and over time many people in
Persia would come to remember even Alexander the Great as an
emperor or king of Rome. Within the empire, Roman law in Latin
continued to be the basis of litigation and was employed in some
other government activities and in military administration. If in
day-to-day affairs it was supplanted by Greek, many formal documents continued to be written in Latin. Late in the sixth century,
a manual of military drill and tactics written entirely in Greek still
gave the words of command as transliterated Latin.[23]

Tradition was important. Rome and the Romans were special,
chosen above other cities and peoples to expand and rule a vast
empire. The new Rome of Constantinople was blessed even more

through its devotion to the one true God. It fostered and protected civilization, as well as Christianity in its correct form, and also maintained just law and kept order, which in turn aided prosperity. The emperor, or at least the idea of the emperor and his authority, was central to this, placed there by God, recipient of the taxes that paid for this system and the army to protect it. The emperor, his ministers and generals, the bishops, and the wider population all looked out on the world certain of the superiority of their empire. Outside was barbarism, no law or bad law, and with rare exceptions superstition, paganism, or heresy. The Persian empire was less barbarous and more civilized than anyone else, but being more advanced and civilized than the rest still left them markedly inferior to Rome.

The Sasanian Persians thought much the same about themselves. They were the centre of the world, leaders in the struggle on earth between the truth and the lie. The Romans were less chaotic and primitive than other peoples while remaining markedly inferior. The king of kings was meant to personify justice and the rule of good law. His ministers and commanders, including the regional kings, were similarly expected to govern well and fairly. Alongside them was the parallel hierarchy of priests and high priests, with the mobad of mobads at its head. Despite the seeming equivalence in a spiritual sense of his title, he was no more the equal of the king of kings than a bishop was the equal of the emperor, and there were several strains of Zoroastrianism rather than a single uniform doctrine. Sasanian monarchs made clear that they were divinely appointed and from the beginning maintained a priestly role. Priests sometimes acted as agents of the state, just as bishops sometimes did in the Roman empire.

In Persia, minority religions, including Christians and the Jewish community, were organized and had recognized leaders to help ensure that they paid their taxes and obeyed the king of kings. Persecutions occurred but were not constant and tended to target the leaders. There is every sign that the various traditions revering Mithra, rather than the other Zoroastrian deities, remained as strong in some areas as they had always been under the Arsacids. The Sasanian empire developed a substantial administrative, judicial, and financial bureaucracy, as well as a more structured Zoroastrian church, although it is less clear how long this took. As far as we can tell from the limited evidence, by the late fourth century if not before, a Sasanian king of kings presided over a far more centralized state than any of his Arsacid predecessors. He also maintained a substantially greater full-time army, supplemented in more traditional ways during major wars by the contingents of kings, nobles, and allies. In time, permanent garrisons and fortifications significantly strengthened the empire's frontiers.[24]

In so many ways, the Roman and Persian empires had become alike by the end of the fifth century. Each was ruled by a single monarch, who maintained substantial armed forces and presided over a bureaucracy that by ancient standards was substantial and reasonably efficient. Each also had something like an established church which was recognized by and supported the monarch, even if there were other religious groups within the empire. Even the difficulties they faced were similar, with frontiers threatened by raids and invasions, disputes within the religious organizations, and competition for influence and power between ministers, generals, and other supposed servants of the monarch and state. Succession to the throne was a regular problem, and an emperor or king of kings might be murdered or challenged by a rival backed by an army. In the case of the Persians, the field of potential challengers was at least restricted to members of the royal line, unlike the Romans, where almost anyone within the senior ranks of the army might be proclaimed.

Neither system was perfect, and civil conflicts continued to break out. For all the similarities between the two empires, each was the product of a distinct society, culture, and tradition, so that, while they did much the same sort of things, they tended to do them differently, in the way that seemed most natural to them. Sasanian monarchs never adopted a single capital equivalent to Constantinople, instead moving between two or more royal cities in the traditional way, influenced by geography and climate. Even the points of greatest similarity may not have come from direct emulation. In earlier centuries, Romans had disdained the complex ceremony and pomp of eastern royal courts, only to embrace such things under the tetrarchy and afterwards. While it is possible that at times there was direct copying of institutions, symbols, and ideas by one empire from the other, most of the similarities probably were created independently in reaction to similar circumstances.

A king of kings and an emperor could address each other as brother in a way unimaginable earlier, and diplomats talked of the empires as equals and natural friends, or as the two eyes of the world or two lamps illuminating it. Such language was the sign of changed times, employed to ease negotiations and in the hope that it would make it more palatable for the other side to accept the desired agreement. The fifth century saw a peace between Rome and Persia that was broken only by rare moments of tension and brief, limited conflicts. Nothing comparable to this had lasted so long since the first century, nor would it happen again. It occurred because it was convenient to leaders on both sides, and it was never tested by too great a crisis or a monarch desperate for glory on a scale unavailable elsewhere. Both empires were faced with plenty of more pressing threats than competing with the other for dominance.

In the first years of the fifth century, Arcadius wanted to do everything to ensure that, in the event of his own death, his infant son Theodosius II would succeed him and then stay emperor. Although not mentioned in the meagre contemporary sources, later historians state that he appealed to Yazdgerd I of Persia to act as guardian to the boy and protect his rights. The king of kings agreed, although in practical terms all this meant was sending an envoy to live in the imperial household at Constantinople. The Roman prince did not go to Persia, as so many Arsacids had gone to Rome in earlier times, and the extent of Persian influence on the child or on subsequent events was probably limited. Theodosius II succeeded and enjoyed a long reign, so we cannot say how far Yazdgerd I might have been willing to go to ensure that this occurred and protect his ward in other circumstances. No doubt the Persian promise was a factor in securing the boy's rule, if one among many, and was unlikely to have been the most significant.[25]

There was a brief conflict between Theodosius II and Persia around the time of Yazdgerd I's death in 420, although the timing may have been coincidental and had more to do with the Sasanian belief that the Romans were focused on the planned expedition against the Vandals and therefore more likely to back down. The interests of individual monarchs and their empires were the driving force in international relations, and the language of brotherhood and friendship readily switched to threats and boasts of strength according to circumstances. Even so, Arcadius's appeal to his Persian counterpart and Yazdgerd I's favourable response do highlight the changing mood and the growing acceptance of a more or less equal balance of power between the two empires.

15

SOLDIERS, WALLS, AND GOLD

LATE FIFTH TO EARLY SIXTH CENTURIES

HOWEVER GRUDGINGLY, THE ROMANS AND PERSIANS BECAME willing to see each other as equals, or almost equals, which was not something they would even consider with their other neighbours. Yet leaders and peoples did not need to be so strong or civilized to pose a threat. The two empires had frontiers that were long, and there were never sufficient resources to be strong everywhere. Settled populations, with the prosperity encouraged by the stable rule of emperor or king of kings, offered very tempting targets for small and large bands of warriors, just as they had always done. The raid remained the most common form of warfare, and this would hold true throughout much of the Middle Ages. As always, any successful attack encouraged more and larger onslaughts in the future.

No one seems to have inspired as much terror in the settled populations of either empire than the various groups known to others as Huns. Ammianus was one of many authors to stress their ugliness as well as their savagery, although oddly enough no literary source mentions the practice of binding a child's skull to distort its shape seen in a substantial minority of the remains in Hunnic graves. As is the case with so many peoples from the ancient world, the Huns never set down their own story, so they are only ever described as outsiders and usually as savage enemies. The label Hun was applied widely and freely, much like names such as Scythian or Celt in earlier periods, making it very hard to understand the true identities of various groups and their relationship with each other. Similarly, attempts to identify nomadic warriors mentioned in Chinese sources with tribes appearing further west—generations, sometimes centuries, later—are intriguing but involve considerable leaps of faith. The simple truth is that relatively little is known for certain about the Huns or to what extent any of the groups to appear were ethnically based. Leaders like Attila proved highly successful at absorbing others—for instance, Goths and other Germanic peoples, most of them settled in agricultural communities—and included contingents of these in his armies. An army of 'Huns' may often have included a wide variety of warriors, with only some, perhaps a minority, fighting in the traditional way of nomadic horse-archers.[1]

The Chionitae or 'Red Huns' have already appeared in our story during the siege of Amida in 359 and continued to play a role for some time. Sometimes they are referred to as Kushans, since they had seized the territory of the old Kushan kingdom, which is another reminder of the vagueness of ethnic terms used to describe other peoples. At some point, the Hephthalites or 'White Huns' appeared on the north-eastern frontiers of Sasanian Persia. One source described them as being lighter skinned than other Huns, which might explain the name, unless he was simply rationalizing from one to the other. All groups labelled as Huns appear to have begun as nomadic societies that produced warriors who covered ground quickly, using surprise and ambush as much as direct force. They were horsemen and archers, just like the Saka and others from earlier periods, including the first Arsacids. By the fourth century, Huns tended to wield an especially powerful composite bow, usually asymmetric, the stave above the warrior's hand longer than below, so that it was easier to handle on horseback. This was designed to drive an arrow with great force at relatively close range rather than pepper the target from a distance. Tactics were essentially the same as those used by horse-archers in the past: wearing the enemy down and avoiding close contact until these enemies were scattered or otherwise weakened. In essence, this was the well-established way of fighting for the steppe peoples. In the right circumstances, it continued to prove devastatingly effective, while the strategic mobility of bands of horsemen meant that their raids could reach deep and often surprise the defenders, spreading terror over a wide area. Even when leaders took over settled populations and the nomads began to become more settled in their lifestyle, they are still depicted as fighting in the same manner.[2]

There were three ways of dealing with such a threat, or indeed one posed by any other tribal people tempted to attack. The first was to bribe them, sending gold or whatever else the leaders valued. Perhaps this was presented as gifts or as payment for some service, but in essence it was the same as the Anglo-Saxon kingdoms of England paying Danegeld to keep Viking armies away, or small businesses giving protection money to the mafia. Once the principle was established, ending such payment was likely to provoke an especially ferocious onslaught as reprisal. There was also never anything to prevent arbitrary increases in the amount demanded, while by its nature, a willingness to pay encouraged other war-leaders in other regions to seek a similar deal.

In contrast, the second option was to use military force to dominate the potential raiders. This was likely to be more expensive in the short term but offered glory and was clearly a more honourable way to deal with the threat. Yet it was not always easy to strike a decisive blow against any Huns, even when they had become more settled, and there was always the risk that they would outwit and maul, or even destroy, an invading force. At best they might be persuaded or forced to submit, but such an object lesson was likely to need repeating in the future, not least because burning crops and seizing livestock were bound to fuel hatred and the desire for revenge.

Finally, there was the option of defence and fortification to protect vulnerable communities from raids, making it as difficult as possible for attackers to reach their targets and then return home with their loot. By its very nature, this was another costly solution, since anything built had to be maintained and garrisoned for as long as the threat persisted. It also meant putting in place defences to protect every vulnerable region; otherwise, attackers simply sought out the gaps and weak spots. None of the options was cheap, and none was guaranteed to work on its own. Throughout their history, the Romans, the Parthians, and the Persians made use of all three methods, usually in combination, the emphasis varying depending on the wider condition of the empire at the time.

Roman walls and frontier systems are well-documented, even if scholars continue to debate the question of what they were designed to achieve and how well they did it. By the end of the fifth century, Hadrian's Wall, by far the most famous military monument left by the Romans, had not been under imperial control or fully maintained for generations. The same was true of the ditches, stockades, and lines of forts along the Rhine and much of the Danube or in North Africa, although efforts were made to protect the areas on and behind the Danube that were still under control. Cities there were heavily fortified, Constantinople most of all. Even so, in the early sixth century a great wall was constructed some forty-three miles (sixty-five kilometres) west of the imperial capital, stretching from one side of the peninsula to the other. Known as the Anastasian Wall after the emperor who had it built, like any other fortification, it was only useful if it was kept in a good state and properly garrisoned and supported by other troops, and this was only possible if the resources and determination of central government were devoted to the task. During the course of the fifth century, most of the forts and fortlets on the desert frontier of the Syrian and Arabian provinces, the old line of the Strata Diocletiana, were allowed to decay. The majority of these bases were abandoned, while the remainder appear to have been manned by no more than token garrisons.[3]

In contrast, the Persians created a number of new defensive systems, although since these are only known through archaeology it is hard to know which monarchs were responsible and the sequence in which they were created and developed. Most striking of all is the Gorgan Wall, which lay east of the Caspian Sea running for some 130 miles (195 kilometres) from its shore to the mountains; the considerable variation in the depth of the Caspian Sea over the centuries means that we cannot be certain where the shoreline lay in the fifth century or judge how much of the wall now lies beneath its waters. In recent years, archaeological explorations of the fortification have made clear that it is Sasanian and have given remarkable insights into its construction. The engineers appear to have begun by digging a deep ditch along most of the length of the planned wall. They then diverted water from the closest rivers to fill this as a moat. The spoil from the excavations was mixed with some of this water to make clay, which was turned into bricks, which were then baked in ovens built at short intervals along its length. Each brick was some 16 x 16 x 4 inches (40 x 40 x 10 centimetres) in size and weighed about forty-four pounds (twenty kilograms). There is no sign of any foundations, but the wall itself was very regular: six feet six inches (two metres) wide and at the very least ten feet (three metres) high. Very few of the bricks remain in place, having been stolen and reused over the centuries, like the vast majority of the stones of Hadrian's Wall.[4]

There are other similarities with the earlier Roman structure, for the Persian wall also had forts along its length, thirty of which have been identified. Geophysical work at one of them located six barrack blocks, each with twenty-four pairs of rooms, or even more if the strongly built structures had more than one storey. Those undertaking the fieldwork suspect that there were originally eight such blocks and—on the basis that the other, similarly sized forts had a comparable layout, and drawing parallels with Rome—suggested a garrison size for the entire wall of some thirty thousand men. Curiously enough, that is similar to the theoretical troop numbers for the forts of Hadrian's Wall at their height. However, unlike Roman army bases of the first to third centuries, the surveyed Persian fort showed little or no trace of other buildings, such as granaries, hospitals, headquarters, or houses. Even more distinctive are the large, strongly fortified enclosures dubbed 'campaign bases' by the team working on the wall. Some forty hectares or so in size, these show no traces of internal buildings, although work in one revealed what appeared to be bases for rows of tents, with slight ditches to help keep them drained.[5]

The Gorgan Wall is testament to the immense effort Sasanian monarchs were willing to devote to securing a frontier area, and there are signs of increased cultivation of the land to its south which suggest that it was successful. Although none match it in sheer scale, the Gorgan Wall was far from unique, and the Sasanians constructed several other lines of fortification, most notably to the west of the Caspian Sea to guard the narrow coastal plain, and also in the passes through the Caucasus. Designs and material vary. One wall was strengthened by a large number of towers, something so far unknown on the Gorgan Wall. Some structures began as mud brick, only to be replaced in stone or fired bricks at some later stage. All appear to have been first erected in the fifth or early sixth centuries and demonstrate the engineering skill of the Sasanians; for instance, one weak sector of the Gorgan Wall was reinforced by damming a river to create a lake.[6]

Yet for all that we have learned in recent years about these Sasanian frontier fortifications, many mysteries remain. Some are minor: the Gorgan Wall was wide enough to have had a walkway on top, but we do not know whether it actually had one—a subject that remains debated with regard to Hadrian's Wall. The forts along it suggest a highly organized and permanent garrison, presumably of full-time soldiers, and this is also true for the other frontier lines. At least some were infantrymen, to act as guards to the forts and walls themselves, although a significant proportion were surely cavalry or capable of fighting on horseback as well as on foot. Around a quarter of the Hadrian's Wall garrisons were horsemen in the second and third centuries, and the traditional emphasis on cavalry in Persian and Parthian warfare makes it likely that the numbers were as high or higher along their frontiers. Walls were never meant to be impenetrable barriers but bases for aggressive defence, patrolling, and diplomacy, and cavalry significantly increased the reach of the garrison and its speed of response.[7]

The large 'campaign bases' lack internal buildings, which does not suggest permanent occupation by the sort of numbers they were capable of accommodating. Archaeologists working on them have wondered whether they were built to shelter the men who built the wall in the first place or for troops to protect the labourers.

Another idea was that these were used by field armies assembled whenever it was felt necessary to bolster the garrisons on the wall itself or to mount a campaign beyond it, and it is perfectly possible that the bases were used both during the initial building phase and later on. Given the substantial scale of the walls and towers forming these enclosures, they were designed to be used for a long time, even if only occasionally. They have much in common with the vast, high-walled enclosure at Qaleh Iraj not far from modern Tehran, the construction of which has now been dated to the Sasanian era sometime around the late fourth or early fifth century. Its curtain wall still stands in places almost 50 feet (14.97 metres) high, had towers to provide even higher platforms, and was wide enough at the base to accommodate hundreds of rooms. Covering some 175 hectares, it dwarfs any Roman military base, or indeed any other similar structure from the Classical world. Positioned in the empire's heartland, it is far from any external threat but lies close to several of the major routes leading to different regions. The suggestion that this was a secure and very grand gathering place when the king of kings mustered a great army makes a good deal of sense.[8]

On a lesser, if still substantial scale, the campaigning bases served a similar purpose, as walled enclosures became tented cities for leaders, soldiers, horses, and other animals. Perhaps they also acted as depots, where food and fodder could be gathered in advance, as well as equipment—for instance, arrows, which were bulky and likely to be needed in great quantity on any campaign. The sixth-century Roman historian Procopius claimed that when a Persian army mustered, each man dropped an arrow into a basket and retrieved one when the army broke up at the end of a campaign, so that the ones left over were seen as an indication of casualties. In contrast to the Roman emperor by this time, the king of kings led any major campaign in person, and judging from stories of the harem being captured after defeats, much of the royal court usually accompanied him. This, and the space required for mounts and other animals, makes it difficult to judge the maximum number of fighting men as opposed to non-combatants who might have sheltered within the walls of Qaleh Iraj or the campaign bases. Depending on circumstances, each place could also function as a mustering point and base for smaller field forces rather than for their full capacity.[9]

The emergence of all this archaeological evidence in recent years has overthrown many long-standing assumptions about the Sasanian state and its military organization. In the main, these ideas had been based on the literary, and therefore Roman, sources. The new evidence allows us to make better sense of the information from elsewhere, including the Greco-Roman literature, and gain a far better appreciation of the Sasanian empire's strength. The scale and sophistication of frontier defences like the Gorgan Wall came as a surprise, even though there was plenty of evidence for large-scale engineering projects, such as canal and irrigation systems and the construction of cities and palaces. These show the same technical skill and ability to gather and direct a very large labour force. It is interesting that the engineers working on the Gorgan Wall made such use of canals, since this was something very well-understood by the Sasanians. Just who provided the labour force is unknown, and that we cannot say whether the work was predominantly or entirely civilian, or whether the troops who would form the first garrisons played a role.

These garrisons suggest that the Sasanian king of kings maintained tens of thousands of full-time soldiers at all times, assuming estimates for the garrison of the Gorgan Wall were reflected in other frontier installations. There is no direct reference to so many professional soldiers in the Roman sources, which may simply be because the Romans never encountered them since they never reached these areas. Stripping other frontiers of troops to send to the west would have been very dangerous for any Sasanian monarch to contemplate. If anything, the sheer scale of these frontier works act as a reminder that the Romans were just one of the threats faced by the Sasanians—and the Parthians before them—and rarely the most serious one.

On the whole, scholars have assumed that the Sasanians, like the Arsacids before them, did not maintain a large standing army and instead raised troops for each campaign, combining royal troops, contingents provided by local kings (although there were fewer of these as time passed), the household troops of the great noble families, and allied contingents, who also often served under the command of their own leaders. All of these elements do appear in the armies of the fifth and sixth centuries. Just as the king of the Chionitae served Shapur II at Amida, there is plentiful evidence for other allied contingents, often described as Huns. The continued prominence of families like the Suren, Karen, and Mihran is also clear. Clay seals, which survive in some quantity even though the official letters and documents they once marked have been lost, bear the names of men from these and the other Arsacid great families, while later tradition portrays them as providing almost all the senior ministers and army commanders. At times one individual or clan became more dominant, but the picture is of constant competition to gain influence and to serve the king of kings in the most senior and distinguished roles. These families continued to dominate their old heartlands, where royal cities were rare, and provided substantial numbers of soldiers when requested. Overall, the evidence from the frontiers reveals that there were far more professional soldiers, presumably in the service of the king of kings, which may mean that the royal component of the army was larger and consisted of more permanent units than we have assumed. In the sixth century, Procopius mentions an elite body of cavalry called 'the Immortals'—a name invoking the ten thousand picked infantry of fifth-century-BC Achaemenid kings, although whether the Romans or Sasanians were trying to invoke the Classical past is hard to say. There may well have been other substantial contingents of professional soldiers available to form the nucleus of a field army.[10]

The Romans of the sixth century—including Procopius, who served on the staff of a leading general and saw Persian armies at first hand—remained unimpressed with Sasanian infantry, at least when it came to pitched battles. If there were drilled and disciplined infantrymen in the service of the king of kings, then these were either kept in distant garrisons or formed no more than a small minority of the foot soldiers in any field army. There is little mention of war elephants in the sources for the fifth century, although they reappear in the sixth. Instead, cavalry dominated

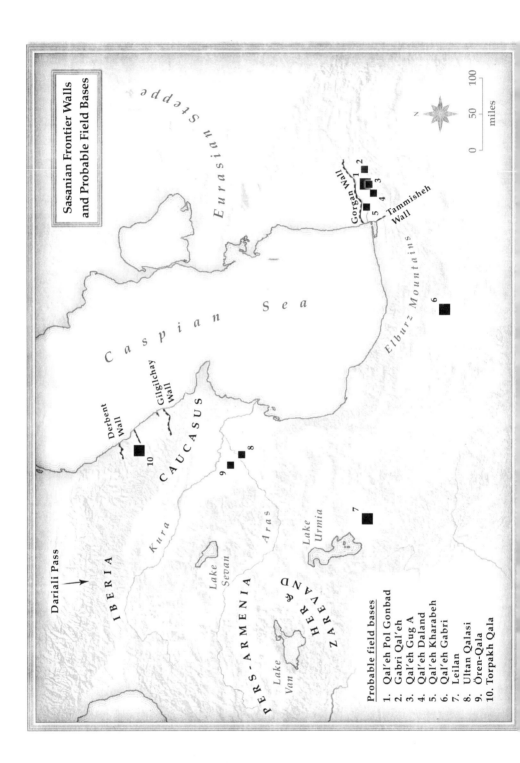

Sasanian Frontier Walls
and Probable Field Bases

Eurasian Steppe

Gorgan Wall
Tammisheh
Wall

Caspian Sea

Elburz Mountains

Gilgilchay
Wall

Derbent
Wall

C A U C A S U S

Kura

Darial Pass

I B E R I A

Lake
Sevan

Lake
Van

P E R S - A R M E N I A

Aras

ZAREVAND & HER

Lake
Urmia

Probable field bases
1. Qal'eh Pol Gonbad
2. Gabri Qal'eh
3. Qal'eh Gug A
4. Qal'eh Daland
5. Qal'eh Kharabeh
6. Qal'eh Gabri
7. Leilan
8. Ultan Qalasi
9. Ören-Qala
10. Torpakh Qala

N

0   50   100

miles

Persian field armies, and the only ones who really mattered on the battlefield were the close-formation, armoured horsemen, with lighter troops marginalized to a support role. The standard horseman wore armour from head to toe and, at least in the front ranks, was likely to ride an armoured horse. Yet unlike the cataphracts of earlier centuries, he was first and foremost an archer. Persian cavalry were known for the rapidity with which they shot arrows from their composite bows. Combined with massed formations, this meant sending a focused cloud of arrows at their opponents, often for a long time, wearing them down before closing to fight with a kontos or more often a straight longsword or heavy club. Discipline was important, the units acting as formations rather than individuals and each one maintaining its place in the line, giving mutual support. Sasanian tactics were careful and deliberate. They liked to attack the Romans near noon, believing them to be less able to cope with the heat and at their weakest after taking an early breakfast. The Sasanians aimed at hammering an enemy for some time with close-range arrow fire before mounting a controlled attack. Nothing, especially pursuit, was supposed to be done too quickly or at all recklessly.[11]

The trend for Roman and Sasanian methods of waging war to grow ever more alike was especially pronounced in the sixth century. Overall, the Roman army continued to be composed predominantly of close-order infantry. However, many of these were employed as more or less fixed garrisons, so that an army operating on campaign tended to have a higher proportion of cavalry. At the end of the century, the *Strategikon*, a military manual attributed to the emperor Maurice, could envisage a field force entirely of horsemen, even though it expected most armies to be a balanced mixture of horse and foot. In battle, the infantry formed dense blocks, behind which retreating cavalry could rally. The front ranks had large shields and spears, as well as helmets and cuirasses, but to the rear some of the men were archers, shooting over the heads of those in front. While infantry formations did play an important role in some of the battles of this era, whether against the Persians or other opponents, they do not seem ever to have attacked and instead were there to resist any onslaught from the enemy. The offensive arm was the cavalry, fighting in close formation, with the men and sometimes the horses armoured. A range of weapons were employed, but many units had the first few ranks equipped with composite bows. They carried fewer arrows than their Sasanian counterparts and were unable to shoot as quickly, although they believed that their missiles struck with greater force. An enemy was to be weakened with arrows before a charge went in, but on balance the Romans stressed shock action more than the Sasanians, although this was really a question of degree. Both emphasized the need for good order and discipline, even if this proved harder to achieve in practice than in theory. Like the Persians, the Romans also made considerable use of allied contingents, especially Huns and others who fought in a similar style.[12]

Tactically, Roman and Sasanian armies appear evenly matched, with, if anything, a slight advantage to the latter. The same was true of siege warfare, and sieges remained far more common than open battle. During assaults, the main attacks had to be launched on foot, and Roman infantry played a full part in these. For the Sasanians, many cavalrymen may have fought dismounted, although it is just possible that Persian infantry was entrusted with and capable of performing more aggressive actions at sieges compared to pitched battles. If anything, the Persian siege-craft appears more effective than Roman, even though the advantage was not so great that it was decisive. Sieges remained difficult, time-consuming enterprises, costly in material and lives, where success was never guaranteed. Little is known about the engineers who supervised these works on either side. The Romans had long since abandoned the practice of building marching camps on campaign, so these later generations of soldiers had less practice at digging and building than their predecessors. Engineers tended to be specialists, recruited and paid by the state, for too much was at stake if they got things wrong. There were no solid lines of fortification where Roman and Sasanian territory met, although there does appear to have been a ditch and rampart for long stretches in the south, where the Persian empire's directly governed land edged on the desert. Yet there were heavily fortified cities, which needed to be garrisoned and their defences maintained.

No form of security came cheaply, and just like the Roman emperor, the king of kings spent far more on defence and warfare than anything else. Large numbers of full-time soldiers needed to be fed, equipped, and rewarded, whether through salary or payment in kind. Wars to dominate an opponent were sometimes profitable, but conquest was rare in this period, so it did not provide a way to let the army pay for itself. In each empire, the bureaucratic system to raise income from taxation, tolls, and other levies to support the army was far from perfect, making the task harder. There is evidence that some of the noblemen and other leaders within the Sasanian empire were paid—or awarded the revenue from the local regions—in set amounts for each soldier they were obliged to provide to the king of kings, but that some took the income without actually maintaining the full complement of men. Similar peculation had long been common within the Roman empire.

By the end of the fifth century, the Romans appear to have abandoned conscription, something always difficult to enforce, and relied instead upon volunteers to provide soldiers. This meant that service had to be made attractive to draw good recruits in sufficient numbers. Even so, some units were most likely heavily under-strength for long periods of time, which meant a saving for the state, assuming that the Romans were not—like the Persians—paying commanders for troops who did not exist. There are signs that many of the limetanei were allowed to become something like part-time soldiers. Papyri show that many of the men in one unit stationed in Egypt were actively engaged in other trades. The state paid them less while allowing them to support themselves and their families by other means. These soldiers were still probably an adequate force for local policing or to perform a static role in the unlikely event of war, but they would have been more difficult to integrate into a field army. Egypt was one of the least vulnerable parts of the empire, at least when it came to the risk of major invasion, so perhaps it was felt less important to maintain the limetanei there in a state of constant readiness. More than likely the treatment of these units varied from province to province, depending on the local situation.[13]

Standing armies are and were by their very nature expensive, and wealthy though the Roman and Sasanian empires were, their resources were far from unlimited, even when those resources were managed efficiently. Since we know far more about the Romans, it is easier to see corruption, incompetence, and neglect on their side, but there is no reason to believe that the Sasanians were very different in these regards, while both empires were periodically weakened by internal power struggles. Each empire possessed a sophisticated military machine that could be highly effective in pitched battle and was skilled in attacking or defending fortifications, as well as waging war through raids. Each army had at least a core of soldiers who were highly trained, disciplined, and obedient to command, and each had the capacity to supply field forces on campaign. No system is perfect, so some contingents and entire armies were less organized and efficient than the ideal.

Estimates for the total number of soldiers in the Roman empire vary, although some scholars argue for a force of over three hundred thousand men, close to the total force for the entire united empire in the first and early second centuries. While these scholars would admit that this was a theoretical number for the men who should have been in service, there remains a tendency to assume that units were normally at something close to their full strength. Since this does not appear to have been true in the more stable days of the principate, it seems even less likely for the fifth and sixth centuries. Even scholars inclined to such high estimates of the size of the army in this period acknowledge that the vast majority of soldiers were tied to one station as garrison troops or their supports. Field armies tended to be small, equivalent to the sort of force a single military province might have fielded in the first or second century. The *Strategikon* considered a force of fifteen thousand to twenty thousand men to be an unusually large army, although it is clear from historical narratives that the biggest Roman armies were invariably those tasked with facing the Sasanians. Even so, neither the Roman forces nor the Persians facing them ever appear to have been huge.[14]

Some long-standing trends became even more pronounced in the fifth and sixth centuries. In the days of Augustus and his successors, the empire struggled to find sufficient resources to deal with two major conflicts simultaneously—major in the sense that they required substantial resources of men and material from outside the province involved. Ultimately, as the chaos of the third century degraded the effectiveness of the army and profoundly changed the command structure of the provinces and their garrisons, any major war required the emperor to supervise the war effort in person. Experiments with more than one emperor followed, although there never seem to have been quite enough troops, resources, and emperors—or that rarest of commodities, trusted commanders—to deal with every crisis that popped up. Part of this was the difficulty of winning conflicts quickly, as seen in the six-year struggle with the Goths that began in 376. Similarly, through the centuries, Arsacid and Sasanian monarchs frequently sought peace with Rome so that they could deal with threats elsewhere, most notably on their other frontiers. Sheer distance was part of this—armies could not switch quickly from one front to another when they were on opposite sides of the empire—but it was also a question of resources.

In the fifth or early sixth century, the Sasanians invested heavily in frontier defences like the Gorgan Wall. This was expensive in the short term and created ongoing costs in the long term, while hopefully reducing the amounts needing to be spent on aggressive campaigns or subsidies to the tribes. All three methods of dealing with threats continued to be used, and it was more a question of changing balance. Royal revenue and resources did not substantially increase during these years. Considerable effort was made to profit from the long-distance trade from India and beyond. Even though the collapse of the western Roman empire drastically reduced the markets for such goods, profits were still substantial, well worth competition to control them; we read of Sasanian merchants excluding their Roman counterparts from most Indian ports. Both empires did their best to dominate the communities around the Arabian Gulf and on the east coast of Africa, competing to control and benefit the most from the trade routes. In the sixth century, Roman monks managed to smuggle silkworms from China back to the empire, although it would be a while before their cultivation led to a substantial industry producing homegrown silk. Imperial authorities benefitted from all this trade, even if much of the effort, and probably profit, went to the entrepreneurs responsible.[15]

Wealthy though the empires were, their resources struggled to match their military ambitions, and they came under particular pressure whenever threats increased, more than one threat flared up at the same time, or conflicts proved difficult to win. One alternative to funding and doing everything themselves was to rely on allies beyond the borders. Subsidies to aid them were considerably cheaper than fighting wars directly, but this came with a lack of control. Allies could prove ineffective, fickle, or suddenly hostile. Both Romans and Sasanians came to rely heavily on Arab groups in the southern desert. For the Romans, this probably allowed the neglect of the old line along the Strata Diocletiana, whereas the Sasanians appear to have maintained a linear defence on their side. In the past, scholars were content to speak of two major powers among the Arab tribes, the pro-Sasanian Lakhmids and pro-Roman Ghassanids, but it is now clear that this is far too simplistic. Instead, the empires tied themselves to dynastic houses, who managed to establish a degree of control over large numbers of other groups. In contrast, the annexation of most of Armenia and parts of the Iberian and Georgian kingdoms by the Sasanians removed the allies and gave the Persians direct control of and responsibility for threats to the key routes through the mountains, hence the subsequent construction of frontier defences. As had been seen in 395, failure to defend the passes permitted raiders like the Huns to attack into both Roman and Persian territory.[16]

A theme running throughout the fifth century and beyond was the Sasanian assertion that since the defences in this region protected both empires, the Romans should help to maintain them. This was not entirely new, since centuries before, Vespasian had declined an Arsacid request for similar cooperation, but now, with Armenia partitioned, the borders of the two empires were joined and the threat was more immediate to both. Again and again, Sasanian ambassadors asked the Roman emperor to contribute. Sending troops was mentioned, and one source speaks of an agreement for each empire to provide the other with three hundred fully equipped cavalry on request, but this appears to be garbled, since this is an oddly small number. More practically, the king of kings wanted gold, ostensibly to help meet the cost of frontier defence. Opinion is divided over whether there was ever a formal treaty in which the Romans promised to meet this demand on a regular or even annual basis. Several payments are recorded, and each side may have presented them differently. For the Roman emperor, this was a mark of goodwill and friendship on a fitting scale for the only other civilized empire in the world, but it was not tribute paid to a stronger rival and potential enemy as the price of peace. The Sasanians understandably presented it as just that, at least to the home audience, and were skilled at pressing hardest for such gifts when the Romans were preoccupied with other problems, most notably the disastrous expeditions against the Vandals in the fifth century.[17]

The Sasanians were not always in a position to take advantage of Roman weakness, having many problems of their own during the course of the fifth century. Yazdgerd I was dubbed 'the sinner' in later tradition, apparently for offending some of the vested interests within his empire, especially the high priests and the main noble clans, who, apart from the Suren, did not figure much in his reign. Following his death in 420, there was a power struggle to determine who would succeed him. One son was proclaimed king and swiftly killed. His replacement came from a different branch of the Sasanian royal house but in turn failed to last very long before he was overthrown and another son of Yazdgerd I, Bahrām V, became king of kings. Unlike his father, who had treated religious minorities well, he began to persecute Christian leaders, many of whom fled to the Roman empire. Persian demands to have them returned were rebuffed, leading to the brief conflict of 420–421, while the Romans were preoccupied with the west. After a few Sasanian victories, peace was negotiated, and among other things, the Romans made one of their contributions to the defence of the Caspian Gates. The Persian Christians returned home with the promise that they would not be arrested, and official suspicion of them was greatly reduced a few years later when a Persian church was created, separate from Rome, a divide reinforced when doctrinal differences grew more significant in later years.[18]

Bahrām V also attempted to impose Zoroastrianism on the Armenians in a bid to bring them under greater control, something which few Armenian kings, let alone outsiders, had ever managed to achieve. The result was rebellion, until a mixture of force and compromise brought some degree of stability. There was also warfare against 'Huns', perhaps Hephthalites, in the north-east of the empire. His son Yazdgerd II succeeded to the throne in 438 and a little later began a war with the Romans, who once again were focused on attempts to deal with the Vandals. After two years of very limited fighting, a Roman general was sent as envoy and approached in such a respectful way, coming on foot and with little or no escort, that a peace was accepted: both sides pledged not to build any new fortified places near the frontier between the two empires nor to suborn each other's Arab allies further south. Another reason the king of kings accepted this deal was that conflict had broken out with the same Huns who had fought against his father. After several years of fighting, they were again persuaded to submit, allowing Yazdgerd II to turn to a fresh rebellion in Armenia, fuelled by efforts to convert the population. The rebels suffered a major defeat in 451, but there was little relief, as the Huns returned to the warpath and others threatened the lands east of the Caspian Sea. Most likely this means that the Gorgan Wall had not yet been built, and it helps to explain why it was felt necessary. Years of campaigning proved indecisive, and Yazdgerd II died in 457.[19]

Two of the dead monarch's sons competed to succeed him, backed by different factions within the noble families. One of them was crowned and ruled for almost two years before he was defeated and executed, when his brother Peroz became king of kings, backed in particular by the Mihran family, who over time supplanted the Suren in monopolizing high office. Peroz managed to put down a rebellion in Albania and made some concessions in the hope of settling Armenia into a better state, but he was to be repeatedly challenged by nomad groups—especially the Hephthalites, although other sources speak of Kidarite Huns. Rumours and reports of these campaigns reached the Romans, even though they may not fully have understood the details of the conflict. In 469, Peroz and his army suffered a heavy defeat after the Huns feigned flight, luring them into a trap. Procopius says that the king of kings agreed to prostrate himself before the Hephthalite king as a sign of submission, for the Persian magi had told him that he could pretend to perform the act at dawn, when it was normal for him to bow before the rising sun. Whether or not this was simply a tall tale of the Persians'—for the Romans—proverbial cunning, Peroz paid the enemy a large sum of gold, swore to keep the peace, and left one of his sons as surety.[20]

Rebellions erupted once more in Armenia and Georgia, partly inspired by factional struggles within the nobility of each region. The rebels allied with each other, but the bond proved fragile. After heavy campaigning, the Georgians capitulated, but a victory over the Armenians failed to end resistance altogether, and around 482 Peroz's attentions turned back to the Hephthalites. Once again, he advanced against them with an army, and once again he failed to understand that when a nomadic army retreated, it need not be a sign of fear. In 484, he fell into another ambush—literally, according to Procopius, who claimed that the Huns dug deep trenches which they concealed with brushwood. The king of kings was killed, along with most of his sons and many noblemen. Before this last campaign, there is a reasonable chance that it was Peroz who ordered the building of the Gorgan Wall, given the trouble the region was causing him. His offensive may have been launched from it, perhaps even using one or more of the campaign bases as the starting point. Like other Arsacids and Sasanians—and indeed the Achaemenid Cyrus the Great—Peroz paid the price for underestimating the skill of nomadic warriors.[21]

Peroz's brother Balash was proclaimed in his place. He paid a large sum to the Hephthalites to buy peace and made concessions in Armenia—including the demolition of fire temples recently set up there and granting the Christian population freedom to worship—to end the rebellion. A challenger soon appeared—perhaps another brother or son of Peroz—and was defeated, ironically enough with the aid of the former Armenian rebels. In 488, Kavadh I, the son left as hostage with the Hephthalites, returned with an army composed of Hunnic allies and discontented noblemen and overthrew his uncle. Just as the empire's political leaders were divided, members of the religious hierarchy, who often came from the same families, faced a major crisis with the emergence of a movement known as the Mazdakites. Details are unclear from the wealth of subsequent condemnation, and they are much debated by scholars, but presumably the leader, Mazdak, preached what he presented as a purer, reformed version of the Zoroastrian faith. It is hard to know what to make of claims that he and his followers believed that property, including wives, should be held in common, but one aspect of the cult may well have been a rejection of the traditional class system, which largely kept families in the same status generation after generation. Kavadh I seems to have favoured the movement, so much so that, in 496, he was deposed and imprisoned by more traditionally minded figures at court. His brother was named king of kings but did not last long. Kavadh I escaped, one story claiming that he did so disguised as one of his wives who had visited him faithfully. She donned his clothes and took his place in his cell to hide his escape for as long as possible. He went back to the Hephthalites, who backed him with an army, so that he returned to reclaim the throne in 498. This support from the Hephthalites came at an immense price, which, after so many years of defeat and infighting, royal funds were unable to meet. Kavadh I sent envoys to the Romans asking that they make a new contribution to the defence of the northern passes.[22]

The emperor Anastasius I refused to give a gift and instead offered a loan, until his advisors convinced him that even this was unwise. Their view was that it was not in Constantinople's interest to ensure good relations between the Sasanians and Hephthalites. Kavadh I's problems grew as fresh rebellion broke out in Armenia and there were risings in other parts of the empire. The king of kings needed to assert his authority and most of all was desperate for funds, and his mind soon turned to an attack on the Roman provinces. In the past, threats and limited military action had forced concessions from the Romans, and if this did not, then a more concerted effort offered the prospect of rich plunder from the many cities of the region. Kavadh I moved first against the Armenian rebels, beating them into submission and recruiting a sizeable contingent to reinforce his army and act as hostages. He persuaded the Hephthalites to send him more men and the other rebel groups in the empire to join his army, promising recompense from the spoils of victory. By the summer of 502, he was ready, and he turned a pacification expedition to Persian-controlled Armenia into a sudden invasion of the Roman province of Armenia.[23]

The Romans were not ready. In the short term this was probably because they did not think that Kavadh I was strong enough to attack them. More importantly, a century of largely unbroken peace had fostered complacency. City walls and other defences were neglected and left unrepaired, and garrisons had been depleted as troops were needed elsewhere or simply considered an expensive and non-essential luxury. Kavadh I took two of the main cities in Roman Armenia, helped by the probable treachery of a commander, who defected and acquired two Persian wives before he was allowed to return to the empire at the end of the war. The king of kings then surprised the Romans again by heading south instead of west and attacking Amida, which led to another epic siege. Soldiers are barely mentioned in our sources, but the civilian volunteers managed a stubborn and skilful defence. Rather than repeat the fatal mistake made during the fourth-century siege, the defenders used a tunnel to undermine the Persians' siege mound.* Yet Kavadh I was determined, even though summer had passed and autumn was waning, making conditions for the besiegers ever harder. After ninety-seven days and considerable loss of life, the Sasanians stormed Amida, sacking the city. Most of the survivors were taken off as slaves, and only a few were left to support the garrison installed by the king of kings. Only then, with a major victory and some plunder—if nowhere near enough to solve his financial problems—Kavadh I withdrew to pass the rest of the winter. He had made his determination very clear.[24]

Yet Anastasius I still did not back down and instead mustered a large force—probably the largest seen in the east since Julian's expedition—with troops drawn from his main field armies. One source gives a total of fifty-two thousand men, although most scholars see this as too high and suggest somewhere between thirty thousand and forty thousand as a more likely total. No overall

---

*See pp. 315–317.

commander was appointed, partly because the troops were not envisaged as a single field force and partly because of the inherent reluctance of emperors to entrust any general with too much power. A glance at some of the men holding more or less equal authority helps to illustrate the dangers of this. One of them was the former son-in-law of a western emperor—not that the western empire existed anymore. Another was Justin, who would in fact be proclaimed emperor when Anastasius I died in 518. Then there was an officer who in just a few years' time rebelled in an unsuccessful bid to seize the imperial purple. A couple of senior men were noted as descendants of Goths who had not gone to the west. Like many army officers, they were of 'barbarian' stock, although there is no indication that this made them any more or less capable and loyal. Their soldiers were also very mixed. Many would prove to be poorly disciplined, although this was widespread and not associated with any particular troop type or ethnic group.[25]

The Roman counter-offensive achieved very little, the movements of the various columns were poorly co-ordinated and sometimes lacking in determination. A siege of Amida was begun, then abandoned when news came that another force was threatened, but by the time the relief force arrived, they discovered that the others had fled in great haste. The siege was renewed without success, and no more was achieved in a more determined effort to take Nisibis, which had always proved a tough nut for any attacker to crack. Several engagements ended in Roman defeats, and near the end of the summer Kavadh I and his main army struck again, but they found that this time the defenders were better prepared. While the king of kings won some minor victories, the main cities such as Constantia, Edessa, and Callinicum defied him, which meant that he withdrew at the end of the year without getting much of the treasure he needed to make the war worthwhile. Arab allies raided the southern Syrian provinces and plundered widely, largely because many troops had been moved from there to support the main Roman effort in Mesopotamia. The war was not going as either side had hoped.

Anastasius I greatly improved the situation by appointing an overall commander to supervise the war effort, choosing a man with an administrative background rather than campaigning experience. He proved competent and gave a far greater sense of purpose to operations, which soon became more aggressive. Matters improved for the Romans even more when, early in 504, Kavadh I was forced to turn and deal with heavy attacks on his northern frontier—probably from the Sabir Huns, yet another nomadic group. In the absence of the king of kings and his army, the Sasanians were no longer capable of major offensives in Mesopotamia. One Roman column drove towards Amida, then retreated when a Persian army closed with them. The Romans became cornered and were forced into a battle, where to everyone's surprise they routed their opponents, breaking the poor run of Roman field forces up to this point in the war.

Amida was besieged again and staunchly defended by its Persian garrison, helped by the fact that little or no damage had been done to its fortifications when the city had fallen in 502. Sasanian engineers blocked a Roman attempt to undermine the walls, intercepting the attackers' tunnel before it had reached them and flooding it before sealing it off. Just like Kavadh I, the Romans stuck with the siege well beyond the usual campaigning season, relying now on blockade and convinced that the defenders would soon run out of food. They were right, but the Persians bluffed well, and when negotiations for surrender began, they hid their precarious situation. A Sasanian army of twenty thousand—all that could be massed in the absence of Kavadh I—approached the Romans, hoping to begin negotiations concerning the city and its garrison and, perhaps, the wider conflict. The Romans agreed to let a convoy of food pass into Amida as a gesture of goodwill but took care to ensure that one general was absent when the oath was taken to keep to these terms. This man then ambushed and destroyed the convoy. Similar behaviour on the part of the Sasanians would doubtless have been presented as shameful treachery rather than a clever stratagem.

Even so, the city continued to hold out, and as winter closed in, many of the Roman troops had had enough and marched home. The Persian field army threatened again, and the siege was brought to a close by negotiation at the beginning of 505. All of the Sasanian troops in the city were allowed to go free with their belongings, as the Romans effectively bought Amida back for one thousand pounds of gold. When they got into the city, the attackers were dismayed to discover that there was only sufficient food remaining in store for the garrison to have survived for another week at most.[26]

Negotiations to end the war, rather than simply the siege, took more than a year to complete, partly because of the time needed for messages to go back and forth. There were no major offensives on either side, and although the Arab confederates of both empires happily raided each other and sometimes struck more settled territory, this was seen as different and almost inevitable. In Mesopotamia, Anastasius I ordered the construction of a new, major, fortified city at Dara, barely fifteen miles from Nisibis on the main route into the Roman province. This was in direct violation of the earlier agreement, although, since the two empires were still at war, that scarcely mattered at the moment. In the longer term, the Sasanians saw it was a provocation, especially when a commander and troops were permanently stationed there. Work went on shielded by the main Roman field army. The defences of other cities were also repaired and reinforced. Kavadh I initially rejected the peace terms on offer, but he was in no position to renew the war on a large scale, nor was there much prospect of the easy plunder that would make such an effort worthwhile. The talks continued, each side trying to secure favourable terms.

In the end, Anastasius I paid Kavadh I a considerable sum of gold, and a seven-year peace was declared. The agreement held, and, although not formally renewed, peace lasted for the best part of two decades before it broke down altogether. From then onwards, relations between Rome and Persia were dominated by intense rivalry and warfare. Thus, the Anastasian War, as it is known, with hindsight marked a turning point after the remarkably peaceful fifth century. Although relatively brief compared with what was to come, it saw sieges of major cities, subterfuge, and treachery on both sides and left a legacy of suspicion. The two eyes of the world would struggle to live in harmony and illuminate each other in the generations to come.

16

WAR AND ETERNAL PEACE

518–c. 600

ONCE AGAIN, THERE WERE SIGNS THAT A PROLONGED PERIOD of peace between the two empires was coming to an end. No single factor made this happen; it was a combination of domestic politics, shifts elsewhere, and the personality of leaders and advisors. This did not mean that frequent war was inevitable from now on, but it did make it more likely whenever one side or the other scented an opportunity. Each new war left grievances, or the sense of lost prestige, which meant that the loser was more than likely to seize a suitable chance to set things right. In a sense, whenever domestic politics made war with the other empire attractive, and a ruler's forces were not already fully committed on other fronts, there was a good chance that an emperor or king of kings would seek to take advantage of any perceived weakness, however temporary, on the part of his rival.

Anastasius I died on 9 July 518. He had no son, and although his three nephews had been shown some favour, this had stopped well short of marking out any of them, or indeed anyone else, as the heir. Instead, after behind-the-scenes wrangling, the commander of the imperial bodyguard, a man named Justin, was proclaimed as emperor. One source alleged that he took money meant to bribe

the officers and soldiers on behalf of another candidate and instead gave it to them in his own name. His accession was certainly
a surprise, but everything was arranged quickly and without major
conflict. In many ways an elderly military man, Justin—in his late
sixties—was fairly typical of the compromise candidates chosen
when there was no more obvious successor.[1]

Tales of the humble origins of men who became emperor need
to be taken with more than a pinch of salt, meaning little more
than that they came from outside the established elite. Yet the nature
of the empire since the third century did allow for some remarkable
careers, and Justin's was one of the most spectacular. Born in Latin-
speaking Illyricum, his Greek was originally poor and never acquired
the polish and sophistication expected of the well-educated, even
though decades spent with guard units in and around the palace
must have meant that he became fluent. Procopius's claim that he was
illiterate and needed a stencil so that his pen could follow the shapes
to sign documents is surely a slander, though perhaps near the end
of his life his hand became unsteady. Although he had no son of his
own, Justin early on showed great favour to his nephew Justinian,
who followed him to Constantinople. Service in the various guard
units brought rapid promotion, and Justinian received far more of
the education his uncle lacked.[2]

At some point Justin adopted Justinian, and the latter may well
have assisted in securing the imperial throne in 518. By 521 he was
consul, a symbolic and highly prestigious revival of the ancient republican magistracy, and was clearly the foremost assistant and
obvious successor to his uncle. During these years he also married, although his choice of bride was surprising, then and now.
Theodora came from a family associated with the circus, for the
lavish chariot races and other entertainments staged there—by
this era no longer including gladiators—required a large industry to support them. Her father supervised the care of animals,
while Theodora and her sisters performed as entertainers on stage.
This was not an honourable occupation, and in the public mind,
women who sang, danced, or otherwise performed were assumed
to double as prostitutes. Procopius, who loathed Theodora, gave
in his *Secret History* a detailed and scurrilous account of her early

life, lambasting her for her lustful nature that drove her to do more than was necessary; one claim was that before she reached puberty she was already performing sex acts for money. Much of what he wrote was surely gossip or his own invention, but even a source favourable to her accepted that she had been a prostitute, but that, after finding her faith, she had attained properly Christian heights of virtue and piety. A special law was required to allow Justinian to marry her, because aristocrats since the early principate had been forbidden to wed those of dishonourable professions or low social status. Justinian made Theodora a wife rather than a mistress and later made her his empress and gave her a very public role. This is hard to explain unless there was a deep emotional bond between them, for she possessed no important political connections.[3]

Justin's influence over Justinian was considerable from the start. Justinian is said to have faced opposition from Justin's wife to his marriage to Theodora, but not from the emperor himself once his wife died. Procopius certainly viewed the reigns of uncle and nephew as essentially the same regime. The accession of a new emperor or king of kings naturally led to diplomatic exchanges between the two empires, all conducted with elaborate ceremony. A detailed description of the reception of a Sasanian embassy to Constantinople was set down during Justinian's reign, giving us insight into the intricacies of the process. Everything was regulated from the moment the Persian ambassador and his entourage crossed the border. It was stipulated that he bring only essential staff, in case this was a surprise attack masquerading as an embassy. The Persians were greeted at each stage of the journey, accommodation and transport laid on for them in suitable style through the provinces and then across the sea to Constantinople. Once there, the process began with a formal reception, then a first audience with the emperor. The ambassador was to prostrate himself before the ruler of the Roman world, be formally accepted, and give his gifts, but he was not permitted to discuss anything at this stage. Apart from the etiquette and ceremony, the account reminds the emperor to ask about the health of the king of kings and his family on multiple occasions and sometimes about the welfare of the ambassador and senior Persian officials known to him from experience or by reputation. The tone of each exchange was determined by whether or not the two empires were currently at peace or at war, but it was assumed that they would exchange ambassadors in either case. Diplomacy was meant to encourage peace by displaying the power and dignity of each side, but it always acknowledged that war could and did break out.[4]

Although new rulers were naturally inclined to assert their strength, at first the peace that had concluded the Anastasian War continued under Justin. An Arab leader allied to Persia raided Roman territory, taking prisoner two senior Roman officers as well as other captives. He was seen as a free agent, not a mere puppet of the king of kings, so although the Romans responded militarily and eventually by ransoming the officers, this was not taken as a breach of the peace between the empires. Of more serious concern was the allegiance of the kingdoms of the Caucasus. The greater part of Armenia, Iberia, Georgia, and Lazica, which lay on the east shore of the Black Sea, had been under Sasanian overlordship for several generations and sometimes under direct rule. These regions had never been easy to control and bring under central government, for either the empire or regional kings. The Persians made repeated attempts to spread Zoroastrianism—both out of a sense that this was right and to integrate the population into the empire—but this prompted resistance and rebellion. Moderation and force calmed these situations for a while before the resentment built up afresh.[5]

Around 521 or 522, the king of the Lazi died, and his son and successor rejected Persian rule and fled to Constantinople, announcing that he wished to become a Christian. Justin welcomed him, and after he was baptized, the king was married to the daughter of a senator and sent home with money and other gifts. Kavadh I sent an embassy to protest the new alliance represented by all this, stating that the region had long been recognized as part of his empire. Justin ignored this and responded by declaring that he could not deny anyone's sincere wish to worship God. Neither empire was willing to go to war over the issue, but relations soured. Around this time, Roman envoys also tried to persuade one of the Hunnic leaders of the region to the north into

alliance with Rome and hostility to Persia. After negotiations, the
Hun changed his mind and allied more closely with Kavadh I.
However, the earlier diplomatic efforts were then put to good use
by the Romans, who revealed the discussions to the Persians to ex-
pose the shifting loyalties of the leader in question. The Sasanians
attacked and killed him.[6]

By this time, Kavadh I was an old man and increasingly concerned about the succession, since he favoured his youngest son,
Khusro I, over two older brothers. Around 525, another embassy
was dispatched to Constantinople, this time with a proposal echoing
Arcadius's appeal to Yazdgerd I to protect the infant Theodosius II.
Kavadh I went further by suggesting that Justin adopt Khusro I as
his son, ensuring that the Romans would support the latter's claim,
at the very least with diplomatic pressure and perhaps even with
money and military force if necessary. Justin and Justinian were
keen on the idea, until a senior advisor warned them that adoption by the emperor in Constantinople would give the Sasanian
prince and his descendants a claim to rule the Roman empire. No
source hints that this was ever Kavadh I's intention, and modern
historians are quick to point out the unlikelihood of Khusro I or
any other Sasanian actually being able to win acceptance as emperor. This is surely true, although it is far less certain whether all
Romans at the time would have considered it to be wholly impossible. Some very unlikely men had become emperors since the third
century, and the empire itself had divided, the west had fallen, and
the east had changed profoundly in ways that earlier generations
surely had not imagined. Caution among senior ministers about
the proposal was understandable, for at the very least such a claim
might have offered the Persians an additional grievance to revive
in every negotiation in the future or even provide a pretext for war.

Instead of full adoption as his son, Justin was persuaded to offer the lesser honour of adoption 'by the spear', something usually
reserved for the kings of tribal peoples to cement an alliance. This
was essentially an honorary status and did not in any way commit
the Romans to active financial or military support of the emperor's
'son'. Negotiations continued and were well advanced, with lega-
tions composed of very senior figures meeting on the borders of

the empire and Khusro I waiting near Nisibis to undergo whatever formal ceremony was necessary to complete the agreement. Over time, the Sasanians realized the implications of what was being offered and surely saw treating the son of the king of kings like some petty warlord as a clear insult. Other grievances re-emerged, the defection of the king of the Lazi was brought up, and the mood soured. The delegations went home without an agreement and with Khusro I and Kavadh I understandably offended.[7]

Around this time, Kavadh I renewed his efforts to bring the kingdoms of the Caucasus more fully under his control, once again encouraging the adoption of Zoroastrianism. This political and religious pressure prompted the king of Iberia to approach Justin for support against the Persians. This was agreed but proved harder to deliver in a meaningful way. The emperor did not want to send his own soldiers, and his agents had difficulty recruiting bands of Huns to fight alongside the Iberians. The king and his supporters were soon driven out of Iberia and took refuge in Lazica. More effort was made to defend Lazica as the Persians followed up their success, but it was always hard to wage war in this mountainous country. Two forts on the border were garrisoned by the Romans but could not be supplied, so they were abandoned and occupied by the Sasanians. Probably in 528 a stronger force was sent, but a divided command meant that it achieved nothing. The Persians were left in control of Iberia—as far as that was ever possible—and of the two forts in Lazica.[8]

In 527, Justin died and was succeeded by Justinian. One of his earliest acts was to strengthen the defences of Roman Armenia, creating several new commands and bringing in more troops. Around the time of the accession, an Arab leader allied to the Sasanians launched raids into Roman Mesopotamia, but this was as usual interpreted as an independent act on his part. Partly in response, some effort was made to improve defences along vulnerable sections of the frontier, most notably turning Palmyra into a fortress city. Belisarius, a protégé of Justinian and a commander who was to figure prominently in the wars of his reign, was sent to build from scratch a new outpost south of Dara but was driven off by the Persians. Kavadh I renewed Persian demands for Roman gold

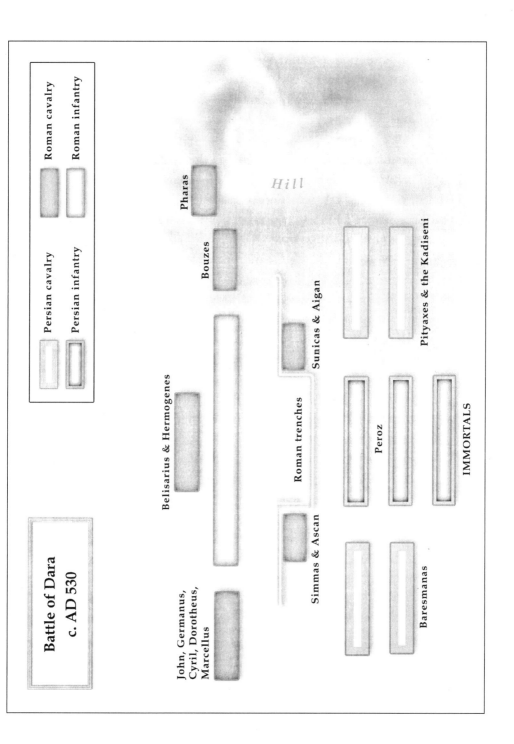

Battle of Dara
c. AD 530

Persian cavalry
Persian infantry
Roman cavalry
Roman infantry

Hill

Pharas

Bouzes

Belisarius & Hermogenes

John, Germanus,
Cyril, Dorotheus,
Marcellus

Simmas & Ascan

Roman trenches

Sunicas & Aigan

Peroz

Baresmanas

IMMORTALS

Pityaxes & the Kadiseni

to help pay for the defences in the passes of the Caucasus and to the east of the Caspian Sea, and there was back-and-forth negotiation for some time without resolving any of the major points of contention. Kavadh I openly threatened invasion if his terms were not met.[9]

In June 530, a large Persian army, allegedly numbering some forty thousand men, crossed the border and advanced on Dara. Belisarius had an army half the size at the city and chose to risk battle in the open, albeit close to the city's walls. The bulk of his troops were infantrymen, poorly trained and inexperienced, so that he had little confidence in them. A system of trenches was dug in front of their positions to make it very hard for the enemy to charge the formations of foot soldiers. Crossing places were set at regular intervals, and in the centre the ditches projected forward in an inverted U shape. Kavadh I did not go on campaign in person, since he was now about eighty, and instead had given command to a member of the Mihran family. For a day, the Sasanian general studied the Roman position, and there were skirmishes and single combats—a bath attendant of one of the Roman officers is said to have fought and killed two Persian opponents. By the next day, ten thousand more infantry had arrived from Nisibis to reinforce the Sasanians, who then waited for the noon heat before launching their attack. Archers on both sides showered the enemy with arrows for a long time; the Romans were helped because the wind was strong and blew towards the Persians. Nothing was decided by this exchange, which often seems to have been the case in this period, largely because both sides were well protected by their armour and most of the shooting was done at fairly long range. As the Sasanians closed to hand-to-hand combat, there was heavy fighting, and small numbers of Roman horsemen, chiefly allied Huns and Heruli, made a series of decisive charges, hitting the Persians in the flank.

Neither side's infantry played any active role in the battle. The Roman foot, sheltered by the ditches, offered a secure base and rallying point for their cavalry and may have added to the volume of missiles sent at the enemy but otherwise did nothing. Belisarius and his officers marshalled their outnumbered horsemen well, shifting fresh reserves to deal with any breakthrough. The Romans exploited the concealment offered by a hill, and their better knowledge of the routes across the trenches, to launch devastating flank charges. At times there is something of a medieval feel to Procopius's narrative of the battle, for instance when a Roman officer—in fact a Hun— killed first the standard-bearer of the Sasanian commander of the left wing and then the commander himself. When the Persian cavalry retreated, the infantry panicked and were cut down as they fled, until Belisarius recalled his men, reluctant to let them pursue too far and fall into disorder. He had won a clear victory—the greatest won in a pitched battle against the Sasanians that any Roman could remember—and did not want to risk losing all that he had gained by chasing the enemy and falling into an ambush.[10]

There was more good news for Justinian when a Persian attack into Armenia was also beaten back. Their hand strengthened by these successes, Roman envoys went to Kavadh I seeking a resumption of peace. The king of kings repeated his demand for gold, saying that with the Romans being so aggressive from their forward base at Dara, he now had to maintain an army to face them as well as another to hold the northern border. In 531, Justinian's repression of other religions provoked a violent rebellion by the Samaritans, some of whom appealed to Kavadh I for aid. Persuaded by an Arab leader of the poor state of Roman defences in southern Mesopotamia, the king of kings abandoned diplomacy for the moment and instead in the spring sent a big raid up the Euphrates, hoping to do well from plunder and extortion. The entire army was mounted, with fifteen thousand Sasanians and five thousand Arab allies, hoping to surprise the defenders by following a route not used by a major army for generations.[11]

Results were disappointing, and the Roman reaction came quicker than expected. Belisarius hurried to the theatre with a small force, then outmanoeuvred the attackers until enough Roman reinforcements arrived to deal with them. The great raid was forced to retreat, and there the campaign might have ended, save for the fact that the Roman troops were desperate to fight. Procopius says that Belisarius was unwilling to continue, but he could not control his ill-disciplined men, who wanted revenge and believed that the Sasanians were running in panic. The Romans attacked near Callinicum on Good Friday, 18 April 531, hungry from fasting and weary from the pace of their pursuit. Even the wind was against them this time, blowing their own arrows back and adding force to those shot by the Persians. The Sasanians made better use of their reserves and broke through, on the left, causing the Roman line to collapse. Belisarius rallied some of the infantry into dense blocks with their backs to a river and held out until the Sasanians withdrew. While the raid had failed to yield Kavadh I any worthwhile profits, the battle had dented Roman confidence at a time when it had been riding high. Justinian ordered an investigation into what had happened and, as a result of this, recalled Belisarius to Constantinople. The Sasanian commander was also sacked at the end of the campaign.[12]

There were fresh attempts by the Romans to negotiate, which came to nothing as Kavadh I ordered an attack against Osrhoene and later against Roman Armenia, his invasion force advancing northwards from Mesopotamia. This led to the hard-fought siege of the principal Roman stronghold at Martyropolis, which drifted on into the winter months. Making no headway, and hearing that Kavadh I had succumbed to old age, the Persian army eventually withdrew. Khusro I, more concerned with securing his hold on the throne in the face of a brother's rival claim than with fighting the Romans, tried to revive the peace talks. Justinian prevaricated, hoping to benefit from the new Sasanian monarch's weakness, even though he also had little desire to continue the war. After a while, a three-month truce was agreed, which led to more serious talks. While this was in force, a band of Sabir Huns who had been recruited by Kavadh I, but who arrived too late for the war, felt that such courtesies were none of their business and raided the Roman provinces so that they did not have to return home empty-handed. Taking the defenders by surprise, they plundered widely, and only a few strays were caught by the Romans and defeated as they withdrew. Investigations swiftly cleared the Persians of any complicity, and the talks continued.[13]

In 532, after a good deal of haggling and changes of mind, a treaty was agreed between Khusro I and Justinian. As a one-off payment, rather than an annual obligation, the Romans paid 110 *centenaria* of gold.* They also withdrew the commander stationed at Dara, along with his troops, back to Constantia, deeper within the province. Any captives and hostages on each side were returned, as were almost all of the forts and other strongholds taken during the war, including the two in Lazica occupied by the Persians. The rhetoric of brotherhood between emperor and king of kings was given full rein, for it was 'written in our ancient records that we are brothers of one another', with promises of aid if the other was ever in need in the future. Not content with a limited term of friendship, this was declared an eternal peace, and it was widely celebrated on both sides.[14]

Both sides were satisfied with the agreement and, at least for the moment, sincere in their desire for peace. Khusro I received a much-needed injection of funds, as well as the prestige of receiving tribute from the Romans, at least as far as his own people were concerned. As part of securing his hold on power against potential rivals from within the family, he also suppressed the Mazdakite movement, executing many of its leaders and the most prominent adherents. Later tradition remembered his long reign as a golden age, when the empire was strong and justly ruled and the power of the king of kings throughout his lands increased. The army grew in size and quality, relying heavily on the lesser nobility and local landlords taken directly into royal service and expected to train for war, while four permanent commands in the west, north, east, and south were created. Similar reorganization improved the administrative, judicial, and financial structures, increasing central control. Scholars used to argue that Khusro I pushed back the power of the great noble clans, but this was most likely little more than what any strong monarch had done in the past. Seals from official documents show that most of the senior commands, notably the generals of the four districts, continued to be held by members of the old established clans—like the Mihran, Karen, and Suren— who often still used the Parthian language alongside the Persian, and who also reappear in all their importance in subsequent reigns.

---

*A measure of about one hundred pounds weight.

Khusro I's later fame probably meant that reforms and good practices from other periods came to be associated with him, so that it is very hard to know precisely what changes he made and how deep these went. Yet the picture of overall strength of the empire at the height of his reign is justified.[15]

Justinian was also a great reformer, building on the work done under Theodosius II by ordering the collation of Roman laws issued since Hadrian and of the answers given by respected jurists to thorny questions. He was also a great builder; Procopius devoted a book to his projects, many of them improving the defences on the frontiers and of cities. Most famously, Justinian commissioned Saint Sophia in Constantinople, the great cathedral built to replace a far more modest church destroyed by fire. Its immense dome—which was part of a rebuilding late in Justinian's reign, following damage from an earthquake—is one of the greatest achievements of Roman engineering. He also was the first emperor in a long time to expand the empire, bringing back under his rule territory lost since the collapse of the west.[16]

None of this happened instantly, nor was it all inevitable, for at the start of 532, as the negotiations leading to the eternal peace were continuing, Justinian's reign almost came to an abrupt end. The main circus factions, supporters of the Green and Blue teams of charioteers, were rioting in what had begun as protests against punishment of some of their members convicted of violent crimes but swiftly turned political in the so-called Nika riots. (Supporters urging on their favourite in the races used to shout out 'Nika', or 'victory', and during the riots it became a slogan.) There were calls for the dismissal or death of several senior ministers, and there is every sign that influential figures were working behind the scenes to overthrow Justinian and replace him. Unable to control the violence with the palace troops, the emperor was said to have planned to flee from his capital, until his nerve was stiffened by Theodora, who told him that 'empire was a good burial shroud'. Instead of fleeing, Justinian had Belisarius and another commander bring their soldiers into the city, notably the *bucellarii* or 'biscuit men', the picked cavalry regiments maintained by senior officers. These hardened professionals quickly routed the rioters. Many died, others were executed—including some of those thought to be exploiting the situation for political gain—and imperial control was restored by force.[17]

Secure for the moment both from internal threats and from fresh conflict with Persia, in 533 Justinian sent the rehabilitated Belisarius with an army of fifteen thousand men against the Vandal kingdom of Africa. Success was rapid, astoundingly so given the disastrous expeditions of the fifth century, for the attack came when much of the Vandals' strength was committed elsewhere. Two years later, Justinian rewarded his general with a consulship and a triumph, leading the Vandal king as a captive through Constantinople. The spoils on display were lavish, including gold and ornaments from the Jewish Temple in Jerusalem taken originally at the time of its destruction in 70 and later by the Vandals when they sacked Rome in 455.

Encouraged by this success, Justinian subsequently sent Belisarius to Sicily, which again fell fairly quickly, and later to Italy, while another expedition landed in Spain. These later campaigns were harder. Only a small part of Visigothic Spain was taken, and while most of Italy fell, this was only after decades of fighting, first against the Ostrogoths and then the Lombards and others. The cost was enormous in manpower and money. Army pay was often very late indeed, which rarely helped morale and provoked several mutinies. Attempts to skimp on the defences and garrisons of Africa led to more fighting against the tribes along the borders. In each area, the prolonged warfare inflicted great hardships on the civilian population, who, even in Italy, were not always persuaded that they were better off under their liberators. Even so, during Justinian's reign most of the lands around the Mediterranean were brought back into the empire, as was the city of Rome itself. This was done in stages, and the emperor's ambitions developed and increased with each success. The desire to regain as much lost territory as possible may have been there from the start, but there is little hint that Justinian worked to a coherent plan. This was opportunistic, and the opportunity came in the first place because there was peace with Persia, so resources could be employed in the west.[18]

The eternal peace had taken some three and a half years to negotiate and lasted barely seven and a half years. There was tension before this, and we hear of raids against Roman communities by Arab leaders allied to the Sasanians, but negotiations prevented this turning into conflict between the empires. Similarly, when rivalry between leaders allied to each empire turned into open war, it did not mean that the empires would be drawn into conflict. Yet Khusro I could see that Justinian was preoccupied with the west and that the defences of Rome's eastern provinces were weaker than they once were. In addition, he received appeals for aid from leaders in Roman Armenia, who resented the imposition of more direct control and the presence of garrisons that had come from the recent reorganization of the region. The king of kings sensed weakness and thought of the great wealth of the cities in the Roman provinces. The attraction of maintaining the peace with his 'brother' Justinian faded. As far as we can tell, he still had to pay the annual tribute to the Hephthalite Huns agreed by his father, Kavadh I, while the costs of maintaining armies and defences remained. Even if only some of the reforms attributed to Khusro I were under way at this stage of his reign, they were not cheap.[19]

Persian diplomacy became more aggressive as Khusro I sought a pretext for invasion and began to prepare his expedition. Justinian sent a letter urging his 'brother' not to break the treaty. No answer was returned, until in May 540 Khusro I led a great army up the Euphrates. The strongest cities in his path were ignored and do not appear to have possessed sufficient garrisons to harass his progress. He attacked Sura, whose Roman commander was killed in the fighting. His name was Arsaces, which suggests that he was Armenian. In spite of his loss, the Sasanians were repulsed, but in subsequent negotiations the Persians tricked the local bishop and got men inside the city, which then swiftly fell. It was sacked, its population taken captive but ransomed when two centenaria was promised by another bishop, although not in the event delivered. Another city paid two thousand pounds of silver to dissuade Khusro I from attacking. When Roman envoys came, the king of kings offered to withdraw altogether from Roman territory for ten centenaria in gold. In the meantime, he sacked Beroea, and some of the garrison there subsequently defected to the Persians, a sign of the poor motivation of many limetanei at this time.[20]

Justinian was unwilling to pay for peace, so the king of kings pushed on towards the Mediterranean coast. At Antioch, the population was encouraged by the arrival of six thousand Roman troops, so much so that their leaders dismissed Khusro I's fresh demand for ten centenaria to leave them unmolested. Yet the old vulnerability of the city's walls had only been made worse by a recent earthquake, and they were not in a good enough state to cope with a full-scale assault. Antioch's citizens did their best to resist but were swiftly overwhelmed. The Roman regular troops played little part in the fighting and marched out of one side of the city as the Persians swarmed over the walls on the opposite side. In normal times, Antioch's population numbered several hundred thousand, perhaps as many as half a million, but a good number had already fled. Even so, the captives and plunder from the sack of Antioch were the greatest won by any Persian army in recent conflicts. One church was spared after treasure had been handed over, but the rest of the city was burned or otherwise destroyed.

Khusro I pressed on to the sea, bathing in the Mediterranean, before beginning the march back to his own empire. Along the way, he extorted money from city after city, none of them willing to face assault. Already, Roman ambassadors had come and eventually agreed to pay fifty centenaria straightaway, with five more every year in the future, ostensibly to pay for the soldiers and defences needed to protect the passes through the Caucasus. To save a little face, this was declared not to be tribute. As the Sasanian army withdrew, Justinian's written agreement to the deal reached Khusro I, which should have brought the peace treaty into effect. Perhaps too elated by all his success, the king of kings could not resist besieging Dara. A Persian attempt to undermine the walls was thwarted by a Roman countermine, but the citizens were still willing to hand over one thousand pounds of silver to persuade Khusro I to depart. All in all, this had been by far the most successful and profitable campaign waged by a Sasanian king for many generations. Using some of the spoils, a new city was built near Ctesiphon and the other royal cities to accommodate the prisoners taken. The king of kings decided to call it Veh-Antioch-Khusro, or 'the better Antioch of Khusro', to remind everyone of what he had done. Later tradition claimed that the new city was designed as a replica of the old one. Yet for all this success, Khusro I had given up the very favourable peace terms offered by a desperate Justinian.[21]

Belisarius was recalled from the ongoing war in Italy to take command in the east, but he struggled to achieve much with the forces available. Most of the troops were demoralized, while many of the officers and allied leaders struggled to work together or obey orders. The Romans raided Assyria, taking one small fortified city before they withdrew. Khusro I and his main army were not in the area to oppose them, making this modest achievement even less impressive. Instead, the king of kings had gone to the north, having announced that he planned to wage war against the Huns who had recently attacked Iberia. In fact, he had received an appeal for aid from the king of Lazica, who had repented of his alliance with Rome. Partly this was the familiar dislike for any strong central government, made worse by the misbehaviour of the main Roman commander of the region. When the Persians advanced into Lazica, the king greeted Khusro I as liberator. After a sharp fight, the main Roman base at the newly built city of Petra was captured, persuading other garrisons to withdraw. However, for all this success, the news of the Roman attack on Assyria caused discontent among many Persians, especially those with family in the area, and was enough to hurry the withdrawal of the main Persian army.[22]

Late in 541, an epidemic appeared in Egypt, apparently brought by travellers coming from the African kingdoms in the south. In the months that followed, the disease spread throughout the Roman empire and well beyond, although that is less well-recorded. It would return on multiple occasions in the decades to come, with many local outbreaks. The descriptions of Procopius and others make clear that it was a form of bubonic plague, which does not mean that other diseases such as typhus did not also flourish in the conditions created by the epidemic. Comparisons have often been drawn with the Black Death in fourteenth-century Europe, and the Justinianic plague is included with this and the early twentieth-century pandemic in Asia as the three most severe plagues in history. Not all scholars agree, and certainty is impossible since we lack detailed statistics about population levels before and after the outbreaks to measure the death toll and trace its wider economic and social consequences. Thus it is hard to say just how much impact it had, at least on long-term demographics, or to compare its cost to the Antonine plague or any of the other plagues that ravaged the ancient world. Clearly, this was an awful experience for many, and the death toll, at least in the crowded cities, was appalling. Yet not all those who contracted the disease died; Justinian became very ill but recovered and lived on for many years. There is no impression that armies or administrations were catastrophically damaged by plague deaths, which does not mean that, in some places at some times, it did not make things very difficult by killing or weakening experienced and well-trained personnel.[23]

In 542, Khusro I once again attacked across the Euphrates, singling out for punishment the bishop who had failed to pay him the promised ransom money in 540. The bishop's city was forced to hand over treasure in recompense but managed to hold out against an attack. Khusro I was eager to reach cities not plundered in the earlier campaign. He had his eyes on Jerusalem and all its wealth, only to be blocked by Belisarius at the head of a large Roman field force. After negotiations, the king of kings agreed to withdraw if unhindered by the Romans, but he broke the agreement—or at least the Roman understanding of it—by seizing Callinicum on his way past, the city's defences too dilapidated to make its defence practical. He then returned to his own empire, in part nervous of the spreading plague. Late in the summer, Justinian ordered a number of commanders, some of them from the southern front, to advance into Persian Armenia. Eventually some thirty thousand Roman troops were concentrated, heavily outnumbering the Sasanian defenders. They captured a number of cities, until success made them overconfident and careless. The Sasanian commander lured them into a skilful ambush and won a great victory.[24]

The next year Khusro I again attacked, this time moving on Osrhoene and besieging Edessa. Yet after two months the city continued to resist, and the king of kings accepted payment of five centenaria to leave. Although welcome, the returns on his offensives had diminished since the glory days of 540, and Khusro I was more inclined to see the benefits of peace. After prolonged negotiation, a five-year truce was declared in 545, after the Romans agreed to pay twenty centenaria as a one-off gift. In the main, this held in Mesopotamia and the south, although Khusro I was accused of trying to seize Dara by treachery, strengthening an ambassador's escort with troops in the hope that all would be admitted to the city, just as the author of the text describing the etiquette for diplomatic exchanges had feared. In the event, the party was not admitted, and the attempt failed. This was not seen as ending the truce, nor was the resumption of war in the Caucasus, where the Lazi had decided that Sasanian occupation was worse than Roman rule, especially since it meant that their access to the Black Sea and its trade was greatly reduced. As Christians, they also resented efforts to convert them to Zoroastrianism, leading to rebellion in 547.[25]

Khusro I saw the war as an opportunity to gain ground in the wider region, including taking some of the other kingdoms around the Black Sea. Justinian sent aid to the Lazi, prompting the Persians to commit more troops, commanded by a member of the Mihran family. Over time, the Romans and their allies gained the advantage, invading Iberia. Another Persian army was sent to the region, only be severely defeated. The Persians still held Petra, something that prompted the king of the Lazi to complain to Justinian, who sacked his commander on the spot and sent another. Some neighbouring communities went further, deciding that they did not care for a Roman presence and switching sides, and fortunes swayed back and forth. In 551, the five-year truce ended and was renewed for another five years, but it was not extended to Lazica, where the war continued to rage without either side securing a permanent advantage. Elsewhere, Arab allies fought each other and occasionally raided the empires themselves, and both of the great powers involved themselves in affairs down as far as the Arabian Gulf, imperial competition fuelling local ambitions and rivalries.

Negotiations for a formal peace took a long time, as they usually did, each side hoping that they could gain enough advantage in Lazica or elsewhere to secure better overall terms. Yet Justinian was still too heavily involved in the west to be able to wage a war with all his might against Persia, while Khusro I was becoming more and more concerned by the Hephthalites. Eventually, over the winter of 561–562, an agreement was reached and a fifty-year peace declared, which was to bind not simply the two empires but also their Arab allies. Lazica was acknowledged as Roman, although the status of a region that the Romans considered to be part of the kingdom while the Persians did not was left unclear. In addition to other clauses regulating the exchange of ambassadors and trade, the Sasanians were no longer to complain about Dara, since the Romans agreed that it would not house more than a minimal garrison. Yet the key to the whole settlement was that once again the Romans had bought peace. They promised to pay thirty thousand gold coins every year (probably equivalent to five hundred pounds of gold), and the first seven years were to be paid immediately and more to come in lump advances at stipulated intervals. Justinian also agreed to pay much smaller subsidies to a number of Arab leaders, who in return promised not to raid Roman territory.[26]

All in all, Khusro I had done better out of this deal than Justinian, although probably not quite as well as he had hoped at times when the war looked particularly favourable. At the same time, he had significantly increased Persian influence in southern Arabia as far as the Arabian Gulf and finally defeated the Hephthalite Hunnic kingdom on his north-eastern border. This was achieved through alliance with the Turkic tribes who had been pressing against the lands of the Hephthalites from the other direction. As had so often been the case in the past, the relief was temporary, and by around 570 he was at war with the Western Turks, as the new, and more eagerly aggressive, nomads established themselves on his borders. In due course, the Romans were able to ally with the Turks and encourage their attacks.

Justinian lost prestige by accepting a permanent liability to pay the Persians, no matter that this was supposed to be funding for defences of mutual benefit. The war in Italy continued to rage, other conquests were challenged, and there were serious attacks against the Balkan provinces. A widower since 548, the emperor was in his eighties and increasingly seen as weak. There was an unsuccessful plot to assassinate him in the autumn of 562, in the aftermath of which Belisarius was disgraced and stripped of assets as well as his household troops. This was more because of his enduring fame, recent disappointing performance on the Balkan frontier, and rivalries within the senior ranks of the army than any actual involvement in the conspiracy. Other commanders had to suppress a new outbreak of rioting by the circus factions in 565, the task being done with thoroughness and considerable brutality. Justinian died that same year, succeeded by his nephew Justin II, since he had no son of his own. There were a few arrests and executions, but on the whole the transition went smoothly.[27]

At first, Justin II dutifully sent the gold due to Khusro I, but at the same time he revived the question of the disputed territory near Lazica and ceased to pay the subsidies promised to Persia's Arab allies. After diplomatic attempts to persuade him to change his mind, the Arab groups began predatory raids, while a wider conflict developed between the Arab allies of each side. In 569, Justin II refused to pay the next instalment of the money due to the Sasanians and sent ambassadors to the Turks, seeking alliance. Many of the inhabitants of Persian Armenia had grown dissatisfied with Persian rule, especially what they saw as the renewed encroachment of Zoroastrianism, and they appealed to the Romans to support them. With this assurance, they rebelled in 571, killing the Sasanian governor—a member of the Suren clan who was accused of seducing the wives of a number of leading noblemen. Many Iberians also defected to Rome. A year later, Justin II decided to resort to all-out war, even though he had not really prepared for major operations. A commander named Marcian was ordered to attack and plunder Persian territory, and in 573 the Romans tried and failed once again to capture Nisibis. They were then routed by a Sasanian counter-offensive, which followed up its success by capturing Dara.

News of this loss was thought to be the cause of Justin II's complete mental collapse, one source claiming that he started making animal noises. His wife, the niece of Theodora, appealed for a truce from Khusro I, declaring that it would be dishonourable for such a great king to wage war on a defenceless woman and sweetening the offer with a payment in gold. On these terms, a truce was declared for a year, and a senior court official, Tiberius II, was declared Caesar and co-ruler, since it had become clear that Justin II was not going to recover, even though he lived on for five years and had occasional lucid moments. Khusro I was persuaded to prolong the truce for three years but not to have it extended to Armenia, where the war continued. A large Sasanian army recovered all of the territory in rebellion and then attacked into the Roman province. Unable to take the key cities, the Persians drove into Cappadocia, only to suffer defeat. Khusro I lost a good deal of his personal baggage, although the old man rode out through the mountains on an elephant at the head of most of his troops. In the aftermath, he was more willing to negotiate, but fighting continued with varying fortunes.[28]

Justin II finally died in 578, the same year that Tiberius II appointed a new commander for the eastern armies, a man named Maurice, who later as emperor wrote or commissioned the *Strategikon*. He proved an active and able commander and won success after success, helped by the death of Khusro I in 579, which distracted the Persians from the war effort. However, a Roman appeal to return to peace on the basis of the old treaty foundered when Khusro I's son Hormizd IV refused to hand back Dara. The war continued, and the Romans won more victories. By 581, Maurice began an offensive aimed at reaching Ctesiphon, and although this did not go so well and had to be abandoned when the Persians attacked Edessa and forced him to return to protect it, this was a sign of greatly renewed Roman confidence and wider ambition. The disappointment was temporary, for when the Persians attacked again the next spring, Maurice defeated them in battle. By now, Tiberius II was in poor health and concerned about the future. Maurice was recalled to Constantinople, betrothed to one of the emperor's daughters, and proclaimed as Caesar. Tiberius II died a few months later, from illness or perhaps poison.[29]

Maurice was forty-three when his reign began, and, following the precedent of the last two centuries, he no longer went on campaign but spent most of his time in or near Constantinople and entrusted the war to subordinates. On the whole these did well, more often raiding Persian territory than defending against Sasanian raids. Some of this success came because Hormizd IV was fighting the Turks and sent his best troops and commander to that front. There were successes and some—though fewer—defeats, but none in themselves decisive. The war went on, and for the moment the Romans chose to reject Sasanian appeals for peace. This determination to secure better terms was a gamble, for Maurice had inherited a treasury that was already struggling to meet all of its commitments, not least the cost of maintaining the western provinces and the ongoing war with Persia. The struggle against the Sasanians had sucked resources—men, money, and attention—away from other frontiers, leading to setbacks in the Balkans in particular, where the Avars and various Slavic peoples threatened to overrun the frontier regions. Apart from this, the decades of plague, earthquakes, fires, and other natural disasters surely had some effect on trade and revenue, even if it cannot be measured and was temporary. Throughout his reign, Maurice was always short of funds, and attempts to improve the situation meant that he acquired a reputation for greed. One desperate measure was to reduce soldiers' pay, which prompted a number of mutinies, the most serious in the east, where some five thousand troops operated independently for some time, even defeating a Sasanian raiding band. The situation seemed ripe for a serious civil war and challenge to his rule, but luck, skill, and concessions prevented this and eventually brought the mutineers back under imperial control.[30]

In 589, Maurice decided on one great effort in the hope of winning enough of a victory to secure a favourable peace. One attack was launched from Mesopotamia, another went from Armenia into Persian Armenia, backed by renewed effort in Lazica, and a raid into Persian territory was made by the Iberians. Hormizd IV does not appear to have campaigned in person, but by this time his ablest general, Bahrām Chobin, had defeated the Turks and was sent to face the Romans and their allies. He won several small successes but then suffered a battlefield defeat at the hands of the Romans and their Lazi allies. The king of kings was so enraged by the news that he sacked and publicly humiliated his general. It proved a grave mistake, for the disgraced general rebelled, determined to oust the king of kings and seize power himself.

As far as we know, Bahrām Chobin had no blood connection to the Sasanian royal house, and if any existed it can only have been extremely distant. Most likely he was a member of one of the established Parthian noble families. Thus, for the first time since Ardashir I had killed the last of the Arsacids, someone from outside the direct Sasanian royal line was proclaimed as king of kings and began to mint his own coins. Plenty of noblemen and their household troops rallied to him, and more soon joined them, whereas support for Hormizd IV dwindled. As the rebel army approached Ctesiphon, senior courtiers decided that the king of kings was a lost cause. Hormizd IV was dethroned and executed, and his son Khusro II proclaimed in his place, but this did not deter Bahrām Chobin. Within days, the forces of each side met in battle. Those loyal to the young king of kings were routed, and Khusro II fled to the Roman empire, appealing to Maurice to restore him to power, promising to give over territory and be 'a son' to the Roman, with a pact of peace between them 'until death'. Eventually Maurice agreed, the news encouraging the many noblemen within the Persian empire inclined to back Khusro II over the usurper.[31]

Aided by a Roman army, Khusro II returned to his homeland, rallying more and more supporters as he came, while others continued to support his rival. Bahrām Chobin showed some of his accustomed skill as a commander, and there was hard fighting in this Persian civil war before Khusro II emerged triumphant. The defeated general took refuge among the Turks but was murdered before he could think of returning. In 591, the victorious Khusro II confirmed the terms of the peace with Maurice, who had expressed his delight in the success of his Persian 'son'. Dara was handed back, as were Martyropolis in Roman Armenia and other lands ceded from Persian Armenia, with some, such as Iberia, most likely being partitioned between the two empires. For the first time in generations, the Romans did not have to pay for peace, at least in a formal sense. The prolonged conflict had strained the empire's already tight finances, but at least it was over, which gave Maurice the opportunity to work on other problems.[32]

With hindsight, it is striking how little had been achieved by either side after decades of warfare. The Romans did well at the end, but only because of the chance that brought about Bahrām Chobin's unprecedented revolution. Overall, the Roman empire had held on to the gains made under Justinian around the Mediterranean and after the treaty held more territory in the east than had been the case for centuries. These last gains had come at the expense of the Sasanian empire, which had also lost some ground to the Turks, although it still held on to the gains made in the south under Khusro II. As the sixth century came to a close, both empires remained larger and more powerful than any of the individual nations or leaders on their borders. As had always been the case, both faced several active or potential threats, which meant that it was rarely possible to employ their full strength against any one opponent. On the whole, the war-making capacity of the Romans and Sasanians was closely matched, neither possessing a marked strategic or tactical advantage. Each empire was capable of fielding substantial numbers of well-disciplined soldiers led by reasonably capable officers. Their armies and ways of fighting continued to be very similar, at least in the wars fought against each other. Similarly, the administrative and financial systems of each empire continued to function efficiently enough to maintain control and support warfare.

There was more continuity than change in these institutions, but this was as true of weaknesses as of strengths. Persia was racked by major civil wars in the years ushering in the sixth century and as it ended. The Roman empire was spared full-scale internal warfare, even though the potential for this was demonstrated on several occasions. Culturally, the Roman empire had changed a good deal, most of all as its sense of identity became ever more exclusively Christian, reducing the importance of older Greco-Roman culture.

Justinian barred 'pagan' education, closing down the philosophical schools of Athens. This prompted one group of scholars to travel to the Sasanian court, hoping to find a true philosopher-king in the person of Kavadh I or his son. They seem to have been disappointed or simply homesick, for Khusro I secured their safe return to live—but not teach—in the Roman empire during one of his treaties with Justinian.

Such cultural changes did not really alter the way that either side conducted diplomacy or waged war. Yet in other ways religion had an important political dimension. Time and again, the encouragement of Zoroastrianism provoked rebellion in Armenia and the kingdoms of the Caucasus. As Christians—or, in the case of the king of Lazica, a convert—the leaders in this area found it easier to appeal to the Christian emperor in Constantinople. Yet it was not simple, and at other times political concerns prompted them to oppose the Christian Romans and seek aid from the Zoroastrian Persians. Part of this was the ongoing differences over doctrine within the wider Christian community, which readily tended to create distinct church hierarchies and reinforce political and ethnic differences. Although Justinian was particularly severe against doctrines that he considered to be heretical within the empire, he and other emperors tended to be far less fussy when seeking alliance with groups outside.

Even so, not all Christians were discontented under Sasanian rule. Some kings of kings were harsher, some more well-disposed, and the same was surely true of their generals, ministers, and regional officials and indeed of the priests of the Zoroastrian church. Khusro II took a Christian as a wife and was particularly tolerant of Christian groups, even leading to a later, implausible tradition that he became a convert. Episodes of persecution tend to be more prominent in our sources than longer periods of goodwill. Justinian's severity prompted the revolt of the Samaritans and was also felt by Jewish, polytheistic, and heretical communities at times, but usually there was far less tension. The savagery of that rebellion and indeed the upheaval and lasting trauma caused by the Mazdakite movement in Persia were considerable, but there is no hint that either empire was often plunged into religious crisis.[33]

All in all, the closing years of the sixth century give the impression of two broadly stable empires, each still strong and neither side dominating. In the shorter term, the Sasanians or Romans could gain an advantage, winning over allies and winning battles, without fundamentally altering the balance of power. Maurice was able to turn round decades of Sasanian success because of the power struggle in Persia, but if Khusro II had made some concessions, none fatally weakened his power in relation to the Romans. With the exception of Khusro I's invasion in 540, none of the Sasanian successes had ever brought substantial profit from plunder and captives. Roman payments, whether lump sums or annual, were more useful and did not incur the cost or risks of mounting a campaign. This gold greatly eased the tight finances for the king of kings but was not in itself essential. At the same time, the cost to the Romans was only a small part of their budget. Prestige of giving or receiving tribute was more important to each side, as was the memory of war and treaties. The frequency of the former in the sixth century created a more hostile attitude on both sides, for all the talk of brotherhood between the rulers. In the main, Khusro II's goodwill towards Maurice would hold, even though the old roots of rivalry between the empires remained.

17

HIGH TIDE

c. 600–621

THE ROMANS AND SASANIANS SPENT MOST OF THE FIFTH century at peace, only to spend most of the sixth century at war. This succession of conflicts was hard-fought, even though objectives were limited on both sides. In the main, fighting occurred in the kingdoms of the Caucasus, in the frontier zone of Mesopotamia, and in the deserts of the south, although there the fighting was mainly done by allied leaders whose agendas were never altogether aligned with those of the emperor in Constantinople or the king of kings. Khusro I bathed in the Mediterranean in 540, and Maurice later planned a drive on Ctesiphon, although this did not take place. Neither man was thinking in terms of permanent conquest, and instead these attacks were meant to win glory, bring plunder, and put pressure on the other side. As striking as the frequency of military operations is the number of embassies going back and forth between the leaders of the two empires. They communicated a lot, far more often and with greater courtesy than in earlier periods. Demands and threats preceded the wars, which were in turn concluded by negotiated settlements sealed by concessions from the party felt to be weaker. Sometimes wars were avoided altogether because an agreement was reached before fighting began.

Both empires understood that the other was strong and that any military advantage they possessed was never sufficient to think in terms of major territorial gain through conquest, at least for the moment. Instead, they aimed to improve their position, reinforcing an advantage if they possessed one or creating one if they felt weaker. At the very least, it was better to maintain the status quo than to let the other empire grow even stronger. The Romans and Sasanians competed to dominate as many of the allied kingdoms on their borders as they could; control in the truest sense was rarely possible, most of all in the kingdoms of the Caucasus. Overall, the advantage swayed back and forth during each war and in the resulting treaties, without either side making substantial, permanent gains. In Mesopotamia, the key remained the fortified cities, especially those commanding the main communication routes, which allowed the passage of armies, individuals, and goods. Once again, neither side did enough to alter the balance permanently by taking and holding on to any of these. For the Sasanians, profit was a central objective, whether with demands of payment from the emperor as the price for maintaining or granting peace, through extortion during invasions, or by plundering the communities who refused to pay. Kavadh I and Khusro I acquired injections of wealth in this way, which surely helped them to fund their army and government. However, most campaigns yielded only meagre profits, while the subsidies paid by the Roman emperor were not large enough to relieve the king of kings of financial worries.

All in all, the succession of conflicts between Romans and Sasanians in the sixth century achieved remarkably little compared to the cost for both sides. Neither secured any deep, permanent advantage, for the two empires remained closely matched when it came to resources and military power. The cost of this warfare is hard to measure—much like the impact of the waves of plague—but there are signs of decline. While Antioch remained one of the greatest cities of its day, it was less splendid and had a smaller population after the depredations of the Sasanians in 540 and, more importantly, a succession of severe earthquakes. The Roman empire had not gained significantly greater sources of income during the sixth century, so paying for the defence of reconquered territory in Africa, Italy, and Spain in addition to the frontiers on the Danube and in the east was a burden the state struggled to meet. There was certainly no spare capacity to permit any fresh overseas adventures, and the overall urge of the emperor and his advisors was towards caution. Maurice's *Strategikon* may have kept traditional commands and the long-standing emphasis on discipline and drill, but it made clear that a wise general risked battle only when absolutely necessary and only with as many advantages on his side as possible. Ideally, wars were won by stratagem, deceit, and stealth to reduce friendly losses and minimize the risk of defeat.[1]

At the start of the seventh century, neither empire enjoyed a certain and decisive advantage over the other. Yet the wider world was changing, and this is reflected in the enemies discussed in the *Strategikon*, each of whom had to be dealt with in different ways. Most prominent are the Avars and the Turks, grouped together as Scythian peoples (and also under the less ancient, if equally vague, label of Huns). They were nomads, originally from the steppes, although like Attila's people they had come to rule large areas of territory and the settled populations living there. The *Strategikon* expected them to wear body armour and sometimes have armoured horses, although still to fight mainly as horse-archers, moving quickly, surprising the enemy, attacking at his weakest points, and ruthlessly pursuing anyone who fled. Ethnographic inquiry for its own sake was not the purpose of a military manual intended to show how to defeat various races, so that other activities and accomplishments of these peoples were dismissed with the claim that their sole concern was warfare. It was an admission that these were formidable opponents, most of all because they had come together under strong leaders.[2]

The origins of both Avars and Turks lay far to the east, probably on the borders of China, where, by the early seventh century, the Tang dynasty was consolidating and expanding the Chinese empire after centuries of civil war and internal chaos. Since both groups appeared far to the west during the later sixth century, their migrations cannot have been wholly caused by this resurgence in Chinese strength. As always, the details are elusive, and what was most likely a complex story of rivalries within the tribes as well as external competition and pressure from a resurgent Chinese empire cannot be reconstructed in anything save the vaguest terms. Nor is it absolutely certain when each group first arrived: the Avars to the north of the Black Sea and the Turks on the Sasanians' northern and eastern borders. The various Huns already there were displaced, destroyed, or absorbed.[3]

Each group acknowledged the leadership of a warlord, khan, or king, someone with the power of an Attila, although the Turks soon split into two loosely aligned halves, with one khan in the west and another in the east. Those in the east were directly in contact with the recovering might of China, while in the west they lived beside the Sasanian empire and had diplomatic contact with the Romans and occasionally military contact with them in the Caucasus. The Avars were pushing into Western Europe as Attila had done, and they confronted the Franks and Lombards as well as the Romans. With them or ahead of them came various Slavic groups who accepted the authority of the Avar khan, even if they were not directly ruled by him. As ever, the settled communities of the Roman, Sasanian, and indeed Chinese empires were tempting targets for raids and extortion, for warlords needed glory and plunder to maintain their leadership. What varied was the capacity of the settled empires to deal with them, which inevitably depended on their other commitments, making it hard to judge whether the big successes of the Avars and Turks came because they were strong or their opponents weak, or more probably a mixture of both. At the very least, by the start of the seventh century it was obvious to everyone that the Avars posed a major problem for the Romans, as did the Turks for the Sasanians.

Some of the other innovations of this era were introduced by this latest wave of migration. The *Strategikon* makes clear that the stirrup was standard issue to Roman cavalrymen, who in this era were drawn from a wide range of nationalities. The stirrup appears to have been invented on the steppes and was probably first seen in the west when the Avars arrived, although it is unclear when the Romans and the Sasanians copied it. In time, its use would lead to changes in the design of the saddle, the four-horned type in use since at least the third century BC being replaced by other patterns, since the horns were no longer necessary. Stirrups help a rider to jump and make it easier to train recruits to a functional level of horsemanship. They were not necessary for shock action, something a wide variety of ancient cavalry had repeatedly shown; Parthian, Roman, and Sasanian cataphracts were capable of performing without them. At best, the Avars and other steppe peoples gained an initial advantage in their first contacts with the Romans and Sasanians, which was soon lost as the latter adopted stirrups as well. A bigger advantage came, as it had always done, because, like all the warrior nomads of the steppes, they were excellent horsemen and archers. There is not the slightest sign that the introduction of the stirrup changed the tactics of Roman or Sasanian cavalry to any significant degree. The only specific use mentioned in the *Strategikon* was the recommendation that a medic should bring both stirrups to one side of the saddle so that he could ride supporting a wounded soldier in front of him, each man with one foot in a stirrup.[4]

The nomads also brought with them the knowledge of how to design and operate a new form of artillery, although in this case the invention originated in China many centuries earlier. Traditional Greek and Roman catapults were torsion engines, their power derived from twisting a cord of sinew or hair, storing the energy in springs held by washers, then releasing it to shoot a missile with great force. Such machines were complex to manufacture and maintain, while the strength of the metals involved placed limits on the size of these ballistae. The Chinese innovation had the brilliance of simplicity and made much larger engines practical—and hence used heavier stones as missiles—and is more familiar to us from the medieval name, the trebuchet. A tall stand supported a long throwing arm mounted on a pivot. There was a sling on one end, and this was hauled downwards and a missile placed into it. A large team of men then took up the ropes attached to the opposite end and at a command pulled it down as hard as they could, lobbing the missile high. Much later, counterweights would come into use, adding far more force to the throw, but even the early version could be constructed quickly and hurl stones heavy enough to damage fortifications. These engines made the Avars more of a threat to walled cities, and the design was so simple compared to earlier artillery that other 'tribal' armies copied them almost as quickly as the Romans did. Sasanian use is not well-attested but is very likely. As with the stirrup, any advantage for the first to adopt the new technology swiftly dissipated as it was copied by others.[5]

The Roman and Sasanian empires were larger, better organized, and wealthier than anyone else apart from each other at the start of the seventh century. Tang China was an exception, but since it was not in direct contact with the Sasanians, it was not a competitor. Yet the Avars and Turkish confederations were strong, and—as with other groups in the past—never had to face the entire war effort of the Romans or Sasanians. This was a difficult time to rule either empire, especially for Khusro II, king of kings through a civil war fought with Roman assistance. Sasanian Persia remained divided for some time. There was a rebellion focusing on Persian Armenia in the north, largely led by men who had backed Khusro II in the civil war. To the south, relations with Arab leaders proved difficult, especially when Khusro II turned against the current king from the Lakhmid dynasty, a line favoured for generations.

In addition, there was faction fighting at the heart of the empire. Two brothers-in-law of Hormizd IV had rebelled against him and fought for his son Khusro II in the civil war, and they had initially done well under the new king's rule. The chronology is murky, but at some point, Khusro II's attitude towards them changed, and he condemned them for murdering his father, even though this was the basis of his own elevation. One was executed; the other escaped and started a revolt to take the throne for himself. He managed to rally aggrieved groups in the north, including significant numbers of noblemen from the Parthian aristocratic houses, but his claim to rule is unclear, although at best was based on a fairly distant connection to the Sasanian royal family. This fresh civil war lasted for several years, until Khusro II finally prevailed, probably around 601. Around the same time, the Turks turned on each other in their own civil war, relieving the threat to the Sasanian empire's eastern and northern borders, at least in the short term.[6]

Maurice soon had problems of his own. As we have seen, his government was always short of funds, and he gained a reputation for greed. On one occasion, he was jeered and pelted by a mob, angry because there was a food shortage in Constantinople. It was believed that he was not doing enough to help and may even have contributed to the crisis. Others resented his indulgence of close family members, granting them senior posts and making them very wealthy. All the while, the Avars and Slavs raided heavily, reaching the Black Sea coast and lands not far from Constantinople itself. Although he no longer commanded in the field, Maurice directed the wars of his reign skilfully and took a personal interest in establishing best practice in the army, most obviously writing or commissioning the *Strategikon*. Yet the reform of the conditions of service in the army—which reduced pay but supposedly compensated the troops by increasing other allowances—continued to provoke resentment even after the mutiny in the east had come to an end. Even so, there were successes in the Balkans in a series of gruelling campaigns that did much to re-establish a defensible frontier, with the Avars being dissuaded from fresh attacks by a mixture of force and bribery. There were also successes against the Slavs and, as the summer of 602 drew to a close, Maurice ordered his field army to stay on campaign north of the Danube rather than return to billets in the cities for the winter. The *Strategikon* claimed that it was best to fight the Slavs in winter, because a people who relied on ambush found this much harder to achieve when trees were bare of leaves and woodland offered less concealment.[7]

In practical terms, the order made sense. The Slavs were already reeling from a succession of Roman offensives, and indeed there may have been a lull in operations which perhaps gave officers and men too much time to think. Yet spending the winter in tents was not a pleasant prospect, and, for whatever reasons, pent-up resentments boiled over, stoked by an ambitious officer named Phocas. He was proclaimed emperor and, once he felt secure, marched on Constantinople. Maurice had very few troops at his disposal, and there was no prospect of summoning sufficient reinforcements to make a difference before Phocas and his army arrived, while most of the city's population were hostile or indifferent. Struggling even to rally all of his ministers and faced with riots, in November 602 Maurice and his family removed their

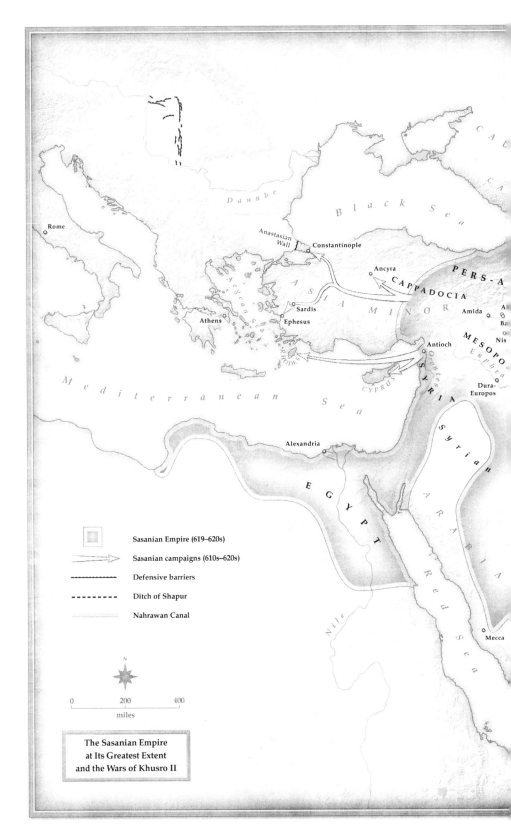

Rome

Danube

Black Sea

Anastasian
Wall ⌐ Constantinople

Ancyra

PERS-A

CAPPADOCIA

Amida
Ba
Nis

MESOPO

A S I A

M I N O R

Sardis

Athens

Ephesus

Antioch

Euphra

Aegean Sea

CYPRUS

SYRIA

Dura-
Europos

Orontes

M e d i t e r r a n e a n   S e a

Syrian

Alexandria

E
G
Y
P
T

Red

A
R
A
B
I
A

Nile

Sea

Mecca

☐ Sasanian Empire (619–620s)

⟶ Sasanian campaigns (610s–620s)

‒‒‒‒‒‒ Defensive barriers

┄┄┄┄ Ditch of Shapur

──────── Nahrawan Canal

N

0   200   400

miles

**The Sasanian Empire
at Its Greatest Extent
and the Wars of Khusro II**

Volga

Aral
Sea

Jaxartes

STEPPE

Caspian Sea

Amu Darya (Oxus)

SOGDIA

Samarkand

Bukhara

Dariali
Fort

Derbent
Wall

Derbent

T'bilisi

Torpakh
Qala

Gilgilchay
Wall

ALBANIA

KOPET DAG

Atrak

BACTRIA

Merv

Balkh

HINDU KUSH

Rag-e-
Bibi

Begram

Peshawar

Viranshar

Gorgan &
Tammisheh
Walls

Gabri
Qal'eh

KHORASSAN

ELBURZ MTS

Takht-e
Suleiman

Qal'eh Pol
Gonbad

Dasht
Qal'eh

Neyshabur

Ghulbiyan

Bisotun

Qal'eh
Gabri

ZAGROS MTS

Herat

Helmand

Ctesiphon

Eyvan-e
Karkha

Gondeshapur

Isfahan

Tigris

Susa

Shushtar

Naqsh-e
Rostam

Estakhr

Bishapur

Gur

Darabgird

Persian Gulf

Indus

SINDH

Kush

Strait of Hormuz

Ed-Dur

Ratto
Kot

PENINSULA

Arabian

Sea

YEMEN

imperial regalia and tried to escape. No one resisted as Phocas and his army entered Constantinople, and he was crowned as emperor. Maurice and his family managed to cross the Bosporus to Chalcedon, only to be arrested. On 27 November, the deposed emperor and his sons were executed, and their severed heads paraded through Constantinople. Key allies were killed or stripped of office and forced to retire—making someone take holy orders was a common means of removing them from politics in this era. Only a handful of the most senior figures managed to change sides.[8]

Phocas was emperor, the first usurper to win power for generations (although a good number had tried to mount a coup and failed). Not everyone accepted him, and a general called Narses on the eastern frontier refused to acknowledge him and was supported by his troops. For the moment, he did not have wider support or the momentum to mount a direct challenge. Other senior figures watched and waited. Phocas was suspicious and cruel, ordering further executions. In 603, the circus factions rioted in Constantinople, and in the years to come the violence of these groups throughout the cities of the east had an ever more political tone. Phocas had the leader of the Greens arrested and burned alive. At some point, perhaps in 605, an attempted coup was discovered at court, prompting another spate of executions, including Maurice's widow and daughters and most remaining male and female relatives.

As his regime was collapsing around him, Maurice had reached out for support to Khusro II, the 'son' he had helped back to power after he had fled from a similar rising in the Sasanian empire. One of Maurice's actual sons, Theodosius, was sent with a delegation to travel to the king of kings. It is unclear how far they got. Phocas's regime maintained that Theodosius and all the other key figures among the envoys were caught and killed. As had long been normal, the new emperor sent his own ambassador to announce his coronation to the Sasanian ruler and present suitable gifts as a mark of goodwill and respect. The Roman embassy reached Ctesiphon in 603, where all the well-established protocols were broken. Khusro II sent back a brusque reply making clear that he did not accept Phocas as a legitimate emperor and complaining of the murder of the true emperor, Maurice. Phocas's envoy was imprisoned, and public mourning for Maurice declared, if it was not already under way. As the Roman had once offered him sanctuary and then sent soldiers to restore him to power, the king of kings announced that he would seek vengeance from the new regime through war. A youth was produced and declared to be Theodosius, the legitimate heir to the imperial purple. No one knows whether he was an imposter (which most scholars assume) or whether Maurice's son had somehow escaped, but it helped to present the Sasanian armies as liberators rather than invaders.[9]

Khusro II owed his throne to Maurice's support, as well as the backing of many aristocrats within his own empire, some of whom had subsequently turned into enemies. The price of Roman support had been a treaty ceding territory and giving up the claim to Roman subsidies. In the past, each side had accepted that treaties were temporary, whatever the claims about their duration, and that, if circumstances ever became more favourable, they could use threats or actual force to make a new, more advantageous deal. In 603, the circumstances were certainly good as far as Khusro II was concerned. He had quelled all internal resistance, the threat posed by the Turks had sharply diminished, and the Romans looked weak. There was trouble in Roman Armenia, stirred up by doctrinal differences between the majority of Christians there and the official position of the empire. Phocas was a new emperor, and there was no certainty that his rule would last as opposition grew. At the very least, the Roman war effort was likely to be weakened by the divisions within the empire.

From a pragmatic point of view, this was a perfect opportunity for Khusro II to set things right by waging war on the Romans until they were willing to accept a new settlement weighted in Persia's favour. This was good for the king of kings himself, repairing any harm his reputation had suffered through granting concessions to Maurice, and would more generally make his empire stronger. There were other practical concerns. Should Phocas cement his hold on power—or another, stronger usurper supplant him—there was a long track record of new regimes in Constantinople seeking glory and popularity by aggression against the Sasanian empire.

Maurice had been a known quantity with no reason for souring relations with Persia. Phocas was unknown, simultaneously vulnerable and potentially hostile, especially if Khusro II found himself in a weaker position in the years to come.

Khusro II was a human being as well as king of kings, and with the very limited sources at our disposal it is impossible to judge the balance between emotion and calculation in his motives. His revulsion at the fate of Maurice and his family may have been genuine or politically convenient or a mixture of both. This is all the harder to judge since it is uncertain whether Theodosius was actually Maurice's son, and more importantly whether the king of kings believed that he was (even if wrongly) or was simply pretending. Almost certainly Khusro II's thinking and intentions changed during the course of the long war that now broke out. It was to prove unlike anything that had happened in all the seven centuries since Sulla had met the envoy of the Arsacid king, but no one knew that at the beginning.

The war began much as other wars between the two empires had begun in the last century, with Sasanian field armies attacking in Mesopotamia and Armenia. Khusro II led the attack on Mesopotamia in person. Roman resistance was poorly co-ordinated because Phocas's commander was engaged with Narses. The latter refused to join the Sasanians but does not seem to have opposed them either. Phocas's general did confront Khusro II's main force, only to take a mortal wound as his army was routed. After this there is little sign of any significant Roman force in this area either willing or capable of facing the Sasanians in the open field. The king of kings left a force to besiege Dara and marched on Edessa, where the population opened its gates. Theodosius was either already there or came with the Sasanians and was accepted by the citizens as the son of Maurice. Khusro II arranged a lavish coronation ceremony for him in the Roman fashion. In a few other places, his presence with the Sasanians was enough to persuade cities to surrender from the beginning or after only brief resistance. Others were unconvinced or unwilling to view the Sasanians as merely auxiliaries in a Roman civil war. That meant a succession of sieges, with determined resistance by Roman garrisons or the civil population when no soldiers were present. Having made peace with the Avars, Phocas managed to muster another army to go to the area, but this too was defeated, and the Sasanians left to conduct their sieges. The principal target in the first campaign was Dara, which fell in 604 after holding out for nine months.

Roman resistance was better organized in Armenia, where there is more talk of counter-attacks, skirmishes, and battles in addition to sieges. Partly this was a reflection of the rugged terrain, which limited the routes practical for large forces, and the climate, which restricted campaigning to the spring and summer under most circumstances. After an initial rebuff, the Sasanians resumed the offensive in 604, and the tide began to turn very much in their favour. A Roman army was defeated in battle, and in the aftermath a large number of Armenians who had fought with them were massacred. At first the Sasanians withdrew to their empire, usually to neighbouring Atropatene, for each winter, but as victory followed victory they took and held more and more forts and fortresses in Armenia. Theodosiopolis, Satala, and several other cities surrendered or were taken by force.[10]

No Roman army had appeared to retake Dara, or for that matter to retake the initiative in Mesopotamia, where the Sasanian offensive soon resumed. One by one, other cities fell, as Persian siege-craft and persistence starved them into submission, convinced them to surrender, or stormed those who would not. Carrhae, Circesium, Callinicum, and Amida were lost to the Sasanians, and by early 610 not a single city east of the Euphrates remained under Roman control. Unlike earlier conflicts, the captured cities were garrisoned and held, for this was no grand raid to plunder and extort. Some places were looted and some captives transported deep within the empire for resettlement, but the Sasanians did not withdraw and instead consolidated their control over the conquered territory. Edessa—which in the past had defied every attacker—was also taken, since apparently up to this point it had remained under Roman control even after the friendly reception of the Persians.

One reason for these successes was that Phocas's regime was crumbling, for in 608 a far better organized and serious challenger appeared. The Elder Heraclius was exarch of North Africa—a

post created in the sixth century as effective overall governor of
the military and civilian authorities in each of the recovered western provinces. His family originated in Armenia and perhaps also
had some connection to Cappadocia, although such things meant
relatively little in the mixed aristocracy of the Roman empire,
especially in the high command of the army. He had enjoyed a
respectable enough career as an officer in Maurice's campaigns,
receiving several promotions culminating in the appointment to
Africa. He had no connection to the imperial family, not that this
had mattered in the Roman empire for a very long time. Having
secured the support of the key leaders in his own province, and
probably covertly reaching out to some outside it, he had himself
and his son and namesake declared consul. Since it was normal for
a new emperor to become consul at the start of his reign, this was
a blatant rejection of Phocas, as was the minting of coins bearing
their names and images.[11]

In 609, forces loyal to the two Heraclii overran Egypt. Much
of the population was sympathetic, and the chief resistance came
from a commander loyal to Phocas. Neither side seems to have
disposed of particularly large armies, but this was often true in
Rome's civil wars and did not render them any less decisive. The
Heraclii won, occupying Alexandria and holding it against a
counter-attack. In 610, Heraclius the Younger sailed with a fleet
and army to Constantinople, landing in October. After a brief fight,
Phocas's forces collapsed and surrendered or fled. The emperor
was caught and executed, along with many of his close advisors,
and Heraclius the Younger was crowned as sole emperor, for his
father vanishes from the record and had perhaps died or was too
elderly to play any active role. His son was about thirty-five and
immediately married his fiancée, daughter of a wealthy landowner
from the North African province. She and Heraclius's mother had
been held in a nunnery at Constantinople by order of Phocas,
presumably as hostages. Establishing a dynasty was important, especially for someone who had fought his way to power. Before the
end of the year, Phocas's brother made a bid for the throne but
was soon murdered. That did not mean that no other challenges

would emerge, as for the second time in a decade a usurper had overthrown and killed the reigning emperor.[12]

Phocas had withdrawn relatively few Roman troops away from the war with the Sasanians to face Heraclius. To have done so risked worse defeats in a foreign war, which would only have damaged his reputation—already shaky because the war was going badly—and perhaps he was also unsure how loyal his soldiers would prove. Either way, not enough were sent to Egypt to defeat Heraclius, and the civil war was lost. This was an age of comparatively small field armies, so even the troops that were sent—probably several thousand, if fewer than ten thousand—reduced the military capability of the forces facing the Sasanians on the border of the Syrian province and others. Even more important was the shift in attention of the emperor and his senior commanders and ministers away from the struggle with Persia to the civil war, for every emperor knew that he was far more likely to die at the hands of internal enemies than foreign invaders. Phocas tried to juggle both threats and ended up failing to deal with either of them.

In 610, the Sasanians crossed the Euphrates and in August took the fortress city of Zenobia. As had been shown in the past, once through the frontier zone, the going became easier for an invader. Antioch fell in October, within days of Heraclius's coronation, and Apamea, Emesa, and many lesser cities also succumbed before the end of the month. Seventy years after Khusro I had bathed in the Mediterranean, the Sasanians were back. His grandson was unwilling to plunder and withdraw. Having reached so deep into Roman territory, he planned to stay, just as he had done in Mesopotamia. This was a reflection of Roman weakness and Sasanian confidence, for he effectively had cut the Romans' eastern provinces into two halves, so that communication between Asia Minor and Palestine was only possible by sea.[13]

One of the first things Heraclius did as emperor was to reach out to the king of kings and send an embassy to announce the death of Phocas—and hence vengeance for Maurice—and his own accession. The gifts accompanying the envoys were even more lavish than usual, reflecting just how badly the war was going for the

Romans in Armenia and Syria. Apart from asking for recognition, Heraclius hoped to open negotiations to end the war. Past experience suggested that such a process could take time, proceeding by fits and starts, and would no doubt mean making substantial concessions, given Persian dominance, but this was the way that all wars between the two empires eventually ended.

Khusro II refused to recognize Heraclius as emperor, stating that the true emperor was Theodosius and making it clear that he felt it his right to pronounce on the legitimacy of the rule of any Roman emperor.* Since Khusro II was effectively overlord of the real emperor, the offerings brought by the pretender were not gifts but his by right. To drive home his point, the king of kings had the Roman ambassadors executed. Even compared to the treatment of Phocas's envoys, this was a dreadful act for most cultures in the ancient world and a staggering break with all the elaborate diplomatic protocols of the last few centuries for communication between the two eyes of the world. In the past, each side had sometimes rejected approaches from the other and often prevaricated, but throughout the conflicts of the sixth century they had kept the channels of communication open. For the next few years, the two empires did not talk to each other, nervous about the fate of any envoys. The rules of the game had changed very suddenly.[14]

Khusro II's aims are unclear. Understandably happy with the ongoing success of his armies, he was confident of his strength and Roman weakness and saw no reason why this should change in the immediate future. Other leaders, whether Roman emperors or kings of kings, had in the past ridden their luck as far as they felt it would go, continuing to wage war and pushing for ever greater victories in the hope of making the ultimate settlement very favourable to them. Whatever the extent of his ambitions at the start of the war, Khusro II was now set on substantial territorial gains. Considerable efforts were made to placate the populations of captured cities so that they were willing to accept Sasanian rule. Recent emperors, including Maurice, had replaced many local

---

*It is well worth bearing this incident in mind before dismissing the worries expressed by Justin's ministers at the proposal to adopt Khusro I.

bishops and other clergy with men more in keeping with the orthodox doctrine approved by Constantinople. Khusro II reversed this and restored the original incumbents or found replacements with similar views, pleasing the majority of the population. It may have helped that he was on the side of Theodosius, so that occupied cities could choose to believe that they were still part of the Roman empire, but there is not enough evidence to show us how far this was pressed. Nor is it known what plans Khusro II had for his emperor, or whether he hoped to bring some or all of the Roman empire under his indirect control, effectively ruling through an emperor or sub-king. This is not just because of a lack of evidence. When Khusro II scorned Heraclius's approach, he made no public demands. Put simply, neither Heraclius nor anyone else on the Roman side knew what the king of kings wanted or whether there was any way to buy peace.

The year 611 did not begin well for Heraclius, and to add to his other worries, in April Constantinople was hit by an especially severe earthquake, something readily interpreted as God's punishment. By that time, a Sasanian army had driven deep into Cappadocia, surprising and capturing its capital, Caesarea. Unlike recent campaigns, the Persians appear to have bypassed other strongholds, and once they had taken this big and well-fortified city they used it as a base for raiding the countryside. The sources suggest that this was not a very large army. Sasanian manpower was stretched thin completing the conquest and subjugation of other areas. They had an advantage over the Romans, but resources were limited, and they could not deploy superior numbers everywhere at the same time.

A Roman army began to blockade Caesarea, which at least curbed the raids, even though progress in the siege was slow. Better news came when Heraclius's cousin managed to defeat a Sasanian force in a pitched battle near Emesa in Syria. Losses were heavy on both sides, but with any sort of victory so rare, this success was much celebrated. In a break with long-standing tradition, Heraclius left Constantinople and visited his commander and the troops blockading Caesarea in early spring 612. After he had left, the Romans were greatly embarrassed when the Sasanian commander and his men sallied out, cut through the siege lines, and escaped to Armenia. Heraclius blamed the commander on the spot for this failure: the former son-in-law of Phocas and one of the handful of men who had made the transition from one regime to the next. Feigning continued respect, the emperor brought the commander before a gathering of senators and stripped him of his rank and his household troops (bucellarii) and had him ordained as a priest.[15]

In 613, Heraclius went further than merely visiting one of his armies on campaign and took command in Syria himself, directing two field armies. Both appear to have joined together to engage the Sasanians somewhere near Antioch. Again there was heavy and costly fighting, until Persian reinforcements tipped the balance and forced the Romans to retreat. The Sasanians continued to press them, and the Romans continued to withdraw. Heraclius had displayed much of the same energy and military skill he had shown in the civil war, but it was not enough to stop the confident, well-led, and skilful Persians, who continued to gain ground. In 614, a Sasanian army went south and stormed Jerusalem after a siege lasting just over twenty days. The city was sacked, assaulting troops running amok as they so often did when forced to capture a stronghold by direct assault.

This was a shock to the entire population of the empire and to Christian communities beyond it on the same scale as the sack of Rome by the Goths in its time, for the most sacred place in the Christian world had fallen to the soldiers of a pagan king. Some relics had been saved before the siege began, but more were captured, including a fragment of the true cross. This was an appalling, humiliating blow for all Romans and especially their emperor. Stories circulated of the horrors of the siege, growing with the telling. The Sasanians appear to have selected some captives for deportation but left the remainder, and for the moment they moved their army to Caesarea Maritima on the coast of Palestine. In the aftermath, violence broke out between Christians and Jews at Jerusalem and then over a wider area, a feature in many provinces over the next few years. In the long run, the Sasanian occupying army tended to side with the Christian majority on the pragmatic basis that this was the best way to keep order.[16]

By the end of 614, the Sasanians had made even more gains and were well-placed to mount further advances, as they controlled the land routes to the south and to the north-west via the Cilician Gates. Khusro II's confidence was high, and, as the successes kept on coming, his ambitions seem to have expanded. He certainly made no effort to reopen negotiations, since he surely believed that his advantage would only increase in the years to come. In contrast, Heraclius faced a dire prospect, for even though he had shown considerable ability as commander and was risking his life in the field as no eastern emperor had done since the fourth century, his armies were still being forced back everywhere. The Roman military system was under immense pressure, with heavy losses as soldiers were killed, crippled, or captured, or they dispersed or deserted. Additionally, the established system of commands, recruitment, training, and billeting was dislocated. At other times, such weakness had invited the appearance of one or more challenges for the throne, but so far these had not emerged. Heraclius's wife had given him a daughter and in 612 produced a son, Heraclius Constantine, who was crowned as co-emperor before he was a year old. Parading his infant heir in so public a way was surely meant to assure people that he and his family had a future as rulers.

To achieve this, he needed to turn the tide in the war. Sources say that Heraclius and his staff studied military manuals and history of past campaigns to learn from best practice and ensure that his reformed armies were drilled in the right way and aware of the most effective tactics. There is certainly a strong correlation between the course of subsequent campaigns and the advice of the *Strategikon*. The system of raising recruits was reformed as part of rebuilding the Roman army, relying more on conscripts from the empire itself, since in the current situation it was harder than usual to hire warriors from outside. All this cost money at a time when the loss of so many cities and districts had substantially reduced tax revenue. Salaries for soldiers and civil servants were halved and paid in a new, adulterated silver coinage, the *hexagram*, as part of a wider devaluation of currency. The new hexagrams were heavy coins, rather crudely manufactured by Roman standards, and if their silver content was low, at least each man received more of them as pay than of the old, smaller, more valuable coins. Perhaps this helped mollify everyone, or perhaps the sheer scale of the Persian threat prevented too much resentment, for there is no trace of unrest similar to that provoked when Maurice reduced army pay. The empire was certainly doing its best to rally everyone against the invader; sometimes a truly desperate situation makes internal disputes and rivalries unimportant. A hexagram series minted after the fall of Jerusalem bore the slogan 'God help the Romans' (*Deus aduita Romanis*), and Heraclius increasingly appealed to his soldiers' Christian faith above calls to defend their homeland and families. In time, he began to assure them that death in battle against the pagan enemy was the same as a martyr's death, assuring them of rewards in heaven.[17]

Heraclius was beginning to rebuild his strength, but none of this was instantaneous, and for the moment the Sasanian advances were too strong to block. In 615, a general named Shahen marched into Asia Minor and pushed as far as Chalcedon on the Bosporus, within sight of Constantinople itself—but not within reach, for the Sasanians did not have boats at their disposal to cross the strait in any force. Yet the shock was enormous, for if Goths, Huns, and others had threatened the imperial capital in the past, no Parthian or Persian army had ever before reached so deep into Roman territory. Khusro II had still issued no specific demands as his price for peace, but Heraclius had to hope that terms were possible. He sent gifts to Shahen and his senior commanders, followed by a bounty for the Sasanian soldiers. Then he went in person to negotiate with the Sasanian general, albeit from the partial safety of a ship moored just offshore. Shahen was willing to listen, since after all, this was how wars ended, even if the process was often protracted with truces and renewed hostilities before a final peace was agreed to and honoured by both sides. More importantly, he knew that the Sasanians held all the advantages and that it was up to the Romans to beg for peace.[18]

That is just what they did, and the result was a letter written by the Senate—and not Heraclius, who still had not been recognized as emperor by Khusro II—to the king of kings. In tone the document was unlike anything ever sent by the Senate in Constantinople, let alone the old Senate in Rome, to any foreign leader. The senators appealed to Khusro II's wondrous clemency and blamed the foul Phocas for his murder of Maurice and his family. Heraclius had overthrown this criminal, then reluctantly been persuaded to become emperor in his stead, but he had been unable to seek recognition from the king of kings until much later than was proper because of the civil war. All this grovelling was meant to persuade Khusro II to receive the distinguished Roman envoys and treat them as ambassadors. That was all that was asked specifically, and the pleas to resolve the differences between the two empires were left very vague. Theodosius was not mentioned, but there was sufficient vagueness in speaking of Maurice and his family to suggest that the Romans were open to recognizing the young man as his son and then as legitimate emperor. This was the price that Heraclius at least implied he was willing to pay to end the war, and that was why the final letter was made on behalf of the Senate.

Shahen was a servant of the king of kings and had no authority to speak for him on such a question. Therefore, he sent a report to Khusro II asking for instructions. In the meantime, a small Roman field force began to raid Persian Armenia. For all their strength, the Sasanian armies could not be strong everywhere after overrunning so much territory. Shahen was ordered east to deal with this problem and spent the rest of the year fruitlessly chasing the raiding force. Although the Romans had achieved very little, this was at least a small success at a time when these were very rare. Meanwhile, Khusro II said that he would accept the Senate's ambassadors. Once they had arrived, he changed his mind, although since little is known about whatever negotiations occurred, the reason is unclear. The Roman ambassadors were imprisoned, and the prospect of peace vanished once again. Heraclius and his advisors still did not know just what Khusro II wanted from them, but since they had all but specifically offered to accept Theodosius, it was surely clear that the king of kings wanted a fundamental change from the long-term coexistence of two more or less equal empires.

Some relief for the Romans was provided by Turkish raids into the north-eastern regions of Khusro II's empire, something made easier because most of his best commanders and troops were facing the Romans. The next few years are very poorly documented. The Sasanians appear to have restored the situation in the region, most likely with the traditional mixture of force, diplomacy, and bribery. If the Turkish raids slowed their advance in the west, then this did not last long. Egypt was invaded, and by 619 Alexandria fell to the Sasanians, which meant that Rome's richest province and a major source of the grain that fed the population of Constantinople had gone. To all intents and purposes, much of Asia Minor was under Sasanian control. Heavy blows like this had brought about the fall of the western Roman empire, most of all the loss of Africa, with its grain and manpower, to the Vandals. Heraclius was left as ruler of Greece, parts of Thrace, the Balkans, the Aegean islands, and North Africa. Around this time, the Visigothic king conquered the Roman enclaves in Spain, and there was trouble in Italy. The Roman empire seemed to be in retreat almost everywhere, and there seemed no reason why the eastern empire would not fall. A story later circulated that Heraclius considered shifting the seat of government away from Constantinople to Africa and perhaps even began to make preparations before he was dissuaded.[19]

In contrast, Khusro II was riding high. His armies had overrun Egypt, Palestine, Syria, and Asia Minor, so he controlled more territory than any of his Arsacid or Sasanian predecessors and ruled over virtually all the lands controlled by the Achaemenid kings at the zenith of their power. According to Greco-Roman sources, recovering the old empire had been a goal—or at least a boast and a useful negotiating tool—of earlier kings of kings. There is no mention of this in the sources for Khusro II, but for the moment his success spoke for itself, while his unwillingness to seek a negotiated peace makes clear that he wanted to achieve even more. Just how much more is impossible to say, but his actions do suggest that at the very least he intended to reduce the Roman empire to a husk of its former self, no longer an equal of the Sasanians but a subordinate neighbour. Perhaps he wished for its eradication, although there is no clear evidence for this. Nor is the fate of Theodosius known, for he simply vanishes from the record. He may have died; apart from all the risks of life in the ancient world, there were fresh outbreaks of plague, some of them severe. Whatever happened to Theodosius, after the early years Khusro II did not make any great effort to establish his protégé as the Roman empire's ruler, in stark contrast to Maurice's military aid to him all those years before. One reason may have been that Theodosius did not win very much support from within the Roman empire. We do not hear of any senior Roman officer or official defecting to the Sasanians—or to the Sasanian-supported Theodosius—in the years of heaviest defeats. Even though, to observers, the Persians surely seemed bound to win, the Roman empire did not fracture.

Khusro II's victories were both startling and without precedent. Far less territory in provinces and allied kingdoms was overrun by the Parthians in 40 BC, and they were evicted from those gains much sooner. Khusro II's campaigns were more methodical, breaking through the hard crust of the Roman frontier, systematically reducing all the fortified cities, and then expanding to province after province. All this was achieved with essentially the same military resources as had been available to his predecessors. Khusro II does not appear to have had substantially more soldiers than earlier kings, nor did his forces possess any new tactical or technical advantage. Although he had acquired far more territory, this could not be exploited immediately to produce large numbers of additional troops. His campaigns surely paid for themselves, as his armies fed off the produce of the former Roman provinces, but only because he was able to build on each success, allowing more victories in the future.

Nothing is taken away from the skill of the Sasanian commanders and armies in these years to say that so much of what they achieved was made possible by Roman weakness. For generations, any difference in strength between the two empires was slight, and there is no sign at all that this had changed in 602. Phocas's usurpation and subsequent insecurity created an opportunity, rendering Roman military efforts poorly co-ordinated and lacking in spirit. The rise of Heraclius added to this fragility, and, even though he proved a far more active, able, and determined leader than Phocas, he inherited a very poor position, with his armies at a significant disadvantage when facing the Persians. This was enough of a margin to give the Sasanians more opportunities, which in turn made it harder for the Romans to recover.

Khusro II and his armies achieved an incredible amount with fairly modest resources. His field armies were in better shape than their opponents, but they were not vast in number, nor could they increase quick enough to keep pace with the need to control and defend all the new conquests. It was simply not possible to recruit and train large numbers of good soldiers quickly, and it was these men who formed the core of the field armies. Both sides faced this problem. For the moment, the Sasanians had a clear advantage in morale and in numbers. In a sense, it was a race to win the overwhelming victory that would cripple or destroy the Roman empire before the Romans recovered enough strength to stop them. This was a gamble, but sometimes in the past empires had crumbled remarkably quickly when faced with attacks by relatively small armies. Khusro II felt that the risk was well worth the potential gain. Every success can only have reinforced his belief that he really could win a complete victory over Rome and end the rivalry of so many centuries.

18

TRIUMPH AND DISASTER

621–632

By 621, Khusro II ruled over more territory than any Arsacid or Sasanian king of kings had done in the past. Whether he knew or cared, he had largely recovered all the lands once ruled by the Achaemenids and possessed much of Alexander the Great's short-lived empire. Syria and Egypt, which had been under Roman rule for so many centuries, were now governed by Khusro II's commanders. There is no sign of concerted, organized resistance to Sasanian rule in these regions after the initial conquest. At the start, the occupying army asked little of the conquered population, encouraging daily life to continue largely as before. On the whole, local elites, the aristocrats and landowners, were willing to accept the new power, just as in the past their equivalents in western provinces had accepted the rule of a Gothic or Vandal warlord as king in place of the rule of a distant Roman emperor. The same families transitioned from one regime to the next, retaining their privileged position and helping the occupying power to keep order and control the wider population.

Fighting was not an attractive option, since it offered no realistic prospect of success and was likely to provoke savage reprisals. The early centuries of the Pax Romana had demilitarized much of the empire, a process taken even further after so many generations of civil wars made emperors reluctant to permit a situation where provincial populations could readily be armed and organized under any circumstances. In the sixth and seventh centuries, the Roman and Sasanian empires each had a hard outer crust, but once through this fortified and defended zone, the interior was vulnerable and largely unprotected.

As a system, this offered a basic level of security to the empire at an acceptable cost, since maintaining substantial numbers of troops throughout the interior, ready in case they were needed, was prohibitively expensive. More importantly from the perspective of an emperor or king of kings, the existence of such armies would have made internal challenges far more likely by providing would-be usurpers with ready access to military force. That risk was far greater and more immediate than the potential threat of a foreign army breaching the outer defences of the empire and reaching the interior. If such an invasion occurred, then in due course an army could be gathered and sent to the region to evict them, if they had not already withdrawn with their plunder. The system assumed that there would be enough time to deal with the problem, and that the great resources which each empire could draw upon in the long run would allow them to drive back any invader eventually, or at least secure an acceptable peace through bribery and concessions. Time was valuable, and if the frontier zone could not keep every invasion out, it was intended to slow the enemy down and provide precious time to react.

Khusro II's campaigns revealed inherent weaknesses in this approach. The fortified frontier zone gave the Romans time just as it was designed to do, but the politics of a divided empire meant that this time was devoted primarily to internal power struggles. For years, responses to the Sasanian attacks, and indeed attacks by Avars and Slavs across the Danube, were poorly co-ordinated and under-resourced. Faced with such lacklustre resistance, Khusro II ordered his armies to grind their way through this outer layer in years of grim, attritional warfare. If an account by someone like Ammianus or Procopius existed for this era, these operations would be better understood and more stress would be placed on these early campaigns, dominated by the siege of walled city after walled city. Roman weakness provided the opportunity, but Sasanian skill and determination captured the frontier zone and opened the way for the subsequent successes. There was still some fighting as Khusro II's armies pushed into the interior of the Roman empire, especially to take the many walled cities of Syria and Palestine, which offered even more opportunity for the Romans to react. Yet having been granted all this time to gather field forces to oppose the invaders, the Romans remained too preoccupied by other concerns to achieve very much. Syria and Palestine fell, and so did Egypt.

The situation in Asia Minor was more complicated. Sasanian armies overran much of Cilicia in the south and marched through most of the wider region, but it is less clear how much territory they physically occupied. The region is best described as contested, with the balance of power steadily swinging more and more in the favour of the Persians. Around 619, the Roman mint at Nicomedia stopped issuing coins, a trend seen in all the mints in other provinces taken by the Persians. There was still a Roman presence in Asia Minor, but it was shrinking. In the Balkans, Avars and Slavs continued to raid deep into Roman territory, attacking the major city of Thessalonica, while Slavic pirates were active in the Aegean, reaching as far as Crete.[1]

Heraclius's empire seemed to be crumbling around him, and he faced added personal tragedy when his wife died. Khusro II still refused to negotiate, which made the decision to keep fighting easier. Late in 621, the emperor withdrew outside Constantinople to spend months planning and preparing for an offensive. Peace was bought in the Balkans and more soldiers recruited, equipped, and paid, all of this partly funded by requisitioning silver plates and ornaments from churches. In April 622, Heraclius went to Bithynia, where he trained and drilled a field army. There are no reliable figures for the number of troops mustered. Some scholars suggest an army of some fifteen thousand to twenty thousand men, making it an unusually large, though conceivably big, army by the standards of the *Strategikon*, and this may be correct, or the emperor may have had fewer soldiers with him. It is safe to say that this was not a massive army and that the Sasanians enjoyed a significant numerical advantage overall in Asia Minor and the surrounding areas, although not necessarily in each encounter. They also had the confidence of almost two decades of victories over the Romans.[2]

After months of rigorous training, Heraclius led his army to war in person. A poet spoke of his need to dye his dark army boots red with Persian blood, while the emperor assured his men that God was on their side and would grant them victory. Heraclius was in his late forties, still fit and active, and he set a personal example in the hard marching campaign that followed, for he relied on speed and surprise to help even the odds against him. An early success came when Arab auxiliaries serving with the Romans killed or captured a scouting party of other Arab tribesmen serving with the Sasanians. The prisoners were enlisted in the Roman army, and Heraclius kept moving, outmanoeuvring each attempt by the Persians to intercept or block them. There were skirmishes, mostly won by the Romans, which helped to boost morale. Eventually there was a full-scale encounter. The Sasanian commander laid an ambush, but Heraclius discovered the plan and set his own ambush. When the Persians emerged from cover, the Romans deliberately fled, luring the pursuing Persians into a trap and routing them. In the aftermath, the main Sasanian force withdrew.[3]

This was a victory, and all the more wonderful for the Romans because it was the first in a very long time. It boosted the prestige of the emperor, encouraged the wider public, and gave confidence and experience of success to the soldiers who had served in the campaign. It was a gamble for the emperor to take the field in person for the second time. Had he failed, the damage to his credibility would have been considerable. However, given how badly the war was going, this was far less of a risk than usual, since his prestige would also have suffered if subordinates he appointed had been defeated. All in all, the risk was worth taking, as few other options were left, and he got away with it. Yet in practical terms the campaign achieved very little. Essentially a large-scale raid, no territory was recovered, and the losses inflicted on the Sasanians were modest. Such a minor success made no real difference to the wider strategic dominance of Khusro II's armies or the precarious state of Heraclius's empire. This point was reinforced before the year was out, when he had to rush back to Constantinople to deal with a new crisis.

Peace with the Avars and their Slavic allies had broken down when the latter once again attacked Thessalonica. There were not the resources to drive them back, since the pick of the emperor's remaining troops were in Asia Minor. Heraclius fell back on the tried and trusted methods of negotiation and bribery. In 623, a meeting was arranged between the envoys of the Avar khan and the emperor and court in person. It was to take place between Constantinople and the long wall higher up the peninsula, and the willingness of Heraclius to go there to meet mere ambassadors gives an idea of the weakness of his negotiating position. Just before the conference, Heraclius scented a trap and galloped from the scene before bands of warriors could surround his party. He escaped, along with some of his staff, but the imperial regalia fell into enemy hands, and large numbers of civilians were captured.

In spite of this humiliating flight, Heraclius remained desperate to buy peace from the Avars and seems to have decided that the treachery could be accepted as an understandable ploy; in the past both Romans and Sasanians had seized enemy leaders who had come to negotiate, and it was seen as all part of the game. The Avar khan had the advantage and knew it, so he extracted an immense price in return for withdrawing. Each year the Romans were to pay him two hundred thousand gold solidi (roughly 2,700 pounds in weight in normal times, although lighter coins were minted in bulk for the occasion), and as the three main hostages he was sent Heraclius's illegitimate son, his nephew (also illegitimate), and the son of a senior official. Of the warlords of Europe, only Attila at the height of his power had extorted wealth on this scale from the Romans.[4]

Heraclius bought time, for there could be little doubt that the Avars and their allies would return when it suited them. For the moment, he was free to resume the offensive against the Sasanians. There is no hint in our sources that Khusro II had encouraged the Avar khan in his attack, although within a few years there was certainly diplomatic contact and a loose alliance between the two. Nor is there any information about the activities of the army Heraclius had left in Asia Minor during 623, which suggests that there was little or no fighting as Sasanian forces resumed their advance, pushing as far as Ancyra. Late in the year, the Persians landed on Rhodes and captured the island and its cities in their only significant maritime achievement during the conflict. Heraclius's empire continued to shrink, and with it the resources to wage war. Just as the Sasanians would look to the Avars as useful allies, the emperor planned to approach the khan of the Western Turks for aid against the Persians. Such an alliance could not be formed quickly, if only because of the great distances the Roman envoys needed to travel simply to begin discussions, but Heraclius was planning ahead. For so rational a man, a few of his choices in these years appear strange. In 622 or 623, he took his niece as his new bride, despite the deep disgust such an incestuous union provoked in many of his subjects. The emperor seems to have believed that he could get away with whatever he decided to do, but at least he was showing confidence that there would be a future for him and the Roman empire.[5]

In the spring of 624, Heraclius returned to Asia Minor to take command of his field army. He claimed to have attempted to open negotiations with the king of kings only to receive an insulting letter in return. In this, Khusro II called himself 'Lord and king of all the earth' and dismissed Heraclius as a 'foolish and worthless servant', while boasting of all his own victories, which the Christian God had done nothing to prevent. Constantinople was doomed to fall, for their Christ, 'who was not able to save himself from the Jews', could not save them from Khusro II's might. Heraclius could bring his family and be settled on an estate granted by the king of kings but could not hope to escape in any other way.

The message was stark and uncompromising, which conformed to the refusal to negotiate in the years since 603. However, the tone is so insulting that most scholars assume the letter was actually concocted by Heraclius and his advisors, not least because they made it public straightaway. Certainly, the sheer arrogance of its language made clear to the emperor's subjects that no compromise was possible with such an enemy, and more importantly that any man who dared to deny the power of the Almighty God in this way was doomed to defeat. From now on, the tendency for Heraclius to assure his soldiers that they were fighting for their God and would be martyrs if they fell increased. Faith offered hope in a conflict that must otherwise have seemed hopeless, for Khusro II had every reason to be confident. For the first time since the initial campaigns, the king of kings planned to accompany one of his armies in the field in 624, probably to drive further into Asia Minor and eventually to Constantinople itself.[6]

Heraclius began his offensive at Caesarea in Cappadocia, then marched quickly north-east into Armenia. The move caught the Sasanians by surprise, and he drove deep into the regions long held by the Persians, raiding and ravaging fields but not stopping to engage in sieges. There was no concerted opposition at this stage, and the first real confrontation came when he turned south into Atropatene, where Khusro II was beginning to muster a large force for his planned campaign. The king of kings was not ready to fight, which suggests that substantial contingents had not yet arrived, so that he had nothing like the forty thousand men claimed in Roman sources. After his advance guard was defeated by the Romans, Khusro II retreated, his army dispersing, destroying crops as it went to deprive the enemy of supplies. At first Heraclius did not pursue and instead went to the city of Ganzak, which surrendered to him. He gave his soldiers a few days of rest, then led them to Thebarmais, which housed one of the most sacred fire temples in the Sasanian empire, having been founded by Ardashir I in the earliest days of the dynasty. Khusro II in his flight had removed many of the temple treasures and taken part of the sacred flame away before leaving. His example, combined with the preparations of the Romans to begin a formal siege, swiftly convinced the defenders to capitulate. Heraclius did not harm the people, but he burned the temple complex to the ground. Excavation has shown the thoroughness of the damage, as well as providing a cache of several hundred clay seals used on official documents stored there.[7]

The Romans were soon on the move again. They had long since passed through the fortified and defended frontier zone of the Sasanian empire and for the moment could run amok in the vulnerable interior. Heraclius's men marched through Media and Atropatene, plundering as they went, but not facing any substantial resistance. He did not intend to return to Roman territory for the winter and instead, after a debate with his officers and a period of rest and prayer for the army, went to Albania in the Caucasus. Some of the local leaders accepted alliance with the Romans, others had to be threatened, but he was able to find sufficient secure billets to house his troops during the winter months. The prisoners with the column would have been a burden to feed and guard, so late in the year he let them go free to find their own way home.

Heraclius's campaign in 624 had been another grand raid, this time far bolder because he led his men so deep into the Sasanian empire and did not return to Roman territory at the end of it. Khusro II and his commanders were taken by surprise and wrong-footed so badly that they did not recover before the winter weather shut down operations for the year. This was a more spectacular success for the Romans than the offensive in 622, although based on the same principles of hard marching and skilful manoeuvring to outwit the enemy rather than defeating them through direct confrontation. If the *Strategikon* is any indication, then two-thirds or even more of Heraclius's troops were infantrymen, which meant that the speed of his army was not inherent but based on tight discipline and inspirational leadership. Earlier training was reinforced by experience, confidence, and hundreds of miles of hard travel through rough country, buoyed by the sense of success, since they were always advancing. The nature of these campaigns reinforces the sense that the emperor led a fairly modest army, quite probably even smaller than the 'big' armies envisaged by the *Strategikon*.

The Roman offensive had shocked the Sasanians, inflicting an embarrassing retreat on Khusro II himself. Heraclius's men lived off the land, consuming or destroying all the produce and livestock they could find. The impact was terrible on the communities within their reach, and the agricultural system was disrupted even more when the Romans took captives and held them for months before releasing them, temporarily depleting the labour force. Yet the Roman army was relatively small, and, although it moved quickly, the area laid waste was limited, the devastation and resultant hardships essentially local. Compared to the conquests made by Khusro II's armies in the war so far, the damage inflicted was minimal. Added to that, surprise would be harder to achieve from now on, since the Sasanians knew where Heraclius was wintering and could better deduce where he might go once the spring arrived.

The king of kings reverted to his policy of previous years and decided to let his commanders run the war under his distant supervision. Three senior generals, each with a field army, were summoned from elsewhere with the aim of cornering and destroying Heraclius and his men. This took time and meant stripping troops from all over the conquered Roman provinces. Completing the conquest of Asia Minor ceased to be the immediate priority, as the basic problem of resources asserted itself once again. Khusro II simply did not have enough reliable troops to be strong everywhere at the same time. There are also signs that funding the war effort was becoming a strain. Later tradition would remember the king as greedy because he was always raising money. Just as Heraclius had drawn treasures from the church to pay for the war, the Sasanians began to confiscate wealth from the churches within their conquered territory. Khusro II's armies had done wonders to conquer so much with limited resources. They needed to do even more to win the final victory.[8]

Inevitably, Sasanian preparations took time, for the sheer distances involved meant that there were delays as orders were dispatched and troops and resources gathered and then moved to the theatre of operations. Shahen, the same general who had negotiated with Heraclius at the Bosporus, appears to have held overall command and is said to have led a force of some thirty thousand men. Distance and the difficulty of communication in a landscape shaped by mountains and rivers made it hard to exert close control on the other two armies, a situation perhaps made worse by competition among the three commanders. For years they had operated largely independently, as each one overran different regions of the Roman empire.

Heraclius moved first, before the Sasanians were ready, and once again he moved fast and went in an unexpected direction.

Early in 625, he began another foray into Atropatene, dodging one of the Persian armies. However, many of his officers were unhappy with the risks he was running, and pressure from the allied contingents from the Caucasian kingdoms forced him to change his plans and retreat. The Sasanian army followed him, and a second general with his troops got ahead of the Romans and tried to block their path. Heraclius turned on the pursuing army, launching a succession of small attacks to stop it in its tracks. Then he bypassed them and hurried back to Atropatene. Belatedly, the two Persian armies joined together and followed him. Heraclius pretended to be afraid of their combined might and led them on. Learning that Shahen and the third Sasanian army was en route to reinforce the others, he decided to risk battle with his pursuers before this happened.

Heraclius let the two Sasanian armies approach his camp, then retreated during the night, force marching to get away. His opponents sensed fear, not realizing that he was heading for a patch of open ground well-suited to Roman tactics. Once there, Heraclius set up camp on a convenient hilltop, rested his men, and waited. Shahen was close now, within a day or two's march, but the two other generals scented the chance to win glory without his help. The Sasanians hurried in pursuit, vying to be the first to catch the demoralized enemy, only to discover the Romans deployed and ready for battle. Unnerved by this unexpected confidence, and hastily formed into their own battle line, the Sasanians were routed with heavy losses, including one of the generals. Shahen arrived too late to assist and was in turn attacked by the Romans and put to flight.

With the three enemy field armies dispersed for the moment, Heraclius was free to move at will and returned to ravaging enemy territory. After a while, a Sasanian army put together from the survivors of the defeats began to shadow him as he marched north-east. Many of Heraclius's Caucasian allies decided to leave and marched back to their own homelands in Iberia and Lazica, encouraging the pursuers, who closed the distance. Both sides deployed in battle lines facing each other. Heraclius was willing to let the Persians attack him, but they remained cautious after the earlier defeats and did not move. For a day, the rival armies stared

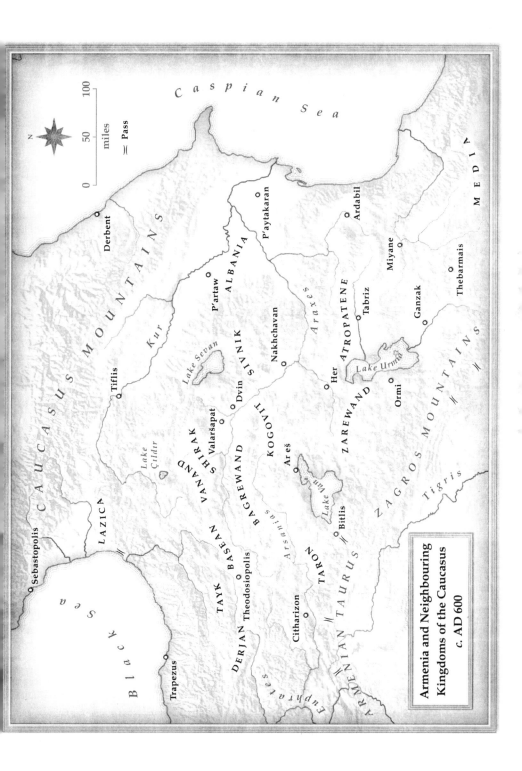

Armenia and Neighbouring
Kingdoms of the Caucasus
c. AD 600

Caspian Sea

MEDIA

Derbent

P'aytakaran

Ardabil

ALBANIA

P'artaw

Miyane

Thebarmais

CAUCASUS MOUNTAINS

Kur

ATROPATENE

Tabriz

Ganzak

Tiflis

Lake Sevan

SIVNIK

Nakhchavan

Her

Lake Urmia

Ormi

Dvin

ZAREWAND

Araxes

Valaršapat

KOGOVIT

ZAGROS MOUNTAINS

SHIRAK

BAGREWAND

Lake Çıldır

Ares

Tigris

VANAND

Lake Van

LAZICA

BASEAN

Arsanias

Sebastopolis

TAYK

Theodosiopolis

Bitlis

TARON

Citharizon

ARMENIAN TAURUS

DERJAN

Black Sea

Trapezus

Euphrates

at each other without either side advancing. At dusk, the Romans withdrew with such confidence and in such good order that the Sasanians did not follow. The year was coming to a close, and Heraclius decided not to winter for a second time deep in enemy territory, and so he headed for Armenia. The Persians followed him at a distance. There were skirmishes, with the Romans more than holding their own, and eventually Heraclius settled down into winter quarters in Roman Armenia—or at least a region that had been Roman until the conquests of Khusro II.

Fighting did not end, despite the season. Shahen had been re-called and command passed to Shahrbaraz, the general of the south and a member of the Mihran clan. Given some six thousand elite horsemen, most likely from units maintained by the king of kings, he decided to raid the lines of the Roman army. Heraclius discovered what was happening and ambushed the Sasanian advance guard. The sources claim only a single man escaped capture or death to bring the news to Shahrbaraz, but the report was soon followed by the appearance of Roman troops all around them. In the one-sided fight that followed, the Sasanian force was destroyed, although its commander managed to ride to safety. The Roman army was able to spend the rest of the winter unmolested.

Once again, Heraclius and his army had marched a long way, surprising the enemy with their speed and willingness to take unexpected, difficult routes. They had faced a succession of Sasanian armies, fighting and winning battle after battle. All of this was good, for it demonstrated the confidence and skill of the emperor and his army and also dented the prestige of the king of kings. The success hinted to the populations of the wider region—especially the Caucasian kingdoms, with their largely Christian populations—that Persian dominance need not prove permanent and that the Romans might return. Yet this was still a raid, plundering and laying waste without conquering any territory. In the end, Heraclius felt unable to stay in hostile territory and had returned to the Roman empire to pass the winter. For all the losses inflicted on the Sasanians, their armies still possessed a great numerical advantage over the Romans, while their confidence would recover. Luck as well as skill had helped the Romans survive and succeed in hostile territory, but, in the end, numbers would tell: militarily, the advantage remained very much in Khusro II's favour. Yet Heraclius had survived and delayed the Sasanian drive to the coast of Asia Minor and Constantinople, and that was something. More important in the longer run was the good progress of his negotiations with the Western Turks, and his presence in Media and Atropatene may have helped to convince the khan that an alliance with Rome might be worthwhile.

Khusro II decided on a massive effort to end the war, raising a great army from his empire and its allies. He also appears to have reached an agreement with the Avars, who, since the departure of Heraclius on distant campaigns, had begun to question the benefits of maintaining the peace. A joint attack towards Constantinople was agreed for the coming summer. Before that, two Sasanian field forces would confront Heraclius, destroying his army or at the very least preventing it from helping Constantinople or disrupting the offensive in any significant way.[9]

Heraclius left winter quarters earlier than expected, giving him a substantial lead before the Sasanian armies began their pursuit. The Romans marched into Mesopotamia, past Amida, and then turned back to make a show of force and slow the pursuers. The Persians dismantled the bridge at Samosata, but Heraclius and his men managed to ford the Euphrates in time before the waters were swollen by the melting of the winter snows in the highlands to the north. Shahrbaraz followed, and an attempt to check him at another river line initially went badly, until the Romans managed to rally, get organized, and beat back the enemy. Heraclius is supposed to have fought with great heroism, defeating a giant of a Persian who attacked him, then driving across a bridge from which the panicking enemy leapt like frogs into the water. Shahrbaraz disengaged and gave up the chase, letting the Roman army march away. Safe for the moment, Heraclius sent some of his troops back to strengthen the garrison of Constantinople.

Once again, Heraclius and his army had survived, but they lacked the strength to confront the main Sasanian army, which in due course drove through Asia Minor and reached the coast at Chalcedon in June. Shahrbaraz was in charge of this main effort, but for all his resources he had few boats at his disposal, so he would be largely an observer as the Avars and allied tribes closed on Constantinople. These would besiege the city and loot it once it had fallen. The khan led a very large army, which Roman sources estimated at some eighty thousand men. Constantinople had formidable defences, but the walls were extensive at some three and a half miles long on the landward side, and with twelve thousand defenders supported by whatever civilian volunteers were available, the Romans could not be strong everywhere. Making use of siege towers, assault sheds, and artillery, including trebuchets, the Avars were well-organized and equipped—if not as skilled in siege-craft as the Sasanians. As usual, the Romans were keen to negotiate, and throughout the siege there was a back-and-forth exchange of envoys, although the talks came to nothing.[10]

On 29 July 626, the Avars closed with the city walls, parading their numbers to convince the Romans that resistance was futile. The attack began two days later, all along the landward wall, probing for a weak spot while wearing out the defenders. Later, boatloads of Slavic warriors began to threaten the weaker seaward walls, doing their best to keep to the shallowest water, where Roman warships could not go. A delegation went to see the khan, who had three Sasanian ambassadors sitting beside him as he spoke to the Romans, who were made to stand. Unluckily for the Persians, their boat was caught by a Roman warship on their way back across the Bosporus. One ambassador was promptly beheaded, while the second had his hands chopped off. The severed head was suspended around the second ambassador's neck, and he was sent back in this state to the khan. After that, the Romans took the third ambassador by boat over to the shore held by the Sasanian army and made a great show of his execution. Such appalling savagery was presumably meant to show the defenders' resolve, but it outraged, rather than dismayed, the attackers. The khan made a formal protest at the barbarous treatment of his guests.

The siege continued, the intensity of the attacks increasing as siege-works were completed, but the defenders held on. They were buoyed by their faith in God's protection and by the favour of the Virgin Mary, praying to her to intercede with her son on their behalf. There was a major success at sea, when Roman warships intercepted and burned or sank a fleet of boats ferrying soldiers across the water. Opinion is divided over whether this was a serious attempt to get Persian troops across the Bosporus to join the siege or an assault by Slavic tribesmen against the city. Attacks continued, and in one pause the Avars and the Sasanians each took position to parade their full might in plain view in the hope of overawing the defenders. A great assault was launched by the Avars and Slavs and was beaten back.

On 8 August, the khan began to withdraw his army. All his attacks had failed, and he could not feed his great host for much longer if they stayed concentrated around the city. He sent word warning the Romans not to dare to harry his men and pulled back slowly, burning churches, other buildings, and anything they could not carry off, including the bulk of their own siege equipment. A little later, the Sasanian army also retired from Chalcedon, and finally, once they were sure that the siege was over, the inhabitants of Constantinople held a service to celebrate their deliverance, with particular thanks being offered to the Virgin Mary, who was presented as the protector of the city. This was an important moment in the growing reverence accorded to her.

Khusro II's grand offensive had failed, although it had been close. In the meantime, Shahen had led another army in pursuit of Heraclius. Weakened by the detachment of several thousand men to reinforce Constantinople, the Romans retreated, managing to keep ahead of the larger Sasanian force and winning a few small encounters. Eventually there was a battle, which the Romans won, pursuing the fleeing enemy and inflicting heavy losses. Shahen escaped, but according to one source his spirit was broken and he died soon afterwards. Khusro II publicly blamed the commander for his failure, and another version of the story claims that he had Shahen executed. There was even worse news for the king of kings when the Western Turks launched heavy raids into his empire, easily crossing frontier lines depleted of soldiers and ravaging Albania and Atropatene with fire and sword. When Khusro II sent envoys in the hope of buying the invaders off and giving him some breathing space, he received a blunt reply. The khan was an ally of the Roman emperor and was himself 'king of the north and lord of the whole earth', while Khusro II was a mere regional governor. Unless the Persians submitted, the khan promised to devastate their lands just as the Persians had laid waste the Roman empire. Khusro II responded in turn with reminders of past alliance, his own strength, and threats of what he might do in reprisal. He continued to dismiss Heraclius, calling him the 'castrated one'. As the year closed, the Turks withdrew for the winter, but the respite was temporary.[11]

Later Arabic tradition depicted an increasingly tyrannical and suspicious Khusro II as his great plans started to crumble around him. In one tradition, he grew to distrust Shahrbaraz, still in command of the largest field army, and sent a secret letter ordering his execution. The general discovered the contents of the letter—in some versions, after it had been intercepted by Heraclius—and faked another which ordered the deaths of many of his senior officers. He showed this to them, convincing his army to support him instead of the king of kings, and continued to be in secret contact with Heraclius and held back from the war. Certainly, Shahrbaraz and his troops played little or no part in operations for the next year or so. Some scholars are inclined to see the story of the letters as later, romantic invention, and at the very least there is surely some embellishment in the account. Whatever the truth, Khusro II does not appear to have been able to count on his general from this point on.[12]

In 627, the Turks returned, rapidly overrunning the Derbent Wall on the west of the Caspian Sea and storming through the pass it protected. The Sasanians simply did not have enough troops left available to stop them. Heraclius went to Lazica, evicting the weak Persian forces there without much difficulty. He then marched to an agreed rendezvous with the Turks outside Tiflis, the capital of Iberia. The Roman emperor met the Turkish khan, the two men embracing, then—at least according to a Roman source—the warlord prostrated himself before Heraclius, and, seeing this, his entire army did the same. Yet the gestures were not all one-sided. Heraclius took off his imperial crown and placed it on the khan's head, then presented him with imperial robes, as well as pearl earrings more fitting to Turkish tradition. The alliance was to be cemented through marriage, as Heraclius pledged his daughter to become the khan's bride. She was not present, so for the moment the groom-to-be had to make do with a portrait, but agreement was reached for her to travel to him in two years' time. The unprecedented willingness of a Roman emperor to marry his child to a warlord, however powerful, is a reminder of just how desperate the Romans' fight for survival had been in recent years. Securing the assistance of tens of thousands of Turkish warriors at last turned the tide in favour of the Romans.[13]

In spite of witnessing the splendour of the Roman and Turkish armies and the enthusiasm of their leaders for the new alliance, the defenders of Tiflis were not cowed. The combined armies besieged the city but could not take it—and it only fell some time later. Instead, the new allies ravaged the surrounding lands, a task the Turks in particular were better suited to perform. As the summer drew to a close, the khan tarried a little longer before he withdrew to pass the winter in his own lands, while Heraclius took the Roman army south into Mesopotamia, where it was possible, if still unusual, for an army to stay in the field throughout the winter months. Some Turkish auxiliaries may have accompanied him as he crossed the Zagros mountains towards the Tigris, but the sources are confused. In December 627, a Sasanian army had gathered to confront the plundering Roman column, but outside Nineveh, Heraclius lured the Persians onto ground of his own choice and attacked. Surprise was helped by thick morning mist, but even so the battle proved a hard one. The Sasanian general and most of his senior officers fell in the fighting, and overnight the Persian army grudgingly withdrew, for the moment leaderless.[14]

Maurice had once contemplated a drive on Ctesiphon until he was called away, but now Heraclius led his army towards this greatest city of the Sasanian empire. In the path lay Dastagerd, a favourite palace of Khusro II where he had spent recent months. On 23 December, the king of kings had his servants pack as much of his treasure and other important belongings as possible onto pack elephants, camels, and mules. A day later he and his family slipped away, leaving orders for the rest to follow. Once at Ctesiphon, he desperately began to organize its defences, summoning troops from all quarters to come to him.

At Dastagerd, Heraclius found that Khusro II had gone, but in spite of the attempted evacuation, vast quantities of luxuries remained to be plundered. Alongside all the silks and splendours were three hundred Roman standards captured in earlier campaigns. The emperor paused, resting his weary soldiers; around this time, they slaughtered as food the collection of game animals kept at a royal precinct for hunting. Returning to the traditional pattern of warfare between the two empires, an embassy went to the king of kings, urging him to open peace talks rather than force more fighting and more destruction when both sides had suffered enough: 'Let us extinguish the fire before it consumes everything.' Khusro II refused and did his best to conscript any men he could find, taking them from the royal household and those of his noblemen. His officials were ruthless in their methods for obtaining this manpower and the funds to pay and equip them. Enthusiasm for the war had evaporated and may never have been high once it was clear this was meant to destroy the Roman empire rather than simply assert Persian dominance and extort concessions.[15]

A conspiracy was formed between senior officers and court officials, with the more or less active participation of Kavadh, one of Khusro II's sons. They reached out to Heraclius, wanting to know whether he was genuine in his desire for a peaceful settlement, assuming the obstacle posed by the king of kings could be removed. The Roman army had not pushed closer to Ctesiphon and was instead plundering the wider area, targeting in particular anywhere with a royal connection. A patrol caught the envoys and brought them to the emperor, who welcomed them and gave them the assurances they had sought. They returned, and the conspirators promptly acted, arresting Khusro II. Kavadh II was crowned king of kings in his place on 25 February 628. Three days later, the new monarch's brothers were executed as potential rivals. The father was shot with arrows, the traditional and honourable method of killing a dethroned king.[16]

Khusro II had had one of the most remarkable careers of any Sasanian—or, for that matter, Arsacid—ruler. Forced into exile as a youth, he had returned with Roman aid, won a civil war, and fought to establish himself against all his rivals. The murder of his former ally Maurice prompted him to go to war against the Romans, whether through genuine outrage or as a useful pretext is uncertain. Either way, he did spectacularly well and dreamed of extinguishing the old rival once and for all. He almost succeeded, but in the end his resources were stretched too thin. This gave the Romans a chance, and the talent of Heraclius and the hard marching and fighting of his soldiers brought the Roman empire back from the brink. Barely a year and a half after the Avars had failed at Constantinople, the man who had expanded the Sasanian empire to its greatest extent was overthrown, condemned for his 'crimes', and executed.

Heraclius and his army had withdrawn before the conspirators acted, so it was two months before he learned that they had succeeded and wished to talk. The war was not over, and there was bound to be a prolonged period of negotiation to hammer out the details, not least how the great swathes of conquered Roman territory could be returned. However, Heraclius was satisfied to give the new regime the chance to establish sufficient control to permit it to deliver on any promises made in the ultimate agreement. A letter from Kavadh II addressed Heraclius as brother, formally marking an end to the shattering of diplomatic norms under his father. This was too late for the imprisoned Roman envoys from the earlier attempts at negotiation. One had died of disease, and the survivors had been killed on Khusro II's orders during the last days of his rule.[17]

Eventually the terms were agreed, with Kavadh II promising to return the conquered Roman provinces and all prisoners still held by the Sasanians, as well as the relics carried off from Jerusalem. Yet when the king of kings sent orders for Shahrbaraz and his army to withdraw from the occupied territory, the general refused to obey. Presumably he wished to protect his own position and status, as well as life, but it is impossible to understand his motives without knowing whether he had been in secret communication with Heraclius in the preceding years. There was no obvious way for the court in Ctesiphon to enforce its orders, and before they could work out what to do, Kavadh II died, perhaps during an outbreak of plague. His infant son Ardashir III was proclaimed as king of kings in the autumn of 628, but Shahrbaraz was not impressed and led his army to Ctesiphon, defeating the troops loyal to the new regime. Ardashir III was executed along with his key supporters, and Shahrbaraz crowned as king of kings in April 630, only the second man from outside the Sasanian family to ascend the throne. He was murdered within a matter of months, as was a nephew of Khusro II who briefly won support. The killing of the other sons of Khusro II in 628 meant that there were no obvious male heirs, so another convention was broken when his daughter Boran became the first woman to rule the empire. She died within a year, apparently of natural causes. A sister succeeded her, but did not last long, and the same was true of the three men who barely claimed power long enough to mint coins before they died. Only in 632 did Yazdgerd III, a grandson of Khusro II, bring a measure of stability.[18]

This confusion and internal disorder meant that the Sasanians were in no position to resume the struggle with Rome, but it also meant that the implementation of the peace treaty took some time. Shahrbaraz maintained good relations with the Romans and staged his coup with Roman approval and probably direct military aid. He ordered the withdrawal of remaining Sasanian troops from conquered territory and returned the relics during his brief reign. In the main, the garrisons obeyed and communities reverted to their old allegiance to Rome, but there was some fighting. Edessa had to be besieged before the Sasanian troops there agreed to leave. Reoccupation of the town led to a massacre of the Jewish population and other perceived collaborators. However, one of the Jewish citizens escaped and brought the news to Heraclius, who ordered the killing to stop. The returned relics were brought first to Constantinople, and it was probably not until March 630 that Heraclius took them back to Jerusalem, making sure to enter the city humbly, walking on foot rather than riding surrounded by the pomp of the imperial court. The world appeared to be returning to its natural state.[19]

Khusro II's war with the Romans was unlike any of the earlier conflicts between the Romans and Sasanians, or for that matter the Parthians. For more than twenty-five years, the two empires fought with an intensity that had no precedent, in campaigns covering a wider area than ever before. The principal reason for this was Khusro II's greater ambition. He scented an opportunity, which for a long time appeared fully vindicated as the Roman defensive zone was overrun and interior provinces conquered. Then it had collapsed around him in just a few years, as Heraclius kept the Romans in the war and began to strike back. These reverses, combined with the strain of maintaining the war effort on such a scale, led to Khusro II's abrupt fall. The king of kings had come closest to complete victory in 626 through cooperation with the Avars. In turn, the Romans had turned the war in their favour through alliance with the Turks. Neither empire had quite enough power on its own to defeat the other, making the role of these tribal confederations critical to the outcome. Yet Khusro II could readily have obtained a very favourable peace through negotiation at several stages and was unwilling even to test the water. Heraclius, realizing how close his empire had come to destruction, was satisfied with far less when the situation was reversed.

This was to be the last war between Sasanians and Romans, although no one could have guessed this at the time. Each empire had faced periods of civil war and instability before, only to recover, its strength and prosperity reduced but still substantial. In 630, the two empires were once again fairly well-balanced in relation to each other. There were encouraging signs for the Sasanians when the Western Turkish confederation collapsed almost as suddenly as the Hunnic confederation had fallen apart after the death of Attila. In this case, it began with successes won by Chinese armies far to the east, who had been encouraged to act by the knowledge that so many Turkish warriors had been drawn off to fight against the Sasanians. These defeats discredited the current Turkish leadership, and unity collapsed for more than a generation—and with it the immediate threat to the kingdoms of the

Caucasus and the Sasanian empire. The planned marriage between the khan and Heraclius's daughter never took place.

Both empires began to recover from the ordeal of such prolonged and costly warfare. Neither was as strong as before. Rome had lost ground in Italy and all its lands in Spain, had seen the Balkan frontier overrun several times, and now had to restore its administration in the recovered provinces in the east as captives returned from long exile. The war had disrupted the economic life of the empire and uprooted populations, which were also struck by several outbreaks of plague. The Sasanians were riven by internal power struggles, which as always tended to loosen central control over their vast empire and especially the regions on the fringes. Both sides needed time to restore and rebuild their strength. It was not to be.

19

ON THAT DAY ALL BELIEVERS SHALL REJOICE

632–C. 700

KHUSRO II's WAR WITH ROME HAD SURPASSED ALL THE PREVI-
ous conflicts between the two empires for its intensity and length
and the sheer devastation it caused. Yet for all the spectacular
Sasanian successes of the first twenty years or so, the conflict ended
in defeat and a negotiated settlement, which essentially restored the
pre-war borders of each empire. Khusro II was already dead before this was confirmed, overthrown once the war had turned sour
and the strain of feeding it with money and men no longer seemed
bearable. His son Kavadh II began to settle with the Romans, halt-
ing all major offensive operations, but it was not until Shahrbaraz
seized power that the treaty was confirmed and the process of
implementing the agreements got under way. Shahrbaraz's assassination within a matter of months did not reignite the war between
the two empires, although it is harder to say how much it im-
peded the process of restoring land and captives. There seem to
have been Roman troops in Sasanian territory for some time afterwards, although there is no indication that they took an active role
in the power struggles that followed, as successive regimes tried

to establish themselves, let alone assert their rule over the entire empire.

As the eventual losers of the war, the Sasanians were in the weaker position. Shahrbaraz was only the third man from outside the royal house of Sasan to be proclaimed as king of kings, even if briefly. Khusro II's daughter Boran, who succeeded him, may well have been little more than a figurehead for a group of senior courtiers, since the empire had no tradition of female rule. Even so, she was depicted on coins minted during her reign. Coins bearing the name of her sister Āzarmēdukht, whose reign as queen was even briefer, have the image of a male ruler. This is unlikely to have been a deliberate attempt to present her as male, for the coins were those of another ruler, quickly overstruck by the new regime, and it was easier to change the name than the picture.[1]

Little is known about any of these short-lived rulers and the regimes backing them. There was usually at least one pretender at large somewhere in the empire, although the difference between a usurper and legitimate ruler was wafer thin at this time. Whole sections of the empire, especially on the fringes, appear more or less independent of central government, controlled by regional leaders able to impose some sort of authority at a local level. Had a strong king of kings emerged and lasted for some time, then no doubt his regime would have asserted itself over most or all of the former empire. For the moment, it was a matter of starting to recover from the impact of the great war, and everything suggests that local and central authorities alike were doing their best. The fire temple destroyed by Heraclius's army in 624 was soon rebuilt, its flame relit. At heart, much of the population still had faith in their traditions, beliefs, laws, and the idea of the rule of a king of kings from the house of Sasan, even if they were less convinced by the claims of particular rulers at that time. There is no real sign of a widespread longing for change or disillusion with the world as it was.[2]

Much the same was true within the Roman empire, and Heraclius had the advantage of greater security, since, for the moment, he faced no serious internal challenge. He also had come out of the war as victor, which helped to buoy spirits within his empire, even though the costs of enduring and finally winning the war far outweighed any profits from the victory. Some of this was tangible: the damage to cities, disruption to farming and trade, or the replacement for years on end of the Roman organs of government with those of the occupying Sasanians. There was also the blow to Rome's reputation from defeat after defeat in the early years. In the third century, Zenobia's forces had overrun Egypt, although whether this was remembered as part of a civil war or as a foreign invasion by Palmyra is unclear. Since then, the province had been secure, again apart from occasional outbursts of civil war. Syria and Palestine were more exposed, and some of their districts had faced plenty of raids, some of them large-scale. Time and again over the centuries, cities had fallen, substantial numbers of people had been transported to Persia as captive labour, and enemies—whether Sasanian, or tribal allies, or Huns—had plundered widely. Civilian populations suffered the most in these circumstances, as they always did. Yet until Khusro II's war they had not been subject to conquest by a foreign enemy that surely appeared permanent. In the long run, the emperor had forced the invaders to leave and had restored imperial administration, but only after years of occupation.[3]

The Roman empire was still strong, but was less strong than it had once been, and its vulnerability to a heavy attack had been made all too plain by the spectacular successes of Khusro II. Many Christians were inclined to see defeat and failure as punishment for the sins of society or individuals. By extension, success demonstrated God's approval. This perhaps created a willingness to accept disasters as avoidable if only people behaved properly, making these disasters easier to understand without doubting the fundamental strength of a state led by an emperor at Constantinople who acted as God's agent on earth. Phocas could be blamed for many of the defeats, and Heraclius's piety as much as his talent taken as the reason for eventual victory. Yet Christians also believed that the world would one day perish, to be replaced by a better, perfect existence purged of sin and its consequences. Rome's empire—even if ruled from Constantinople—was a beacon of civilization and faith on earth, but it would not last forever, and the apocalypse would one day come. This meant that disasters, whether natural or through war, could be seen as signs of the end of the world or simply as more burdens to bear. No one could be sure, although particular dates and dreadful events tended to encourage predictions of impending cataclysm. Such ideas were not the sole preserve of Christians in this era, and similar fears emerged in those of other faiths, including Zoroastrians. These were uncertain times, not least because of the periodic outbreaks of plague. Many people believed that the world as they knew it might come to an apocalyptic end and that this might happen during their lifetime. Most also understood that it might not, and that things could equally continue for years or generations much as they were.[4]

Heraclius had brought the empire back from what must have seemed the very brink of destruction, reclaimed all the lost territory, and returned the looted relics to Jerusalem. Sasanian occupation had exacerbated doctrinal divisions between Christians, and in some areas it had greatly heightened tension between Christian and Jewish communities over the latter's real or imagined collaboration with the invaders. Such splits within and between communities were a long-standing feature of many Roman provinces, and although the current spate of violence was unusually bad, it was still not so serious as to pose a major threat to imperial stability. Constantinople's desire to enforce its view on doctrinal matters remained strong, and Heraclius was bolder in his actions in some areas. In 632, he ordered the forced baptism of some or all of the Jewish population in the African provinces, although the details and scale of both the intention and the implementation are obscure. There were limits to what the central government could achieve, especially since its resources remained very thinly stretched. Heraclius had won the war with a small field army and had struggled to pay them. Estimates of the total number of troops available to the empire range from fifty thousand to one hundred thousand, with the vast majority tied down as garrisons. While smaller than the army in earlier periods, this was still a considerable total to supply and pay, and the sums had to be met from regular taxation, which could not be expected to revert to pre-war levels instantly. Pay seems often to have been in arrears, and there was little or no capacity to increase the size of the army.[5]

Although Romans and Sasanians were now at peace with each other, that did not mean there was no more fighting. The Sasanians had their civil wars, and both empires had other frontiers and other antagonists. Groups of warriors usually described as Arabs or Saracens launched a number of raids into the territories of both empires. This was nothing new. Sometimes such bands had come as allies of one of the big empires, and sometimes they freelanced. Romans and Sasanians alike had devoted considerable effort in the past to creating fortified lines and stationing troops to deter or deal with attacks of this sort. Militarily it was rarely possible to stop the raiders coming in, but there was a better chance of catching them as they went home laden with plunder and inflicting a defeat that might act as a deterrent to others. As we have seen, more reliance was placed on winning allies among the leaders of the Arab tribes, promoting their interests and power so that they were better placed to restrain others and deal with counter-attacks from the other empire's allies. In addition, these leaders supplied each empire with significant numbers of warriors to serve with the field armies. Arabs played a prominent role in Heraclius's campaigns and those of his Sasanian opponents, excelling as scouts and raiders and also serving in the main battle line when necessary.[6]

This was part of a wider picture of Roman and Sasanian diplomacy and intervention reaching far beyond their formally governed provinces. During the sixth century, this activity spread down as far as the Arabian Gulf and the west coast of Africa. A strong kingdom in what is now Yemen was led by a dynasty and an elite who at some point had converted to Judaism. Allied to the Sasanians, this kingdom was attacked by Axum, the equally powerful, sophisticated, and Christian kingdom in Ethiopia, which was encouraged and partly financed by the Romans. The invasion was a success, although the general in command split from his king and set up his own independent regime. This was a reminder that although the great empires were involved, neither was in control of events, for the leaders of the region were never mere pawns but were independent players in their own right. The profits from the spice trade and the wider sea trade to the east helped to fund any regime able to dominate the region, and this was one of the motives for Roman intervention.[7]

Outside aid and encouragement helped to escalate competition between leaders and states without ever making it fit neatly into the aims of the king of kings or the emperor in Constantinople. Similarly, the allied leaders closer to the borders of each empire were never reduced to simple subordinates willing to obey orders. Maurice had turned on the Jafnid king in circumstances that are obscure, although this group of tribes, often known as the Ghassanids, appears on the whole to have returned to an alignment with Rome by the time of Heraclius. Khusro II executed the last king of the Lakhmid line and instead imposed direct rule. This continued a trend towards physical occupation of the lands along the Persian Gulf and government through officials of the Sasanian empire rather than local leaders, although inevitably the officials had to deal with chieftains in the area. Up to this point, the largest groupings of Arab communities in the wider area were those created by the lines of kings backed by each empire. No Arab leader had so far managed to bring together large numbers of groups, unlike some of the warlords among the Huns, Germanic tribes, and especially the Avars and Turks. This was a sparsely populated region, not subject to substantial migration from outside.[8]

There was a tendency for the Romans (and many later peoples) to equate Arabs with nomadic groups. Travelling bands—whether pastoralists arriving with their herds and tents, merchants, or raiders—were very visible as different to the settled population when they appeared in an area and then moved on. Such groups were Arabs, but they were not the only Arabs of the ancient world, simply the ones most likely to draw attention in Greco-Roman sources. Many people who spoke Arabic languages lived in static communities, wherever the land was better and the water supply permitted marginal land to be tended and to yield a worthwhile harvest. There were villages, towns, and cities, with organized governments that in some cases grouped together into bigger kingdoms, mostly some distance from the lands of either empire. There were Arabs who were farmers as well as pastoralists, and there were traders, craftsmen, and men who might embark on long journeys for business without being nomads.

Nomads and settlements were not exclusive and interacted as a matter of routine and tradition, sometimes violently, but more often to mutual benefit. There were also substantial communities of Arabs—in the sense of people speaking an Arabic language—in cities throughout Roman Palestine, Syria, and beyond, and in the Sasanian empire. This had been true from the start of the period and had only increased as the centuries passed. Arabs were subjects of the emperor and the king of kings, as well as represented among people and groups from outside the empires. Many were Christian, some were Jewish. They were not automatically strangers, nor were they united. Only outsiders grouped them all together as Arabs. Once, Palmyra—as Pliny had put it, standing between two empires—had played a critical role in linking the provinces with communities and trade from far afield. Yet with Palmyra long since relegated to no more than another Roman garrison city, the connections had become smaller scale and spread over a wider area.

Arabs, as the Romans and Sasanians saw them, were not united nor ever likely to come together under a charismatic leader as other tribal peoples had done. Some communities were at times hostile and were dealt with in the usual ways: by threats, by bribes and diplomacy, and by direct violence when necessary. Better yet, a hostile leader or group was most easily dealt with by persuading or cajoling another leader or group to oppose them. Arabs were not perceived as a major adversary, so the *Strategikon* did not bother to discuss them at all in the section on dealing with likely enemies. That did not mean that the Romans had learned nothing about them as opponents in all the long centuries of contact. Belisarius based one strategic decision on the knowledge that the Persians' Arab allies were celebrating a religious festival, which meant that they would not take the field for several months. Yet the Roman experience of Arab leaders was of raiders, enemies who moved fast and crossed deserts far more easily than a regular army could. They were fierce, savage, but had no skill or appetite for siegecraft and could not hold on to ground. Their attacks were to be

AVAR KHAGANATE

B Y Z A N T I N E   E M

Franks

AQUITAINE

Bla

Lombards

Constantinople

Visigoths

Toledo

SARDINIA

SICILY

Ghazwat al-Sav
Battle of the M.
634

Mediter
ranean Sea

CRETE

Carthage

Sbeitla
647

Qayrawan
670

Tripoli
647

Barqa
644

Alexandria

Fustat

Tangiers

I S L A M I C

Bab
Fo
64

Gadamis

EGYP

FAZZAN

Asw
64

M A K

Dongola

A L

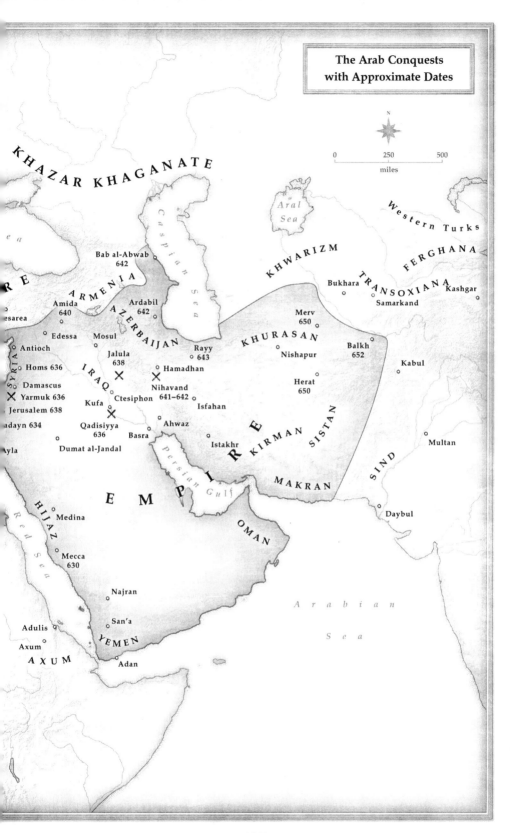

The Arab Conquests
with Approximate Dates

N

0   250   500
miles

KHAZAR KHAGANATE

Aral Sea

Western Turks

Caspian Sea

KHWARIZM

FERGHANA

Bab al-Abwab
642

ARMENIA

TRANSOXIANA

Kashgar

Bukhara

Samarkand

Amida
640

Ardabil
642

AZERBAIJAN

Merv
650

esarea

Edessa

Mosul

Rayy
643

KHURASAN

Balkh
652

Antioch

Jalula
638

Nishapur

Kabul

Homs 636

IRAQ

Hamadhan

Herat
650

Damascus

Ctesiphon

Nihavand
641–642

Yarmuk 636

Kufa

Isfahan

Jerusalem 638

adayn 634

Qadisiyya
636

Ahwaz

E

Multan

Ayla

Basra

Istakhr

KIRMAN

SISTAN

SIND

Dumat al-Jandal

Persian Gulf

MAKRAN

E   M   P   I   R   E

Daybul

HIJAZ

Medina

OMAN

Red Sea

Mecca
630

Najran

Arabian

San'a

Sea

Adulis

Axum

YEMEN

AXUM

Adan

SYRIA

endured, however frightful: one story claims that a pagan Arab leader ordered the mass sacrifice of four hundred captured girls. However savage, these were not conquerors who threatened to occupy settled provinces but plunderers who usually were willing to let captives be ransomed.[9]

From the perspective of the Arab communities, both empires were known quantities, more or less distant, and, depending on their own circumstances, seen as a threat, a potential friend, or a business opportunity. Some men had fought against one of the empires or had served in their armies, and plenty had visited the empires in search of pasture for the nomads or to trade, or they had met with folk who came from the empire on similar tasks. All felt in some way, however small, the ripples caused by generations of interventions by the two empires in the affairs of their communities. They were part of the wider economies of Rome and Persia in some senses and sheltered in others. The successive plagues that ravaged the urbanized hearts of the empires did not spread as easily among the smaller and more scattered Arab communities. For the inhabitants of Arabia itself, the hand of Persia was felt far more directly, as the Sasanians campaigned and did their best to absorb much of the region. They were closer, aggressive, and as a result tended to be resented even more than the distant Romans.

Our sources for the histories of the cities and tribes of Arabia during these centuries are meagre, which makes it difficult to trace developments in the region. Arab groups and leaders tend to appear in Greek and Roman sources when they became involved with one or both of the great powers. Nor does the situation improve as much as we would like with the appearance of the Prophet Muhammed, even though this led to profound changes far beyond Arabia. The earliest Muslim sources, most of all the Qur'an, were written to inspire and instruct the faithful and not to satisfy the curiosity of historians. The histories of Muhammed's life, career, and the rise of the caliphs who followed him were set down centuries later, influenced by the passage of time and the political and religious disputes of the writers' own era. Like so many of the Greco-Roman sources for our topic, these Muslim sources are often vague, unreliable on details, and prone to exaggeration.

They allow us to trace the overall course of events while leaving doubts about chronology and many of the details, which makes explaining what happened far harder. This means that there must be a considerable degree of guesswork about any reconstruction of these years and very little certainty.[10]

Muhammed was probably born around 570, although some scholars would argue that the true date was a little earlier, and perhaps even as early as 552. He and his family came from and lived in Mecca, a city engaged in commerce, as were many in the wider region. There was a strong tradition that Muhammed was a merchant who went on several long journeys, including visits to Syria some six hundred miles from his home at its closest point. Another tradition held that he was a shepherd, and perhaps both are true. Mecca contained a well-known shrine to a god, probably Hubal, which attracted pilgrims from elsewhere. The government of the city appears to have been strong and stable, which helped to foster trade and wider prosperity, but Mecca and its leaders remained essentially local in importance.[11]

Around 610, Muhammed began to preach in his home city, explaining that his message had come in a series of revelations, beginning with a visit from the angel Gabriel. He taught that there was only one God and instructed a steadily growing band of followers in the true way to honour and worship Him. By 622, there was friction with the authorities in Mecca, prompting Muhammed and his community to leave and travel the two hundred or so miles to Medina (at the time called Yathrib), where they settled. This was known as the *hijra* and in time became the first year of a new system of dating. There were still enemies, and Muhammed and his followers fought against them, skirmishing and raiding camps and villages. Most of the time they won, and the ranks of his followers continued to grow. Those who fought him were defeated, but individuals and peoples who submitted were welcomed into his community as equals. Eventually he was strong enough to march on Mecca, defeating its leaders in battle and destroying the shrine they protected in 628 or possibly a year or two later.[12]

There were other leaders at the head of bands of warriors, some of whom, later dubbed false prophets in the Muslim tradition, may have based their leadership in part on religious claims. This means that some of the raids against the Romans or Sasanians in the early years may have been conducted by these groups, or they may simply have been part of the traditional pattern of opportunistic raiding rather than coming from members of Muhammed's community. With each empire focused on fighting the other and its major allies, defences elsewhere were neglected as troops were drawn away for the main effort. The aftermath of the war was also a time of disorder, as the Romans began to reoccupy the territory lost during the war and the Sasanians turned to fighting each other for power. In 629, a Roman field force intercepted and defeated an Arab band that do appear to have been part of Muhammed's following. Yet such failures were rare, and in 630 several large cities and groups in Arabia allied with Muhammed. Soon most of his rivals had been defeated or had chosen to join him. Some fully became part of the community of the faithful (umma), while others submitted and paid tribute.[13]

Former enemies played prominent roles in the campaigns to come, and for some time, warriors of other faiths served under Muslim leadership, and provision was made for them to receive a fair share of the spoils. Monotheists, whether Christian or Jewish—or those from other cults who held one god to be supreme over all others—were most readily accepted. During the great conflict between Romans and Sasanians, Muhammed and his followers' sympathies lay far more with Rome. The Qur'an speaks of a Roman defeat, but then of their eventual victory 'in a few years' and says that 'on that day all Believers shall rejoice.' This is generally believed to refer to Heraclius's final victory after the early disasters in the war with Khusro II. The Sasanians were a bigger threat, but they were also polytheists, and Zoroastrianism—with its highly structured society that preserved social distinctions—was in direct contrast to the far more egalitarian community created by Muhammed. The Romans, on the other hand, worshipped the true God, even if they were misguided in their understanding. Later Muslim tradition tended to present Heraclius himself favourably, even claiming that he privately acknowledged Muhammed and his message but was unable to share this understanding with his subjects.[14]

Sympathy for the Romans and hostility to the Sasanians only went so far, and attacks on both began before the death of Muhammed in 632. Some allies chose this moment to break away from the community, leading to a period of internal fighting until control was restored by the first of the caliphs. Under these men, the Arab advance gathered pace, striking simultaneously at both of the great empires. Yet this was no vast invasion by a huge horde of warriors. In the earlier days, Muhammed had sometimes led no more than a few hundred men. By now, Arab armies numbered in thousands, and more than one could be fielded simultaneously. They appear to have been a mix of the true Bedouin nomads, most if not all riding horses or occasionally camels, and men who fought on foot, many of them drawn from the cities and other settled communities. Armour was rare, equipment light, and the emphasis on rapid movement and surprise. Several of the commanders who appear in these years were exceptionally talented, and each success added to the confidence and cohesion of the armies.[15]

Opposing them were relatively small numbers of Romans, and many of the early encounters were likely little more than large skirmishes. As in the past, Romans and Sasanians alike relied on Arab allies to defeat Arab enemies, partly because they tended to be best able to chase and fight them and partly because few good-quality regular troops were available. The later Muslim tradition depicted the Roman and Sasanian forces arrayed against the Arab attackers as huge, but this must be set alongside the tendency of Greco-Roman sources to claim that they were usually vastly outnumbered. There is a good chance that the Arab forces often were outnumbered, albeit by far less of a margin than the later sources would claim. Even so, they tended to win most of the encounters against Romans and Persians, allowing the raids to drive ever deeper into provincial territory, yielding more plunder and attracting more warriors to the cause.

It may have taken a while for the Romans to realize that this was turning into a major problem. Even then, Heraclius had limited resources, and there were only so many troops that could be sent to the area, even if he could find the supplies they required or the money to pay them. When units in Africa were ordered to move to the east, the governor, backed by the senior bishop, refused to obey, presumably feeling that they were needed where they were. By 636, the Romans had gathered a substantial field army, drawing on mobile units from Syria, the neighbouring provinces, and the empire's reserves. Heraclius did not command in person, presumably because of his age and health, although perhaps this was another reflection that the war did not seem as critical as the one against the Sasanians. Instead, he supervised from a distance. Nor did he make any spiritual appeal to the troops, as he had done during the war with Khusro II. There are no reliable numbers for the army, although the fifteen thousand to twenty thousand of the *Strategikon* is once again a guide to its likely maximum size. It was probably smaller, perhaps significantly so, and included Arab allies and a substantial contingent of Armenian troops among the regulars. As a force, it had had little time to train together, so it was far less of a practiced and confident team than the army Heraclius had led in the later stages of the war with Persia. A divided command did not help matters, and there were questions over the loyalty of one general, unless this was invented in the aftermath to deflect blame from the emperor.

The Muslim army was smaller than its opponents but was based around men used to working together. In July 636, the two sides closed with each other near Yarmuk, to the east of the Golan Heights. Roman doctrine continued to see battle as a last resort, to be joined only when the advantages were overwhelmingly in their favour, and sought instead to wear the enemy down using surprise and ambush. The Arabs fought in a similar way, so the encounter spread over several weeks in a series of rapid marches and skirmishes. During this time, the Arab leaders consistently out-thought their Roman counterparts, then out-manoeuvred and out-fought them. In the end the Romans were routed, their army destroyed or dispersed. There was no prospect of massing another field army of any size or quality in the area for years, if at all, so that this and the earlier encounters effectively removed the Romans' capacity to face the Arabs in the open anywhere in Syria, Palestine, or Mesopotamia. There were still garrisons, but none were large or of high quality, and no commander was left on the spot with the authority and ability to co-ordinate the defences. Heraclius withdrew to Asia Minor and began creating a new frontier line there. The provinces to the south were largely left to their own devices.[16]

These were all regions with fresh memories of Sasanian occupation, and once again city by city they faced the choice of whether to resist or come to terms with the new invaders. Some resisted, hoping that the Arabs were no more inclined towards sieges than in the past, and would threaten for a while and then leave, especially once winter arrived. They were wrong. Homs (formerly Emesa) held out for the winter of 636–637, then negotiated a settlement with a written treaty guaranteeing their lives, property, laws, and continued practice of their Christian faith. The price was 110,000 gold coins. Other cities made similar deals, encouraged when they saw that the Arab armies honoured the bargains. Chalkis in Syria negotiated a year-long truce, promising to surrendered if they were not relieved in that time. The Arabs honoured their side of the bargain, holding off for a year, and the city duly surrendered at the end of twelve months. Jerusalem lasted longer, capitulating in 638 after a two-year blockade. Arab armies were now better organized and more determined, able to stay in one place for a long time, but they still were reluctant to mount direct assaults on well-fortified cities unless there was no other choice. Caesarea Maritima on the coast only fell in 641, helped by its position, which made it easier to bring in supplies by sea. It had to be stormed, and in the aftermath all of the seven thousand troops and volunteer defenders unable to escape were executed.[17]

The Arab conquests were not bloodless and at times showed all the savagery typical of ancient warfare. Nor were they unopposed. From the start, the Roman response was poorly co-ordinated and lacking in strength, but all the sources suggest that the mobile units fought hard and did not simply give in. Similarly, the leaders in the cities considered their options. They did not welcome the invaders but accepted the reality of Arab might and, as time passed, realized that these were no mere raiders. It helped that the long-term contacts with Arab merchants and the presence of Arab speakers in many communities made these new conquerors familiar, in some senses less alien than the Sasanians. As important was the willingness of Arab commanders to negotiate and accept submission, just as Muhammed had done in his campaigns. They, too, were helped by familiarity from past contacts, especially with cities inland.

It was also far easier for them to deal with Christian and Jewish communities—the People of the Book, as they would become known. At this stage, these groups did not have a deep-seated hatred for Muslims, nor did Muslims hate them in turn. The Sasanians had largely respected the faiths of the conquered provincial communities, but with the Arab conquests the respect came more easily and naturally. Perhaps it was easier for Christian groups whose doctrine differed from the one proclaimed at Constantinople to submit, although on the whole all groups accepted that resistance was unlikely to succeed. Church life continued; bishops remained public figures with influence within their communities. In Jerusalem, the Arabs built a small prayer house on the site once occupied by Herod's Temple. This seems to have been vacant land, for there does not appear to have been a church on this spot; the Church of the Holy Sepulchre remained the pre-eminent Christian site in the city. Caliph Umar, the current leader of the movement, visited the city a little later and was careful to show respect. While this had much to do with the reverence for Jerusalem and for Jewish and Christian tradition embodied from the start in the teachings of Muhammed, it also made political sense. The Arab occupiers did not alienate the conquered people as long as they submitted and paid the agreed tribute.[18]

As Syria, Palestine, and then Mesopotamia fell to the Muslim armies, so did large swathes of Sasanian territory. Like the Romans, the Sasanians resisted, sending what troops were available against the invaders. Yet their war effort was hampered even more by divisions within the empire, which had already fragmented. Yazdgerd III had to be crowned in Persis in 632, presumably because his supporters did not have a secure hold over Ctesiphon until a few years later. The early fighting against the Arabs was small-scale, and the Sasanians had a few successes, even if the overall trend was of defeat. After a while, the Persians gathered a substantial field army, only to see it shattered in January 638 at Qadisiyya, an

Arab victory as important as the one at Yarmuk. Ctesiphon and the other royal cities around it fell to the Muslims in 640 as they overran much of what is now Iraq. Communities there reacted just like the ones in the Roman provinces—and much as they had done during the war with Rome—with very few fighting to the death and most seeking terms. Yazdgerd III escaped from Ctesiphon before it fell but in the subsequent pursuit had to abandon most of his baggage. He retired deeper into his empire, going first to the old heartland of his family. In the years that followed, he did his best to rally support to protect the remainder of his empire and in the hope of retaking what had been lost, but he was unable to turn the tide.[19]

The Arab armies continued to advance. In 640 they invaded Egypt, and the progression there was the same as everywhere else, with initial resistance by Roman garrisons, then some hard fighting before these troops were soundly defeated and organized resistance at a provincial level ceased, after which the invaders dealt with each community individually. Alexandria fell, and even though a few years later a Roman fleet managed to retake the great city, they could not hold it. Egypt, the great breadbasket of the eastern empire and a major source of imperial revenue, was forever lost to the Romans. Initial Arab offensives in Armenia failed, but their raids into Asia Minor became larger and more frequent, and sometimes their armies had enough confidence to winter in Roman territory. At the same time, more and more of the Sasanian empire was taken. Media fell around the same time as Egypt, Persis at the end of the decade. Yazdgerd III fled ever further east but was so discredited that he was challenged by a group of officials supported by local noblemen. Defeated in 650, he was killed a year later, one story claiming that the man who did it did not even know that this was the king of kings. From Egypt, the Arab armies pushed to the west along the African coast and built fleets to reach into the Mediterranean. Islands were raided, some overrun, and the first of a succession of major attacks against Constantinople launched in 654.[20]

By this time, the Sasanian empire was no more. Several sons of Yazdgerd III fled to China asking for aid against the Arabs. The eldest was recognized as the Sasanian monarch by the Chinese emperor, even though all he was able to control was a small area dubbed the 'Persian Area Command' around Sistan. A statue depicting him declared him to be 'Peroz, King of Persia, Grand General of the Right Courageous Guard and Commander-in-Chief of Persia'. A son succeeded him, and the line continued for some time, serving with their retainers as Chinese generals and dreaming of taking back all that they had lost. In 710, a Sasanian 'Bonnie Prince Charlie' tried to do just that, only to fail. Memory lasted longer, until the community of Persian exiles and royalty living in China eventually faded away as a distinct group. In their old empire, resistance to the Arab invaders did not end with the exile of the Sasanian royal house, but it was regional and disunited. Some leaders fought for a long time and won significant victories, while others came to terms with the Muslims. The men in control of the defences around the Caspian Sea did a deal with the Arabs to continue to guard these vulnerable frontiers instead of paying tribute. Most of the major Parthian clans eventually came to an accommodation with the new overlords and were allowed to keep their lands and status in return for loyalty to the caliphs, just as they had once transferred allegiance from the Arsacid dynasty to the house of Sasan. Yet that had been a transition from one ruling family to another, while the empire remained essentially the same. Now, more than eight centuries after Arsaces I had carved out an empire from the waning Seleucids, something very different had taken shape.[21]

At the same time, the Roman empire continued, but as a shadow of its former self. Later in the seventh century, an Arab army overran all of the remaining African provinces, with the now familiar pattern of initial resistance that was beaten down, after which each community made its own decisions and eventually was either defeated or, most often, came to terms with the invaders. There was a longer, tougher fight with the neighbouring Berber groups, who for generations had asserted their independence from the Romans and Vandals with great determination. Emperors continued to rule from Constantinople and would do so until it fell to the Ottoman Turks in 1453, but by the end of the seventh century the lands they controlled had shrunk to a remnant. Most of Asia Minor and Armenia remained more or less under Roman control for some time, even if they were vulnerable to Arab attacks, as were the islands in the Mediterranean. Cyprus was invaded twice in the seventh century, plundered, and much of its population carried off as slaves. There was still a Roman presence in the Balkans, doing its best to hold back successive enemies, joined in time by the Bulgars. By medieval standards, the emperor was head of a sizeable and reasonably wealthy kingdom, but it was little more than that, simply one kingdom among many.[22]

The change that occurred in the seventh century was one of the great revolutions in the history of the world. With hindsight, it all seems to have happened incredibly quickly, with the Romans losing Palestine, Syria, and Egypt in little more than a decade, and the entire Sasanian empire collapsing in similar fashion almost as swiftly. The impression is reinforced by the poverty of the sources and the difficulty of tracing what happened in any detail, and ten or fifteen years was not a short time for those living through all this. This conflict was quickly decisive compared to many wars in the ancient world, although similar to the recent collapse of Roman defences under Khusro II's onslaught and the subsequent rapid downfall of his empire so soon after it had seemed to be on the very brink of victory. Rapid is a relative term. Although the Sasanians took much territory in a fairly short time, like the Arabs, they had to fight for a lot of it. Neither the two great empires nor the Muslim armies who then overthrew them fielded vast numbers of soldiers. Small armies decided these great wars.

Given the scale of the revolution, understanding how and why it happened is obviously of immense interest, but the questions are easier to ask than they are to answer. It was surely no coincidence that the Romans and Sasanians struggled to deal with a new threat when it emerged so soon after the titanic, exhausting, and ultimately futile war they had just waged against each other. They were weary, resources of men and material were in short supply, and the Sasanians were politically divided. Neither side appeared to take the Arab challenge seriously, greatly underestimating its potential. At first, this did not seem a life-and-death struggle comparable to the recent conflict between the two empires. Familiar with fighting each other and well aware of the threats posed by groups like the Avars, Turks, and before them the Huns, the Romans and Sasanians had not had to deal with a challenge on this scale and from this direction before. The Arabs surprised them and proved not to be susceptible to bribery or as easy to divide as other tribes. Both empires struggled to adapt, and even though they did win some small successes and divert more resources to the problem, they did not do so fast enough and well enough to cope. Some of this was due to the cost of the recent war between them and some of it a sign of long-term decline.[23]

Roman and Sasanian mistakes and weaknesses are one thing, but usually it is wiser to ask why a side won rather than why its opponents lost. There had been sudden revolutions in the past, for instance when the first Achaemenids rebelled and took over an empire of which they had been part. The analogy Alexander's Macedonians provide is in some ways closer, when a fringe people of the Achaemenid empire in just a generation made themselves strong enough to overthrow it. Warlords like Attila created unity among disparate and fractious tribes, so that in a short time they overran huge swathes of territory, extorting tribute from emperors in Italy and Constantinople. The Achaemenid empire lasted a long time, whereas Alexander's fractured after his death and Attila's short-lived regime fell apart even more quickly. Muhammed began and his followers spread something very different, establishing a faith that would become one of the world's great religions. Yet not all the warriors who served with the Arab armies were Muslims, especially in the early days. Such men fought for a fair share of the plunder, to be on the winning side, and through alliance or kinship. Still, the core of the army and all of its leaders were believers, which gave a unity to the enterprise unlike anything a mere warlord could provide.

The Arab armies and their leaders proved themselves to be very good. Early on, the armies most likely included men who had served with the Romans and Sasanians, especially during the recent war. That meant that they understood well how the soldiers of the empires fought. They had also passed through many parts of the empire, so they knew the best routes and had a sense for the lie of the land. Through this mix of experience and the confidence and momentum gained as they won victory after victory, these armies became highly formidable. Another aspect of Muhammed's message was that it taught individuals how to conduct their own lives and how to treat others. This gave a consistency to the behaviour of individual generals as they fought campaigns hundreds of miles or sometimes more than a thousand miles away from the guiding hand of the caliph. Ruthlessness could be appropriate, as with all ancient cultures, and determined enemies had to be fought at all costs. Yet it was better to have them submit than to kill them, and it was best of all if they willingly joined the community of the faithful, but this was not essential.

The Arab empire that emerged in the seventh century was composed overwhelmingly of non-Muslims and remained like this for some time. Conversion was gradual and never universal. Christians and Jews continued in their own faith for generations, and this was accepted as long as they obeyed and paid their tribute or, more rarely, served with the army. Some Zoroastrians resisted the Muslim takeover fiercely until they were eradicated. Yet even there, many chose a path of acceptance and were permitted to follow their own beliefs and practices, with some fire temples remaining active. Parthian clans remained powerful in their old fiefs for a very long time, preserving their version of traditional Persian religion. Only gradually did more and more of the elite and the wider population convert to Islam.

The story of these conquests, and the development of the kingdoms that emerged, is far too big a theme to describe here. Yet it is best to see these changes first and foremost as the product of Arab victories rather than of Roman and Sasanian defeats. Success on such a scale does not simply happen, however vulnerable the established powers may have been. The spread of the Arab armies was made easier by the internal disputes over the succession to Heraclius, where the death of the son from his first marriage brought to the fore the questionable status of the children produced by his marriage to his niece. For a decade or so, the Roman war effort was rendered more feeble than it would otherwise have been, which no doubt made easier the Muslim conquest of North Africa. Yet Arab expansion was in turn delayed by several periods of bitter infighting over how best to fulfil the Prophet's vision for his community and the future, which in time led to the Shia and Sunni divide that fundamentally shaped subsequent history. These power struggles over succession gave the Romans some breathing space without allowing them to take back any of the lands already lost. By now, there were severe limits to how far the Roman empire could recover, for it simply lacked the resources and skill to expand once more, which meant that its successes had little lasting impact. Over time, the Arab dynasties of the Muslim empire would lose out to other lines of kings, some from Iran and more founded by outsiders, especially the Turks. Yet for a while, the caliphs presided over a realm bigger than that ruled by the Arsacids or Sasanians. The former were largely forgotten, but memories of the good and bad Sasanian monarchs survived. In contrast, after Heraclius, Roman emperors—and the Arabs continued to call them Romans—were seen as villains and enemies. Hostility and hatred between Christian, Muslim, and Jew would grow, not universally but becoming ever more common and more bitter as the centuries passed.[24]

Even before this, the shape of the political world had changed profoundly as the Muslim Arabs conquered Persia and the greater part of the eastern Roman empire, and in time they took more of Spain than Justinian's armies had proved capable of doing. Even though neither empire was at the height of its power when these invasions occurred—and, more immediately, both were exhausted from decades of all-out conflict begun by Khusro II—the Arab success remains spectacular. This was not a victory of a mighty empire over weaker states, whether in numbers or in wealth and technology. Over time, as the Arabs created an empire of their own, they would start to enjoy some of the advantages held in the past by the Romans and Sasanians, but this was not true at the beginning. Simply possessing riches, territory, and manpower has never been enough unless these are employed efficiently, and neither the Romans nor the Sasanians were at their best in the decades after

630. Success encourages success, and the early victories won by Arab armies fuelled the confidence to go on and do more. Chance played a part—as the Romans had always said it did in war—and it is wrong to see what happened as inevitable or the Arab conquests as easy, any more than the rise of Rome or of the Arsacids was smooth and natural. These were hard-fought wars won by well-led, highly motivated, skilful, and lucky armies.

By ancient standards, including those of the wars between Romans and Persians, the Arab conquests were not unusually brutal. Raiding by its nature tended to be savage, with murder, rape, abduction, and cruelty all common, while the storming of a city often led to even greater slaughter. Yet there was not massacre and destruction for the sake of it, for the victors wished to benefit from the wealth and prosperity of the conquered lands, much like the warlords who had overrun the western Roman empire—or for that matter the Romans, the Arsacids, and the Sasanians in their own eras of conquest. Occupation by the Arabs was rarely so oppressive as to become intolerable—again much like the situation in Europe in the fifth century and afterwards. On the whole, day-to-day life changed very little in districts of the former Roman and Persian empires, especially in the early years of Arab occupation. Taxes and tribute were paid to new authorities, but daily life largely continued, most of all with respect to faith and public worship, for religious change was gradual. There was some settlement, which meant the confiscation of land for the new communities, but it was limited in scale.

One of the main reasons the Muslim Arabs were able to create such a vast empire so quickly was that they asked relatively little of their new subjects, at least at first. The same had been true in the past of the Romans, Parthians, Persians, and, on a smaller scale, the warlords who had carved up the western Roman empire. The Muslims took over communities long accustomed to central authority, which was usually distant and had long since demilitarized, so that wars were waged by armies organized by the imperial authorities, ideally occurring a long way away. Once this central government was gone, with little or no prospect of its return in the immediate future, civilian populations did not feel themselves capable of opposing the military might of the conqueror, so they accepted the invader.

There was pragmatism on both sides. The Arab armies lacked the numbers to hold down a large population purely by force, which made it sensible to treat subject populations well. The latter, in turn, could see that they were given more day-to-day freedom if they complied with the demands of the conquerors. Once again, this was much the same as the behaviour of Gothic, Vandal, and other warlords in the west, for much the same reason. While it is an oversimplification, more of the existing culture and infrastructure survived in the lands overrun by the Arabs compared to the conquests of tribal groups in Europe. Some of this was cultural, for at least at first the Arabs had a good deal more in common with their new subjects. As importantly, they represented a much larger and more coherent new regime, united by faith, and politically they brought together far larger sections of the former Roman and Sasanian provinces than anyone was able to do in the west. Most areas were also part of older traditions of civilization, much of it predating the Greeks and Romans. In that sense, the Dark Ages proved less dark in the Muslim world compared to the Christian kingdoms in Europe, as old knowledge was preserved and new ideas developed.

THE RIVALRY BETWEEN Rome and Parthia-Persia had come to an end, as the first empire shrank to a pale shadow of its former might and the other vanished altogether. The last great war between them—some would see it as the last great war before antiquity became the medieval world—left them exhausted, and within a few years the Arab armies had triumphed over them. Almost eight centuries of competition were over, and the two lights or eyes of the world had ceased to shine.

CONCLUSION

THE ARAB CONQUESTS BROUGHT TO AN END OVER FOUR CENTU-
ries of competition between the Romans and the Sasanians, and
nearer seven centuries when the Arsacid Parthians are included.
Politically, the change was seismic. Even after the loss of Italy and
the western provinces, the Roman empire in the east was very big,
both economically and militarily stronger than any of its neighbours—including Sasanian Persia, even if the difference between
the two was far narrower than it had been in the past. Similarly,
the Sasanians controlled more territory and wealth than any people on their borders except the Romans. Such inherent advantage
had never guaranteed victory in a war, let alone on the battlefield,
but it did mean that the great empires were harder to damage in a
way that permanently and critically degraded their strength.

Yet in spite of these impressions of continued might, the Arab
conquests swept away the Sasanians, left the Roman empire a
shadow of its former self, and did all this very quickly, in just a
couple of decades. The speed of this collapse was only partly a reflection of timing. Exhausted after Khusro II's war, the two empires
were particularly vulnerable at just the moment when the Arabs
attacked. Each was weary, the Sasanians coping with defeat and absorbed by bitter infighting, and the Romans knowing their victory

had come only after long years of humiliating losses and disaster. Khusro II's armies had achieved spectacular success as they overran so much of the Roman empire, and then they experienced a just as spectacular and even more rapid defeat that cost them the war. The seesawing fortunes of both sides in this final conflict exposed more serious, longer-term vulnerabilities, which meant that neither empire was able to make good use of its full resources. The Persians almost won and the Romans finally did, but only through alliance with the Avars and Turks, respectively. Such alliances were able to shift the balance in one side's favour far more dramatically than a similar alliance would have done in the past.

All in all, while the balance of power between the two empires remained close at the start of the seventh century—just as it had always been, especially since the collapse of the western Roman empire—each side was long past the height of its power. Civil war and internal power struggles were old problems for both empires, sometimes kept in check for decades, even generations, but always capable of breaking out once more. In addition, since the early sixth century, the two empires had fought each other more often than in the past and had faced numerous other enemies, including at times large and powerful groups of tribes. Rarely were any of these wars profitable for the Romans or Sasanians, at least on a sufficient scale to cover their costs. Although some specialists on this period will disagree, it is hard to avoid the impression of long-term decline in the power and efficiency of both empires. Strong rulers—men like Khusro I and Justinian—tended to do better than weaker, less secure monarchs, and studying the powerful reigns gives an impression of greater strength for each empire than is justified.

Given the populations and wealth of the empires, the Roman and Persian armies were small, especially in terms of the good-quality troops suitable to serve in field armies. Both empires relied on troops who were effectively professionals and who tended to be drawn from certain narrow sections of society and received prolonged training. This gave little room to increase numbers quickly, hence the tendency for both to hire warriors from outside each empire whenever they wanted to expand their armies, assuming such warriors were available and could be kept under control. Most of the time, they were willing to be hired and proved loyal to their employer, but neither was guaranteed. In wars between the two empires the system worked reasonably well, but it was difficult to face another opponent or opponents simultaneously. While this had long been a problem, it does appear worse in this era. If a war went badly, it took far longer for either empire to rebuild its military strength.

The Romans and the Parthians, and then Sasanians, were rivals for a huge span of history. Neither destroyed the other or permanently took the greater part of the other's territory to reduce them to no more than a local power. During the many conflicts, each empire spent a great deal on fortifications, garrisons, field armies, and the material of war. For much of the period, the biggest armies deployed by either the Romans or the Parthians-Sasanians were raised to fight the other. Thus, there was great expenditure of effort, resources, and, to an extent, blood over many generations for modest gain.

This raises the possibility that the rivalry between the two great empires was a burden which over time weakened both of them. It would not be the sole cause of decline, since there were foreign wars against many other opponents as well as internal power struggles, all of which were costly. Civil war was especially damaging, since inevitably the empire bore the cost of both winning and losing each struggle, while the insecurity of emperors or kings of kings encouraged a state system designed principally to keep them in power over any other concern. There were also other trends within society, not to mention the impact on economic activity of natural disasters and the succession of plagues to sweep through the lands from the second century onwards. All of these contributed to weakening both empires, even if they are hard to measure and in most respects would have occurred even if the two empires had maintained unbroken peace with the other.

The question is whether the competition between the Romans and the Parthians and Sasanians in the long run damaged both sides, playing a significant—if not necessarily central—part in eroding their strength and rendering them incapable of meeting the challenge of the Arab conquests. There is no real doubt that both were weak in the immediate aftermath of Khusro II's war, at the very moment the Arabs were uniting under the new faith. Working back, the frequent conflicts of the sixth century can also be seen as damaging both sides, devouring resources for little permanent gain and interfering with the social and political structures of the Arab communities, perhaps encouraging them to unite. Yet how far back can such an argument be projected, especially since the fifth century had seen notably good relations between Sasanians and Romans? It is evident that in seven centuries neither empire managed to destroy the other, and at the end of it all the Persian empire was a memory and the Roman empire severely and permanently reduced. From that long-term perspective, the rivalry could be seen as futile, even self-harming.

Care is needed, since similar logic would suggest that a person who lives to 100 has failed when he or she does not manage to survive to be 110. The sheer duration of the rivalry between the two empires is in itself important, for it testifies to their longevity. After the first encounter with the Romans at the start of the first century BC and the period of heavy conflict later in that century, the Parthians continued to hold on to their empire until 224, and the house of Sasan reigned over what was territorially the same empire for another four hundred years and more. During the same time, Rome's republic turned into the principate, changed profoundly in the course of the third century, and later divided into eastern and western halves before the east survived the collapse of the west.

None of this should be taken for granted. There were many changes during these centuries but as much, if not more, continuity, so that these were recognizably the same empires. The success of Roman civilization is familiar to us, even if in popular consciousness the later periods and the rule of the emperors in Constantinople are less familiar and not what most people think of when they think of the Romans. Arsacid Parthia controlled a huge empire for four and a half centuries, for the last three with Rome as a rival. The entire history of the Sasanian dynasty was played out with the Romans as competitors, an ever-present factor in the decisions made by each monarch.

Few other empires of comparable size have lasted as long. During that time, the Roman empire and the Parthian-Sasanian empire gave their substantial populations stability, prosperity, long-distance trade on a grand scale, the rule of law, and encouraged cultural sophistication to a degree rare in the ancient world. That they also gave them long periods of civil war, outbreaks of religious and other oppression, and a fairly constant societal inequality does not change all this. These were large and highly successful states for an exceptionally long time.

The theme of this book has been the rivalry between the two empires, and it is now worth considering what was at stake in this before rushing to judgement about the benefits and costs for each side. In just a few years, Alexander the Great conquered virtually all of what would one day be Rome's eastern provinces as well as the lands later ruled by the Arsacids and the Sasanians. Only a few areas did not fall to him. He was about to push to the Arabian Gulf when he died. His attitude towards the kingdoms of the Caucasus is less certain, as up to that point he had shown little interest in the area. In time, Arab armies would take much of Alexander's empire, but it took them longer, and they soon began to split up into separate kingdoms.

Alexander's success enthralled Greeks and Romans alike for its speed and sheer scale, whatever their feelings about Alexander himself. For the Romans, almost any military operation east of the Mediterranean led their minds swiftly to the incredible adventure of the Macedonian king all those years before. Familiarity all too easily makes people forget that something was exceptional. Arguably the Mongols of Genghis Khan conquered as much— perhaps even more—land as quickly, but no one else in human history has achieved success on this scale and had it last as a single entity even as long as the brief life of Alexander's empire. Hitler's Operation Barbarossa saw the Wehrmacht and its allies advancing vast distances in a short time and inflicting appalling casualties on the enemy—and less than four years later the Red Army was in Berlin. Throughout history, empires have risen and fallen, and sometimes the collapse has happened quickly, but only Alexander has conquered and taken over as big a state as Achaemenid Persia so quickly. More often, empires are weakened and fragment or collapse over time.

The Romans had the model of Alexander to inspire them, as the poets in particular so often made clear. Crassus, Antony, Augustus, Caius Caesar, Trajan, Caracalla, Julian, and plenty of other Roman leaders were likened to Alexander—sometimes by themselves. None of them actually won victories in the east on a comparable scale, and certainly none of them conquered Parthia or, in the later era, Sasanian Persia. Harder to say is whether any of them actually wanted to copy Alexander in such a literal sense or actively planned to overthrow Rome's eastern rival.

Crassus's objectives for his expedition into Parthia are uncertain, since they ended in disaster at an early stage of the campaign. What most likely began as an intervention in a Parthian civil war surely had changed into something else, but there are many objectives—some very ambitious—that fall short of outright conquest of all or most of the Arsacid empire. The story—if it is not apocryphal—of Crassus boasting that he would dictate terms at Seleucia does suggest that he aimed to defeat rather than destroy the Parthians, imposing a treaty on them favourable to Rome and no doubt personally glorious and profitable to himself. Antony's grand expedition in 36 BC also failed too early to make clear his ultimate objective, but it appears to have been aimed at forcing regional kings to submit and perhaps replacing them with candidates of his own. The subsequent Donations of Alexandria, where he gave Parthia to one of his children by Cleopatra, is a bizarre episode in so many ways, and there was never any attempt to implement it in reality. Even so, making a son king of Parthia suggests that Antony envisaged an ideal world where Parthia existed, albeit as an ally ruled by his child rather than by an Arsacid.

In the second century, Trajan enjoyed more success than either Crassus or Antony before his eastern campaigns turned sour. He created provinces in Armenia, Mesopotamia, and Assyria. The precise extent of this Assyrian province is unclear, but it would still have left the greater part of the Parthian empire under the rule of the king of kings, ideally the man appointed by Trajan. Lucius Verus took a little territory, and Septimius Severus significantly more to form his Mesopotamian province. Both men marched to Ctesiphon and back, asserting dominance and forcing the Parthians to accept Roman-imposed peace terms in what were relatively swift campaigns. Neither man showed the slightest sign of wanting more than limited territorial gain. None of these were attempts to destroy the Parthian empire as the Romans had once destroyed the Carthaginian empire (and even then, within a generation they had founded their own Roman colony on the ruins of the old city).

There really is very little sign that any Roman ever seriously planned to conquer Parthia. Julius Caesar might be seen as an exception, for the expedition he planned but never launched was conceived on a grand scale. However, he also set aside three years for the operation, including a preliminary campaign on the Danube against the Dacians. This time frame suggests that his objective was a massive demonstration of force, either to persuade the king of kings to submit or even to replace him with a man more friendly to the Romans and to Caesar. If Caesar did expect to conquer Parthia in this time, it would imply a staggering ignorance of geography on the part of a man who had spent a decade overrunning Gaul.[1]

Such ignorance—for not only Caesar but all of Rome's elite, no matter how well-educated—is accepted by scholars arguing for the very limited ability on the part of Rome's leaders to plan at the higher levels. For them, limited, confused, and false perceptions of the lands beyond the empire combined with an ideology of expansion and glory to shape Roman decision-making in ways that would seem crude by any modern standards. To an extent this is artificial, since more might be learned through comparison with eighteenth- or nineteenth-century states and empires rather than the world of the late twentieth and early twenty-first centuries.

All in all, while such views have helped to illuminate neglected aspects of Roman ways of thinking and acting and focused discussion of the army and its uses in many beneficial ways, they lack credibility, especially when pushed to an extreme. On campaign, Roman armies proved perfectly capable of finding their way around, even outside the frontiers of the empire. We should remember that Alexander and the Hellenistic kingdoms had left a good deal of geographical information about the lands that subsequently became Parthian. Over time, as campaigns tended to be fought in much the same areas, more knowledge was acquired.[2]

This did not mean that no mistakes were ever made when it came to intelligence gathering, or that armies never got lost. War is a complicated business, where much can go wrong, and plenty of modern travellers manage to get themselves lost in spite of all the benefits of detailed maps. A fair reading of the ancient sources, and in particular examination of what the armies actually did, makes it clear that the Romans—and for that matter the Parthians and Sasanians—were fully capable of planning operations, organizing supply, and moving large numbers of troops over considerable distances. They also showed an awareness of the wider geography, especially the crucial political geography of potential allies and likely enemies who needed to be taken into account. Underestimating the ability of the ancients to behave rationally and in a practical way is rarely justified.

Nor should the enthusiasm of poets and the boasts of official statements ever be taken as representing the sum total of Roman thoughts on any matter or be understood any more literally than the propaganda of more modern leaders and states. Human beings are rarely so simple in their outlook. The Romans certainly believed conquest and the profits and glory that came with it to be good, admirable things. They created an empire through conquest and never seriously questioned that this was a justifiable thing to do because it benefitted Rome. Glory and reputation mattered to individual aristocrats and perhaps even more for emperors. It was vital for any emperor to be seen as a victor.

These were concerns, and important ones, but they were never the only motivations, nor were views about war, glory, and empire so purely monolithic. An emperor could be a victor and a glorious leader because under him the empire was so strong that no one dared to oppose it. Peace based on Roman might was perfectly acceptable and did not require an actual war. Only what was seen as a major provocation, which implied lack of respect for Rome, or still worse an actual defeat, called for a firm reply and perhaps war. In the same way, under the republic and afterwards, aggressive warfare and especially expansion was not constant. At times it was common, but at other times it was not. The Romans did not take every opportunity to fight a new war, let alone every opportunity to annex territory. Under the principate, after the burst of expansion under Augustus, wars of conquest were rare. Clearly, the desire for glory could be, and usually was, overtaken by other considerations.

If any Roman leaders thought seriously about the conquest of Parthia or Persia, then they did amazingly little to achieve it. There were long periods of peace and stability when resources could have been drawn from all over the empire to mount an all-out invasion, but this did not happen. While it was understandable for Shapur I to boast that Gordian III and Valerian brought most of the races of the empire against him, this was far from true. Therefore, if the Romans are seen as desiring the destruction of their eastern neighbour, we must conclude that the circumstances were never right for the attempt to be made, and then repeated if it failed. This suggests other concerns, whether threats on other frontiers, worries about internal stability, or an appreciation of the sheer cost in men and money of such an enterprise.

There is also the question of deterrence, as Romans soon realized that both the Arsacids and Sasanians were formidable opponents and that their empire was extensive, which meant that it could not be easily overrun. Julius Caesar is said to have planned a very cautious approach in his projected eastern war, learning about the Parthians before risking battle, for Carrhae had shown—as would later encounters—that there was a real risk of serious losses and defeat. It would have been strange indeed if the Romans—or at least most Romans, particularly among the elite—did not become aware of these factors, whatever the boasts of propaganda. On balance, it is much simpler to conclude that a desire to conquer Parthia-Persia was never foremost in the mind of Roman commanders.[3]

Simply because of the nature of our sources, Parthian—and subsequently Sasanian—ambitions are inevitably harder to study than Roman ones, which makes it even less practical to assess their attitudes to warfare and their knowledge of geography. With the exception of Khusro II's war, no king of kings ever threatened

Constantinople, let alone Italy or the west, or attempted to destroy the Roman empire. Some Arsacid and some Sasanian monarchs laid claim to the old Achaemenid empire, at least according to Greco-Roman sources. In some ways, Babylonia—with its cities and their Greek, Aramaic-speaking, and Jewish populations—had more in common with wider Syria than either had with the lands around them, so that it could seem more natural for them all to belong to the same kingdom than to be separate. Although united under the Achaemenids and the Seleucids (and later under the Arabs), these regions in fact remained separate throughout the period. In 41–40 BC, Parthian armies did overrun Syria and Palestine but were expelled within a couple of years. No Parthian or Sasanian army mounted a serious attempt to take them again until Khusro II's war in the seventh century. Similarly, with the possible exception of Trajan, the Romans never made any attempt to occupy Babylonia on a permanent basis.

Objectives on both sides were limited. This was not about destroying the rival empire but about winning a big enough advantage to make gains in the peace treaty which everyone expected to bring the war to an end. Some of these gains were territorial. During the course of the second century, the Roman frontier advanced in Mesopotamia, reaching the Tigris as well as pushing further down the Euphrates. In one sense, Dio Cassius was right to see this as a provocation to the Arsacids and then the Sasanians, but Severus's claim that it was a bulwark to the Roman provinces also had some truth, and a Roman presence in this area was maintained until the very end of the rivalry, with only a few interruptions.

Conflict concerned itself with relatively minor improvements of each side's position in the area. After the death of Julian, Jovian's peace settlement with Shapur II was criticized because it gave up two key cities, Nisibis and Singara, along with other concessions. Later, Dara became a bone of contention for the Sasanians, including whether a Roman commander and his troops were stationed there or further back. Threats were made and wars fought with the aim of shifting the balance along this frontier zone, but the practical advantages were never more than local. The Sasanians in particular saw invasions as profitable enterprises as well as aggressive bargaining. Neither side planned attacks into the other's lands in order to capture and hold on to territory, with the exception of key frontier cities.

The rivalry over Armenia began earlier and lasted as long as any other source of contention, extending to the neighbouring kingdoms in the Caucasus, especially in the later centuries, but in many ways this competition followed the same basic pattern. With Mesopotamia, Armenia offered the best routes for armies travelling from one empire's territory to the other. That meant that it could be seen as an opportunity to strike at the rival and as a pathway for the enemy to launch its own attack. Either way, whereas better to have a friendly ruler in control of Armenia, one actively hostile was threatening. Both the Romans and the Parthians—and in due course the Sasanians—often intervened in Armenia, not least because of the kingdom's volatile politics. Sometimes this led to direct confrontation between the forces of the two empires. Less often, it expanded into a wider war between them on other fronts as well.

The sense of limited objectives is nowhere clearer than in Armenia and the Caucasus. The desire to feel secure was central to both sides, which usually meant feeling dominant so that the rival would be deterred from confrontation or lose if it ever developed. This sense of strength and security was sought by both sides through a mixture of direct control, alliance, and maintenance of a strong military presence on the border. Each empire always competed with the other, since there was a good chance that if one felt too dominant then the other would feel threatened. Neither could afford to devote all its resources all of the time to its rivalry with the other, while an added element of uncertainty came from the ongoing competition among the monarchs and aristocrats of Armenia itself, and similarly those of Iberia, Lazica, and the other neighbours. The imperial rivalry was just one strand in this unending struggle for dominance within the kingdoms. Local ambition was fuelled by competition between Rome and Parthia-Persia and in turn often stirred up hostility between the great powers. Even the conquest and partition of Armenia did not put an end to this.

Wars were limited in their objectives and in their scale. Neither side showed any desire to escalate conflicts into a struggle to the death. Although occasionally very large armies were assembled—for instance, when a Roman emperor decided to come to the east in person—much of the actual fighting was done on a smaller scale. Even when the Romans assembled big armies, these tended to operate as several distinct columns rather than one great host. The Arsacids and Sasanians acted in the same way, and large battles were rare events, unlike sieges. Campaigns tended to be about manoeuvre, and throughout the period, but especially in the last few centuries, raiding was the most common way to put pressure on the enemy. Although the sixth century saw the most frequent conflict between the two powers, it was also probably the time when the modest objectives of both sides are most clear.

The Parthians and Sasanians were formidable adversaries, fielding very effective armies, but it is hard to see Roman reluctance to attempt all-out conquest as beginning at a tactical or even strategic level. Carrhae was a disaster, as was Antony's expedition to Media, while in between Ventidius routed two Parthian armies. Certainly, the legionary who stood on his two feet and carved out the empire with his gladius fought in a very different way to a Parthian horse-archer, for the latter could keep out of harm's way and kill from a distance. This did not mean that the Roman tactical system had met its match. After all, neither legionaries nor horse-archers were ever supposed to fight on their own but rather in large numbers and with the support of other troop types, which meant that the situation was far more complicated.

The story of the conflicts between the Romans, the Parthians, and the Persians is one of ongoing adaptation and innovation. Both sides learned from the other, trying to shift the odds in their favour. Well-balanced, all-arms Roman forces proved very hard for the Parthians to deal with in later generations. Over time, the two sides became more and more alike, so that the difference between the armies of the sixth and seventh centuries was slight, coming in matters of detail rather than overall style of fighting.

Tactically, the advantage between the two sides ebbed and flowed, with neither gaining a decisive edge for very long. Strategically, it was much the same, especially once the Sasanians proved themselves as adept as the Romans in siege-craft, after which both sides were capable of taking strongly fortified cities. In the main, conquered territory was readily consolidated. There is no sign of long-term resistance to Roman rule in Mesopotamia, just as cities taken by war or treaty by the Sasanians appear to have accepted this new reality—in some cases because new citizens were brought in. The rebellions against Trajan in 116 need not mean that, in time, areas such as Babylonia could not have become reconciled to Roman rule.

That the Romans never conquered these regions had little to do with tactical and strategic capability. It did have a lot to do with the sheer scale of the task. Conquering substantial parts of the Parthian-Sasanian empire would have required very large numbers of troops and a willingness to wage war and enforce occupation over a long period of time. Trajan tried but was too old, although it is harder to say whether he gave up on the idea because of failing health or whether giving up was the trigger for his rapid decline. No one else really tried, whether because calculation swiftly led to the conclusion that such a project was too expensive, too difficult, or simply impractical in the foreseeable future, or more likely because the prospective advantages did not match the risks and cost. Instead, there was limited war with limited objectives, both sides seemingly understanding the rules and stepping back from pushing the other too far.

Many wars were fought, however limited they were in scale and objectives, but even though they figure prominently in our sources, they were rarer than we might expect. The first century was a time of almost unbroken peace, with Nero's war in Armenia the only major exception. This conflict was very much a limited war, interrupted by frequent negotiation, and with a minor exception restricted to Armenia itself. If the second century saw grander campaigns, with two conflicts started by the Romans and one by the Parthians, it still meant barely a decade of fighting compared to some ninety years of peace.

In the third century and some of the fourth century, warfare between the empires became a good deal more common, only to be very rare indeed in the fifth century, then frequent after that.

The overall pattern is of long periods of essentially peaceful coexistence, which sometimes broke down. Whether from coincidence, their own agenda, or the side effects of Rome's lack of internal stability, the era of the Sasanians witnessed far more conflict than that of the Arsacids. Even so, until the time of Khusro II, the Sasanians sought glory, profit, and the preservation or improvement of their position along the frontiers with the Roman provinces. They did not actively seek any greater outcome than this.

This was about dominance rather than conquest, and dominance in turn has a lot to do with perception. Throughout these seven centuries, both empires felt it necessary to demonstrate their might, to feel that they were strong and have others believe it as well. This was important for Rome's elite under the republic and then for the emperors, and it was equally important for the king of kings, but there was always more than one audience.

The first was the peoples living outside the empire or near its borders. These needed to be convinced that the empire was so strong that it was far better to be its friend than its enemy. Ideally, this made everyone compliant, discouraging the rival empire from seeking confrontation, and making allies and provincial populations eager to please. Impressing this audience meant possessing substantial military forces and appearing willing and able to use them, and sometimes having to wage war as proof.

A second group was the population of the empire, especially the elite who were more significant politically. A ruler needed to assure this audience that he was a great and strong leader and that they were all part of the greatest empire in the world. In the main, most of this audience was far away from any actual conflict, which made it easier for a regime to exaggerate any achievements and present a treaty that was reasonably fair, or even involved concessions, as an unambiguous triumph.

On the whole, the system worked for both empires, allowing most rulers a measure of security from internal threats and avoiding conflict with the other empire unless it seemed advantageous. There was good deal of bluster and sabre-rattling in all periods, each side revelling in proclamations of its overwhelming supremacy, even in diplomatic exchanges. Both sides knew the rules, imposing limits on their response. Simultaneously, a Roman emperor and a king of kings could each assure their own subjects that they were strong, and that the other man and his empire were weak and feeble, without this requiring an attempt to prove the claim by going to war. This was yet another way in which the two sides became so alike.

A relationship based on continuous restatement of strength tended to lend particular importance to symbols and to otherwise unimportant places in border or contested areas. Armenia mattered because it was large and allowed travel from one empire to the other along certain routes. Ideally, each side preferred to see the region as more under their control than under that of their rival, since that secured their nearest provinces and left them with the sense that they had the option of using Armenia to attack should they choose. Yet compromise was possible. Nero's treaty was artificial, which did not prevent it from keeping the peace for more than a generation, since it satisfied both sides. It was also the result of almost a decade of fighting, sometimes sporadic, sometimes intense, but always limited in scale and with frequent negotiations to resolve matters. Perceptions of strength were subject to near-constant challenge, which could lead to actual war as in this case.

The stakes in this warfare were usually fairly small, which does not mean that they were unimportant. A series of failures could escalate, encouraging the rivals to seek even more of an advantage, which risked discrediting the leader of the losing side or creating a sudden reversal of fortune. Personal involvement in a campaign was risky for an emperor or a king of kings if things did not go at least well enough to be presented as a success. Balance between the two empires was generally fairly even. The Romans took and held on to more territory over the course of this rivalry than the other empire, but they did not develop any greater advantage. Most wars saw successes and failures for both sides and ended with a readjustment of the relationship between the two empires which was usually slight. In essence, it was a game, played to broadly understood and honoured rules and with a rematch whenever one side scented the chance to do better than last time.

Opportunities often came when the other empire was faced with a serious military problem on another frontier, and even more often during times of internal upheaval. This in turn meant that as long as both empires were stable and successful, the chances of them going to war with each other were substantially reduced. In contrast, whenever either or both were rent by civil war or had suffered heavy losses in distant fighting, there was a far stronger chance of the Romans and Parthians or Persians going to war with each other. Prolonged peace between the two empires tended to encourage more peace, while outbreaks of war encouraged further warfare, especially whenever one side did well enough to shatter the other's cherished belief in its superiority. In the third and fourth centuries, and again in the sixth and seventh, there was always a fairly recent pretext for a new conflict. At other times, all the old insults and humiliations had been more or less avenged, so that it took a bigger crisis, rather than simply rivalry, to lead to open war. Mutual weakness was no assurance of peace, since an emperor or king of kings might feel the need for glory to strengthen his position and judge that the rival empire was weaker for the moment.

Wars between the empires were expensive and only occasionally were victories great enough to make substantial profits. At the same time, maintaining sufficient military strength and securing alliances with kings and leaders in the border areas also cost a good deal in gold and resources. There was never any sign of moving away from the ongoing rivalry and assertions of dominance—something extraordinarily unlikely in the ancient world, or indeed for most of human history. Neither empire's military existed for the sole purpose of opposing the other, for each had plenty of other opponents. Nor did the scale of the threat change fundamentally in the third century AD with the rise of the Sasanians, something asserted by many scholars who study the later Roman empire. No ancient sources claim that the Roman state and military had to reform to meet this 'new' threat or that the Sasanians after Ardashir I and Shapur I were always as aggressive and successful. The Roman empire and army certainly changed, but the causes must be sought elsewhere, and any suggestion that these became better organized for war on a large scale should be treated with extreme caution. The cost of maintaining the army as a share of imperial income may have increased without producing a more effective or larger force. Paying for a standing army was always expensive for the Romans, and the military arrangements of the Parthians and Sasanians were similarly costly.

Yet the rulers of both empires were willing to foot the bill for maintaining their strength in relation to the other and indeed on a smaller scale against the other peoples with whom they had contact. Some rulers bolstered their position and others were discredited through fighting the other empire. Most had smaller gains or losses. From either side's perspective, the other empire was a famous and worthy opponent—indeed the most famous and worthy available. The other empire was also a coherent state far larger than anyone else with whom they had to deal, which meant that it was easier to negotiate with them than with lots of different warlords and chieftains. A treaty agreed between the empires was more likely to be honoured for longer than one where minor shifts in tribal politics could easily lead to fresh hostility. Even so, domestic concerns played a major role in decisions made by emperors and kings of kings alike, so that relations with the other empire could still shift suddenly for reasons that had nothing to do with anything the other one had done.

Especially in the later period, there are signs of complacency in the way each thought of the other, which only reinforced this sense. Thus, Kavadh I or Khusro I could see that the Romans were preoccupied elsewhere and sense a chance to adjust the current balance of power in their favour—and perhaps make a quick profit—by threatening or actually waging war. The Romans acted in the same way, for instance when they knew the Sasanians had problems on their northern and eastern frontiers. In each case, they read the situation, decided that they had a short-term advantage, and tried to make the most of it, but so many generations of limited war made them believe that nothing too terrible could happen if things went wrong. At the very worst, they might suffer a blow to their prestige and have to accept a less favourable treaty—but only for the moment, until the advantage shifted in their favour once again.

Limited war and limited objectives reduced the risks of conflict for both empires. Most of the time this helped foster good relations between them, especially under the principate when the Romans generally felt more secure and had less to prove, but also later, if rarely for so long a period. Peace was normal—wary, watchful peace based on a sense of each empire's military might—and warfare occasional. For centuries, both empires flourished, benefiting from the stability each one promoted, not least because this encouraged trade. At times this broke down, and there was always a danger that one war led to another, so that conflict became almost—if not quite—normal in the third century, for parts of the fourth, and from the early sixth century until the end. Hostility can become a habit very quickly, making each side more suspicious of anything the other one does and readier to see the need to strike back. Even so, for a very long time these wars remained focused on the frontier regions, not always small-scale but with restricted objectives.

Near the end, Khusro II broke the rules by refusing to negotiate, partly because his success revealed that the Romans were much weaker than everyone had believed—perhaps including the king of kings himself—so that there really was a good chance of total victory. It was a misjudgement, but not so very different from the decisions made by earlier leaders to prolong a war—albeit far less ambitious in its aim—past a point where it proved to their advantage. A system based on ongoing competition and frequent restatements of power, sometimes extending to waging war, always ran the risk of spiralling into escalating conflict unlikely to benefit either side.

Yet for centuries it had more or less worked. Two aggressive empires lived alongside one another, always posturing and sometimes fighting but within mutually accepted restrictions that prevented permanent, let alone all-out, war aimed at destroying the other. It was not perfect, but it was unlike any other relationship in the ancient world, and if it finally ended, like the empires themselves, it was remarkably successful for a very long time. Both empires prospered without the need for fresh conquests. Each maintained powerful military forces, backed by fortifications, other support, and networks of allies, for emperor and king of kings alike were expected to be mighty in war. These armies acted as deterrents, and the system was based on shows of strength to dissuade attack. Any perceived crack in this façade risked a renewal of war, which in turn carried dangers, since any serious defeat would weaken the perception even more. As a result, the empires postured and competed and sometimes came to blows until each one was satisfied that an acceptable balance had occurred. There is no sign that the cost of maintaining peace through strength against the other—and against lesser rivals on other frontiers—in the long run placed too heavy a burden on the finances and resources of either empire.

Once again, the sheer duration of the rivalry and of each empire makes it difficult to accept that competition was an ultimately unsustainable burden to either. Taking this longer perspective, it is striking how often the two empires preferred the wary standoff of peace to the alternative of conflict. All of which reinforces a sense that the leaders on both sides acted rationally, deciding what was in their best interests and trying to achieve it, in ways that would challenge some of the more simplistic understandings of ancient ideology and thought. That is not to say that individuals did not sometimes act out of lust for glory or out of fear and ambition, just as leaders in other eras and cultures have done. There was emotion as well as calculation in this long story. Both were usually present, and sometimes 'rational' calculations were based on wholly mistaken beliefs of the nature of the world and of the enemy. That again says no more than that the emperors, monarchs, and other players were human. Some were more able, some luckier—that very Roman concept—than others.

Whatever their faults and merits, the two empires survived and prospered for centuries. Whether because or in spite of the talents and actions of their leaders—usually a mixture of both—the Romans and Parthians and Persians coexisted for an immensely long period of time. The willingness of both sides to accept restraints on their competition surely made a significant contribution to their success. While it is hard to prove that the rivalry benefitted both empires and contributed to their success and longevity, it certainly does not appear to have been a major source of weakness.

ACKNOWLEDGEMENTS

The idea for writing this book developed some years ago, partly because other books made me consider some episodes in this story and raised many more questions than I could readily answer. Parthians and Persians tend to be covered separately, and consideration of their relationship with the Romans either concerned with limited periods of time or so very broad-brush that it allowed for sweeping statements. No one had looked at the rivalry as a whole in this sort of detail, but this seems the best way of understanding the unique relationship between the Romans and their most powerful neighbour.

The topic is vast, and, as always, I have relied on the work of many, many scholars, whose books, articles, and ideas have made this book possible. This is particularly true for this topic, since it has meant covering some periods less familiar to me, while I can claim no expertise in Iranian studies and no knowledge whatsoever of the languages of some of the sources, since my background is with the Greco-Roman material. There is a great deal of marvellous scholarship by specialists in this field and in other topics. The endnotes will lead a reader into this great body of work, each work cited offering references to other books and articles. My most sincere thanks goes out to all the many scholars whose work has informed and inspired me during the course of writing this book.

Most of the work has been done during the Covid pandemic, a time of lockdowns and travel restrictions. I should also like to thank the staff at the ICS Library in London, who have done their utmost to give readers access to the collection whenever this was possible.

I also wish to thank the family and friends who have read all or part of the manuscript and provided many a helpful comment. Kevin Powell was as thorough as ever in his analysis, something especially useful in a book like this which covers such a long period of time. Dorothy King listened to many ideas at great length and commented with many, many sharp and well-informed insights, as she has done on so many aspects of the ancient world. Geoffrey Greatrex often pointed me in the right direction, and the frequency with which his works are referenced will show the influence he has had on my understanding of the subject. Also, late in the stage of writing, I attended a conference on strategy in the ancient world at the US Marine Corps University—a session postponed for two years because of the pandemic. The papers and especially the enthusiasm of the discussions and informal conversations with the group assembled there not only acted as tonic but helped me test some ideas and provided other insights. To all of these folk, I am very grateful.

ILLUSTRATION CREDITS

1. Author's photo.
2. © José Luiz Bernardes Ribeiro / CC BY-SA 4.0, Wikimedia Commons.
3. © The Trustees of the British Museum.
4. Author's photo.
5. Yale University Art Gallery / Wikimedia Commons.
6. Author's photo.
7. Following Hadrian / Wikimedia Commons.
8. Bequest of Joseph H. Durkee, 1898 / The Met Museum.
9. Gift of Martin A. Ryerson / Art Institute Chicago.
10. Author's photo.
11. Author's photo.
12. Classical Numismatic Group, Inc. / Wikimedia Commons.
13. imageBROKER / Alamy Stock Photo.
14. Author's photo.
15. Author's photo.
16. Author's photo.
17. Found in the Forum Boarium (Rome), 15th century / Wikimedia Commons.
18. Author's photo.
19. Author's photo.
20. Author's photo.
21. © Livius.Org / Jona Lendering.
22. © Livius.Org / Jona Lendering.
23. Artaban V. Vers 230 / Wikimedia Commons.
24. Lebrecht Music & Arts / Alamy Stock Photo.
25. Yale University Art Gallery.

BIBLIOGRAPHY

Crook, J., Lintott, A., & Rawson, E., eds. *The Cambridge Ancient History*. Vol. 9, *The Last Age of the Roman Republic 146–43 BC* (1994)

Bowman, A., Champlin, E., & Lintott, A., eds. *The Cambridge Ancient History*. Vol. 10, *The Augustan Empire 43 BC–AD 69* (1996)

Bowman, A., Garnsey, P., & Rathbone, D., eds. *The Cambridge Ancient History*. Vol. 11, *The High Empire AD 70–192* (2000)

Bowman, A., Cameron, A., & Garnsey, P., eds. *The Cambridge Ancient History*. Vol. 12, *The Crisis of Empire AD 193–337* (2005)

Cameron, A., & Garnsey, P., eds. *The Cambridge Ancient History*. Vol. 13, *The Late Empire* (1998)

Cameron, A., Ward-Perkins, B., & Whitby, M., eds. *The Cambridge Ancient History*. Vol. 14, *Late Antiquity: Empire and Successors AD 425–600* (2000)

Yarshater, E., ed. *The Cambridge History of Iran*. Vol. 3 (1–2), *The Seleucid, Parthian and Sasanian Periods* (1983)

Aliev, A., Gadjiev, M., Gaither, M., Kohl, P., Magomedov, R., & Aliev, I. 'The Ghilghilchay Defensive Long Wall: New Investigations'. *Ancient East and West* 5 (2006): 143–177

Allen, J. *Hostages and Hostage-Taking in the Roman Empire* (2006)

Anthony, S. *Muhammad and the Empires of Faith* (2020)

Aperghis, G. *The Seleukid Economy: The Finances and Financial Administration of the Seleukid Empire* (2004)

Arce, I. 'Transformation Patterns of Roman Forts in the Limes Arabicus from Severan to Tetrarchic and Justinianic Periods'. In Hodgson, Bidwell, & Schachtmann (2017), 121–130

Ash, R. 'An Exemplary Conflict: Tacitus' Parthian Battle Narrative (*Annals* 6. 34–35)'. *Phoenix* 53 (1999): 114–135

Austin, N., & Rankov, B. *Exploratio: Military and Political Intelligence in the Roman World from the Second Punic War to the Battle of Adrianople* (1995)

Balogh, D., ed. *Hunnic Peoples in Central and South Asia: Sources for Their Origins and History* (2020)

Barnes, T. *Ammianus Marcellinus and the Representation of Historical Reality* (1998)

———. *The New Empire of Diocletian and Constantine* (1982)

Bennett, J. *Trajan: Optimus Princeps* (1997)

Bigwood, J. 'Queen Mousa, Mother and Wife(?) of King Phaatakes of Parthia: A Re-evaluation of the Evidence'. *Mouseion* 3.4 (2004): 35–70

Bingen, J. *Hellenistic Egypt: Monarchy, Society, Economy, Culture* (2007)

Birley, A. *Hadrian: The Restless Emperor* (1997)

———. *Marcus Aurelius: A Biography* (rev. ed., 1987)

———. *Septimius Severus: The African Emperor* (1999)

Bishop, M. '*Praesidium*: Social, Military, and Logistical Aspects of the Roman Army's Provincial Distribution During the Early Principate'. In Goldsworthy & Haynes (1999), 111–118

Bishop, M., & Coulston, J. *Roman Military Equipment from the Punic Wars to the Fall of Rome* (2nd ed., 2006)

Blockley, R. 'Ammianus Marcellinus on the Persian Invasion of AD 369'. *Phoenix* 42 (1988): 244–260

———. 'Subsidies and Diplomacy: Rome and Persia in Late Antiquity'. *Phoenix* 39 (1985): 62–74

Bowersock, G. 'Augustus and the East: The Problem of Succession'. In *Caesar Augustus: Seven Aspects*, edited by F. Millar & E. Segal, 169–188 (1990)

———. *Empires in Collision in Late Antiquity* (2012)

———. *Julian the Apostate* (1978)

———. 'Mavia, Queen of the Saracens'. In *Studien zur antiken Sozialgeschichte: Festschrift Friedrich Vittinghoff*, edited by W. Eck, H. Galstere, & H. Wolff, 477–495 (1980)

Braund, D. 'Dionysiac Tragedy in Plutarch, Crassus'. *Classical Quarterly* 43 (1993): 468–474

Breeze, D. *The Frontiers of Imperial Rome* (2011)

Brunt, P. *Italian Manpower 225 BC–AD 14* (1971)

Burns, T. *Barbarians Within the Gates of Rome: A Study of Roman Military Policy and the Barbarians, ca. 375–425 AD* (1994)

Callieri, P. 'Cultural Contacts Between Rome and Persia at the Time of Ardashir I (c. AD 224–240)'. In Sauer (2019), 221–238

Campbell, B. 'War and Diplomacy: Rome and Parthia, 31 BC–AD 235'. In *War and Society in the Roman World*, edited by J. Rich & G. Shipley, 213–240 (1993)

Campbell, D. 'What Happened at Hatra?: The Problem of the Severan Siege Operations'. In Freeman and Kennedy (1986), 1:51–58

Canepa, M. 'Sasanian Rock Reliefs'. In Potts (2013), 856–877

———. *The Two Eyes of the Earth: Art and Ritual of Kingship Between Rome and Sasanian Iran* (2009)

Casey, P. 'Justinian, the Limetanei, and Arab-Byzantine Relations in the Sixth Century'. *Journal of Roman Archaeology* 9 (1996): 214–222

Chi, J., & Heath, S., eds. *Edge of Empires: Pagans, Jews, and Christians at Roman Dura-Europos* (2012)

Connolly, P. 'The Roman Saddle'. In *Roman Military Equipment: The Accoutrements of War*, edited by M. Dawson, 7–27 (1987)

Corby, M. 'Hadrian's Wall and the Defence of North Britain'. *Archaeologia Aeliana*, series 5, vol. 39 (2010): 9–13

Corey Brennan, T. 'Sulla's Career in the Nineties: Some Reconsiderations'. *Chiron* 22 (1992): 103–158

Coulston, J. 'Roman, Parthian and Sassanid Tactical Developments'. In Freeman & Kennedy (1986), 2:59–75

Croke, B. 'Justinian's Constantinople'. In Maas (2005), 60–86

Crow, J. 'Recent Research on the Anastasian Wall in Thrace and Late Antique Linear Barriers Around the Black Sea'. In Hodgson, Bidwell, & Schachtmann (2017), 131–138

Dabrowa, E. 'The Arsacids and Their State'. In *Altertum und Gegenwart*, edited by R. Rollinger et al., 21–52 (2012)

———. 'The Frontier in Syria in the First Century AD'. In Freeman & Kennedy (1986), 1:93–108

———. 'The Parthian Aristocracy: Its Social Position and Political Activity'. *Parthica* 25 (2013): 53–62

———. 'Parthian-Armenian Relations from the 2nd Century BCE to the Second Half of the 1st Century CE'. *Electrum* 28 (2021): 41–57

———. 'Tacitus on the Parthians'. *Electrum* 24 (2017): 171–189

Daryaee, T. 'From Terror to Tactical Usage: Elephants in the Parthia-Sasanian Period'. In Sarkhosh Curtis et al. (2016), 36–41

———. *Sasanian Persia: The Rise and Fall of an Empire* (2007)

Debevoise, N. *A Political History of Parthia* (1938)

Dennis, G., trans. *Maurice's Strategikon: Handbook of Byzantine Military Strategy* (1984)

Dodgeon, M., & Lieu, S. *The Roman Eastern Frontier and the Persian Wars.* Vol. 1, AD 226–363 (1991)

Donner, F. 'The Background to Islam'. In Maas (2005), 510–533

Drinkwater, J. *Nero: Emperor and Court* (2019)

Dubs, H. 'An Ancient Military Contact Between Romans and Chinese'. *American Journal of Philology* 62 (1941): 322–330

————. 'A Roman City in Ancient China: A Reply to Professor Carmann'. *Journal of Asian Studies* 22 (1962): 135–136

Duncan-Jones, R. 'The Impact of the Antonine Plague'. *Journal of Roman Archaeology* 9 (1996): 108–138

Dyson, S. *The Creation of the Roman Frontier* (1985)

Eddy, S. *The King Is Dead: Studies in the Near Eastern Resistance to Hellenism 334–31 BC* (1961)

Edwell, P. *Between Rome and Persia: The Middle Euphrates, Mesopotamia and Palmyra Under Roman Control* (2008)

————. 'The Euphrates as a Boundary Between Rome and Parthia in the Late Republic and Early Empire'. *Antichthon* 47 (2013): 191–206

————. *Rome and Persia at War: Imperial Competition and Contact 193–363 CE* (2021)

El-Cheikh, N. 'Muhammad and Heraclius: A Study in Legitimacy'. *Studia Islamica* 89 (1999): 5–21

Ellerbrock, U. *The Parthians: The Forgotten Empire* (2021)

Engels, D. 'Middle Eastern "Feudalism" and Seleucid Dissolution'. In *Seleucid Dissolution: The Sinking of the Anchor*, edited by K. Erikson & G. Ramsay, 19–36 (2011)

Fabian, L. 'Bridging the Divide: Marriage Politics Across the Caucasus'. *Electrum* 28 (2021): 221–244

Farrokh, K. *The Armies of Ancient Persia: The Sasanians* (2014)

Ferguson, J. 'China and Rome'. In *Aufstieg und Niedergang der römischen Welt*, II.9, 581–603 (1978)

Fink, R. *Roman Military Records on Papyrus* (1971)

Fisher, G. *Between Empires: Arabs, Romans and Sasanians in Late Antiquity* (2011)

Fisher, G., & Wood, P. 'Writing the History of the "Persian Arabs": The Pre-Islamic Perspective on the "Nasrids" of al-Hirah'. *Iranian Studies* 49 (2016): 247–290

Fitzpatrick, M. 'Provincializing Rome: The Indian Ocean Trade Network and Roman Imperialism'. *Journal of World History* 22 (2011)

Flemming, R. 'Galen and the Plague'. In *Galen's Treatise Περὶ Ἀλυπίας (de indolentia) in Context: A Tale of Resilience*, edited by C. Petit, 219–244 (2019)

Fonara, C. 'Julian's Persian Expedition in Ammianus and Zosimus'. *Journal of Hellenic Studies* 111 (1991): 1–15

Freeman, P. 'The Annexation of Arabia and Imperial Grand Strategy'. In Kennedy (1996), 91–118

Freeman, P., & Kennedy, D., eds. *The Defence of the Roman and Byzantine East*. 2 vols. (1986)

Fuhrmann, C. *Policing the Roman Empire: Soldiers, Administration and Public Order* (2012)

Galikowski, M. 'Palmyra as a Trading Centre'. *British Institute for the Study of Iraq* 56 (1994): 27–33

Gariboldi, A. 'The Birth of the Sasanian Monarchy in Western Sources'. In Sarkhosh Curtis, et al. (2016), 47–52

Gaslain, J. 'Some Aspects of Political History: Early Arsacid Kings and the Seleucids'. In Sarkhosh Curtis et al. (2016), 3–7

Ghodrat-Dizaji, M. 'Disintegration of Sasanian Hegemony over Northern Iran (AD 623–643)'. *Iranica Antiqua* 46 (2011): 315–329

Goldberg, C. 'Decimation in the Roman Republic'. *Classical Journal* 111 (2015–2016): 141–164

Goldsworthy, A. *Antony and Cleopatra* (2010)

———. *Augustus: From Revolutionary to Emperor; First Emperor of Rome* (2014)

———. *The Fall of the West (How Rome Fell)* (2009)

———. *Hadrian's Wall: Rome and the Limits of Empire* (2018)

———. *In the Name of Rome* (2003)

———. *Pax Romana: War, Peace and Conquest in the Roman World* (2016)

———. *The Roman Army at War: 100 BC–AD 200* (1996)

Goldsworthy, A., & Haynes, I. *The Roman Army as a Community in Peace and War*. Journal of Roman Archaeology Supplementary Series no. 34 (1999)

Gowing, A. 'Tacitus and the Client Kings'. *Transactions of the American Philological Association* 120 (1990): 315–331

Gradoni, M. 'The Parthian Campaigns of Septimius Severus: Causes, and Roles in Dynastic Legitimation'. In *The Roman Empire During the Severan Dynasty: Case Studies in History, Art, Architecture, Economy and Literature*, edited by E. De Sena, 3–23 (2013)

Grainger, J. *Nerva and the Roman Succession Crisis of AD 96–99* (2003)

Grant, M. *Cleopatra* (1971)

Greatrex, G. 'Roman Frontiers and Foreign Policy in the East'. In *Aspects of the Roman East: Papers in Honour of Professor Fergus Millar FBA*, edited by R. Alston, 103–173 (2007)

———. *Rome and Persia at War: 502–532* (1998)

Greatrex, G., & Bardill, J. 'Antiochus the "Praepositus": A Persian Eunuch at the Court of Theodosius II'. *Dumbarton Oaks Papers* 50 (1996): 171–197

Greatrex, G., & Greatrex, M. 'The Hunnic Invasion of the East of 395 and the Fortress of Ziatha'. *Byzantion* 69 (1999): 65–75

Greatrex, G., & Lieu, N. *The Roman Eastern Frontier and the Persian Wars*. Vol. 2, AD 363–630 (2002)

Greenhalgh, P. *Pompey: The Roman Alexander* (1980)

Gregoratti, L. 'Corbulo Versus Vologaeses: A Game of Chess for Armenia'. *Electrum* 24 (2017): 107–121

———. 'The Importance of the Mint of Seleucis on the Tigris for Arsacid History: Artabanus and the Greek Parthian Cities'. *Mesopotamia* 47 (2012): 129–136

———. 'Parthian Women in Flavius Josephus'. In *Jüdisch-hellenistische Literatur in ihrem interkulturellen Kontext*, edited by M. Hirschberger, 183–192 (2012)

Griffin, M. 'Review of W. Eck, A. Caballos, & F. Fernandez, *Das Senatus Consultum de Cn. Piso Patre*'. *Journal of Roman Studies* 87 (1997): 249–263

Gruen, E. 'Herod, Rome, and the Diaspora'. In Jacobson & Kokkinos (2009), 13–27

Grünewald, T. *Bandits in the Roman Empire: Myth and Reality*. Translated by J. Drinkwater (2004)

Guey, J. 'Autour des Res Gestae Divi Saporis 1: Deniers (d'or) et (de compte) anciens'. *Syria* 38 (1961): 261–274

Haldon, J. *The Byzantine Wars: Battles and Campaigns of the Byzantine Era* (2001)

Hause, S., & Tucker, D. 'The Final Onslaught: The Sasanian Siege of Hatra'. *Zeitschrift für Orient-Archäologie* 2 (2009): 106–139

Heather, P. *The Fall of the Roman Empire: A New History* (2005)

———. *The Goths* (1996)

———. *Goths and Romans: 332–489* (1991)

———. *Rome Resurgent: War and Empire in the Age of Justinian* (2018)

Hekster, O., & Zair, N. *Rome and Its Empire* (2008)

Hodgson, N. 'The End of the Ninth Legion'. *Britannia* 52 (2021): 97–118

———. *Hadrian's Wall: Archaeology and History at the Limit of Rome's Empire* (2017)

Hodgson, N., Bidwell, P., & Schachtmann, J., eds. *Roman Frontier Studies 2009: Proceedings of the XXI International Congress of Roman Frontier Studies (Limes Congress) Held at Newcastle upon Tyne in August 2009* (2017)

Hölbl, G. *A History of the Ptolemaic Empire*. Translated by T. Saavedra (2001)

Holden, P. 'Mediterranean Plague in the Age of Justinian'. In Maas (2005), 134–160

Horbury, W. *The Jewish War Under Trajan and Hadrian* (2014)

Howard-Johnston, J. 'The India Trade in Late Antiquity'. In Sauer (2019), 284–304

———. *The Last Great War of Antiquity* (2021)

———. 'The Official History of Heralius' Persian Campaigns'. In *The Roman and Byzantine Army in the East*, edited by E. Dabrowa, 57–87 (1994)

———. 'Pride and Fall: Khusro II and His Regime, 626–628'. In *La Persia e Bisanzio: Atti dei Convegni Lincei 2002*, edited by G. Gnoli, 93–113 (2003)

Hoyland, R. *In God's Path: The Arab Conquests and the Creation of an Islamic Empire* (2013)

Huff, D. 'The Functional Layout of the Fire Sanctuary at Takht-I Sulaiman'. In *Current Research in Sasanian Archaeology, Art and History*, edited by D. Kennet & P. Luft, 1–13 (2008)

Hughes, I. *Belisarius: The Last Roman General* (2009)

Humfress, C. 'Law and Legal Practice in the Age of Justinian'. In Maas (2005), 161–184

Huyse, P. *Die Dreisprachige Inschrift Sabuhrs I. an Der Ka'ba-i Zardust (SKZ)*. 2 vols. (1999)

Intagliata, E. *Palmyra After Zenobia:* AD 273–750 (2018)

Isaac, B. *The Limits of Empire* (rev. ed., 1992)

Jacobson, D., & Kokkinos, N., eds. *Herod and Augustus: Papers Presented at the IJS Conference, 21st–23rd June 2005* (2009)

James, S. *Excavations at Dura-Europos 1928–1937: Final Report VII—the Arms and Armour and Other Military Equipment* (2004)

———. 'Of Colossal Camps and a New Roman Battlefield: Remote Sensing, Archival Archaeology and the "Conflict Landscape" of Dura-Europos, Syria'. In *Understanding Roman Frontiers*, edited by D. Breeze & I. Oltean, 328–345 (2015)

———. *The Roman Military Base at Dura-Europos, Syria: An Archaeological Visualization* (2019)

———. 'Stratagems, Combat and "Chemical Warfare" in the Siege Mines at Dura-Europos'. *American Journal of Archaeology* 115 (2011): 69–101

Jones, A. *The Later Roman Empire: 284–602* (1964)

Jones, K. 'Marcus Antonius' Median War and the Dynastic Politics of the Near East'. In Schlude & Rubin (2017), 51–63

Juntunen, K. 'Ancient Elegeia: Battlefield or Roman Outpost? From Written Sources to Archaeological Evidence'. In *Proceedings of the 24th International Limes Congress, Serbia, 2018* (forthcoming)

Kaegi, W. *Byzantium and the Early Islamic Conquests* (1992)

———. *Heraclius, Emperor of Byzantium* (2003)

———. *Muslim Expansion and Byzantine Collapse in North Africa* (2010)

Kagay, D. 'The Traction Trebuchet: A Triumph of Four Civilizations'. *Viator* 31 (2000): 433–486

Keaveney, A. 'The King and the War-Lords: Romano-Parthian Relations Circa 64–53 BC'. *American Journal of Philology* 103 (1982): 412–428

———. 'Roman Treaties with Parthia Circa 95–Circa 64 BC'. *American Journal of Philology* 102 (1981): 195–212

———. *Sulla: The Last Republican* (2nd ed., 2005)

———. 'Sulla's Cilician Command: The Evidence of Apollinaris Sidonius'. *Historia* 54 (1995): 29–36

Keitel, E. 'The Role of Parthia and Armenia in Tacitus Annals 11 and 12'. *American Journal of Philology* 99 (1978): 462–473

Kelly, C. *Attila the Hun: Barbarian Terror and the Fall of the Roman Empire* (2008)

Kennedy, D. '"European" Soldiers and the Severan Siege of Hatra'. In Freeman & Kennedy (1986), 2:397–409

———, ed. *The Roman Army in the East.* Journal of Roman Archaeology Supplementary Series no. 18 (1996)

Kennedy, D., & Riley, D. *Rome's Desert Frontier from the Air* (1990)

Keppie, L. *Legions and Veterans: Roman Army Papers, 1971–2000* (2000)
———. 'Legions in the East from Augustus to Trajan'. In Freeman & Kennedy (1986), 2:411–429
Krebs, C. *A Most Dangerous Book: Tacitus's* Germania *from the Roman Empire to the Third Reich* (2011)
Kuhrt, A. *Persian Empire: A Corpus of Sources from the Achaemenid Period*. 2 vols. (2007)
Kulikowski, M. *Rome's Gothic Wars* (2007)
———. *The Triumph of Empire: The Roman World from Hadrian to Constantine* (2016)
Labbaf-Khaniki, M. 'Long Wall of Asia: The Backbone of Asian Defensive Landscape'. In vol. 2 of *Proceedings of the 10th International Congress on the Archaeology of the Ancient Near East*, edited by R. Salisbury, F. Höflmayer, & T. Bürge, 113–121 (2018)
Lander, J. 'Did Hadrian Abandon Arabia?'. In Freeman & Kennedy (1986), 2:447–453
Latham, J., & Patterson, W. *Saracen Archery: A Mameluk Work, c. 1368* (1970)
Lawrence, D., & Wilkinson, T. 'The Northern and Western Borderlands of the Sasanian Empire: Contextualising the Roman/Byzantine and Sasanian Frontier'. In Sauer (2019), 99–125
Lee, A. 'The Empire at War'. In Maas (2005), 113–133
———. *From Rome to Byzantium* AD *363–565: The Transformation of Ancient Rome* (2013)
Lendon, J. *Soldiers and Ghosts: A History of Battle in Classical Antiquity* (2005)
Lenski, N. *The Failure of Empire: Valens and the Roman State in the Fourth Century* AD (2002)
Lepper, F. *Trajan's Parthian War* (1948)
Lerner, J. 'Mithridates I and the Parthian Archer'. In Schlude & Rubin (2017), 1–24
Leslie, D., & Gardiner, K. 'Chinese Knowledge of Western Asia During the Han'. *T'oung Pao* 68 (1982): 254–308
Levick, B. 'Pliny in Bithynia—and What Followed'. *Greece and Rome* 26 (1979): 119–131
———. *Tiberius the Politician* (1999)
———. *Vespasian* (2nd ed., 2020)
Levithan, J. *Roman Siege Warfare* (2013)
Lewin, A. 'The New Frontiers of Late Antiquity in the Near East from Diocletian to Justinian'. In *Frontiers in the Roman World*, edited by O. Hekster & T. Kaizer, 234–263 (2011)
Lieu, S., & Mikkelsen, G., eds. *Silk Road Studies*. Vol. 18, *Between Rome and China: History, Religions and Material Culture of the Silk Road* (2016)
Linderski, J. 'Two Quaestorships'. *Classical Philology* 70 (1975): 35–38

Lintott, A. *The Constitution of the Roman Republic* (1999)

Llewellyn-Jones, L. *Persians: The Age of the Great Kings* (2022)

Luce, T. 'Livy, Augustus, and the Forum Augustum'. In *Augustus*, edited by J. Edmondson, 399–415 (2009)

Ma, J. 'Peer Polity Interaction in the Hellenistic Age'. *Past and Present* 180 (2003): 9–39

Maas, M., ed. *The Cambridge Companion to the Age of Justinian* (2005)

MacMullen, R. *Enemies of the Roman Order* (1966)

Maenchen-Helfen, O. *The World of the Huns: Studies in Their History and Culture* (1973)

Marshall, A. 'The *Lex Pompeia de provinciis* (52 BC) and Cicero's *Imperium* in 51–50 BC: Constitutional Aspects'. In *Aufstieg und Niedergang der römischen Welt*, I.1, 887–921 (1972)

Mattern, S. 'The Defeat of Crassus and the Just War'. *Classical World* 96 (2003): 387–396

———. *Rome and the Enemy: Imperial Strategy in the Principate* (1999)

Matthews, J. 'The Origin of Ammianus'. *Classical Quarterly* 44 (1994): 252–269

———. *The Roman Empire of Ammianus Marcellinus* (1989)

Matyszak, P. *Mithridates the Great: Rome's Indomitable Enemy* (2008)

Maxfield, V. 'Ostraca and the Roman Army in the Eastern Desert'. In *Documenting the Roman Army: Essays in Honour of Margaret Roxan*, edited by J. Wilkes, 153–173 (2003)

Mayor, A. *The Poison King: The Life and Legend of Mithridates, Rome's Deadliest Enemy* (2010)

McLaughlin, R. *The Roman Empire and the Indian Ocean: The Ancient World Economy and the Kingdoms of Africa, Arabia and India* (2014)

———. *The Roman Empire and the Silk Routes: The Ancient World Economy and the Empires of Parthia, Central Asia and Han China* (2019)

Mennen, I. *Power and Status in the Roman Empire* (2011)

Mielczarek, M. *Cataphracti and Clibinarii: Studies in the Heavy Armoured Cavalry of the Ancient World* (1993)

Millar, F. 'Paul of Samosata, Zenobia, and Aurelian: The Church, Local Culture and Political Allegiance in Third Century Syria'. In F. Millar, *Rome, the Greek World and the East*. Vol. 3, *The Greek World, the Jews and the East*, edited by H. Cotton & G. Rogers, 243–273 (2006)

———. *The Roman Near East* (1993)

Minns, E. 'Parchments of the Parthian Period from Avroman in Kurdistan'. *Journal of Hellenic Studies* 35 (1915): 22–65

Mitchell, S. 'Legio VII and the Garrison of Augustan Galatia'. *Classical Quarterly* 26 (1976), 298–308

Monferrer-Sala, J. '"New Skin for Old Stories": Queens Zenobia and Māwiya, and Christian Arab Groups in the Eastern Frontier During the 3rd–4th

Centuries CE'. In *Mapping Knowledge: Cross-Pollination in Late Antiquity and the Middle Ages*, edited by C. Burnett & P. Mantas-Espana, 71–98 (2014)

Mordechai, L. 'Antioch in the Sixth Century: Resilience or Vulnerability?'. In *Environment and Society in the Long Later Antiquity*, edited by A. Izdebski & M. Mulryan, 25–41 (2018)

Mordechai, L., Eisenberg, M., Newfield, T., Izdebski, A., Kay, J., & Poinar, H. 'The Justinianic Plague: An Inconsequential Pandemic?'. *Proceedings of the National Academy of Sciences of the United States of America* 51 (2019): 25546–25554

Morely, C. 'The Arabian Frontier: A Keystone of the Sasanian Empire'. In Sauer (2019), 268–283

Murdoch, A. *The Last Pagan: Julian the Apostate and the Death of the Ancient World* (2003)

Nabel, J. 'The Seleucids Imprisoned: Arsacid-Roman Hostage Submission and Its Hellenistic Precedents'. In Schlude & Rubin (2017), 25–50

Nappo, D., & Zerbini, A. 'Trade and Taxation in the Egyptian Desert'. In *Frontiers in the Roman World: Proceedings of the Ninth Workshop of the International Network, Impact of Empire (Durham, 16–19 April 2009)*, edited by O. Hekster & T. Kaizer, 61–77 (2011)

Nemati, M., Mousavinia, M., & Sauer, E. 'Largest Ancient Fortress of South-West Asia and the Western World?: Recent Fieldwork at Sasanian Qaleh Iraj at Pishva, Iran'. *Journal of the British Institute of Persian Studies* 58 (2020): 190–220

Olbrycht, M. 'Arsacid Iran and the Nomads of Central Asia—Ways of Cultural Transfer'. In *Complexity of Interaction Along the Eurasian Steppe Zone in the First Millennium CE*, edited by J. Bremmann & M. Schmauder, 333–390 (2015)

———. 'Dynastic Connections in the Arsacid Empire and the Origins of the House of Sasan'. In Sarkhosh Curtis et al. (2016), 23–35

———. 'The Genealogy of Artabanos II (AD 8/9–39/40), King of Parthia'. *Miscellanea Anthropologica et Sociologica* 15 (2014): 92–97

Osgood, J. *Caesar's Legacy: Civil War and the Emergence of the Roman Empire* (2006)

Overtoom, N. 'The Parthians' Unique Mode of Warfare: A Tradition of Parthian Militarism and the Battle of Carrhae'. *Anabasis* 8 (2017): 97–122

———. 'The Power Transition Crisis of the 160s–130s BCE and the Formation of the Parthian Empire'. *Journal of Ancient History* 7 (2019): 111–155

———. *Reign of Arrows: The Rise of the Parthian Empire in the Hellenistic Middle East* (2020)

Pamuk, S., & Shatzmiller, M. 'Plagues, Wages and Economic Change in the Islamic Middle East, 700–1500'. *Journal of Economic History* 74, no. 1 (2014): 196–229

Patterson, L. 'Minority Religions in the Sasanian Empire: Suppression, Integration and Relations with Rome'. In Sauer (2019), 181–198

Pékary, T. 'Le "tribut" aux Perses et les finances de Philippe l'Arabe'. *Syria* 38 (1961): 275–283

Pernet, L. 'Fighting for Caesar: The Archaeology and History of Gallic Auxiliaries in the 2nd–1st Centuries BC'. In *Julius Caesar's Battle for Gaul: New Archaeological Perspectives*, edited by A. Fitzpatrick & C. Haselgrove, 179–196 (2019)

Petersen, L. *Siege Warfare and Military Organization in the Successor States (400–800 AD): Byzantium, the West and Islam* (2013)

Pohl, W. 'Justinian and the Barbarian Kingdoms'. In Maas (2005), 448–476

Pollard, N. 'The Roman Army as "Total Institution" in the Near East?: Dura-Europos as a Case Study'. In Kennedy (1996), 211–227

———. *Soldiers, Cities and Civilians in Roman Syria* (2000)

Potter, D. *Constantine the Emperor* (2013)

———. 'Emperors, Their Borders and Their Neighbours: The Scope of Imperial *Mandata*'. In Kennedy (1996), 49–66

———. 'The Inscriptions on the Bronze Herakles from Mesene: Vologeses IV's War with Rome and the Date of Tacitus' *Annales, Zeitschrift für Papyrologie und Epigraphik* 88 (1991): 277–290

———. 'Palmyra and Rome: Odaenathus' Titulature and the Use of *Imperium Maius*'. *Zeitschrift für Papyrologie und Epigraphik* 113 (1996): 271–285

———. *The Roman Empire at Bay* (2004)

Potts, D., ed. *The Oxford Handbook of Ancient Iran* (2013)

———. 'Sasanian Iran and Its Northeastern Frontier: Offense, Defense, and Diplomatic Entente'. In *Empires and Exchanges in Eurasian Late Antiquity: Rome, China, Iran, and the Steppe, ca. 250–750*, edited by N. di Cosmo & M. Maas, 287–301 (2018)

Pourshariati, P. *The Decline and Fall of the Sasanian Empire: The Sasanian-Parthian Confederacy and the Arab Conquest of Iran* (2008)

Rahim Shayegan, M. *Arsacids and Sasanians: Political Ideology in Post-Hellenic and Late Antique Persia* (2011)

Rankov, B. 'The Governor's Men: The *Officium Consularis*'. In Goldsworthy & Haynes (1999), 15–34

Rekavandi, H. O., Sauer, E., Wilkinson, T., & Nokahdeh, J. 'The Archaeology of Sasanian Frontier Troops: Recent Fieldwork on Frontier Walls in Northern Iran'. In Hodgson, Bidwell, & Schachtmann (2017), 145–150

Rezakhani, K. 'From the Kushans to Western Turks'. In *King of the Seven Climes: A History of the Ancient Iranian World (3000 BCE–651 CE)*, edited by T. Daryaee, 199–226 (2017)

Rich, J. 'Augustus, War, and Peace'. In *The Representation and Perception of Roman Imperial Power: Proceedings of the Third Workshop of the*

International Network, Impact of Empire (Roman Empire, c. 200 BC–AD 476), edited by L. de Blois, P. Erdkamp, O. Hekster, G. de Kleijn, & S. Mols, 329–357 (2003)

———. 'The Parthian Honours'. *Papers of the British School at Rome* 66 (1998): 71–128

Richmond, I. 'Palmyra Under the Aegis of Rome'. *Journal of Roman Studies* 53 (1963): 43–54

Ridgway, W. 'Euripides in Macedon'. *Classical Quarterly* 20 (1926): 1–19

Romer, F. 'Caius' Military Diplomacy in the East'. *Transactions of the American Philological Association* 109 (1979): 199–214

Rose, C. 'The Parthians in Augustan Rome'. *American Journal of Archaeology* 109 (2005): 21–75

———. '"Princes" and Barbarians on the Ara Pacis'. *American Journal of Archaeology* 94 (1990): 453–467

Rosenstein, N. *Imperatores Victi* (1990)

———. 'Marriage and Manpower in the Hannibalic War: *Assidui, Proletarii* and Livy 24. 18. 7–8'. *Historia* 51 (2002): 163–191

———. *Rome and the Mediterranean 290 to 146 BC: The Imperial Republic* (2012)

Ross, S. *Roman Edessa: Politics and Culture on the Eastern Fringes of the Roman Empire, 114–242 CE* (2001)

Rubin, Z. 'Diplomacy and War in the Relations Between Byzantium and the Sassanids in the Fifth Century AD'. In Freeman & Kennedy (1986), 2:677–695

Saddington, D. 'Client Kings' Armies Under Augustus: The Case of Herod'. In Jacobson & Kokkinos (2009), 303–323

Said, E. *Orientalism* (1978)

Salway, B. 'What's in a Name? A Survey of Roman Onomastic Practice from c. 700 BC to AD 700'. *Journal of Roman Studies* 84 (1994): 124–145

Sampson, G. *The Defeat of Rome: Crassus, Carrhae and the Invasion of the East* (2008)

Sarantis, A. 'Waging War in Late Antiquity'. In *War and Warfare in Late Antiquity*, edited by A. Sarantis & N. Christie, 1–98 (2013)

Sarkhosh Curtis, V. 'The Iranian Revival in the Parthian Period'. In Sarkhosh Curtis & Stewart (2007), 7–25

Sarkhosh Curtis, V., & Magub, A. *Rivalling Rome: Parthian Coins and Culture* (2020)

Sarkhosh Curtis, V., Pendleton, E., Alram, M., & Daryaee, T., eds. *The Parthian and Early Sasanian Empires: Adaptation and Expansion* (2016)

Sarkhosh Curtis, V., & Stewart, S., eds. *The Age of the Parthians* (2007)

Sauer, E., ed. *Sasanian Persia: Between Rome and the Steppes of Eurasia* (2019)

Sauer, E., & Nokandeh, J. 'Forts and Megafortresses, Natural and Artificial Barriers: The Grand Strategy of the Sasanian Empire'. In *Proceedings of the International Congress of Young Archaeologists 2015*, edited by M. Kharanaghi, M. Khanipour, & R. Naseri, 236–256 (2018)

Sauer, E., Nokandeh, J., Pitskhelauri, K., & Rekavandi, H. O. 'Innovation and Stagnation: Military Infrastructure and Shifting Balance of Power Between Rome and Persia'. In Sauer (2019), 241–267

Sauer, E., Nokandeh, J., & Rekavandi, H. O., eds., *Ancient Arms Race: Antiquity's Largest Fortresses and Sasanian Military Networks of Northern Iran*. 2 vols. (2022)

Sauer, E., Rekavandi, H. O., Wilkinson, T., & Nokandeh, J. *Persia's Imperial Power in Late Antiquity: The Great Wall of Gorgān and the Frontier Landscapes of Sasanian Iran* (2013)

Schlude, J. *Rome, Parthia, and the Politics of Peace: Origins of War in the Ancient Middle East* (2020)

Schlude, J., & Overman, J. 'Herod the Great: A Near Eastern Case Study in Roman-Parthian Politics'. In Schlude & Rubin (2017), 93–110

Schlude, J., & Rubin, B., eds. *Arsacids, Romans, and Local Elites: Cross-Cultural Interactions of the Parthian Empire* (2017)

Schlude, J., & Rubin, B. 'Finding Common Ground: Roman-Parthian Embassies in the Julio-Claudian Period'. In Schlude & Rubin (2017), 65–91

Schörle, K. 'Palmyrene Merchant Networks and Economic Integration into Competitive Markets'. In *Sinews of Empire*, edited by H. Teigan & E. Seland, 147–154 (2017)

Schürer, E., Vermes, G., & Millar, F. *The History of the Jewish People in the Age of Jesus Christ*. Vol. 1 (1973)

Scullion, S. 'Euripides and Macedon, or the Silence of the Frogs'. *Classical Quarterly* 53 (2003): 389–400

Seager, R. 'Perceptions of Eastern Frontier Policy in Ammianus, Libanius and Julian'. *Classical Quarterly* 47 (1997): 253–268

———. *Pompey the Great: A Political Biography* (2nd ed., 2002)

———. *Tiberius* (2nd ed., 2005)

Seaver, J. 'Publius Ventidius: Neglected Roman Military Hero'. *Classical Journal* 47 (1952): 275–280

Seland, E. 'Ancient Trading Networks and New Institutional Economics: The Case of Palmyra'. In *Antike Wirtschaft und ihre kulturelle Prägung— The Cultural Shaping of the Ancient Economy*, edited by K. Droß-Krüpe, S. Föllinger, & K. Ruffing, 223–234 (2016)

———. *Ships of the Desert and Ships of the Sea: Palmyra in the World Trade of the First Three Centuries* CE (2016)

Shavarebi, E. 'Historical Aspects, Iconographical Factors, Numismatic Issues, Technical Elements: How to Obtain a Convincing Chronology for the Rock Reliefs of Ardashir I'. *Anabasis* 5 (2014): 108–122

Shaw, B. 'Bandits in the Roman Empire'. *Past & Present* 105 (1984)

Sherwin-White, A. 'Ariobarzanes, Mithridates, and Sulla'. *Classical Quarterly* 27 (1977): 173–183

———. *The Letters of Pliny: A Historical and Social Commentary* (1966)

———. *The Roman Citizenship* (1973)

———. *Roman Foreign Policy in the East: 168 BC to AD 1* (1983)

Shoemaker, S. *The Apocalypse of Empire: Imperial Eschatology in Late Antiquity and Early Islam* (2018)

Sidebottom, H. *The Mad Emperor: Heliogabalus and the Decadence of Rome* (2022)

Sidnell, P. *Warhorse* (2007)

Simpson, A. 'The Departure of Crassus for Parthia'. *Transactions and Proceedings of the American Philological Association* 69 (1938): 532–541

Sommer, M. *Palmyra: A History* (2017)

Southern, P. *Empress Zenobia: Palmyra's Rebel Queen* (2008)

Southern, P., & Dixon, K. *The Late Roman Army* (1996)

Stephenson, P. *New Rome: The Roman Empire in the East AD 395–700* (2021)

Stockton, D. *Cicero: A Political Biography* (1971)

Strauss, B. *The War That Made the Roman Empire: Antony, Cleopatra and Octavian at Actium* (2022)

Strootman, R. 'The Seleucid Empire Between Orientalism and Hellenocentrism: Writing the History of Iran in the Third and Second Centuries BCE'. *Nāme-ye Irān-e Bāstān: The International Journal of Ancient Iranian Studies* 11, no. 1–2 (2011/2012): 17–35

Strugnell, E. 'Thea Musa, Roman Queen of Parthia'. *Iranica Antiqua* 43 (2008): 275–298

Swain, S. 'Greek into Palmyrene: Odaenathus as "Corrector Totius Orientis"'. *Zeitschrift für Papyrologie und Epigraphik* 99 (1993): 157–164

Syme, R. *Emperors and Biography: Studies in the Historia Augusta* (1971)

———. *The Roman Revolution* (1960)

Tao, W. 'Parthia in China: A Re-examination of the Historical Records'. In Sarkhosh Curtis & Stewart (2007), 87–104

Temin, P. 'The Economy of the Early Roman Empire'. *Journal of Economic Perspectives* 20 (2006): 133–151

Thomas Parker, S. 'New Research on the Roman Frontier in Arabia'. In Hodgson, Bidwell, & Schachtmann (2017), 139–144

Thompson, E. *The Huns*. Revised and edited by P. Heather (1996)

Thorley, J. 'The Development of Trade Between the Roman Empire and the East Under Augustus'. *Greece and Rome* 16 (1969): 209–223

———. 'The Roman Empire and the Kushans'. *Greece and Rome* 26 (1979): 181–190

———. 'The Silk Trade Between China and the Roman Empire at Its Height, Circa AD 90–130'. *Greece and Rome* 18 (1971): 71–80

Tomber, R. 'Pots, Coins and Trinkets in Rome's Trade with the East'. In *Rome Beyond Its Frontiers: Imports, Attitudes and Practices*. Journal of Roman Archaeology Supplementary Series no. 95, edited by P. Wells, 87–104 (2013)

Treadgold, W. *Byzantium and Its Army: 284–1081* (1995)

Ward, A. *Marcus Crassus and the Late Roman Republic* (1977)

Ward-Perkins, B. *The Fall of Rome and the End of Civilization* (2005)

Warmington, B. *Nero: Reality and Legend* (1969)

Watson, A. *Aurelian and the Third Century* (1999)

Welles, C. 'The Epitaph of Julius Terentius'. *Harvard Theological Review* 34, no. 2 (1941): 79–102

Wellesley, K. *The Year of the Four Emperors* (3rd ed., 2000)

Wheeler, E. 'The Army and the *Limes* in the East'. In *A Companion to the Roman Army*, edited by P. Erdkamp, 234–266 (2007)

———. 'The Laxity of the Syrian Legions'. In Kennedy (1996), 229–276

Whitby, M. *The Emperor Maurice and His Historian Theophylact on Persian and Balkan Warfare* (1988)

Whitehouse, D., & Williamson, A. 'Sasanian Maritime Trade'. *Iran* 11 (1973): 29–49

Whittaker, C. 'Indian Trade Within the Roman Imperial Network'. In *Rome and Its Frontiers: The Dynamics of Empire* (2004), 163–180

Williams, S. *Diocletian and the Roman Recovery* (1985)

Williams, W. 'Caracalla and Rhetoricians: A Note of the *cognitio de Goharienis*' *Latomus* 33 (1974): 663–667

Winsbury, R. *Zenobia of Palmyra: History, Myth and the Neo-classical Imagination* (2012)

Wintjes, J. 'Field Officers: Principate'. In *The Encyclopedia of the Roman Army*. Vol. 2, edited by Y. Le Bohec, 399–402 (2015)

Wolfram, H. *The Roman Empire and Its Germanic Peoples*. Translated by T. Dunlap (1997)

Young, G. *Rome's Eastern Trade: International Commerce and Imperial Policy, 31 BC–AD 305* (2001)

Zadorojniy, A. 'Tragic and Epic in Plutarch's Crassus'. *Hermes* 125 (1997): 169–182

Zanker, P. *The Power of Images in the Age of Augustus*. Translated by A. Shapiro (1988)

NOTES

INTRODUCTION

1. For an introduction to the wider issues of the Roman empire and its nature, see A. Goldsworthy, *Pax Romana: War, Peace and Conquest in the Roman World* (2016), esp. 63–86 for a discussion of Caesar in Gaul.

2. For discussion of the particular role played by Tacitus's *Germania* in German consciousness, see C. Krebs, *A Most Dangerous Book: Tacitus's Germania from the Roman Empire to the Third Reich* (2011).

3. Estimates based on suggestions for the Seleucids, the predecessors to the Parthians, in G. Aperghis, *The Seleukid Royal Economy: The Finances and Financial Administration of the Seleukid Empire* (2004), 35–58. The chart on p. 56 brings together two systems of estimating the population of each region. Taking the areas under Parthian-Sasanian rule gives ranges of 9.5 to 12 million and 11.75 to 14 million in each case. Apart from everything else, not all of these areas neatly fit the territory of the later period. For instance, substantial parts of populous Mesopotamia were occupied by the Romans for much of this period. All estimates for ancient populations need to be taken with more than a pinch of salt.

4. One of the most influential studies of more recent Western perceptions of the peoples of Asia remains E. Said, *Orientalism* (1978), which is often cited in ways that the author himself finds highly surprising—see the preface to the 2003 and the afterword to the 1995 editions. His theme is essentially the nineteenth and twentieth centuries, and the conditions he highlights, notably the economic and military dominance of colonial powers in this period, do not reflect in any way the relationship between the Romans and Parthians-Sasanians. Ancient historians are now more inclined to be aware of the dangers of seeing everything from a Western—or Roman—perspective and do their best to avoid this. See, for instance, D. Kennedy, 'Parthia and Rome: Eastern Perspectives', in *The Roman Army in the East*, Journal of Roman Archaeology Supplementary Series no. 18, ed. D. Kennedy (1996), 67–90, esp. 67–69 with references to other works. Some go further and import baggage from postcolonial studies into their analysis of the ancient world, something inherently risky.

5. For a sensible analysis and also a good survey of the debate, see G. Greatrex, 'Roman Frontiers and Foreign Policy in the East', in *Aspects of the Roman East: Papers in Honour of Professor Fergus Millar FBA*, ed. R. Alston (2007), 103–173.

CHAPTER 1: FELIX

1. Plutarch, *Sulla* 5. 3–6 for the full account. Livy, *Pers.* 70 simply states that Parthian ambassadors came to Sulla seeking friendship with the Roman people, as does Rufus Festus, *Breviarum* 15. Justin, *Epitome* 38. 1. 1–5. 9 deals with the Cappadocian background but does not mention Sulla or the Parthian embassy; Velleius Paterculus 2. 24. 3 notes that Sulla made the first diplomatic contact with the Parthians, but oddly dates this to several years later.

2. In general, see N. Debevoise, *A Political History of Parthia* (1938), 46–47; and for more detailed discussion, including the complex question of dating the encounter, see A. Sherwin-White, 'Ariobarzanes, Mithridates, and Sulla', *Classical Quarterly* 27 (1977): 173–183; A. Sherwin-White, *Roman Foreign Policy in the East 168 BC to AD 1* (1983), 218–220; A. Keaveney, 'Roman Treaties with Parthia Circa 95–Circa 64 BC', *American Journal of Philology* 102 (1981): 195–212, esp. 195–199; A. Keaveney, 'Sulla's Cilician Command: The Evidence of Apollinaris Sidonius', *Historia* 54 (1995): 29–36; A. Keaveney, 'The King and the War-Lords: Romano-Parthian Relations Circa 64–53 BC', *American Journal of Philology* 103 (1982): 412–428; for the subsequent relationship, T. Corey Brennan, 'Sulla's Career in the Nineties: Some Reconsiderations', *Chiron* 22 (1992): 103–158. Dating of the meeting between Sulla and Orobazus depends on the chronology of the disputed succession in Cappadocia and the dating of his praetorship, both complex issues and impossible to resolve with the current evidence.

3. For Sulla's early life and its context, see A. Keaveney, *Sulla: The Last Republican*, 2nd ed., (2005), 11–21.

4. A. Lintott, *The Constitution of the Roman Republic* (1999), 135–136, suggests that the number of quaestors may have risen to twelve each year before Sulla raised the number to twenty during his dictatorship. On Sulla, see Plutarch, *Sulla* 3–4; Sallust, *Jugurthine War* 105. 1–113. 6.

5. Plutarch says that Sulla claimed voters wanted him to be aedile so rejected him as praetor, *Sulla* 5. 1–2, and uses a hostile source accusing him of bribing his way to success a year later.

6. Corey Brennan (1992), 137–144 notes the pressures on available magistrates.

7. On prorogation of magistrates, see Lintott (1999), 113–114; for an overview of the Roman political system in this period, see Goldsworthy (2016), 21–35.

8. On available manpower, see Sherwin-White (1983), 9–10 and more generally P. Brunt, *Italian Manpower 225 BC–AD 14* (1971).

9. Sherwin-White (1983), 11–15, 52–55 on Rome's focus on the western Mediterranean.

10. For discussion see S. Dyson, *The Creation of the Roman Frontier* (1985).

11. On the demands of military service and available manpower, see N. Rosenstein, *Rome and the Mediterranean 290 to 146 BC: The Imperial Republic* (2012), 94–96, 112–116; and N. Rosenstein, 'Marriage and Manpower in the Hannibalic War: *Assidui, Proletarii* and Livy 24. 18. 7–8', *Historia* 51 (2002): 163–191; on conquest and its impact in general, see Goldsworthy (2016), 37–61.

12. J. Ma, 'Peer Polity Interaction in the Hellenistic Age', *Past and Present* 180 (2003): 9–39.

13. See Goldsworthy (2016), 133–145.

14. Murder of the legate Cnaeus Octavius, see Polybius 31. 2. 1–11, 11. 1–3; Appian, *Syrian Wars* 46.

15. On the bequest, Strabo, *Geog.* 13. 4. 2, Justin, *Epitome* 36. 4. 5, with full discussion in Sherwin-White (1983), 80–84. For the political violence in Rome, see A. Lintott in *The Cambridge Ancient History* (hereafter *CAH²*), vol. 9, *The Last Age of the Roman Republic* 146–43 BC, eds. J. Crook, A. Lintott, & E. Rawson (1994), 61–77.

16. For the war in Asia and the establishment of the province, see Sherwin-White (1983), 84–92.

17. See Dyson (1985), 161–164; human sacrifice, Plutarch *Moralia* 284 A–C.

18. For a survey of the Social War, see E. Gabba in *CAH²* 9:104–128.

19. Plutarch, *Sulla* 5. 7–7. 1.

20. For a survey of these events, see R. Seager in *CAH²* 9:165–181.

CHAPTER 2: KING OF KINGS

1. N. Debevoise, *A Political History of Parthia* (1938) remains a good starting place for approaching Parthian history, and see also A. Bivar, 'The Political History of Iran Under the Arsacids', in *The Cambridge History of Iran*, vol. 3, part 1, ed. E. Yarshater (1983), 21–99, and S. Hauser, 'The Arsacids (Parthians)', in *The Oxford Handbook of Ancient Iran*, ed. D. Potts (2013), 728–750. For the Achaemenids, see L. Llewellyn-Jones, *Persians: The Age of the Great Kings* (2022).

2. Tablet 330 in Sachs-Hunger Collection, translation from A. Kuhrt, *Persian Empire: A Corpus of Sources from the Achaemenid Period*, 2 vols. (2007), 447–448, cited with discussion in P. Briant, *Darius in the Shadow of Alexander*, trans. J. Todd (2015), 60–64. On the impact of Macedonian occupation on Zoroastrianism, see S. Eddy, *The King Is Dead: Studies in the Near Eastern Resistance to Hellenism 334–31 BC* (1961), esp. 3–80.

3. For a good discussion, see D. Engels, 'Middle Eastern "Feudalism" and Seleucid Dissolution', in *Seleucid Dissolution: The Sinking of the Anchor*, ed. K. Erikson & G. Ramsay (2011), 19–36; in general, see E. Bickerman, 'The Seleucid Period', in Yarshater (1983), 3–20, and R. Strootman, 'The Seleucid Empire Between Orientalism and Hellenocentrism: Writing the History of Iran in the Third and Second Centuries BCE', *Nāme-ye Irān-e Bāstān: The International Journal of Ancient Iranian Studies* 11, no. 1–2 (2011/2012): 17–35.

4. V. Sarkhosh Curtis, 'The Iranian Revival in the Parthian Period', in *The Age of the Parthians*, eds. V. Sarkhosh Curtis & S. Stewart (2007), 7–25, esp. 7–8; N. Overtoom, *Reign of Arrows: The Rise of the Parthian Empire in the Hellenistic Middle East* (2020), 75–85.

5. Overtoom (2020), 79–80.

6. On the name, see V. Sarkhosh Curtis & A. Magub, *Rivalling Rome: Parthian Coins and Culture* (2020), 3; sources for the start of the dynasty, Arrian, Parthica Frag. 30 = Photius, *Bibliographica* 58, and Justin, *Epitome* 41. 1. 10–12, 5. 1–10; on the probability that one of the two brothers in Arrian is mythical, see

E. Dabrowa, 'The Arsacids and Their State', in *Altertum und Gegenwart*, eds. R. Rollinger et al. (2012), 21–52, esp. 26–27.

7. See Sarkhosh Curtis (2007), 7–9; J. Gaslain, 'Some Aspects of Political History: Early Arsacid Kings and the Seleucids', in *The Parthian and Early Sasanian Empires: Adaptation and Expansion*, eds. V. Sarkhosh Curtis et al. (2016), 3–7, esp. 3–5. On the different traditions of the Parthians compared to some Iranians, see Eddy (1961), 81–92.

8. Overtoom (2020), 89–90, 94–107, esp. 101–102; on the evidence for capture of Seleucus II, see J. Nabel, 'The Seleucids Imprisoned: Arsacid-Roman Hostage Submission and Its Hellenistic Precedents', in *Arsacids, Romans, and Local Elites: Cross-Cultural Interactions of the Parthian Empire*, eds. J. Schlude & B. Rubin (2017), 25–50, esp. 26–28; for Antiochus III's campaign, the main account is Polybius 10. 27. 1–31. 13 and 49. 1–15, 11. 39. 1–16 for subsequent operations in Bactria, all with Overtoom (2020), 107–130.

9. Overtoom (2020), 131–173 for a detailed assessment of the limited evidence.

10. Justin, *Epitome* 36. 1. 1–6, 38. 9. 1–10, with Overtoom (2020), 176–188, for the campaign and aftermath; on hostages in general, see Nabel (2017).

11. Sarkhosh Curtis (2007), 8–11; J. Lerner, 'Mithridates I and the Parthian Archer', in Schlude & Rubin (2017), 1–24.

12. Justin, *Epitome* 38. 10. 1–39. 1; Josephus, *Jewish Antiquities* (hereafter *AJ*) 13. 236–239; Diodorus Siculus 34/35. 1, 16, 17. 1–2; with Overtoom (2020), 191–215.

13. Overtoom (2020), 228–245; N. Overtoom, 'The Power Transition Crisis of the 160s–130s BCE and the Formation of the Parthian Empire', *Journal of Ancient History* 7 (2019): 111–155.

14. Sarkhosh Curtis (2007), 12–13; for a detailed discussion of memory of the Achaemenids, see M. Rahim Shayegan, *Arsacids and Sasanians: Political Ideology in Post-Hellenic and Late Antique Persia* (2011), esp. 228–247 on the title 'king of kings'.

15. Bivar (1983), 41–45.

CHAPTER 3: WARS AND RUMOURS OF WARS

1. There is a good discussion in Sherwin-White (1983), 102–158, and accessible biographies of Mithridates VI are P. Matyszak, *Mithridates the Great: Rome's Indomitable Enemy* (2008), and A. Mayor, *The Poison King: The Life and Legend of Mithridates, Rome's Deadliest Enemy* (2010).

2. Plutarch, *Lucullus* 11. 1 for 'kicking the enemy in the guts'.

3. For the war, see Sherwin-White (1983), 159–185; for negotiations between Romans and Parthians, see Keaveney (1981), 195–212, esp. 199–202, and J. Schlude, *Rome, Parthia, and the Politics of Peace: Origins of War in the Ancient Middle East* (2020), 29–41; quote 'too many for an embassy' in Plutarch, *Lucullus* 27. 4.

4. For Pompey's early life, see P. Greenhalgh, *Pompey: The Roman Alexander* (1980) and R. Seager, *Pompey the Great* (2nd ed., 2002), 1–39.

5. On Pompey's activities in the east, see Sherwin-White (1983), 186–234; Seager (2002), 53–62.

6. Dio 37. 5. 4–5; Plutarch, *Pompey* 36. 2; on the confused situation in the wider region, see P. Edwell, 'The Euphrates as a Boundary Between Rome and Parthia in the Late Republic and Early Empire', *Antichthon* 47 (2013): 191–206.

7. Keaveney (1981), 204–212; Keaveney (1982), 412–428; Schlude (2020), 42–59.

8. Plutarch, *Pompey* 38. 2; Dio 37. 6. 1–2.

9. Plutarch, *Lucullus* 30. 2–31. 1; on frontiers in this era, see S. Dyson, *The Creation of the Roman Frontier* (1985), esp. 122–171 on the frontier in Gaul.

10. Sherwin-White (1983), 271–279; Schlude (2020), 60–62; Keaveney (1982), 412–417; on Ptolemy, see A. Goldsworthy, *Antony and Cleopatra* (2010), 78–80, 96–104.

11. Crassus and property and views on wealth, see Plutarch, *Crassus* 2. 1–8; for his life, see A. Ward, *Marcus Crassus and the Late Roman Republic* (1977), 46–82.

12. Ward (1977), 83–98, with Appian, *Civil Wars* 1. 14. 120 for the mass crucifixion.

13. Ward (1977), 273–285.

14. Debevoise, (1938), 75–78; Bivar (1983), 48–49; with Dio 39. 56. 2; Justin, *Epitome* 42. 4. 1.

15. Plutarch, *Crassus* 16. 3–5; with other sources and discussion in A. Simpson, 'The Departure of Crassus for Parthia', *Transactions and Proceedings of the American Philological Association* 69 (1938): 532–541; and more recently and briefly, Schlude (2020), 62–65.

16. Cicero, *Ad Atticum* 4. 13 for the contemporary account and *De divinatione* 1. 29–30.

17. G. Sampson, *The Defeat of Rome: Crassus, Carrhae and the Invasion of the East* (2008), 94–95, 101–106, argues that the Parthian civil war was fundamental to Crassus's concept of the war.

18. On the influence of drama and especially Euripides's *Bacchae* on Plutarch, see D. Braund, 'Dionysiac Tragedy in Plutarch, Crassus', *Classical Quarterly* 43 (1993): 468–474, and A. Zadorojniy, 'Tragic and Epic in Plutarch's Crassus', *Hermes* 125 (1997): 169–182.

19. Plutarch, *Crassus* 17. 4, 20. 1, 25. 2.

20. Note the contrast with the similarly elderly Pompey in 49 BC, who threw himself into the training exercises of his soldiers: Plutarch, *Pompey* 64. 1–2; on the 54 BC campaign, see Plutarch, *Crassus* 17. 1–4, with Sherwin-White (1983), 281–284.

21. Plutarch, *Crassus* 17. 4–8; Dio 40. 13. 3; Cicero discovered that his predecessor as governor of Cilicia had sent orders to cities requiring them to billet troops over winter but soon made clear that he preferred to be paid to cancel the obligation: Cicero, *Ad Att.* 5. 21; for provincial government in this era, Goldsworthy (2016), 107–132, provides an introduction.

CHAPTER 4: THE BATTLE

1. Plutarch, *Crassus* 19. 1–3, with Sherwin-White (1983), 284–287; Schlude (2020), 65–67.

2. Plutarch, *Crassus* 18. 1–2; Dio 40. 16. 1–3.

3. Dio 15. 1–6 on the Parthian army, with useful comments in Kennedy (1996), 67–90, esp. 83–84; M. Mielczarek, *Cataphraci and Clibinarii: Studies in the Heavy Armoured Cavalry of the Ancient World* (1993); and Overtoom (2020), 37–52.

4. P. Sidnell, *Warhorse* (2007), 20–21, 35, 85 on development of the saddle; for the detailed reconstruction of the Roman saddle derived from this type, see P. Connolly, 'The Roman Saddle', in *Roman Military Equipment: The Accoutrements of War*, ed. M. Dawson (1987), 7–27.

5. See M. Olbrycht, 'Arsacid Iran and the Nomads of Central Asia—Ways of Cultural Transfer', in *Complexity of Interaction Along the Eurasian Steppe Zone in the First Millennium CE*, eds. J. Bremmann & M. Schmauder (2015), 333–390, esp. 369–374.

6. Plutarch, *Crassus* 21. 6–7, 27. 1–2; Justin, *Epitome* 41. 2. 5; Josephus, *AJ* 17. 23, with N. Overtoom, 'The Parthians' Unique Mode of Warfare: A Tradition of Parthian Militarism and the Battle of Carrhae', *Anabasis* 8 (2017): 97–122, esp. 97; Caesar, *Bellum Gallicum* (hereafter *BG*) 6. 13, where the common folk in Gaul were treated 'virtually as slaves'.

7. Plutarch, *Crassus* 21. 1–5, emphasizing that Orodes II did not treat the threat posed by Crassus lightly and also stressing the strength and ability of Surena. The assumption that there were only ten thousand Parthians at Carrhae is often made: examples include Sherwin-White (1983), 287–288, n. 44; Kennedy (1996), 84; and Bivar (1983), 52–53, all assume this, as does A. Goldsworthy, *The Roman Army at War 100 BC–AD 200* (1996), 187. Sampson (2008), 112–113, discusses the strategy, with criticism in Overtoom (2017), 109, n. 62.

8. Plutarch, *Crassus* 19. 3–6; Dio 40. 17. 1–19. 4; Caesar, *BG* 1. 39–41.

9. Plutarch, *Crassus* 21. 1–7; Dio 40. 20. 1–21. 1.

10. Plutarch, *Crassus* 31. 7 claims that there were twenty thousand dead and ten thousand prisoners taken in the whole campaign. This would include the garrisons, and in addition there were survivors who reached Syria and reformed a small army (Appian, *Civil Wars* [hereafter *BC*] 2. 18); it is claimed that ten thousand escaped to Syria. As stated earlier, no total is given for Surena's army, other than Velleius Paterculus 2. 46. 4, who exaggerates by saying 'innumerable forces of cavalry'. The Romans appear to have felt that only many years of successful, hard campaigning turned soldiers into true veterans: Caesar, *BG* 8. 8. On the variable size of legions on campaign in this period, see Goldsworthy (1996), 22–23. For Cassius and the date of his quaestorship, see J. Linderski, 'Two Quaestorships', *Classical Philology* 70 (1975): 35–38.

11. Plutarch, *Crassus* 23. 1–4.

12. Plutarch, *Crassus* 23. 4–6. Dio's version of the battle is briefer and appears to differ from the sequence of events in Plutarch. Dio 40. 21. 2–3 claims that Publius Crassus took the initiative and, seeing a small number of Parthians, launched an attack with part of the Roman army. Most likely this is simply a result of condensing the events of the battle, and in general Plutarch's narrative is more plausible.

13. Plutarch, *Crassus* 23. 6. Dio 40. 21. 2 oddly claims that the Parthians hid in woodland, which is highly unlikely in this area, as well as in folds in the ground, which makes much more sense.

14. Plutarch, *Crassus* 23. 7–24. 4. Lucullus had encountered Armenian cataphracts and outmanoeuvred and routed them using a combination of cavalry and legionaries, Plutarch, *Lucullus* 28. 2–4. However, the Armenians do not

appear to have employed large numbers of horse-archers and certainly did not co-ordinate cataphracts and horse-archers as well as the Parthians.

15. J. Latham & W. Patterson, *Saracen Archery: A Mameluk Work, c. 1368* (1970), 142. For discussion of confrontations between infantry and cavalry, see Goldsworthy (1996), 228–235.

16. Caesar, *Bellum Civile* 3. 53, with Goldsworthy (1996), 185–186.

17. Plutarch, *Crassus* 24. 5–25. 1, with Overtoom (2017), 99–101.

18. Plutarch, *Crassus* 25. 2–3; Publius in Gaul, see Caesar, *BG* 1. 52, where he commanded cavalry but gave an order for the third line of legionary cohorts to advance, (2. 34, 3. 7–11) where he was given command of a legion on detached service, and (3. 20–27) where he fought a campaign as independent commander; on Gallic cavalry as auxiliaries in this era, see L. Pernet, 'Fighting for Caesar: The Archaeology and History of Gallic Auxiliaries in the 2nd–1st Centuries BC', in *Julius Caesar's Battle for Gaul: New Archaeological Perspectives*, eds. A. Fitzpatrick & C. Haselgrove (2019), 79–196.

19. Plutarch, *Crassus* 26. 1–3.

20. Plutarch, *Crassus* 25. 3–12.

21. Plutarch, *Crassus* 26. 1–6.

22. Plutarch, *Crassus* 27. 1–2; Dio 40. 22. 1–5; on the proper behaviour of a general facing defeat, see N. Rosenstein, *Imperatores Victi* (1990), 114–151, and Goldsworthy (1996), 163–165.

23. Plutarch, *Crassus* 27. 3; Dio 40. 24. 1–3, claiming that the Parthians were running low on arrows and that in many cases bowstrings had snapped. This was a long engagement by any standard.

24. Plutarch, *Crassus* 27. 3–8; Dio 40. 25. 1–2.

25. Plutarch, *Crassus* 28. 1–29. 1; Dio 40. 25. 3–5.

26. Plutarch, *Crassus* 29. 1–31. 6; Dio 40. 26. 1–27. 4.

27. Plutarch, *Crassus* 33. 1–4; Dio 40. 27. 3; cf. Appian, *Mithridatic Wars* 21 for the same punishment inflicted on a Roman; on Euripides in Macedonia, see W. Ridgway, 'Euripides in Macedon', *Classical Quarterly* 20 (1926): 1–19; S. Scullion, 'Euripides and Macedon, or the Silence of the Frogs', *Classical Quarterly* 53 (2003): 389–400.

28. Plutarch, *Crassus* 32. 1–5.

29. Appian, *BC* 2. 18 claims that fewer than ten thousand soldiers mustered in Syria, while Dio 40. 28. 1 notes that the province was effectively without a governor or garrison.

30. For casualties at Arausio of eighty thousand soldiers and forty thousand servants and slaves, see Livy *Periochae* 67, citing Valerius Antias as source; Appian, *Mithridatic Wars* 89 gives no overall figure for losses at Zela in 67 BC but states that the dead included twenty-four tribunes (the entire complement of four legions) and 150 centurions (equivalent to all the officers of two and a half legions). Caesar had fifteen cohorts of legionaries plus auxiliary troops massacred in the winter of 54–53 BC, see Caesar, *BG* 5. 26–37. On the subsequent importance of Carrhae, see S. Mattern, 'The Defeat of Crassus and the Just War', *Classical World* 96 (2003): 387–396.

31. For Pompey's career and the political context in these years, see R. Seager, *Pompey the Great: A Political Biography* (2nd ed., 2002), 125–151.

32. Lucan, *Pharsalia* 1. 125–126.

33. For the appointment of provincial governors at this time, see D. Stockton, *Cicero: A Political Biography* (1971), esp. 225–226; for a detailed discussion

of his appointment, see A. Marshall, 'The *Lex Pompeia de provinciis* (52 BC) and Cicero's *Imperium* in 51–50 BC: Constitutional Aspects', in *Aufstieg und Niedergang der römischen Welt* I.1 (1972), 887–921.

34. For Cicero's time in Cilicia, see Stockton (1971), 227–253, and Goldsworthy (2016), 107–130.

35. Dio 40. 28. 1–29. 3; Cicero, *Ad Familiares* 2. 10. 2, 15. 1. 2, 3. 1, 4. 7; *Ad Atticum* 5. 18. 1–2, 20. 3, 21. 2. On the overall situation, see Kennedy (1996), 67–90, esp. 77–79; Sherwin-White (1983), 292–297.

36. Cicero, *Ad Atticum* 5. 20–21; *Ad Familiares* 2. 10, 15. 4; Dio 40. 30. 1–2.

CHAPTER 5: INVASIONS

1. According to Plutarch, *Caesar* 32, Julius Caesar quoted the poet Menander in Greek, *aneristho kubos*, rather than the more famous Latin *iacta alea est*. For other versions of the episode, see Suetonius, *Caesar* 31–32; Appian, *BC* 2. 35.

2. Envoy to Orodes II, Caesar, *Civil War* 3. 82; Dio 41. 55, 42. 2; Lucan, *Pharsalia* 2. 633, 637. Pompey considered fleeing to Parthia: Plutarch, *Pompey* 76. 4; Quintilian 3. 8. 33; Appian, *BC* 2. 83; Dio 42. 2. 5; Velleius Paterculus 2. 53. 1; Florus 2. 13, 51. For overviews of the situation in the east in these years, see Debevoise (1938), 104–108; Sherwin-White (1983), 289–302; Schlude (2020), 76–84.

3. Cicero, *Ad Familiares* 12. 19 = Shackleton Bailey (hereafter SB) 205, and *Ad Atticum* 14. 9; mentioning Pacorus, Dio 47. 27; Appian, *BC* 4. 58–59.

4. Cicero, *Ad Familiares* 15. 1 (SB 104), 2. 3 (SB 105); on Antony in 41–40 BC, see Josephus, *AJ* 14. 314–316, and 14. 301–312 (quote from Loeb translation); and for discussion, J. Osgood, *Caesar's Legacy: Civil War and the Emergence of the Roman Empire* (2006), 105–106.

5. Plutarch, *Antony* 26–27; Appian, *BC* 5. 1, 8–9; Dio 48. 24. 2; Josephus *AJ* 15. 89.

6. On Pacorus, see Debevoise (1938), 104 and fn. 43.

7. On Caesar's planned expedition, see Dio 43. 51, 45. 3; Suetonius, *Divine Julius* 44. 3; and *Augustus* 8; Appian, *BC* 2. 110, 3. 91; Plutarch, *Brutus* 22.

8. Dio 48. 24. 4–25. 1, 26. 5; with R. Syme, *The Roman Revolution* (1960), 223; and discussion of the campaign and its context in Kennedy (1996), 67–90, esp. 77–81; Osgood (2006), 185, 225–228.

9. Josephus, *AJ* 14. 330–376; *Jewish War* 1. 248–279; with Osgood (2006), 185–186; E. Schürer, G. Vermes, & F. Millar, *The History of the Jewish People in the Age of Jesus Christ* (1973), 1:278–286.

10. For this period see Goldsworthy (2010), 261–281.

11. J. Seaver, 'Publius Ventidius: Neglected Roman Military Hero', *Classical Journal* 47 (1952): 275–280, 300.

12. Dio 48. 39. 2–41. 6, 49. 19. 1–20. 5; Plutarch, *Antony* 34; Aulus Gellius, *Attic Nights* 15. 4; Frontinus, *Strat.* 1. 1. 6, 2. 2. 5, 2. 5. 36–37; with Sherwin-White (1983), 303–306; Debevoise (1938), 114–120.

13. Justin, *Epitome* 42. 11–16, 5. 1; Dio 49. 23; Plutarch, *Crassus* 33; *Antony* 37.

14. Mattern (2003), 387–396, esp. 392.

15. Operations against the Iberians, see Sherwin-White (1983), 307–308. The subordinate was named Publius Candidius Crassus, but was no relation

of Marcus Licinius Crassus. On the army gathered for Antony's expedition, see Plutarch, *Antony* 37; Appian, *BC* 2. 110; Velleius Paterculus 2. 82. 1–2. For discussion, see P. Brunt, *Italian Manpower 225 BC–AD 14* (1971), 503–504; Sherwin-White (1983), 311, fn. 37. L. Keppie, 'Mark Antony's Legions', in *Legions and Veterans: Roman Army Papers 1971–2000* (2000), 75–96.

16. Suetonius, *Divine Julius* 44. 3.

17. Dio 49. 25. 1–3; Plutarch, *Antony* 38; Strabo, *Geog.* 11. 13. 3–4; Frontinus, *Strat.* 1. 1. 6; with Sherwin-White (1983), 308–311, and Pelling in *CAH²*, vol. 10, *The Augustan Empire 43 BC–AD 69*, eds. A. Bowman, E. Champlin, & A. Lintott, (1996), 32. On the campaign and with a very different interpretation, see K. Jones, 'Marcus Antonius' Median War and the Dynastic Politics of the Near East', in Schlude & Rubin (2017), 51–63.

18. Plutarch, *Antony* 38; Dio 49. 25. 3; with Sherwin-White (1983), 311–315, and slow pace of baggage, see Goldsworthy (1996), 287–296.

19. Plutarch, *Antony* 38; Dio 49. 25. 3–26. 1.

20. Plutarch, *Antony* 39; Dio 49. 26. 1–27. 1. On decimation, see C. Goldberg, 'Decimation in the Roman Republic', *Classical Journal* 111 (2015–2016): 141–164.

21. Plutarch, *Antony* 40–42; Dio 49. 27. 2–28. 1.

22. Plutarch, *Antony* 42–43; Dio 49. 29. 1.

23. Plutarch, *Antony* 44–45; Dio 49. 29. 2–4.

24. Plutarch, *Antony* 45.

25. Velleius Paterculus 2. 82. 2; Plutarch, *Antony* 46–48.

26. On losses, see Plutarch, *Antony* 49–51; Velleius Paterculus 2. 82. 3; Dio 49. 31. 1–3; with Sherwin-White (1983), 320–321. Livy, *Pers.* 130 also claims that eight thousand men died 'in storms' during the march through Armenia but does not give a figure for overall casualties. He also accuses Antony of ordering the march so that he could winter with Cleopatra.

27. Plutarch, *Antony* 36, 52–53; Dio 49. 33. 1–3, 39. 1–40. 2; with Jones (2017), 58–59.

28. On the Donations, see Plutarch, *Antony* 54; Dio 49. 41. 1–6; with Pelling in *CAH²* 10:40–41; Osgood (2006), 338–339; M. Grant, *Cleopatra* (1971), 162–175; J. Bingen, *Hellenistic Egypt: Monarchy, Society, Economy, Culture* (2007), 78–79; G. Hölbl, *A History of the Ptolemaic Empire*, trans. T. Saavedra (2001), 244–245; for an up-to-date account of the war of 31–30 BC, see B. Strauss, *The War That Made the Roman Empire: Antony, Cleopatra and Octavian at Actium* (2022).

CHAPTER 6: EAGLES AND PRINCES

1. For the story of Augustus's career, see A. Goldsworthy, *Augustus: From Revolutionary to Emperor; First Emperor of Rome* (2014) as an introduction to the vast literature on the subject.

2. Suetonius, *Augustus* 29; P. Zanker, *The Power of Images in the Age of Augustus*, trans. A. Shapiro (1988) remains the best starting place for consideration of Augustus's public image.

3. Dio 69. 6. 3.

4. On Tiridates, see Dio 51. 18. 2–3, 53. 33. 2; Justin, *Epitome* 42. 5. 6–9. The sources for Tiridates are confused and contradictory, especially over chronology,

so that what follows is conjectural. For discussion, see Debevoise (1938), 136–140; Sherwin-White (1983), 322–323; and Bivar (1983), 65–66.

5. For the killing of the harem, see Isadore of Charax, *Parthian Way-Stations* 1; for the four queens/wives named in text probably dated to 21–20 BC, see E. Minns, 'Parchments of the Parthian Period from Avroman in Kurdistan', *Journal of Hellenic Studies* 35 (1915): 22–65.

6. Horace, *Odes* 3. 5. 2–12 (Loeb translation, slightly modified); cf. Horace, *Odes* 1. 2. 22, 51–52, 3. 6. 9–12; Propertius 3. 4. For the role of warfare in Augustus's public image and the popularity of attacking Parthians, Britons, and Indians, see J. Rich, 'Augustus, War, and Peace', in *The Representation and Perception of Roman Imperial Power: Proceedings of the Third Workshop of the International Network, Impact of Empire (Roman Empire, c. 200 BC–AD 476)*, eds. L. de Blois et al. (2003), 329–357; J. Edmondson, ed., *Augustus* (2009), 137–164, esp. 143–148. For discussion of how far the poet's opinions on this matter reflected opinion more generally, see Schlude (2020), 92–102; and S. Mattern, *Rome and the Enemy: Imperial Strategy in the Principate* (1999), 186–188. On the captives and the romantic if unlikely theory that some ended up in China, see H. Dubs, 'An Ancient Military Contact Between Romans and Chinese', *American Journal of Philology* 62 (1941): 322–330, and 'A Roman City in Ancient China: A Reply to Professor Carmann', *Journal of Asian Studies* 22 (1962): 135–136.

7. L. Keppie, 'Legions in the East from Augustus to Trajan', in Freeman & Kennedy (1986), 2:411–429; S. Mitchell, 'Legio VII and the Garrison of Augustan Galatia', *Classical Quarterly* 26 (1976): 298–308.

8. On royal forces, see D. Saddington, 'Client Kings' Armies Under Augustus: The Case of Herod', in *Herod and Augustus: Papers Presented at the IJS Conference, 21st–23rd June 2005*, eds. D. Jacobson & N. Kokkinos (2009), 303–323.

9. Dio 51. 16. 2, where Augustus returned a prince to Media Atropatene, but refused a similar request from Armenia, because of the killing of Romans.

10. Josephus, *AJ* 15. 18–19; *Jewish War* 1. 284; with J. Schlude & J. Overman, 'Herod the Great: A Near Eastern Case Study in Roman-Parthian Politics', in Schlude & Rubin (2017), 93–110, esp. 99–105; and in general E. Gruen, 'Herod, Rome, and the Diaspora', in Jacobson & Kokkinos (2009), 13–27.

11. Ten legions concentrated, but then divided into several columns because they were too unwieldy, Velleius Paterculus 2. 113; more dangerous to wage war against Parthia than in Europe, see Sherwin-White (1983), 328–334.

12. Dio 54. 9. 1–6; with B. Levick, *Tiberius the Politician* (1999), 24–27; R. Seager, *Tiberius* (2nd ed., 2005), 13–14.

13. Dio 54. 8. 1–3; Velleius Paterculus 2. 100. 1; Livy, *Pers.* 141; Suetonius, *Augustus* 21. 3; with Sherwin-White (1983), 323–326; and Debevoise (1938), 140–141.

14. *Res Gestae* 29; on the awards, see J. Rich, 'The Parthian Honours', *Papers of the British School at Rome* 66 (1998): 71–128; with Gruen in *CAH²* 10:159–160; and C. Rose, 'The Parthians in Augustan Rome', *American Journal of Archaeology* 109 (2005): 21–75.

15. For the Forum and Temple of Mars Ultor, see T. Luce, 'Livy, Augustus, and the Forum Augustum', in Edmondson (2009), 399–415.

16. See Rose (2005), 22–26; Rich (1998), 97–115.

17. For Musa, see Josephus, *AJ* 18. 39–43, which is gossipy and garbled; with J. Bigwood, 'Queen Mousa, Mother and Wife(?) of King Phaatakes of

Parthia: A Re-evaluation of the Evidence', *Mouseion* 3.4 (2004): 35–70; E. Strugnell, 'Thea Musa, Roman Queen of Parthia', *Iranica Antiqua* 43 (2008): 275–298; L. Gregoratti, 'Parthian Women in Flavius Josephus', in *Jüdisch-hellenistische Literatur in ihrem interkulturellen Kontext*, ed. M. Hirschberger (2012), 183–192, esp. 184–186; and J. Schlude & B. Rubin, 'Finding Common Ground: Roman-Parthian Embassies in the Julio-Claudian Period', in Schlude & Rubin (2017), 65–91, esp. 72–78. While it is generally assumed that the woman described by Josephus and the one depicted on coins are one and the same, we really do not know, and it is possible that they were in fact mother and daughter. Sibling marriage was a good deal more common than union between mother and son.

18. *Res Gestae* 32. 4–5; Velleius Paterculus 2. 94. 4; Justin 42. 5. 12; Strabo, *Geog.* 6. 4. 2, 16. 1. 28; Tacitus, *Annals* 2. 1; Suetonius, *Augustus* 21. 3; with Schlude (2020), 100–101; and J. Allen, *Hostages and Hostage-Taking in the Roman Empire* (2006), 84–87.

19. See Allen (2006), esp. 52–55; on the Ara Pacis, see Rose (2005), 36–44, modifying earlier view in C. Rose, '"Princes" and Barbarians on the Ara Pacis', *American Journal of Archaeology* 94 (1990): 453–467.

20. Josephus, *AJ* 18. 42–43 reports that it was said that mother and son were lovers and makes no mention of marriage; on Tiberius, see G. Bowersock, 'Augustus and the East: The Problem of Succession', in *Caesar Augustus: Seven Aspects*, eds. F. Millar & E. Segal (1990), 169–188.

21. Dio 55. 10. 17–21, 55. 10A. 3–9; Josephus, *AJ* 18. 39–43; Tacitus, *Annals* 2. 4; *Res Gestae* 27; Ovid, *Ars Amatoria* 1. 177–229; Velleius Paterculus 2. 101. 1–3; with F. Romer, 'Caius' Military Diplomacy in the East', *Transactions of the American Philological Association* 109 (1979): 199–214.

22. Velleius Paterculus 2. 102. 1–3; Dio 55. 10a. 5–10; Suetonius, *Augustus* 65. 1–2; Tacitus, *Annals* 1. 3; Strabo, *Geog.* 11. 14. 6.

23. Josephus, *AJ* 18. 43; *Res Gestae* 32, which probably refers to Phraataces.

CHAPTER 7: BETWEEN TWO GREAT EMPIRES

1. For the main narrative, see Tacitus, *Annals* 2. 1–3; with Debevoise (1938), 151–153; Suetonius, *Tiberius* 16 notes that the Parthian envoys were sent to see Tiberius, then on campaign on the German frontier. Tacitus, *Annals* 2. 1–3; with Josephus, *AJ* 18. 45–50, who similarly claimed that Vonones was unpopular because of his time as a hostage in Rome. For discussion of the origins of Artabanus, see M. Olbrycht, 'The Genealogy of Artabanos II (AD 8/9–39/40), King of Parthia', *Miscellanea Anthropologica et Sociologica* 15 (2014): 92–97.

2. Tacitus, *Annals* 2. 4, 56–58, 68; Suetonius, *Tiberius* 49. 2; *Caius* 1–2; for thorough discussion of the trial of Piso and the text of the Senate's decree, see M. Griffin, 'Review of W. Eck, A. Caballos, & F. Fernandez, *Das Senatus Consultum de Cn. Piso Patre*', *Journal of Roman Studies* 87 (1997): 249–263.

3. Tacitus, *Annals* 1. 11 for the advice to keep the empire within its boundaries, with the cynical Tacitus speculating whether this was motivated by fear or envy.

4. U. Ellerbrock, *The Parthians: The Forgotten Empire* (2021), 49–50; L. Gregoratti, 'The Importance of the Mint of Seleucis on the Tigris for Arsacid History: Artabanus and the Greek Parthian Cities', *Mesopotamia* 47 (2012): 129–136, esp. 130–133.

5. For the narrative, see Josephus, *AJ* 18. 310–379, with 374 noting the ongoing intercommunal tension in Seleucia; with Bivar (1983), 69–74. On the Jewish nobleman with five hundred horsemen, Josephus, *AJ* 17. 23–27. On banditry within the Roman empire, see R. MacMullen, *Enemies of the Roman Order* (1966), 192–212, 255–268; B. Shaw, 'Bandits in the Roman Empire', *Past & Present* 105 (1984): 3–52; T. Grünewald, *Bandits in the Roman Empire: Myth and Reality*, trans. J. Drinkwater (2004); C. Fuhrmann, *Policing the Roman Empire: Soldiers, Administration and Public Order* (2012); and Goldsworthy (2016), 217–244.

6. Suetonius, *Tiberius* 25. 1; on the relationship between the Arsacid king and the nobility, see E. Dabrowa, 'The Parthian Aristocracy: Its Social Position and Political Activity', *Parthica* 25 (2013): 53–62.

7. Tacitus, *Annals* 6. 31–36; with R. Ash, 'An Exemplary Conflict: Tacitus' Parthian Battle Narrative (*Annals* 6. 34–35)', *Phoenix* 53 (1999): 114–135; Debevoise (1938), 156–159.

8. Tacitus, *Annals* 6. 36–37, 41–44; with Gregoratti (2012), 129–136; E. Dabrowa, 'Parthian-Armenian Relations from the 2nd Century BCE to the Second Half of the 1st Century CE', *Electrum* 28 (2021): 41–57, esp. 50–51; and more generally on marriage ties and politics in the wider region, see L. Fabian, 'Bridging the Divide: Marriage Politics Across the Caucasus', *Electrum* 28 (2021): 221–244.

9. Josephus, *AJ* 18. 101–105.

10. Tacitus, *Annals* 11. 8–10; with Debevoise (1938), 166–171; Bivar (1983), 74–75; E. Keitel, 'The Role of Parthia and Armenia in Tacitus Annals 11 and 12', *American Journal of Philology* 99 (1978): 462–473; E. Dabrowa, 'Tacitus on the Parthians', *Electrum* 24 (2017): 171–189. Raid on villages near Zeugma: Philostratus, *Life of Apollonius* 1. 31, 37.

11. Tacitus, *Annals* 2. 42, 11. 8; with A. Gowing, 'Tacitus and the Client Kings', *Transactions of the American Philological Association* 120 (1990): 315–331; and F. Millar, *The Roman Near East* (1993), 52–53.

12. Tacitus, *Annals* 11. 10, 12. 10–14; with Debevoise (1938), 172–174.

13. Tacitus, *Annals* 12. 44–47; Josephus, *AJ* 20. 73–96; with Debevoise (1938), 174–177.

14. Tacitus, *Annals* 12. 50–51.

15. Tacitus, *Annals* 13. 6–8, 34–35; with B. Isaac, *The Limits of Empire* (rev. ed., 1992), 24–25; and E. Wheeler, 'The Laxity of the Syrian Legions', in Kennedy (1996), 229–276, both arguing that the stereotype of poor-quality legions in the east is not based on fact and that the training programme was normal. For Corbulo's career, see A. Goldsworthy, *In the Name of Rome* (2003), 263–289.

16. Tacitus, *Annals* 13. 9.

17. Tacitus, *Annals* 13. 34, 36; Frontinus, *Strat.* 4. 1. 21, 28.

18. Tacitus, *Annals* 13. 37–39.

19. Tacitus, *Annals* 13. 39–41; Dio 52. 19. 1–20. 1.

20. Frontinus, *Strat.* 2. 9. 5; Tacitus, *Annals* 13. 41, 14. 23–25.

21. Tacitus, *Annals* 14. 23–26; with A. Barrett, 'Annals 14. 26 and the Armenian Settlement of AD 60', *Classical Quarterly* 29 (1979): 465–469.

22. Tacitus, *Annals* 15. 1–6.

23. Tacitus, *Annals* 15. 7–8.

24. Tacitus, *Annals* 15. 9.

25. Tacitus, *Annals* 15. 9–17.
26. Tacitus, *Annals* 15. 17–18, 24–29; for analysis of the campaigns, see B. Warmington, *Nero: Reality and Legend* (1969), 85–100; J. Drinkwater, *Nero: Emperor and Court* (2019), 131–152; L. Gregoratti, 'Corbulo Versus Vologaeses: A Game of Chess for Armenia', *Electrum* 24 (2017): 107–121.
27. Tacitus, *Annals* 15. 29–31; Dio 52. 23. 1–6, 53. 1–7.1; Pliny, *Natural History* (hereafter *NH*) 30. 6.
28. See discussion in Schlude (2020), 127–134.
29. In general, see J. Coulston, 'Roman, Parthian and Sassanid Tactical Developments', in Freeman & Kennedy (1986), 2:59–75.
30. Tacitus, *Annals* 2. 56.
31. Suetonius, *Vespasian* 6; Tacitus, *Histories* 4. 51.
32. Dio 52. 17. 5–6.

CHAPTER 8: GOOD AT BUSINESS

1. The number of centurions in a legion depended on the size and organization of its first cohort, but was in theory fifty-nine or sixty, with possibly another in charge of the legion's cavalry. This suggests c. 1,800 legionary centurions at the start of the second century AD, with a similar or slightly higher total for the auxilia, although the status of these was lower. There were also the praetorians, urban cohorts, and vigils in Rome, and centurions in the fleet, notably commanding a ship of any size. For general discussion of centurions and their status and background, see Goldsworthy (1996), 13–15; and J. Wintjes, 'Field Officers: Principate', in *The Encyclopedia of the Roman Army*, vol. 2, ed. Y. Le Bohec (2015), 399–402.
2. On intelligence gathering, see N. Austin & B. Rankov, *Exploratio: Military and Political Intelligence in the Roman World from the Second Punic War to the Battle of Adrianople* (1995), 21–22, 102–107; and B. Rankov, 'The Governor's Men: The *Officium Consularis*', in A. Goldsworthy & I. Haynes, *The Roman Army as a Community in Peace and War*, Journal of Roman Archaeology Supplementary Series no. 34 (1999), 15–34.
3. Quote from Josephus, *Jewish War* 7. 224 (Loeb translation).
4. Josephus, *Jewish War* 7. 219–243 for the full narrative of this episode.
5. For discussion of communication between emperor and governor, see D. Potter, 'Emperors, Their Borders and Their Neighbours: The Scope of Imperial *Mandata*', in Kennedy (1996), 49–66; and more generally, Goldsworthy (2016), 309–384 for an introduction to the debate over Roman frontiers.
6. M. Bishop, '*Praesidium*: Social, Military, and Logistical Aspects of the Roman Army's Provincial Distribution During the Early Principate,' in Goldsworthy & Haynes (1999), 111–118.
7. Greatrex (2007), 103–173, esp. 104–116.
8. Josephus, *AJ* 18. 312–313; Matthew 2. 1; Philostratus, *Life of Apollonius of Tyana* 19–40; *Life of Saint Thomas*.
9. In general, see R. McLaughlin, *The Roman Empire and the Silk Routes: The Ancient World Economy and the Empires of Parthia, Central Asia and Han China* (2019); R. McLaughlin, *The Roman Empire and the Indian Ocean: The Ancient World Economy and the Kingdoms of Africa, Arabia and India* (2014); and the

papers in S. Lieu & G. Mikkelsen, eds., *Silk Road Studies*, vol. 18, *Between Rome and China: History, Religions and Material Culture of the Silk Road* (2016). On military monitoring and Egypt, see D. Nappo & A. Zerbini, 'Trade and Taxation in the Egyptian Desert', in *Frontiers in the Roman World: Proceedings of the Ninth Workshop of the International Network, Impact of Empire (Durham, 16–19 April 2009)*, eds. O. Hekster & T. Kaizer (2011), 61–77, esp. 72–24; see also V. Maxfield, 'Ostraca and the Roman Army in the Eastern Desert', in *Documenting the Roman Army: Essays in Honour of Margaret Roxan*, ed. J. Wilkes (2003), 153–173, esp. 154–156, 164–167.

10. G. Young, *Rome's Eastern Trade: International Commerce and Imperial Policy, 31 BC–AD 305* (2001), 90–186; M. Fitzpatrick, 'Provincializing Rome: The Indian Ocean Trade Network and Roman Imperialism', *Journal of World History* 22 (2011): 27–54, on the wider context and the advantages of transport by sea.

11. Young (2001), 47–50, 66–69, 165–166, 210–212.

12. McLaughlin (2019), 1–11.

13. McLaughlin (2019), 29–73; D. Leslie & K. Gardiner, 'Chinese Knowledge of Western Asia During the Han', *T'oung Pao* 68 (1982): 254–308; W. Tao, 'Parthia in China: A Re-examination of the Historical Records', in Sarkhosh Curtis & Stewart (2007), 87–104; and J. Thorley, 'The Silk Trade Between China and the Roman Empire at Its Height, Circa AD 90–130', *Greece and Rome* 18 (1971): 71–80.

14. Sima Qian, *Shifi* 123. 3172. 3; Tao (2007), 89–95.

15. See Thorley (1971), esp. 73–76; Bivar (1983), 191–209; Ptolemy, *Geog.* 1. 11. 6–7; with Young (2001), 190–191. On India, see R. Tomber, 'Pots, Coins and Trinkets in Rome's Trade with the East', in *Rome Beyond Its Frontiers: Imports, Attitudes and Practices*, Journal of Roman Archaeology Supplementary Series no. 95, ed. P. Wells (2013), 87–104; C. Whittaker, 'Indian Trade Within the Roman Imperial Network', in *Rome and Its Frontiers: The Dynamics of Empire* (2004), 163–180; Pliny, *NH* 12. 84.

16. Pliny, *NH* 6. 26, 12. 41.

17. See Young (2001), 201–207; Fitzpatrick (2011), 31–35.

18. The wider context is well explored in Fitzpatrick (2011).

19. Reweaving silk: Pliny, *NH* 6. 20; with McLaughlin (2019), 6–8, 42–46; and in general Thorley (1971), 75–79.

20. J. Ferguson, 'China and Rome', *Aufstieg und Niedergang der römischen Welt*, II.9 (1978), 581–603; J. Thorley, 'The Development of Trade Between the Roman Empire and the East Under Augustus', *Greece and Rome* 16 (1969): 209–223; and Young (2001), esp. 27–89, 187–200; Tao (2007), 99–100; McLaughlin (2019), 192–198 for speculative discussion.

21. McLaughlin (2019), 49–56.

22. Young (2001), 201–220; Fitzpatrick (2011), 35–42.

23. E.g., Thorley (1971), 75–76, 79.

24. On the imperial economy in general, see P. Temin, 'The Economy of the Early Roman Empire', *Journal of Economic Perspectives* 20 (2006): 133–151.

25. Debevoise (1938), xlii, 119, 204; Ellerbrock (2021), 140–143.

26. J. Amussen, 'Christians in Iran', in Yarshater (1983), 924–927; R. Emmerick, 'Buddhism Among Iranian Peoples', in Yarshater (1983), 949–964.

27. Ellerbrock (2021), 261–263.

CHAPTER 9: GLORY AND TEARS

1. Tacitus, *Histories* 1. 4; for narrative of the Year of Four Emperors, see K. Wellesley, *The Year of the Four Emperors* (3rd ed., 2000); on the law, see M. Griffin in *CAH²*, vol. 11, *The High Empire AD 70–192*, eds. A. Bowman, P. Garnsey, & D. Rathbone, (2000), 10, 11–12.

2. B. Levick, *Vespasian* (2nd ed., 2020), 4–15; Suetonius, *Vespasian* 4. 3.

3. Bivar (1983), 86–87; Debevoise (1938), 213–219; Ellerbrock, (2021), 59–62, summarizing the main analyses of coin series.

4. On the family, see J. Bennett, *Trajan: Optimus Princeps* (1997), 11–19. Friction with the Parthians and this period in general, see Pliny, *Pan.* 14; Aurelius Victor, *Caes.* 9. 12; with Schlude (2020), 140–155, esp. 146–147.

5. Dio 66. 19. 3b–c; Tacitus, *Histories* 1. 2; Suetonius, *Nero* 57. 2; for Domitian, see Schlude (2020), 149–150.

6. On the eastern frontiers, see E. Wheeler, 'The Army and the *Limes* in the East', in *A Companion to the Roman Army*, ed. P. Erdkamp (2007), 234–266; E. Dabrowa, 'The Frontier in Syria in the First Century AD', in Freeman & Kennedy (1986), 1:93–108, esp. 98–99.

7. Wheeler (2007), 243.

8. Alans, see Josephus, *Jewish War* 7. 244–251; Suetonius, *Domitian* 2. 2; Dio 65 (66. 15. 3); Dacia, Dio 67. 6. 1–7. 4.

9. For this period, see J. Grainger, *Nerva and the Roman Succession Crisis of AD 96–99* (2003); Bennett (1997), 42–52.

10. The letters from Pliny's legateship in Bithynia were published as book ten of his correspondence. Since Pliny died in office, the release of these letters presumably was done with Trajan's approval and may have been intended as a model for proper behaviour by a governor and fitting diligence for a good emperor. See A. Sherwin-White, *The Letters of Pliny: A Historical and Social Commentary* (1966), 526–555.

11. A good survey of these campaigns and commemoration is Bennett (1997), 85–103, 148–160.

12. For discussion of the many complexities of the annexation, see P. Freeman, 'The Annexation of Arabia and Imperial Grand Strategy', in Kennedy (1996), 91–118.

13. J. Thorley, 'The Roman Empire and the Kushans', *Greece and Rome* 26 (1979): 181–190.

14. F. Lepper, *Trajan's Parthian War* (1948) remains the most thorough discussion of the many problems associated with this conflict because of the paucity of sources; Bennett (1997), 183–193. See also B. Levick, 'Pliny in Bithynia—and What Followed', *Greece and Rome* 26 (1979): 119–131.

15. Dio 68. 17. 1–18. 1, 23. 1–2.

16. Dio 68. 18. 2, 19. 1–20. 4; with Bennett (1997), 192–195.

17. Discussion in Lepper (1948), 46–48, 136–148; and Bennett (1997), 194–196; including Arrian, *Parthica* 5. 85, 87. The fragments of the *Parthica* are conveniently collected and translated in Lepper (1948), 225–253.

18. S. James, 'Of Colossal Camps and a New Roman Battlefield: Remote Sensing, Archival Archaeology and the "Conflict Landscape" of Dura-Europos, Syria', in *Understanding Roman Frontiers*, eds. D. Breeze & I. Oltean (2015), 328–345; Dio 68. 22. 3; on imperial titles and salutations, see Lepper (1948), 31–53.

19. Dio 68. 21. 1–3, 24. 1–25. 6; with S. Ross, *Roman Edessa: Politics and Culture on the Eastern Fringes of the Roman Empire, 114–242 CE* (2001), 30–34.

20. Dio 68. 26. 1–4, 26. 4, 27. 1–28. 3.

21. Dio 68. 28. 4–30. 1.

22. For a thorough recent examination of the Jewish rebellions, see W. Horbury, *The Jewish War Under Trajan and Hadrian* (2014), 164–277; Dio 68. 33. 1.

23. Dio 68. 30. 1–3, 75. 9. 6; with Lepper (1948), 88–96; Bennett (1997), 199–201; Schlude (2020), 161–162; Debevoise (1938), 234–239.

24. Dio 68. 31. 1–4, 33. 1–3, 69. 1. 1–2. 6; with A. Birley, *Hadrian: The Restless Emperor* (1997), 75–84; Bennett (1997), 201–204.

25. Dio 68. 17. 1; for discussion, see Lepper (1948), 158–213; Schlude (2020), 162–165; B. Campbell, 'War and Diplomacy: Rome and Parthia, 31 BC–AD 235', in *War and Society in the Roman World*, eds. J. Rich & G. Shipley (1993), 213–240, esp. 234–238.

26. Dio 68. 6. 1–7. 5.

27. Mattern (1999) is the most thorough examination of glory and images of strength in the context of foreign relations.

28. Dio 69. 2. 3; J. Lander, 'Did Hadrian Abandon Arabia?', in Freeman & Kennedy (1986), 2:447–453; and for Hadrian in general, see Birley (1997); for the Jewish rebellion, see Horbury (2014), 278–428.

29. Birley (1997), 289–297; Scriptores Historiae Augustae (hereafter SHA), *Antoninus Pius* 2. 3–6.

30. D. Potter, 'The Inscriptions on the Bronze Herakles from Mesene: Vologeses IV's War with Rome and the Date of Tacitus' *Annales*', *Zeitschrift für Papyrologie und Epigraphik* 88 (1991): 277–290.

31. M. Bishop, *Lucius Verus and the Roman Defence of the East* (2018), 61–81; P. Edwell, *Rome and Persia at War: Imperial Competition and Contact 193–363 CE* (2021), 42–46.

32. Versions of the fate of the legate were mocked in Lucian, *How to Write History* 25–26, but the text does not make clear what actually happened. For discussion, see N. Hodgson, 'The End of the Ninth Legion', *Britannia* 52 (2021): 97–118, esp. 102, citing K. Juntunen, 'Ancient Elegeia: Battlefield or Roman Outpost? From Written Sources to Archaeological Evidence', in *Proceedings of the 24th International Limes Congress, Serbia, 2018* (forthcoming).

33. The best attempt to reconstruct the conflict is Bishop (2018), 83–115.

34. R. Duncan-Jones, 'The Impact of the Antonine Plague', *Journal of Roman Archaeology* 9 (1996): 108–138; and R. Flemming, 'Galen and the Plague', in *Galen's Treatise Περὶ Ἀλυπίας (de indolentia) in Context: A Tale of Resilience*, ed. C. Petit (2019), 219–244; on the triumph and aftermath, see Bishop (2018),117–125.

35. Galen, *Ind.* 2. 6–7. For Marcus Aurelius, see A. Birley, *Marcus Aurelius: A Biography* (rev. ed., 1987), esp. 140–210.

36. For the narrative, see A. Birley, *Septimius Severus: The African Emperor* (1999), 89–120. On the eastern frontier, see Edwell (2021), 46–48; Schlude (2020), 167–168; and M. Gradoni, 'The Parthian Campaigns of Septimius Severus: Causes, and Roles in Dynastic Legitimation', in *The Roman Empire During the Severan Dynasty: Case Studies in History, Art, Architecture, Economy and Literature*, ed. E. De Sena (2013), 3–23.

37. Dio 75. 1. 1–2. 3, 76. 9. 1–13. 1; on aspects of the siege of Hatra, see D. Campbell, 'What Happened at Hatra?: The Problem of the Severan Siege Operations', in Freeman and Kennedy (1986), 1:51–58; and D. Kennedy,

'"European" Soldiers and the Severan Siege of Hatra', in Freeman and Kennedy (1986), 2:397–409.

38. Dio 75. 3. 2–3.

39. Dio 72. 36. 4.

CHAPTER 10: DYNASTIES

1. Dio 77. 15. 2–4, 17. 4; Herodian 3. 14. 1–3, 15. 1–3; SHA, *Severus* 19. 14.

2. Dio 78. 2. 1–3. 3; Herodian 4. 4. 1–3–5. 7; SHA, *Caracalla* 2. 5–11; *Geta* 6. 1–2.

3. Dio 78. 15. 2–7, 17. 3–4. For a discussion of Caracalla's style of rule, see D. Potter, *The Roman Empire at Bay* (2004), 140–146; and see G. Fowden in *CAH²*, vol. 12, *The Crisis of Empire AD 193–337*, eds. A. Bowman, A. Cameron, & P. Garnsey (2005), 545–547. For an example of Caracalla's method of hearing a petition, see *Supplementum Epigraphicum Graecum* (hereafter SEG) 17. 759; with discussion in W. Williams, 'Caracalla and Rhetoricians: A Note of the *cognitio de Gohairienis*', *Latomus* 33 (1974): 663–667. Vestal Virgins, see Dio 78. 16. 1–3. Extension of citizenship: Dio 78. 9. 5; and SHA, *Caracalla* 5. 8; with A. Sherwin-White, *The Roman Citizenship* (1973), 275–287, 380–394; Potter (2004), 138–139.

4. Dio 78. 18. 1, 19. 1–2, 20. 1–21. 1, 22. 1–23. 2, 79. 1. 1. 3. 3; Herodian 4. 7. 3–7, 8. 6–11. 9; SHA, *Caracalla* 6. 1–6; for discussion, see Potter (2004), 141–144; Millar (1993), 142–146; B. Campbell in *CAH²*, 12:18–19.

5. Debevoise (1938), 263–266; Schlude (2020), 170–171 for the campaign.

6. SHA, *Caracalla* 6. 5–7. 1; Dio 79. 4. 1–6. 5, 11. 1–21. 5; Herodian 4. 12. 1–15. 9, 5. 1. 1–2. 6; SHA, *Macrinus* 2. 1–4; with Potter (2004), 145–147.

7. Herodian 4. 15. 4; Dio 79. 26. 2–27. 3.

8. Dio 79. 30. 2–41. 4; Herodian 3. 2. 1–5. 1; for discussion, see Millar (1993), 119–120, 145–147, 300–309; Potter (2004), 148–152.

9. Dio 80. 7. 1–4, 11. 1–21. 3; Herodian 5. 5. 6–7. 2; SHA, *Elagabalus* 3. 4–5, 4. 1–2, 6. 78. 3, 15. 6, 18. 3; Potter (2004), 153–157; for an up-to-date analysis of Elagabalus, see H. Sidebottom, *The Mad Emperor: Heliogabalus and the Decadence of Rome* (2022).

10. Dio 80. 17. 2–21. 3, 81. 4. 2–5. 2; Herodian 5. 7. 1–8. 10, 6. 1. 4–10; SHA, *Elagabalus* 13. 1–17. 3; for discussion of the reign, see R. Syme, *Emperors and Biography: Studies in the Historia Augusta* (1971), 146–162; Potter (2004), 158–166; and Campbell in *CAH²*, 12:22–27.

11. Dio 80. 4, 1–2; Herodian 6. 2. 1–7. 6; Zonaras 12. 15; for Maximinus, see Syme (1971), 179–193; Herodian 6. 8. 1–8; SHA, *Maximinus* 2. 1–5. 1 on Maximinus and 'humble origins'; Herodian 6. 9. 1–8 on the murder of Alexander; SHA, *Maximinus* 7. 1–6.

12. Dio 80. 3. 1–2, 4. 1–2; Herodian 6. 2. 1–2, 6–7.

13. R. Frye in Yarshater (1983), 116–124; T. Daryaee, 'Ardaxšīr and the Sasanians' Rise to Power', *Anabasis* 1 (2010): 236–255; M. Olbrycht, 'Dynastic Connections in the Arsacid Empire and the Origins of the House of Sasan', in Sarkhosh Curtis et al. (2016), 23–35.

14. Agathius 2. 27. 1–5; Syncellus, 440, 11–441, 2; both of which are conveniently presented and translated in M. Dodgeon & S. Lieu, *The Roman Eastern Frontier and the Persian Wars*, vol. 1, AD 226–363 (1991), 9–10. See

also A. Gariboldi, 'The Birth of the Sasanian Monarchy in Western Sources', in Sarkhosh Curtis et al. (2016), 47–52.

15. Olbrycht (2016), 23–28.

16. Olbrycht (2016), 27–28, 30–31.

17. On the many problems of the date, sequence, and symbolism of the rock reliefs of this period, see E. Shavarebi, 'Historical Aspects, Iconographical Factors, Numismatic Issues, Technical Elements: How to Obtain a Convincing Chronology for the Rock Reliefs of Ardashir I', *Anabasis* 5 (2014): 108–122; P. Callieri, 'Cultural Contacts Between Rome and Persia at the Time of Ardashir I (c. AD 224–240)', in *Sasanian Persia: Between Rome and the Steppes of Eurasia*, ed. E. Sauer (2019), 221–238.

18. Olbrycht (2016), 30–31.

19. Ammianus Marcellinus 23. 6. 6; dismissed by Gariboldi (2016), 50, but viewed as plausible by Olbrycht (2016), 31.

20. Olbrycht (2016), 27–32.

21. T. Daryaee, 'From Terror to Tactical Usage: Elephants in the Parthia-Sasanian Period', in Sarkhosh Curtis et al. (2016), 36–41; Tacitus, *Annals* 15. 15 for Vologaeses I riding on an elephant.

22. For a detailed discussion of the relationship between Sasanian kings and the Parthian noble clans, see P. Pourshariati, *The Decline and Fall of the Sasanian Empire: The Sasanian-Parthian Confederacy and the Arab Conquest of Iran* (2008), esp. 33–82.

23. See Callieri (2017), 221–238.

24. Sources for a Persian attack on the Roman provinces c. 238: see Dodgeon & Lieu (1991), 32–33.

CHAPTER 11: AND THE CAESAR LIED AGAIN

1. The most relevant sections of this inscription, the Greek version known as the *res gestae divi Saporis*, are conveniently translated in Dodgeon & Lieu (1991): 2. 1. 3, 2. 3, 3. 1. 4, 2. 6, with quote from p. 34. It is found in full in P. Huyse, *Die Dreisprachige Inschrift Sabuhrs I. an Der Ka'ba-I Zardust (SKZ)*, 2 vols. (1999).

2. M. Canepa, *The Two Eyes of the Earth: Art and Ritual of Kingship Between Rome and Sasanian Iran* (2009), 54–55 on the emphasis on Iran and non-Iran.

3. Note the sensible caution in Edwell (2021), 76.

4. For sources, see Dodgeon & Lieu (1991), 32–33: 1. 4. 4–5, 1. 5. 1; for the archaeology, see S. Hause & D. Tucker, 'The Final Onslaught: The Sasanian Siege of Hatra', *Zeitschrift für Orient-Archäologie* 2 (2009): 106–139.

5. *SEG* 7 (1934), 743b, lines 17–19, for the attack and *L'Année épigraphique* (1948), 124, for the memorial to Terentius.

6. See S. James, *The Roman Military Base at Dura-Europos, Syria: An Archaeological Visualization* (2019), 3, 63, 85, 254, 230, who points out that it is unlikely that his memorial came from the house where it was found. For earlier interpretations, see C. Welles, 'The Epitaph of Julius Terentius', *Harvard Theological Review* 34, no. 2 (1941): 79–102. See also on equipment and uniform, S. James, *Excavations at Dura-Europos 1928–1937: Final Report VII–the Arms and Armour and Other Military Equipment* (2004), 62–65.

7. Fink, *Roman Military Records* 50, 194, n. 11; also in Dodgeon & Lieu (1991), 328–331, esp. 331, n. 4; with James (2019), 241–242, 245–250.

8. Fink, *Roman Military Records* 1; on equipment, see M. Bishop & J. Coulston, *Roman Military Equipment from the Punic Wars to the Fall of Rome* (2nd ed., 2006), 128–198; and James (2004), esp. 242–254.

9. This point is very well made by James (2019), 250–258.

10. For contrasting views, see N. Pollard, 'The Roman Army as "Total Institution" in the Near East?: Dura-Europos as a Case Study', in Kennedy (1996), 211–227; and N. Pollard, *Soldiers, Cities and Civilians in Roman Syria* (2000); see also P. Edwell, *Between Rome and Persia: The Middle Euphrates, Mesopotamia and Palmyra Under Roman Control* (2008), 115–148.

11. The papers gathered in J. Chi & S. Heath, eds., *Edge of Empires: Pagans, Jews, and Christians at Roman Dura-Europos* (2012) offer a good and splendidly illustrated introduction to the mixed community in the city.

12. Edwell (2008), 63–87, 135–139.

13. Dodgeon & Lieu (1991) 2. 1. 1–3. 4 gather the sources for Gordian's Persian expedition and its aftermath; for discussion, see Edwell (2021), 74–81. Shapur's inscription describes Gordian's army and defeat in lines 6–9.

14. On the money paid to Shapur I, see T. Pékary, 'Le "tribut" aux Perses et les finances de Philippe l'Arabe', *Syria* 38 (1961): 275–283; and J. Guey, 'Autour des Res Gestae Divi Saporis 1: Deniers (d'or) et (de compte) anciens', *Syria* 38 (1961): 261–274.

15. For the rock reliefs in general, see M. Canepa, 'Sasanian Rock Reliefs', in Potts (2013), 856–877; and Canepa (2009), 53–68.

16. For an overview of these emperors, see J. Drinkwater in *CAH²*, 12:33–39.

17. Edwell (2021), 67–70; Canepa (2009), 71–75; and Canepa (2013), 866–870.

18. For sources, see Dodgeon & Lieu (1991) 3. 1. 1–2. 5. Shapur's account is in lines 10–19. On Dura-Europos, see Edwell (2008), 91, 235, n. 131; and James (2004), 23–24.

19. Edwell (2021), 90–97; Ammianus Marcellinus 23. 5. 3 for the story of the actress warning the theatre audience of Persian attack.

20. James (2004), 24–25, 30–31.

21. For the siege, see James (2004), 31–39; and S. James, 'Stratagems, Combat and "Chemical Warfare" in the Siege Mines at Dura-Europos', *American Journal of Archaeology* 115 (2011): 69–101.

22. James (2004), 69–70, 129–134; and in general Mielczarek (1993), esp. 41–67, 73–85.

23. For Valerian, see Drinkwater in *CAH²*, 12:41–44.

24. Sources for the campaign in Dodgeon & Lieu (1991) 3. 2. 6–4. 2; Shapur's account lines 19–37. For discussion, see Edwell (2021), 100–107.

25. Canepa (2013), 865–873; on captives being mutilated and abandoned, Ammianus Marcellinus 19. 6. 2.

CHAPTER 12: A BRILLIANT QUEEN AND THE RESTORER OF THE WORLD

1. Dodgeon & Lieu (1991) 3. 3. 4–4. 1 for sources, and discussion in Edwell (2021), 112–114.

2. See Drinkwater in *CAH²*, 12:44–48.

3. For more detail on the wider period and a range of interpretations, see Potter (2004), 217–298; A. Goldsworthy, *The Fall of the West (How Rome Fell)* (2009), 86–153; and especially M. Kulikowski, *The Triumph of Empire: The Roman World from Hadrian to Constantine* (2016), 98–193.

4. Goldsworthy (2016), 309–384.

5. Both Potter (2004) and Kulikowski (2016) are inclined to view many changes in this period as improvements; see also B. Campbell in *CAH²*, 12:110–127.

6. For a good survey of senatorial careers in this era, see I. Mennen, *Power and Status in the Roman Empire* (2011), 49–81.

7. Mennen (2011), 193–246.

8. A good overview is provided in P. Southern & K. Dixon, *The Late Roman Army* (1996).

9. On equipment, see Bishop & Coulston (2006), 149–232.

10. See E. Sauer et al., 'Innovation and Stagnation: Military Infrastructure and Shifting Balance of Power Between Rome and Persia', in Sauer (2019), 241–267; and O. Hekster & N. Zair, *Rome and Its Empire* (2008), 31–44.

11. Potter (2004), 137–139, 172, 272–273; M. Corbier in *CAH²*, 12:327–439.

12. M. Sommer, *Palmyra: A History* (2017), 120, 145–148.

13. For differing views, see S. Swain, 'Greek into Palmyrene: Odaenathus as "Corrector Totius Orientis"', *Zeitschrift für Papyrologie und Epigraphik* 99 (1993): 157–164; with D. Potter, 'Palmyra and Rome: Odaenathus' Titulature and the Use of *Imperium Maius*', *Zeitschrift für Papyrologie und Epigraphik* 113 (1996): 271–285.

14. Pliny, *NH* 5. 88; with I. Richmond, 'Palmyra Under the Aegis of Rome', *Journal of Roman Studies* 53 (1963): 43–54; M. Galikowski, 'Palmyra as a Trading Centre', *British Institute for the Study of Iraq* 56 (1994): 27–33; Sommer (2017), 53–91.

15. Sommer (2017), 91–105; with E. Seland, *Ships of the Desert and Ships of the Sea: Palmyra in the World Trade of the First Three Centuries CE* (2016), esp. 10–25.

16. E. Seland, 'Ancient Trading Networks and New Institutional Economics: The Case of Palmyra', in *Antike Wirtschaft und ihre kulturelle Prägung—The Cultural Shaping of the Ancient Economy*, eds. K. Droß-Krüpe, S. Föllinger & K. Ruffing (2016), 223–234; Seland, *Ships* (2016), 28–61, esp. 75–88.

17. *Inscriptions grecques et latines de la Syrie* 17. 1. 241; with Seland, *Ships* (2016), 64–74.

18. K. Schörle, 'Palmyrene Merchant Networks and Economic Integration into Competitive Markets', in *Sinews of Empire*, eds. H. Teigan & E. Seland (2017), 147–154.

19. For sources, see Dodgeon & Lieu (1991) 4. 1. 1–4. 4.

20. *CISem.* 2. 3946; with Potter (1996), 272–274.

21. Sommer (2017), 139–169; with sources in Dodgeon & Lieu (1991) 4. 5. 1–11. 5.

22. For biographies, see P. Southern, *Empress Zenobia: Palmyra's Rebel Queen* (2008); and R. Winsbury, *Zenobia of Palmyra: History, Myth and the Neoclassical Imagination* (2012); and more briefly for her career, see Potter (2004), 266–272.

23. For cataphracts, see Festus, *Brev.* 24; Zosimus 1. 50. 2–4, 53. 1–3.

24. F. Millar, 'Paul of Samosata, Zenobia, and Aurelian: The Church, Local Culture and Political Allegiance in Third Century Syria', in *Rome, the Greek World and the East*, vol. 3, *The Greek World, the Jews and the East*, eds.

H. Cotton & G. Rogers (2006), 243–273, with 265, fn. 146, for the law protecting right of asylum in synagogues.

25. Dodgeon & Lieu (1991) 3. 3. 3.

26. Potter (2004), 302–314.

27. Goldsworthy (2009), 95–99; M. Edwards in *CAH²* 12:573–588.

28. Potter (2004), 241–244, 254–255; G. Clarke in *CAH²* 12:625–647.

29. For a detailed biography, see A. Watson, *Aurelian and the Third Century* (1999).

30. Dodgeon & Lieu (1991) 4. 8–11. 1.

31. On Palmyra in later years, see E. Intagliata, *Palmyra After Zenobia:* AD *273–750* (2018); on Carus, see Dodgeon & Lieu (1991) 5. 1. 6–2. 1.

CHAPTER 13: SIEGES AND EXPEDITIONS

1. For discussion, see Frye (1983), 127–132.

2. J. Duchesne-Guillemin in Yarshater (1983), 874–886.

3. In general, see S. Williams, *Diocletian and the Roman Recovery* (1985); and T. Barnes, *The New Empire of Diocletian and Constantine* (1982).

4. Potter (2004), 280–290, 294–298.

5. For sources, see Dodgeon & Lieu (1991) 5. 2. 3–5. 2; for discussion, see Edwell (2021), 220–226, 238–252.

6. Edwell (2021), 226–238; Isaac (1992), 161–218; for analysis and excellent pictures, see D. Kennedy & D. Riley, *Rome's Desert Frontier from the Air* (1990); and for placing the frontier works in this region in the context of other frontiers, see D. Breeze, *The Frontiers of Imperial Rome* (2011), 118–132.

7. For a good survey of the army in this period, see Southern & Dixon (1996).

8. Tacitus, *Germania* 41; Dio 72. 11. 2–3 for restrictions on entry points into the provinces on other frontiers.

9. Frye (1983), 131–132.

10. The literature on Constantine is vast, but good starting places are D. Potter, *Constantine the Emperor* (2013); Potter (2004), 340–439; SHA, *Severus* 29. 2.

11. On Christianity and the role of religion in the relationship between Rome and Persia, see Edwell (2021), 259–291. On the claims made by the charlatan Metrodorus, see Ammianus Marcellinus 25. 4. 23; Credenus, *Chronicle* 1, 516, 12–517, 15.

12. Ammianus Marcellinus 17. 5. 3–15 for the exchange of letters and ambassadors.

13. On the Battle of Singara, see Edwell (2021), 305–309; with sources in Dodgeon & Lieu (1991) 7. 3. 4.

14. Dodgeon & Lieu (1991) 7. 4. 1–6. 4; with Edwell (2021), 296–315.

15. For an excellent analysis of the sieges in this era, see J. Levithan, *Roman Siege Warfare* (2013), 170–204.

16. For sources, see Dodgeon & Lieu (1991) 7. 1. 3, 4. 5–5. 1, 5. 5; on the end of the Kushano-Sasanian dynasty, see Bivar (1983), 209–213.

17. See J. Matthews, *The Roman Empire of Ammianus Marcellinus* (1989); J. Matthews, 'The Origin of Ammianus', *Classical Quarterly* 44 (1994): 252–269; and T. Barnes, *Ammianus Marcellinus and the Representation of Historical Reality* (1998), 1–10.

18. Ammianus Marcellinus 17. 5. 1–3, 14. 3, 18. 5. 5–6. 5, 17–18; with Edwell (2021), 315–320.

19. Ammianus Marcellinus 18. 6. 5–7. 3.

20. Ammianus Marcellinus 18. 7. 3–8. 14.

21. Ammianus Marcellinus 18. 9. 1–4, 19. 2. 14; for a detailed analysis of the siege, see Levithan (2013), 187–195; with Edwell (2021), 320–326.

22. For the narrative of the siege, see Ammianus Marcellinus 19. 1. 1–9. 9; and for discussion, R. Blockley, 'Ammianus Marcellinus on the Persian Invasion of AD 369', *Phoenix* 42 (1988): 244–260.

23. Ammianus Marcellinus 20. 6. 1–8.

24. Ammianus Marcellinus 20. 7. 1–17.

25. Ammianus Marcellinus 20. 11. 1–31; with Edwell (2021), 326–334, on the wider campaign; and R. Seager, 'Perceptions of Eastern Frontier Policy in Ammianus, Libanius and Julian', *Classical Quarterly* 47 (1997): 253–268, esp. 253–262.

26. Ammianus Marcellinus 21. 6. 6–7. 7.

27. On Julian's beliefs, see G. Bowersock, *Julian the Apostate* (1978), 12–20, 61–65; Potter (2004), 496–499, 508–509; and G. Fowden, 'Julian, Philosopher and Reformer of Polytheism' in *CAH²*, vol. 13, *The Late Empire*, eds. A. Cameron & P. Garnsey (1998), 212–233. In general A. Murdoch, *The Last Pagan: Julian the Apostate and the Death of the Ancient World* (2003).

28. Edwell (2021), 212–233; C. Fonara, 'Julian's Persian Expedition in Ammianus and Zosimus', *Journal of Hellenic Studies* 111 (1991): 1–15; on Julian's relationship with the past, see J. Lendon, *Soldiers and Ghosts: A History of Battle in Classical Antiquity* (2005), 290–309.

29. On the sources for the campaign, see Dodgeon & Lieu (1991), 231–274; with main narrative Ammianus Marcellinus 21. 12. 1–25. 8. 18; and discussion in Matthews (1989), 130–179; and Edwell (2021), 354–384. On army numbers, Ammianus Marcellinus 23. 3. 5, 24. 7. 4, 25. 7. 2; and Zosimus 3. 13.

30. Ammianus Marcellinus 22. 9. 1–10. 7.

31. For discussion of Julian's behaviour during sieges, see Lendon (2005), 292–300; and Levithan (2013), 196–204.

32. Ammianus Marcellinus 25. 3. 1–23; with Potter (2004), 518; and N. Lenski, *The Failure of Empire: Valens and the Roman State in the Fourth Century AD* (2002), 14, for the date.

33. Ammianus Marcellinus 25. 9. 1–13 on the handover of Nisibis and other territory.

CHAPTER 14: THE TWO EYES OF THE WORLD

1. Ammianus Marcellinus 25. 7. 14.

2. On the Carthaginian indemnity, see Polybius 15. 18. 1–8; Livy 30. 37. 1–6.

3. Ammianus Marcellinus 30. 6. 1–6.

4. Peter Patricius, 'Fragment 13', quoted with translation in Dodgeon & Lieu (1991) 5. 4. 2; and Theophylact Simonat(t)a 4. 11. 2–3 (trans. Whitby).

5. Collected sources in G. Greatrex & N. Lieu, *The Roman Eastern Frontier and the Persian Wars*, vol. 2, *AD 363–630* (2002), 21–30.

6. For sources, see n. 5, and especially Ammianus Marcellinus 27. 12. 1–18, 30. 1. 1–2. 5.

7. For narrative, see Goldsworthy (2009), 245–263. And for greater detail, Lenski (2002); P. Heather, *Goths and Romans 332–489* (1991); P. Heather, *The*

Goths (1996); H. Wolfram, *The Roman Empire and Its Germanic Peoples*, trans. T. Dunlap (1997); M. Kulikowski, *Rome's Gothic Wars* (2007); and T. Burns, *Barbarians Within the Gates of Rome: A Study of Roman Military Policy and the Barbarians, ca. 375–425 AD* (1994).

8. On nomenclature, see B. Salway, 'What's in a Name? A Survey of Roman Onomastic Practice from c. 700 BC to AD 700', *Journal of Roman Studies* 84 (1994): 124–145.

9. See Frye (1983), 140–143.

10. Greatrex & Lieu (2002), 14–15 for sources; with G. Bowersock, 'Mavia, Queen of the Saracens', in *Studien zur antiken Sozialgeschichte: Festschrift Friedrich Vittinghoff*, eds. W. Eck, H. Galstere, & H. Wolff (1980), 477–495. For discussion of her identity and the similarities drawn with Zenobia in the later tradition, see J. Monferrer-Sala, '"New Skin for Old Stories": Queens Zenobia and Māwiya, and Christian Arab Groups in the Eastern Frontier During the 3rd–4th Centuries CE', in *Mapping Knowledge: Cross-Pollination in Late Antiquity and the Middle Ages*, eds. C. Burnett & P. Mantas-Espana (2014), 71–98.

11. For sources, see Greatrex & Lieu (2002), 17–19; with G. Greatrex & M. Greatrex, 'The Hunnic Invasion of the East of 395 and the Fortress of Ziatha', *Byzantion* 69 (1999): 65–75.

12. On this period, see Goldsworthy (2009), 285–313; P. Heather, *The Fall of the Roman Empire: A New History* (2005), esp. 191–299.

13. Goldsworthy (2009), 335–352, on Britain.

14. Heather (2005), 300–348; and C. Kelly, *Attila the Hun: Barbarian Terror and the Fall of the Roman Empire* (2008) for more detail.

15. Heather (2005), 191–250, and in general for the question of the causes of Rome's fall. See also B. Ward-Perkins, *The Fall of Rome and the End of Civilization* (2005).

16. For Aetius's career and its context, see I. Hughes, *Aetius: Attila's Nemesis* (2012).

17. Heather (2005), 300–304, 385–407.

18. Goldsworthy (2009), 363–369.

19. For a good survey of the different fortunes of the east and west, see P. Heather, *Rome Resurgent: War and Empire in the Age of Justinian* (2018), 19–68.

20. For the period, see A. Lee in *CAH²*, vol. 14, *Late Antiquity: Empire and Successors AD 425–600*, eds. A. Cameron, B. Ward-Perkins, & M. Whitby (2000), 33–52.

21. For a detailed introduction to the structures of government, see A. Jones, *The Later Roman Empire: 284–602* (1964), 321–606; on Constantinople, see B. Croke, 'Justinian's Constantinople', in *The Cambridge Companion to the Age of Justinian*, ed. M. Maas (2005), 60–86.

22. Suetonius, *Tiberius* 25. 1; on faith and division, see P. Allen in *CAH²*, 14:811–834; circus factions repairing the walls, see Kelly (2008), 102–103.

23. For the manual, see G. Dennis, trans., *Maurice's Strategikon: Handbook of Byzantine Military Strategy* (1984).

24. See Duchesne-Guillemin (1983), 874–906, on religion; and N. Miri, 'Sasanian Administration and Sealing Practices', in Potts (2013), 909–991; on the relationship between kings and priests, see L. Patterson, 'Minority Religions in the Sasanian Empire: Suppression, Integration and Relations with Rome', in Sauer (2019), 181–198.

25. Greatrex & Lieu (2002), 32–33, for sources; with G. Greatrex & J. Bardill, 'Antiochus the "Praepositus": A Persian Eunuch at the Court of Theodosius II', *Dumbarton Oaks Papers* 50 (1996): 171–197.

CHAPTER 15: SOLDIERS, WALLS, AND GOLD

1. Ammianus 31. 2. 1–12; see also E. Thompson, *The Huns*, rev. and ed. P. Heather (1996), 56–59; and on Hunnic appearance, see O. Maenchen-Helfen, *The World of the Huns: Studies in Their History and Culture* (1973), 358–375; and especially for sources, D. Balogh, ed., *Hunnic Peoples in Central and South Asia: Sources for Their Origins and History* (2020).

2. Procopius, *Wars* 1. 3. 1–2 on the Hephthalites.

3. On the Anastasian Wall, see J. Crow, 'Recent Research on the Anastasian Wall in Thrace and Late Antique Linear Barriers Around the Black Sea', in *Roman Frontier Studies 2009: Proceedings of the XXI International Congress of Roman Frontier Studies (Limes Congress) Held at Newcastle upon Tyne in August 2009*, eds. N. Hodgson, P. Bidwell, & J. Schachtmann (2017), 131–138. On the Strata Diocletiana, see P. Casey, 'Justinian, the Limitanei, and Arab-Byzantine Relations in the Sixth Century', *Journal of Roman Archaeology* 9 (1996): 214–222; A. Lewin, 'The New Frontiers of Late Antiquity in the Near East from Diocletian to Justinian', in Hekster & Kaizer (2011), 234–263; I. Arce, 'Transformation Patterns of Roman Forts in the Limes Arabicus from Severan to Tetrarchic and Justinianic Periods', in Hodgson, Bidwell, & Schachtmann (2017), 121–130; and S. Thomas Parker, 'New Research on the Roman Frontier in Arabia', in Hodgson, Bidwell, & Schachtmann (2017), 139–144.

4. E. Sauer et al., *Persia's Imperial Power in Late Antiquity: The Great Wall of Gorgān and the Frontier Landscapes of Sasanian Iran* (2013); and more generally on Sasanian frontier defences, see A. Aliev et al., 'The Ghilhilchay Defensive Long Wall: New Investigations', *Ancient East and West* 5 (2006): 143–177; and M. Labbaf-Khaniki, 'Long Wall of Asia: The Backbone of Asian Defensive Landscape', in *Proceedings of the 10th International Congress on the Archaeology of the Ancient Near East*, eds. R. Salisbury, F. Höflmayer, and T. Bürge (2018), 2:113–121. Not released until after this book was complete, E. Sauer, J. Nokandeh, & H. O. Rekavandi, eds., *Ancient Arms Race: Antiquity's Largest Fortresses and Sasanian Military Networks of Northern Iran*, 2 vols. (2022), will provide the most up-to-date study of these topics.

5. H. O. Rekavandi et al., 'The Archaeology of Sasanian Frontier Troops: Recent Fieldwork on Frontier Walls in Northern Iran', in Hodgson, Bidwell, & Schachtmann (2017), 145–150, esp. 146–147. For introductions to Hadrian's Wall, see N. Hodgson, *Hadrian's Wall: Archaeology and History at the Limit of Rome's Empire* (2017); and A. Goldsworthy, *Hadrian's Wall* (2018).

6. D. Lawrence & T. Wilkinson, 'The Northern and Western Borderlands of the Sasanian Empire: Contextualising the Roman/Byzantine and Sasanian Frontier', in Sauer (2019), 99–125.

7. See M. Corby, 'Hadrian's Wall and the Defence of North Britain', *Archaeologia Aeliana* series 5, vol. 39 (2010): 9–13.

8. M. Nemati, M. Mousavinia, & E. Sauer, 'Largest Ancient Fortress of South-West Asia and the Western World?: Recent Fieldwork at Sasanian Qaleh Iraj at Pishva, Iran', *Journal of the British Institute of Persian Studies* 58 (2020):

190–220; see also E. Sauer & J. Nokandeh, 'Forts and Megafortresses, Natural and Artificial Barriers: The Grand Strategy of the Sasanian Empire', in *Proceedings of the International Congress of Young Archaeologists 2015*, eds. M. Kharanaghi, M. Khanipour, & R. Naseri (2018), 236–256.

9. Procopius, *Wars* 1. 18. 51–53.

10. Pourshariati (2008), esp. 59–83, 98–101; Immortals, see Procopius, *Wars* 1. 14. 31, 44–45; on the army in general in light of the recent archaeological finds, see G. Greatrex, *Rome and Persia at War: 502–532* (1998), 52–59; and Sauer et al. (2019), 241–267.

11. Maurice, *Strategikon* 9. 1.

12. Dennis (1984) offers the text in translation; Procopius, *Wars* 1. 18. 33–34 on the difference between Roman and Persian archery; see also Greatrex (1998), 31–40.

13. Pourshariati (2008), 88–94; on the Roman army at this time, see W. Tread-gold, *Byzantium and Its Army: 284–1081* (1995), 43–64, 87–98; and on limitanei, Jones (1964), 659–663.

14. Greatrex (1998), 33.

15. Procopius, *Wars* 1. 20. 1–12, 8. 17; in general, see McLaughlin (2014); and especially D. Whitehouse & A. Williamson, 'Sasanian Maritime Trade', *Iran* 11 (1973): 29–49; and C. Morely, 'The Arabian Frontier: A Keystone of the Sasanian Empire', in Sauer (2019), 268–283; and J. Howard-Johnston, 'The India Trade in Late Antiquity', in Sauer (2019), 284–304.

16. For discussion, see G. Fisher, *Between Empires: Arabs, Romans and Sasanians in Late Antiquity* (2011).

17. E.g., Z. Rubin, 'Diplomacy and War in the Relations Between Byzantium and the Sassanids in the Fifth Century AD', in Freeman & Kennedy (1986), 2:677–695; and R. Blockley, 'Subsidies and Diplomacy: Rome and Persia in Late Antiquity', *Phoenix* 39 (1985): 62–74; for the promise of soldiers, see Joshua Stylites 8.

18. Pourshariati (2008), 59–70; Frye (1983), 143–152; L. Patterson, 'Minority Religions in the Sasanian Empire: Suppression, Integration and Relations with Rome', in Sauer (2019), 181–198, esp. 187–193.

19. Procopius, *Wars* 1. 2. 11–13; with other sources in Greatrex & Lieu (2002), 36–43; on the context of Sasanian problems in the north-east, see D. Potts, 'Sasanian Iran and Its Northeastern Frontier: Offense, Defense, and Diplomatic Entente', in *Empires and Exchanges in Eurasian Late Antiquity: Rome, China, Iran, and the Steppe, ca. 250–750*, eds. N. di Cosmo & M. Maas (2018), 287–301.

20. Procopius, *Wars* 1. 3. 1–22, with 17–22 for the ploy; Pourshariati (2008), 70–75.

21. Procopius, *Wars* 1. 4. 1–35; on the building of the Gorgan Wall, see Rekavandi et al. (2017), 145.

22. Frye (1983), 149–152; Yarshater in Yarshater (1983), 991–1024; Pourshariati (2008), 82–83; Procopius, *Wars* 1. 6. 1–9 for a version of Kavadh's escape from prison.

23. For the Anastasian War, see Greatrex & Lieu (2002), 62–81 for sources; Greatrex (1998), 72–119, for narrative and analysis on which my description draws heavily; advice given to Anastasius, see Procopius, *Wars* 1. 7. 1–2.

24. Greatrex (1998), 84, on the absence of Roman soldiers in the narrative of Amida.

25. Joshua Stylites 54 gives the highest figure; see discussion in Greatrex (1998), 96; on the commanders, see Procopius, *Wars* 1. 8. 1–3.

26. Joshua Stylites 80 for the Roman deception; Roman surprise at the amount of food left in Amida, see Procopius, *Wars* 1. 9. 20–23.

CHAPTER 16: WAR AND ETERNAL PEACE

1. Malalas 410–411.

2. Procopius, *Secret History* 2. 6; a similar story was told about the fifth-century Gothic king Theodoric, see Anonymous Valesianus 79.

3. Procopius, *Secret History* 2. 9. 1–30; with A. Cameron in *CAH²*, 14:64.

4. Constantine VII Porphyrogenitus, *De Ceremoniis* 89–90 (398–410), translated in Greatrex & Lieu (2002), 124–128; with discussion in Heather (2018), 211–212.

5. Greatrex (1998), 139–159.

6. For sources, see Greatrex & Lieu (2002), 79–80, 82.

7. For the sources, see Greatrex & Lieu (2002), 81; with the main account Procopius, *Wars* 1. 11. 1–30; with discussion in Greatrex (1998), 134–138; and Heather (2018), 91–93. The latter believes that the refusal of Kavadh I's request was deliberate provocation on Justin and Justinian's part.

8. Sources in Greatrex & Lieu (2002), 82; with Greatrex (1998), 139–147.

9. Sources in Greatrex & Lieu (2002), 83–88; with Greatrex (1998), 148–165.

10. Procopius, *Wars* 1. 13. 12–14. 55; with Greatrex (1998), 168–185; I. Hughes, *Belisarius: The Last Roman General* (2009), 53–59; and J. Haldon, *The Byzantine Wars: Battles and Campaigns of the Byzantine Era* (2001), 28–35, for analysis.

11. Greatrex (1998), 185–192.

12. Procopius, *Wars* 1. 16. 1–18. 56; with Greatrex (1998), 193–212.

13. Malalas 472–473; Procopius, *Wars* 1. 21. 28.

14. Malalas 18. 44; with Greatrex (1998), 213–221.

15. Frye (1983), 153–162; T. Daryaee, *Sasanian Persia: The Rise and Fall of an Empire* (2007), 28–30, for the more traditional view; with Pourshariati (2008), esp. 83–118, for a more nuanced assessment. On the training of the army, employing evidence mainly from the later Sasanian era, see K. Farrokh, *The Armies of Ancient Persia: The Sasanians* (2014), 80–100.

16. The collection of papers in Maas (2005) offers very good introductions to a range of themes, notably C. Humfress, 'Law and Legal Practice in the Age of Justinian', 161–184. See also A. Lee, *From Rome to Byzantium* AD 363–565: *The Transformation of Ancient Rome* (2013), 241–300.

17. Procopius, *Wars* 11. 24; *Secret History* 12. 12; with Heather (2018), 109–114, P. Stephenson, *New Rome: The Roman Empire in the East* AD 395–700 (2021), 196–198.

18. In general, see Hughes (2009), 70–182, 202–230; Heather (2018), 269–302; A. Lee, 'The Empire at War', in Maas (2005), 113–133; W. Pohl, 'Justinian and the Barbarian Kingdoms', in Maas (2005), 448–476.

19. For sources, see Greatrex & Lieu (2002), 97–103.

20. For the letter, see Procopius, *Wars* 2. 4. 14–26, and the whole campaign 2. 4. 1–14. 7; with other sources in Greatrex & Lieu (2002), 103–108.

21. The much later Arab tradition reflected in Tabari 1. 898/157–158 claimed that the captives from Antioch were given new houses in streets identical to their old homes in every way.

22. Procopius, *Wars* 2. 14. 8–19. 49.

23. Procopius, *Wars* 2. 22. 1–23. 21; P. Holden, 'Mediterranean Plague in the Age of Justinian', in Maas (2005), 134–160, is a good survey of the extensive literature on the subject. For differing views on its impact, contrast S. Pamuk & M. Shatzmiller, 'Plagues, Wages and Economic Change in the Islamic Middle East, 700–1500', *Journal of Economic History* 74, no. 1 (2014): 196–229; with L. Mordechai et al., 'The Justinianic Plague: An Inconsequential Pandemic?', *Proceedings of the National Academy of Sciences of the United States of America* 51 (2019): 25546–25554.

24. Procopius, *Wars* 2. 20. 1–21. 34, 24. 1–25. 35; and other sources in Greatrex & Lieu (2002), 109–112.

25. Procopius, *Wars* 2. 26. 1–30. 48; with Greatrex & Lieu (2002), 113–118.

26. Greatrex & Lieu (2002), 118–133; with the treaty given in Menander, Frag. 6. 314–397, 132–133.

27. Hughes (2009), 231–241; Heather (2018), 269–271; Cameron in *CAH*², 14:82–85; M. Whitby in *CAH*², 14:86–87.

28. Greatrex & Lieu (2002), 135–150, for sources; with Stephenson (2021), 220–222; Frye (1983), 158–160; Whitby in *CAH*², 14:91–94.

29. Greatrex & Lieu (2002), 151–166; Whitby in *CAH*², 14:95–98.

30. For sources, see Greatrex & Lieu (2002), 167–175; Whitby in *CAH*², 14:99–104; in general M. Whitby, *The Emperor Maurice and His Historian Theophylact on Persian and Balkan Warfare* (1993), 276–304.

31. Frye (1983), 62–166; Pourshariati (2008), 118–130, identifying Bahrām as from the Mihran house.

32. Stephenson (2021), 226–228.

33. Frye (1983), 161–162.

CHAPTER 17: HIGH TIDE

1. Stephenson (2021), 234; with more detail in L. Mordechai, 'Antioch in the Sixth Century: Resilience or Vulnerability?' in *Environment and Society in the Long Later Antiquity*, eds. A. Izdebski & M. Mulryan (2018), 25–41.

2. *Strategikon* 11. 2; for useful survey of the military situation in the period, see A. Sarantis, 'Waging War in Late Antiquity', in *War and Warfare in Late Antiquity*, eds. A. Sarantis & N. Christie (2013), 1–98.

3. Heather (2018), 284–287, on early Roman contact with the Avars; more generally, Whitby (1988), 80–89, 109–137; on the Turks, see A. von Gabain, in Yarshater (1983), 613–624; and K. Rezakhani, 'From the Kushans to Western Turks', in *King of the Seven Climes: A History of the Ancient Iranian World (3000 BCE–651 CE)*, ed. T. Daryaee (2017), 199–226.

4. *Strategikon* 1. 2, 2. 9.

5. D. Kagay, 'The Traction Trebuchet: A Triumph of Four Civilizations', *Viator* 31 (2000): 433–486; and for a slightly different view, L. Petersen, *Siege Warfare and Military Organization in the Successor States (400–800 AD): Byzantium, the West and Islam* (2013), 406–424.

6. Frye (1983), 165–167; Pourshariati (2008), 130–140.

7. *Strategikon* 11. 4; on Maurice's difficulties, see Whitby in *CAH²*, 14:99–108.

8. For more detail, see Stephenson (2021), 236–238; J. Howard-Johnston, *The Last Great War of Antiquity* (2021), 8–18.

9. Howard-Johnston (2021), 18–22; Greatrex & Lieu (2002), 182–184; Frye (1983), 166–168; with Canepa (2009), 126–127.

10. Sources in Greatrex & Lieu (2002), 184–187; for detailed discussion, see Howard-Johnston (2021), 22–36.

11. W. Kaegi, *Heraclius, Emperor of Byzantium* (2003), 19–48; Howard-Johnston (2021), 39–48.

12. Kaegi (2003), 48–57; Howard-Johnston (2021), 49–71.

13. Greatrex & Lieu (2002), 187–189.

14. Kaegi (2003), 58–68; Howard-Johnston (2021), 72–81.

15. Kaegi (2003), 67–72; Howard-Johnston (2021), 80–85.

16. Greatrex & Lieu (2002), 189–193; Kaegi (2003), 73–83; Howard-Johnston (2021), 87–102.

17. Kaegi (2003), 87–91; J. Howard-Johnston, 'The Official History of Heralius' Persian Campaigns', in *The Roman and Byzantine Army in the East*, ed. E. Dabrowa (1994), 57–87, esp. 84.

18. Greatrex & Lieu (2002), 193–195; Kaegi (2003), 83–86; Howard-Johnston (2021), 103–120, on the negotiations.

19. Kaegi (2003), 88, on the plan to move to Africa; on the course of the war and the fall of Egypt, see Greatrex & Lieu (2002), 195–197; Kaegi (2003), 91–99; Howard-Johnston (2021), 113–133.

CHAPTER 18: TRIUMPH AND DISASTER

1. Howard-Johnston (2021), 205–206, 211, fn. 69.

2. Kaegi (2003), 100–112; Howard-Johnston (2021), 192–195.

3. Sources for this campaign, see Greatrex & Lieu (2002), 198–199. For narrative and analysis of the campaign, see Kaegi (2003), 112–118; and Howard-Johnston (2021), 196–200. These provide the most detailed and convincing reconstruction of the war, so I have generally followed their analysis. However, the nature of the sources means that certainty is often impossible on details and chronology, let alone the motivations and strategic thinking on each side.

4. Kaegi (2003), 118–121; Howard-Johnston (2021), 200–213.

5. Kaegi (2003), 106–107, 260–261; Stephenson (2021), 241–242.

6. Kaegi (2003), 122–124; Howard-Johnston (2021), 215–217.

7. For the campaign, see sources in Greatrex & Lieu (2002), 200–202; with Kaegi (2003), 125–128; Howard-Johnston (2021), 217–229; on the temple, see D. Huff, 'The Functional Layout of the Fire Sanctuary at Takht-I Sulaiman', in *Current Research in Sasanian Archaeology, Art and History*, eds. D. Kennet & P. Luft (2008), 1–13.

8. For the second year of campaigning, see sources in Greatrex & Lieu (2002), 202–205; with Kaegi (2003), 129–132; Howard-Johnston (2021), 229–245.

9. For sources, narrative, and analysis, see Greatrex & Lieu (2002), 205–209; with Kaegi (2003), 133–141; Howard-Johnston (2021), 246–268.

10. For the siege, see Howard-Johnston (2021), 268–284.

11. Sources for the final stages of the war, see Greatrex & Lieu (2002), 209–225.

12. Kaegi (2003), 148–151, accepts the story as basically credible, while Howard-Johnston (2021), 267–268, suggests Roman disinformation; on Shahrbaraz and his background, see Pourshariati (2008), 142–146.

13. Howard-Johnston (2021), 295–303.

14. On the final campaign, see Kaegi (2003), 156–174; Howard-Johnston (2021), 304–314.

15. J. Howard-Johnson, 'Pride and Fall: Khusro II and His Regime, 626–628', in *La Persia e Bisanzio: Atti dei Convegni Lincei 2002*, ed. G. Gnoli (2003), 93–113, on Khusro's last years.

16. Howard-Johnston (2021), 314–320; Pourshariati (2008), 153–160.

17. On the negotiations, see Greatrex & Lieu (2002), 226–228; Kaegi (2003), 174–180; Howard-Johnston (2021), 321–328.

18. Frye (1983), 170–172; Kaegi (2003), 180–191; Howard-Johnston (2021), 336–346.

19. Kaegi (2003), 201–207; Howard-Johnston (2021), 346–359.

CHAPTER 19: ON THAT DAY ALL BELIEVERS SHALL REJOICE

1. T. Daryaee, *Sasanian Persia: The Rise and Fall of an Empire* (2007), 35–36.

2. M. Ghodrat-Dizaji, 'Disintegration of Sasanian Hegemony over Northern Iran (AD 623–643)', *Iranica Antiqua* 46 (2011): 315–329 in general, and 320–321 for the rebuilding of the fire temple destroyed by Heraclius.

3. Kaegi (2003), 192–228, on the state of the empire and Heraclius's activities in the years between the war with Persia and the Arab invasion.

4. For fears in the early sixth century, see Greatrex (1998), 5–7, 43; S. Shoemaker, *The Apocalypse of Empire: Imperial Eschatology in Late Antiquity and Early Islam* (2018), esp. 64–89.

5. Kaegi (2003), 91; W. Kaegi, *Muslim Expansion and Byzantine Collapse in North Africa* (2010), 84–85, on the forced baptism; W. Kaegi, *Byzantium and the Early Islamic Conquests* (1992), 39–43, discusses the size of the Roman army at this time.

6. Kaegi (1992), 52–59.

7. In general, see L. Conrad in *CAH²*, 14:678–700; R. Hoyland, *In God's Path: The Arab Conquests and the Creation of an Islamic Empire* (2013), 8–30, esp. 21–27.

8. Fisher (2011); and G. Fisher & P. Wood, 'Writing the History of the "Persian Arabs": The Pre-Islamic Perspective on the "Nasrids" of al-Hirah', *Iranian Studies* 49 (2016): 247–290.

9. Procopius, *Wars* 2. 16. 1–19 for Belisarius's awareness of an Arab festival; Greatrex & Lieu (2002), 86, for sources; with Greatrex (1998), 152, for the alleged sacrifice of girls in 529.

10. For an up-to-date discussion of the sources for the life of Muhammed and his world and how to approach them, see S. Anthony, *Muhammad and the Empires of Faith* (2020); see also F. Donner, 'The Background to Islam' in Maas (2005), 510–533.

11. Anthony (2020), 59–82.

12. Hoyland (2013), 36–39.

13. Donner (2005), 526; Kaegi (1992), 68–74.

14. On the mixed composition of the early Muslim armies, see Hoyland (2013), 56–65; on apparent sympathy for Rome in the struggle with Persia, Qur'an 30. 2–4; on the positive tradition about Heraclius, see N. El-Cheikh, 'Muhammad and Heraclius: A Study in Legitimacy', *Studia Islamica* 89 (1999): 5–21.

15. Hoyland (2013), 31–55, on the early campaigns and the many problems of chronology; with Kaegi (1992), 79–111, for more emphasis on conflict with the Romans.

16. On the Yarmuk campaign, see Kaegi (1992), 112–146; Haldon (2001), 56–66; on the refusal of his governor in Africa to send troops to the east, see Kaegi (2003), 233–234.

17. In general, see Kaegi (1992), 147–180, with 159 for Chalkis; and Hoyland (2013), 46–49.

18. Hoyland (2013), 47–48.

19. Daryaee (2007), 37–38; Hoyland (2013), 49–54; Pourshariati (2008), 161–181, esp. 213–220; Hoyland (2013), 82–91.

20. For Egypt, see Hoyland (2013), 66–78.

21. Frye (1983), 172–177; Daryaee (2007), 37–38; and Pourshariati (2008), esp. 260–318.

22. On the Arab conquest of Africa, see Kaegi (2010), esp. 92–115, on the balance of power at the start of the period; with Hoyland (2013), 78–81, 90–93.

23. For one view emphasizing the post-war weakness in both empires, see G. Bowersock, *Empires in Collision in Late Antiquity* (2012), 55–77; see also Kaegi (1992), 236–287.

24. Heraclius and the problem of succession and the campaigns of this era, see Stephenson (2021), 256–273.

CONCLUSION

1. Plutarch, *Caesar* 58 claimed that Caesar planned to defeat the Parthians and then march back via Europe, conquering Scythians, Germans, and various others on the way before crossing the Rhine into Gaul. If there is any truth in the story, which seems unlikely since it is not mentioned by Cicero or anyone else writing nearer the time, then this can be seen to support a very poor understanding of the distances involved. We do know that Caesar named magistrates for three years as the period of his planned absence.

2. For a fuller discussion of the question of maps and understanding of geography, see Greatrex (2007), 103–173, esp. 130–142.

3. Suetonius, *Julius Caesar* 44. 3.

INDEX

Adrian Goldsworthy received his DPhil in ancient history from Oxford and has taught at Cardiff University, King's College, and the University of Notre Dame in London. The author of numerous books, including *Pax Romana*, *How Rome Fell*, *Caesar*, *Hadrian's Wall*, and *Philip and Alexander*, he lives in South Wales, UK.